CLYMER®

SUZUKI

1500 INTRUDER/BOULEVARD C90 • *1998-2009*

The world's finest publisher of mechanical how-to manuals

P.O. Box 12901, Overland Park, Kansas 66282-2901

Copyright ©2011 Penton Business Media, Inc.

FIRST EDITION
First Printing October, 2007

SECOND EDITION
First Printing June, 2011

Printed in U.S.A.

CLYMER and colophon are registered trademarks of Penton Business Media, Inc.

ISBN-10: 1-59969-413-1

ISBN-13: 978-1-59969-413-9

Library of Congress: 2011927467

AUTHOR: Clymer Staff.

TECHNICAL PHOTOGRAPHY: George Parise with assistance from Curt Jordan, Jordan Engineering, Oceanside,CA.

TECHNICAL ILLUSTRATIONS: Errol McCarthy.

WIRING DIAGRAMS: Bob Meyer and Rick Arens.

EDITOR: Rick Arens and James Grooms.

PRODUCTION: Adriane Roberts.

TOOLS AND EQUIPMENT: K & L Supply Co. at www.klsupply.com.

COVER: Mark Clifford Photography at www.markclifford.com. Motorcycle courtesy of Bert's Mega Mall, Covina, CA.

CLYMER®

Publisher Ron Rogers

EDITORIAL

Editorial Director
James Grooms

Editor
Steven Thomas

Associate Editor
Rick Arens

Authors
Michael Morlan
George Parise
Ed Scott
Ron Wright

Technical Illustrators
Steve Amos
Errol McCarthy
Mitzi McCarthy
Bob Meyer

SALES

Sales Manager–Marine
Jay Lipton

Sales Manager–Powersport/I&T
Matt Tusken

CUSTOMER SERVICE

Customer Service Manager
Terri Cannon

Customer Service Representatives
Karen Barker
Dinah Bunnell
Suzanne Johnson
April LeBlond
Sherry Rudkin

PRODUCTION

Director of Production
Dylan Goodwin

Production Manager
Greg Araujo

Senior Production Editor
Darin Watson

Production Editor
Adriane Roberts

Associate Production Editor
Ashley Bally

P.O. Box 12901, Overland Park, KS 66282-2901 • 800-262-1954 • 913-967-1719

More information available at *clymer.com*

CONTENTS

QUICK REFERENCE DATA

MOTORCYCLE INFORMATION

MODEL:_____ YEAR:_____

VIN NUMBER:_____

ENGINE SERIAL NUMBER:_____

CARBURETOR SERIAL NUMBER OR I.D. MARK:_____

WHEEL AND TIRE SPECIFICATIONS

Item	Specification
Wheel size	
Front	
1998-2001 models	16 × MT 3.50
2002-on models	16 × MT 3.50, 16M/C × MT 3.50
Rear	15M/C × MT 5.00
Wheel runout limit	
Axial	2.0 mm (0.08 in.)
Radial	2.0 mm (0.08 in.)
Axle runout limit	
Front	0.25 mm (0.010 in.)
Rear	0.25 mm (0.010 in.)
Tire Size	
Front	
1998-2001 models	150/80-16 71H
2002-on models	150/80-16 71H, 150/80-16M/C 71H
Rear	180/70-15M/C 76H
Tire tread minimum depth	
Front	1.6 mm (0.06 in.)
Rear	2.0 mm (0.08 in.)
Tire pressure (cold)*	
Front	
Solo	200 kPa (29 psi)
Rider and passenger	200 kPa (29 psi)
Rear	
Solo	250 kPa (36 psi)
Rider and passenger	250 kPa (36 psi)

*Tire inflation pressure is for original equipment tires. Aftermarket tires may require different inflation pressure. The use of tires other than those specified by the manufacturer may cause instability.

RECOMMENDED LUBRICANTS AND FLUIDS

Fuel octane	
U.S., California and Canada models	
Pump octane: (R+M) / 2	87
Research octane	91
All models except U.S., California and Canada	
1998 models	85-95
1999-on models	91
Fuel tank capacity (including reserve)	
1998-1999 models	15.5 liters (4.1 gal.)
2000-2004	15.0 liters (4.0 gal.)
2005-on	14.0 liters (3.7 gal.)
Engine oil	
Classification	API SF, SG or SH, SJ with JASO MA rating
Viscosity	SAE 10W-40

(continued)

RECOMMENDED LUBRICANTS AND FLUIDS

Engine oil (continued)	
Capacity	
Oil change only	3.7 liters (3.9 qt.)
Oil and filter change	4.3 liters (4.5 qt.)
When engine completely dry	5.0 liters (5.3 qt.)
Brake/Clutch fluid	DOT 4
Fork oil	
Viscosity	SS-08 fork oil or an equivalent #10 fork oil
Capacity per leg	
1998-2004 models	439 ml (14.8 oz.)
2004-on models	416 ml (14.1 oz.)
Final drive gear oil	
Type	SAE 90 hypoid gear oil meeting API GL-5 certification
Final drive capacity	200-220 ml (6.8-7.4 oz.)

MAINTENANCE AND TUNE-UP SPECIFICATIONS

Item	Specification
Battery	
Type	
1998-2004 models	FTH 16 BS-1 Maintenance free (sealed)
2005-on models	FTZ 16 BS-1 Maintenance free (sealed)
Capacity	
1998-2004 models	12 volt 50.4 kC (14 amp hour)/10 HR
2005-on models	12 volt 64.8 kC (18 amp hour)/10 HR
Spark plug	
Type	
Standard	NGK: DPR7EA-9, Denso: X22EPR-U9
Cold	NGK: DPR8EA-9 or DPR9EA-9; Denso: X24EPR-U9 or X27EPR-U9
Gap	0.8-0.9 mm (0.02-0.035 in.)
Spark-test gap	Over 8 mm (0.3 in.)
Idle speed	
1998-2000 Switzerland and Austria models	950-1050 rpm
All 1998-2000 models except Switzerland and Austria	900-1100 rpm
2001-on models	900-1100 rpm
Fast idle speed (2005-on models)	1400-2000 rpm when engine is cold
Throttle cable free play	2.0-4.0 mm (0.08-0.16 in.)
Auto-decompression cable free play	1.0 mm (0.04 in.)
Auto-decompression solenoid clearance	6.0 mm (0.24 in.)
Throttle position sensor	
Output voltage @ idle	Approx. 1.12 volts
Output voltage variance	0.064-0.096 volts
Ignition timing*	
1998-2004 models	2° BTDC @ 1000 rpm
2005-on	9° BTDC @ 1000 rpm
Compression pressure (at sea level)	
Standard	1000-1400 kPa (145-203 psi)
Service limit	800 kPa (116 psi)
Maximum difference between cylinders	200 kPa (29 psi)
Engine oil pressure @ 60° C (140° F)	350-650 kPa (51-94 psi) @ 3000 rpm
Brake pedal height	98 mm (3.86 in.)
Shift pedal height	82 mm (3.23 in.)
Wheel runout limit	
Axial	2.0 mm (0.08 in.)
Radial	2.0 mm (0.08 in.)
Shock absorber spring preload	
Standard preload (spring length)	222 mm (8.74 in.)
Maximum preload (min. spring length)	217 mm (8.54 in.)
Minimum preload (max. spring length)	227 mm (8.94 in.)

*Not adjustable.

MAINTENANCE AND TUNE UP TORQUE SPECIFICATIONS

Item	N•m	in.-lb.	ft.-lb.
Bleed valve	7.5	66	–
Brake disc bolt	23	–	17
Brake hose banjo bolt	23	–	17
Clutch hose banjo bolt	23	–	17
Cylinder head cover bolt			
6 mm	10	89	–
8 mm	25	–	18
Expansion chamber bolt	23	–	17
Exhaust header bolt/nut	23	–	17
Final drive drain bolt	23	–	17
Front axle	65	–	48
Front axle clamp bolt	23	–	17
Front caliper housing bolt			
1998-2001 models	33	–	24
2002-on models	35	–	26
Front caliper mounting bolt	35	–	26
Handlebar clamp bolt			
1998-2004 models	16	–	12
2005-on models	23	–	17
Handlebar holder nut			
1998-2004 models	50	–	37
2005-on models	70	–	52
Handlebar weight bolt	50	–	37
Lower fork bridge clamp bolt	23	–	17
Muffler bracket bolt/nut	23	–	17
Muffler/exhaust pipe clamp bolt/nut	23	–	17
Muffler hanger bolt/nut	23	–	17
Oil drain bolt	21	–	15
Oil filter union	15	–	11
Oil gallery plug			
Main oil gallery	18	–	13
6 mm	10	89	–
8 mm	10	89	–
12 mm	21	–	15
14 mm	23	–	17
16 mm	35	–	26
Oil hose banjo bolt	26	–	19
Rear axle nut	110	–	81
Rear caliper bracket bolt/nut	60	–	44
Rear caliper mounting bolt	35	–	26
Rear caliper housing bolt			
1998-2001 models	33	–	24
2002-on models	21	–	15
Rear master cylinder pushrod locknut	18	–	13
Spark plug	18	–	13
Upper fork bridge clamp bolt			
2005-on models	23	–	17

CHAPTER ONE

GENERAL INFORMATION

This detailed and comprehensive manual covers 1998-2009 Suzuki 1500 Intruder/Boulevard C90 models.

Step-by-step procedures and hundreds of original photographs and illustrations created during a complete disassembly of the motorcycle guide the reader through every job.

Whether it is routine maintenance, troubleshooting or a major overhaul, Clymer manuals provide reliable information to perform the job. Accurate, clear and concise text, combined with detailed illustrations and photography, make it possible for the novice enthusiast to safely and enjoyably service their motorcycle. While at the same time, those with more experience rely on the in-depth coverage to tackle complicated procedures.

MANUAL ORGANIZATION

A shop manual is a tool and, as in all Clymer manuals, the chapters are thumb-tabbed for easy reference. Main headings are in the table of contents and index. Frequently used specifications and capacities from the tables at the end of each individual chapter are listed in the *Quick Reference Data* section at the front of the manual. Specifications and capacities are provided in metric and U.S. Standard units of measure.

Some procedures refer to headings in other chapters or sections of the manual. When a specific head-ing is called out in a step, it will be italicized as it appears in the manual. If a sub-heading is indicated as being "in this section" it is located within the same main heading. For example, the sub-heading *Handling Gasoline Safely* is located within the main heading *SAFETY*.

This chapter provides general information on shop safety, tool basics and tool use, service fundamentals and shop supplies. Refer to **Tables 1-5** at the end of the chapter for vehicle dimensions, weight, and general shop service information.

Refer to Chapter Two for troubleshooting information. The procedures present typical symptoms and steps to pinpoint and repair the problem.

Refer to Chapter Three for routine lubrication and maintenance procedures.

Subsequent chapters describe specific systems such as the engine, transmission, clutch, drive system, fuel and exhaust systems, electrical system, suspension, brakes and body/frame.

WARNINGS, CAUTIONS AND NOTES

The terms WARNING, CAUTION and NOTE each have specific meanings in this manual.

A WARNING emphasizes areas where injury or even death could result from negligence. Mechanical damage may also occur. WARNINGS *are to be taken seriously*.

A CAUTION emphasizes areas where equipment damage could result. Disregarding a CAUTION could cause permanent mechanical damage, though injury is unlikely.

A NOTE provides additional information to make a step or procedure easier or clearer. Disregarding a NOTE could cause inconvenience, but would not cause equipment damage or injury.

SAFETY

Refer to the following guidelines to safely service the motorcycle.

1. Do not operate the motorcycle in an enclosed area. The exhaust gasses contain carbon monoxide, an odorless, colorless and tasteless poisonous gas. Carbon monoxide levels build quickly in small, enclosed areas and can cause unconsciousness and death in a short time. Always properly ventilate the work area or operate the motorcycle outside.

2. *Never* use gasoline or any extremely flammable liquid to clean parts. Refer to *Handling Gasoline Safely* and *Cleaning Parts* in this section.

3. *Never* smoke or use a torch in the vicinity of flammable liquids, such as gasoline or cleaning solvent.

4. If welding or brazing on the motorcycle, remove the fuel tank to a safe distance at least .50 ft. (15 m) away.

5. Avoid contact with engine oil and other chemicals. Most are carcinogens. Wash your hands thoroughly after coming in contact with engine oil. If possible, wear disposable gloves.

6. Use the correct type and size of tools to avoid damaging fasteners.

7. Keep tools clean and in good condition. Replace or repair worn or damaged equipment.

8. When loosening a tight fastener, consider what would happen if the tool slips.

9. When replacing fasteners, make sure the new fasteners are the same size and strength as the original ones.

10. Keep the work area clean and organized.

11. Wear eye protection *any time* the safety of the eyes is in question. This includes procedures that involve drilling, grinding, hammering, compressed air and chemicals.

12. Wear the correct clothing for the job. Tie up or cover long hair so it does not get caught in moving equipment.

13. Do not carry sharp tools in clothing pockets.

14. Always have an approved fire extinguisher available. Make sure it is rated for gasoline (Class B) and electrical (Class C) fires.

15. Do not use compressed air to clean clothes, the motorcycle or the work area. Debris may be blown into eyes or skin. *Never* direct compressed air at any-

one. Do not allow children to use or play with any compressed air equipment.

16. When using compressed air to dry rotating parts, hold the part so it does not rotate. Do not allow the force of the air to spin the part. The air jet is capable of rotating parts at extreme speed, which may damage the part. The part may disintegrate and cause injury.

17. Do not inhale the dust created by brake pad and clutch wear. These particles may contain asbestos. In addition, some types of insulating materials and gaskets may contain asbestos. Inhaling asbestos particles is hazardous to health.

18. Never work on the motorcycle while someone is working under it.

19. When placing the motorcycle on a stand, make sure it is secure before walking away or working under it.

Handling Gasoline Safely

Many people forget gasoline is hazardous because it is so common. Gasoline is a volatile flammable liquid and is one of the most dangerous items in the shop. Keep in mind when working on the machine, gasoline is always present in the fuel tank, fuel line and throttle body. To avoid an accident when work-

ing on or around the fuel system, carefully observe the following precautions:

1. *Never* use gasoline to clean parts. Refer to *Cleaning Parts* in this section.
2. When working on the fuel system, work outside or in a well-ventilated area.
3. Do not add fuel to the fuel tank or service the fuel system while the motorcycle is near open flames, sparks or where someone is smoking. Gasoline vapor is heavier than air; it collects in low areas and is more easily ignited than liquid gasoline.
4. Allow the engine to cool completely before working on any fuel system component.
5. Store gasoline in an approved storage container.
6. Immediately wipe up spilled gasoline with rags. Store the rags in a metal container with a lid until they can be properly disposed of, or place them outside in a safe place for the fuel to evaporate.
7. Do not pour water onto a gasoline fire. Water spreads the fire and makes it more difficult to put out. Use a class B, BC or ABC fire extinguisher to extinguish the fire.
8. Always turn off the engine before refueling. Do not spill fuel onto the engine or exhaust system. Do not overfill the fuel tank. Leave an air space at the top of the tank to allow room for the fuel to expand due to temperature fluctuations.

Cleaning Parts

Cleaning parts can be a tedious job. However, with the proper supplies the task can be much easier. Many types of chemical cleaners and solvents are available for shop use. Cleaning parts is an important part of a successful repair. Note the following:

1. Observe the product label before using any chemical. Note if it is poisonous and/or flammable.
2. Do not mix cleaning solvent types unless called for. If mixing chemicals is required, measure the proper amounts according to the manufacturer.
3. Work in a well-ventilated area.

4. Wear chemical-resistant gloves.
5. Wear safety glasses.
6. Wear a vapor respirator if the instructions call for it.
7. Wash your hands and arms thoroughly after cleaning parts.
8. Keep chemical products away from children and pets.
9. Thoroughly clean all oil, grease and cleaner residue from any part that must be heated.
10. Use a nylon brush when cleaning parts. Metal brushes may cause a spark.
11. When using a parts washer, only use the solvent recommended by the manufacturer. Make sure the parts washer is equipped with a metal lid that will lower in case of fire.

Warning Labels

The motorcycle may be equipped with labels affixed to various locations. Refer to these labels for safety, operating and service instructions. Refer to owner's manual for label description and location. If a label(s) is missing, contact a dealership for a replacement(s).

SERIAL NUMBERS

Serial numbers are located on the frame, engine, transmission and carburetor or throttle body. Record these numbers in the *Quick Reference Data* section in the front of the manual. Have these numbers available when ordering parts.

The vehicle identification number (VIN) is located on the right frame downtube (**Figure 1**). The frame serial number (**Figure 2**) is stamped into the right side of the steering head.

The engine serial number (**Figure 3**) is stamped into a raised pad on the rear of the engine.

FASTENERS

> *WARNING*
> *Do not install fasteners with a strength classification lower than the originals. Doing so may cause equipment failure and/or damage.*

> *CAUTION*
> *Make sure fasteners are not mismatched or cross-threaded by starting all fasteners by hand. If a fastener is hard to start or turn, determine the cause before tightening. Inspect unidentified fasteners carefully.*

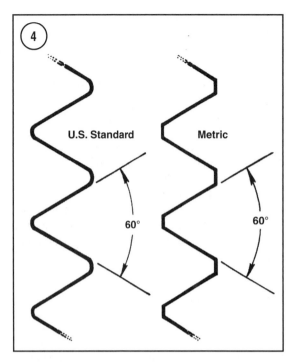

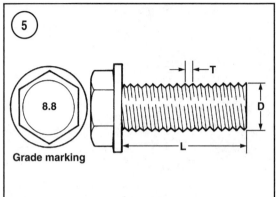

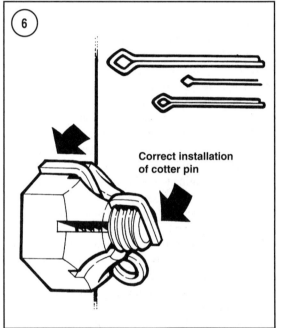

Threaded Fasteners

Tighten most threaded fasteners by turning them clockwise (right-hand threads). If the normal rotation of the component would loosen the fastener, it may have left-hand threads. If a left-hand threaded fastener is used, it is noted in the text.

Two dimensions are required to match the thread size of the fastener: the number of threads in a given distance and the outside diameter of the threads. The measurement across two flats on a nut or bolt indicates the wrench size.

The models covered in this manual use metric fasteners (**Figure 4**). Metric fasteners are classified by their length (L, **Figure 5**), diameter (D) and distance between thread crests (pitch) (T). The numbers, 8-1.25 × 130, may identify a typical bolt. This indicates the bolt has a diameter of 8 mm, the distance between thread crests is 1.25 mm and the length is 130 mm. The internal diameter and the thread pitch identify nuts.

If there is a number on the top of a metric fastener (**Figure 5**), this indicates the strength grade. Higher numbers are stronger. Typically, unnumbered fasteners are the weakest.

Torque Specifications

To ensure a successful repair, install and tighten fasteners as specified. An accurate torque wrench is necessary to perform many of the procedures.

Torque specifications are in the text and/or tables for most fasteners. If a fastener does not have a man-ufacturer provided specification, refer to **Table 5** at the end of this chapter for torque recommendations. Refer to *Threaded Fasteners* in this section to determine the fastener size. Refer to *Tools* in this chapter for torque wrench information.

Self-Locking Fasteners

Several types of bolts, screws and nuts incorporate a system to create interference between the fasteners. The most common types are the nylon insert nut or a dry adhesive coating on the threads of a bolt.

Self-locking fasteners provide increased holding strength due to their vibration resistance. Generally, self-locking fasteners should not be reused. The locking materials are distorted after the initial installation and removal. If necessary, discard and replace self-locking fasteners after removing them. Do not install standard fasteners in place of self-locking fasteners.

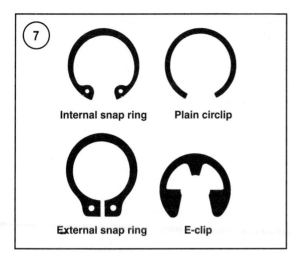

Internal snap ring   Plain circlip

External snap ring   E-clip

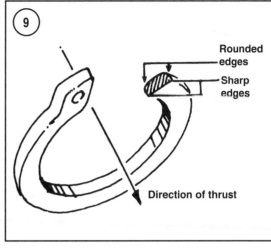

Rounded edges

Sharp edges

Direction of thrust

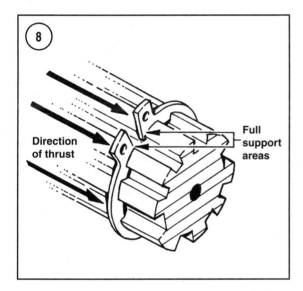

Direction of thrust

Full support areas

Washers

Typically, washers are either flat washers or lockwashers. Flat washers are discs with a hole to fit a screw or bolt. Lockwashers are split rings used to prevent a fastener from working loose. When tightened, they tension the fastener. Flat washers can act as spacers and/or seals, or can help distribute fastener load to prevent component damage. Make sure lockwashers are installed in the correct locations, as they can damage soft material surfaces.

As with fasteners, when replacing washers make sure the replacements are of the same design and quality as the originals.

Cotter Pins

A cotter pin is a split metal pin inserted into a hole or slot to prevent a fastener from loosening. A common place to use a cotter pin is with a castellated (slotted) nut on the rear axle. When installing a cotter pin, make sure the diameter and length is correct for the hole in the fastener. After correctly tightening the fastener and aligning the holes, insert the cotter pin through the hole and bend the ends over the fastener (**Figure 6**). Unless instructed, never loosen a tightened fastener to align the holes. If the holes do not align, tighten the fastener just enough to achieve alignment.

Snap Rings

Snap rings (**Figure 7**) are circular-shaped metal retaining clips. They are required to secure parts and gears in place on parts such as shafts, pins or rods. External snap rings are used to retain items on shafts. Internal type snap rings secure parts within housing bores. In some applications, in addition to securing the component(s), snap rings of varying thickness also determine endplay. These are often called selective snap rings.

Snap rings can be machined and stamped-type snap rings. Machined snap rings (**Figure 8**) can be installed in either direction, because both faces have sharp edges. Stamped snap rings (**Figure 9**) have a sharp and a round edge. When installing a stamped snap ring in a thrust application, it typically must be installed with the sharp edge facing away from the part producing the thrust.

Observe the following when installing snap rings:
1. Wear eye protection when removing and installing snap rings.
2. Remove and install snap rings with snap ring pliers. Refer to *Tools* in this chapter.
3. In some applications, it may be necessary to replace snap rings after removing them.
4. Compress or expand snap rings just enough to install them. If overly expanded, they lose their retaining ability.
5. After installing a snap ring, make sure it seats completely.

E-Clips

E-clips are required in some applications to secure rod and shaft components. Remove E-clips with a flat blade screwdriver by prying between the shaft and E-clip. To install an E-clip, center it over the shaft groove and push or tap it into place.

SHOP SUPPLIES

Lubricants and Fluids

The following section describes the types of lubricants most often required. Make sure to follow the manufacturer's recommendations for lubricant types.

Engine oils

Engine oil for four-stroke motorcycle engines is classified by three standards: the American Petroleum Institute (API) service classification, the Society of Automotive Engineers (SAE) viscosity rating and the Japanese Automobile Standards Organization (JASO) T 903 Standard rating. Always use the oil recommended by the manufacturer.

The API service classification indicates the oil meets specific lubrication standards. The first letter in the classification *S* indicates that the oil is for gasoline engines. The second letter indicates the standard the oil satisfies. Viscosity is an indication of the oil's thickness. Thin oils have a lower number while thick oils have a higher number. Engine oils fall into the 5- to 50-weight range for single-grade oils. Multigrade oils are identified by a *W* after the first number, which indicates the low-temperature viscosity.

JASO classifications are: MA (high friction applications) and MB (low friction applications). Only oil that has passed JASO standards can carry the JASO certification label.

The manufacturer recommends SF or SG oil with an SAE viscosity rating of 10W-40 for the models covered in this manual.

Grease

Grease is lubricating oil with thickening agents added to it. Grease maintains its lubricating qualities better than oil on long, strenuous rides. Furthermore, water does not wash grease off parts as easily as it does oil.

The National Lubricating Grease Institute (NLGI) grades grease. Grades range from No. 000 to No. 6, with No. 6 being the thickest. Typical multipurpose grease is NLGI No. 2. For specific applications, manufacturers may recommend water-resistant type grease or one with an additive such as molybdenum disulfide (MoS_2).

When grease is called for in a procedure, unless otherwise indicated, use Suzuki Super Grease A (part No. 99000-25030) or an equivalent water-resistant, lithium-based grease.

If a procedure calls for moly oil, use a 50:50 mixture of engine oil and Suzuki Moly Paste (part No. 99000-25140).

Brake fluid

Brake fluid is a hydraulic fluid used to transmit hydraulic pressure (force) to the wheel brakes. The Department of Transportation (DOT) classifies brake fluid and the classification is on the fluid container.

When adding brake fluid, only use the fluid recommended by the manufacturer. All models covered in this manual call for DOT 4 brake fluid in both the brake and clutch systems.

Do not mix brake fluid types or classifications. Silicone-based (DOT 5) fluid is not compatible with other types or in systems it was not designed for.

Brake fluid will damage any plastic, painted or plated surface it contacts. Use extreme care when working with brake fluid and wash any spills immediately with soap and water.

Hydraulic brake systems require clean and moisture free brake fluid. Never reuse brake fluid. Keep containers and reservoirs properly sealed.

Cleaning Solvents and Degreasers

Many chemicals are available to remove oil, grease and other residue from the motorcycle. Note all use and disposal recommendations before using any cleaning solvent. Refer to *Safety* in this chapter.

Use brake parts cleaner to clean brake system components. Brake parts cleaner leaves no residue. Use electrical contact cleaner to clean electrical connections and components without leaving any residue. Carburetor cleaner is a powerful solvent used to remove fuel deposits and varnish from fuel system components. Use this cleaner carefully, as it may damage finishes.

Generally, use degreasers to remove heavy grease accumulation from engine and frame components. Make sure the degreaser is compatible with rubber/plastic components and will not damage finishes.

Gasket Sealant

Sealant can be used in combination with a gasket or seal. In other applications, such as between crankcase halves, only sealant is required. Follow the manufacturer's recommendation for sealant type and application. Use extreme care if choosing a sealant other than the type originally recommended. Before applying any sealant, clean all old gasket residue from the mating surfaces. Remove all gasket material from blind threaded holes to avoid inaccurate bolt torque. Clean mating surfaces with an aerosol parts cleaner and a lint-free cloth to ensure the application area is clean.

Refer to the following sealant recommendations for the models covered in this manual:
1. Suzuki Bond 1207B (part No. 99000-31140): a silicon-based sealant for vibration-prone, high-heat applications.
2. Suzuki Bond 1215 (part No. 99000-31110): UK, Australia and Europe models.
3. Suzuki Bond 1216 (part No. 99104-31160): a silicon-based sealant for high-crankcase pressure applications.

Gasket Remover

Aerosol gasket remover can help remove stubborn gaskets. This product can speed up the removal process and prevent damage to the mating surface that may be caused by using a scraping tool. Most gasket removers are caustic. Follow the gasket remover manufacturer's instructions for use.

Threadlock Compound

A threadlock compound is a fluid applied to the threads of fasteners. When the fluid dries it becomes a solid filler between the threads. This makes it difficult for the fastener to work loose from vibration or heat expansion and contraction. Some threadlock compounds also act as fluid seals.

Before applying a threadlock compound, remove any old compound from both thread areas and clean them with aerosol parts cleaner. Use the compound sparingly. Excess fluid can run into adjoining parts.

Threadlock compounds are available for various applications depending on their strength and temperature specifications. Follow the manufacturer's recommendations and always use the correct compound or its equivalent.

Refer to the following compound recommendations and descriptions for the models covered in this manual:
1. Suzuki Thread Lock Super 1303 (part No. 99000-32030): a high-strength, retaining type compound.
2. Suzuki Thread Lock 1333B (part No. 99000-32020): a medium-strength, bearing and stud lock.
3. Suzuki Thread Lock Super 1322 (part No. 99000-32110) UK, Europe and Australia models.

4. Suzuki Thread Lock 1342 (part No. 99000-32050): low-strength compound recommended for frequently removed parts.
5. Suzuki Thread Lock Super 1360 (part No. 99000-32130): medium-strength, high temperature compound.

TOOLS

Most of the procedures in this manual can be performed with hand tools and test equipment familiar to the home mechanic. Always use the correct tools for the job at hand. Keep tools organized and clean. Store them in a tool chest with related tools organized together.

Quality tools are essential and a good investment. Look for tools made from high-strength alloy steel that are light, easy to use and wear resistant. A polished working surface without sharp edges makes the tool comfortable to use and easy-to-clean.

Some of the procedures in this manual specify special tools. In many cases, the tool is illustrated in use. Those with a large tool kit may be able to use a suitable substitute or fabricate a replacement. However, in some cases, the specialized equipment or expertise may make it impractical for the home mechanic to attempt the procedure. When necessary, such operations come with the recommendation to have a dealership or specialist perform the task. It may be less expensive to have a professional perform these jobs, especially when considering the cost of equipment. Each person will have to evaluate his or her unique circumstance to determine a course of action.

When purchasing tools, consider the tool's potential frequency of use. If you are just starting to build a tool kit, consider purchasing a basic tool set from a quality tool supplier. These sets are available in many tool combinations and offer substantial savings when compared to individually purchased tools. As work experience grows and tasks become more complicated, add specialized tools.

The tool manufacturer's part number is provided for many of the tools mentioned in this manual. These part numbers are correct at the time of first edition publication. The publisher cannot guarantee the part numbers or tools listed in this manual will be available in the future. Check with a dealership before ordering tools.

Screwdrivers

Screwdrivers of various lengths and types are mandatory for the simplest tool kit. The two basic types are the slotted tip (flat blade) and the Phillips tip. These are available in sets that often include an assortment of tip sizes and shaft lengths.

Make sure the size of the tip conforms to the size and shape of the fastener. Use them only for driving screws. Never use a screwdriver for prying or chiseling metal. Repair or replace worn or damaged screwdrivers. A worn tip may damage the fastener, making it difficult to remove.

Phillips-head screws are often damaged by incorrectly fitting screwdrivers. Quality Phillips screwdrivers are manufactured with their crosshead tip machined to Phillips Screw Company specifications. Poor quality or damaged Phillips screwdrivers can back out (camout) and round over the screw head. In addition, weak or soft screw materials can make removal difficult.

An effective screwdriver for Phillips screws is the ACR Phillips II screwdriver. Anti-camout ribs on the driving faces or flutes of the screwdriver's tip (**Figure 10**) improve the driver-to-fastener grip. ACR Phillips II screwdrivers are designed for ACR Phillips II screws, but they work well on all common Phillips screws. ACR Phillips II screwdrivers are available in different tip sizes and interchangeable bits to fit screwdriver bit holders.

Another way to prevent camout and to increase the grip of a Phillips screwdriver is to apply valve grinding compound or Permatex Screw & Socket Gripper onto the screwdriver tip. After loosening/tightening the screw, clean the screw recess to prevent possible contamination.

Wrenches

Box-end, open-end and combination wrenches (**Figure 11**) are available in a variety of types and sizes.

The number stamped on the wrench refers to the distance between the work areas. This size must match the size of the fastener head.

The box-end wrench is an excellent tool because it grips the fastener on all sides. This reduces the chance of the tool slipping. The box-end wrench is designed with either a 6- or 12-point opening. For stubborn or damaged fasteners, the 6-point provides superior holding because it contacts the fastener across a wider area at all six edges. For general use, the 12-point works well. It allows the wrench to be removed and reinstalled without moving the handle over such a wide arc.

An open-end wrench is fast and works best in areas with limited overhead access. It contacts the fastener at only two points and is subject to slipping if under heavy force, or if the tool or fastener is worn. A box-end wrench is preferred in most instances, especially when breaking loose and applying the final tightness to a fastener.

The combination wrench has a box-end on one end and an open-end on the other. This combination makes it a convenient tool.

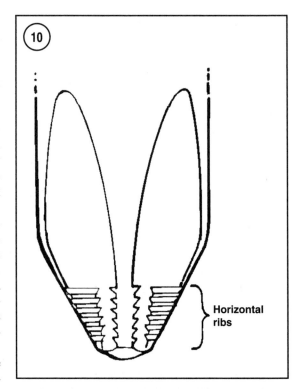

Horizontal ribs

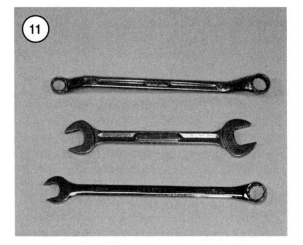

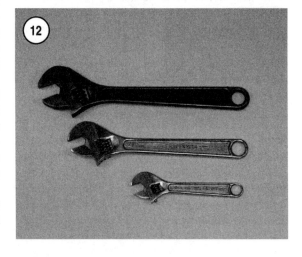

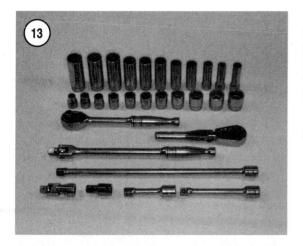

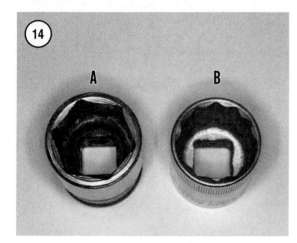

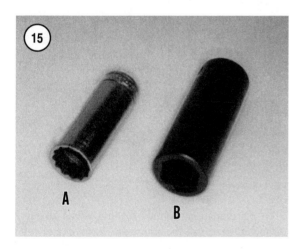

Adjustable wrenches contact the fastener at only two points, which makes them more subject to slipping off the fastener. Because one jaw is adjustable and may become loose, this shortcoming is aggravated. Make certain the solid jaw is the one transmitting the force.

Socket Wrenches, Ratchets and Handles

WARNING
Do not use hand sockets with air or impact tools because they may shatter and cause injury. Always wear eye protection when using impact or air tools.

Sockets that attach to a ratchet handle (**Figure 13**) are available with 6-point (A, **Figure 14**) or 12-point (B) openings and different drive sizes. The drive size indicates the size of the square hole that accepts the ratchet handle. The number stamped on the socket is the size of the work area and must match the fastener size.

As with wrenches, a 6-point socket provides superior-holding ability, while a 12-point socket needs to be moved only half as far to reposition it on the fastener.

Sockets are designated for either hand or impact use. Impact sockets are made of thicker material for more durability. Compare the size and wall thickness of a 19-mm hand socket (A, **Figure 15**) and the 19-mm impact socket (B). Use impact sockets when using an impact driver or air tools. Use hand sockets with hand-driven attachments.

Various handles are available for sockets. Use the speed handle for fast operation. Flexible ratchet heads in varying lengths allow the socket to be turned with varying force and at odd angles. Extension bars allow the socket setup to reach difficult areas. The ratchet is the most versatile. It allows the user to install or remove the nut without removing the socket.

Sockets combined with any number of drivers make them undoubtedly the fastest, safest and most convenient tool for fastener removal and installation.

Impact Drivers

WARNING
Do not use hand sockets with air or impact tools because they may shatter and cause injury. Always wear eye protection when using impact or air tools.

An impact driver provides extra force for removing fasteners by converting the impact of a hammer

Adjustable Wrenches

An adjustable wrench, or Crescent wrench, (**Figure 12**) can fit nearly any nut or bolt head that has clear access around its entire perimeter. An adjustable wrench is best used as a backup wrench to keep a large nut or bolt from turning while the other end is being loosened or tightened with a box-end or socket wrench.

blow into a turning motion. This makes it possible to remove stubborn fasteners without damaging them. Impact drivers and interchangeable bits (**Figure 16**) are available from most tool suppliers. When using a socket with an impact driver, make sure the socket is designed for impact use. Refer to *Socket Wrenches, Ratchets and Handles* in this section.

Allen Wrenches

Use Allen or setscrew wrenches (**Figure 17**) on fasteners with hexagonal recesses in the fastener head. These wrenches are available in L-shaped bar, socket and T-handle types. A metric set is required when working on most motorcycles. Allen bolts are sometimes called socket bolts.

Torque Wrenches

Use a torque wrench with a socket, torque adapter or similar extension to tighten a fastener to a measured torque. Torque wrenches come in several drive sizes (1/4, 3/8, 1/2 and 3/4) and have various methods of reading the torque value. The drive size indicates the size of the square drive that accepts the socket, adapter or extension. Common methods of reading the torque value are the deflecting beam, the dial indicator and the audible click (**Figure 18**).

When choosing a torque wrench consider, the torque range, drive size and accuracy. The torque specifications in this manual provide an indication of the range required.

A torque wrench is a precision tool that must be properly cared for to remain accurate. Store torque wrenches in cases or separate padded drawers within a toolbox. Follow the manufacturer's instructions for their care and calibration.

Torque Adapters

Torque adapters or extensions extend or reduce the reach of a torque wrench. The torque adapter shown in **Figure 19** is used to tighten a fastener that cannot be reached because of the size of the torque wrench head, drive, and socket. If a torque adapter changes the effective lever length (**Figure 20**), the torque reading on the wrench will not equal the actual torque applied to the fastener. It is necessary to recalibrate the torque setting on the wrench to compensate for the change of lever length. When using a torque adapter at a right angle to the drive head, calibration is not required, because the effective length has not changed.

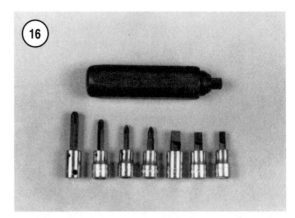

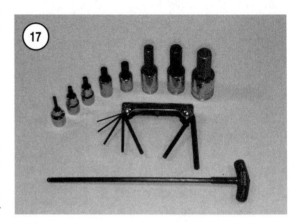

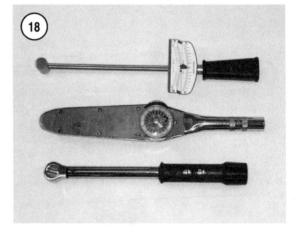

To recalculate a torque reading when using a torque adapter, use the following formula and refer to **Figure 20**:

$$TW = \frac{TA \times L}{L + A}$$

TW is the torque setting or dial reading on the wrench.

TA is the torque specification and the actual amount of torque that is applied to the fastener.

A is the amount that the adapter increases (or in some cases reduces) the effective lever length as measured along the centerline of the torque wrench.

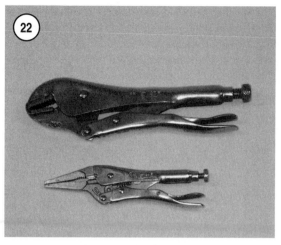

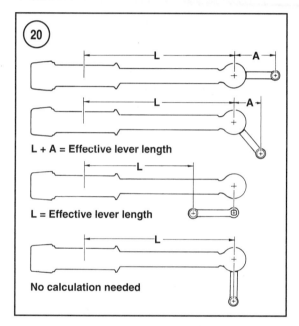

$L = 14$ in.

$$TW = \frac{20 \times 14}{14 + 3} = \frac{280}{17} = 16.5 \text{ ft.-lb.}$$

In this example, set the torque wrench to the calculated torque value of 16.5 ft.-lb. Although the torque wrench is set to 16.5 ft.-lb., the applied torque is 20 ft.-lb. When using a beam-type wrench, tighten the fastener until the pointer aligns with 16.5 ft.-lb.

Pliers

Pliers come in a wide range of types and sizes. Pliers are useful for holding, cutting, bending, and crimping. Do not use them to turn fasteners. **Figure 21** and **Figure 22** show several types of useful pliers. Each design has a specialized function. Slip-joint pliers are general-purpose pliers used for gripping and bending. Diagonal cutting pliers are needed to cut wire and can be used to remove cotter pins. Use needlenose pliers to hold or bend small objects. Locking pliers (**Figure 22**), sometimes called Vise-Grips, are used to hold objects very tightly. They have many uses ranging from holding two parts together, to gripping the end of a broken stud. Use caution when using locking pliers because the sharp jaws damage the objects they hold.

Snap Ring Pliers

> *WARNING*
> *Snap rings can slip and fly off when removing and installing them. In addition, the snap ring pliers' tips may break. Always wear eye protection when using snap ring pliers.*

Snap ring pliers are specialized pliers with tips that fit into the ends of snap rings to remove and install them.

L + A = Effective lever length

L = Effective lever length

No calculation needed

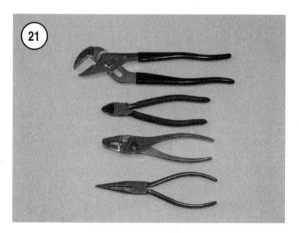

L is the lever length of the wrench as measured from the center of the drive to the center of the grip.

The effective length is the sum of L and A.

Example:

$TA = 20$ ft.-lb.

$A = 3$ in.

Snap ring pliers (**Figure 23**) are available with a fixed action (either internal or external) or convertible (one tool works on both internal and external snap rings). They may have fixed tips or interchangeable ones of various sizes and angles. For general use, select convertible type pliers with interchangeable tips (**Figure 23**).

Hammers

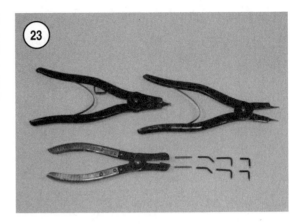

WARNING
Always wear eye protection when using hammers. Make sure the hammer face is in good condition and the handle is not cracked. Select the correct hammer for the job and make sure to strike the object squarely. Do not use the handle or the side of the hammer to strike an object.

Various types of hammers are available to fit a number of applications. Use a ball-peen hammer to strike another tool, such as a punch or chisel. Use soft-faced hammers when a metal object must be struck without damaging it. *Never* use a metal-faced hammer on engine and suspension components because damage occurs in most cases.

MEASURING TOOLS

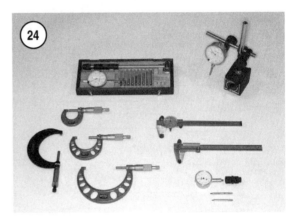

The ability to accurately measure components is essential to perform many of the procedures described in this manual. Equipment is manufactured to close tolerances, and obtaining consistently accurate measurements is essential to determine which components require replacement or further service.

Each type of measuring instrument (**Figure 24**) is designed to measure a dimension with a certain degree of accuracy and within a certain range. When selecting the measuring tool, make sure it is applicable to the task.

As with all tools, measuring tools provide the best results if cared for properly. Improper use can damage the tool and cause inaccurate results. If any measurement is questionable, verify the measurement using another tool. A standard gauge is usually provided with micrometers to check accuracy and calibrate the tool if necessary.

Precision measurements can vary according to the experience of the person taking the measurement. Accurate results are possible only if the mechanic possesses a feel for using the tool. Heavy-handed use of measuring tools produces inaccurate results. Hold the tool gently by the fingertips to easily feel the point at which the tool contacts the object. This

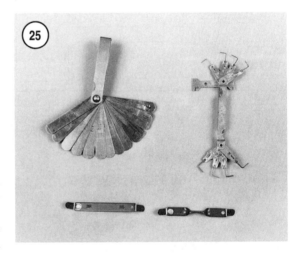

feel for the equipment produces measurements that are more accurate and reduces the risk of damaging the tool or component. Refer to the following subsections for specific measuring tools and their use.

Feeler Gauge

Use feeler, or thickness, gauges (**Figure 25**) for measuring the distance between two surfaces.

A feeler gauge set consists of an assortment of steel strips of graduated thickness. Each blade is marked

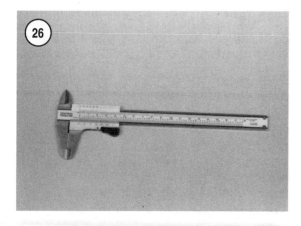

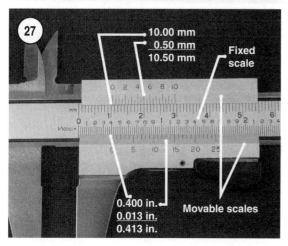

10.00 mm
0.50 mm
10.50 mm

Fixed scale

0.400 in.
0.013 in.
0.413 in.

Movable scales

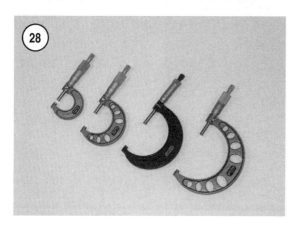

with its thickness. Blades can be of various lengths and angles for different procedures.

A common use for a feeler gauge is to measure valve clearance. Use wire (round) type gauges to measure spark plug gap.

Calipers

Use calipers (**Figure 26**) to obtain inside, outside and depth measurements. Although not as precise as a micrometer, they typically measure to within 0.05

mm (0.001 in.). Most calipers have a range up to 150 mm (6 in.).

Calipers are available in dial, vernier or digital versions. Dial calipers have a dial readout that provides convenient reading. Vernier calipers have marked scales that must be compared to determine the measurement. The digital caliper uses a liquid-crystal display (LCD) to show the measurement.

Properly maintain the measuring surfaces of the caliper. There must not be any dirt or burrs between the tool and the measured object. Never force the caliper to close around an object. Close the caliper around the highest point so it can be removed with a slight drag. Some calipers require calibration. Always refer to the manufacturer's instructions when using a new or unfamiliar caliper.

To read a vernier caliper, refer to **Figure 27**. The fixed scale is marked in 1 mm increments. Ten individual lines on the fixed scale equal 1 cm. The moveable scale is marked in 0.05 mm (hundredth) increments. To obtain a reading, establish the first number by the location of the 0 line on the movable scale in relation to the first line to the left on the fixed scale. In this example, the number is 10 mm. To determine the next number, note which of the lines on the movable scale align with a mark on the fixed scale. A number of lines will seem close, but only one will align exactly. In this case, 0.50 mm is the reading to add to the first number. The result of adding 10 mm and 0.50 mm is a measurement of 10.50 mm.

Micrometers

Use a micrometer for linear measurement. Most of the procedures in this manual call for an outside micrometer to measure the diameter of cylindrical components and material thickness. When combined with a telescoping gauge or small hole gauge, a micrometer can obtain inside diameter measurements.

A micrometer's size indicates the minimum and maximum size of a part it can measure. The usual sizes (**Figure 28**) are 0-25 mm (0-1 in.), 25-50 mm (1-2 in.), 50-75 mm (2-3 in.) and 75-100 mm (3-4 in.).

Micrometers covering a wider range of measurements are available. These use a large frame with interchangeable anvils of various lengths. This type of micrometer makes it more flexible, but its overall size may make it less convenient.

Adjustment

Before using a micrometer, check its adjustment as follows:
1. Clean the anvil and spindle faces.

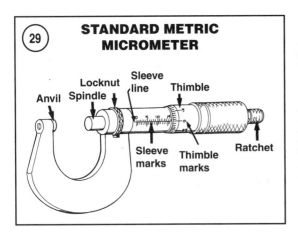

STANDARD METRIC MICROMETER

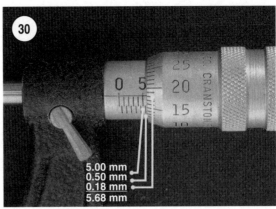

5.00 mm
0.50 mm
0.18 mm
5.68 mm

2A. To check a 0-25 mm or 0-1 in. micrometer:
  a. Turn the thimble until the spindle contacts the anvil. If the micrometer has a ratchet stop, use it to ensure the proper amount of pressure is applied.
  b. If the adjustment is correct, the 0 mark on the thimble aligns exactly with the 0 mark on the sleeve line. If the marks do not align, the micrometer is out of adjustment.
  c. Follow the manufacturer's instructions to adjust the micrometer.

2B. To check a micrometer larger than 25 mm or 1 in., use the standard gauge supplied by the manufacturer. A standard gauge is a steel block, disc or rod that is machined to an exact size.
  a. Place the standard gauge between the spindle and anvil and measure its outside diameter or length. If the micrometer has a ratchet stop, use it to ensure the proper amount of pressure is applied.
  b. If the adjustment is correct, the 0 mark on the thimble aligns exactly with the 0 mark on the sleeve line. If the marks do not align, the micrometer is out of adjustment.
  c. Follow the manufacturer's instructions to adjust the micrometer.

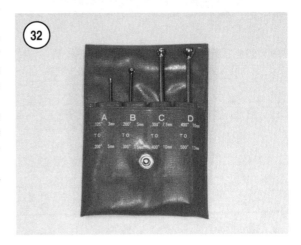

Care

Micrometers are precision instruments. Store and use them as follows:

1. Store micrometers in protective cases or separate padded drawers in a toolbox.

2. When in storage, make sure the spindle and anvil faces do not contact each other or another object. If they do, temperature changes and corrosion may damage the contact faces.

3. Do not clean a micrometer with compressed air. Dirt forced into the tool will cause wear.

4. Lubricate micrometers with a lightweight tool oil to prevent corrosion.

Reading

The standard metric micrometer (**Figure 29**) is accurate to one one-hundredth of a millimeter (0.01 mm). The sleeve line is graduated in millimeter and half millimeter increments. The marks on the upper half of the sleeve line equal 1.00 mm. Each fifth mark above the sleeve line is identified with a number. The number sequence depends on the size of the micrometer. A 0-25 mm micrometer, for example, will have sleeve marks numbered 0 through 25 in 5 mm increments. This numbering sequence continues with

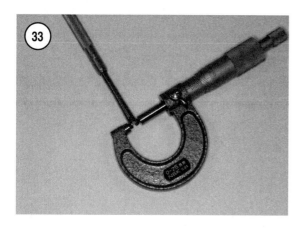

1. Read the upper half of the sleeve line and count the number of lines visible. Each upper line equals 1 mm.

2. See if a half-millimeter line is visible on the lower sleeve line. If so, add 0.50 mm to the reading in Step 1.

3. Read the thimble mark that aligns with the sleeve line. Each thimble mark equals 0.01 mm. If a thimble mark does not align exactly with the sleeve line, estimate the amount between the lines. For accurate readings in two-thousandths of a millimeter (0.002 mm), use a metric vernier micrometer.

4. Add the readings from Steps 1-3.

Telescoping and Small Hole Gauges

Use telescoping gauges (**Figure 31**) and small hole gauges (**Figure 32**) to measure bores. Neither gauge has a scale for direct readings. Use an outside micrometer to determine the reading.

To use a telescoping gauge, select the correct size gauge for the bore. Compress the movable post and carefully insert the gauge into the bore. Carefully move the gauge in the bore to make sure it is centered. Tighten the knurled end of the gauge to hold the movable post in position. Remove the gauge and measure the length of the posts. Telescoping gauges are typically used to measure cylinder bores.

To use a small hole gauge, select the correct size gauge for the bore. Carefully insert the gauge into the bore. Tighten the knurled end of the gauge to carefully expand the gauge fingers to the limit within the bore. Do not overtighten the gauge because there is no built-in release. Excessive tightening can damage the bore surface and the tool. Remove the gauge and measure the outside dimension (**Figure 33**). Small hole gauges are typically used to measure valve guides.

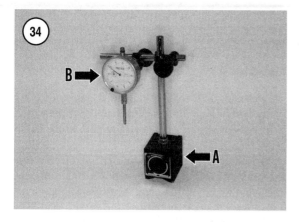

Dial Indicator

A dial indicator (**Figure 34**) is a gauge with a dial face and needle used to measure variations in dimensions and movements. Measuring brake rotor runout is a typical use for a dial indicator.

Dial indicators are available in various ranges and graduations and with three basic types of mounting bases: magnetic (A, **Figure 34**), clamp, or screw-in stud. When purchasing a dial indicator, select one with a continuous dial (B, **Figure 34**).

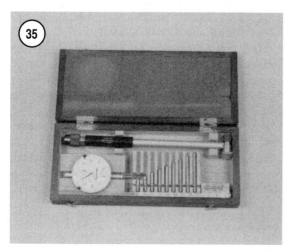

larger micrometers. On all metric micrometers, each mark on the lower half of the sleeve equals 0.50 mm.

The tapered end of the thimble has 50 lines marked around it. Each mark equals 0.01 mm. One complete turn of the thimble aligns its 0 mark with the first line on the lower half of the sleeve line or 0.50 mm.

When reading a metric micrometer, add the number of millimeters and half-millimeters on the sleeve line to the number of one one-hundredth millimeters on the thimble. To read a standard metric micrometer, refer to **Figure 30** and perform the following:

Cylinder Bore Gauge

A cylinder bore gauge is similar to a dial indicator. The gauge set shown in **Figure 35** consists of a dial indicator, handle and different length adapters (anvils) to fit the gauge to various bore sizes. The bore gauge is used to measure bore size, taper and out-of-round. When using a bore gauge, follow the manufacturer's instructions.

Compression Gauge

A compression gauge (**Figure 36**) measures combustion chamber (cylinder) pressure, usually in psi or kg/cm². The gauge adapter is either inserted or screwed into the spark plug hole to obtain the reading. Disable the engine so it does not start and hold the throttle in the wide-open position when performing a compression test.

Multimeter

A multimeter (**Figure 37**) is an essential tool for electrical system diagnosis. The voltage function indicates the voltage applied or available to various electrical components. The ohmmeter function tests circuits for continuity and measures the resistance of a circuit.

Some manufacturers' specifications for electrical components are based on results using a specific test meter. Results may vary if a meter not recommended by the manufacturer is used. Such requirements are noted when applicable.

Each time an analog ohmmeter is used or if the scale is changed, the ohmmeter must be calibrated. Refer to the manufacturer's instructions.

ELECTRICAL SYSTEM FUNDAMENTALS

A thorough study of the many types of electrical systems used in today's motorcycles is beyond the scope of this manual. However, an understanding of voltage, resistance and amperage is necessary to perform basic diagnostic tests.

Refer to Chapter Two for troubleshooting information. Refer to Chapter Nine for specific system test procedures.

Voltage

Voltage is the electrical potential or pressure in an electrical circuit and is expressed in volts. The more pressure (voltage) in a circuit, the more work can be performed.

Direct current (DC) voltage means the electricity flows in one direction. All circuits powered by a battery are DC circuits.

Alternating current (AC) means the electricity flows in one direction momentarily and then switches to the opposite direction. Alternator output is an example of AC voltage. This voltage must be changed

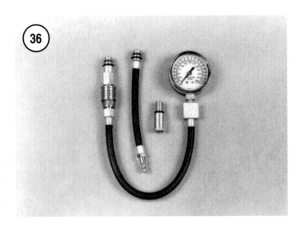

or rectified to direct current to operate in a battery-powered system.

Resistance

Resistance is the opposition to the flow of electricity within a circuit or component. It is measured in ohms. Resistance causes a reduction in available current and voltage.

Resistance is measured in an inactive circuit with an ohmmeter. The ohmmeter sends a small amount of current into the circuit and measures how difficult it is to push the current through the circuit.

An ohmmeter, although useful, is not always a good indicator of a circuit's actual ability under operating conditions. This is because of the low voltage (6-9 volts) the meter uses to test the circuit. The voltage in an ignition coil secondary winding can be several thousand volts. Such high voltage can cause the coil to malfunction, even though it tests acceptable during a resistance test.

Resistance generally increases with temperature. Perform all testing with the component or circuit at room temperature. Resistance tests performed at high temperatures may indicate high resistance readings and cause unnecessary replacement of a component.

Amperage

Amperage is the unit of measurement for the amount of current within a circuit. Current is the actual flow of electricity. The higher the current, the more work can be performed up to a given point. If the current flow exceeds the circuit or component capacity, it will damage the system.

SERVICE METHODS

Most of the procedures in this manual are straightforward and can be performed by anyone reasonably competent with tools. However, consider personal

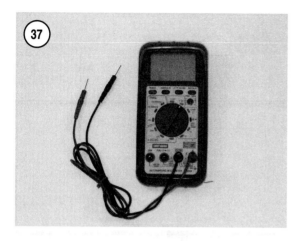

capabilities carefully before attempting any operation involving major disassembly.

1. In this manual, the term *Front* refers to the front of the motorcycle. The front of any component is the end closest to the front of the motorcycle. *Left* and *right* refer to the position of the parts as viewed by the rider sitting on the seat facing forward.

2. Whenever servicing an engine or suspension component, secure the motorcycle in a safe manner.

3. Tag all similar parts for location and mark all mating parts for position. Record the number and thickness of any shims when removing them. Identify parts by placing them in sealed and labeled plastic sandwich bags.

4. Label disconnected wires and connectors with masking tape and a marking pen. Connectors must be reconnected to their mates. Do not rely on memory alone.

5. Protect finished surfaces from physical damage or corrosion. Keep gasoline and other chemicals off painted surfaces.

6. Use penetrating oil on frozen or tight bolts. Avoid using heat where possible. Heat can warp, melt or affect the temper of parts. Heat also damages the finish of paint and plastics.

7. When a part is a press fit or requires a special tool for removal, the information or type of tool is identified in the text. Otherwise, if a part is difficult to remove or install, determine the cause before proceeding.

8. To prevent objects or debris from falling into the engine, cover all openings.

9. Read each procedure thoroughly and compare the illustrations to the actual components before starting the procedure. Perform the procedure in sequence.

10. Recommendations are occasionally made to refer service to a dealership or specialist. In these cases, it may be more economical to have a specialist perform the task.

11. The term *replace* means to discard a defective part and replace it with a new part. *Overhaul* means

to remove, disassemble, inspect, measure, repair and/or replace parts as required to recondition an assembly.

12. Some operations require using a hydraulic press. If a press is not available, have these operations performed by a shop equipped with the necessary equipment. Do not use makeshift equipment that may damage the motorcycle or parts.

CAUTION
Do not direct high-pressure water at steering bearings, fuel hoses, wheel bearings, suspension and electrical components. Water may force grease out of the bearings and possibly damage the seals.

13. Repairs are much faster and easier if the motorcycle is clean before starting work. Degrease the motorcycle with a commercial degreaser; follow the directions on the container for the best results. Clean all parts with cleaning solvent when removing them.

14. If special tools are required, have them available before starting the procedure. When special tools are required, they are described at the beginning of the procedure.

15. Make diagrams of similar-appearing parts. For instance, crankcase bolts are often not the same lengths. Do not rely on memory alone. Carefully laid out parts can become disturbed, making it difficult to reassemble the components correctly.

16. Make sure all shims and washers are reinstalled in the same location and position.

17. Whenever rotating parts contact a stationary part, look for a shim or washer.

18. Use new gaskets if there is any doubt about the condition of old ones.

19. Replace self-locking fasteners. Do not install standard fasteners in place of self-locking ones.

20. Use grease to hold small parts in place if they tend to fall out during assembly. Do not apply grease to electrical or brake components.

Heating Components

WARNING
Wear protective gloves to prevent injury when heating parts.

A heat gun or propane torch is required to disassemble, assemble, remove and install many parts and components in this manual. Read the safety and operating information supplied by the manufacturer of the heat gun or propane torch while also noting the following:

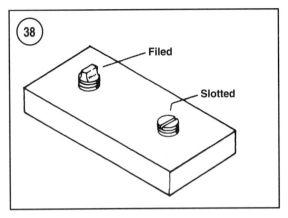

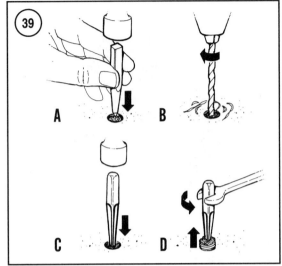

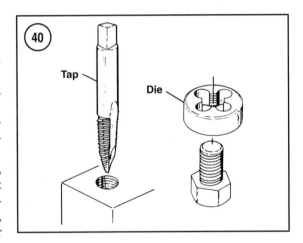

CAUTION
Do not use a welding torch when heating parts in this manual. A welding torch applies excessive heat to a small area very quickly, which can damage parts in a short time.

1. The work should be clean and dry. Wipe up all grease, oil and other fluids from parts.

2. Never use a gas torch near the battery, fuel tank, fuel lines or other flammable materials.

3. Check for leaking or damaged fuel system components. Repair or remove these parts before beginning work.

4. Before heating a part installed on the motorcycle, check areas around the part and those *hidden* that could be damaged or possibly ignite Do not heat surfaces than can be damaged by heat. Shield materials, such as cables and wiring harnesses, near the part or area to be heated.

5. Before heating a part, read the procedure through to see what other tools, such as a hammer and bearing driver, will be required and have them at hand. This will allow you to work quickly while the part is at its optimum temperature.

6. The amount of heat required to loosen or install a critical part is listed in the text. To avoid damaging a part, monitor temperature with heat sticks or an infrared thermometer if possible. Another way, though not as accurate, is to place tiny drops of water on the part. When the water starts to sizzle, bead and jump, the part is hot enough.

7. Keep the heat in motion to prevent overheating.

8. When the temperature is monitored, the careful use and application of the heat should not be injurious to the part. However, before heating other parts not recommended in the text, consider the effects of heat applied to the part.

9. Remove all combustible components and materials from the work area.

10. When using a heat gun, remember that the heat is flameless and can be in excess of 540° C (1000° F).

11. Have an ABC fire extinguisher near the job.

12. Always wear protective goggles and gloves when heating parts.

Removing Frozen Fasteners

If a fastener cannot be removed, several methods may be used to loosen it. First, apply penetrating oil liberally and let it penetrate for 10-15 minutes. Rap the fastener several times with a small hammer. Do not hit it hard enough to cause damage. Reapply the penetrating oil if necessary.

For frozen screws, apply penetrating oil as described. Then insert a screwdriver into the slot and rap the top of the screwdriver with a hammer. This loosens the rust so the screw can be removed in the normal way. If the screw head is too damaged to use this method, grip the head with locking pliers and twist the screw out.

Avoid applying heat unless specifically instructed. Heat may melt, warp or remove the temper from parts.

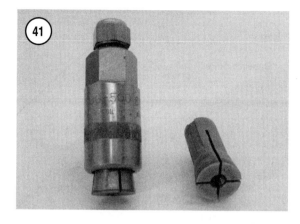

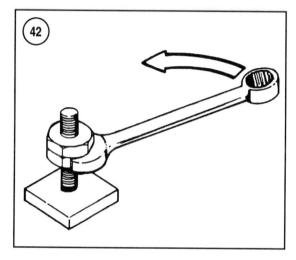

insert. Follow the manufacturer's instructions when installing their insert.

Stud Removal/Installation

A stud removal tool (**Figure 41**) is available from most tool suppliers. This tool makes the removal and installation of studs easier. If one is not available, thread two nuts onto the stud and tighten them against each other. Remove the stud by turning the lower nut (**Figure 42**).

1. Measure the height of the stud above the surface.
2. Thread the stud removal tool onto the stud and tighten it, or thread two nuts onto the stud.
3. Remove the stud by turning the stud remover or the lower nut.
4. Remove any threadlock compound from the threaded hole. Clean the threads with an aerosol parts cleaner.
5. Install the stud removal tool onto the new stud, or thread two nuts onto the stud.
6. Apply threadlock compound to the threads of the stud.
7. Install the stud and tighten with the stud removal tool or the top nut.
8. Install the stud to the height noted in Step 1 or its torque specification.
9. Remove the stud removal tool or the two nuts.

Removing Broken Fasteners

If the head breaks off a screw or bolt, several methods are available for removing the remaining portion. If a large portion of the remainder projects out, try gripping it with locking pliers. If the projecting portion is too small, file it to fit a wrench or cut a slot in it to fit a screwdriver (**Figure 38**).

If the head breaks off flush, use a screw extractor. To do this, center punch the exact center of the remaining portion of the screw or bolt (A, **Figure 39**). Drill a small hole into the screw (B, **Figure 39**) and tap the extractor into the hole (C). Back the screw out with a wrench on the extractor (D, **Figure 39**).

Repairing Damaged Threads

Occasionally, threads are stripped through carelessness or impact damage. Often the threads can be repaired by running a tap (for internal threads on nuts) or die (for external threads on bolts) through the threads (**Figure 40**). To clean or repair spark plug threads, use a spark plug tap.

If an internal thread is damaged, it may be necessary to install a Helicoil or some other type of thread

Removing Hoses

When removing stubborn hoses, do not exert excessive force on the hose or fitting. Remove the hose clamp and carefully insert a small screwdriver or pick tool between the fitting and hose. Apply a spray lubricant under the hose and carefully twist the hose off the fitting. Clean any corrosion or rubber hose material from the fitting with a wire brush. Clean the inside of the hose thoroughly. Do not use any lubricant when installing the hose (new or old). The lubricant may allow the hose to come off the fitting, even with the clamp secure.

Bearings

Bearings are precision parts and require proper lubrication and, in some cases, maintenance. Replace damaged bearings immediately. While bearings are normally removed only when damaged, there may be times when it is necessary to remove a bearing in good condition. However, improper bearing removal can damage the bearing and possibly the shaft or case.

Bearing replacement procedures are included in individual chapters where applicable; however, use the following procedures as a guideline.

Removal

1. When using a puller to remove a bearing from a shaft, take care that the shaft is not damaged. Always place a piece of metal between the end of the shaft and the puller screw. In addition, place the puller arms next to the inner bearing race. See **Figure 43**.

2. When using a hammer to remove a bearing from a shaft, do not strike the hammer directly against the shaft. Instead, use a brass or aluminum spacer between the hammer and shaft (**Figure 44**). Make sure to support both bearing races with wooden blocks as shown.

3. The ideal method of bearing removal is with a hydraulic press. Note the following when using a press:

   a. Always support the inner and outer bearing races with a suitable size wooden or aluminum spacer (**Figure 45**). If only the outer race is supported, pressure applied against the balls and/or the inner race will damage them.

   b. Always make sure the press ram (**Figure 45**) aligns with the center of the shaft. If the ram is not centered, it may damage the bearing and/or shaft.

   c. The moment the shaft is free of the bearing, it drops to the floor. Secure or hold the shaft to prevent it from falling.

Installation

Unless otherwise specified, install bearings with the manufacturer's mark or number facing outward.

1. When installing a bearing into a housing, apply pressure to the *outer* bearing race (**Figure 46**). When installing a bearing onto a shaft, apply pressure to the *inner* bearing race (**Figure 47**).

2. When installing a bearing as described in Step 1, always use some type of driver. Never strike the bearing directly with a hammer or it will damage the bearing. When installing a bearing, use a piece of pipe or a driver with a diameter that matches the bearing inner race. **Figure 48** shows the correct way to use a driver and hammer to install a bearing.

3. Step 1 describes how to install a bearing into a case half or over a shaft. However, when installing a bearing over a shaft and into a housing at the same time, a tight fit is required for both outer and inner bearing races. In this situation, install a spacer underneath the driver tool so pressure is applied evenly across both races. Refer to **Figure 48**. If the outer race is not supported as shown, the balls will push against the outer bearing race and damage it.

Interference fit

1. Follow this procedure when installing a bearing over a shaft. When a tight fit is required, the bear-

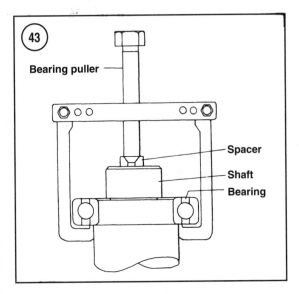

43

Bearing puller

Spacer

Shaft

Bearing

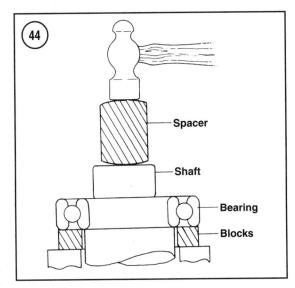

44

Spacer

Shaft

Bearing

Blocks

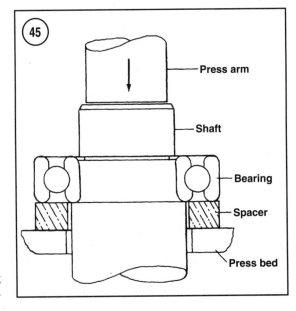

45

Press arm

Shaft

Bearing

Spacer

Press bed

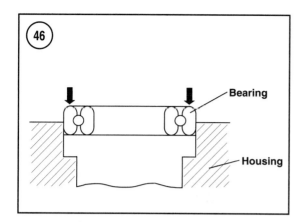

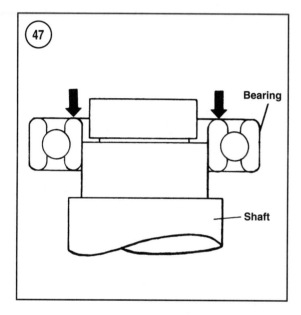

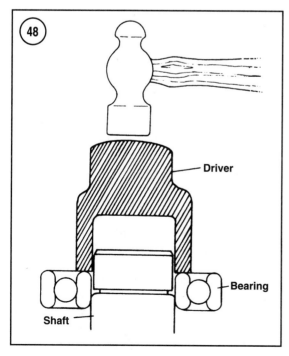

ing inside diameter is smaller than the shaft. In this case, driving the bearing onto the shaft using normal methods may cause bearing damage. Instead, heat the bearing before installation. Note the following:

a. Secure the shaft so it is ready for bearing installation.

b. Clean all residues from the bearing surface of the shaft. Remove burrs with a file or sandpaper.

c. Fill a suitable pot or beaker with clean mineral oil. Place a thermometer rated above 120° C (248° F) in the oil. Support the thermometer so it does not rest on the bottom or side of the pot.

d. Remove the bearing from its wrapper and secure it with a piece of heavy wire bent to hold it in the pot. Hang the bearing in the pot so it does not touch the bottom or sides of the pot.

e. Turn the heat on and monitor the thermometer. When the oil temperature rises to approximately 120° C (248° F), remove the bearing from the pot and quickly install it. If necessary, place a socket on the inner bearing race and tap the bearing into place. As the bearing chills, it tightens on the shaft, so installation must be done quickly. Make sure the bearing is installed completely.

2. Follow this step when installing a bearing into a housing. Bearings are generally installed in a housing with a slight interference fit. Driving the bearing into the housing using normal methods may damage the housing or cause bearing damage. Instead, heat the housing before the bearing is installed. Note the following:

a. Wash the housing thoroughly with detergent and water. Rinse and rewash as required to remove all traces of oil and other chemical deposits.

b. Heat the housing to approximately 100° C (212° F) in an oven or on a hot plate. Do not heat the housing with a propane or acetylene torch. To check the temperature, fling tiny drops of water on the housing. If they sizzle and evaporate immediately, the temperature is correct. Heat only one housing at a time.

c. Remove the housing from the oven or hot plate, and hold onto the housing with welding gloves.

d. Hold the housing with the bearing side down and tap the bearing out. Repeat for all bearings in the housing.

e. Before heating the bearing housing, place the new bearing in a freezer if possible. Chilling a bearing slightly reduces its outside diameter while the heated bearing housing assembly is slightly larger due to heat expansion. This makes bearing installation easier.

f. While the housing is still hot, install the new bearing(s) into the housing. Install the bearings by hand, if possible. If necessary, lightly tap the bearing(s) into the housing with a driver placed on the outer bearing race (**Figure 49**). Do not install new bearings by driving on the inner bearing race. Install the bearing until it seats completely.

Seal Replacement

Seals (**Figure 50**) contain oil, water, grease or combustion gasses in a housing or shaft. Improperly removing a seal can damage the housing or shaft. Improperly installing the seal can damage the seal. Note the following:

1. Prying is generally the easiest and most effective method of removing a seal from the housing. However, always place a rag underneath the pry tool (**Figure 51**) to prevent damage to the housing. Note the seal's installed depth or if it is installed flush.

2. Pack waterproof grease into the seal lips before the seal is installed.

3. In most cases, install seals with the manufacturer's numbers or marks facing out.

4. Install seals with a socket or driver placed on the outside of the seal as shown in **Figure 52**. Drive the seal squarely into the housing until it is to the correct depth or flush (**Figure 53**) as noted during removal. Never install a seal by hitting against the top of it with a hammer.

STORAGE

Several months of non-use can cause a general deterioration of the motorcycle. This is especially true in areas of extreme temperature variations. This deterioration can be minimized with careful preparation for storage. A properly stored motorcycle is much easier to return to service.

Storage Area Selection

When selecting a storage area, consider the following:

1. The storage area must be dry. A heated area is best but not necessary. It should be insulated to minimize extreme temperature variations.

2. If the building has large window areas, mask them to keep sunlight off the motorcycle.

3. Avoid buildings in industrial areas where corrosive emissions may be present. Avoid areas close to saltwater.

4. Consider the area's risk of fire, theft or vandalism. Check with an insurer regarding motorcycle coverage while in storage.

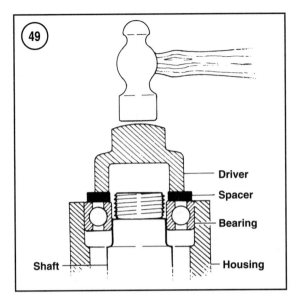

Driver
Spacer
Bearing
Shaft
Housing

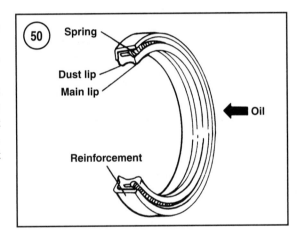

Spring
Dust lip
Main lip
Oil
Reinforcement

Preparing the Motorcycle for Storage

The amount of preparation a motorcycle should undergo before storage depends upon the expected length of non-use, storage area conditions and personal preference. Consider the following list the minimum requirement.

1. Wash the motorcycle thoroughly. Make sure all dirt, mud and road debris is removed.

2. Start the engine and allow it to reach operating temperature. Drain the engine oil regardless of the riding time since the last service. Fill the engine with the recommended type and quantity of oil.

3. Fill the fuel tank with fuel mixed with a fuel stabilizer. Mix the fuel and stabilizer in the ratio recommended by the stabilizer manufacturer. Run the engine for a few minutes so the stabilized fuel can enter the fuel injection system.

4. Remove the spark plugs and pour a tablespoon (45-60 ml) of engine oil into the cylinders. Place a rag over the openings and slowly turn the engine over to distribute the oil. Reinstall the spark plugs.

5. Remove the battery. Store the battery in a cool and dry location. Charge the battery once a month.
6. Cover the muffler and intake openings.
7. Apply a protective substance to the plastic and rubber components. Make sure to follow the manufacturer's instructions for each type of product being used.

8. Place the motorcycle on its centerstand. Rotate the front tire periodically to prevent a flat spot from developing and damaging the tire.
9. Cover the motorcycle with old bed sheets or something similar. Do not cover it with any plastic material that traps moisture.

Returning the Motorcycle to Service

The amount of service required when returning a motorcycle to service after storage depends on the length of non-use and storage conditions. In addition to performing the reverse of the above procedure, make sure the brakes, clutch, throttle and engine stop switch all work properly before operating the motorcycle. Refer to Chapter Three and evaluate the maintenance schedule to determine which areas require service.

Table 1 VEHICLE DIMENSIONS AND WEIGHT (APPROXIMATE)

Overall length	2525 mm (99.4 in.)
Overall width	
1998-2004 models	965 mm (38.0 in.)
2005-on models	
Australia	995 mm (39.2 in.)
All 2005-on models except Australia	1020 mm (40.2 in.)
Overall height (VL1500 and C90 models)	
1998-2004	1165 mm (45.9 in.)
2005-on	1125 mm (44.3 in.)
Overall height (C90T and C90SE models)	
2006-on	1422 mm (56.0 in.)
Seat height	700 mm (27.6 in.)
Wheelbase	1700 mm (66.9 in.)
Ground clearance	
1998-2004 models	145 mm (5.7 in.)
2005-on models	140 mm (5.5 in.)
Dry weight (VL1500 and C90 models)	
1998-2001	296 kg (653 lb.)
2002-2004	299 kg (659 lb.)
2005-on	302 kg (666 lb.)
Dry weight (C90T and C90SE models)	
2006-on	316 kg (697 lb.)

Table 2 DECIMAL AND METRIC EQUIVALENTS

mm	in.	Nearest fraction	mm	in.	Nearest fraction
1	0.0394	1/32	26	1.0236	1 1/32
2	0.0787	3/32	27	1.0630	1 1/16
3	0.1181	1/8	28	1.1024	1 3/32
4	0.1575	5/32	29	1.1417	1 5/32
5	0.1969	3/16	30	1.1811	1 3/16
6	0.2362	1/4	31	1.2205	1 7/32
7	0.2756	9/32	32	1.2598	1 1/4
8	0.3150	5/16	33	1.2992	1 5/16
9	0.3543	11/32	34	1.3386	1 11/32
10	0.3937	13/32	35	1.3780	1 3/8
11	0.4331	7/16	36	1.4173	1 13/32
12	0.4724	15/32	37	1.4567	1 15/32
13	0.5118	1/2	38	1.4961	1 1/2
14	0.5512	9/16	39	1.5354	1 17/32
15	0.5906	19/32	40	1.5748	1 9/16
16	0.6299	5/8	41	1.6142	1 5/8
17	0.6693	21/32	42	1.6535	1 21/32
18	0.7087	23/32	43	1.6929	1 11/16
19	0.7480	3/4	44	1.7323	1 23/32
20	0.7874	25/32	45	1.7717	1 25/32
21	0.8268	13/16	46	1.8110	1 13/16
22	0.8661	7/8	47	1.8504	1 27/32
23	0.9055	29/32	48	1.8898	1 7/8
24	0.9449	15/16	49	1.9291	1 15/16
25	0.9843	31/32	50	1.9685	1 31/32

Table 3 CONVERSION FORMULAS

Multiply:	By:	To get the equivalent of:
Length		
Inches	25.4	Millimeter
Inches	2.54	Centimeter
Miles	1.609	Kilometer
Feet	0.3048	Meter
Millimeter	0.03937	Inches
Centimeter	0.3937	Inches
Kilometer	0.6214	Mile
Meter	3.281	Feet
Fluid volume		
U.S. quarts	0.9463	Liters
U.S. gallons	3.785	Liters
U.S. ounces	29.573529	Milliliters
Liters	0.2641721	U.S. gallons
Liters	1.0566882	U.S. quarts
Liters	33.814023	U.S. ounces
Milliliters	0.033814	U.S. ounces
Milliliters	1.0	Cubic centimeters
Milliliters	0.001	Liters
Torque		
Foot-pounds	1.3558	Newton-meters
Foot-pounds	0.138255	Meters-kilograms
Inch-pounds	0.11299	Newton-meters
Newton-meters	0.7375622	Foot-pounds
Newton-meters	8.8507	Inch-pounds
Meters-kilograms	7.2330139	Foot-pounds
Volume		
Cubic inches	16.387064	Cubic centimeters
Volume (continued)		
Cubic centimeters	0.0610237	Cubic inches

(continued)

Table 3 CONVERSION FORMULAS (continued)

Multiply:	By:	To get the equivalent of:
Temperature		
Fahrenheit	(°F − 32) × 0.556	Centigrade
Centigrade	(°C × 1.8) + 32	Fahrenheit
Weight		
Ounces	28.3495	Grams
Pounds	0.4535924	Kilograms
Grams	0.035274	Ounces
Kilograms	2.2046224	Pounds
Pressure		
Pounds per square inch	0.070307	Kilograms per square centimeter
Kilograms per square centimeter	14.223343	Pounds per square inch
Kilopascals	0.1450	Pounds per square inch
Pounds per square inch	6.895	Kilopascals
Speed		
Miles per hour	1.609344	Kilometers per hour
Kilometers per hour	0.6213712	Miles per hour

Table 4 TECHNICAL ABBREVIATIONS

A	Ampere
AC	Alternating current
A.h.	Ampere hour
C	Celsius
cc	Cubic centimeter
CDI	Capacitor discharge ignition
CKP sensor	Crankshaft position sensor
cm	Centimeter
cu. in.	Cubic inch and cubic inches
cyl.	Cylinder
DC	Direct current
ECM	Electronic control module
EOT sensor	Engine oil temperature sensor
F	Fahrenheit
fl. oz.	Fluid ounces
ft.	Foot
ft.-lb.	Foot-pounds
gal.	Gallon/gallons
GP sensor	Gear position sensor
HO2 sensor	Heated oxygen sensor
hp	Horsepower
Hz	Hertz
IAP sensor	Intake air pressure sensor
IAT sensor	Intake air temperature sensor
in.	Inch and inches
in.-lb.	Inch-pounds
in. Hg	Inches of mercury
kg	Kilogram
kg/cm^2	Kilogram per square centimeter
kgm	Kilogram meter
km	Kilometer
km/h	Kilometer per hour
kPa	Kilopascals
kW	Kilowatt
L	Liter and liters
L/m	Liters per minute
lb.	Pound and pounds
m	Meter
mL	Milliliter
mm	Millimeter

(continued)

Table 4 TECHNICAL ABBREVIATIONS (continued)

MPa	Megapascal
N	Newton
N•m	Newton meter
oz.	Ounce and ounces
p	Pascal
PAIR	Pulsed secondary air injection
psi	Pounds per square inch
pt.	Pint and pints
qt.	Quart and quarts
rpm	Revolution per minute
STP sensor	secondary throttle position sensor
STV	Secondary throttle valve
STVA	Secondary throttle valve actuator
TDC	Top dead center
TO sensor	Tip over sensor
TP sensor	Throttle position sensor
TPC valve	Tank pressure control valve
V	Volt
VAC	Alternating current voltage
VDC	Direct current voltage
W	Watt

Table 5 TORQUE RECOMMENDATIONS*

Thread diameter	N•m	in.-lb.	ft.-lb.
5 mm			
Bolt and nut	5	44	–
Screw	4	35	–
6 mm			
Bolt and nut	10	88	–
Screw	9	80	–
6 mm flange bolt and nut	12	106	–
6 mm bolt with 8 mm head	9	80	–
8 mm			
Bolt and nut	22	–	16
Flange bolt and nut	27	–	20
10 mm			
Bolt and nut	35	–	26
Flange bolt and nut	40	–	30
12 mm			
Bolt and nut	55	–	40.5

*Torque recommendations for fasteners without a specification. Refer to the torque specification table at the end of each applicable chapter for specific applications.

CHAPTER TWO

TROUBLESHOOTING

The troubleshooting procedures described in this chapter provide typical symptoms and logical methods for isolating the cause(s). There may be several ways to solve a problem, but only a systematic approach will be successful in avoiding wasted time and possibly prevent unnecessary parts replacement. Gather as much information as possible to aid in diagnosis. Never assume anything and do not overlook the obvious. Make sure the kill switch is in the run position and there is fuel in the tank.

An engine needs three basics to run properly: correct air/ fuel mixture, compression, and a spark at the correct time. If any one of these is missing, the engine will not run.

Learning to recognize symptoms makes troubleshooting easier. In most cases, expensive and complicated test equipment is not needed to determine whether repairs can be performed at home. On the other hand, be realistic and do not start procedures that are beyond your experience and available equipment. If the motorcycle requires the attention of a professional, describe symptoms and conditions accurately. The more information a techni-

cian has available, the easier it is to diagnose the problem.

STARTING THE ENGINE

Starting System Operation

WARNING
The warning lights should turn off after a few seconds or after the engine starts. If a light stays on, turn the engine off and check the oil level as described in Chapter Three.

The starting system includes an interlock system that interrupts current flow to the starter relay and the auto-decompression relay. The position of the sidestand, clutch lever, and gear selector affect starting.

The engine will not crank and the auto-decompression solenoid will not operate unless the transmission is in neutral and the clutch disengaged, or the transmission is in gear, with the clutch disengaged and the sidestand up.

Starting Procedure

Cold engine

1. Shift the transmission into neutral.
2. Make sure the engine stop switch (A, **Figure 1**) is in the run position.
3. On 1998-2004 models, pull the starter knob (**Figure 2**) all the way out to the fully on position.
4. Turn the ignition switch on.
5. The following indicator lights turn on when the ignition switch is on:
   a. The neutral indicator light (when the transmission is in neutral).
   b. Oil pressure warning light.
   c. Fuel level warning light (carbureted models).

> *NOTE*
> *When a cold engine is started with the throttle open and the starter knob on, a lean mixture will result and cause hard starting.*

6. Completely close the throttle. Pull in the clutch lever and press the starter button (B, **Figure 1**).
7A. On 1998-2004 models, perform the following:
   a. Once the engine has started, adjust the starter knob to keep the engine idling between 1000 and 1500 rpm.
   b. After approximately 30 seconds, press the starter knob off. In cold weather, the starter knob may need to remain on for a slightly longer period.
7B. On 2005-on models, let the engine run until it warms up.
8. The engine is warm when it cleanly responds to the throttle.

Warm or hot engine

1. Shift the transmission into neutral.
2. Turn the ignition switch on.
3. On 1998-2004 models, press the starter knob to its fully off position.
4. Make sure the engine stop switch (A, **Figure 1**) is set to run.
5. Pull in the clutch lever, open the throttle slightly and press the starter button (B, **Figure 1**).

Flooded engine

If the engine will not start and if a strong gasoline smell is present, the engine is probably flooded. To start a flooded engine:
1. Turn the engine stop switch (A, **Figure 1**) off.

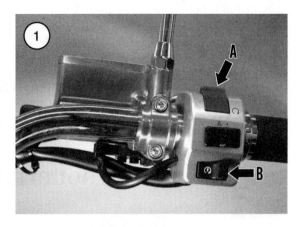

2. On 1998-2004 models, make sure the starter knob (**Figure 2**) is in its fully closed position.
3. Open the throttle fully.
4. Turn the ignition switch on and operate the starter button for five seconds.
5. Wait ten seconds, and set the engine stop switch to run.
6. Open the throttle slightly and press the starter button.
7. If the engine starts but idles roughly, vary the throttle position slightly until the engine idles and responds smoothly.

ENGINE WILL NOT START

Identifying the Problem

The first step in troubleshooting a no start condition is to narrow the possibilities by following a specific troubleshooting procedure, while never overlooking the obvious. Many times, a starting problem is simple, such as a disconnected or damaged wire.

If the engine does not start, perform the following steps. If the engine fails to start after performing these checks, refer to the troubleshooting procedures indicated in the steps. If the engine starts, but

idles roughly, refer to *Engine Performance* in this chapter.

1. Refer to *Starting The Engine* in this chapter to make sure all switches and starting procedures are correct.

2. If the starter does not operate, refer to *Electrical Systems* in this chapter.

3. If the starter operates, and the engine seems flooded, refer to *Flooded Engine* in this chapter.

4. Make sure the tank has sufficient fuel. Turn the ignition switch on and check the fuel level warning light. The fuel level is low if the warning light remains on.

5. Test the ignition system by performing the *Spark Test* in this section.

6. Check engine compression as described in Chapter Three.

Spark Test

WARNING
Disable the fuel delivery system during a spark test to prevent fuel from entering the cylinders while cranking the engine. Place the tester away from the spark plug hole to prevent fuel vapors from being ignited.

WARNING
Do not hold the spark plugs, tester, wire or connector. Serious electrical shock may result.

Use a new spark plug or spark tester (Motion-Pro part No. 08-0122) or an equivalent tool to perform this test.

1. Remove the steering head and upper covers as described in Chapter Fifteen.

2. Disconnect the fuel pump connector (**Figure 3**, 1998-2004 models; **Figure 4**, 2005-on models).

3. Remove the spark plugs as described in Chapter Three.

4. Set the spark tester gap to the 8.0 mm (0.3 in.) range and insert the spark tester into the spark plug cap. Touch the tester base to a good engine ground. Position the tester so the electrode can be seen.

5. Shift the transmission into neutral, turn the ignition switch on, and place the engine stop switch in the run position.

6. Operate the starter button to turn the engine over. A fat blue spark must be evident across the tester terminals.

7. Repeat this test for the other cylinder.

8. If the spark is good, the ignition system is functioning properly. Check for one or more of the following possible malfunctions:
   a. Obstructed or faulty fuel system component.
   b. Engine damage or low compression.
   c. Engine flooded.

9. If the spark was weak or if there was no spark in one or both cylinders, refer to Chapter Ten.

Engine is Difficult to Start

1. After attempting to start the engine, remove one of the spark plugs as described in Chapter Three and check for the presence of fuel on the plug tip. Note the following:
   a. If no fuel is visible on the plug, remove the other spark plug. If there is no fuel on this plug, perform Step 2.
   b. If there is fuel on the plug tip, go to Step 5.
   c. If there is an excessive amount of fuel on the plug, check for a clogged or plugged air filter, incorrect fast idle valve operation/adjustment or incorrect throttle valve operation (stuck open).

2A. On carbureted models, perform the *Fuel Pump Volume Test* described in Chapter Eight.
   a. If the fuel output is low, replace the fuel pump.
   b. If fuel output is within specification, proceed to Step 5.

2B. On fuel injected models, perform the *Fuel Pump Operation Test* in Chapter Nine. Note the following:

    a. If the fuel pump operation is correct, go to Step 3.

    b. If the fuel pump operation is faulty, test the fuel pump relay and the tip over sensor as described in Chapter Nine. If both of these components are within specification, replace the fuel pump.

3. Perform the *Fuel Pump Discharge Test* described in Chapter Nine.

    a. If the fuel output is low, replace the fuel pump.

    b. If fuel output is within specification, proceed to Step 4.

4. Perform the *Fuel Pressure Test* described in Chapter Nine.

    a. If fuel pressure is within specification, proceed to Step 5.

    b. If fuel pressure is low, check for a leak in the fuel system, a clogged fuel filter, or faulty pressure regulator or fuel pump.

5. Perform the spark test as described in this chapter. Note the following:

    a. If the spark is weak or if there is no spark, go to Step 6.

    b. If the spark is good, go to Step 7.

6. If the spark is weak or if there is no spark, check the following:

    a. Fouled spark plug(s).

    b. Damaged spark plug(s).

    c. Loose or damaged spark plug wire(s).

    d. Loose or damaged ignition coil/plug cap(s).

    e. Damaged ECM.

    f. Damaged crankshaft position sensor.

    g. Faulty direct ignition coil(s).

    h. Damaged engine stop switch.

    i. Damaged ignition switch.

    j. Dirty or loose-fitting electrical connectors.

7. If the engine turns over but does not start, the engine compression is probably low. Check for the following possible malfunctions:

    a. Leaking cylinder head gasket.

    b. Incorrect valve clearance.

    c. Bent or stuck valve(s).

    d. Worn valve guide(s).

    e. Incorrect valve timing.

    f. Worn cylinders and/or pistons rings.

    g. Improper valve-to-seat contact.

    h. Air in the hydraulic lifters.

    i. Faulty auto-decompression solenoid or relay.

    j. Auto-decompression cable needs adjusting.

    k. Defective igniter or ECM.

8. If the spark is good, try starting the engine by following normal starting procedures. If the engine starts but then stops, check for the following conditions:

    a. Incorrect fast idle valve operation (fuel injected models).

    b. Faulty needle valve (carbureted models).

    c. Clogged fuel tank breather hose or fuel hose.

    d. Clogged TPC valve and fuel vapor separator (Chapter Eight).

    e. Contaminated fuel.

    f. Clogged fuel filter.

    g. Defective fuel pump.

Engine Does Not Crank

If the engine will not turn over, check for one or more of the following:

1. Blown fuse.
2. Discharged battery.
3. Defective starter, starter relay or starter switch.
4. Faulty starter clutch.
5. Seized pistons(s).
6. Seized crankshaft bearings.
7. Broken connecting rod.
8. Locked-up transmission or clutch assembly.

ENGINE PERFORMANCE

Refer to the following checklists if the engine runs but is not operating at peak performance. Where ignition timing is mentioned, remember that it cannot be adjusted. If the ignition timing is incorrect, a part within the ignition system is faulty. Check individual ignition system components and replace any faulty part.

Engine Will Not Idle

1. Clogged air filter element.
2. Incorrect idle speed adjustment.
3. Incorrect throttle cable free play.
4. Air in hydraulic valve lifters or defective lifter.
5. Worn valve guide.
6. Worn rocker arm or shaft.
7. Fouled or improperly gapped spark plug(s).
8. Faulty ignition system component.
9. Defective fuel pump.
10. Throttle valves not synchronized.
11. Incorrect float chamber fuel level (carbureted models).
12. Clogged carburetor jet or fuel injector.
13. Vacuum leak: leaking head gasket or intake manifold(s).
14. Low engine compression.

Poor Overall Performance

1. Securely support the motorcycle with the rear wheel off the ground and spin the rear wheel by hand. If the wheel spins freely, perform Step 2. If the wheel does not spin freely, check for the following conditions:
   a. Dragging rear brake.
   b. Excessive rear axle torque.
   c. Damaged rear axle/bearing.
   d. Damaged final drive.
2. Check clutch operation. If the clutch slips, refer to *Clutch* in this chapter.
3. Test ride the motorcycle and accelerate lightly. If the engine speed increases according to throttle position, perform Step 4. If the engine speed does not increase, check for one or more of the following problems:
   a. Clogged air filter or air ducts.
   b. Restricted fuel flow.
   c. Pinched fuel tank breather hose.
   d. Clogged or damaged muffler.
4. Check for one or more of the following problems:
   a. Low engine compression.
   b. Worn or fouled spark plugs.
   c. Incorrect spark plug heat range.
   d. Clogged jet(s) or fuel injector(s).
   e. Incorrect ignition timing due to a faulty ignition component or damaged igniter/ECM.
   f. Incorrect oil level (too high or too low).
   g. Contaminated oil.
   h. Worn or damaged valve train assembly.
   i. Engine overheating. See *Engine Overheats* in this section.
5. If the engine knocks when it accelerates or when running at high speed, check for one or more of the following possible malfunctions:
   a. Incorrect type of fuel.
   b. Lean fuel mixture.
   c. Advanced ignition timing due to a damaged ignition system component.
   d. Excessive carbon buildup in the combustion chamber(s).
   e. Worn pistons and/or cylinder bores.

Poor High Speed Performance

1. Weak valve springs.
2. Worn camshaft.
3. Improper valve timing.
4. Spark plug gap too narrow.
5. Insufficiently advanced ignition timing.
6. Defective ignition coil.
7. Faulty signal generator/crankshaft position sensor.
8. Faulty igniter/ECM.
9. Clogged air filter element.

10. Clogged fuel line.
11. Low fuel level in float bowl (carbureted models).
12. Air in hydraulic valve lifters.
13. Faulty fuel pump.

Engine Lacks Power

1. Weak valve springs.
2. Improperly timed valves.
3. Valve not seating.
4. Worn cylinder or piston rings.
5. Fouled or incorrect spark plug.
6. Clogged air filter.
7. Incorrect fuel level in float bowl (carbureted models).
8. Throttle valves not synchronized.
9. Intake manifold air leak.
10. Engine oil level too high.
11. Faulty ignition coil.
12. Faulty igniter/ECM.
13. Faulty signal generator/crankshaft position sensor.
14. Faulty fuel pump.

Engine Overheats

1. Excessive carbon on piston crown or combustion chamber.
2. Low oil level.
3. Oil not circulating properly.
4. Improper oil viscosity.
5. Intake air leak.
6. Dragging brake(s).
7. Clutch slipping.
8. Improper spark plug heat range.
9. Fuel Injected models:
   a. Short in the intake air pressure sensor or its wire.
   b. Short in the intake air temperature sensor or its wire.
   c. Defective fuel injector.
   d. Defective engine oil temperature sensor.

Engine Backfires

1. Improper ignition timing caused by faulty ignition system component.
2. Incorrect throttle valve adjustment.
3. Lean fuel mixture.

Engine Misfires During Acceleration

1. Improper ignition timing caused by faulty ignition system component.
2. Excessively worn or defective spark plug(s).
3. Incorrect throttle valve adjustment.

ENGINE NOISES

A strange noise is often the first evidence of an internal engine problem. An unusual knocking, clicking or tapping sound may be an early sign of pending trouble. While engine noises can indicate problems, distinguishing a normal noise from an abnormal one can be difficult. Professional mechanics often use a mechanic's stethoscope to isolate engine noises. A length of vacuum hose, held with one end in the area of the noise and the other end held near your ear (not directly on your ear), may also be used. If necessary, have an experienced mechanic diagnose any unusual noise.

Consider the following when troubleshooting engine noises:

1. A knocking or pinging during acceleration may be caused by the use of a lower octane fuel than recommended. It may also be caused by poor fuel, the wrong spark plug heat range or carbon buildup in the combustion chamber. Refer to *Heat Range* and *Compression Test* in Chapter Three.

2. Slapping or rattling noises at low speed or during acceleration may be caused by excessive piston-to-cylinder clearance (piston slap). Piston slap is easier to detect when the engine is cold and before the pistons have expanded. Once the engine has warmed up, piston expansion reduces piston-to-cylinder clearance.

3. A knocking or rapping while decelerating is usually caused by excessive connecting rod bearing clearance.

4. A persistent knocking and vibration during every crankshaft rotation is usually caused by worn connecting rod or main bearing(s). This can also be caused by broken piston rings or damaged piston pins.

5. A rapid on-off squeal indicates a compression leak around the cylinder head gasket or spark plug(s).

Valve Clatter

1. Air trapped in hydraulic lifter.
2. Defective hydraulic lifter.
3. Auto-decompression cable needs adjustment.
4. Weak or broken valve spring.
5. Worn rocker arm and/or shaft.
6. Worn camshaft journal.

Piston Noise

1. Worn piston or cylinder.
2. Excessive carbon in the combustion chamber.
3. Worn piston ring or ring groove.

4. Worn piston pin or piston pin bore.

Crankshaft Noise

1. Noisy bearings.
2. Worn connecting rod bearing.
3. Worn crankshaft bearing.
4. Excessive thrust clearance.

Cam Chain Noise

1. Chain stretch beyond service limit.
2. Worn cam chain sprocket.
3. Faulty cam chain tensioner.

Clutch Noise

1. Worn mainshaft spline.
2. Worn clutch hub spline.
3. Worn plain plate teeth.
4. Distorted friction disc or plain plate.
5. Worn clutch release bearing.
6. Weak clutch damper.

Transmission Noise

1. Worn gear.
2. Worn mainshaft or countershaft spline.
3. Worn primary drive gear.
4. Worn bearing.

ENGINE LUBRICATION

Insufficient engine lubrication quickly leads to engine seizure. Check the engine oil level before each ride and top off the oil as described in Chapter Three. Oil pump service is addressed in Chapter Five.

Oil Consumption High or Engine Smokes Excessively

1. Too much engine oil in engine.
2. Worn valve guides or valve stems.
3. Worn valve stem seals.
4. Worn or damaged piston rings.
5. Scuffed or scored cylinder walls.
6. Worn or damage piston oil ring.

Oil Leaks

1. Clogged air filter housing breather hose.
2. Loose engine parts.
3. Damaged gasket sealing surfaces.

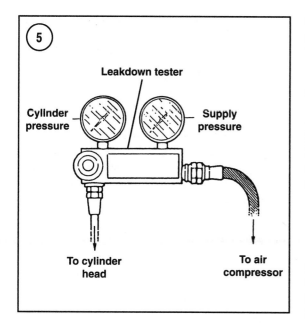

⑤

Leakdown tester

Cylinder pressure

Supply pressure

To cylinder head

To air compressor

Low Oil Pressure

1. Low oil level.
2. Worn or damaged oil pump.
3. Clogged oil pump screen.
4. Clogged oil filter.
5. Clogged oil cooler.
6. Internal oil leaks.
7. Incorrect type of engine oil.
8. Oil pressure relief valve stuck open.
9. Worn crankshaft bearings or incorrect oil clearance.

High Oil Pressure

1. Clogged oil filter.
2. Clogged oil cooler.
3. Clogged oil gallery or metering orifices.
4. Incorrect type of engine oil.

No Oil Pressure

1. Damaged oil pump.
2. Low oil level.
3. Damaged oil pump drive shaft.
4. Damaged oil pump drive sprocket.
5. Incorrect oil pump installation.

Oil Level Too Low

1. Insufficient amount of oil.
2. Worn piston rings.
3. Worn cylinder(s).
4. Worn valve guides.
5. Worn valve stem seals.

6. Piston rings incorrectly installed during engine overhaul.
7. External oil leaks.

Oil Contamination

1. Stuck or misadjusted float allowing engine to flood (carbureted models).
2. Oil and filter not changed at specified intervals or when operating conditions demand more frequent changes.

CYLINDER LEAKDOWN TEST

While a compression test (Chapter Three) can identify a weak cylinder, a leakdown test can determine where the compression leak occurs. With a leakdown tester and an air compressor (**Figure 5**), perform the test by applying compressed air through the cylinder head and then measuring the leak rate percentage.

1. Run the engine until it is warm. Then turn the engine off.
2. Remove the air filter housing (Chapter Eight). Secure the throttle in its wide-open position.
3. Set the rear cylinder to top dead center on the compression stroke as described in *Camshaft, Removal* in Chapter Four.

> *WARNING*
> *Remove any tools attached to the end of the crankshaft. The crankshaft may spin when compressed air is applied to the cylinder. To prevent the engine from turning over, shift the transmission into top gear and have an assistant apply the rear brake.*

4. Remove the spark plug from the rear cylinder.
5. Thread the tester's adapter into the rear cylinder spark plug hole following the manufacturer's instructions. Connect the leakdown tester onto the adapter. Connect an air compressor hose onto the tester's fitting.
6. Apply compressed air to the leakdown tester and perform a cylinder leakdown test following the manufacturer's instructions. Read the leak percentage on the gauge. Note the following:
   a. On a new or rebuilt engine, a loss of 0 to 5 percent is desirable. A loss of 6 to 14 percent is acceptable and indicates the engine is in good condition.
   b. Also note the difference between cylinders. On a used engine, a difference of 10 percent or less between cylinders is satisfactory.
   c. If the difference between cylinders exceeds 10 percent, the engine is in poor condition and requires further inspection, and possible engine repair.

2

7. With air pressure still applied to the combustion chamber, listen for air escaping from the following areas. If necessary, use a stethoscope:
   a. Air leaking through the exhaust pipe indicates a leaking exhaust valve.
   b. Air leaking through the air intake system indicates a leaking intake valve.
   c. Air leaking through the crankcase breather suggests worn piston rings or a worn cylinder bore.
8. Remove the leakdown tester and repeat these steps for the front cylinder.

CLUTCH

Refer to Chapter Six for clutch service.

Clutch Lever Hard to Pull In

If the clutch lever is hard to pull in, check the following:
1. Insufficient hydraulic fluid.
2. Air in the hydraulic lines.
3. Damaged clutch lifter bearing.

Rough Clutch Operation

Rough operation can be caused by an excessively worn, grooved or damaged clutch hub and/or clutch housing slots.

Clutch Slip

If the engine speed increases without an increase in motorcycle speed, the clutch is probably slipping. Some main causes of clutch slip are:
1. Weak or damaged clutch springs.
2. Worn plain plates or friction discs.
3. Damaged pressure plate.
4. Damaged clutch release mechanism.
5. Clutch contaminated by engine oil additive.

Clutch Drag

If the clutch will not disengage or if the motorcycle creeps with the transmission in gear and the clutch disengaged, the clutch is dragging. Some main causes of clutch drag are:
1. Clutch hydraulic fluid leak.
2. Warped clutch plates.
3. Unevenly worn clutch springs.
4. Damaged clutch lifter assembly.
5. Loose clutch nut.

6. Damaged pressure plate, clutch hub splines or clutch housing slots.

TRANSMISSION

Transmission symptoms are sometimes hard to distinguish from clutch symptoms. Common transmission symptoms and their possible causes are listed below. Refer to Chapter Seven for transmission service procedures. Before working on the transmission, make sure the clutch and gearshift linkage assemblies are working properly.

Jumps Out of Gear

1. Improperly adjusted shift pedal position.
2. Loose or damaged shift drum stopper lever.
3. Bent or damaged shift fork(s).
4. Bent shift fork shaft(s).
5. Damaged shift drum grooves.
6. Worn gear dogs or slots.
7. Worn shift cam.

Transmission Will Not Shift

1. Bent shift pedal or linkage.
2. Stripped shift lever splines.
3. Damaged shift lever linkage.
4. Improperly adjusted shift pedal.
5. Broken shift cam or shift cam plate.
6. Bent shift fork.
7. Broken shift shaft return spring.

Excessive Gear Noise

1. Worn bearings.
2. Worn or damaged gears.
3. Excessive gear backlash.

ELECTRICAL TESTING

This section covers general electrical testing and tool use. Refer to *Electrical Systems* in this chapter and to Chapter Ten for component/system specific procedures.

Start troubleshooting by analyzing the symptom and all possible causes systematically. Do not overlook the possibility of a simple cause like a blown fuse, poor ground or a separated/damaged electrical connector. Test the simplest and most obvious items first and try to make tests at easily accessible points on the motorcycle. Use the wiring diagrams at the end of the manual to determine how the circuit works by tracing the current path from the power source

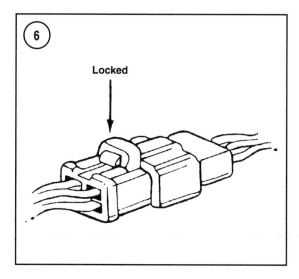

Locked

1. Check the main fuse (Chapter Ten). If the fuse is blown, replace it.

2. The various circuit fuses are mounted in the fuse box behind the speed sensor cover (Chapter Ten). Inspect the fuse protecting the suspect circuit. Replace the fuse as necessary.

3. Inspect the battery (Chapter Ten). Make sure it is fully charged. Make sure the battery leads are clean and securely attached to the battery terminals.

4. Disconnect each electrical connector in the suspect circuit. Never pull the electrical wires when disconnecting an electrical connector. Only pull the connector housings.

5. Examine each connector half carefully. Connectors are often the weak link in the electrical system. This is especially true on high-mileage machines or those exposed to water. Check for the following:

   a. Bent or damaged terminals that will not connect to their mates in the other half of the connector, thereby causing an open circuit.

   b. Make sure each terminal is pushed all the way into the connector and secure. If not, carefully push it in with a narrow blade screwdriver and make sure it locks in place.

   c. Check the wires for damage where they enter the connector and attach to their terminals.

   d. Make sure the connectors are clean and each electrical terminal is corrosion free. If necessary, clean and pack the connectors with dielectric grease to prevent future contamination.

   e. Push the connector halves together so they fully engage and lock together (**Figure 6**).

through the circuit components to ground. Also, check any circuits sharing the same fuse, ground or switch. If the other circuits work properly and the shared wiring is good, the cause must be in the wiring used only by the suspect circuit. If all related circuits are faulty at the same time, the probable cause is a poor ground connection or a blown fuse(s).

While referring to the following procedures, perform the tests in sequence. Each test presumes the components tested in the earlier steps are working properly. Tests can yield invalid results if performed out of sequence.

Electrical Component Replacement

Most motorcycle dealerships and parts suppliers will not accept the return of any electrical part. If the exact cause of an electrical system malfunction cannot be determined, have a dealership retest the specific system to verify the test results. If a new electrical component is installed and the system still does not work, the unit, in all likelihood, cannot be returned for a refund.

Consider any test results carefully before replacing a component that tests only slightly out of specification, especially for resistance. A number of variables can affect test results dramatically. These include: the test meter's internal circuitry, ambient temperature, and the conditions under which the machine has been operated. All instructions and specifications have been checked for accuracy. However, successful test results depend, to a great degree, upon individual accuracy.

Preliminary Checks and Precautions

Perform the following before starting any electrical troubleshooting:

Intermittent Problems

Intermittent problems can be difficult to locate. For example, vibration while riding can be hard to duplicate during testing. To locate and repair intermittent problems, you will need to simulate the condition in the shop to test the components. Note the following:

1. Vibration is a common problem with loose or damaged electrical connectors.

   a. Perform a continuity test as described in the appropriate service procedure, or in *Continuity Test* (this section).

   b. Lightly pull or wiggle the connectors while repeating the test. Do the same when checking the wiring harness and individual components, especially where the wires enter a housing or connector.

   c. A change in meter readings indicates a poor connection. Find and repair the problem or replace the part. Check for wires with cracked or broken insulation.

2. Heat can cause problems with connectors or joints that have loose or poor connections. As these connections heat up, the connection or joint expands and separates, causing an open circuit. Other heat related problems can occur when solid state devices heat up and fail when warm, but otherwise operate normally.

   a. Troubleshoot the problem to isolate it to a specific area or component.
   b. To check a connector, perform a continuity test as described in the appropriate service procedure, or in *Continuity Test* (this section). Then repeat the test while heating the connector with a heat gun. If the meter reading was normal (continuity) when the connector was cold, then fluctuated or read infinity with heat applied, the connection is bad.
   c. To check a component, allow the engine to cool. Then start and run the engine. Note operational differences when the engine is cold and hot.
   d. If the engine will not start, isolate and remove the component, first test it at room temperature, and then after heating it with a heat gun. A change in meter readings indicates a temperature problem.

CAUTION
A heat gun will quickly heat components. Do not apply direct heat or exceed 60° C (140° F) for any electrical component.

3. If the problem occurs when riding in wet conditions, or in areas with high humidity, start and run the engine in a dry area. Then, with the engine running, spray water onto the suspected component. Often times, water related problems repair themselves after the component heats up enough to dry itself, further complicating diagnosis.

Back Probing a Connector

Some tests, such as voltage or peak voltage tests, require back probing a connector. In these instances, insert a small wire, or a back probe pin, into the connector at the indicated terminal. Connect the multimeter test probe(s) to the back probe pin(s). The pin(s) must not exceed 0.5 mm (0.02 in.) in diameter.

Make sure the back probe pin contacts the metal part of the terminal. Exercise caution so the pin does not deform either the male or female terminals in the connector.

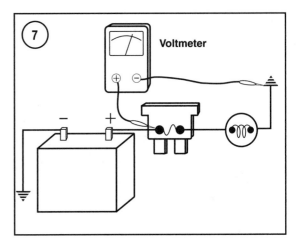

Test Light or Voltmeter

Use a test light to check for voltage in a circuit by attaching one lead to ground and the other lead to various points along the circuit. The bulb lights when voltage is present.

Use a voltmeter to determine how much voltage is present in any given circuit. When using a voltmeter, attach the positive test lead to the component or wire and the negative test lead to a good ground (**Figure 7**).

Voltage test

Unless otherwise specified, make voltage tests with the electrical connectors connected. Insert the test probes into the backside of the connector and make sure the test lead touches the electrical terminal.

Always check both sides of a connector, as one side may be loose or corroded thus preventing electrical flow through the connector.

1. Attach the voltmeter negative test lead to a good ground (bare metal). Make sure the part used for the ground is not insulated with a rubber gasket or rubber grommet.
2. Attach the voltmeter positive test lead to the point (electrical connector, etc.) being tested (**Figure 7**).
3. Turn the ignition switch on. If using a test light, the test light will come on if voltage is present. If using a voltmeter, note the voltage reading. The reading should be within one volt of battery voltage. If the voltage is less, a problem exists in the circuit.

Voltage drop test

The wires, cables, connectors, and switches in the electrical circuit are designed to carry current with low resistance. This ensures current can flow through the circuit with a minimum loss of voltage. Voltage drop indicates where there is resistance in a circuit.

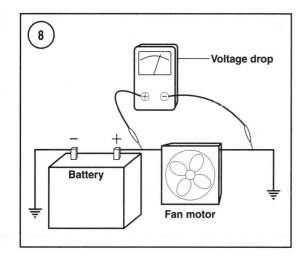

A higher-than-normal amount of resistance in a circuit decreases the flow of current, and causes the voltage to drop between the source and destination. The greater the resistance in a circuit, the greater the voltage drop reading.

Use a voltmeter to measure voltage drop when current is running through the circuit. If the circuit has no resistance, there is no voltage drop and the voltmeter should indicate 0 volts. A voltage drop of 1 or more volts indicates a circuit with excessive resistance.
1. Connect the voltmeter positive test lead to the end of the wire or device closest to the battery.
2. Connect the voltmeter negative test lead to the ground side of the wire or device (**Figure 8**).
3. Turn the components in the circuit on.
4. The voltmeter should indicate zero volts. If it reads one volt or more, a problem exists within the circuit. A voltage drop reading of 12 volts indicates an open in the circuit.

Testing for a short

1. Remove the blown fuse from the fuse panel.
2. Connect the test light or voltmeter across the fuse terminals in the fuse panel. Turn the ignition switch on and check for battery voltage.
3. With the test light or voltmeter attached to the fuse terminals, wiggle the wiring harness of the suspect circuit at 15.2 cm (6 in.) intervals. Start next to the fuse panel and work away from the panel.
4. Watch the test light or voltmeter while moving along the harness. If the test light blinks or if the needle on the voltmeter moves while wiggling the when the harness, there is a short-to-ground at that point.

Peak voltage testing

A peak voltage test checks the voltage output of a component at normal cranking speed. This test mea-

sures a component's output voltage under operating conditions.

Peak voltage specifications are minimum values. If the measured voltage meets or exceeds this specification, the test results are satisfactory. In some instances, the measured voltage may exceed the minimum specification.

Use the multicircuit tester (Suzuki part No. 09900-25008) with the peak voltage adapter, or an equivalent multimeter and peak voltage adapter, to perform a peak voltage test. Refer to the tool manufacturer's instructions.

Self-powered Test Light

Use a self-powered test light to check for circuit continuity as follows:
1. Touch the test leads together to make sure the light bulb turns on. If not, correct the problem before using the test light in a test procedure.
2. Disconnect the motorcycle's battery or remove the fuse(s) protecting the test circuit. Do not test powered circuits or solid state devices with a self powered test light.
3. Select two points within the circuit where there should be continuity.
4. Attach one lead of the self-powered test light to each point.
5. If there is continuity, the self-powered test light bulb will turn on.
6. If there is no continuity, the self-powered test light bulb will not come on indicating an open circuit.

Ohmmeter

> *CAUTION*
> *Never connect an ohmmeter to a circuit that has power applied to it. Always disconnect the battery negative cable before using an ohmmeter.*

An ohmmeter measures the resistance (in ohms) to current flow in a circuit or component.

Ohmmeters may be analog (needle scale) or digital (LCD or LED readout). Most ohmmeters have a switch to select different resistance ranges, while others are auto-ranging. If the resistance range must be set, make sure the correct range is selected. The analog ohmmeter also has a set-adjust control to zero or calibrate the meter. Digital ohmmeters do not require calibration.

To use an ohmmeter, connects its test leads to the terminals or leads of the test circuit. If an analog meter is used, calibrate it by touching the test leads together and turning the set-adjust knob until the meter reads zero. When the leads are uncrossed, the needle should move to the infinite resistance range.

During a continuity test, a reading of infinity indicates there is an open in the circuit or component. Zero resistance indicates continuity and no measured resistance.

If the meter needle falls between these two ends of the scale, this indicates the actual resistance to current flow present in the circuit. To determine the resistance, multiply the meter reading by the ohmmeter scale. For example, a meter reading of 5 multiplied by the R × 1000 scale is 5000 ohms of resistance.

Continuity test

Perform a continuity test with an ohmmeter to determine the integrity of a circuit or component. A circuit with continuity forms a complete circuit. An incomplete or open circuit has a problem in either the circuit's wiring, connectors or components.

A self powered test light may also be used to check for continuity.
1. Disconnect the negative battery cable.
2. Attach one test lead to one end of the part of the circuit to be tested.
3. Attach the other test lead to the other end of the part or the circuit to be tested.
4. On a complete circuit, an ohmmeter reads zero or very low resistance indicating continuity. A reading of infinite resistance indicates no continuity and the circuit is open. A self-powered test light comes on if the circuit is complete.

Ammeter

Use an ammeter to measure the flow of current (amps) in a circuit. When connected in series in a circuit (**Figure 9**), the ammeter determines if current is flowing through the circuit and if the current is excessive. Current flow is often referred to as current draw. Comparing actual current draw in the circuit or component to the manufacturer's specified current draw provides useful diagnostic information.

Jumper Wire

A jumper wire is a simple way to bypass a potential problem and isolate it to a particular point in a circuit. If a faulty circuit works properly with a jumper wire installed, an open exists between the two jumper points in the circuit.

To troubleshoot a device like a lamp with a jumper wire, first use the jumper to determine if the problem is on the ground side or the load side. Test the ground by connecting a jumper between the lamp and a good ground. If the lamp comes on, the problem is the connection between the lamp and ground. If the lamp

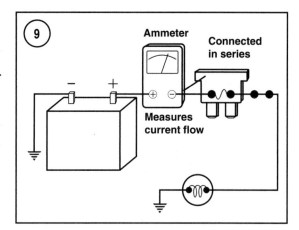

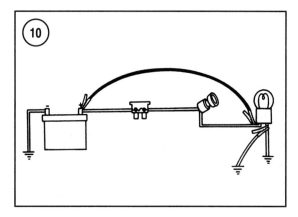

does not come on with the jumper installed, the problem is between the lamp and the power source.

To isolate the problem, connect the jumper between the battery and the lamp as shown in **Figure 10**. If it comes on, the problem is between these two points. Next, connect the jumper between the battery and the fuse side of the switch. If the lamp comes on, the switch is good. By successively moving the jumper from one point to another, the problem can be isolated to a particular place in the circuit.

Pay attention to the following when using a jumper wire:
1. Make sure the jumper wire gauge (thickness) is the same as that used in the circuit being tested. A smaller gauge wire will rapidly overheat and could melt.
2. Install insulated boots over alligator clips. This prevents accidental grounding, sparks or possible shock when working in cramped quarters.
3. Jumper wires are temporary test measures only. Do not leave a jumper wire installed; this creates a fire hazard.
4. When using a jumper wire, always install an in-line fuse/fuse holder to the jumper wire.
5. Never use a jumper wire across any load (a component that is connected and turned on). This would result in a direct short and will blow the fuse(s).

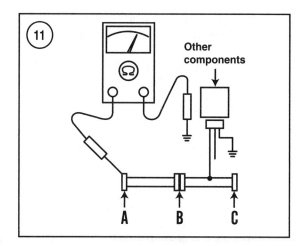

6. Perform the *Stator Resistance Test* (Chapter Ten). If stator resistance is out of specification, replace the stator.

7. Perform the *No-load Voltage Test* (Chapter Ten). If the voltage is out of specification, the alternator is faulty. Replace the stator and retest. If the problem persists, the rotor is faulty.

8. Perform the *Regulator/Rectifier Voltage Test* (Chapter Ten). If any test is out of specification, replace the regulator/rectifier.

9. Inspect the charging system wiring for a short or for corroded connectors.

   a. Repair the wiring or connector.

   b. If the wiring is good, replace the battery.

Short-to-Ground Test

1. Disconnect the negative battery cable.

2. Disconnect the electrical connector from each end of the suspect circuit (A and C, **Figure 11**).

3. If the circuit branches off to include other component(s), disconnect the electrical connector(s) of those components as well.

4. Connect an ohmmeter test probe to a terminal in one end of the circuit (A, **Figure 11**). Connect the other ohmmeter test lead to a good ground.

5. If continuity is indicated, a short-to-ground exists between A and C in **Figure 11**.

6. Disconnect connector B, and check the continuity between A and ground (**Figure 11**). If continuity is present, the short is between points A and B. If no continuity is found, the short is between B and C.

ELECTRICAL SYSTEMS

Refer to Chapter Ten for component specific testing. Refer to *Electrical Testing* in this chapter for general information.

Charging System

A malfunction in the charging system generally causes an undercharged battery.

1. Check the connections at the battery. If polarity is reversed, check for a damaged regulator/rectifier.

2. Check for loose or corroded battery cable connectors.

3. Check battery condition. Clean and recharge as required.

4. Perform the *Current Draw Test* (Chapter Ten). If current draw is excessive, check for a short in the wiring harness.

5. Perform the *Regulated Voltage Test* (Chapter Ten). If voltage is within specification, the battery is faulty.

Ignition System (Carbureted Models)

1. Check the main and ignition fuses (Chapter Ten).

2. Check the battery as described in Chapter Ten.

3. Check all ignition system connectors for loose or corroded terminals.

4. Perform the igniter input voltage test (Chapter Ten).

   a. If the input voltage is less than battery voltage, check for a faulty ignition switch, broken wire or poor connection in the circuit.

   b. If input voltage is within specification, proceed to Step 5.

5. Perform the ignition coil peak voltage test (Chapter Ten).

   a. If peak voltage is less than specified, proceed to Step 6.

   b. If peak voltage equals or exceeds specification, check the spark plugs. Replace the plugs as necessary. If the plugs are in good condition, proceed to Step 6.

6. Perform the ignition coil resistance test (Chapter Ten).

   a. If either resistance is out of specification, replace the ignition coil.

   b. If both resistance reading are within specification, proceed to Step 7.

7. Perform the signal generator peak voltage and resistance tests (Chapter Ten).

   a. If peak voltage and/or resistance is out of specification, replace the signal generator.

   b. If both values are within specification, check the igniter connectors. If they are in good condition, replace the igniter.

Ignition System (Fuel Injected Models)

Refer to *Diagnostic System Troubleshooting* in Chapter Nine.

Starting System

Starter does not operate

1. Check the main fuse (Chapter Ten).
2. Check the battery as described in Chapter Ten.
3. With the transmission in neutral and engine stop switch in the run position, disengage the clutch and turn the ignition switch on. Listen for the operation of the starter relay. The relay should click.
   a. If the relay clicks, perform Step 4.
   b. If a click is not heard, perform Step 5.
4. Perform the *Starter Operation Test* (Chapter Ten).
   a. If the motor does not run, replace it.
   b. If the motor runs, check the starter lead for a loose or corroded connection. If the starter motor lead is in good condition, perform Step 5.
5. Perform the starter relay test (Chapter Ten).
   a. If the relay is out of specification, replace the relay.
   b. If the relay tests within specification, check for poor contacts at the starter relay.
6. Check the continuity of the ignition switch (Chapter Ten).
7. Check the continuity of the engine stop switch (Chapter Ten).
8. Check the continuity of the clutch switch (Chapter Ten).
9A. On carbureted models, check the continuity of the neutral switch (Chapter Ten).
9B. On fuel injected models, check the gear position sensor by performing the gear position sensor voltage and continuity tests (Chapter Ten).
10. Inspect the turn signal/sidestand relay (Chapter Ten).
11. Check the continuity of the starter button (Chapter Ten).
12. Check the wiring and each connector in the starting circuit.

Slow starter operation

1. Perform the *Starter Operation Test* (Chapter Ten). Replace the starter if it does not operate properly.
2. Watch the auto-decompression solenoid while pressing the starter button.
   a. If the solenoid operates when the button is pressed, proceed to Step 3.
   b. If the solenoid does not operate when the button is pressed, proceed to Step 4.
3. Adjust the auto-decompression cable (Chapter Three). Check the solenoid operation by repeating Step 2. If the solenoid operates but the starter is still sluggish, the auto-decompression solenoid is faulty.

4. Perform the *Auto-decompression Solenoid Test* (Chapter Ten). Replace the solenoid if it fails either portion of the test.
5. Perform the *Auto-decompression Relay Continuity Test* (Chapter Ten). Replace the relay if it is faulty.
6. Check for poor contacts in the circuit wiring.
7. Replace the igniter.

STEERING AND SUSPENSION

Steering is Stiff

1. Incorrect steering stem adjustment (too tight).
2. Improperly installed upper or lower fork bridge.
3. Damaged steering stem.
4. Damaged steering head bearings.
5. Tire pressure too low.
6. Worn or damaged tire.

Handlebar Vibration

1. Front fork legs not balanced.
2. Damaged fork leg.
3. Damaged front axle.
4. Loose steering head bearings.
5. Worn or incorrect tire.
6. Incorrect tire pressure.
7. Worn steering stem bearing or race.

Motorcycle Steers to One Side

1. Bent front or rear axle.
2. Bent frame or fork(s).
3. Worn or damaged wheel bearings.
4. Worn or damaged swing arm pivot bearings.
5. Damaged steering head bearings.
6. Bent swing arm.
7. Incorrectly installed wheels.
8. Front and rear wheels are not aligned.
9. Uneven front fork adjustment.
10. Front fork legs positioned unevenly in the fork bridges.

Suspension Noise

1. Loose fasteners.
2. Damaged front fork or rear shock absorber.
3. Low fork oil level.
4. Worn swing arm or suspension linkage bearings.

Wheel Vibration

1. Loose wheel axle or axle clamp bolt(s).
2. Loose or damaged wheel bearing(s).
3. Damaged wheel(s).

4. Damaged tire(s).
5. Unbalanced tire and wheel assembly.
6. Loose swing arm pivot bolt.
7. Loose or damaged swing arm or suspension linkage bearings.
8. Loose fasteners.
9. Incorrect fork oil level.

Hard Suspension (Front Fork)

1. Bent axle.
2. Excessive tire pressure.
3. Damaged steering head bearings.
4. Incorrect steering head bearing adjustment.
5. Bent fork tube.
6. Binding slider.
7. Incorrect weight fork oil.
8. Too much fork oil.
9. Plugged fork oil passage.
10. Worn or damaged fork tube bushing or slider bushing.
11. Damaged damper rod.

Hard Suspension (Rear Shock Absorber)

1. Excessive rear tire pressure.
2. Bent or damaged shock absorber.
3. Incorrect shock adjustment.
4. Damaged shock absorber bushing(s).
5. Damaged shock absorber collar(s).
6. Damaged swing arm or suspension linkage bearings.
7. Damaged swing arm or suspension linkage component.
8. Poorly lubricated suspension components.

Soft Suspension (Front Fork)

1. Insufficient tire pressure.
2. Insufficient fork oil level.
3. Incorrect fork oil viscosity.
4. Weak or damaged fork springs.

Soft Suspension (Rear Shock Absorber)

1. Incorrectly adjusted rear shock.
2. Insufficient rear tire pressure.
3. Weak or damaged shock absorber spring.
4. Damaged shock absorber.
5. Leaking damper unit.

SHAFT DRIVE

Noisy Secondary Gear or Final Drive Assembly

1. Insufficient oil level.

2. Worn or damaged drive or driven gears.
3. Excessive backlash.
4. Improper tooth contact.
5. Damaged bearings.
6. Weak damper spring.
7. Worn or damaged cam dog surface.

Noisy drive shaft

1. Damaged universal joint.
2. Damaged drive shaft splines.
3. Shaft insufficiently lubricated.

Engine Power Not Reaching Rear Wheel

1. Broken drive shaft.
2. Broken or damaged gear teeth.
3. Broken or damaged input/output cam dog.
4. Weak damper spring.

Oil Leak from Secondary Gearcase or Final Drive

1. Damaged oil seals.
2. Damaged O-rings.
3. Loose gearcase bolts.

BRAKE SYSTEM

Inspect the brake system frequently and address any problems immediately. Refer to Chapter Fourteen for brake service. Refer to Chapter Three for brake maintenance.

Brake Drag

1. Warped or damaged brake disc.
2. Brake caliper not sliding correctly on slide pins.
3. Sticking or damaged brake caliper pistons.
4. Contaminated brake pads and disc.
5. Plugged master cylinder port.
6. Contaminated brake fluid and hydraulic passages.
7. Restricted brake hose joint.
8. Loose brake disc mounting bolts.
9. Damaged or misaligned wheel.
10. Incorrect wheel alignment.
11. Incorrectly installed brake caliper.
12. Poorly lubricated brake-lever or brake-pedal.

Brake Grab

1. Damaged brake pad pin. Look for steps or cracks along the pad pin surface.
2. Contaminated brake pads and disc.

3. Incorrect wheel alignment.
4. Warped brake disc.
5. Loose brake disc mounting bolts.
6. Brake caliper not sliding correctly.
7. Mismatched brake pads.
8. Damaged wheel bearings.

Brake Squeal or Chatter

1. Contaminated brake pads and disc.
2. Incorrectly installed brake caliper.
3. Warped brake disc.
4. Damaged wheel bearing.
5. Mismatched brake pads.
6. Incorrectly installed brake pads.
7. Contaminated brake fluid.
8. Clogged master-cylinder return port.
9. Loose front or rear axle.

Soft or Spongy Brake Lever or Pedal

1. Air in brake hydraulic system.
2. Low brake fluid level.

3. Leaking brake hydraulic system.
4. Clogged brake hydraulic system.
5. Worn brake caliper seals.
6. Worn master cylinder seals.
7. Sticking caliper piston.
8. Sticking master cylinder piston.
9. Damaged front brake lever.
10. Damaged rear brake pedal.
11. Contaminated brake pads and disc.
12. Excessively worn brake disc or pad(s).
13. Warped brake disc.

Hard Brake Lever or Pedal Operation

1. Clogged brake hydraulic system.
2. Sticking caliper piston.
3. Sticking master cylinder piston.
4. Glazed or worn brake pads.
5. Mismatched brake pads.
6. Damaged front brake lever.
7. Damaged rear brake pedal.
8. Brake caliper not sliding correctly.
9. Worn or damaged brake caliper seals.

CHAPTER THREE

LUBRICATION AND MAINTENANCE

This chapter covers lubrication, maintenance, and tune-up procedures. A properly maintained motorcycle is critical to achieving a long service life. A poorly maintained machine may be unreliable and/or unsafe.

If a procedure requires more than minor disassembly, a reference to the appropriate chapter is provided. Refer to the Index to quickly locate the desired section.

Refer to **Table 1** at the end of this chapter for the maintenance schedule. If the motorcycle is operated in extreme conditions, consider shortening the service interval. If the motorcycle is operated infrequently, refer to the time-based intervals. Refer to **Tables 2-5** for specifications.

CYLINDER FIRING ORDER

The rear cylinder is No. 1; the front cylinder is No. 2. The cylinder firing order is rear to front (1-2).

ENGINE ROTATION

During engine operation, it rotates counterclockwise when viewed from the left (alternator) side. Use the flywheel bolt to rotate the crankshaft manually, and always turn the crankshaft counterclockwise in the direction of operation.

TUNE-UP

Refer to **Table 4** for tune-up specifications.

Service or check the following items in order as described in this chapter:
1. Air filter.
2. Spark plugs.
3. Compression test.
4. Engine oil and filter.
5. Throttle valve synchronization.
6. Brake system.
7. Suspension components.
8. Tires and Wheels.
9. Final drive.
10. Fasteners.

AIR FILTER

The air filter removes dirt and debris from the incoming air. Regular air filter service is critical in preventing engine wear. Remove, clean, and inspect the air filter at the interval specified in **Table 1**. Replace the air filter if it is soiled, severely clogged or damaged.

Replace the air filter at the recommended interval (**Table 1**).
1. Remove the upper covers (Chapter Fifteen).
2. Remove the air filter screws (**Figure 1**) and lift the element (**Figure 2**) from the air filter housing.

3. If necessary, clean the interior of the air filter housing (**Figure 3**) with a shop rag and solvent.

4. Remove the housing drain plug (**Figure 4**) and drain away any accumulated moisture or debris.

5. Cover the housing opening with a clean shop cloth to prevent debris entry.

6. Gently tap the element to loosen dirt.

CAUTION
In the next step, do not apply compressed air directly at the filter, otherwise dirt will be forced into the element.

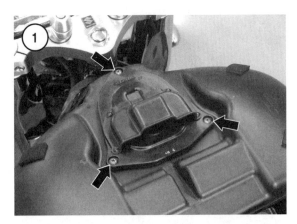

7. Apply compressed air at an angle to the *outside* of the air filter element (**Figure 5**) and blow away all loosened dirt.

8. Carefully inspect the filter element. If it is torn or broken in any area, replace the air filter. If the element is in good condition, return it to use until the time interval for replacement is reached.

9. Install the filter by reversing the removal procedures.

COMPRESSION TEST

Use a compression gauge (**Figure 6**) and perform a compression test to determine the condition of the rings, head gasket, pistons, and cylinders. Record the compression readings in the maintenance log at the end of this manual to provide an ongoing record. By comparing current readings with previous ones, a developing problem may be indicated. An engine with low compression or a large difference between cylinders cannot be tuned properly. Refer to **Table 4** for the compression specification.

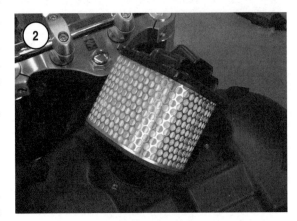

1. Make sure the battery is fully charged to ensure proper cranking speed.

2. Warm the engine to normal operating temperature and turn the engine off.

3. Remove the spark plugs as described in *Spark Plugs* in this chapter.

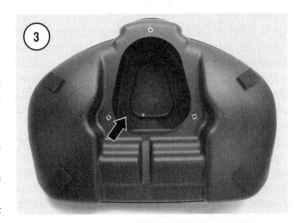

WARNING
Disable the fuel system to prevent fuel from entering the cylinders when the engine is turned over.

4. Disconnect the fuel pump connector (carbureted models: **Figure 7**; fuel injected models: **Figure 8**).

5. Screw the compression gauge into one cylinder following the manufacturer's instructions (**Figure 9**). Make sure the gauge properly seats.

6. Set the engine stop switch to run and turn the ignition switch on.

7. Open the throttle completely and use the starter

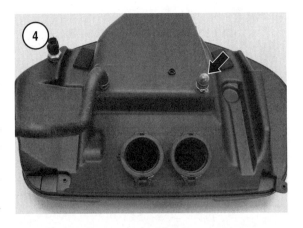

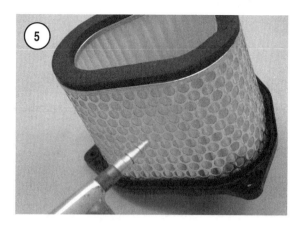

3

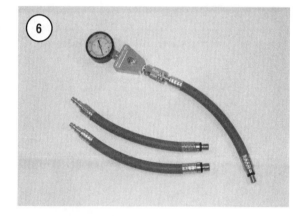

button to crank the engine while observing the gauge. Record the reading and cylinder number after there is no further rise in pressure. Maximum pressure should be achieved in approximately 5 seconds.

8. Repeat Steps 5-7 for the other cylinder.

9. Compare the maximum reading for each cylinder with the specification. If the reading is below the service limit, perform the following:

    a. Pour about a teaspoon of oil into the cylinder and turn the engine over once to distribute the oil.

    b. Reinstall the compression gauge and repeat the test. If the reading increases significantly, piston ring and/or cylinder wear is indicated. If the reading did not increase, valve wear is indicted.

10. Also note the difference between the two cylinders. If the readings exceed the maximum difference between cylinders specification, further engine diagnosis may be required. Refer to *Cylinder Leakdown Test* in Chapter Two.

11. If a compression reading exceeds the specification, check for carbon buildup in the combustion chamber.

12. Connect the fuel pump connector.

13. Install the spark plugs as described in this chapter.

SPARK PLUGS

Removal/Installation

1. Remove the upper covers (Chapter Fifteen).

2. Remove the cylinder head side cap from the cylinder (Chapter Four).

> *CAUTION*
> *Dirt around the spark plug can fall into the engine and cause damage.*

3. Blow away all loose dirt from the top surface of the cylinder head cover.

4. Grasp the spark plug cap (A, **Figure 10**), and carefully pull it straight up and off the spark plug (**Figure 11**).

5. Label the spark plug cap with its cylinder number.

6. Use compressed air to blow debris from the spark plug well.

7. Install a rubber insert spark plug socket onto the spark plug. Make sure it correctly seats on the plug. Install the socket handle and turn the spark plug out about halfway.

8. Use compressed air to blow out the spark plug well and remove any debris that was trapped below the spark plug hex fitting.

9. Remove the spark plug. Mark the spark plug with its cylinder number.

10. Repeat Steps 2-9 for the remaining spark plug.

11. Inspect the plugs as described in this section.

12. Inspect the spark plug caps for damage. Replace if necessary.

13. Measure, and if necessary adjust the spark plug gap as described in this section.

14. Reverse the preceding steps to install the spark plugs. Note the following:

    a. Screw the spark plug into the cylinder head by hand until the plug bottoms. Tighten the plug (**Figure 11**) to 18 N•m (13 ft.-lb.).

    b. Refer to the marks made during removal and install each spark plug cap (A, **Figure 10**) onto the correct spark plug. Press the spark plug cap firmly onto the spark plug. Rotate the assembly slightly in both directions and make sure it is securely attached to the plug.

Gap

Use a spark plug gapping tool, and a wire feeler gauge to measure and adjust the gap. Carefully gap the spark plug to ensure a reliable spark. Refer to **Table 4** for the plug gap specification.

1. If installed, unscrew the terminal nut from the end of the plug.

2. Insert a wire feeler gauge between the center and side electrodes of the plug (**Figure 12**). If the gap is correct, a slight drag is felt as the wire is pulled through the gap. If there is no drag or if the gauge will not pass through, bend the side electrode with a gaping tool (**Figure 13**) and set the gap to specification.

Type

Refer to **Table 4** for the recommended spark plugs.

Spark plugs are available in different heat ranges (**Figure 14**). A plug with an incorrect heat range can

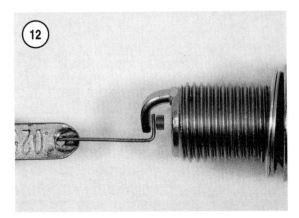

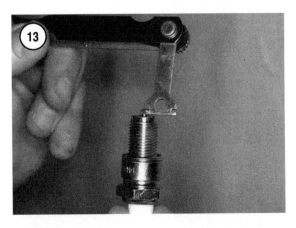

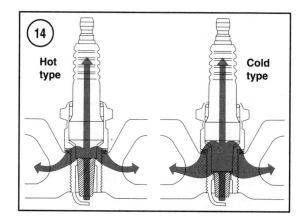

Hot type / Cold type

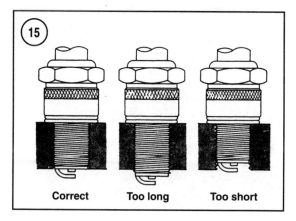

Correct   Too long   Too short

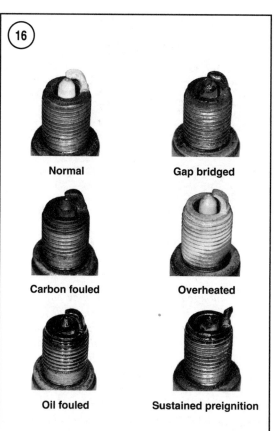

Normal   Gap bridged

Carbon fouled   Overheated

Oil fouled   Sustained preignition

foul or overheat. A hot plug may cause preignition and engine damage. Do not change the spark plug heat range to compensate for adverse engine operating conditions.

If all engine systems are working correctly and operating conditions warrant, use a hot plug for low speeds and low temperatures, and use a cold plug for high speeds, high engine loads and high temperatures.

A plug's operating temperature should be hot enough to burn off unwanted deposits but not so hot that it damages the plug or causes preignition. To determine if plug heat range is correct, remove each spark plug and examine the insulator.

When replacing plugs make sure the reach (**Figure 15**) is correct. A longer than standard plug could interfere with the piston and cause engine damage.

Inspection

Inspect the spark plugs for excessively worn electrodes, signs of overheating or damaged porcelain. Replace worn or damaged plugs.

Reading the spark plugs can provide information about spark plug operation, air/fuel mixture composition, and engine conditions (such as oil consumption or pistons). Before checking the spark plugs, operate the motorcycle under a medium load for approximately 6 miles (10 km). Avoid prolonged idling before shutting off the engine. Remove the spark plugs as described in this chapter. Examine each plug and compare it to those shown in **Figure 16**.

Normal condition

A light tan- or gray-colored deposit on the firing tip, and no abnormal gap wear or erosion indicates good engine, ignition and air/fuel mixture conditions. The heat range is correct. Check the plug gap and reinstall the plug.

Carbon fouled

Soft, dry, sooty deposits covering the firing end of the plug are evidence of incomplete combustion. If the deposits are excessive, the plug may misfire. One or more of the following conditions can cause carbon fouling:
1. Rich air/fuel mixture.
2. Cold spark plug heat range.
3. Clogged air filter.
4. Failed or improperly operating ignition component.
5. Low engine compression.
6. Prolonged idling.

Oil fouled

An oil fouled plug has a black insulator tip, a damp oily film over the firing end, and a carbon layer over the nose. Common causes for this condition are:

1. Incorrect air/fuel mixture.
2. Faulty fuel injection system.
3. Low idle speed or prolonged idling.
4. Ignition component failure.
5. Spark plug heat range too cold.
6. Engine still being broken in.
7. Valve guides worn.
8. Piston rings worn or broken.

Gap bridging

Deposit build up between the electrodes reduces the gap and may eventually close it. Check for excessive carbon and/or oil in the combustion chamber.

Overheating

Badly worn electrodes and premature gap wear are signs of overheating, along with a gray or white-blistered porcelain insulator surface. This condition may be the result of using a plug with the incorrect heat range (hot). If the spark plug heat range is correct, consider the following causes:

1. Lean air/fuel mixture.
2. Faulty fuel injection operation.
3. Improperly operating ignition component.
4. Engine lubrication system malfunction.
5. Cooling system malfunction.
6. Engine air leak.
7. Improper spark plug installation (overtightening).
8. No spark plug gasket.

Worn out

Corrosive combustion gasses and ignition voltage eventually wear down the electrodes. A worn spark plug requires more voltage to fire and may misfire under high loads. Replace worn plugs.

Preignition

Melted electrodes are the result of preignition. Check for improper throttle body mounting, intake manifold leaks or advanced ignition timing. The plug heat range may also be too hot. Find the cause of the preignition before returning the engine to service.

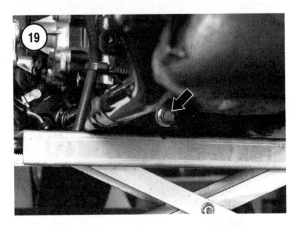

ENGINE OIL AND FILTER

> *WARNING*
> *Prolonged contact with oil may cause skin cancer. Wear fluid resistant gloves to prevent contact. If necessary, wash your hands thoroughly with soap and water as soon as possible after handling or coming in contact with engine oil.*

Refer to **Table 1** for the recommended oil and filter change interval. If the motorcycle is operated in extreme conditions, reduce the service interval. If the

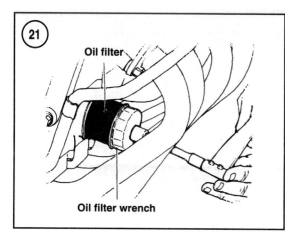

Oil filter

Oil filter wrench

machine is used infrequently, consider using a time based service schedule.

Refer to **Table 3** for oil specifications. Refer to Chapter One for general lubricant information.

Oil Level Check

1. Securely support the motorcycle in an upright position on a level surface.
2. Start the engine and warm it up for several minutes.
3. Shut off the engine and let the oil settle for approximately three minutes.

CAUTION
Do not perform an oil level reading with the motorcycle on the sidestand. The oil will flow away from the window, giving a false reading.

4. Have an assistant sit on the bike to hold it vertically.
5. Check the engine oil level in the oil inspection window (A, **Figure 17**). The oil level must be between the full and low lines on the clutch cover.
6. If necessary, adjust the oil level by performing the following:

a. Remove the speed sensor cover (B, **Figure 17**) as described in *Clutch Cover Removal* (Chapter Six).
b. If the oil level is low, remove the oil filler cap (**Figure 18**). Insert a small funnel into the filler neck. Add oil to correct the level.
c. If the oil level is too high, remove the oil filler cap and draw out the excess oil with a syringe or suction pump.

7. Inspect the O-ring seal on the oil filler cap. Replace the O-ring if it is damaged or hard.
8. Install the oil filler cap.
9. Recheck the oil level.

Oil and Filter Change

NOTE
Do not discard oil in the trash, or pour it onto the ground or down a storm drain. Pour used oil into plastic containers and dispose of it properly. Many service stations and oil retailers accept used engine oil for recycling.

1. Remove the speed sensor cover (B, **Figure 17**) as described in *Clutch Cover Removal* (Chapter Six).
2. Start the engine and warm it up for several minutes. Warming the engine heats up the oil so it flows freely, and carries out contaminants and sludge.
3. Shut the engine off. Securely support the motorcycle in an upright position on a level surface.
4. Place a drain pan under the oil drain bolt (**Figure 19**).
5. Remove the drain bolt and gasket from the bottom of the oil pan.
6. Loosen the oil filler cap (**Figure 18**). This speeds up the flow of oil.
7. Allow the oil to completely drain.
8. If necessary, inspect the drained oil for contamination.

WARNING
Make sure the exhaust system has cooled before oil filter removal. If necessary, protect your hands accordingly.

9. To replace the oil filter, perform the following:
a. Move the drain pan under the oil filter (**Figure 20**).
b. With a socket-type oil filter wrench (**Figure 21**, typical), turn the filter *counterclockwise* until oil begins to run out. When the oil stops dripping, loosen and remove the filter.
c. Hold the filter over the drain pan and pour out any remaining oil. Place the old filter in a plastic bag. Dispose of the old filter properly.

d. Thoroughly clean the oil filter mounting surface (A, **Figure 22**) on the crankcase to prevent oil leaks.

e. Apply a light coat of clean engine oil to the oil filter seal.

f. Install the oil filter onto the threaded oil pipe (B, **Figure 22**) and tighten the filter by hand until the seal contacts the crankcase.

g. With the oil filter wrench, tighten the filter an additional one to two turns.

10. Inspect the drain bolt gasket for damage. Replace the gasket if necessary.

11. Install the drain bolt (**Figure 19**) and gasket. Tighten the oil drain bolt to 21 N•m (15 ft.-lb.).

12. With a funnel, add the quantity of oil specified in **Table 3** through the oil fill hole.

13. Remove the funnel and install the oil filler cap securely.

14. Start the engine and let it idle.

15. Check the oil filter and drain plug for leaks. Tighten either if necessary.

16. Turn off the engine and check the engine oil level as described in this section. Adjust the oil level if necessary.

ENGINE OIL PRESSURE TEST

1. The following Suzuki tools, or their equivalents, are required to check the oil pressure:

   a. Oil pressure gauge hose: part No. 09915-74520.

   b. Oil pressure gauge adapter: part No. 09915-74532.

   c. Gauge (high pressure): part No. 09915-77330.

2. Securely support the motorcycle on a level surface.

3. Check the engine oil level as described in this chapter. Add oil if necessary.

4. Place a drain pan under the main oil gallery plug to catch the oil that drains out during the test.

5. On the right crankcase, remove the main oil gallery plug (**Figure 23**). It is behind the oil pressure switch and to the rear of the oil filter fitting.

6. Install the adapter into the main oil gallery. Install the hose and gauge into the adapter. Make sure the fitting is secure and route the hose away from the exhaust pipe.

7. Start the engine and warm it up. Operate the engine at 2000 rpm for 10-20 minutes.

8. Increase engine speed to 3000 rpm. The oil pressure should be within the range specified in **Table 4** when the oil temperature is 60° C (140° F).

9. If the oil pressure is lower than specified, check the following:

   a. Clogged oil filter.

   b. Oil leaking from an oil passageway.

   c. Damaged oil seal(s).

   d. Defective oil pump.

   e. Excessive engine bearing clearances.

   f. Combination of the above.

10. If the oil pressure is higher than specified check the following:

   a. Oil viscosity too high (drain the oil and install the proper oil).

   b. Clogged oil passageway.

   c. Combination of the above.

11. Shut off the engine and remove the gauge.

12. Apply a light coat of gasket sealer to the main oil gallery plug. Then install the plug (**Figure 23**) into the crankcase. Tighten it to 18 N•m (13 ft.-lb.).

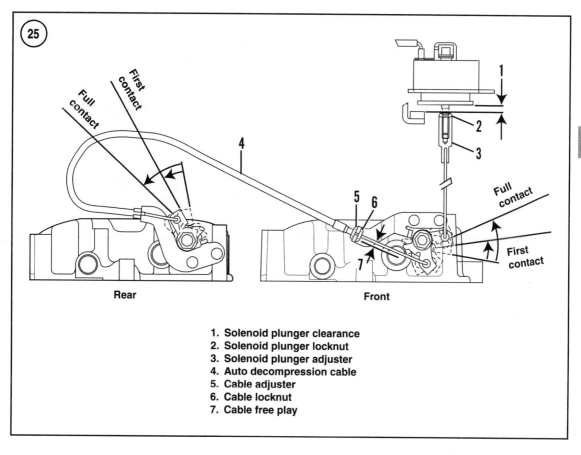

1. Solenoid plunger clearance
2. Solenoid plunger locknut
3. Solenoid plunger adjuster
4. Auto decompression cable
5. Cable adjuster
6. Cable locknut
7. Cable free play

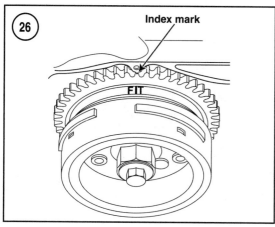

13. Check oil level and adjust if necessary.

FUEL FILTER (1998-2004 Models)

Removal/Inspection/Installation

1. Remove the rider's seat (Chapter Fifteen).
2. Disconnect the fuel hose from the input fitting (A, **Figure 24**) on the filter.
3. Disconnect fuel hose from the filter's output fitting (B, **Figure 24**). Note that the arrow on the filter points in the direction of fuel flow (toward the fuel pump).

4. Bend the clamp arms (C, **Figure 24**) away from the fuel filter and remove the filter.
5. Inspect the fuel filter for cracks or clogs. Replace the filter if it appears dirty or rusty.
6. Install the fuel filter by reversing the removal procedure.
    a. Position the filter so its arrow points in the correct direction of fuel flow.
    b. Make sure each hose is securely connected to the correct fitting.

AUTO-DECOMPRESSION CABLE ADJUSTMENT

Refer to **Figure 25**.
1. Remove the rider's seat and upper covers (Chapter Fifteen).
2. Remove the cylinder head side cap from each head (Chapter Four).
3. Remove the air filter housing (Chapter Eight).
4. Remove the alternator cover (Chapter Five).
5. Set the front cylinder to TDC on the compression stroke by performing the following:
    a. Use the flywheel bolt to rotate the engine counterclockwise until the front cylinder TDC mark (F|T) on the flywheel aligns with the index mark on the crankcase (**Figure 26**).

b. Move the front cylinder auto-decompression lever (A, **Figure 27**) rearward. If it moves through its full range of movement, the front cylinder is set to TDC on the exhaust stroke. Set it to the compression stroke by rotating the engine an additional 360° counterclockwise until the front cylinder TDC mark aligns with the crankcase mark.

6. Loosen the cable locknut (B, **Figure 27**) and loosen the locknut on the auto-decompression solenoid plunger (2, **Figure 25**).

7. Turn the solenoid plunger adjuster (3, **Figure 25**) so there is sufficient slack in the cable (4).

8. Rotate the front (A, **Figure 27**) and rear (B, **Figure 10**) auto-decompression levers until they just contact their respective exhaust rocker arms. Have an assistant hold the levers in this position.

9. Turn the cable adjuster (C, **Figure 27**) until the cable free play (7, **Figure 25**) equals the auto-decompression cable free play specified in **Table 4**.

10. Tighten the cable locknut (B, **Figure 27**) securely.

11. While still holding the levers in their first contact positions, turn the auto-decompression solenoid adjuster (3, **Figure 25**) until the clearance (1) between the plunger and its stopper equals the auto-decompression solenoid clearance specified in **Table 4**.

12. Tighten the plunger locknut (2, **Figure 25**).

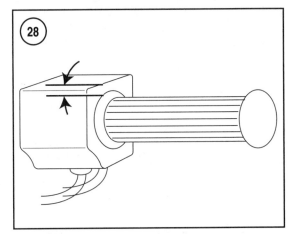

THROTTLE CABLE FREE PLAY

Check the throttle cable free play at the specified interval. Measure throttle cable free play (**Figure 28**) at the end of the throttle grip. Make minor adjustments at the throttle grip. If the free play cannot be properly adjusted at the throttle grip, perform a major adjustment at the throttle pulley. If the free play still cannot be adjusted to specification due to cable stretch, replace them.

Check

1. Shift the transmission into neutral. Start the engine and let it idle.

2. Once the engine is warm, slowly twist the throttle grip to raise the engine speed. Note the amount of rotational movement needed to increase engine speed off idle. This is throttle cable free play. It should be within specification (**Table 4**).

> *WARNING*
> *With the engine running at idle speed, turn the handlebars from side to side. If the idle speed increases during this movement, either the throttle cables need adjusting or they are incorrectly*

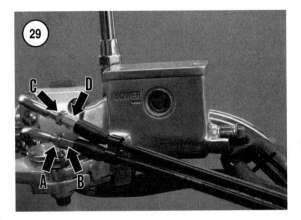

routed through the frame. Correct this problem immediately. Do not ride the motorcycle in this unsafe condition.

3. With the engine still idling, turn the handlebar from lock to lock. Idle speed should not change.

Minor Adjustment

1. Loosen the return cable locknut (A, **Figure 29**) and turn the adjuster (B) all the way in toward the throttle housing.

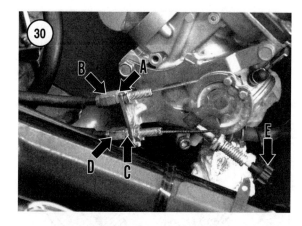

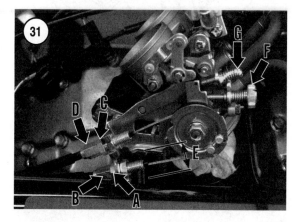

7. Start the engine and recheck the free play.

Major Adjustment (Fuel Injected Models)

1. Remove the air filter housing (Chapter Eight).
2. At the throttle pulley, loosen the locknut (A, **Figure 31**) on the return cable and turn the cable adjuster (B) to obtain sufficient slack.
3. Loosen the pull cable locknut (C, **Figure 31**).
4. Turn the pull cable adjuster (D, **Figure 31**) in or out until the throttle cable free play at the throttle grip (**Figure 28**) is within specification (**Table 4**).
5. Hold the pull cable adjuster (D, **Figure 31**) and tighten its locknut (C) securely.
6. While holding the throttle grip fully closed, turn the return cable adjuster (B, **Figure 31**) and check the return cable deflection (E). Continue to adjust the return cable until its deflection equals 1.0 mm (0.04 in.).
7. Tighten the return cable locknut (A, **Figure 31**) securely.
8. Start the engine and recheck the free play.

ENGINE IDLE SPEED

WARNING
With the engine running at idle speed, turn the handlebars from side to side. If the idle speed increases during this movement, either the throttle cables require adjusting or they are incorrectly routed through the frame. Correct this problem before adjusting the idle speed.

Before adjusting idle speed, clean or replace the air filter, test the engine compression, and synchronize the throttle valves (this chapter). Idle speed cannot be properly adjusted if these items are not within specification. Refer to the procedures described in this chapter.

1. Securely support the motorcycle on a level surface.
2. Make sure the throttle cable free play is adjusted correctly (this chapter).
3. Remove the upper cover from the left side (Chapter Fifteen).
4. Connect a tachometer to the engine following the manufacturer's instructions.
5. Start the engine and allow it to reach normal operating temperature. With the engine at idle, turn the throttle stop screw (E, **Figure 30**: carbureted models; F, **Figure 31**: fuel injected models) on the left side until the idle speed is within specification (**Table 4**).

2. Loosen the pull cable locknut (C, **Figure 29**). Turn its adjuster (D, **Figure 29**) until throttle cable free play is within the range specified in **Table 4**.
3. Hold the pull cable adjuster (D, **Figure 29**) and tighten its locknut (C) securely.
4. Hold the throttle grip closed and turn out the return cable adjuster (B, **Figure 29**) until resistance is felt.
5. Hold the adjuster and tighten the return cable locknut (A, **Figure 29**).
6. Start the engine and recheck the free play.

Major Adjustment (Carbureted Models)

1. Remove the air filter housing (Chapter Eight).
2. At the throttle pulley, loosen the locknut (A, **Figure 30**) on the return cable and turn the cable adjuster (B) to obtain sufficient slack.
3. Loosen the pull cable locknut (C, **Figure 30**).
4. Turn the pull cable adjuster (D, **Figure 30**) in or out until the throttle cable free play at the throttle grip (**Figure 28**) is within specification (**Table 4**).
5. Hold the pull cable adjuster (D, **Figure 30**) and tighten its locknut (C) securely.
6. With the throttle grip closed, turn the return cable adjuster (B, **Figure 30**) until resistance is felt. Hold the adjuster and tighten the return cable locknut (A, **Figure 30**).

6. Rev the engine a few times and make sure the speed returns to the set speed. Readjust, if necessary.

7. Shut off the engine.

FAST IDLE SPEED (FUEL INJECTED MODELS)

1. Remove the upper covers (Chapter Fifteen).

2. Connect a tachometer to the engine. Start the engine and allow it to reach operating temperature.

3. Set the idle speed to 1000 rpm.

4. Inspect the throttle position sensor as described in Chapter Nine. In necessary, adjust the sensor.

5. Turn off the engine.

6. Refer to *Throttle Position Sensor Output Voltage Test* in Chapter Nine and measure TPS output voltage when the throttle is closed. Record the reading. This reading is the output voltage at idle.

7. Turn the ignition switch off and remove the air filter housing (Chapter Eight).

8. Manually move the secondary throttle valves to the fully open position (**Figure 32**). Repeat Step 6, and measure the TPS output voltage while the secondary throttle valves are held open. Record this reading. This reading is the output voltage at STV open.

9. Subtract the idle reading (Step 6) from the STV open reading (Step 8). The difference is the TPS output voltage variance. The variance should be within the range specified in **Table 4**.

10. If the variance is out of specification, adjust the fast idle screw (G, **Figure 31**), and repeat Step 8 and Step 9. Continually adjust the fast idle screw and retest until the output voltage variance is within the specified range.

11. Once variance is within specification, let the engine completely cool down.

12. Start the engine and note the idle speed. If should equal the fast idle speed specified in **Table 4**. If it does not, check for a short in the oil temperature circuit or in the secondary throttle valve actuator circuit.

THROTTLE VALVE SYNCHRONIZATION

Carbureted Models

Use a vacuum balancer gauge (Suzuki part No. 09913-13121), or its equivalent, to perform this procedure.

1. Balance the vacuum gauges following the manufacturer's instructions.

2. Remove the carburetors (Chapter Eight).

3. On non-California models, remove the cap from the vacuum fitting on the each carburetor. On

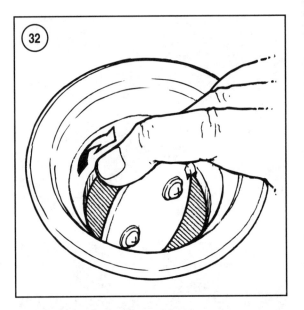

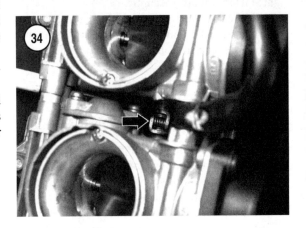

California models, disconnect the EVAP hose from the vacuum fitting on each carburetor.

4. Connect a vacuum gauge to the vacuum fitting (**Figure 33**) on each carburetor.

5. Reinstall the carburetors (Chapter Eight).

6. Connect a tachometer to the engine. Start the engine and adjust idle speed to 1750 rpm with the throttle stop screw.

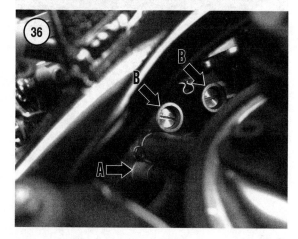

7. Check the position of the balls in the vacuum balancer gauge. If the balls are not at the same level, gradually adjust the synchronizing screw (**Figure 34**) until both balls ride at the same level.

8. Snap the throttle a few times and recheck the gauge. Readjust synchronization if required.

9. Remove the vacuum balancer.

10. Adjust engine idle speed (this chapter).

Fuel Injected Models

A digital vacuum tester or a vacuum balancer gauge (Suzuki part No. 09913-13121), or its equivalent, is needed to perform this procedure.

1. Remove the seats and the upper covers (Chapter Fifteen).

2. Start the engine. Run the engine at idle until it warms to operating temperature.

3. Connect a tachometer to the engine. Use the throttle stop screw to set the idle speed to 1000 rpm. Turn off the engine.

4. Calibrate the vacuum gauge following the tool manufacturer's instructions.

5. Disconnect the 3-pin connector (A, **Figure 35**) from each intake air pressure sensor.

6. Follow the IAP sensor vacuum hose (B, **Figure 35**) from the sensor to its vacuum fitting on the throttle body (A, **Figure 36**). Disconnect the IAP sensor hose from the throttle body fitting and connect the vacuum gauge to this vacuum fitting.

7. Repeat Step 5 and Step 6 for the opposite cylinder.

8. Start the engine and let it idle. If necessary, use the throttle stop screw (F, **Figure 31**) to adjust the idle speed to 1000 rpm.

9. With the engine running at idle, check the gauge readings. When properly balanced, the throttle valves should have equal vacuum in both cylinders. If this is not the case, synchronize the throttle valve by performing either Step 10A or Step 10B.

10A. When using a digital vacuum tester, perform the following:

   a. Turn each idle air screw (B, **Figure 36**) clockwise until it lightly bottoms. Count the number of turns needed to bottom each screw. Record these numbers.

   b. Check the difference between the vacuum in each cylinder.

   c. Gradually turn out the idle air screw on the throttle body with the higher vacuum. Stop when the vacuum equals the vacuum in the other cylinder.

   d. Recheck the synchronization. If still out of specification, remove each idle air screw (B, **Figure 36**). Clean the screws and the throttle body passages with an aerosol carburetor cleaner. Dry them with compressed air and reinstall the screws. Turn them out the number of turns noted in substep a, and recheck.

10B. When using a vacuum balancer gauge, perform the following:

   a. Check the difference between the vacuum in each cylinder.

   b. If the difference is greater than one ball, gradually turn out the idle air screw on the throttle with the higher vacuum. Stop when this higher vacuum equals the vacuum in the other cylinder.

   c. The throttle valves are synchronized when the balls in No. 1 and No. 2 cylinder are at the same level on the vacuum balancer.

11. Snap the throttle a few times and recheck the vacuum readings. Readjust synchronization if required.

12. Check the idle speed. If necessary, use the throttle stop screw to set idle speed to 1000 rpm.

13. Stop the engine and detach the equipment.

14. Reconnect the rear IAP sensor vacuum line (B, **Figure 35**) to the correct throttle body vacuum fitting (A, **Figure 36**). Connect the electrical connector to the IAP sensor (A, **Figure 35**).

15. Repeat Step 14 for the front IAP sensor (**Figure 37**) hose and connector.

16. Install the air filter housing (Chapter Eight).

17. Restart the engine and check the engine idle speed.

18. If necessary, adjust the throttle cable free play as described in this chapter.

FUEL LINE INSPECTION

Inspect the fuel hoses at the intervals specified in **Table 1**.

1. Remove the air filter housing (Chapter Eight).

2. Inspect the fuel hose(s) for leaks, hardness, deterioration or other damage.

3. Make sure the hoses are securely attached to their respective fittings.

4. On fuel injected models, make sure the fuel supply hose is securely attached to its fittings.

5. Replace damaged fuel hose(s) as needed or at the intervals specified in **Table 1**.

EMISSION CONTROL SYSTEMS

PAIR System

The PAIR (air supply) system introduces fresh air into the cylinder exhaust port to reduce unburned fuel emissions.

Inspect all PAIR hoses for deterioration, damage or loose connections at the intervals in **Table 1**. Replace any parts or hoses as required. Check the fittings and tightness of clamps.

If necessary, remove, and inspect the PAIR control valve and the reed valves as described in Chapter Eight.

Evaporative Emission Control System (California Models)

At the service intervals in **Table 1**, check all of the emission control lines and the EVAP canister for loose connections or damage. Also check the EVAP canister housing for damage. Replace any parts or hoses as required. Refer to the vacuum hose routing label (**Figure 38**) inside the toolbox cover and the diagram in Chapter Eight for additional information.

CLUTCH

Fluid Level Check

Maintain the fluid level above the lower mark on the clutch master cylinder reservoir (**Figure 39**). If the clutch fluid level reaches the lower level mark, correct the fluid level by adding new DOT 4 brake fluid.

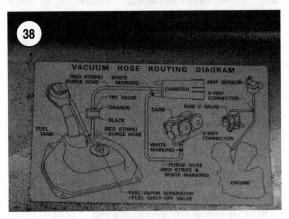

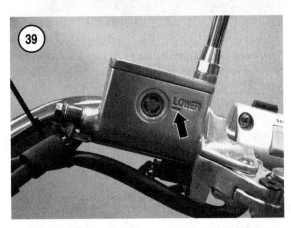

Fluid Change

Brake fluid absorbs moisture from the atmosphere. Change the clutch fluid every two years (Chapter Six).

Clutch Hose

Check the clutch hose between the master cylinder and release cylinder. The manufacturer recommends replacing the clutch hose every four years. If there are any leaks, tighten the connections and bleed the system as described in Chapter Six. If this does not

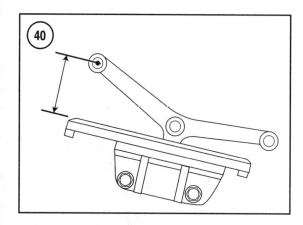

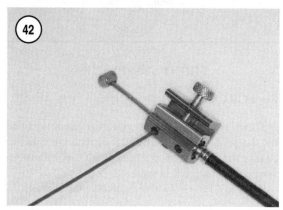

4. Loosen the locknut (A, **Figure 41**) at each end of the shift rod (B).

5. Turn the rod (B, **Figure 41**) until the shift pedal moves to the specified height or to the rider's desired height.

6. Tighten each locknut securely.

CONTROL CABLE LUBRICATION

Lubricate non-nylon lined control cables with a cable lubricant and cable lubricator (**Figure 42**) during cable adjustment or if a cable becomes stiff. During cable lubrication, inspect the cables for fraying, and check the housing for damage. Replace any defective cables immediately.

> *CAUTION*
> *Most nylon-lined cables do not require lubrication. On aftermarket cables, follow the cable manufacturer's instructions.*

1. Disconnect each cable end as described in the relevant chapter.

2. Attach a cable lubricator (**Figure 42**) to a cable end, following the manufacturer's instructions.

3. Insert the lubricant nozzle into the lubricator. Place a shop cloth at the end of the cable(s) to catch the excess lubricant.

4. Press the nozzle and hold it down until the lubricant begins to flow out the other end of the cable. It may be necessary to adjust the lubricator for it to seal properly. If lubricant does not flow out the end of the cable, check the cable for fraying, bending or other damage.

5. Remove the lubricator and wipe off all excess lubricant from the cable. Place a dab of grease onto the cable ends before reconnecting it.

6. Install the cable as described in the appropriate chapter.

7. Adjust the cable as described in this chapter.

stop the leak or if a line is obviously damaged, replace the hose. Then bleed the system.

SHIFT PEDAL HEIGHT

1. Securely support the motorcycle on a level surface.

2. Remove the secondary gear cover (Chapter Seven).

3. Measure the distance from the top of the floorboard to the middle of the shift pedal pin (**Figure 40**). Refer to **Table 4** for the specified shift pedal height.

TIRES AND WHEELS

Refer to Chapter Eleven for tire changing.

Tire Inspection

1. With an accurate tire gauge, check, and if necessary, adjust the tire pressure (**Table 2**) for good performance and tire life. Check tire pressure when the tires are cold; never release air pressure from a warm or hot tire to match the recommended tire pressure. Doing so causes an under-inflated tire.

2. Periodically inspect the tires for the following:

a. Deep cuts or imbedded objects. If a nail or other object is in a tire, mark its location before removal to help locate the hole for repair. If a small object has punctured the tire, air may leak very slowly due to the tendency of tubeless tires to self-seal when punctured. Check the tires carefully.

b. Flat spots.

c. Uneven wear.

d. Cracks.

e. Separating plies.

f. Sidewall damage.

3. Measure the tread depth in the center of the tire (**Figure 43**) using a small ruler or a tread depth gauge. Replace the original equipment tires before the center tread depth wears to the minimum tread depth specified in **Table 2**.

4. Compare the wear in the center of the contact patch with the wear at the edges and note the following:

a. If the tire shows excessive wear at the edge of the contact patch but the wear at the center is normal, the tire has been under-inflated. Under-inflated tires result in higher tire temperatures, hard or imprecise steering and abnormal wear.

b. If the tire shows excessive wear in the center of the contact patch but wear at the edge is normal, the tire has been over-inflated. Over-inflated tires result in a hard ride and abnormal wear. Sustained straight line riding can also wear out the center of the tire.

5. The tires are also designed with tread wear indicators. When these are even with the tread blocks, the tires are no longer safe and must be replaced.

6. Other factors that have an effect on tire wear are:

a. Overloading.

b. Incorrect wheel alignment.

c. Incorrect wheel balance.

d. Worn or damaged wheel bearings.

Wheel Inspection

Frequently inspect the wheel for cracks, warp or dents. A damaged wheel may cause an air leak or steering vibration. If an alloy wheel is damaged, the wheel must be replaced. It *cannot* be repaired.

Wheel runout is the amount of wobble a wheel shows as it rotates. To quickly check runout, support the motorcycle with the wheel off the ground. Slowly turn the wheel while holding a pointer solidly against a fork leg or the swing arm with the other end against the rim. For more precise inspection, remove the wheel, and check the axial and radial runout (**Figure 44**) as described in Chapter Eleven.

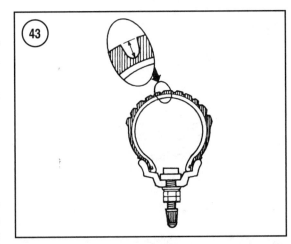

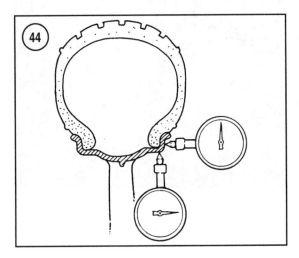

FRONT SUSPENSION

Fork Oil Change

There is no oil change interval recommended for the front fork. Generally, it is recommended to change the fork oil once a year. If the fork oil is contaminated, change it immediately.

Refer to Chapter Twelve to change the fork oil.

Front Fork Inspection

Inspect the front fork at the intervals in **Table 1**.

1. Use a soft wet cloth to wipe the fork tubes to remove any dirt and debris. As this debris moves against the fork seals, it eventually damages the seals and causes an oil leak.

2. Check the fork sliders for any oil seal leaks or damage.

3. Apply the front brake and pump the fork up and down. Check for smooth operation.

4. Refer to the specifications in **Table 5** and check the following fasteners:

a. Lower fork bridge clamp bolt.

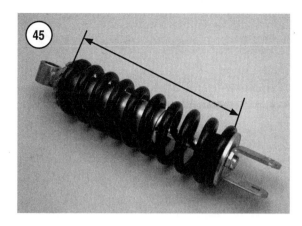

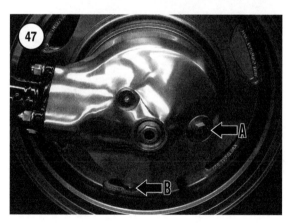

b. Upper fork bridge clamp bolt (fuel injected models).
c. Handlebar clamp bolt.
d. Handlebar holder nut.
e. Front axle.
f. Front axle clamp bolt.

STEERING HEAD

Inspection

1. Securely support the motorcycle on a level surface with the front wheel 20-30 mm (0.8-1.2 in.) off the floor.

2. Check the control cables and wiring harness routing.
3. Grasp the lower end each fork leg. Try to rock the steering head back and forth. Adjust the steering head bearings (Chapter Twelve) if excessive movement is noted.

REAR SUSPENSION

Inspection

1. Securely support the motorcycle with both wheels on the ground. Check the shock absorber by bouncing on the seat several times.
2. Securely support the motorcycle with the rear wheel off the ground.
3. While an assistant steadies the motorcycle, push hard on the rear wheel (sideways) to check for side play in the swing arm bearings.
4. Check the shock absorber for oil leaks or other damage.
5. Check the shock absorber, suspension linkage, rear axle, and swing arm hardware. Make sure all fasteners are tight.

Shock Absorber Adjustment

Set the spring preload by adjusting the spring length (**Figure 45**). A longer spring length provides a softer ride; a shorter spring length provides a stiffer ride. There must be preload on the spring at all times. Never ride the motorcycle without some spring preload. Doing so could cause loss of control. The standard, maximum and minimum preload specifications are in **Table 4**.

1. Securely support the motorcycle on a level surface.
2. Loosen the locknut (A, **Figure 46**).
3. Turn the adjust nut (B, **Figure 46**) clockwise to increase preload or counterclockwise to reduce preload.
4. Hold the adjust nut and tighten the locknut securely.
5. Measure the spring length. It must be between the minimum and maximum length specified in **Table 4**.

FINAL DRIVE

Oil Check

1. Securely support the motorcycle in an upright position on a level surface.
2. Remove the filler bolt (A, **Figure 47**) from the final drive.
3. The oil level should sit at the edge of the filler hole.

4. If the oil level is low, add gear oil until the final drive is full. Refer to **Table 3** for the recommended final drive gear oil.

5. Install the final drive filler bolt with a new O-ring. Tighten the bolt securely.

Oil Change

1. Securely support the motorcycle in an upright position on a level surface. Remove the filler bolt (A, **Figure 47**) to facilitate draining.

2. Place a drain pan under the drain bolt (B, **Figure 47**).

3. Remove the drain bolt and drain the oil from the final drive.

4. Install the final drive drain bolt and tighten it to 23 N•m (17 ft.-lb.).

5. Refer to **Table 3** and add the recommended quantity of final drive gear oil.

6. Check the level of oil in the final drive. Add oil as necessary.

7. Install the final drive filler bolt with a new O-ring. Tighten the bolt securely.

BRAKE SYSTEM

WARNING
Use DOT 4 brake fluid. Do not mix different types of brake fluid as they may not be compatible.

CAUTION
Be careful when handling brake fluid. Do not spill it on painted, plated or plastic surfaces. It may damage these surfaces. Wash the area immediately with soapy water and thoroughly rinse off.

Fluid Level Check

Maintain the fluid level above the lower mark on the reservoir. If the brake fluid level reaches that mark (front: **Figure 48**, rear: **Figure 49**), correct the fluid level by adding new brake fluid.

1. Securely support the motorcycle on level ground.

2A. When adding brake fluid to the front master cylinder, position the handlebars so the master cylinder reservoir is level.

2B. On the rear master cylinder, make sure the top of the reservoir is level.

3. Clean any dirt from the top cover of the master cylinder prior to removing the cover.

4. Remove the top cover, diaphragm plate (front master cylinder) and the diaphragm.

5. Add brake fluid from a sealed brake fluid container.

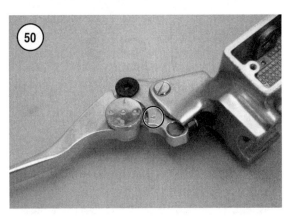

6. Reinstall the diaphragm, diaphragm plate (front master cylinder) and the top cover.

Fluid Change

Brake fluid absorbs moisture from the atmosphere. Drain out the old brake fluid and change it every two years as described in Chapter Fourteen.

Brake Hoses

Check the brake hoses between the master cylinder and each brake caliper. If there are leaks, tighten

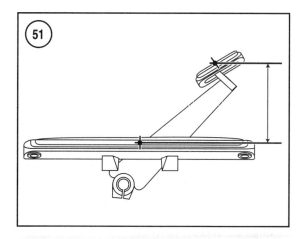

Front Brake Lever Position Adjustment

Adjust the brake lever to hand grip distance to suit rider preference.

1. Push the brake lever forward away from the handle grip.
2. Rotate the adjusting dial until the desired setting is opposite the arrow on the bracket (**Figure 50**). Position No. 1 sets the lever to the furthest position away from the hand grip; position No. 4 sets the lever to the position closest to the grip.
3. Make sure the stop on the brake lever holder engages the detent in the adjusting dial.
4. After adjusting the lever position, spin the wheel and check for any brake drag. Readjust as necessary.

Brake Pedal Height Adjustment

The pedal height is the distance from the top of the brake pedal to the top of the footrest (**Figure 51**). The brake pedal height changes as the brake pads wear. If the brake pedal height is outside the range specified in **Table 4**, adjust the height by performing the following.

1. Securely support the motorcycle on a level surface.
2. Make sure the brake pedal is in the at-rest position.
3. Loosen the rear brake master cylinder locknut (A, **Figure 52**) and turn the pushrod (B) in either direction until the brake pedal height is within the specified range.
4. Tighten the rear master cylinder pushrod locknut (A, **Figure 52**) to the 18 N•m (13 ft.-lb.).

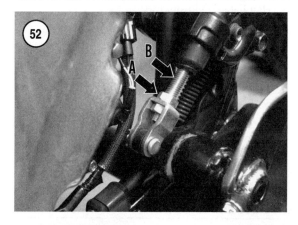

Rear Brake Light Switch Adjustment

1. Turn the ignition switch on.
2. Depress the brake pedal and watch the brake light. The brake light should come on just before pressure is felt at the brake pedal.
3. To adjust the brake light switch, hold the switch body (A, **Figure 53**) and turn the adjusting locknut (B). To make the light come on earlier, turn the adjusting locknut and move the switch body *up*. Move the switch body *down* to delay the light coming on.
4. Make sure the brake light comes on when the pedal is depressed and goes off when the pedal is released. Readjust if necessary.
5. Turn the ignition switch off.

the connections. Then bleed the brakes as described in Chapter Fourteen. If this does not stop the leak or if a line is obviously damaged, replace the hose(s). Then bleed the brakes.

The manufacturer recommends brake hose replacement every four years.

Pad Inspection

Inspect the brake pads for excessive or uneven wear, scoring or contamination of the friction surface. Refer to *Brake Pad Inspection* in Chapter Fourteen.

GENERAL LUBRICATION

Swing arm Bearings

Lubricate the swing arm bearings with grease at the rear suspension inspection intervals in **Table 1**.

Refer to Chapter Thirteen, as the swing arm must be removed.

Steering Head Bearings

Remove, clean and lubricate the steering head bearings with grease at the steering inspection interval in **Table 1**. Refer to Chapter Twelve.

Wheel Bearing Inspection/Lubrication

Regularly inspect and lubricate the wheel bearings as described in Chapter Eleven.

Miscellaneous

Unless otherwise indicated, lubricate the following items with grease.
1. Shift pedal pivot.
2. Brake pedal pivot.
3. Footrest pivot.
4. Clutch lever pivot.
5. Front brake lever pivot.
6. Sidestand pivot.
7. Control cable ends.
8. O-rings and oil seal lips.

FASTENERS

Vibration can loosen many fasteners on a motorcycle. Check the tightness of all fasteners, especially those on:
1. Engine mounting hardware.
2. Engine crankcase covers.
3. Handlebar and front fork.
4. Gearshift lever.
5. Brake pedal and lever.
6. Exhaust system.
7. Lighting equipment
8. Brake system.

Table 1 MAINTENANCE SCHEDULE

Initial 600 miles (1000 km) or 1 month
Change engine oil and replace oil filter
Change the final drive gear oil
Check idle speed; adjust if necessary
Check throttle cable free play; adjust or lubricate as necessary
Check the automatic decompression cable; adjust or lubricate as necessary
Check brake pads for wear
Check brake discs thickness; replace if necessary
Check brake discs for rust and corrosion; clean if necessary
Check steering play; adjust if necessary
Check and tighten all exhaust system fasteners
Check tightness of all chassis fasteners; tighten if necessary
On California models, synchronize the throttle valves
Every 4000 miles (6000 km) or 6 months
Check air filter element for contamination; clean or replace if necessary
Check spark plugs; replace if necessary
Check all fuel system hoses for leakage; repair or replace if necessary
Change engine oil
Check idle speed; adjust if necessary
Check throttle cable free play; adjust or lubricate as necessary
Check the automatic decompression cable; adjust or lubricate as necessary
Bleed the clutch line, and check the fluid level in the clutch master cylinder. Add fluid as necessary
Check the clutch hose for leaks. Repair as necessary
Check brake pads for wear
Check brake discs thickness; replace if necessary
Check brake discs for rust and corrosion; clean if necessary
Check brake system for leaks; repair if necessary
Bleed the brake and check brake fluid level in both reservoirs; add fluid if necessary
Check tire and wheel condition. Check wheel bearings
Lubricate all pivot points
Check tightness of all chassis fasteners; tighten if necessary
(continued)

Table 1 MAINTENANCE SCHEDULE (continued)

Every 7500 miles (12,000 km) or 12 months
  Check air filter element for contamination; clean or replace if necessary
  Replace both spark plugs
  Change engine oil
  Inspect the final drive gear oil. Add or replace the oil as necessary
  Check all fuel system hoses for leaks; repair or replace if necessary
  Check idle speed; adjust if necessary
  Check throttle cable free play; adjust or lubricate as necessary
  Check the automatic decompression cable; adjust or lubricate as necessary
  Inspect the fuel filter; replace as necessary
  Synchronize the throttle valves
  Check EVAP hoses (California models)
  Check PAIR (air supply) hoses
  Bleed the clutch line, and check the fluid level in the clutch master cylinder. Add fluid as necessary
  Check the clutch hose for leaks. Repair as necessary
  Check brake pads for wear
  Check brake discs thickness; replace if necessary
  Check brake discs for rust and corrosion; clean if necessary
  Check brake system for leaks; repair if necessary
  Bleed the brake and check brake fluid level in both reservoirs; add fluid if necessary
  Check tire and wheel condition
  Check front fork operation and for leaks
  Check steering play; adjust if necessary
  Check the operation of the rear suspension. Inspect the shock absorber for leaks
  Check tightness of all chassis fasteners; tighten if necessary
  Check and tighten all exhaust system fasteners
Every 11,000 miles (18,000 km) or 18 months
  All of the checks listed in 4000 miles (6000 km) or 6 month interval, and perform the following
  Replace air filter element
  Change the engine oil and oil filter
Every 15,000 miles (24,000 km) or 24 months
  All of the checks listed in 7500 miles (12,000 km) or 12 month interval
Every 2 years
  Replace the clutch fluid
  Replace the brake fluid
Every 4 years*
  Replace all brake hoses
  Replace all clutch hoses
  Replace all fuel hoses
  Replace the EVAP hoses (California models)

*Manufacturer recommendation.

Table 2 TIRE SPECIFICATIONS

Item	Front	Rear
Tire type	Tubeless	Tubeless
Size		
1998-2001 models	150/80-16 71H	180/70-15M/C 76H
2002-on models	150/80-16 71H, 150/80-16M/C 71H	180/70-15M/C 76H
Minimum tread depth	1.6 mm (0.06 in.)	2.0 mm (0.08 in.)
Inflation pressure (cold)*		
Solo	200 kPa (29 psi)	250 kPa (36 psi)
Rider and passenger	200 kPa (29 psi)	250 kPa (36 psi)

*Tire inflation pressure is for original equipment tires. Aftermarket tires may require different inflation pressure. The use of tires other than those specified by the manufacture may cause instability.

Table 3 RECOMMENDED LUBRICANTS AND FLUIDS

Fuel octane
  USA, California and Canada models
    Pump octane: (R+M) / 2   87
    Research octane   91

(continued)

Table 3 RECOMMENDED LUBRICANTS AND FLUIDS (continued)

All models except USA, California and Canada	
1998 models	85-95
1999-on models	91
Fuel tank capacity (including reserve)	
1998-1999 models	15.5 liters (4.1 gal.)
2000-2004	15.0 liters (4.0 gal.)
2005-on	14.0 liters (3.7 gal.)
Engine oil	
Classification	API SF, SG or SH, SJ with JASO MA rating
Viscosity	SAE 10W-40
Capacity	
Oil change only	3.7 liters (3.9 qt.)
Oil and filter change	4.3 liters (4.5 qt.)
When engine completely dry	5.0 liters (5.3 qt.)
Brake/Clutch fluid	DOT 4
Fork oil	
Viscosity	SS-08 fork oil or an equivalent #10 fork oil
Capacity per leg	
1998-2004 models	439 ml (14.8 oz.)
2004-on models	416 ml (14.1 oz.)
Final drive gear oil	
Type	SAE 90 hypoid gear oil meeting API GL-5 certification
Final drive capacity	200-220 ml (6.8-7.4 oz.)

Table 4 MAINTENANCE AND TUNE-UP SPECIFICATIONS

Item	Specification
Spark plugs	
Type	
Standard	NGK: DPR7EA-9, Denso: X22EPR-U9
Cold	NGK: DPR8EA-9 or DPR9EA-9; Denso: X24EPR-U9 or X27EPR-U9
Gap	0.8-0.9 mm (0.032-0.035 in.)
Spark-test gap	Over 8 mm (0.3 in.)
Idle speed	
1998-2000 Switzerland and Austria models	950-1050 rpm
All 1998-2000 models except Switzerland and Austria	900-1100 rpm
2001-on models	900-1100 rpm
Fast idle speed (2005-on models)	1400-2000 rpm when engine is cold
Throttle cable free play	2.0-4.0 mm (0.08-0.16 in.)
Auto-decompression cable free play	1.0 mm (0.04 in.)
Auto-decompression solenoid clearance	6.0 mm (0.24 in.)
Throttle position sensor	
Output voltage @ idle	Approx. 1.12 volts
Output voltage variance	0.064-0.096 volts
Ignition timing*	
1998-2004 models	2° BTDC @ 1000 rpm
2005-on	9° BTDC @ 1000 rpm
Compression pressure (at sea level)	
Standard	1000-1400 kPa (145-203 psi)
Service limit	800 kPa (116 psi)
Maximum difference between cylinders	200 kPa (29 psi)
Engine oil pressure @ 60° C (140° F)	350-650 kPa (51-94 psi) @ 3000 rpm
Brake pedal height	98 mm (3.86 in.)
Shift pedal height	82 mm (3.23 in.)
Wheel runout limit	
Axial	2.0 mm (0.08 in.)
Radial	2.0 mm (0.08 in.)
Shock absorber spring preload	
Standard preload (spring length)	222.0 mm (8.74 in.)
Maximum preload (min spring length)	217 mm (8.54 in.)
Minimum preload (max spring length)	227 mm (8.94 in.)

*Not adjustable.

Table 5 MAINTENANCE AND TUNE UP TORQUE SPECIFICATIONS

Item	N•m	in.-lb.	ft.-lb.
Bleed valve	7.5	66	–
Brake disc bolt	23	–	17
Brake hose banjo bolt	23	–	17
Clutch hose banjo bolt	23	–	17
Cylinder head cover bolt			
6 mm	10	89	–
8 mm	25	–	18
Expansion chamber bolt	23	–	17
Exhaust header bolt/nut	23	–	17
Final drive drain bolt	23	–	17
Front axle	65	–	48
Front axle clamp bolt	23	–	17
Front caliper housing bolt			
1998-2001 models	33	–	24
2002-on models	35	–	26
Front caliper mounting bolt	35	–	26
Handlebar clamp bolt			
1998-2004 models	16	–	12
2005-on models	23	–	17
Handlebar holder nut			
1998-2004 models	50	–	37
2005-on models	70	–	52
Handlebar weight bolt	50	–	37
Lower fork bridge clamp bolt	23	–	17
Muffler bracket bolt/nut	23	–	17
Muffler/exhaust pipe clamp bolt	23	–	17
Muffler hanger bolt/nut	23	–	17
Oil drain bolt	21	–	15
Oil filter union	15	–	11
Oil gallery plug			
Main oil gallery	18	–	13
6 mm	10	89	–
8 mm	10	89	–
12 mm	21	–	15
14 mm	23	–	17
16 mm	35	–	26
Oil hose banjo bolt	26	–	19
Rear axle nut	110	–	81
Rear caliper bracket bolt/nut	60	–	44
Rear caliper mounting bolt	35	–	26
Rear caliper housing bolt			
1998-2001 models	33	–	24
2002-on models	21	–	15
Rear master cylinder pushrod locknut	18	–	13
Spark plug	18	–	13
Upper fork bridge clamp bolt			
2005-on models	23	–	17

3

CHAPTER FOUR

ENGINE TOP END

This chapter provides procedures for engine top end components. These include the camshafts, valves, pistons, cylinder heads and cylinders. Refer to Chapter Five for crankcase procedures.

When inspecting components, compare measurements to the specifications at the end of this chapter.

CYLINDER HEAD SIDE CAP

Each cylinder head has an inboard and an outboard side cap. Although the caps on one cylinder are similar to their counterparts on the other cylinder, the caps are not interchangeable. If more than one cylinder head side cap is being removed, label it so it can be easily identified for installation.

The outboard cap covers a spark plug and auto-decompression lever. This cap can be removed while the engine is in the frame. The engine must be removed to remove the inboard cap.

Removal/Installation

Refer to **Figure 1**.
1. Perform the following when removing an outboard cap:
   a. Remove the upper cover from the appropriate side of the motorcycle (Chapter Fifteen).
   b. Remove the cylinder head side cap bolts (A, **Figure 2**). Watch for the washer and damper installed beneath each bolt.

c. Remove the outboard cap (B, **Figure 2**). Watch for the spacers (A, **Figure 3**), washers (B), and dampers (C) beneath the cap.
2. Perform the following when removing an inboard cap:
   a. Remove the engine as described in Chapter Five.
   b. Remove the cylinder head side cap bolts (A, **Figure 4**). Watch for the washer and damper installed beneath each bolt.
   c. Removing the inboard cap (B, **Figure 4**) from the cylinder head. Watch for the bushings beneath the cap.
3. Install each side cap by reversing the removal procedure.
   a. Install any removed dampers, spacers, washers or bushings.
   b. Tighten the cylinder head side cap bolts to 25 N•m (18 ft.-lb.).

CYLINDER HEAD COVER

Removal

Refer to **Figure 1**.
1. Remove the engine (Chapter Five). Remove the spark plug from the appropriate cylinder.
2. Remove the inboard cylinder head side cap (B, **Figure 4**, front cylinder shown) from the appropriate cylinder.

3A. Remove the cylinder head cover from the front cylinder by performing the following:

 a. Evenly loosen the cylinder head cover bolts (**Figure 5**) securing the breather cover to the cylinder head cover. Remove the bolts. Discard the gasket washers under the four bolts (A, **Figure 5**) indicated.

 b. Remove the breather cover (B, **Figure 5**) and gasket.

 c. In a crisscross pattern, evenly loosen and remove the remaining cylinder head cover bolts (**Figure 6**). Note the two bolts with a gasket washer. Install new gasket washers beneath these bolts during assembly.

 d. Remove the cylinder head cover from the cylinder head. Watch for the dowels (A, **Figure 7**) and the camshaft end plug (B) beneath the cover.

3B. Remove the cylinder head cover from the rear cylinder by performing the following:

 a. Loosen the rear cylinder head cover plug (A, **Figure 8**).

 b. Evenly loosen the cylinder head cover bolts in a crisscross pattern.

 c. Remove the cylinder head cover bolts. Discard the gasket washers under the bolts (B, **Figure 8**) indicated. Install new gasket washers during installation.

 d. Remove the cylinder head cover from the cylinder head. Watch for the dowels (A, **Figure 9**) and camshaft end plug (B) beneath the cover.

4. If necessary, disassemble and remove the auto-decompression assembly from the cylinder head cover.

Installation

1. Bleed the hydraulic lifters as described in this chapter.

2. Apply Suzuki Bond 1216 to the respective cylinder head cover where shown in **Figure 10**.

3. Apply 50:50 mixture of molybdenum disulfide grease and oil to the camshaft holders (A, **Figure 11**, rear cylinder head shown) in each cylinder head cover.

4A. When installing a front cylinder head cover, perform the following:

 a. Install the dowels (A, **Figure 7**) and camshaft end plug (B) into the cylinder head.

 b. Lower the cylinder head cover onto the front cylinder head. If the cylinder head/cylinder assembly was removed, feed the tensioner lock tool through the rear hole (A, **Figure 12**) in the cover. Make sure the lock tool cable is not caught between the cylinder head and cover.

 c. Install the cylinder head cover bolts shown in **Figure 12**. Install a new gasket washer under the bolts (B and C, **Figure 12**) indicated. Make sure the bolt (B, **Figure 12**) indicated passes through the hole in the exhaust rocker arm shaft.

 d. Evenly tighten the cylinder head bolts in a crisscross pattern. Tighten the bolts securely at this time, but do not fully tighten to final specification yet.

 e. If the head/cylinder assembly was removed, release the cam chain tensioner by pulling out the lock tool. Remove the tool.

 f. Remove the oil plug (D, **Figure 12**) and gasket from the cylinder head cover.

 g. Fill the rocker arm oil gallery through the oil hole (**Figure 13**) with approximately 50 ml (1.7 U.S. oz.) of the specified motor oil.

 h. Install the cylinder head cover oil plug (D, **Figure 12**) with a new gasket. Tighten the plug to 10 N•m (89 in.-lb.).

 i. Set the breather cover (B, **Figure 5**) and a new gasket into place on the front cylinder head cover. Install the remaining cylinder head cover bolts (**Figure 5**). Install new gasket washers (A, **Figure 5**).

 j. In a crisscross pattern, evenly tighten the front cylinder head cover bolts. Tighten the 8-mm bolts to 25 N•m (18 ft.-lb.). Then tighten the 6-mm bolts to 10 N•m (89 in.-lb.).

4B. When installing a rear cylinder head cover, perform the following:

 a. Install the dowels (A, **Figure 9**) and camshaft end plug (B) into the cylinder head.

 b. Lower the cylinder head cover onto the rear cylinder head. If the cylinder head/cylinder assembly was removed, feed the tensioner lock tool through the hole (A, **Figure 14**) in the rear cover. Make sure the lock tool is not caught between the cylinder head and cover.

 c. Install the cylinder head bolts, making sure the bolt indicated (B, **Figure 14**) passes through the hole in the exhaust rocker arm shaft.

 d. Install a new gasket washer under each bolt (B, **Figure 8**) noted during removal.

 e. In a crisscross pattern, evenly tighten the rear cylinder head cover bolts. Tighten the 8-mm bolts to 25 N•m (18 ft.-lb.). Then tighten the 6-mm bolts to 10 N•m (89 in.-lb.).

 f. If the cylinder head/assembly was removed, release the cam chain tensioner in the cylinder by pulling out the lock tool. Remove the tool.

 g. Apply Suzuki Bond 1216 to the threads of the rear cylinder head cover plug. Install the plug (A, **Figure 8**) and tighten to 25 N•m (18 ft.-lb.).

 h. Remove the oil plug (C, **Figure 8**) and its gasket from the cylinder head cover.

 i. Fill the rocker arm oil gallery through the oil hole (**Figure 13**, typical) with approximately

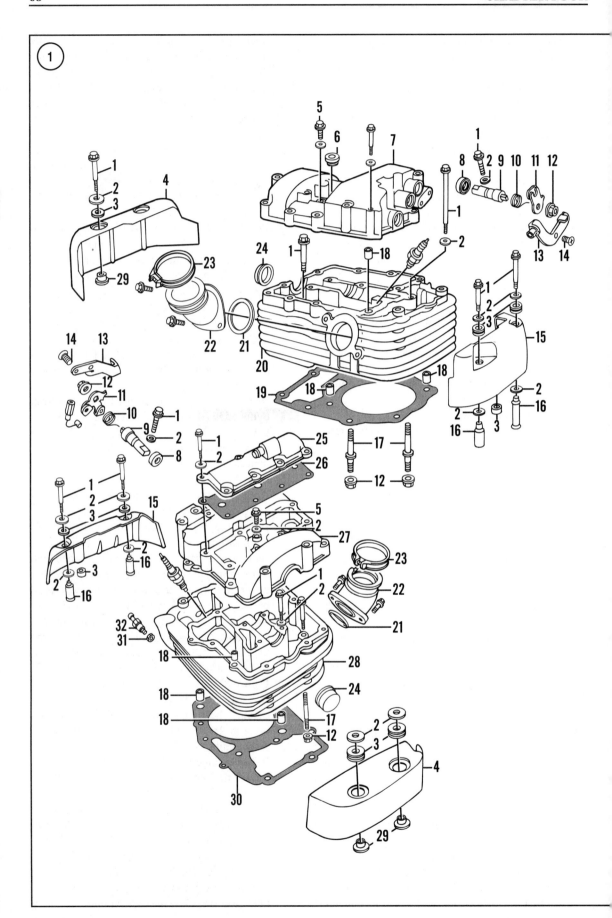

CYLINDER HEAD AND COVERS

1. Bolt
2. Washer
3. Damper
4. Inboard side cap
5 Oil plug
6. Rear cylinder head cover plug
7 Rear cylinder head cover
8. Oil seal
9. Decompression shaft
10. Spring
11. Decompression lever
12 Nut
13. Decompression cable holder
14. Screw
15. Outboard side cap
16. Spacer
17 Stud
18. Dowel
19. Rear head gasket
20 Rear cylinder head
21. O-ring
22. Intake manifold
23. Clamp
24 Plug
25. Breather cover
26. Gasket
27. Front cylinder head cover
28. Front cylinder head
29. Collar
30 Front head gasket
31. Gasket
32. Intake port union

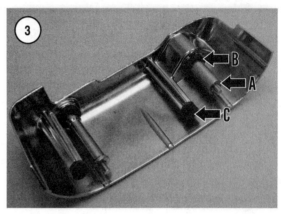

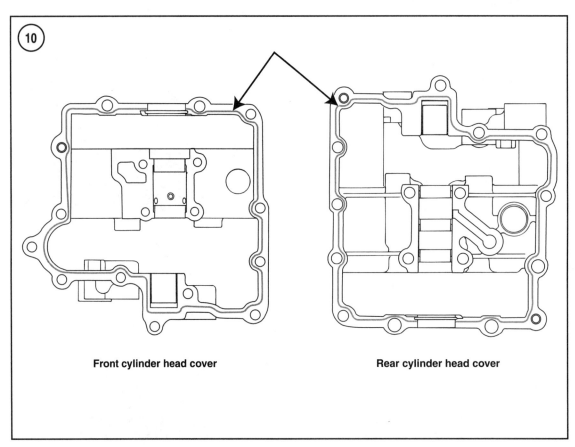

Front cylinder head cover

Rear cylinder head cover

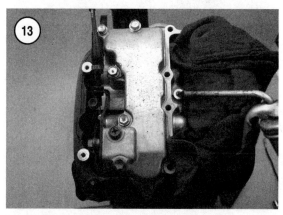

50 ml (1.7 U.S. oz.) of the specified motor oil.

j. Install the cylinder head cover oil plug with a new gasket. Tighten the plug to 10 N•m (89 in.-lb.).

5. Set a damper into each mounting hole in the in-board cylinder head side cap and seat a collar into each damper.

6. Fit the side cap (**Figure 4**) into place on its cylinder head, and install the cylinder head side cap bolts and washers. Tighten the side cap bolts to 25 N•m (18 ft.-lb.).

7. Install the spark plugs. Tighten each spark plug to 18 N•m (13 ft.-lb.).

4

Disassembly

> *CAUTION*
> *Keep the rocker arm and decompression lever assemblies separate. Do not mix parts during assembly.*

Refer to **Figure 1** and **Figure 15**.

1. If disassembling the front cylinder cover, remove the mounting screws (A, **Figure 16**) and the decompression cable holder (B).

2. Remove the intake rocker arm shaft and gasket washer (B, **Figure 11**).

> *CAUTION*
> *Note that the spring washer is on the inboard side of its rocker arm and the thrust washer is on the outboard side. Make sure these are on the correct side during assembly.*

3. Remove the intake rocker arm (C, **Figure 11**) with its spring washer and thrust washer.

4. Remove the exhaust rocker arm plug (**Figure 17**) and its gasket washer.

5. Install a 6-mm bolt (A, **Figure 18**) into the exhaust rocker arm shaft. Pull the bolt and rocker arm shaft from the cylinder head cover. Note the hole (B, **Figure 18**) in the rocker arm shaft.

6. Remove the exhaust rocker arm (C, **Figure 18**) along with its thrust washer and wave washer.

7. Remove the auto-decompression shaft set bolt (A, **Figure 19**) and washer.

8. Remove the auto-decompression shaft (B, **Figure 19**) and spring.

9. Inspect the auto-decompression-shaft oil seal (**Figure 20**) for leaks or damage. Replace the seal if it is damaged or hardened.

Assembly

The manufacturer recommends Suzuki Moly Paste (part No. 99000-251400) as an assembly lube. Some

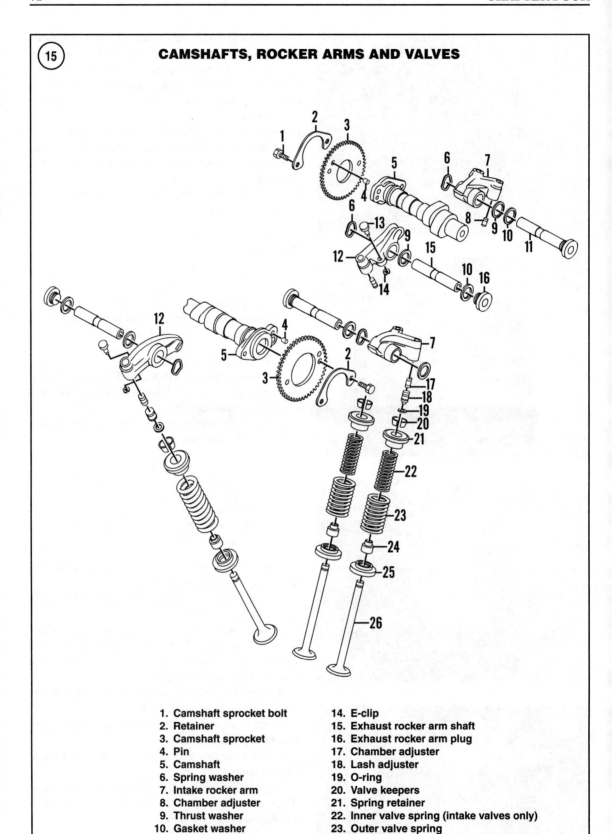

15

CAMSHAFTS, ROCKER ARMS AND VALVES

1. Camshaft sprocket bolt
2. Retainer
3. Camshaft sprocket
4. Pin
5. Camshaft
6. Spring washer
7. Intake rocker arm
8. Chamber adjuster
9. Thrust washer
10. Gasket washer
11. Intake rocker arm shaft
12. Exhaust rocker arm
13. Decompression pin
14. E-clip
15. Exhaust rocker arm shaft
16. Exhaust rocker arm plug
17. Chamber adjuster
18. Lash adjuster
19. O-ring
20. Valve keepers
21. Spring retainer
22. Inner valve spring (intake valves only)
23. Outer valve spring
24. Oil seal
25. Spring seat
26. Valve

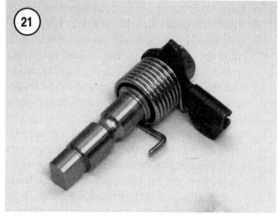

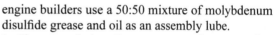

engine builders use a 50:50 mixture of molybdenum disulfide grease and oil as an assembly lube.

1. If removed, install a new auto-decompression shaft oil seal (**Figure 20**).

2. Pack the lips of the oil seal with grease.

3. Lubricate the auto-decompression shaft with an assembly lube.

4. Slide the spring over the auto-decompression shaft so its arm engages the decompression lever (**Figure 21**).

5. Carefully slide the auto-decompression shaft through the oil seal until the lever bottoms. The spring arm must engage the boss (C, **Figure 19**) on the cylinder head.

6. With a new gasket washer, install the auto-decompression shaft set bolt (A, **Figure 19**). Tighten it securely.

7. Turn the cover over and inspect the auto-decompression shaft. If the shaft is correctly installed, the flat on the shaft (**Figure 22**) should be visible and face up out of the cover.

8. Install the exhaust rocker arm by performing the following:

    a. Make sure the 6-mm bolt (A, **Figure 18**) is still in place in the exhaust rocker arm shaft. Lubricate the shaft with an assembly lube.

b. Install the exhaust rocker arm (A, **Figure 23**) with the wave washer (B) on its inboard side. Slide the shaft through the rocker arm, wave washer, and into the cylinder head boss. Make sure the auto-decompression pad on the rocker arm sits against the flat of the auto-decompression shaft (**Figure 22**).

c. While an assistant presses the rocker arm toward the wave washer, pull out the rocker arm shaft far enough so the thrust washer can be installed between the outboard side of the rocker arm and the cover (**Figure 24**). Install the rocker arm shaft until it is completely seated in its boss.

d. Use a punch or drift (**Figure 25**) to align the hole in the rocker arm shaft (B, **Figure 18**) with the cylinder head cover bolt hole. The cover bolt must pass through the exhaust rocker arm shaft during cover installation.

e. Install the exhaust rocker arm shaft plug with its gasket washer (**Figure 17**). Tighten the plug to 28 N•m (21 ft.-lb.).

9. Install the intake rocker arm by performing the following:

a. Make sure the gasket washer is in place on the intake rocker arm shaft.

b. Lubricate the rocker arm shaft with an assembly lube and install the shaft (A, **Figure 26**) into its boss in the cylinder head cover so the bolt slightly protrudes from the boss.

c. Install the thrust washer (B, **Figure 26**) onto the shaft end. If necessary, withdraw the shaft so it and the washer sit flush against the outboard side of the cover.

d. Lubricate the rocker arm bore and the wave washer with an assembly lube.

e. Position the wave washer on the inboard side of the rocker arm.

f. Lower the rocker arm and wave washer assembly into place, press the arm against the wave

washer so the washer compresses against the inboard boss on the cover.

g. Have an assistant install the rocker arm shaft (B, **Figure 11**) through the rocker arm bore, through the wave washer and into the boss in the cover.

h. Install the intake rocker arm shaft into the cover and tighten it to 37 N•m (27 ft.-lb.).

10. If assembling a front cylinder head cover, install the decompression cable holder (B, **Figure 16**). Apply Suzuki Thread Lock 1342 to the threads of the mounting screws (A, **Figure 16**) and tighten the screws securely.

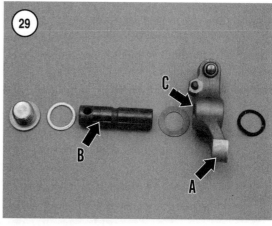

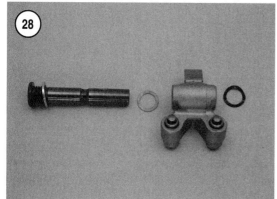

the cover. Replace the cover if any measurement exceeds the service limit.

Rocker arm

1. Remove the intake (**Figure 28**) and exhaust (**Figure 29**) rocker arm assemblies as described in this section.
2. Inspect the rocker arm pad (A, **Figure 29**) where it rides on the cam lobe. If the pad is scratched or unevenly worn, inspect the cam lobe for scoring, chipping or flat spots. If necessary, replace the rocker arm and the camshaft.
3. Inspect the rocker arm shaft (B, **Figure 29**) for cracks, wear or scoring. Measure the outside diameter of the rocker arm shaft.
4. Measure the inside diameter of the rocker arm bore (C, **Figure 29**).
5. Replace any part that is worn or out of specification.

Auto-decompression lever assembly

1. Remove the auto-decompression lever assembly (**Figure 21**) as described in this section.
2. Visually inspect the auto-decompression shaft for signs wear or damage. Pay attention to the flat of the shaft.
3. Inspect the decompression seat on the exhaust rocker arm for wear or damage.
4. Inspect the auto-decompression oil seal (**Figure 20**) in the cylinder head.
5. Replace any worn or damaged part(s).

HYDRAULIC LIFTERS

Inspection

1. Remove the cylinder head cover as described in this chapter.

Inspection

Refer to **Table 2** for specifications.

Cylinder head cover

1. Clean all sealant residue from the cylinder-head mating surface of the cover (**Figure 27**).
2. Set the cylinder head cover on a surface plate or a piece of plate glass.
3. Measure for warp by inserting a feeler gauge between the cylinder head cover mating surface and the surface plate. Measure at several places around

2. Carefully remove the single hydraulic lifter (A, **Figure 30**) from the exhaust rocker arm. Remove both lifters (B, **Figure 30**) from the intake rocker arm. Note each lifter's location.

3. Inspect the lifter for wear or damage. Carefully inspect the lifter where it contacts the valve stem (A, **Figure 31**).

4. Inspect the lifter O-ring (B, **Figure 31**). Replace it if the O-ring is damaged or brittle.

5. Check the oil hole in the lifter. It must be clear and open.

6. Bleed the lifters before reinstalling them in the rocker arms.

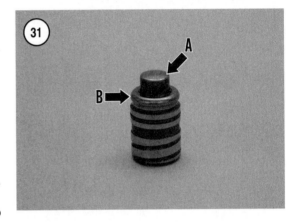

Bleeding

Use the bleeding tool (Suzuki part No. 09913-10740) and kerosene to bleed the lifters.

> *CAUTION*
> *Only use kerosene to bleed the lifters. Any other fluid may cause engine damage.*

1. Fill a transparent container with clean kerosene.

2. Insert the lifter into the bleeding tool (**Figure 32**). Follow the tool manufacturer's instructions.

3. Place the tool and lifter into the kerosene. Keep the lifter upright and completely submerged.

4. Repeatedly press and release the lifter plunger (**Figure 33**). Continue pumping the lifter until air bubbles stop coming from the lifter.

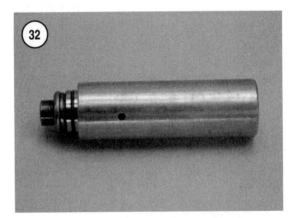

> *CAUTION*
> *Once bled, keep the lifter upright on the bench. If air enters the lifter, repeat the bleeding process.*

> *NOTE*
> *The small amount of kerosene left in the lifter will not contaminate the engine oil.*

5. Remove the lifter from the tool and compress the plunger by hand. The plunger should move smoothly and its stroke must be within the specified range (**Table 2**). If the plunger stroke is excessive, bleed the lifter again and remeasure the stroke. If it is still excessive, replace the lifter.

6. Reinstall the lifter in its original location.

7. Repeat the process for each remaining lifter.

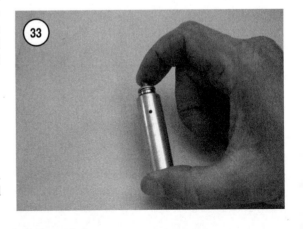

CAMSHAFTS

The chain tensioner lock tool (Suzuki part No. 09918-53810), or its equivalent, is needed to install the camshafts.

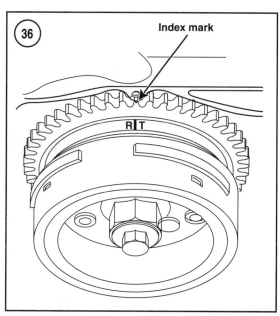

Index mark

R|T

Identification

On 1998-2004 models, identify the camshafts by the mark embossed on their edge (**Figure 3**4); *F* for the front and *R* for the rear. On 2005-on models, identify the front camshaft by the *B* and the rear camshaft by the *C* (**Figure 35**) stamped on the shaft end.

Removal

Refer to **Figure 15**.
1. Remove the engine and the alternator cover (Chapter Five).
2. Remove the cylinder head cover.
3. Remove the spark plugs from both cylinders to ease crankshaft rotation.

> *NOTE*
> *The following step sets the rear cylinder (No. 1) to top dead center (TDC) on the compression stroke. Remove and install the camshafts from both cylinders with the rear cylinder set at TDC.*

4. Set the rear cylinder to TDC on the compression stroke by performing the following:

> *CAUTION*
> *If the front camshaft is removed, hold the front cam chain taut against the timing sprocket when rotating the engine.*

   a. Use the flywheel bolt to rotate the engine counterclockwise, when viewed from the left side, until the *R|T* mark on the flywheel aligns with the index mark on the crankcase (**Figure 36**).
   b. Make sure the rocker arms in the rear cylinder have some play, indicating each valve is closed.
   c. If not, rotate the engine one additional turn (360°) counterclockwise.
   d. Check the rocker arms. They should now have play.

5. Straighten the retainer tab away from the flat of the exposed cam sprocket bolt. Remove the bolt (**Figure 37**).
6. Use the flywheel bolt to rotate the crankshaft counterclockwise, when viewed from the left side, until the remaining cam sprocket bolt is exposed.

7. Bend the retainer tab away from the bolt flat. Remove the remaining cam sprocket bolt (A, **Figure 38**). Then remove the retainer (B).

8. Lift the cam chain (A, **Figure 39**) from the camshaft sprocket (B) and remove the sprocket from the camshaft.

9. Hold the cam chain and remove the camshaft from the cylinder head (**Figure 40**).

10. Use safety wire to secure the cam chain to the engine so the chain will not fall into the crankcase.

11. If necessary, repeat Steps 3-10 and remove the camshaft from the other cylinder head.

Installation

NOTE
If both camshafts are removed, install the rear camshaft first.

1. If not already done, lock the cam chain tensioner in its fully retracted position by performing the following:

   a. Use a long, narrow screwdriver to press the release lever in the tensioner body (**Figure 41**).

   b. While holding the lever in the released position, use a second screwdriver to push the cam chain tensioner plunger to its fully retracted position.

   c. Continue to hold the plunger in its fully retracted position, and insert the chain tensioner lock tool into the gap between the release lever and the tensioner body (**Figure 42**). If necessary, use the first screwdriver to increase this gap to its maximum (**Figure 43**). Then install the tool.

   d. Once the tool is in the gap, release the plunger.

CAUTION
Be careful during the rest of the procedure. If the lock tool is removed before installation is complete, restart the procedure from the beginning.

NOTE
Hold each cam chain taut against its timing sprocket while rotating the engine.

2. Make sure the rear cylinder is still at TDC on the compression stroke. If necessary, use the flywheel bolt to rotate the crankshaft counterclockwise, when viewed from the left side, until the $R|T$ mark on the flywheel aligns with the index mark on the crankcase (**Figure 36**).

3. Apply an assembly lube to the camshaft journals and lobes. Also make sure the tensioner lock tool sits on the rear side of the cam chain tunnel in each cylinder.

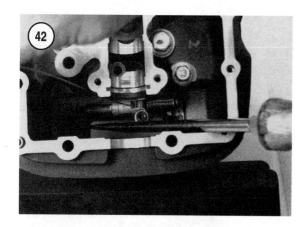

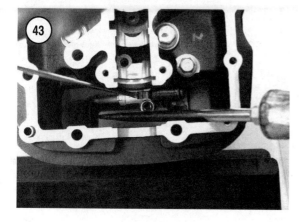

4. Apply a light coat of grease to the locating pin (A, **Figure 35**) and install it into the end of the camshaft.

5. Slide the rear camshaft between the runs of the rear cam chain and seat the camshaft in the rear cylinder head. Position the camshaft so the arrow on the camshaft end points forward and the timing marks align with the upper edge of the cylinder head as shown in **Figure 40**.

NOTE
When installing the camshaft sprocket, be careful so the locating pin is not

knocked from the camshaft. If the pin works loose, it will probably fall into the crankcase, which will have to be disassembled so the pin can be removed.

6. Fit the camshaft sprocket between the cam chain runs and seat the sprocket onto the camshaft. The locating pin on the camshaft must engage the hole in the sprocket (C, **Figure 39**) and the chain must engage the sprocket teeth.

7. Make sure the $R|T$ mark on the flywheel still aligns with the index mark on the crankcase. Make sure the timing arrow on the rear camshaft points forward and aligns with the top edge of the cylinder head. If necessary, realign the camshaft and sprocket by repeating Step 5 and Step 6.

8. Fit a new retainer (A, **Figure 44**) into place on the rear camshaft sprocket. Make sure the lockwasher will cover the locating pin once both cam sprocket bolts have been installed.

9. Apply Suzuki Thread Lock Super 1303 to a cam sprocket bolt and install the bolt (B, **Figure 44**) into the exposed hole in the rear camshaft sprocket. Finger-tighten the bolt at this time.

10. Use the flywheel bolt to rotate the engine until the other cam sprocket bolt hole is exposed. Hold the front cam chain taut against its timing sprocket while rotating the engine.

11. Apply Suzuki Thread Lock Super 1303 to the threads of the other cam sprocket bolt. Install the bolt (A, **Figure 38**) and tighten to 15 N•m (11 ft.-lb.).

12. Bend the tab of the lockwasher against a flat of the bolt head.

13. Use the flywheel bolt to rotate the engine counterclockwise, when viewed from the left side, until the first cam sprocket bolt is exposed. Hold the front cam chain taut against its timing sprocket while rotating the engine.

14. Tighten the first cam sprocket bolt to 15 N•m (11 ft.-lb.). Bend the lockwasher tab against a bolt flat (**Figure 37**).

NOTE
The remaining steps describe the installation of the front camshaft. Both camshafts (front or rear) are installed with the rear cylinder at TDC on the compression stroke.

15. Set the rear cylinder to TDC as follows:
    a. Use the flywheel bolt to rotate the crankshaft counterclockwise, when viewed from the left side, until the $R|T$ mark on the flywheel aligns with the index mark on the crankcase (**Figure 36**).

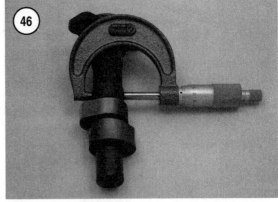

b. Check the timing marks on the rear camshaft. The arrow must point forward and align with the top of the cylinder head as shown in **Figure 39**.

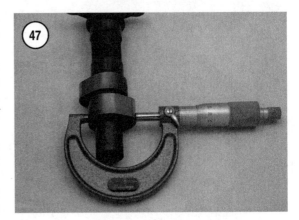

c. If necessary, rotate the crankshaft an additional turn counterclockwise so the R/T aligns with the crankcase mark, and the rear camshaft arrow points forward and aligns with the top of the cylinder head.

16. Apply a light coat of grease to the locating pin (B, **Figure 35**) and install it into the end of the front camshaft.

17. Slide the front camshaft between the runs of the front cam chain and seat the camshaft in the front cylinder head. Position the camshaft so its arrow points forward and the timing marks align with the upper edge of the cylinder head. See **Figure 45**.

18. Complete the camshaft installation by repeating Steps 6-13.

19. Set the rear cylinder to TDC by performing Step 15.

20. The arrow on each camshaft should now point forward and align with the top of the cylinder head. Refer to **Figure 39** (rear cylinder) and **Figure 45** (front cylinder).

21. If any timing arrow does not point forward and align with the top of the cylinder head, the camshaft is incorrectly timed. Remove and reinstall the camshaft(s).

Inspection

Refer to **Table 2** at the end of this chapter for specifications.

1. Inspect the camshaft journals for wear.

2. Measure the outside diameter of each journal (**Figure 46**). Record the measurements. Replace a camshaft if any journal diameter is outside the specified range.

3. Inspect the camshaft lobes for scoring, flat spots or other signs of wear. The lobes should be smooth and the edges should be square. Slight damage can be removed with a silicone carbide oil stone. Initially, use a No. 100-120 grit stone. Then, polish with a No. 280-320 grit stone.

4. Measure the cam lobe height (**Figure 47**). Replace the camshaft is any lobe is worn to the service limit.

5. Place each camshaft on a set of V-blocks and check the runout with a dial indicator.

6. Make sure the locating pin (A or B, **Figure 35**) fits tightly in the end of the camshaft. Replace the pin if it is loose.

7. Inspect the surface of the camshaft holders in the cylinder head (**Figure 48**) and in the cylinder head

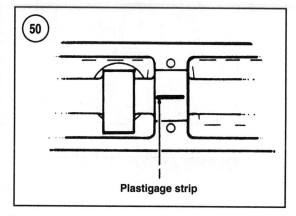

Plastigage strip

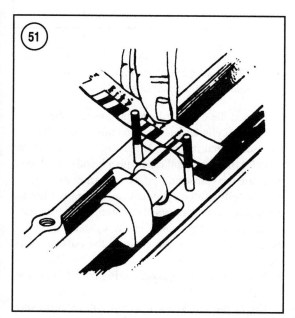

cover (C, **Figure 30**). Replace the cylinder head and cover if the holders are scored or excessively worn.

8. Inspect the teeth on the cam sprocket (**Figure 49**). Also inspect the mounting holes and the locating pin hole in the sprocket. Replace the sprocket if the teeth are excessively worn or if the holes are elongated.

9. Measure the camshaft oil clearance.

Oil clearance

1. Remove all oil and grease from the camshaft journals and from the camshaft holders in the cylinder head and cover.

2. Check the identification marks on the camshaft and set the camshaft into its cylinder head with its lobes facing down. Do not install the sprocket or cam chain.

3. Install the dowels into the cylinder head.

4. Place a strip of Plastigage across each camshaft journal. The Plastigage must parallel the cam centerline (**Figure 50**).

5. Install the cylinder head cover and cover bolts. When checking the front cylinder, install the breather cover and its gasket. Then install the cover bolts.

6. In a crisscross pattern, evenly tighten the cylinder head cover bolts. Tighten the 8-mm bolts to 25 N•m (18 ft.-lb.). Then tighten the 6-mm bolts to 10 N•m (89 in.-lb.).

7. Evenly loosen the cylinder head cover bolts and remove the cover.

8. Measure the width of the flattened Plastigage at its widest point (**Figure 51**). If any measurement exceeds the camshaft oil clearance service limit, check the journal outside diameter measurements taken earlier.

9. If the outside diameter of each camshaft journal is within specification, the cylinder head and cover probably require replacement. Confirm this by checking the camshaft journal inside diameter.

   a. Remove the camshaft from the cylinder head.

   b. Install the cylinder head cover, and tighten the cylinder head cover bolts as described in Step 5 and Step 6.

   c. Measure the inside diameter of each camshaft holder.

   d. Replace the cylinder head and its cover if the camshaft holder inside diameter is not within the specified range.

10. If the oil clearance is within specification, remove all Plastigage from the camshaft and cylinder head cover. Plastigage can plug oil galleries.

CYLINDER AND CYLINDER HEAD ASSEMBLY

Remove and install the cylinder and cylinder head as an assembly. The cylinder head nut on the intake side of the cylinder cannot be properly tightened with the cylinders on the engine.

The photographs in this section show a front cylinder/head assembly. The procedure for the rear assembly is the same.

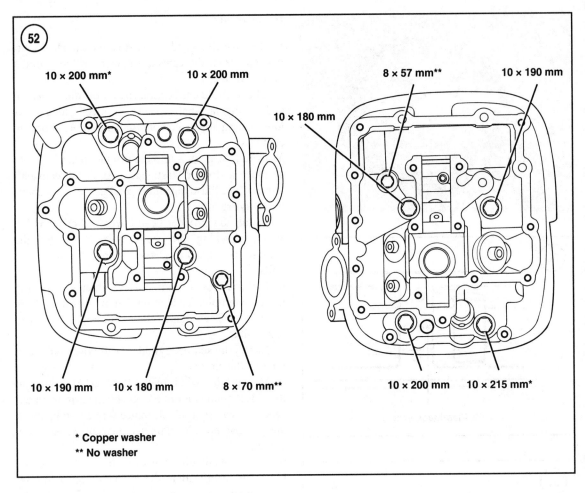

52

10 × 200 mm*   10 × 200 mm   8 × 57 mm**   10 × 190 mm

10 × 180 mm

10 × 190 mm   10 × 180 mm   8 × 70 mm**   10 × 200 mm   10 × 215 mm*

* Copper washer
** No washer

Removal

CAUTION
The cylinder/cylinder head assembly is heavy. Have an assistant help during removal/installation.

1. Remove the cylinder head cover and camshaft as described in this chapter.

NOTE
*The cylinder head bolts are different sizes (**Figure 52**). If both cylinder/head assemblies are being removed, keep the bolts, cylinder, and cylinder head for one assembly separate from the other to prevent mixing parts.*

2. Evenly loosen the 10-mm cylinder head bolts (A, **Figure 53**) in a crisscross pattern. If the cylinder head will be separated from the cylinder, also loosen the 8-mm cylinder head bolt (B, **Figure 53**), but leave it finger-tight.

3. Remove each 10-mm cylinder head bolt and its washer. Note the bolt with the copper washer (**Figure 52**).

CAUTION
The cooling fins are fragile. They may be damaged if tapped or pried too hard.

4. Loosen the cylinder by tapping around the perimeter of the cylinder base with a soft-faced mallet. *Do not* use a metal hammer. If necessary, gently pry the cylinder from the crankcase with a broad-tipped tool.

5. Untie the cam-chain safety wire from the engine.

6. Carefully lift the cylinder/head assembly from the crankcase until it clears the piston. Guide the cam chain through the tunnel in the cylinder head and cylinder, and secure the chain to the outside of the crankcase.

7. Remove the base gasket (A, **Figure 54**) and dowels (B).

8. Cover the crankcase opening with a clean shop cloth to keep debris out of the crankcase.

9. If necessary, repeat this procedure and remove the other cylinder/head assembly.

10. When servicing a rear cylinder/head assembly, remove the No. 22 oil jet (**Figure 55**) and the No. 14 oil jet (**Figure 56**) from the crankcase.

11. Disassemble the cylinder head and cylinder as described in this section.

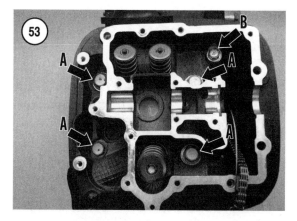

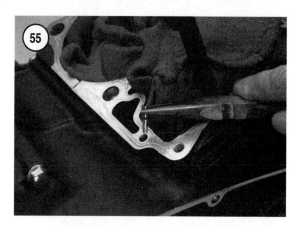

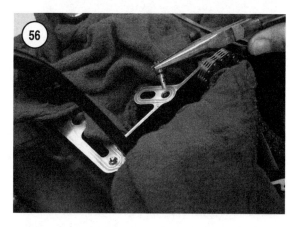

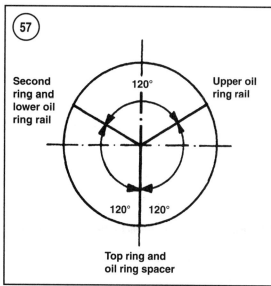

Installation

1. If removed, install the No. 22 oil jet (**Figure 55**) and the No. 14 oil jet (**Figure 56**) into their locations in the crankcase (rear cylinder). Make sure each jet and the oil galleries in the crankcase are clear. Apply engine oil to the O-ring on each oil jet and press the jet into place until it bottoms.

2. Apply a liberal coat of clean engine oil to the cylinder walls, pistons, and rings.

3. Clean the mating surfaces of the cylinder and the crankcase.

4. Applying Suzuki Bond 1207B to the seam where the two crankcase halves join. The sealant should cover approximately 1/2-inch on either side of the seam.

5. Install the dowels (B, **Figure 54**) and a new base gasket (A) onto the crankcase.

6. Make sure the piston ring end gaps are positioned as shown in **Figure 57**.

7. Position the cylinder/head assembly over the crankcase.

8. Lower the assembly while an assistant feeds the cam chain and the rear cam chain guide up through the cam chain tunnel in the assembly. At the same time, make sure the front cam chain guide in the cylinder/head assembly passes down in front of the cam chain.

9. Tie the cam chain safety wire to the outside of the assembly.

10. Have an assistant start the cylinder down over the piston. Manually compress each piston ring as it enters the cylinder. Seat the cylinder on the crankcase.

11. Make sure the cam chain, rear chain guide, and the tensioner lock tool are all positioned correctly in the cam chain tunnel.

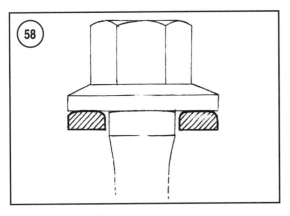

12. Install a washer onto each 10-mm cylinder head bolt. Install a copper washer on the bolt indicated in **Figure 52**. Make sure the rounded side of the washer faces the bolt head as shown in **Figure 58**.

13. Install each 10-mm cylinder head bolt into its correct location as shown in **Figure 52**.

14. Following a crisscross pattern, evenly tighten the 10-mm cylinder head bolts (A, **Figure 53**) in two-to-three stages. Tighten the bolts to 25 N•m (18 ft.-lb.) and then to 37 N•m (27 ft.-lb.).

15. Repeat Steps 2-14, and install the other cylinder head and cylinder assembly.

Disassembly

The chain tensioner lock tool (Suzuki part No. 09918-53810) , or its equivalent, is needed when performing this procedure.

1. Remove the cylinder/cylinder head assembly as described in this section.

2. Refer to *Camshaft, Installation* in this chapter and lock the cam chain tensioner.

3. Remove the 8-mm cylinder head bolt (A, **Figure 59**) from the cylinder head.

4. Remove the cylinder head nuts from the cylinder head stud on the intake side (**Figure 60**) and exhaust side (**Figure 61**) of the cylinder.

5. Loosen the cylinder head from the cylinder by tapping around the perimeter of the cylinder head with a soft-faced mallet.

6. Carefully lift the cylinder head from the cylinder.

7. Remove the cylinder head gasket (A, **Figure 62**) and dowels (B).

8. Remove the front cam chain guide (**Figure 63**) from its seat in the cylinder.

9. Remove the mounting bolts (A and B, **Figure 64**) and lift the cam chain tensioner from the well in the cylinder. Note the tensioner bolt lengths. The longer bolt (A, **Figure 64**) sits in the outboard side of the cam chain tensioner.

10. Inspect the cylinder head, cylinder, and cam chain tensioner as described in this section.

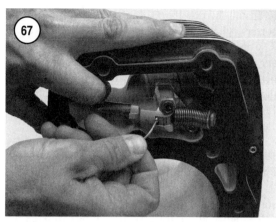

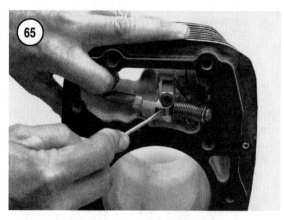

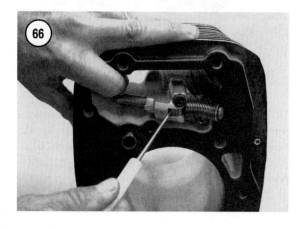

Assembly

Use the tensioner lock tool (Suzuki part No. 09918-53810), or its equivalent, to assemble, and install the cylinder head and cylinder.

1. Set the cylinder upright on the bench.

2. Each cam chain tensioner is identified by an *F* (front) or *R* (rear) embossed on the body. Set the correct cam chain tensioner into position inside the tensioner well in the top of the cylinder (**Figure 64**).

3. Apply Suzuki Thread Lock 1342 to the threads of the cam chain tensioner mounting bolts and install the bolts. Install the long bolt (A, **Figure 64**) on the outboard side of the tensioner. Tighten the bolts to 10 N•m (89 in.-lb.).

4. Lock the cam chain tensioner in the fully-retracted position by performing the following:

   a. Use a small screwdriver to release the lock on the cam chain tensioner and press the plunger toward the tensioner body until the spring is completely compressed (**Figure 65**).

   b. While holding the plunger in the retracted position, use the screwdriver to increase the gap between the tensioner lock and body (**Figure 66**).

   c. Insert the tensioner lock tool into that gap (**Figure 67**) and release the plunger.

NOTE
*The front cam chain guides are not identical. The cam chain guide with the larger knuckle (A, **Figure 68**) goes into the front cylinder and the guide with the smaller knuckle (B) into the rear.*

5. Lower the front cam chain guide into the cylinder until the guide rests in its seat (**Figure 63**).

NOTE
The hole pattern on the front cylinder head gasket differs from the pattern on the rear head gasket. Install each gasket onto the correct cylinder.

6. Install the dowels (B, **Figure 62**) and install the correct cylinder head gasket (A) onto the cylinder.

7. Carefully lower the cylinder head onto the cylinder until the head is seated. Make sure each cylinder head stud passes through its hole in the cylinder. At the same time, have an assistant guide the cable (B, **Figure 59**) of the tensioner lock tool up through the cam chain tunnel as the head is lowered.

8. Install the 8-mm cylinder head bolt (A, **Figure 59**) through the cylinder head and into the cylinder. Finger-tighten the bolt.

9. Install a cylinder head nut onto the cylinder head stud on the exhaust side (**Figure 61**) and the intake side (**Figure 60**) of the assembly. Finger-tighten the nuts.

10. Evenly tighten the cylinder head nuts and the 8-mm cylinder head bolt in two-to-three stages.

11. Tighten the cylinder head nuts and the 8-mm cylinder head bolt to 10 N•m (89 in.-lb.), and then to 25 N•m (18 ft.-lb.).

12. Repeat Steps 2-11, and install the remaining cylinder head onto its cylinder.

Inspection

Refer to **Table 2** for specifications.

Leak test

1. Position the cylinder head so the exhaust ports face up. Pour solvent or kerosene into each exhaust port opening (**Figure 69**).

2. Turn the head over slightly and check each exhaust valve area on the combustion chamber side. On seats in good condition, no fluid will leak past the valve seats. If any area is wet, the valve or valve seat requires service. Remove the valve, and inspect the valve and seat for wear or damage.

3. Pour solvent into the intake ports and check the intake valves.

Cylinder head

1. Remove all traces of gasket residue from the upper and lower gasket surfaces on the cylinder head. Do not scratch the gasket surfaces.

> #### *CAUTION*
> *Cleaning the combustion chamber with the valves removed can damage the valve seat surfaces. A damaged or even slightly scratched valve seat will cause poor valve seating.*

2. *Without removing the valves*, remove all carbon deposits from the combustion chamber (A, **Figure**

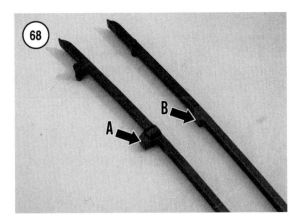

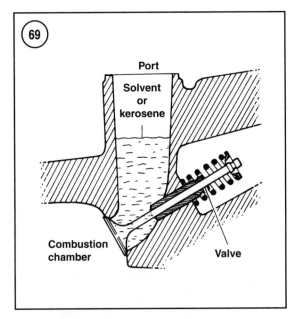

70). Use a fine wire brush dipped in solvent or make a scraper from hardwood. Take care not to damage the head, valves or spark plug threads (B, **Figure 70**).

3. Clean the head in solvent. Blow it dry with compressed air.

4. Examine the spark plug threads in the cylinder head for damage. If necessary, clean the threads with

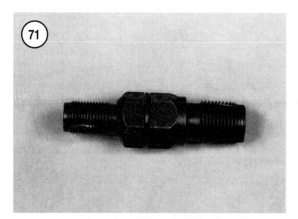

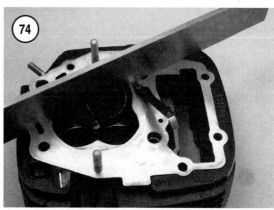

air into the engine. If necessary, remove the intake manifold and discard the O-rings.

7. Check for cracks in the combustion chamber, the intake port, and the exhaust port. Replace a cracked cylinder head.

8. Inspect the internal threads (rear cylinder) or studs (front cylinder) on the exhaust port for damage. If necessary, clean them with a tap. Clean all other bolt holes with a tap to remove debris.

9. Place a straightedge across the gasket surface at several points. Measure warp by attempting to insert a feeler gauge between the straightedge and cylinder head at each location (**Figure 74**). If warp exceeds the limit in **Table 2**, resurface or replace the cylinder head.

10. If necessary, refer to *Valves and Valve Components* is this chapter.

11. If the cylinder head required valve service or was bead-blasted, thoroughly clean the head in solvent, and then with hot soapy water to remove all residual grit.

12. If removed, install the intake manifold with a new intake manifold O-ring. Lubricate each O-ring with grease. Install each intake manifold in its original location. Position each manifold so the arrow on the manifold face points to the top of the cylinder head. Apply Suzuki Thread Lock 1342 to the threads of the manifold bolts (B, **Figure 73**) and tighten them securely.

13. If removed, install the exhaust manifold onto the rear cylinder head. Install a new exhaust gasket and tighten the exhaust manifold bolts to 23 N•m (17 ft.-lb.).

Cylinder

1. Carefully remove all gasket material from the cylinder block gasket surfaces. If necessary, soak the old gasket material in solvent. Do not scratch or gouge the gasket surface.

a spark plug thread tap (**Figure 71**) to remove carbon or true minor thread damage. Apply tap cutting fluid or kerosene to the tap. If thread damage is severe, install a steel thread insert.

5. Examine the piston crown (**Figure 72**). The crown should show no signs of wear or damage. If a crown appears pecked or spongy-looking, also check the spark plug, valves, and combustion chamber for aluminum deposits. If aluminum deposits are noted, the cylinder is overheating due to a lean air/fuel mixture and/or preignition.

6. Inspect the intake manifold (A, **Figure 73**) for cracks or other damage that would allow unfiltered

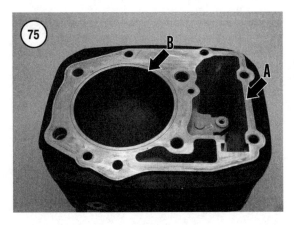

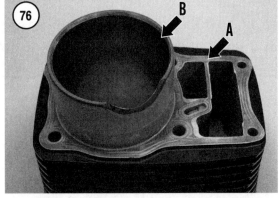

2. Check the mating surfaces on the top (A, **Figure 75**) and bottom (A, **Figure 76**) of the cylinder block for cracks or damage.

3. Inspect the cylinder walls (B, **Figure 75** and B, **Figure 76**) for deep scratches, signs of seizure or other damage.

4. Use a straightedge and flat feeler gauge to check the top of the cylinder block for warp (**Figure 77**). Check this at several places across the cylinder block. Replace the cylinder if warp exceeds the service limit.

5. Measure the cylinder bore inside diameter with a cylinder bore gauge. Measure the bore at the top, middle and bottom of the cylinder as shown in **Figure 78**. At each height, measure the bore across two axes: one parallel to the crankshaft and the other 90° to the crankshaft. Replace the cylinder if the bore is out of specification. Oversized pistons are not available from the manufacturer.

6. Lubricate the cylinder wall with engine oil to prevent rust.

Cam chain tensioner

1. Inspect the cam chain tensioner body and rack for wear or damage.

2. Release the lock (A, **Figure 79**) and press the plunger (B) into the body. It should move smoothly.

3. Replace the tensioner if any damage is noted or if the plunger does not move smoothly.

4. Inspect the sliding surface of the front cam chain guide (**Figure 68**). Replace the guide as necessary.

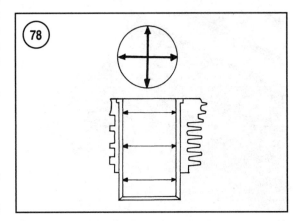

CAM CHAINS AND REAR CHAIN GUIDES

The front cylinder timing sprocket drives the front cam chain and is an integral part of the left side of the crankshaft. The rear cylinder timing sprocket drives the rear cam chain and is splined to the right side of the crankshaft.

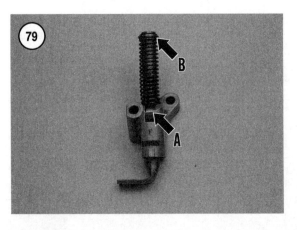

The cam chains do not have replaceable links. Do not cut them. Replacement parts are not available.

Removal/Installation

The rear chain guide in each cylinder is bolted to the crankcase. The rear guide pivots on a bushing in the guide's mounting hole. A washer sits on each side of the guide.

1. Remove the cylinder/cylinder head assembly as described in this chapter.

2A. For the front cylinder, perform the following:

    a. Remove the flywheel and starter clutch gear as described in Chapter Five.

    b. Remove the cam chain guide bolt (A, **Figure 80**) and lift the rear cam chain guide from the tunnel. Watch for the two washers and bushing installed with the guide.

    c. Remove the cam chain (B, **Figure 80**) from the front cylinder timing sprocket and lift the chain from the cam chain tunnel.

2B. For the rear cylinder, perform the following:

    a. Remove the primary drive gear (Chapter Six).

    b. Remove the cam chain guide bolt (A, **Figure 81**) and lift the rear cam chain guide from the tunnel. Watch for the two washers and bushing installed with the guide.

    c. Remove the cam chain (B, **Figure 81**) from the rear cylinder timing sprocket and lift it from the cam chain tunnel.

    d. Slide the rear cylinder timing sprocket (A, **Figure 82**) from the crankshaft taper. Note that the indexing dot on the sprocket aligns with the dot on the crankshaft.

    e. Remove the thrust washer (B, **Figure 82**) from the crankshaft. Note that the chamfered side of the thrust washer faces in toward the crankcase.

3. Installation is the reverse of removal. Note the following:

    a. Install the thrust washer onto the right side of the crankshaft so the washer's chamfered side (**Figure 83**) faces the crankcase.

    b. Install the rear cylinder timing sprocket so its indexing dot aligns with the dot on the crankshaft (**Figure 82**).

    c. Make sure the bushing (A, **Figure 84**) is in place in the rear cam chain guide.

    d. When installing a rear cam chain guide, fit a washer onto each side of the guide.

    e. Apply Suzuki Thread Lock 1342 to the cam chain guide bolt threads, and tighten the bolt to 10 N•m (89 in.-lb.).

Inspection

If the cam chain is severely worn or damaged, the cam chain tensioner may not be working properly; refer to *Cam Chain Tensioner* in this chapter.

1. Clean the cam chain (B, **Figure 84**) in solvent. Blow it dry with compressed air.

2. Check the cam chain for:
   a. Worn or damaged pins and rollers.
   b. Cracked or damaged side plates.

3. If the cam chain is severely worn or damaged, inspect the camshaft sprocket (**Figure 85**) and the timing sprocket (A, **Figure 86**, rear sprocket shown) for the same cylinder. If either sprocket shows signs of wear or damage, replace them both along with the chain.

> *CAUTION*
> *If a cam chain, timing sprocket or cam sprocket in a particular cylinder re-quires replacement, replace all three parts as a set. Do not install a new chain onto a worn sprocket. The old parts will quickly wear out the chain.*

4. Inspect the timing sprocket for worn or damaged teeth (A, **Figure 86**, rear sprocket shown).

5. Inspect the internal splines (B, **Figure 86**) in the rear cylinder timing sprocket. If damage is found, also check the splines on the end of the crankshaft.

6. Inspect the sliding surface of the rear cam chain guide (C, **Figure 84**). Replace the guide as needed.

VALVES AND VALVE COMPONENTS

Refer to **Figure 87**.

A valve spring compressor is required to remove and install the valves.

Valve Removal

1. Remove and disassemble the cylinder/head assembly described in this chapter.

2. Install a valve spring compressor squarely over the valve spring retainer and place the other end of tool against the valve head.

> *CAUTION*
> *To avoid loss of spring tension, do not compress the spring any more than necessary to remove the valve keepers.*

3. Tighten the compressor until the valve keepers separate from the valve stem. Lift the valve keepers out through the compressor with a magnet or needle-nose pliers (**Figure 88**).

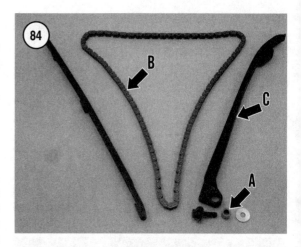

4. Gradually loosen the compressor and remove it from the cylinder head.

> *CAUTION*
> *As each set of valve components is removed, place them in separate containers or sandwich bags. Label each valve set by its cylinder number and as either an intake left, an intake right or an exhaust. Do not intermix valve components.*

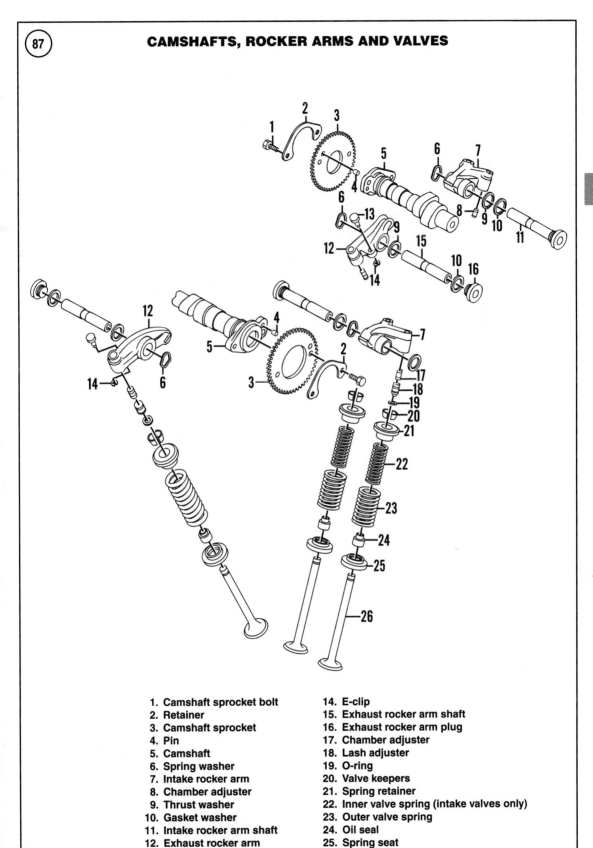

CAMSHAFTS, ROCKER ARMS AND VALVES

1. Camshaft sprocket bolt
2. Retainer
3. Camshaft sprocket
4. Pin
5. Camshaft
6. Spring washer
7. Intake rocker arm
8. Chamber adjuster
9. Thrust washer
10. Gasket washer
11. Intake rocker arm shaft
12. Exhaust rocker arm
13. Decompression pin
14. E-clip
15. Exhaust rocker arm shaft
16. Exhaust rocker arm plug
17. Chamber adjuster
18. Lash adjuster
19. O-ring
20. Valve keepers
21. Spring retainer
22. Inner valve spring (intake valves only)
23. Outer valve spring
24. Oil seal
25. Spring seat
26. Valve

5. Remove the spring retainer (**Figure 89**).

6. When servicing an exhaust valve, remove the single valve spring. When servicing an intake valve, remove both the inner (**Figure 90**) and outer springs (**Figure 91**).

> *CAUTION*
> *Remove any burrs from the valve stem (**Figure 92**) before removing the valve to prevent guide damage.*

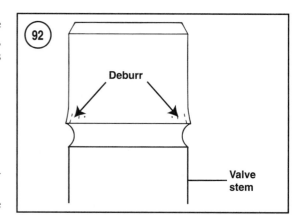

7. Rotate the valve and remove it from the combustion chamber side of the head (**Figure 93**).

8. Pull the oil seal (A, **Figure 94**) from the valve guide. Discard the seal.

9. Remove the spring seat (B, **Figure 94**). Keep the components (**Figure 95**) organized and separated.

10. Repeat Steps 3-10, and remove the remaining valves. Keep all valve sets separate.

Valve Installation

1. Clean the end of the valve guide.

2. Install the spring seat (**Figure 96**) over the valve guide. Do not confuse the valve spring retainer (A, **Figure 95**) with the spring seat (B). The inside diameters are different.

3. Apply molybdenum disulfide oil to a new oil seal

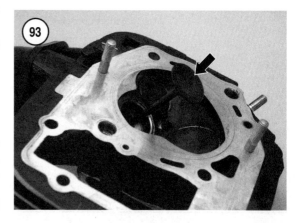

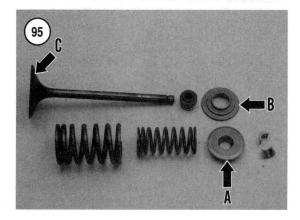

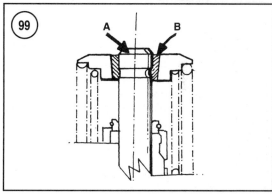

4

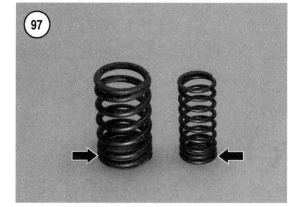

and seat the seal (A, **Figure 94**) onto the end of the valve guide.

4. Coat the valve stem with an assembly lube. Install the valve part way into the guide. Slowly turn the valve (**Figure 93**) as it enters the oil seal and continue turning it until the valve is completely installed.

5. Install a valve spring with its *closer* wound coils (**Figure 97**) facing down into the cylinder head. If the paint mark is still visible on the spring, the end with the paint should face up out of the head.

    a. Install a single valve spring onto an exhaust valve.

    b. Install the outer spring (**Figure 91**) and then the inner spring (**Figure 90**) onto an intake valve.

6. Install the spring retainer (**Figure 89**) and seat it onto the valve spring.

CAUTION
To avoid loss of spring tension, do not compress the springs any more than necessary to install the valve keepers.

7. Compress the valve spring with a valve spring compressor and install the valve keepers (**Figure 88**).

8. Make sure both keepers are seated around the valve stem prior to releasing the compressor.

9. Slowly release the compressor and remove it. Tap the end of the valve stem with a drift and hammer to make sure the keepers are seated (**Figure 98** and **Figure 99**).

10. Repeat Steps 1-9 for the remaining valves.

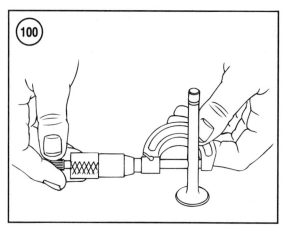

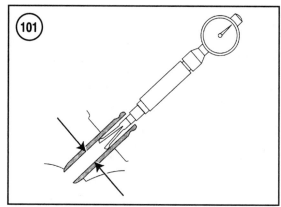

Valve Inspection

When measuring the valves and valve components in this section, compare any measurements to the specifications in **Table 2**. Replace worn, damaged or out of specification parts.

1. Clean valves in solvent. Do not gouge or damage the valve-seating surface.

2. Inspect the valve face (C, **Figure 95**). Remove minor imperfections by lapping the valve as described in this section. If the valve face is excessively pitted or uneven, the valve is not serviceable.

3. Inspect the valve stem for wear and roughness. Measure the valve stem outside diameter with a micrometer (**Figure 100**).

4. Remove all carbon and varnish from the valve guides with a stiff spiral wire brush.

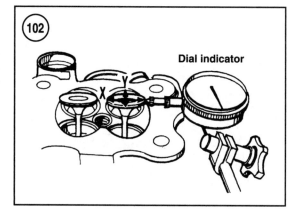

5. Measure the valve guide inside diameter with a small hole gauge (**Figure 101**). Measure the guide at the top, center, and bottom positions. Measure the small hole gauge with a micrometer.

6. Subtract the smaller valve stem outside diameter from the larger valve guide inside diameter. The difference is the valve stem-to-guide clearance. If the clearance is out of specification, determine if the guide, the valve or both are out of specification. If the guide requires replacement, also replace the valve.

7. Measure the valve stem deflection as follows:
   a. Hold the valve approximately 10 mm (0.39 in.) off its seat.
   b. Attach a dial indicator to the valve head (**Figure 102**).
   c. Rock the valve sideways in two directions 90° to each other.
   d. If the valve stem deflection in either direction exceeds the service limit, determine if the guide, the valve or both are out of specification.

8. Check each valve spring as follows:
   a. Inspect the valve spring for visual damage.
   b. Measure the valve spring free length (**Figure 103**).

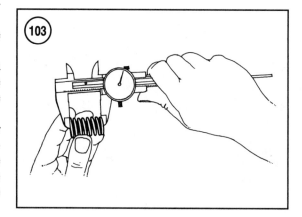

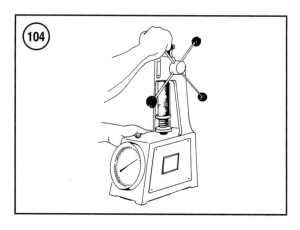

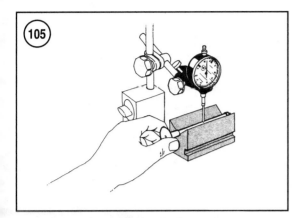

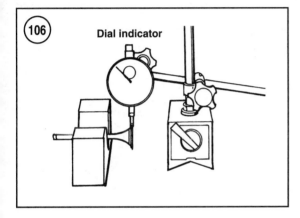

Dial indicator

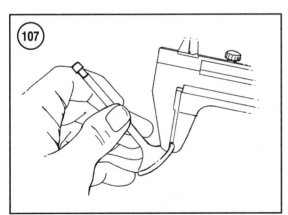

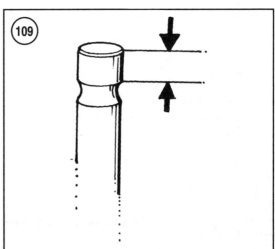

c. Use a scale to measure spring tension (**Figure 104**).

d. Repeat for each valve spring.

9. Check the valve spring seats and valve keepers for cracks or other damage.

10. Check the valve stem runout with a V-block and dial indicator as shown in **Figure 105**. Replace the valve if the valve stem runout exceeds the service limit.

11. Measure valve head radial runout with a dial indicator as shown in **Figure 106**. Replace the valve if its radial runout exceeds the service limit.

12. Measure the valve head thickness (**Figure 107**). Replace the valve if valve head thickness is less than the service limit.

13. Inspect the valve seats (**Figure 108**) as described in this section.

14. Inspect the valve stem end for pitting or wear. If damage is noted, the end may be resurfaced as long as the finished stem end length (**Figure 109**) is not less than the service limit. Replace the valve if stem end length is less than the service limit.

Valve Guide Replacement

Tools

The following Suzuki tools, or their equivalents, are required to replace the guides.

1. Valve guide remover/installer:
   a. Intake: part No. 09916-44910.
   b. Exhaust: part No. 09916-44511.
2. Valve guide bore reamer:
   a. Intake (10.8 mm): part No. 09916-34580.
   b. Exhaust (12.3 mm): part No. 09916-34531.
3. Valve guide reamer:
   a. Intake (5.5 mm): part No. 09916-34550.
   b. Exhaust (7.0 mm): part No. 09916-34520.
4. Valve guide reamer handle: part No. 09916-34542.

Procedure

> *CAUTION*
> *The valve guides are an interference fit in the cylinder head; cooling the guides and heating the head eases installation. Do not use a torch or apply a direct flame to the cylinder head, instead use a shop oven or hot plate. Wear heavy gloves during the following procedure when handling the heated cylinder head.*

1. Place the new valve guides in a freezer.
2. Remove the intake manifold from the cylinder head. When servicing the rear cylinder head, also remove the exhaust manifold.
3. Thoroughly clean the cylinder head before heating it. Note that residual solvent will create an odor during heating.
4. Place the cylinder head in a shop oven and warm it to 100° C (212° F).
5. Using heavy gloves or kitchen pot holders, remove the cylinder head form the oven and place it onto wooden blocks with the combustion chamber facing up.
6. From the combustion side of the head, drive the old valve guide (A, **Figure 110**) from the cylinder head with the valve guide installer/remover (B) and a hammer.
7. Remove and discard the old valve guide.

> *NOTE*
> *Only oversized valve guides are available from the manufacturer.*

8. After the cylinder head has cooled, ream the valve guide bore as follows:
   a. Apply cutting oil to both the valve guide bore and to the appropriate valve guide bore reamer.

> *CAUTION*
> *Always rotate the valve guide reamer clockwise. The valve guide bore will be damaged if the reamer is rotated counterclockwise.*

   b. Insert the valve guide bore reamer from the combustion chamber side and rotate the reamer *clockwise*. Continue to rotate the reamer and work it down through the entire length of the valve guide bore. Continue to apply additional cutting oil during this procedure.
   c. Rotate the reamer *clockwise* until it has traveled all the way through the bore.
   d. Rotate the reamer *clockwise* and completely withdraw the reamer from the valve guide.
9. Reheat the cylinder head as described in Step 4.
10. Using heavy gloves, remove the cylinder head form the oven and place it onto wooden blocks with the combustion chamber facing down.

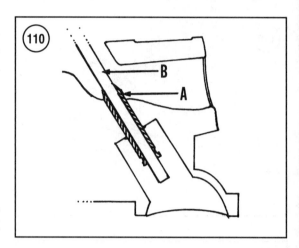

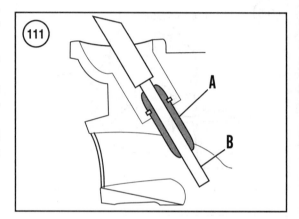

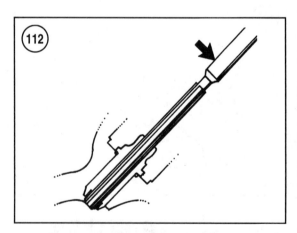

11. Remove one valve guide from the freezer.

> *CAUTION*
> *Failure to lubricate the new valve guide and guide bore will result in damage to the cylinder head and/or valve guide.*

12. Apply clean engine oil to the new valve guide and to the valve guide bore in the cylinder head.
13. From the top side of the cylinder head (camshaft side), drive the new valve guide (A, **Figure 111**) into the cylinder head with the a hammer and the valve

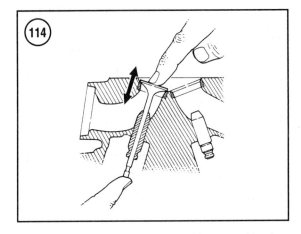

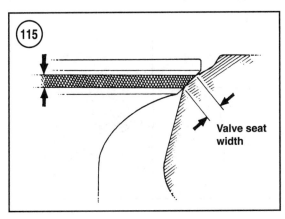

Valve seat
width

b. Insert the valve guide reamer from the combustion chamber side (**Figure 112**) and rotate the reamer *clockwise*. Continue to rotate the reamer and work it down through the entire length of the new valve guide. Continue to apply additional cutting oil during this procedure.

c. Rotate the reamer *clockwise* until it has traveled all the way through the new valve guide.

d. Rotate the reamer *clockwise* and completely withdraw the reamer from the valve guide.

e. Measure the inside diameter of the valve guide with a small hole gauge. Measure the gauge with a micrometer. Compare the measurement to the specification in **Table 2**. Replace the valve guide if it is not within specification.

15. If necessary, repeat Steps 1-14 for any other valve guide.

16. Thoroughly clean the cylinder head and valve guides with solvent. Dry the head with compressed air.

17. Lightly oil the valve guides to prevent rust.

18. Reface the valve seats as described in this section.

19. Install the intake manifold.

a. Install a new O-ring with the intake manifold. Lubricate the O-ring with grease.

b. Position the manifold (A, **Figure 113**) so the arrow points to the top of the cylinder head.

c. Apply Suzuki Thread Lock 1342 to the intake manifold bolts (B, **Figure 113**) and tighten them securely.

20. If servicing the rear cylinder head, also install the exhaust manifold.

a. Install a new exhaust gasket into the exhaust port.

b. Tighten the exhaust manifold bolts to 23 N•m (17 ft.-lb.).

Valve Seat Inspection

1. Remove the valves as described in this section.

2. Thoroughly clean all carbon deposits from the valve face with solvent. Completely dry the valve face.

3. Spread a thin layer of marking compound evenly on the valve face (C, **Figure 95**) and insert the valve into its guide.

4. Support the valve by hand (**Figure 114**), and tap the valve up and down in the cylinder head. Do *not* rotate the valve; a false impression will result.

5. Remove the valve and examine the impression left by the marking compound on both the valve and valve seat. Look for an impression in the dye that is smooth, even, and polished.

6. Measure the valve seat width (**Figure 115**) and compare it with the specification (**Table 2**).

7. If the valve seat is within specification, install the valves as described in this section.

8. If the valve seat is not correct, recondition it as described in this section.

guide installer/remover (B). Drive the valve guide into the bore until the circlip seats completely against the cylinder head.

14. After the cylinder head has cooled, ream the new valve guides as follows:

a. Apply cutting oil to both the new valve guide and to the valve guide reamer.

CAUTION
Always rotate the valve guide reamer clockwise. The valve guide will be damaged if the reamer is rotated counterclockwise.

Valve Seat Reconditioning

Tools

The following Suzuki tools, or their equivalents, are needed to recondition the valve seats. Follow the tool manufacturer's instructions when reconditioning the valve seats.

1. The valve cutter set: part No. 09916-21111.
2. Valve seat cutter N-229 (15°/45°): part No. 09916-27720.
3. Valve seat cutter N-608 (45°): part No. 09916-24935.
4. Solid pilot N-140-5.5: part No. 09916-24480.
5. Solid pilot N-110-1.

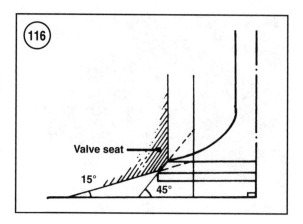

Procedure

The valve seat angles for both the intake and exhaust valves are the same. The valve contact surface is a 45° angle. The area above the contact surface (closest to the combustion chamber) is a 15° angle (**Figure 116**). Refer to **Figure 117** for the appropriate valve seat cutter and solid pilot.

1. Carefully rotate and insert the solid pilot into the valve guide. Make sure the pilot seats correctly.

> *CAUTION*
> *Measure the valve seat contact area in the cylinder head after each cut to make sure the contact area is correct and to prevent excessive material removal. If too much material is removed, the cylinder head must be replaced.*

2. Install the 45° cutter onto the solid pilot. Clean the valve seat with one or two turns (**Figure 118**). Check the seat and if it is still pitted or burned, turn the cutter additional turns until the surface is clean.
3. Inspect and measure the valve seat width as described in this section.
4. If the contact area is too wide or too high on the valve face (**Figure 119**), use the 15° cutter to lower and narrow the contact area.
5. If the contact area is too narrow or too low on the valve face (**Figure 120**), use the 45° cutter to remove a portion of the valve seat material and thus increase the contact area.
6. After the desired valve seat position and width are obtained, use the 45° cutter and *very lightly* clean away any burrs created during the previous cuts. Remove only enough material as necessary.
7. Check the finish for a smooth and velvety surface; it should *not* be shiny or highly polished. The final seating takes place when the engine is first run.
8. Repeat Steps 1-7 for all remaining valve seats.

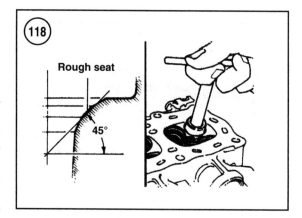

	Intake		Exhaust	
	45°	15°	45°	15°
Valve seat cutter	N-229 or N-608	N-229 or N-212	N-634	N-217
Solid pilot	N-140-5.5	N-140-5.5	N-110-1	N-110-1

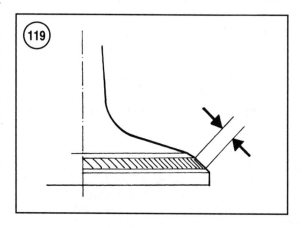

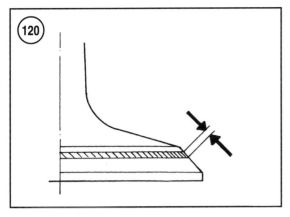

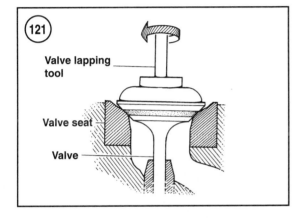

Valve lapping tool

Valve seat

Valve

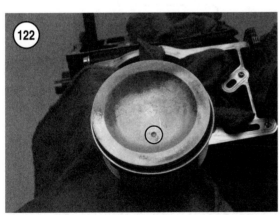

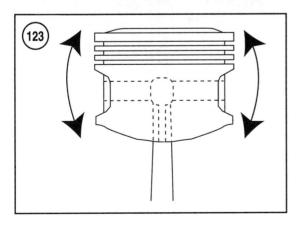

9. Lap the seat and valve as described in this section.

Valve Seat Lapping

Lap the seat surface after reconditioning the valve seat or whenever installing a new valve and valve guide. In cases where the valve has not been reconditioned and the wear or distortion is not excessive, valve lapping can restore the seat surface.

1. Smear a light coating of fine grade valve lapping compound on the seating surface of the valve.
2. Apply molybdenum disulfide oil to the valve stem and insert the valve into the cylinder head.
3. Wet the suction cup of the valve lapping tool and stick it onto the valve head.
4. Lap the valve to the valve seat as follows (**Figure 121**):
   a. Lap the valve by rotating the valve lapping tool between your hands in both directions.
   b. Every 5 to 10 seconds, *stop* and rotate the valve 180° in the valve seat.
   c. Continue lapping until the contact surfaces of the valve and the valve seat in the cylinder head are a uniform gray. Stop as soon as they turn this color to avoid removing too much material.
5. Thoroughly clean the cylinder head and all valve components in solvent, followed by a wash with detergent and hot water.
6. After completing the lapping and reinstalling the valve assemblies, refer to *Cylinder and Cylinder Head Assembly*, and leak test the valve seats.
7. After the cylinder head and valve components are cleaned in detergent and hot water, apply a light coat of engine oil to machined surfaces to prevent rust.

PISTON AND PISTON RINGS

Piston Removal

1. Remove the cylinder/head assembly (this chapter).
2. Mark the top of each piston with an *F* or *R* to correctly identify them during installation.
3. Note that the side of the piston with the index dot (**Figure 122**) faces the exhaust side of the cylinder. If this dot is not clearly visible, mark the exhaust side.
4. Rotate the crankshaft so one piston moves to the top of its stroke. Stuff a shop rag into the crankcase opening beneath the piston so parts cannot fall into the crankcase.
5. Before removing the piston, hold the rod tightly and rock the piston as shown in **Figure 123**. Any rocking motion, not to be confused with the normal sliding motion, indicates wear on the piston pin, rod bushing, pin bore, or more likely, a combination of all three.

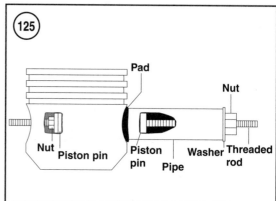

6. Remove the circlip (**Figure 124**) from each side of the piston pin bore. Discard the piston circlips. Install new circlips during assembly.

7. From one side, push the piston pin out of the piston by hand. If the pin is tight, use a fabricated tool (**Figure 125**) to pull the pin from the piston. Do not drive out the piston pin. This action could damage the pin, connecting rod or piston.

8. Lift the piston off the connecting rod.

9. Repeat Steps 2-8 for the other piston.

10. Inspect the pistons as described in this section.

Piston Installation

> *CAUTION*
> *Install each piston onto its original connecting rod. Refer to the marks placed on each piston during removal.*

1. Apply a light coat of an assembly lube to the piston pin, piston bore, and connecting rod bushing.

2. Install a new circlip into one side of the piston. Make sure the circlip end gap is not seated in the piston's notch (**Figure 126**).

3. Slide the piston pin into the piston until the pin is flush with the inside of the piston pin boss (**Figure 127**).

4. Set the piston onto the connecting rod so that the index dot (**Figure 122**) on the piston crown faces the exhaust side of the cylinder.

5. Align the piston pin with the connecting rod bushing. Push the piston pin through the connecting rod until the pin lightly bottoms against the piston pin circlip in the opposite side.

6. Install a *new* piston pin circlip (**Figure 124**) into the piston. Make sure the circlip is properly seated in the piston groove (**Figure 126**).

7. Check the installation of the piston.

8. Repeat Steps 1-7 for the remaining piston.

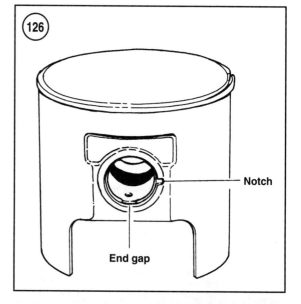

Piston Inspection

1. If necessary, remove the piston rings as described in this section.

> *CAUTION*
> *Be careful not to damage the piston when removing carbon. Do not use a wire brush*

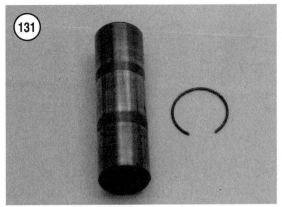

4

wear or damage. If the crown appears pecked or spongy-looking, also check the spark plug, valves, and combustion chamber for aluminum deposits. These deposits indicate the engine is overheating.

4. Examine each ring groove for burrs, dented edges or other damage. Pay particular attention to the top compression ring groove. It usually wears more than the others do. Because the oil rings hold oil, these rings and grooves wear little compared to compression rings and their grooves. If an oil ring groove is worn or if the oil ring assembly is difficult to remove, the piston skirt may be deformed. If necessary, replace the piston.

5. Check the oil control holes (**Figure 129**) in the piston for carbon or oil sludge buildup. Clear them with compressed air.

6. Inspect the piston skirt (**Figure 130**) for cracks or other damage. If a piston shows signs of seizure (bits of aluminum build-up on the piston skirt), replace the piston. If the piston skirt is worn or scuffed unevenly from side-to-side, the connecting rod may be bent or twisted.

7. Check the circlip groove on each side for wear, cracks or other damage. Check the circlip fit by installing a new circlip into each groove, and then attempting to move the circlip from side-to-side. If the circlip has any side play, the groove is worn. Replace the piston.

8. Measure the piston-to-cylinder clearance as described in this section.

9. Measure the piston pin diameter as described in this section.

10. Inspect the piston ring grooves as described in this section.

Piston Pin Inspection

1. Clean the piston pin in solvent and dry it thoroughly.

2. Inspect the piston pin (**Figure 131**) for chrome flaking or cracks. Replace it if necessary.

to clean the piston skirt or ring grooves. Do not remove carbon from the sides of the piston above the top ring or from the top of the cylinder bore. Removal of carbon from these two areas may cause increased oil consumption.

2. Carefully clean the carbon from the piston crown with solvent and a soft scraper. Remark the piston as soon as it is cleaned.

3. After cleaning the piston, examine the crown (**Figure 128**). The crown should show no signs of

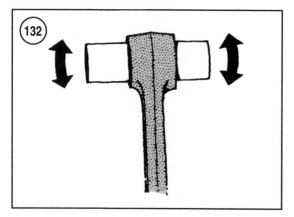

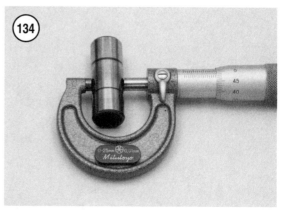

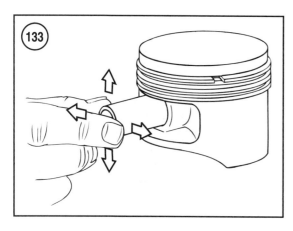

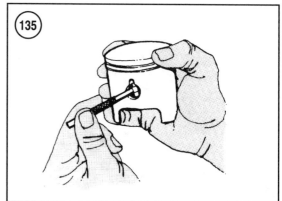

3. Oil the piston pin and install it into the connecting rod. Slowly rotate the piston pin and check for radial play (**Figure 132**).

4. Oil the piston pin and partially install it into the piston. Check the piston pin for excessive play (**Figure 133**).

5. Measure the piston pin outside diameter with a micrometer (**Figure 134**). Measure the diameter at three places along the piston pin. If any measurement is less than the service limit specified in **Table 2**, replace the piston pin.

6. Measure the inside diameter of the piston pin bore (**Figure 135**) with a small hole gauge. Measure the small hole gauge with a micrometer. If the measurement exceeds the service limit specified in **Table 2**, replace the piston.

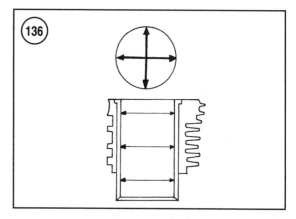

7. Replace the piston pin and/or piston or connecting rod if necessary.

Piston-to-Cylinder Clearance

1. Make sure the piston skirt and cylinder wall are clean and dry.

2. Measure the inside diameter of the cylinder bore with a cylinder bore gauge. Measure the bore at the top, middle, and bottom of a cylinder as shown in **Figure 136**. At each height, measure the bore across

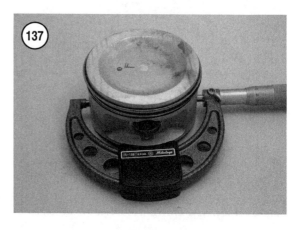

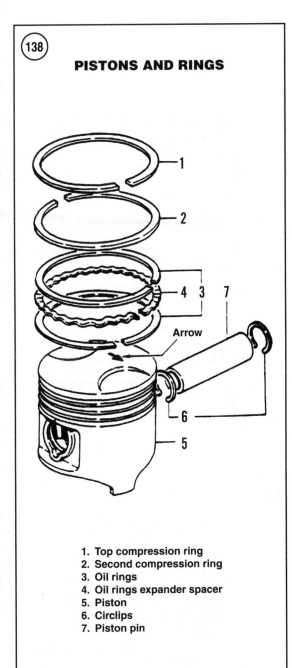

PISTONS AND RINGS

1. Top compression ring
2. Second compression ring
3. Oil rings
4. Oil rings expander spacer
5. Piston
6. Circlips
7. Piston pin

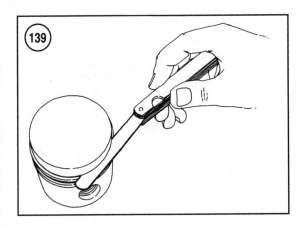

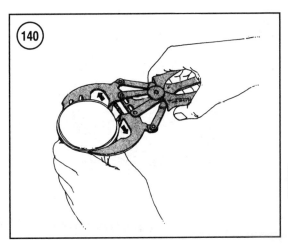

two axes: one parallel to the crankshaft and the other 90° to the crankshaft.

3. Measure the piston outside diameter at a point 16 mm (0.6 in.) from the bottom of the skirt (**Figure 137**).

4. Subtract the piston outside diameter from the largest bore inside diameter; the difference is piston-to-cylinder clearance. If clearance exceeds the service limit specified in **Table 2**, replace the piston and cylinder. The cylinders in this engine cannot be bored or honed.

Piston Ring Removal/Inspection

The piston ring assembly is a three-ring type (**Figure 138**). The top and second rings are compression rings. The lower ring is an oil control ring assembly (consisting of two ring rails and an expander spacer).

When measuring the piston rings and piston in this section, compare the measurements to specifications in **Table 2**. Replace parts that are out of specification or show damage.

1. Measure the side clearance of each compression ring in its groove with a flat feeler gauge (**Figure 139**). If the clearance exceeds the specified service limit, replace the rings. If the clearance is still excessive with the new rings installed, replace the piston.

> *WARNING*
> *The edges of all piston rings are very sharp. Be careful when handling them to avoid cuts.*

> *CAUTION*
> *Store the old rings in the order in which they are removed.*

2. Remove the compression rings with a ring expander tool (**Figure 140**) or by spreading the ring ends by hand (**Figure 141**).

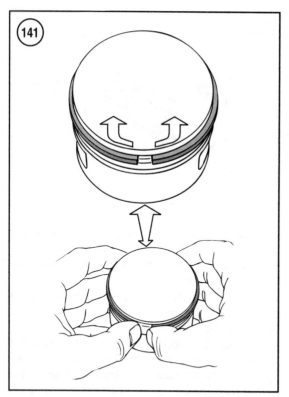

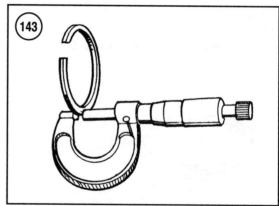

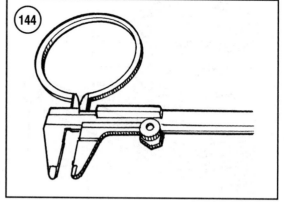

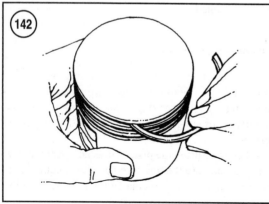

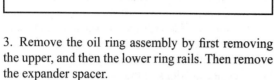

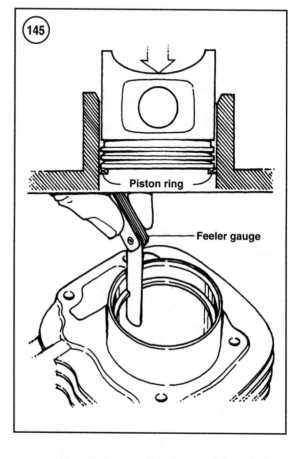

Piston ring

Feeler gauge

3. Remove the oil ring assembly by first removing the upper, and then the lower ring rails. Then remove the expander spacer.

4. Using a broken piston ring, carefully remove carbon and oil residue from the piston ring grooves (**Figure 142**). Do not remove aluminum material from the ring grooves. This will increase ring side clearance.

5. Measure each ring groove width. Measure each groove at several points around the piston. Replace the piston if any groove width is outside the specified range.

6. Inspect the ring grooves carefully for burrs, nicks or for broken or cracked lands. Replace the piston if necessary.

7. Measure the thickness of each compression ring

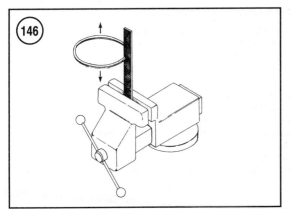

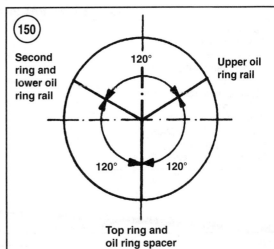

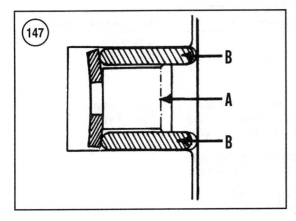

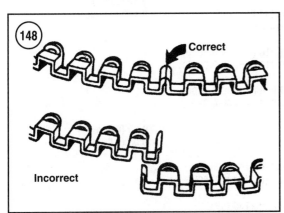

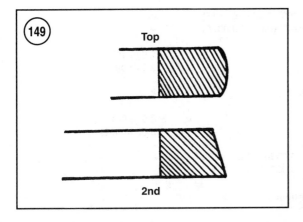

with a micrometer (**Figure 143**). If the thickness is less than specified, replace the ring(s).

8. Measure the free end gap (**Figure 144**). If the free end gap exceeds the service limit, replace the ring(s).

9. Insert the ring into the bottom of the cylinder bore and square it within the cylinder wall with the piston. Measure the end gap with a feeler gauge (**Figure 145**). Replace the rings if the end gap equals or exceeds service limit. Also measure the end gap when installing new piston rings. If the gap on a new compression ring is smaller than specified, hold a small file in a vise, grip the ends of the ring by hand and enlarge the gap (**Figure 146**).

Piston Ring Installation

1. Clean the piston and rings. Dry them with compressed air.

2. Install piston rings as follows:

   a. Install the oil control ring assembly into the bottom ring groove. Install the oil ring expander spacer first (A, **Figure 147**). Then install each ring rail (B). Make sure the expander spacer ends butt together (**Figure 148**). They should not overlap. If reassembling used parts, install the ring rails in their original positions.

   b. Install the 2nd or middle compression ring with the manufacturer's mark facing up. The second ring has a slight taper (**Figure 149**).

   c. Install the top compression ring with the manufacturer's mark facing up.

3. Make sure the rings are seated completely in their grooves all the way around the piston and that the end gaps are distributed around the piston as shown in **Figure 150**. To prevent compression loss, the ring gaps must not align.

4. Refer to *Engine Break-In* (Chapter Five).

Table 1 GENERAL ENGINE SPECIFICATIONS

Engine type	4-stroke, OHC, 3-valve, 45° V-twin
Bore x stroke	96 × 101 mm (3.780 × 3.976 in.)
Displacement	1462 cc (89.2 cu. in.)
Compression ratio	8.5 : 1
Ignition timing	
1998-2004 models	2° BTDC @ 1000 rpm
2005-on	9° BTDC @ 1000 rpm
Firing order	Rear — front (1 — 2)
Engine running rotation	Counterclockwise, viewed from the left side
Cooling system	Air
Lubrication system	Wet sump

Table 2 ENGINE TOP END SPECIFICATIONS

Item	Standard mm (in.)	Service limit mm (in.)
Cylinder head warp	–	0.05 (0.002)
Cylinder head cover warp	–	0.05 (0.002)
Camshaft		
Cam lobe height		
Intake		
1998-2004 models	35.680-35.730 (1.4047-1.4067)	35.38 (1.393)
2005-on models	35.320-35.370 (1.3905-1.3925)	35.02 (1.379)
Exhaust	36.880-36.930 (1.4520-1.4539)	36.58 (1.440)
Camshaft holder inside diameter		
Front head right side, rear head left side	20.012-20.025 (0.7879-0.7884)	–
Front head left side, rear head right side	25.012-25.025 (0.9847-0.9852)	–
Camshaft journal outside diameter		
Front head right side, rear head left side	19.959-19.980 (0.7858-0.7866)	–
Front head left side, rear head right side	24.959-24.980 (0.9826-0.9835)	–
Camshaft runout	–	0.10 (0.004)
Camshaft oil clearance	0.032-0.066 (0.0013-0.0026)	0.150 (0.0060)
Hydraulic tappet plunger stroke	0-0.5 (0-0.02)	
Rocker arm bore inside diameter		
Intake	14.000-14.018 (0.5512-0.5519)	–
Exhaust	16.000-16.018 (0.6299-0.6306)	
Rocker arm shaft outside diameter		
Intake	13.966-13.984 (0.5498-9.5506)	–
Exhaust	15.966-15.984 (0.6286-0.6293)	–
Valves and valve springs		
Valve stem deflection	–	0.35 (0.014)
Valve stem runout	–	0.05 (0.002)
Valve stem outside diameter		
Intake	5.475-5.490 (0.2156-0.2161)	–
Exhaust	6.945-6.960 (0.2734-0.2740)	–
Valve guide inside diameter		
Intake	5.500-5.512 (0.2165-0.2170)	–
Exhaust	7.000-7.015 (0.2756-0.2762)	–
Valve stem-to-guide clearance		
Intake	0.010-0.037 (0.0004-0.0015)	–
Exhaust	0.040-0.070 (0.0016-0.0028)	–
Valve stem end length		
Intake	–	2.5 (0.10)
Exhaust	–	2.2 (0.09)
Valve diameter		
Intake	33 (1.3)	–
Exhaust	40 (1.6)	–
Valve head thickness	–	0.5 (0.02)
Valve head radial runout	–	0.03 (0.001)
Valve seat width		–
Intake	0.9-1.1 (0.035-0.043)	–
Exhaust	1.0-1.2 (0.039-0.047)	–

(continued)

Table 2 ENGINE TOP END SPECIFICATIONS (continued)

Item	Standard mm (in.)	Service limit mm (in.)
Valve seat cutter angle		
Intake	15, 45°	
Exhaust	15, 45°	
Valve spring free length		
Intake		
Inner spring	–	35.0 (1.38)
Outer spring	–	37.8 (1.49)
Exhaust	–	40.6 (1.60)
Valve spring tension		
Intake		
Inner	5.3-6.5 kg @ 28.0 mm (11.68-14.33 lb. @ 1.10 in.)	–
Outer	14.0-14.2 kg @ 31.5 mm (30.87-31.31 lb. @ 1.24 in.)	–
Exhaust	20.3-23.3 kg @ 35.0 mm (44.75-51.37 lb. @ 1.38 in.)	
Cylinder bore diameter	96.000-96.015 (3.7795-3.7801)	–
Cylinder warp	–	0.05 (0.002)
Compression pressure	1000-1400 kPa (145-203 psi)	800 kPa (116 psi)
Compression maximum difference between cylinders	200 kPa	(29 psi)
Piston-to-cylinder clearance	0.02-0.03 (0.0008-0.0012)	0.120 (0.0047)
Piston diameter*	95.975-95.990 (3.7785-3.7791)	95.88 (37.7748)
Piston rings		
Free end gap		
First ring	Approx 13.5 (0.53)	10.8 (0.43)
Second ring	Approx. 14.0 (0.55)	11.2 (0.44)
End gap		
First ring	0.30-0.45 (0.012-0.018)	0.70 (0.028)
Second ring	0.45-0.60 (0.018-0.024)	1.00 (0.039)
Piston ring thickness		
First ring	1.160-1.175 (0.0457-0.0463)	–
Second ring	1.470-1.490 (0.0579-0.0587)	–
Piston ring side clearance		
First	–	0.180 (0.007)
Second	–	0.150 (0.006)
Piston ring groove width		
First	1.210-1.230- (0.0476-0.0484)	–
Second	1.510-1.530 (0.0594-0.0602)	–
Oil	2.810-2.830 (0.1106-0.1114)	–
Piston pin bore inside diameter	23.002-23.008 (0.9056-0.9058)	23.030 (0.9067)
Piston pin outside diameter	22.992-23.000 (0.9052-0.9055)	22.980 (0.9047)

*Measured 16 mm (0.6 in.) from the piston skirt bottom.

Table 3 ENGINE TOP END TORQUE SPECIFICATIONS

Item	N•m	in.-lb.	ft.-lb.
Cam chain guide bolt	10	89	–
Cam chain tensioner mounting bolt	10	89	–
Cam sprocket bolt	15	–	11
Cylinder head bolt			
8 mm		–	
Initial	10	89	–
Final	25	–	18
10 mm			
Initial	25	–	18
Final	37	–	27
Cylinder head cover bolt			
6 mm	10	89	–
8 mm	25	–	18

(continued)

Table 3 ENGINE TOP END TORQUE SPECIFICATIONS (continued)

Item	N•m	in.-lb.	ft.-lb.
Cylinder head cover oil plug	10	89	–
Cylinder head nut			
Initial	10	89	–
Final	25	–	18
Cylinder head side cap bolt	25	–	18
Intake rocker arm shaft	37	–	27
Exhaust manifold bolt	23	–	17
Exhaust rocker arm shaft plug	28	–	21
Rear cylinder head cover plug	25	–	18
Spark plug	18	–	13

CHAPTER FIVE

ENGINE LOWER END

This chapter describes service procedures for the engine lower end components. These include the crankcase, crankshaft, connecting rods, and oil pump. This chapter also includes removal and installation procedures for the transmission shafts, internal shift mechanism and the secondary drive gear assembly. Refer to Chapter Seven to service and inspect these components.

When inspecting the lower end components, compare any measurements to the specifications at the end of this chapter. Replace worn, damaged or out of specification parts.

ENGINE

Precautions and Service Notes

1. The following components can be serviced without removing the engine:
   a. Flywheel.
   b. Starter clutch and gears.
   c. Clutch.
   d. Carburetors or fuel injectors.
   e. Starter.
   f. Secondary driven gear assembly.
2. Use a hydraulic floor jack to support the engine.
3. Two people are needed to remove and install the engine.
4. If necessary, decrease the weight of the engine by removing engine subassemblies first.

5. Loosen tight fasteners with the engine in the frame. For example, the flywheel bolt will be difficult to loosen on the work bench without securing the engine.
6. Label connectors and hoses with tape and a marker before disassembly.
7. Make notes or take photographs of all mounting hardware. Note their positions on the motorcycle and keep the various components separate. **Figure 1** shows the engine mounting hardware for a typical model. The use of some washers and other hardware may differ on some models.
8. Replace all self-locking nuts during engine installation.

Removal

1. Securely support the motorcycle on a level surface.
2. Drain the engine oil and remove the oil filter as described in Chapter Three.
3. Remove the battery and battery box as described in Chapter Ten.
4. Remove the seats, steering head covers, meter cover, and upper covers (Chapter Fifteen). On 2005-on models, remove the mounting bolts and lower the upper cover damper (**Figure 2**) from each side of the frame.
5. Remove the following assemblies:

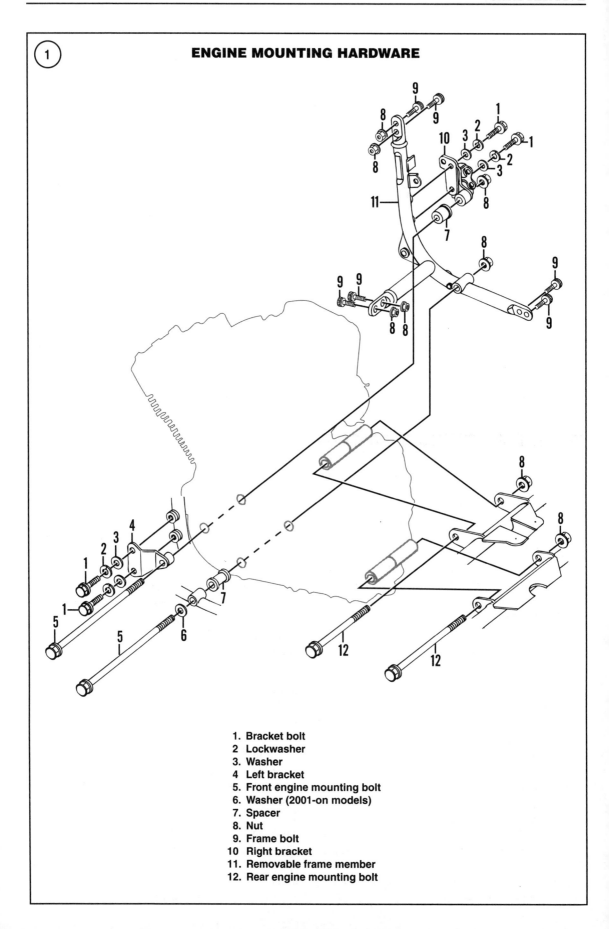

ENGINE MOUNTING HARDWARE

1. Bracket bolt
2. Lockwasher
3. Washer
4. Left bracket
5. Front engine mounting bolt
6. Washer (2001-on models)
7. Spacer
8. Nut
9. Frame bolt
10 Right bracket
11. Removable frame member
12. Rear engine mounting bolt

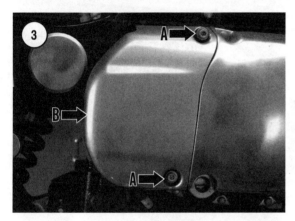

a. Air filter housing and exhaust system (Chapter Eight).

b. On 1998-2004 models, carburetors (Chapter Eight).

c. In 2005-on models, throttle bodies (Chapter Nine).

d. Horn and starter (Chapter Ten). Note that the battery ground wire mounts beneath the lower starter bolt.

e. Secondary gear cover and the shift pedal/footrest (Chapter Seven).

6A. On models without the PAIR System, remove the engine side box (Chapter Eight).

6B. On models with the PAIR system, remove the PAIR system (Chapter Eight or Chapter Nine).

7. Remove the cover bolts (A, **Figure 3**) and lower the speed sensor cover (B) from the clutch cover.

8. Disconnect the following electrical connectors:

a. On 1998-2004 models, disconnect the 3-pin connector from the speed sensor (**Figure 4**).

b. On 2005-on models, disconnect the 3-pin speed sensor connector (A, **Figure 5**).

c. Disconnect the 2-pin rear brake light switch (B, **Figure 5**).

9. Remove the bracket bolt (**Figure 6**), and move the fuse box and relay out of the way.

10. Unscrew the terminal screw (A, **Figure 7**) and disconnect the electrical terminal from the oil pressure switch.

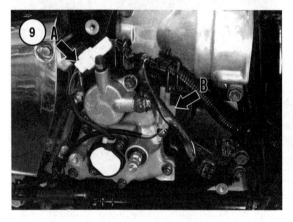

11A. On 1998-2004 models:

  a. Disconnect the neutral switch single-pin connector (A, **Figure 8**) and 2-pin connector (B).

  b. Disconnect the 2-pin signal generator connector (C, **Figure 8**), 3-pin stator connector (D), and the 2-pin sidestand switch connector (E).

11B. On 2005-on models:

  a. Disconnect the 3-pin gear position sensor connector (A, **Figure 9**) and the 2-pin sidestand switch connector (B) from their harness mates. Note how each wire is routed around the clutch release cylinder.

  b. Lift the fuel-tank filler neck. Then disconnect the 2-pin crankshaft position sensor connector (A, **Figure 10**) and 3-pin stator connector (B).

  c. Disconnect the 2-pin engine oil temperature sensor connector (B, **Figure 7**).

12. Remove the clutch release cylinder (Chapter Six). Pull the left clutch push rod (**Figure 11**) from the transmission mainshaft so the rod will not be damaged.

13. Remove the outboard cylinder head side cap (Chapter Four) from each cylinder.

14. Disconnect the cable from each auto-decompression lever by performing the following:

  a. On the rear cylinder, press the auto-decompres-

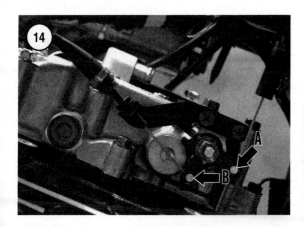

sion lever (A, **Figure 12**) forward and release the cable end (B) from the lever.

b. Hold the auto-decompression plunger (A, **Figure 13**) and remove the plunger limiter bolt (B). Lower the plunger limiter (C, **Figure 13**) from the auto-decompression solenoid.

c. Disconnect the plunger cable end (A, **Figure 14**) from the decompression lever on the front cylinder.

d. Disconnect the auto-decompression cable end (B, **Figure 14**) from the decompression lever.

CAUTION
Oil cooler removal is recommended to provide access to the front of the engine and protect the cooler from damage during engine removal.

15. Remove the oil cooler as described in this chapter.

16. Drain the fluid from the rear brake (Chapter Fourteen) and perform the following:

a. Remove the banjo bolt (**Figure 15**) and disconnect the brake hose from the rear brake master cylinder.

b. Seal the hose end in a plastic bag so brake fluid will not leak onto the motorcycle.

c. Release the holders (**Figure 16** and **Figure 17**) securing the rear brake hose to the engine or removable frame member.

17. Remove the flywheel (this Chapter) and clutch (Chapter Six) to reduce the weight of the engine.

18. Roll a hydraulic jack under the engine. Raise the jack and place tension against the engine to ease mounting bolt removal.

19. Loosen all engine mounting and frame hardware (**Figure 1**).

20. Remove the upper front engine mounting nut (A, **Figure 18**) and the lower front engine mounting nut (A, **Figure 19**). Discard the self-locking nuts.

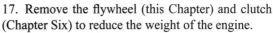

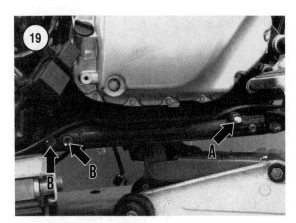

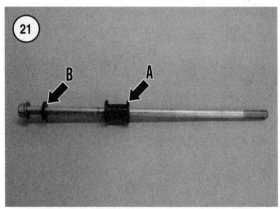

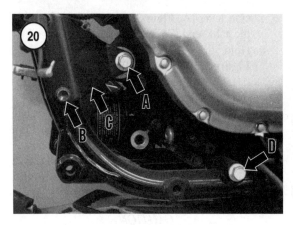

21. Pull the upper front engine mounting bolt (A, **Figure 20**) from the left side. Note the spacer (B, **Figure 18**) between the crankcase and right removable frame downtube.

22. Remove the bracket bolts (B, **Figure 20**) and remove the engine bracket (C) from the left side. Note the washer and lockwasher installed on each bolt.

23. Remove the lower front engine mounting bolt (D, **Figure 20**). Watch for the spacer (A, **Figure 21**) between the engine and the left frame downtube. On 2001-on models, also watch for the washer (B, **Figure 21**).

24. Remove the self-locking nuts from the front frame bolts (**Figure 22**) and the upper frame bolts (A, **Figure 23**), leaving the bolts in place.

25. Remove the front frame bolts (**Figure 22**) and the rear frame bolts (B, **Figure 19**) from the removable frame member.

26. Remove the upper frame bolts (A, **Figure 23**) and lower the removable frame member (B) from the right side (**Figure 24**). The brake pedal, rear brake master cylinder, and reservoir come out with the frame member.

27. Remove the upper rear engine mounting nut (**Figure 25**) and the lower rear engine mounting nut (**Figure 26**). Discard the self-locking nuts.

28. With an assistant steadying the engine, withdraw

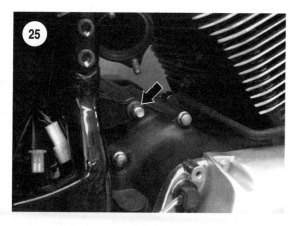

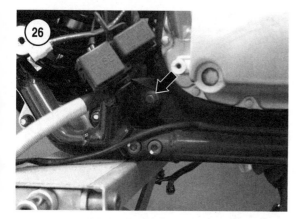

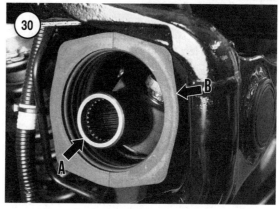

the upper rear engine mounting bolt (**Figure 27**) and the lower rear mounting bolt (**Figure 28**).

29. Lower the jack and the roll the engine forward until the U-joint disengages from the driveshaft (**Figure 29**).

30. Roll the jack and engine from the right side of the frame. Carefully remove the engine from the jack and support the engine on wooden blocks.

Installation

1. Remove the tool box from the right side (Chapter Fifteen).

2. Install the U-joint (A, **Figure 30**) onto the driveshaft in the swing arm. Fit the boot (B, **Figure 30**) onto the swing arm with the *UP* mark facing up.

3. Slide the spacer (**Figure 31**) into the right side of the upper front engine mount.

4. Position the hydraulic jack between the frame.

5. With an assistant, lift the engine and set it onto the jack. Gently raise the jack and roll the engine rearward until the secondary driven shaft engages the U-joint in the swing arm, and the rear engine mounts sit between the frame mounts (**Figure 24**).

6. Install the upper rear engine mounting bolt (**Figure 27**) and the lower rear mounting bolt (**Figure 28**) from the left side.

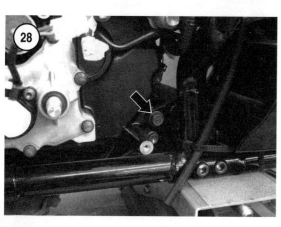

7. Using new self-locking fasteners, install the upper (**Figure 25**) and lower (**Figure 26**) rear engine mounting nuts. Do not tighten the fasteners at this time.

8. Fit the removable frame member into place on the right side. Install the rear frame bolts (B, **Figure 19**), upper frame bolts (A, **Figure 23**), and the front frame bolts (**Figure 22**). Finger-tighten the rear frame bolts.

9. Install new self-locking nuts onto the upper frame bolts (A, **Figure 23**) and the front frame bolts (**Figure 22**). Do not tighten the fasteners at this time.

10. Fit the engine bracket (C, **Figure 20**) onto the left frame member. Install and finger-tighten the engine bracket bolts (B, **Figure 20**). Include a washer and lockwasher on each bolt.

11. Install the lower front engine mounting bolt (D, **Figure 20**) so the spacer (A, **Figure 21**) sits between the engine and left frame member. Include a washer (B, **Figure 21**) on 2001-on models.

12. Install the upper front engine mounting bolt (A, **Figure 20**). Make sure this bolt passes through the spacer (B, **Figure 18**) and the engine bracket on the right side. Install a new self-locking nut (A, **Figure 18**) onto the bolt. Do not tighten the fasteners at this time.

13. Install and finger-tighten the lower front engine mounting nut (A, **Figure 19**). Use a new self-locking nut.

14. Evenly tighten the frame bolts/nuts, the engine bracket bolts, and the engine mounting bolts/nuts. Then tighten to specification as follows:

    a. Tighten the frame bolts/nuts to 50 N•m (37 ft.-lb.).

    b. Tighten the engine bracket bolts (B, **Figure 20**) to 23 N•m (17 ft.-lb.).

    c. Tighten the engine mounting nuts to 79 N•m (58 ft.-lb.).

15. Reinstall the remaining components by reversing Steps 1-17 of *Removal*.

ALTERNATOR COVER

Removal

1. Drain the engine oil and remove the oil filter (Chapter Three).

2. Remove the secondary gear cover and the shift pedal/footrest (Chapter Seven).

3A. On carbureted models, disconnect the 3-pin stator connector (D, **Figure 8**) and the 2-pin signal generator connector (C).

3B. On fuel injected models:

    a. Remove the seats, steering head cover, meter cover, and upper covers (Chapter Fifteen).

    b. Lift the fuel-tank filler neck. Then disconnect the 2-pin crankshaft position sensor connector (A, **Figure 10**) and 3-pin stator connector (B).

35

4. Release any wire holders securing the motorcycle.

5. Remove the alternator cover bolts. Note the wire holder behind the bolts indicated (**Figure 32**).

6. Remove the alternator cover and dowels (A, **Figure 33**). Discard the gasket (B, **Figure 33**).

7. Watch for the torque limiter bushing (**Figure 34**) in the cover.

8. Remove the washer (C, **Figure 33**) from the torque limiter shaft so it will not be lost.

Installation

1. If removed, fit the torque limiter bushing (**Figure 34**) into the alternator cover. Apply an assembly lube to the inside of the bushing.

2. Slip the washer (A, **Figure 35**) onto the torque limiter shaft.

3. Fit the dowels (A, **Figure 33**) into the crankcase and install a new alternator cover gasket (B).

36

> *CAUTION*
> *The alternator magnet is strong and will pull the cover into place. If necessary, use spacers between the cover and the crankcase to prevent pinching your hand.*

4. Position the cover so the stator aligns with the flywheel and set the cover into place (**Figure 36**).

5. Align the dowels with their bosses in the cover. Remove any spacers and set the cover against the gasket (**Figure 32**).

6. Install the alternator cover bolts. Include a wire holder behind the bolts (**Figure 32**) noted during removal.

7. Tighten the bolts to 10 N•m (89 in.-lb.).

37

FLYWHEEL

Removal/Inspection

A rotor remover (Suzuki part No. 09930-30721), or its equivalent, is needed to remove the flywheel.

1. Remove the alternator cover (this chapter).

2. Remove the starter idler gear (B, **Figure 35**) and its shaft (C).

3. Loosen but do not remove the flywheel bolt (A, **Figure 37**). Hold the flywheel flats with an adjustable wrench or hold the flywheel with a universal flywheel holder.

4. Install the rotor remover so its center screw presses against the flywheel bolt.

38

5. Hold the rotor remover (**Figure 38**) and turn its center screw until the flywheel is loose on the crankshaft taper.

5

6. Remove the tool and unscrew the flywheel bolt (A, **Figure 37**). Remove the flywheel (B, **Figure 37**) from the crankshaft.

7. Remove the Woodruff key (A, **Figure 39**) from the crankshaft taper.

8. Inspect the inside of the flywheel for metal debris attached to the magnets (**Figure 40**).

9. Inspect the flywheel keyway (A, **Figure 40**) for wear or damage. If necessary, replace the flywheel.

10. Inspect the one-way clutch rollers (A, **Figure 41**) as described in *Starter Clutch and Gears* in this chapter.

Installation

1. Clean all oil and grease from the crankshaft taper.

2. Install the Woodruff key (A, **Figure 42**) into the crankshaft.

3. Align the keyway in the flywheel with the Woodruff key in the crankshaft. Slide the flywheel onto the crankshaft until the flywheel bottoms against the starter clutch gear. Rotate the flywheel clockwise while pressing toward the crankcase. Make sure the starter gear bearing surface (B, **Figure 39**) engages the rollers of the starter clutch (A, **Figure 41**) on the back of the flywheel.

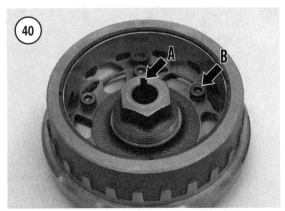

4. Apply Suzuki Thread Lock Super 1303 to the threads of the flywheel bolt and install the bolt (A, **Figure 37**).

5. Hold the flats on the flywheel with a wrench and tighten the flywheel bolt to 160 N•m (118 ft.-lb.).

6. Install the starter idler gear (B, **Figure 35**) and its shaft (C). Make sure the idler gear and torque limiter teeth engage.

7. Install the alternator cover (this chapter).

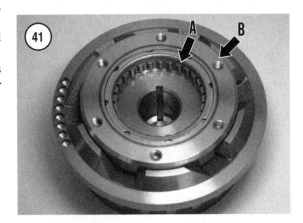

STARTER CLUTCH AND GEARS

Removal

Refer to **Figure 43**.

1. Remove the alternator cover and flywheel (this chapter).

2. If still installed, remove the starter idler gear (B, **Figure 35**) and its shaft (C).

3. Remove the starter clutch gear (A, **Figure 44**) from the crankshaft.

4. Remove the torque limiter (B, **Figure 44**). Watch for the inboard washer (A, **Figure 45**) behind the torque limiter.

5. If necessary, remove the torque limiter bushing (B, **Figure 45**) from the crankcase.

6. Test the starter clutch by performing the following:

    a. Set the flywheel on the bench so the one-way clutch (A, **Figure 41**) faces up.

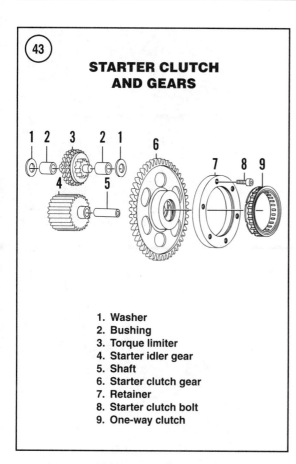

STARTER CLUTCH AND GEARS

1. Washer
2. Bushing
3. Torque limiter
4. Starter idler gear
5. Shaft
6. Starter clutch gear
7. Retainer
8. Starter clutch bolt
9. One-way clutch

b. Set the starter clutch gear onto the one-way clutch so the gear's bearing surface (A, **Figure 46**) rests on the rollers in the one-way clutch.

c. Press the starter clutch gear into the one-way clutch while simultaneously rotating the gear counterclockwise (**Figure 47**).

d. Hold the flywheel. Then rotate the starter clutch gear clockwise and counterclockwise. The gear should rotate freely when turned counterclockwise, but it should lock up when rotated clockwise.

e. Replace the starter clutch if the starter clutch gear rotates freely in both direction or locks up in both directions.

7. Remove the starter clutch gear by lifting it from the starter clutch while simultaneously rotating the gear counterclockwise.

Installation

1. Insert the torque limiter's inboard bushing (**Figure 48**) into the boss in the crankcase.

2. Apply an assembly lube to the inside of the bushing (B, **Figure 45**).

3. Fit the inboard washer onto the torque limiter shaft (A, **Figure 45**) and slide the shaft into the bushing (B, **Figure 44**).

4. Install the starter clutch gear (A, **Figure 44**) onto the crankshaft. The teeth of the starter clutch gear must engage those of the torque limiter.

5. Install the flywheel (this chapter).

6. Install the starter idler gear (B, **Figure 35**) and its shaft (C). Make sure the idler gear and torque limiter teeth engage.

7. Install the washer (A, **Figure 35**) onto the torque limiter and install the alternator cover (this chapter).

Inspection

Use the starter torque limiter holder (Suzuki part No. 09930-73130) and starter torque limiter socket (part No. 09930-73140) to inspect the torque limiter.

1. Inspect the inside of the torque limiter bushings for scratches, scoring or wear. Replace the bushings if any wear is noted.

2. Inspect the starter idler gear teeth (A, **Figure 49**) and torque limiter teeth (B and C) for wear or chipping.

3. Inspect each shaft for scoring or signs of burns.

4. Insert the shaft into the starter idler gear. If noticeable play is noted, replace the gear and its shaft as a set.

5. Inspect the starter clutch gear for worn or chipped teeth (B, **Figure 46**).

6. Inspect the starter clutch bushing (C, **Figure 46**) and its bearing surface (A) for scoring or scratches.

7. Inspect the rollers (A, **Figure 41**) in the one-way clutch for burrs, wear or damage.

8. Check the slip of the torque limiter by performing the following:

  a. Secure the torque limiter holder in a vise.

  b. Insert the torque limiter into the holder (**Figure 50**).

  c. Install the torque limiter socket onto a beam-type torque wrench.

  d. Rotate the torque limiter with the socket. Note the torque specification when the torque limiter slips. Replace the torque limiter if the slip torque is outside the specified range (**Table 1**).

Disassembly

1. Set the flywheel upright on the bench.

2. Evenly loosen and remove the starter clutch bolts (B, **Figure 40**) from the inside of the flywheel.

3. Lift the flywheel away from the starter clutch.

4. Remove the one-way clutch (A, **Figure 41**) from the retainer (B). Note that the side of the one-way clutch with the lip faces the flywheel.

5. Set the new one-way clutch into the retainer so the side with the lip faces the flywheel.

6. Set the retainer onto the back of the flywheel so the retainer's chamfer faces away from the flywheel.

See **Figure 41**. Align the retainer bolt holes with the holes in the flywheel.

7. Invert the assembly and install the starter clutch bolts (B, **Figure 40**). Apply Suzuki Thread Lock Super 1303 to the bolt threads.

8. Evenly tighten the starter clutch bolts in a criss-cross pattern. Tighten the bolts to 26 N•m (19 ft.-lb.).

OIL COOLER

Removal/Installation

Refer to **Figure 51**.

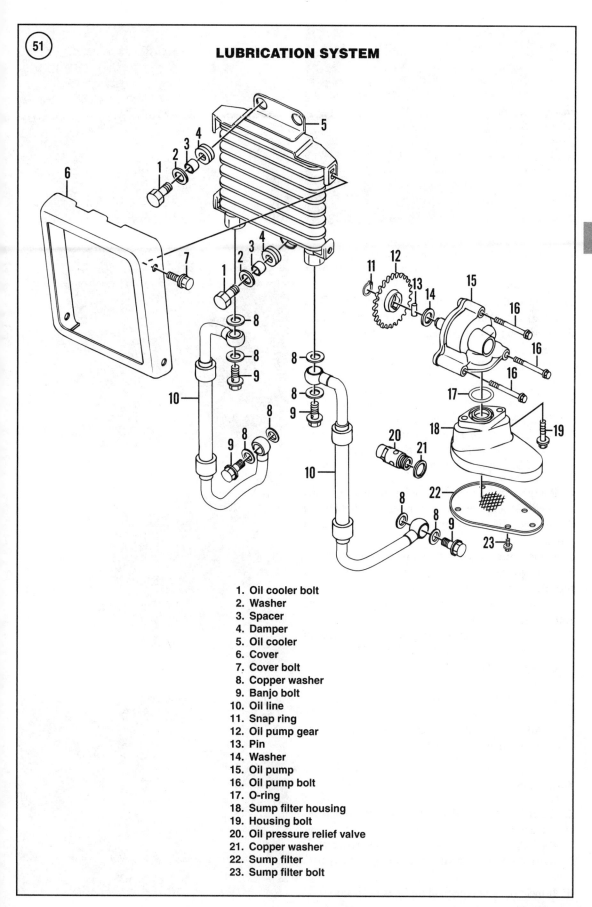

LUBRICATION SYSTEM

1. Oil cooler bolt
2. Washer
3. Spacer
4. Damper
5. Oil cooler
6. Cover
7. Cover bolt
8. Copper washer
9. Banjo bolt
10. Oil line
11. Snap ring
12. Oil pump gear
13. Pin
14. Washer
15. Oil pump
16. Oil pump bolt
17. O-ring
18. Sump filter housing
19. Housing bolt
20. Oil pressure relief valve
21. Copper washer
22. Sump filter
23. Sump filter bolt

1. Remove the battery and battery box (Chapter Ten).
2. Drain the engine oil and remove the oil filter (Chapter Three).
3. Remove the banjo bolt (A, **Figure 52**). Then separate each oil pipe (B) from the crankcase. Watch for the copper washer on each side of the oil pipe fittings.

> *NOTE*
> *On 1998-2000 models, the oil cooler mounting bolts use a washer as shown in **Figure 51**. On 2001-on models, the washer is an integral part of the oil cooler mounting bolt in the two upper oil cooler mounting bolts.*

4. Remove the upper oil cooler mounting bolts (**Figure 53**) and the lower mounting bolt (**Figure 54**). Watch for the damper and spacer in each mount.
5. Remove the oil cooler along with its oil lines.
6. Remove the cover bolts and pull the cover from the oil cooler.
7. Installation is the reverse of removal. Note the following:
   a. Make sure a damper and spacer are in place in each oil cooler mount (A, **Figure 55**).
   b. Install a copper washer onto each side of the oil pipe fittings.
   c. Tighten the banjo bolts (A, **Figure 52**) to 26 N•m (19 ft.-lb.).
   d. Add engine oil (Chapter Three). Start the engine and check for leaks.

Inspection

1. Carefully clean all debris from the oil cooler fins (B, **Figure 55**).
2. Blow the oil cooler clear with compressed air.
3. Use a flat blade screwdriver to straighten any bent fins.
4. Inspect the oil cooler and oil lines for leaks.

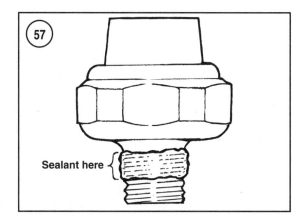

Sealant here

OIL PRESSURE SWITCH

Removal/Installation

1. Disconnect the negative battery cable.
2. Remove the screw (**Figure 56**) and separate the wire from the oil pressure switch.
3. Remove the oil pressure switch from the crankcase.
4. Installation is the reverse of these steps. Note the following:
   a. Apply a light coat of Suzuki 1207B sealant, or its equivalent, to the switch threads where shown in **Figure 57**.
   b. Tighten the oil pressure switch to 14 N•m (10 ft.-lb.).

OIL PRESSURE RELIEF VALVE

Removal/Inspection/Installation

1. Remove the clutch cover (Chapter Six).
2. Remove the oil pressure relief valve (**Figure 58**) from the right crankcase half. Watch for the copper washer installed behind the valve.
3. Inspect the oil pressure relief valve by pushing the piston with a dowel or similar tool (**Figure 59**). Replace the relief valve if the piston does not move smoothly.
4. Install a new copper washer onto the oil pressure relief valve.
5. Install the oil pressure relief valve and tighten to 28 N•m (21 ft.-lb.).

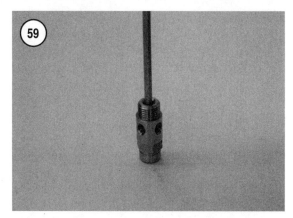

OIL PUMP GEAR

The oil pump is located in the right crankcase half. The oil pump shaft extends out through the right crankcase half. The oil pump gear mounts directly onto the shaft. The oil pump spur gear on the back of the clutch housing drives the oil pump gear.

Removal/Inspection/Installation

1. Remove the clutch (Chapter Six).
2. Stuff a shop rag into the crankcase opening so a dropped part cannot fall into the crankcase.
3. Use snap ring pliers to remove the snap ring (**Figure 60**) from the oil pump shaft.
4. Rotate the oil pump gear so its pin sits horizontally. Then remove the oil pump gear (**Figure 61**) from the pump shaft.
5. Carefully slide the pin (A, **Figure 62**) from the pump shaft and remove the washer (B).
6. Inspect the oil pump gear for chipped or broken teeth (A, **Figure 63**). If damaged, also inspect the oil pump spur gear.

7. Check the boss (B, **Figure 63**) on the inboard side of the oil pump gear.

8. Replace the gear if any damage is noted.

9. Installation is the reverse of removal. Note the following:

    a. Install the oil pump gear so its flat side faces out away from the crankcase. See **Figure 61**.

    b. Make sure the snap ring (**Figure 60**) seats fully in the groove on the pump shaft.

OIL PUMP

The oil pump is located in the right crankcase half. The crankcase must be separated to remove the pump. The oil pump gear and sump filter are replaceable.

Removal/Installation

Refer To **Figure 51**.

1. Remove the engine and separate the crankcase as described in this chapter.

2. Remove the oil pump bolts (**Figure 64**) and lift the oil pump from the right crankcase half.

3. Installation is the reverse of removal. Note the following:

    a. Apply Suzuki Thread Lock 1342 to the threads of the oil pump bolts.

    b. Tighten the oil pump mounting bolts to 10 N•m (89 in.-lb.).

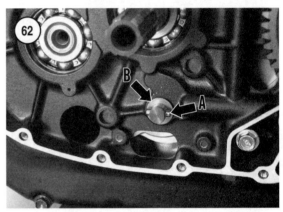

Disassembly/Assembly

1. Remove the sump filter bolts (**Figure 65**) and lift the sump filter from the sump housing.

2. Remove the sump housing bolts (A, **Figure 66**) and pull the sump housing (B) from the oil pump.

3. Remove the O-ring from the sump housing. Install a new O-ring during assembly.

4. Installation is the reverse of removal. Note the following:

    a. Lubricate the new O-ring with grease and install it into the sump housing.

    b. Apply Suzuki Thread Lock 1342 to the threads of the sump housing bolts (A, **Figure 66**) and tighten the bolts to 10 N•m (89 in.-lb.).

    c. Apply Suzuki Thread Lock 1342 to the threads of the sump filter bolts (**Figure 65**) and tighten the bolts to 5 N•m (44 in.-lb.).

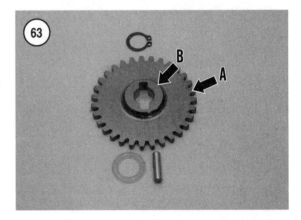

Inspection

1. Rotate the oil pump shaft (C, **Figure 66**). It should turn smoothly without binding or noise.

2. Replace the pump if any noise or binding is noted. No replacement parts are available.

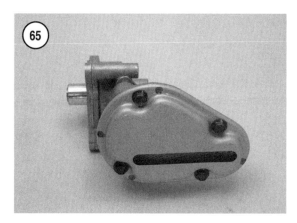

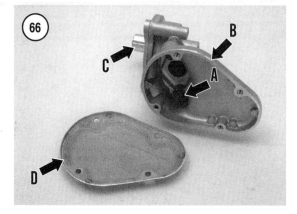

3. Use compressed air to clean the sump filter (D, **Figure 66**). Apply air from the inside of the filter.

4. Inspect the filter for tears or other damage. Replace the sump filter if it contains even small holes.

CRANKCASE

Separating the Crankcase

1. Remove the engine (this chapter).

2. Remove each cylinder/head assembly and remove each piston (Chapter Four).

3. Remove the clutch and primary drive gear (Chapter Six).

4. Remove the flywheel, torque limiter, starter clutch gears, oil pump gear, and the oil pressure relief valve (this chapter).

5. Remove the cam chain and rear cam chain guide from each cylinder (Chapter Four).

> *CAUTION*
> *The countershaft bolt has left-hand threads.*

6. Slide the universal joint onto the secondary driven shaft and hold the universal joint with an adjustable wrench (**Figure 67**). Remove the speed sensor rotor (A, **Figure 68**). Then remove the countershaft bolt (B) and washer.

7. Remove the secondary driven gear assembly and the external shift mechanism (Chapter Seven).

> *NOTE*
> *Make a cardboard template of the left and right crankcase halves. Place a hole in the template that corresponds to each crankcase bolt's location. During disassembly, insert the bolts in the template to identify them during assembly.*

8. Set the crankcase on the bench with the left side facing up. Evenly loosen and remove the crankcase bolts (**Figure 69**). Note the locations of the 6-mm bolts (**Figure 69**).

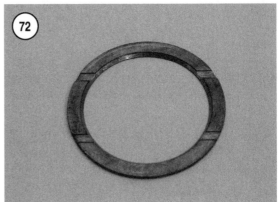

9. Turn the crankcase over so the right side faces up.
10. Evenly loosen and remove the right crankcase
bolts (**Figure 70**). Note the location of the 6-mm bolt
(**Figure 70**).

> *CAUTION*
> *Do not use a metal hammer to separate*
> *the crankcase.*

11. Tap around the perimeter of the crankcase with a
soft-faced mallet.
12. Lift the right crankcase half from the left half.
Watch for the dowels (A, **Figure 71**) and O-ring (B).
Make sure the thrust shim (C, **Figure 71**) remains
with the crankshaft.

Joining the Crankcase

1. Install any removed components into the left
crankcase half as described in *Crankcase Assembly*
(this section).
2. Install the dowels (A, **Figure 71**) and a new O-
ring (B) into the left crankcase half. Apply grease to
the O-ring. Make sure the thrust shim is in place on
the crankshaft (C, **Figure 71**). The grooved side of
the thrust shim (**Figure 72**) must face the crankshaft.
3. Set the right crankcase half face up on the bench.
4. Apply a *thin* layer of Suzuki Bond 1207B to the
crankcase mating surfaces. Completely cover the indicated areas (**Figure 73**).
5. Lower the right crankcase half onto the left half.
6. Install each right crankcase bolt (**Figure 70**)
into its correct location. Evenly tighten the right
crankcase bolts in two-to-three stages following a
crisscross pattern. Do not tighten the bolts to final
specification yet.
7. Turn the crankcase over so the left side faces up.
8. Install each left crankcase bolt (**Figure 69**) into its
correct location. Evenly tighten the left crankcase bolts
in two-to-three stages following a crisscross pattern.

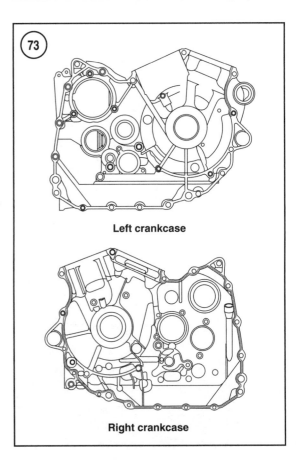

Left crankcase

Right crankcase

9. Tighten the 8-mm left crankcase bolts to 10 N•m (89 in.-lb.), and then to 22 N•m (16 ft.-lb.).

10. Tighten the 6-mm left crankcase bolts (A, **Figure 69**) to 11 N•m (97 in.-lb.).

11. Turn the crankcase over to tighten the right crankcase bolts (**Figure 70**). First tighten the 8-mm crankcase bolts to 10 N•m (89 in.-lb.), and then to 22 N•m (16 ft.-lb.). Tighten the 6-mm crankcase bolt (A, **Figure 70**) to 11 N•m (97 in.-lb.).

12. Install the secondary driven gear assembly and the external shift mechanism (Chapter Seven).

> *CAUTION*
> *The countershaft bolt has left-hand threads. Some click-type torque wrenches only work while tightening clockwise. Check the torque wrench or use a beam-type torque wrench.*

13. Install the speed sensor rotor. Then install the countershaft bolt and washer. Hold the universal joint with an adjustable wrench (**Figure 67**). Tighten the speed sensor rotor (A, **Figure 68**) to 100 N•m (74 ft.-lb.). Tighten the countershaft bolt (B, **Figure 68**) to 60 N•m (44 ft.-lb.).

14. Install the cam chain and rear cam chain guide for each cylinder (Chapter Four).

15. Install the flywheel, torque limiter, starter clutch gears, oil pump gear, and oil pressure relief valve (this chapter).

16. Install the clutch and primary drive gear (Chapter Six).

17. Install each piston and then each cylinder/head assembly (Chapter Four).

18. Install the engine (this chapter).

Crankcase Disassembly

1. Separate the crankcase as described in this section.

2. Lift the crankshaft (D, **Figure 71**) from the left crankcase half. Watch for the thrust shim (C, **Figure 71**) on the right side of the crankshaft.

> *CAUTION*
> *The shift forks and shafts (**Figure 74**) are unique. Mark them during removal so they can be installed in the correct locations.*

3. Remove the countershaft shift-fork shaft (**Figure 75**). Then remove the shift forks from countershaft third gear (A, **Figure 76**) and countershaft fourth gear (B).

4. Remove the mainshaft shift-fork shaft (C, **Figure 76**). Then remove the shift fork (**Figure 77**) from mainshaft second gear.

5. Remove the shift drum (**Figure 78**) from its bearing.

6. Remove the overdrive gear (A, **Figure 79**) and its bushing (B) from the secondary drive gear assembly.

7. Remove the countershaft (A, **Figure 80**) and the mainshaft (B) as a single assembly.

8. Remove the secondary drive gear retainer bolts and the retainer (A, **Figure 81**).

9. Remove the secondary drive gear assembly (**Figure 82**) from the crankcase. Also remove the shims (**Figure 83**) located behind the assembly. Note the number of shims, as they determine the gear lash.

10. Remove the oil pump from the right crankcase half (this chapter).

11. Remove the oil separator bolts (**Figure 84**) and the oil separator from each crankcase half.

12. If still installed, remove the oil jets from the crankcase halves as follows:

  a. Remove the jet retainer (A, **Figure 85**) and pull the piston oil jet (**Figure 86**) from right crankcase half. Repeat for the left crankcase half (**Figure 87**).

  b. Remove the transmission oil jet (**Figure 88**) from the shift mechanism housing in the left crankcase half.

  c. Remove the secondary gear oil jet (**Figure 89**) from the secondary gearcase in the left crankcase half.

  d. Remove the rear cylinder head oil jets from the right crankcase half (**Figure 90** [No. 14] and **Figure 91** [No. 22]).

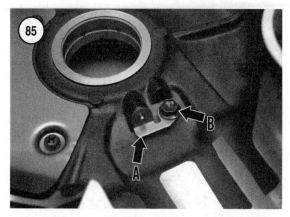

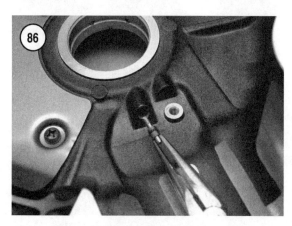

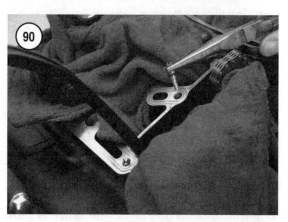

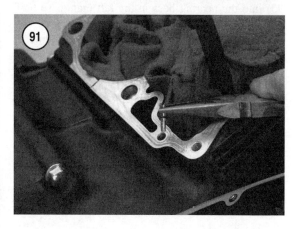

e. Clean each oil jet with solvent and blow it clear with compressed air. Replace the oil jets if they are restricted.

Crankcase Assembly

1. If removed, install a new oil seal into the left crankcase half. Apply grease to the lips of the new seal. Then drive the seal into place with a bearing driver or socket that matches the outside diameter of the seal.
2. Set each crankcase half onto the bench.
3. Install each piston oil jet by performing the following:
    a. Oil and install a new O-ring (**Figure 92**) onto each piston oil jet.
    b. Press a piston oil jet (**Figure 86**) into its housing in the right crankcase half.
    c. Set the oil jet retainer (A, **Figure 85**) into place.
    d. Apply Suzuki Thread Lock 1432 to the threads of the piston oil jet bolt (B, **Figure 85**) and tighten the bolt to 10 N•m (89 in.-lb.).
    e. Repeat for the left crankcase half (**Figure 87**).
4. Apply clean engine oil to the O-ring on each remaining oil jet and install each jet until it bottoms in its gallery.
    a. Seat the transmission oil jet (**Figure 88**) into the shift mechanism housing in the left crankcase half.
    b. Install the secondary gear oil jet (**Figure 89**) into the secondary gearcase in the left crankcase half.
    c. Press the rear cylinder head oil jets (**Figure 90** [No. 14] and **Figure 91** [No. 22]) into the right crankcase half.
5. Set the oil separator (A, **Figure 84**) into place in each crankcase half. Apply Suzuki Thread Lock 1342 to the threads of each oil separator bolt and tighten the bolts to 10 N•m 89 in.-lb.).
6. Install the oil pump (this chapter).
7. Position the left crankcase half on the bench so its inboard side faces up.
8. Install the secondary drive gear shims (**Figure 93**) into the bearing boss in the left crankcase half. See **Figure 83**.
9. Lower the secondary drive gear assembly into its bearing boss (**Figure 82**). Make sure the assembly bottoms against the shims.
10. Set the retainer (A, **Figure 81**) onto the secondary drive gear assembly. Apply Suzuki Thread Lock Super 1303 to the threads of the secondary drive gear retainer bolts. Install and tighten the bolts to 23 N•m (17 ft.-lb.).
11. Mesh the gears of the countershaft (A, **Figure 80**) and mainshaft assemblies (B). Then lower both shafts into the left crankcase half. Make sure each shaft is fully seated in its bearing.
12. Lower the shift drum (**Figure 78**) into its bearings.

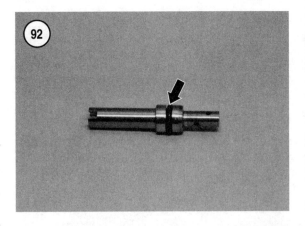

13. Position the mainshaft shift fork as noted during removal and seat the shift fork into the groove in mainshaft second gear (**Figure 77**).
14. Rotate the shift fork around the gear so the fork locating pin engages its groove in the shift drum. Then install the mainshaft shift fork shaft (C, **Figure 76**).
15. Position each countershaft shift fork as noted during removal. Then install a shift fork into the countershaft third gear (A, **Figure 76**) and countershaft fourth gear (B).
16. Rotate each shift fork so its locating pin engages its groove in the shift drum and install the countershaft shift fork shaft (**Figure 75**).

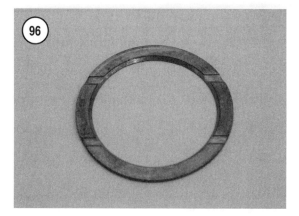

17. Seat the bushing into the overdrive gear (**Figure 94**).

18. Install the overdrive gear (A, **Figure 79**) and bushing (B) onto the secondary drive gear assembly so the slots in the gear (**Figure 95**) engage the dogs (B, **Figure 81**) on the secondary drive output cam. Make sure the teeth of the secondary drive overdrive gear engage the teeth of the countershaft overdrive gear as shown (**Figure 79**).

19. Lower the tapered end of the crankshaft (D, **Figure 71**) into the main bearing in the left crankcase half. Make sure each connecting rod sits in the correct cylinder hole.

20. Install the thrust shim (C, **Figure 71**) onto the right side (splined side) of the crankshaft so the shim's oil grooves (**Figure 96**) face down toward the crankweb.

21. Join the crankcase as described in this section.

Crankcase Inspection

1. Carefully remove all sealant from the crankcase mating surfaces. Do not damage the mating surfaces.

> *CAUTION*
> *When drying the bearings with compressed air, hold the inner race so it will not rotate. Without lubrication the bearings will be damaged if allowed to spin.*

2. Clean the crankcase and bearings with solvent. Thoroughly dry them with compressed air.

3. Clean the crankcase oil passages with compressed air.

4. Inspect the crankcase mating surfaces. They must be free of any damage that could cause an oil leak.

5. Inspect the crankcase halves for cracks and fractures, especially in the lower areas where they are vulnerable to rock damage.

6. Check the areas around the stiffening ribs and bearing bosses for damage. Repair or replaced a damaged crankcase.

7. Check the threaded holes for damage and debris. If necessary, clean or repair the threads with a tap. Coat the tap threads with kerosene or tap fluid before use.

8. Lightly oil the crankcase bearings with engine oil.

9. Rotate the mainshaft (A, **Figure 97**), countershaft (B), and the shift drum bearings (C) slowly by hand. Check each bearing for roughness, pitting, galling, and play. If any bearing is noisy, turns roughly or has excessive play, replace the bearing and its mate in the other crankcase half.

10. Inspect the crankshaft main bearings for wear, scoring or abrasion. Make sure the bearing inserts are locked into place.

Bearing Replacement

Two bearing remover/installers (Suzuki part Nos. 09913-75810 and 09913-75520), or their equivalents, are needed to replace the crankcase bearings.

Before removal, refer to the bearing size codes and identify the bearings. Note each bearing position in the crankcase and record it for proper installation.

1. Remove any bearing retainer.

2. Heat the crankcase half to approximately 95-125° C (203-257° F) in a shop oven or on a hot plate. Do

not heat the crankcase with a torch. This type of localized heating may warp the crankcase.

3. Wearing a pair of suitable gloves for protection, remove the crankcase half from the oven and place it on wooden blocks.

4. Drive the bearing out with an appropriate size bearing driver, socket or a drift.

5. After removing bearings, clean the crankcase half in solvent and dry it thoroughly.

6. Chill the replacement bearings in a freezer for approximately 30 minutes.

7. Heat the crankcase half again to approximately 95-125° C (205-257° F) and install the new bearings.

8. During bearing installation, press on the outer bearing race only. Use a bearing driver or socket that matches the outside diameter of the bearing (A, **Figure 98**).

9. If one bearing requires replacement, also replace its mate in the opposite crankcase half.

10. Install any removed bearing retainers (B, **Figure 98**, typical). Apply Suzuki Thread Lock 1342 to the threads of a bearing retainer bolt(s).

11. Repeat for the other crankcase half.

CRANKSHAFT

Removal/Installation

Refer to **Figure 99**.

1. Separate the crankcase. Remove the crankshaft as described in *Crankcase Disassembly* (this chapter).

2. Inspect the crankshaft and the main bearing inserts as described in this section.

3. Install the crankshaft as described in *Crankcase Assembly* (this chapter).

Inspection

1. Clean the crankshaft thoroughly with solvent and dry it with compressed air. If necessary, clean the oil passages (A, **Figure 100**) with rifle cleaning brushes. Lightly oil the journal surfaces to prevent rust.

2. Blow the oil passages clear with compressed air.

3. Inspect the journals (B, **Figure 100**) for scratches, heat discoloration or other defects. Remove very small scratches with fine emery cloth. Refer more serious damage to a machine shop.

4. Check the crankshaft splines (C, **Figure 100**) for excessive wear or damage.

5. Check the flywheel taper (A, **Figure 101**), threads (B), and Woodruff key slot (C) for damage.

6. Check the timing sprocket (D, **Figure 101**) for excessive wear or tooth damage.

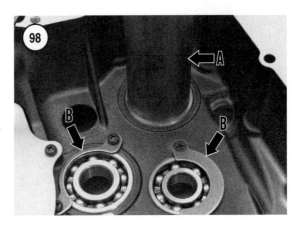

NOTE
New crankshaft main bearing inserts must be honed after installation. If the bearings require replacement, refer this to a machine shop.

7. Inspect the crankshaft main bearing inserts as follows:

   a. Inspect the crankshaft main bearing inserts (**Figure 102**) for wear, scoring or abrasion. If either insert is questionable, replace the entire set.

   b. Clean the crankshaft journals and crankcase main bearings.

   c. Use a bore gauge to measure the inside diameter of each crankshaft main bearing (**Figure 103**). For each bearing, take two measurements – 90° to each other – and record each measurement.

   d. Use a micrometer to measure the outside diameter of each crankshaft journal (**Figure 104**). For each journal, take two measurements – 90° to each other – and record each measurement.

   e. Calculate the crankshaft journal oil clearance by subtracting the crankshaft journal outside diameter from the crankshaft bearing inside diameter.

   f. If the oil clearance is outside the range specified in **Table 1**, either the crankshaft, main bearing inserts or both must be replaced.

Thrust clearance

Check the crankshaft thrust clearance whenever the crankshaft is removed from the crankcase.

1. Set the left crankcase half on the bench so its inboard side face up.

2. Install the tapered end of the crankshaft into its bearing in the left crankcase half. Make sure each connecting rod sits in the correct cylinder hole.

3. Install the thrust shim (C, **Figure 71**) onto the right side (splined side) of the crankshaft so the shim's oil grooves (**Figure 96**) face down toward crankshaft.

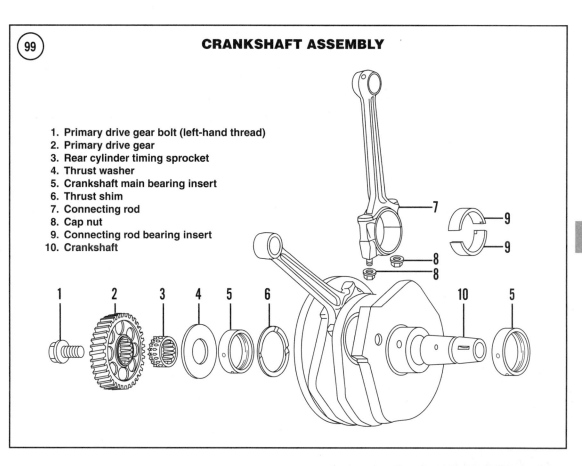

CRANKSHAFT ASSEMBLY

99

1. Primary drive gear bolt (left-hand thread)
2. Primary drive gear
3. Rear cylinder timing sprocket
4. Thrust washer
5. Crankshaft main bearing insert
6. Thrust shim
7. Connecting rod
8. Cap nut
9. Connecting rod bearing insert
10. Crankshaft

5

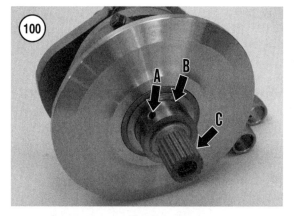

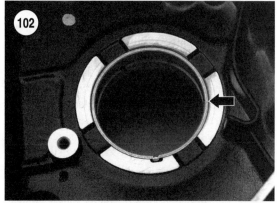

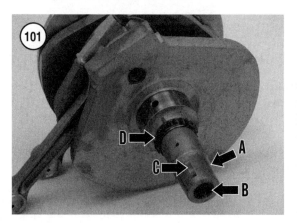

4. Lower the right crankcase half onto the left half. Install and hand tighten the crankcase bolts. Do not apply sealant to the crankcase and do not torque the bolts.

5. Install the thrust washer (A, **Figure 105**) onto the splined end of the crankshaft. The chamfered side of the washer (**Figure 106**) must face the crankshaft.

6. Install the rear cylinder timing sprocket (B, **Figure 105**) onto the crankshaft so the timing dot on the sprocket aligns with the timing dot on the crankshaft.

> NOTE
> *The primary drive gear bolt has left-hand threads.*

7. Install the primary drive gear (A, **Figure 107**) onto the crankshaft. The side with the painted dot should face in. Tighten the primary drive gear bolt (B, **Figure 107**) to 150 N•m (111 ft.-lb.).

8. Use a feeler gauge (**Figure 108**) to measure the clearance between the right crankcase half and the thrust washer. If crankshaft thrust clearance is outside the specified range (**Table 1**), select a new thrust shim by performing the following:

    a. Remove the crankshaft by reversing Steps 1-7. Measure the thickness of the existing thrust shim.

    b. Thrust shims are available in increments of 0.025 mm (0.0010 in.). Select a new shim to bring the thrust clearance within specification. Refer to **Table 4**.

    c. Install the new thrust shim and remeasure the thrust clearance. Repeat as necessary until the thrust clearance is within specification.

    d. Remove crankshaft and reassemble the crankcase as described in this chapter.

CONNECTING ROD

Removal/Installation

1. Remove the crankshaft as described in *Crankcase Disassembly* in this chapter.

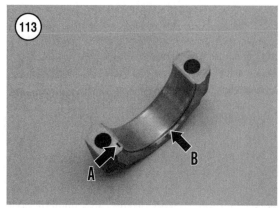

2. Slide the connecting rods to one side. Use a flat feeler gauge to measure the big end side clearance between the connecting rod and the crankshaft (**Figure 109**). Repeat this on the other connecting rod. Compare each measurement to the specification in **Table 1**. If either clearance is outside the range specified, refer to *Inspection* in this section.

> *CAUTION*
> *Before disassembly, mark each connecting rods and its cap so they can be installed in their original locations.*

3. Remove the connecting rod cap nuts (A, **Figure 110**) and cap (B). Then carefully separate the connecting rod from the crankpin. Keep each cap with its connecting rod (**Figure 111**). When a cap is installed on the correct connecting rod, the code portion of the cap aligns with the code portion of the rod to form a complete number. Refer to **Figure 112**.

> *CAUTION*
> *The bearing inserts must be installed in their original locations. Keep each bearing insert in its connecting rod or cap. If the bearing inserts are removed, label the back of the insert to identify the correct cylinder and connecting rod or cap.*

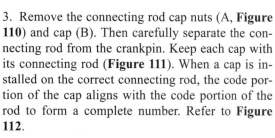

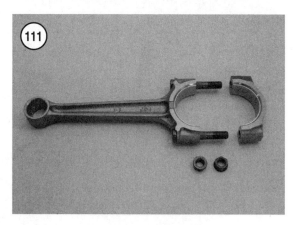

4. Inspect the connecting rods and bearings as described in this section.
5. Install each bearing insert so its tab (A, **Figure 113**) locks in the cutout on the cap or connecting rod. If reusing the bearings, install each insert in its original location.
6. Apply an assembly lube to the crankpin and to the bearing inserts.

> *CAUTION*
> *The connecting rod numeric codes face the intake side of their respective cylinder (**Figure 112**). The rear cylinder*

connecting rod is the left rod (crank-shaft taper side). When rotated so the small end is up, the numeric code (3) should face forward. The front cylinder connecting rod is the right rod (crank-shaft splined end). When rotated so the small end is up, the numeric code (2) should face rearward.

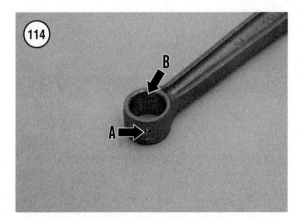

7. Carefully set a connecting rod onto its crankpin so the side with the numeric code faces the intake side of its cylinder.

8. Fit the correct rod cap (B. **Figure 110**) onto the connecting rod. Make sure the cap's numeric code aligns with the code on the connecting rod (**Figure 112**).

9. Apply engine oil to the cap nuts (A, **Figure 110**) and install the nuts onto the bolts. Evenly tighten the cap nuts to 25 N•m (18 ft.-lb.), and then to 51 N•m (38 ft.-lb.).

10. Repeat Steps 7-9 for the remaining connecting rod.

11. Rotate each connecting rod around the crankpin and check for binding.

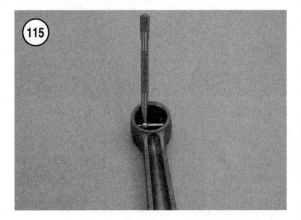

Inspection

1. Check each connecting rod assembly for damage such as cracks or burns.

2. Make sure the small end oil hole (A, **Figure 114**) is open. Clean it out if necessary.

3. Measure the rod small end inside diameter with a small hole gauge (**Figure 115**). Measure the gauge with a micrometer and compare the reading to the service limit in **Table 1**.

4. Check the crankpin (**Figure 116**) for wear, scoring or other damage.

5. Check the piston pin contact surface (B, **Figure 114**) in the small end for wear or abrasion.

6. Oil the piston pin and install it into the connecting rod small end. Rock the pin and check for radial play (**Figure 117**).

7. Have a machine shop check the connecting rods for twisting and bending.

8. Examine the bearing inserts for wear (B, **Figure 113**), scoring or burned surfaces. They are reusable if in good condition. Make a note of the bearing color identification on the side of the insert if the bearing is to be discarded. A previous owner may have used undersize bearings.

9. Compare the connecting rod big end side clearance measurement to the specification in **Table 1**. If the side clearance exceeds the service limit, perform the following:

   a. Measure the width of the connecting rod big end with a micrometer (**Figure 118**). If the

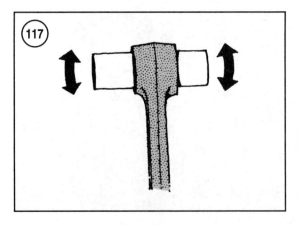

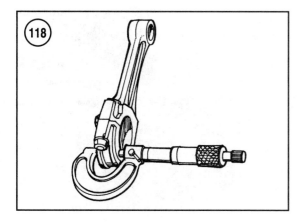

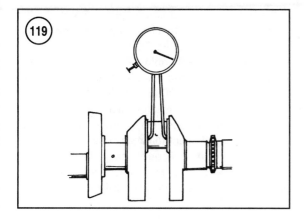

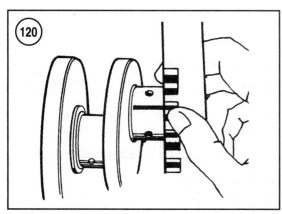

width is less than the value specified in **Table 1**, replace the connecting rod assembly.

b. Measure the crankpin width with a caliper (**Figure 119**) and compare the measurement to the dimension in **Table 1**. If the width is greater than specified, replace the crankshaft.

Oil clearance

1. Check each connecting rod bearing insert for wear or scoring. If the bearing inserts are in good condition they may be reused. If the cap or rod insert is questionable, replace the inserts as a set.

2. Clean the crankpins (**Figure 116**) and check for excessive wear or damage.

3. If removed, install the existing bearing inserts into the connecting rod and cap. Lock the inserts into place (**Figure 113**).

4. Carefully set a connecting rod onto its crankpin so the side with numeric code faces the intake side of its cylinder. The rear connecting rod code should face the front of the engine; the front connecting rod code should face the rear. Refer to **Figure 112**.

5. Lay a piece of Plastigage parallel across the crankpin (**Figure 120**) so it does not lie across an oil hole.

6. Fit the correct rod cap (B, **Figure 110**) onto the connecting rod. Make sure the cap's numeric code aligns with the code on the connecting rod.

7. Apply engine oil to the cap nuts (A, **Figure 110**). Then install the nuts onto the bolts. Evenly tighten the cap nuts to 25 N•m (18 ft.-lb.), and then to 51 N•m (38 ft.-lb.).

8. Repeat Steps 4-7 for the other connecting rod.

9. Loosen the cap bolts. Carefully lift each cap straight up and off the connecting rod.

10. Measure the width of the flattened Plastigage according to the manufacturer's instructions (**Figure 120**). Measure both ends of the Plastigage strip.

a. A difference of 0.025 mm (0.001 in.) or more indicates a tapered journal. Confirm this by measuring the crankpin outside diameter with a micrometer as shown in **Figure 121**.

b. If the connecting rod big end oil clearance is greater than the service limit specified in **Table 1**, select new bearings as described in this section.

11. Remove all of the Plastigage from the crankpins or rod caps. Plastigage can plug the oil holes.

Bearing Selection

1. A numeric code (1, 2 or 3) on the intake side of the connecting rod (**Figure 112**) corresponds to the big end inside diameter.

2. A set of numeric codes (1, 2 or 3) stamped on the crankshaft web corresponds to the crankpin outside diameter (**Figure 122**).

3. Select new bearings by cross-referencing the crankpin outside diameter code in the top row of **Table 2** with the connecting rod inside diameter code in the left column of the table. The intersection of the appropriate row and column indicates the color of the new bearing insert. **Table 3** lists the bearing color, part number, and insert thickness. Always replace all connecting rod bearing inserts as a set.

4. After installing new bearing inserts, recheck the oil clearance. If the clearance is still out of specification, either the crankshaft or the connecting rod is worn to the service limit. Measure the inside diameter of the connecting rod big end and measure the outside diameter of the crankpin. Compare the measurements to the specifications in **Table 1**. Replace the component(s) that is out of specification.

ENGINE BREAK-IN

When replacing top end components or performing major lower end work, break in the engine as though it were new.

During break-in, oil consumption may be higher than normal. Frequently check, and if necessary, correct the oil level (Chapter Three).

During the first 500 miles (800 km) of operation, keep the throttle opening at less than 1/2 throttle. In the period between 500 and 1000 miles (800-1600 km), operate the engine at less than 3/4 throttle.

Vary the engine speed during the break-in period. Avoid prolonged operation at any one engine speed.

After the break-in period, change the engine oil and filter as described in Chapter Three to remove any particles produced during break-in.

Table 1 ENGINE LOWER END SPECIFICATIONS

Item	Standard mm (in.)	Service limit mm (in.)
Connecting rod		
Small end inside diameter	23.015-23.023 (0.9061-0.9064)	23.040 (0.9071)
Big end side clearance	0.10-0.20 (0.004-0.008)	0.30 (0.012)
Big end width	21.95-22.00 (0.864-0.866)	–
Big end oil clearance	0.024-0.042 (0.0009-0.0017)	0.080 (0.0032)
Big end inside diameter		
Code 1	53.000-53.006 (2.0866-2.0868)	–
Code 2	53.006-53.012 (2.0868-2.0871)	–
Code 3	53.012-53.018 (2.0871-2.0873)	–
Crankshaft		
Crankpin width	22.10-22.15 (0.870-0.872)	–
Crankpin outside diameter		–
Standard	49.982-50.000 (1.9678-1.9685)	–
Code 1	49.994-50.000 (1.9683-1.9685)	–
Code 2	49.988-49.994 (1.9680-1.9683)	–
Code 3	49.982-49.988 (1.9678-1.9680)	–
Crankshaft journal outside diameter	51.965-51.980 (2.0459-2.0465)	–
Crankshaft main bearing inside diameter	52.000-52.015 (2.0472-2.0478)	
Crankshaft journal oil clearance	0.020-0.050 (0.0008-0.0020)	0.080 (0.0032)
Crankshaft runout	–	0.05 (0.002)
Crankshaft thrust clearance		
(at right crankcase)	0.05-0.10 (0.002-0.004)	–
Crankshaft thrust bearing thickness	1.925-2.175 (0.0758-0.0856)	
Oil pressure @ 60° C (140° F)	350-650 kPa (51-94 psi) @ 3000 rpm	–
Oil pump reduction ratio	1.154 (76/51 × 31/40)	–
Starter torque limiter slip torque	20-40 N•m (15-30 ft.-lb.)	–

Table 2 CONNECTING ROD BEARING INSERT SELECTION

Connecting rod inside diameter code	Crankpin outside diameter code	1	2	3
1		Green	Black	Brown
2		Black	Brown	Yellow
3		Brown	Yellow	Blue

Table 3 CONNECTING ROD BEARING INSERT DIMENSIONS

Color	Part No.	Specification mm (in.)
Green	12164-38B01-0A0	1.485-1.4888 (0.0585-0.0586)
Black	12164-38B01-0B0	1.488-1.491 (0.0586-0.0587)
Brown	12164-38B01-0C0	1.491-1.494 (0.0587-0.0588)
Yellow	12164-38B01-0D0	1.494-1.497 (0.0588-0.0589)
Blue	12164-38B01-0E0	1.497-1.500 (0.0589-0.0591)

Table 4 CRANKSHAFT THRUST SHIM SELECTION

I.D. Number	Thrust Shim Thickness	Part No.
1	1.925-1.950 (0.0758-0.0768)	12228-38B00-0A0
2	1.950-1.975 (0.0768-0.0778)	12228-38B00-0B0
3	1.975-2.000 (0.0778-0.0787)	12228-38B00-0C0
4	2.000-2.025 (0.0787-0.0797)	12228-38B00-0D0
5	2.025-2.050 (0.0797-0.0807)	12228-38B00-0E0
6	2.050-2.075 (0.0807-0.0817)	12228-38B00-0F0
7	2.075-2.100 (0.0817-0.0827)	12228-38B00-0G0
8	2.100-2.125 (0.0827-0.0837)	12228-38B00-0H0
9	2.125-2.150 (0.0837-0.0846)	12228-38B00-0I0
10	2.150-2.175 (0.0846-0.0856)	12228-38B00-0J0

Table 5 ENGINE LOWER END TORQUE SPECIFICATIONS

Item	N•m	in.-lb.	ft.-lb.
Alternator cover bolt	10	89	–
Connecting rod cap nut			
Initial	25	–	18
Final	51	–	38
Countershaft bolt*	60	–	44
Crankcase bolts			
6 mm	11	97	–
8 mm			
Initial	10	89	–
Final	22	–	16
Engine bracket bolt	23	–	17
Engine mounting bolt/nut	79	–	58
Frame bolt/nut	50	–	37
Flywheel bolt	160	–	118
Oil drain bolt	21	–	15
Oil filter union	15	–	11
Oil gallery plug			
Main oil gallery	18	–	13
6 mm	10	89	–
8 mm	10	89	–
12 mm	21	–	15
14 mm	23	–	17
16 mm	35	–	26

(continued)

5

Table 5 ENGINE LOWER END TORQUE SPECIFICATIONS (continued)

Item	N•m	in.-lb.	ft.-lb.
Oil hose banjo bolt	26	–	19
Oil pump mounting bolt	10	89	–
Oil pressure relief valve	28	–	21
Oil pressure switch	14	–	10
Oil separator bolt	10	89	–
Piston oil jet bolt	10	89	–
Primary drive gear bolt*	150	–	111
Secondary drive gear retainer bolt	23	–	17
Speed sensor rotor bolt	100	–	74
Starter clutch bolts	26	–	19
Sump filter bolts	5	44	–
Sump housing bolts	10	89	–
*Left-hand threads.			

CLUTCH AND PRIMARY DRIVE GEAR

6

This chapter covers the clutch, clutch release mechanism, and the primary drive gear.

When inspecting components in this chapter, compare measurements to the specifications in **Table 1**. Replace worn, damaged or out of specification parts.

CLUTCH HYDRAULIC SYSTEM

The clutch system uses DOT 4 brake fluid. Refer to *Brake Service* in Chapter Fourteen for general information that applies to the clutch system.

Bleeding

Bleed the clutch manually or with a vacuum pump.
1. Remove the secondary gear cover (Chapter Seven).
2. Check the banjo bolt on the release cylinder (A, **Figure 1**) and on the clutch master cylinder (A, **Figure 2**). They must be tight.
3. Remove the dust cap (B, **Figure 1**) from the bleed valve on the release cylinder. Fit a box-end wrench onto the valve.

4. Clean all debris from the top of the clutch master cylinder reservoir. Then remove the top cover (B, **Figure 2**), diaphragm plate, and the diaphragm from the reservoir.
5. Add brake fluid to the reservoir until the fluid level reaches the upper limit. Loosely install the diaphragm and the cover. Leave them in place during this procedure to keep dirt out of the system and so brake fluid cannot spurt from the reservoir.

> *NOTE*
> *As fluid enters the system, the level in the reservoir drops. Add brake fluid as necessary to keep the fluid level 10 mm (3/8 in.) below the reservoir top so air will not enter the system. When using a vacuum pump, check the fluid level in the reservoir often. It will drop rapidly.*

6A. To manually bleed the system, perform the following:
   a. Connect a length of clear tubing to the bleed valve (**Figure 3**) on the release cylinder. Place the other end of the tube into a clean container.

Fill the container with enough fresh brake fluid to keep the hose end submerged. The tube should be long enough so its loop is higher than the bleed valve. This prevents air from being drawn back into the caliper during bleeding.

b. Pump the clutch lever a few times.

c. Apply the clutch lever until it stops and hold it in this position.

d. Open the bleed valve with the wrench. Let the clutch lever move to the limit of its travel. Then close the bleed valve. Do not release the lever while the bleed valve is open.

e. Repeat substeps b-d until the brake fluid flowing from the hose is clear and free of air.

6B. To vacuum bleed the system, perform the following:

a. Assemble the vacuum tool following the manufacturer's instructions.

b. Connect the pump's catch hose to the bleed valve on the release cylinder (**Figure 4**).

c. Operate the vacuum pump to create vacuum in the hose.

d. Use a wrench to open the bleed valve. The vacuum pump should pull fluid from the system. Close the bleed valve before the brake fluid stops flowing from the system (low vacuum pressure) or before the master cylinder reservoir runs empty. Add fluid to the reservoir as necessary.

e. Operate the clutch lever a few times.

f. Repeat substeps c-e until the fluid leaving the bleed valve is clear and free of air bubbles.

7. If the system is difficult to bleed, tap the master cylinder and release cylinder housing with a soft mallet to release trapped air bubbles.

NOTE
Initially bleed the clutch with the clutch lever adjuster set to the No. 4 setting. Once the clutch feels solid, check the feel with the adjuster in several different setting.

8. Test the feel of the clutch lever. It should feel firm and offer the same resistance each time it is operated. If the lever feels soft, air is still trapped in the system. Continue bleeding.

9. When bleeding is complete, disconnect the hose from the bleed valve. Tighten the bleed valve to 7.5 N•m (66 in.-lb.).

10. Add brake fluid to the reservoir and adjust the fluid level.

11. Install the diaphragm, diaphragm plate, and top cap onto the clutch master cylinder. Make sure the cap is secure.

12. Test ride the motorcycle to make sure the clutch operates properly.

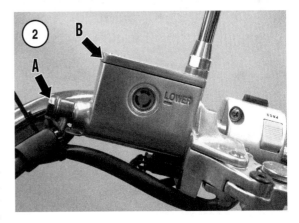

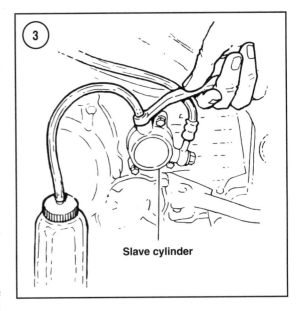

Slave cylinder

Draining

Always drain the brake fluid from the system before disconnecting a clutch hose. Draining reduces the amount of fluid in the system when removing components.

As with brake bleeding, drain the system either manually or with a vacuum pump.

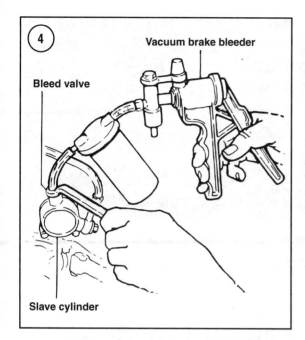

4

Vacuum brake bleeder

Bleed valve

Slave cylinder

7

3A. To manually drain the clutch, perform the following:

   a. Connect a length of clear hose to the bleed valve. Insert the other end into a container (**Figure 3**).

   b. Apply the clutch lever until it stops. Hold the lever in this position.

   c. Open the bleed valve with a wrench and let the lever move to the limit of its travel. Close the bleed valve.

   d. Release the lever, and repeat substep b and substep c until brake fluid stops flowing from the bleed valve.

3B. To drain the clutch with a hand-operated vacuum pump, perform the following:

   a. Connect the pump's catch hose to the bleed valve on the release cylinder (**Figure 4**).

   b. Operate the vacuum pump to create vacuum in the hose.

   c. Use a wrench to open the bleed valve. The vacuum pump should pull fluid from the system.

   d. When fluid has stopped flowing through the hose, close the bleed valve.

   e. Repeat substeps b-d until brake fluid no longer flows from the bleed valve.

CLUTCH COVER

Removal/Installation

1. Remove the mufflers and exhaust pipes (Chapter Eight).

2. Remove the mounting bolts (A, **Figure 5**), and lower the speed sensor cover (B) from the right side.

3. Drain the engine oil (Chapter Three).

4A. On carbureted models, disconnect the 3-pin connector from the speed sensor (**Figure 6**).

4B. On fuel injected models, disconnect the 3-pin speed sensor connector (**Figure 7**).

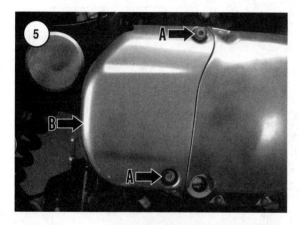

5

6

1. Remove the secondary gear cover (Chapter Seven).

2. Remove the dust cap (B, **Figure 1**) from the bleed valve on the release cylinder. Fit a box-end wrench onto the bleed valve. Remove all dirt from the valve and its outlet port.

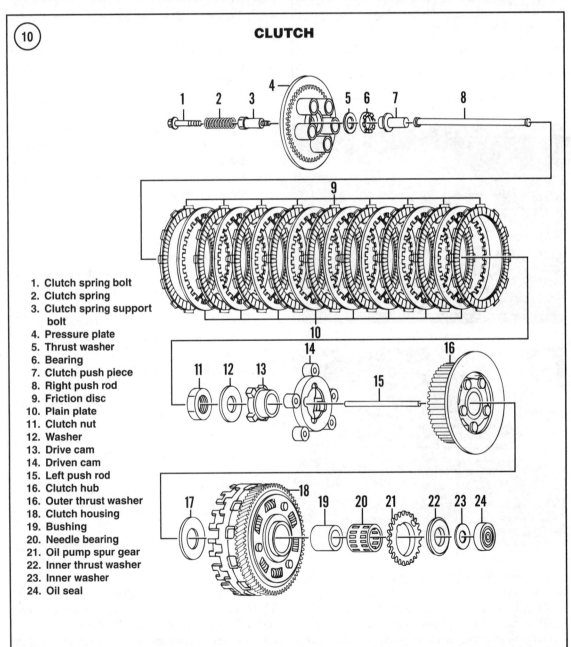

CLUTCH

1. Clutch spring bolt
2. Clutch spring
3. Clutch spring support
   bolt
4. Pressure plate
5. Thrust washer
6. Bearing
7. Clutch push piece
8. Right push rod
9. Friction disc
10. Plain plate
11. Clutch nut
12. Washer
13. Drive cam
14. Driven cam
15. Left push rod
16. Clutch hub
16. Outer thrust washer
18. Clutch housing
19. Bushing
20. Needle bearing
21. Oil pump spur gear
22. Inner thrust washer
23. Inner washer
24. Oil seal

5. Remove the clutch cover bolts. Note the cable holder behind one bolt (A, **Figure 8**) and the gasket washer behind two of the bolts (B). They must be reinstalled behind these bolts during installation.

6. Pull the cover from the crankcase. Remove the dowels (A, **Figure 9**) and gasket (B).

7. If necessary, remove the speed sensor from the cover (Chapter Ten).

8. Install the clutch cover by reversing the removal procedures. Note following:

    a. Install a new cover gasket (B, **Figure 9**).

    b. Install a gasket washer behind the clutch cover bolts (B, **Figure 8**) noted during removal.

    c. Install a cable holder behind the bolt noted (A, **Figure 8**).

CLUTCH

The clutch is a wet multi-plate type. The clutch hub is splined to the right end of the transmission mainshaft. The clutch housing is driven by the primary drive gear and rotates freely on the mainshaft.

Clutch activation is via a hydraulic master cylinder and release cylinder. The movement of the release cylinder acts upon two pushrods, which disengage and engage the clutch.

Removal/Disassembly

The clutch can be serviced with the engine in the frame. Refer to **Figure 10**.

1. Remove the clutch cover as described in this chapter.

2. Evenly loosen the clutch spring bolts in a crisscross pattern. Once all the bolts are loose, remove each bolt (A, **Figure 11**) and the clutch spring.

3. Remove the pressure plate (B, **Figure 11**) from the clutch.

4. Remove the clutch thrust washer (A, **Figure 12**), bearing (B), and clutch push piece (C).

5. Slide the right clutch push rod (**Figure 13**) from the mainshaft.

6. Remove the outside friction disc (A, **Figure 14**). Note that the tabs of this friction disc fit in the short slots (B, **Figure 14**) of the clutch housing. Also note that the tabs of all the other friction discs fit into the long slots (C, **Figure 14**). The tabs of each friction disc must be installed in the correct slots during assembly.

7. Remove the outside plain plate (**Figure 15**).

8. Continue to remove a friction disc, and then a plain plate. Set each part atop the stack as it is removed. The last part removed is a friction disc (A, **Figure 16**).

6

9. Unstake the clutch nut.

10. Hold the clutch hub with a clutch holder and remove the clutch nut (**Figure 17**).

11. Remove the washer (**Figure 18**) from the mainshaft. Note that the concave side of the washer faces in.

12. Remove the clutch hub (**Figure 19**), clutch drive cam, and driven cam.

13. Remove the outer thrust washer (A, **Figure 20**) and the clutch housing (B).

14. Remove the needle bearing (**Figure 21**), bushing (A, **Figure 22**), and inner thrust washer (B). Note that the flat side of the thrust washer faces out.

15. Remove the washer (**Figure 23**) from the mainshaft.

Assembly/Installation

1. Install the washer (**Figure 23**) onto the mainshaft.

2. Lubricate the inner thrust washer with engine oil and install the thrust washer (B, **Figure 22**) onto the mainshaft. The flat side of the thrust washer must face out (chamfered side in).

3. Install the bushing (A, **Figure 22**) and the needle bearing (**Figure 21**). Apply engine oil to each part before installation.

6

4. Install the clutch housing onto the mainshaft (**Figure 24**). Position the housing so the primary driven gear (A, **Figure 24**) engages the primary drive gear (B) and so the oil pump spur gear (C) engages the oil pump gear (D). Rotate the primary drive gear or the oil pump gear as necessary to align the gear teeth. Press the clutch housing onto the mainshaft until the housing bottoms.

5. With a screwdriver, wiggle the oil pump gear and make sure it still engages the oil pump spur gear.

6. Apply engine oil to the outer thrust washer and install the washer (A, **Figure 20**).

7. Install the clutch driven cam (A, **Figure 25**) into the clutch hub (B) so the indexing dot (C) on the driven cam aligns with the dot (D) on the hub.

8. Install the clutch drive cam (A, **Figure 26**) into the driven cam (B) so the indexing dot (C) in the drive cam aligns with the dot (D) on the driven cam.

9. Align the splines of the clutch drive cam with the mainshaft and install the clutch hub/cam assembly (**Figure 19**).

10. Install the washer (**Figure 18**) so its concave side faces in toward the clutch hub.

11. Install a new clutch nut (**Figure 17**) onto the mainshaft.

12. Hold the clutch hub with a clutch holder (**Figure 27**) and tighten the clutch nut to 95 N•m (75 ft.-lb.).

13. Stake the clutch nut (**Figure 28**) into place.

CAUTION
If installing new friction discs, soak them in clean engine oil for approximately 20 minutes.

NOTE
If reinstalling used friction discs and plain plates, install them in the reverse of their removal order.

14. Install the first friction disc (A, **Figure 16**) into the clutch housing so the tabs of the disc fit into the long slots (B) in the clutch housing as noted during removal.

15. Install a plain plate (**Figure 15**) so its splines engage those in the clutch hub.

16. Install the next friction disc. Then install another plain plate. Install the friction disc so its tabs fit in the long slots of the clutch housing.

17. Repeatedly install a friction disc, and then another plain plate until all the plates and discs are installed. End by installing the last friction disc (A, **Figure 14**).

18. Make sure the disc tabs engage the short slots (B, **Figure 14**) in the clutch housing.

19. Install the right clutch push rod (**Figure 13**) and clutch push piece (C, **Figure 12**) into the mainshaft.

20. Install the bearing (B, **Figure 12**) and thrust washer (A) onto the clutch push piece.

21. Install the pressure plate (B, **Figure 11**) so the hole in the plate (C) sits over the small triangle (**Figure 29**) on the clutch hub.

22. Fit a spring over each clutch spring support bolt. Install the clutch spring bolts (A, **Figure 11**) and evenly tighten them in a crisscross pattern to 10 N•m (89 in.-lb.).

Inspection

Inspect all parts and compare measurement to the specifications in **Table 1**. Replace worn, damaged or out of specification parts. If any friction disc is damaged or out of specification, replace all of the discs as a set.

1. If still installed, remove the clutch drive (A, **Figure 26**) and driven cams (B) from the clutch hub.

2. Clean all clutch parts in a petroleum-based solvent such as kerosene. Thoroughly dry them with compressed air.

3. Measure the thickness of each friction disc at several places around the disc as shown in **Figure 30**.

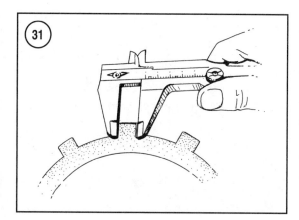

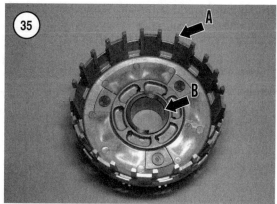

4. Measure the width of all tabs on each friction disc (**Figure 31**).

5. Inspect the friction material for cracks, uneven wear or damage. Also check the disc tabs for surface damage.

6. Check the plain plates for warp with a flat feeler gauge on a surface plate or a piece of plate glass (**Figure 32**).

7. Inspect the plain plates for cracks, damage or color change. Blue discoloration indicates overheated clutch plates.

8. Check the clutch plates for an oil glaze. Remove any buildup by lightly sanding both side of the clutch plate with 400 grit sandpaper placed on a surface plate.

9. Inspect the inner teeth on the clutch plates. The tooth contact surfaces must be smooth.

10. Inspect the splines (**Figure 33**) of the clutch hub for rough spots or chatter marks. Repair minor damage with a file or oil stone.

11. Inspect the ramps, and slots in the drive (A, **Figure 34**) and driven cams (B) for damage or excessive wear. Inspect the bearing surfaces of the drive and driven cams. If either cam is worn, replace both as a set.

12. Inspect the clutch spring support bolts (C, **Figure 34**) for wear. Replace all the bolts if any one is worn. Apply Suzuki Thread Lock Super 1303 to the threads of new clutch spring support bolts and tighten them to 11 N•m (97 in.-lb.).

13. Inspect the slots (A, **Figure 35**) in the clutch housing for cracks, nicks or galling where they contact the friction disc tabs. Inspect both the long and the short slots in the housing. If damage is evident on any slot, replace the housing.

14. Check the bearing surface of the clutch housing (B, **Figure 35**) for signs of wear or damage.

15. Inspect the teeth of the primary driven gear (A, **Figure 36**) and the oil pump spur gear (**Figure 37**). Remove any small nicks with an oil stone. If damage is severe, replace the gear.

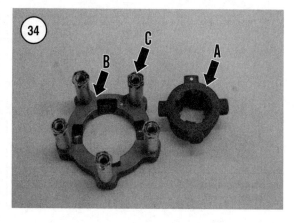

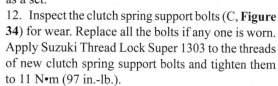

16. Check the clutch housing damper springs (B, **Figure 36**) for cracks or other damage.

17. Install the pin (**Figure 38**) into the clutch housing and install the oil pump spur gear so its cutout (**Figure 39**) engages the pin.

18. Check the needle bearing (A, **Figure 40**). It must turn smoothly without excessive play or noise.

19. Check the inner and outer surfaces of the bushing (B, **Figure 40**) for wear or damage.

20. Install the bushing into the needle bearing. Rotate the bushing and check for wear. Replace either/or both parts if necessary.

21. Inspect the pressure plate (**Figure 41**) for wear or damage.

22. Check the clutch push piece (A, **Figure 42**) for wear or damage. Pay particular attention to the end that rides against the clutch right push rod.

23. Check the clutch push piece bearing (B, **Figure 42**). Make sure it rotates smoothly.

24. Install the bearing and washer onto the push piece. Rotate them by hand and make sure all parts rotate smoothly.

25. Inspect the right clutch push rod (A, **Figure 43**). If the clutch release cylinder has also been removed, inspect the left clutch push rod (B, **Figure 43**) as well. If a rod is bent, replace it. Otherwise it may hang up within the mainshaft channel, causing erratic clutch operation.

26. Measure the free length of each clutch spring (**Figure 44**). Replace all the clutch springs if the free length of any spring is less than the service limit.

CLUTCH MASTER CYLINDER

Refer to **Figure 45**.

Removal

> *CAUTION*
> *Cover the fuel tank and front wheel to protect them from brake fluid spills. Brake fluid will damage paint, plastic, and plated surfaces. Immediately wash any spilled brake fluid from the motorcycle. Use soapy water and rinse the area completely.*

1. If servicing the master cylinder (**Figure 45**), perform the following:

   a. Drain the fluid from the clutch as described in this chapter.

   b. Clean the top of the master cylinder.

   c. Remove the top cover (A, **Figure 46**), diaphragm plate and diaphragm from the master cylinder reservoir.

   d. Place a rag beneath the banjo bolt (B, **Figure 46**). Then remove the bolt. Separate the clutch

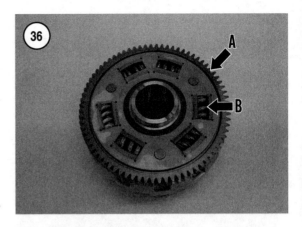

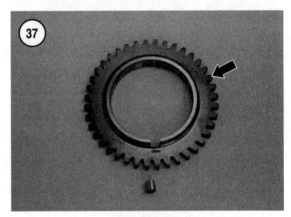

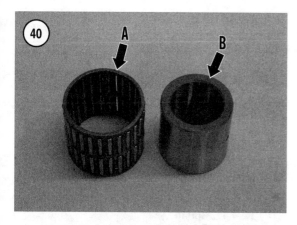

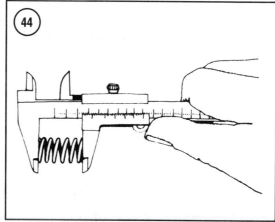

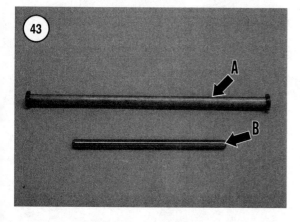

6

hose from the master cylinder. Watch for the two sealing washers, one on each side of the clutch hose fitting.

  e. Seal the loose end of the clutch hose in a plastic bag to prevent brake fluid from leaking onto the motorcycle. Suspend the hose from the handlebar.

2. Disconnect the electrical connector (C, **Figure 46**) from the clutch switch.

3. Loosen the mirror locknut (A, **Figure 47**) and remove the mirror from the clutch lever assembly.

4. Pry the trim caps from the master cylinder clamp bolts, remove the clamp bolts (B, **Figure 47**) and lower the master cylinder from the handlebar. Pour any residual brake fluid from the reservoir.

Installation

1. Set the master cylinder onto the left handlebar so the clamp mating surface (A, **Figure 48**) aligns with the indexing dot (B) on the handlebar.

2. Mount the clamp with the UP mark facing up and install the master cylinder clamp bolts (B, **Figure 47**). Tighten the upper clamp bolt first. Then tighten the lower bolt so there is a gap at the bottom. Tighten the clutch master cylinder clamp bolts to 10 N•m (89 in.-lb.).

3. Connect the electrical connector (C, **Figure 46**) to the clutch switch.

4. Fit the clutch hose onto the master cylinder. Install a new sealing washer onto each side of the hose fitting. Tighten the banjo bolt (B, **Figure 46**) to 23 N•m (17 ft.-lb.).

5. Refill the master cylinder reservoir and bleed the clutch system as described in this chapter.

Disassembly

1. Remove the clutch master cylinder as described in this section.

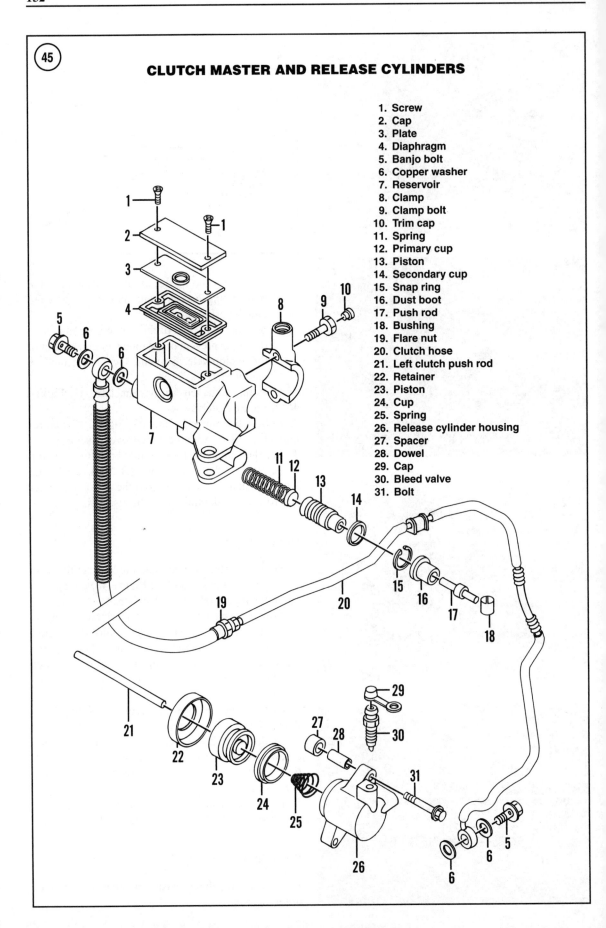

CLUTCH MASTER AND RELEASE CYLINDERS

1. Screw
2. Cap
3. Plate
4. Diaphragm
5. Banjo bolt
6. Copper washer
7. Reservoir
8. Clamp
9. Clamp bolt
10. Trim cap
11. Spring
12. Primary cup
13. Piston
14. Secondary cup
15. Snap ring
16. Dust boot
17. Push rod
18. Bushing
19. Flare nut
20. Clutch hose
21. Left clutch push rod
22. Retainer
23. Piston
24. Cup
25. Spring
26. Release cylinder housing
27. Spacer
28. Dowel
29. Cap
30. Bleed valve
31. Bolt

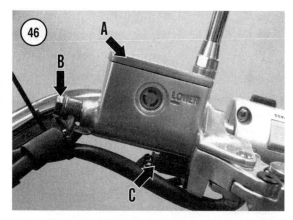

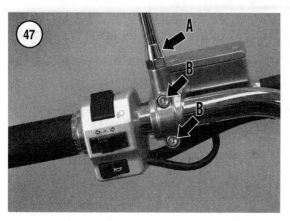

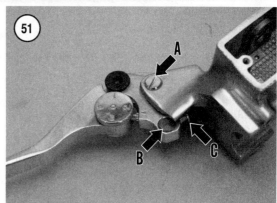

6

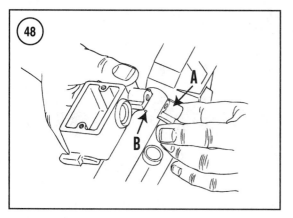

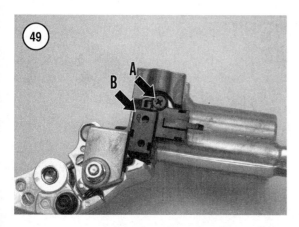

2. Unscrew the mounting screw (A, **Figure 49**). Then remove the clutch switch (B) from the reservoir.

3. Remove the nut (**Figure 50**) from the clutch lever pivot bolt.

4. Remove the clutch lever pivot bolt (A, **Figure 51**) and slide the lever from the master cylinder bracket. Watch for the bushing (B, **Figure 51**) in the clutch lever. Also note that the end of the pushrod (C, **Figure 51**) engages the hole in the bushing.

5. Roll the rubber boot (**Figure 52**) from the cylinder bore and remove the pushrod/boot assembly (**Figure 53**) from the master cylinder. Note that the round end of the pushrod faces the piston.

6. Press the piston into the cylinder bore. Then remove the internal snap ring and washer.

7. Remove the piston (**Figure 54**) and the primary cup/spring assembly (**Figure 55**) from the cylinder bore.

Assembly

1. Soak the new cups in new DOT 4 brake fluid for approximately 15 minutes to make them pliable. Coat all parts and the inside of the cylinder bore with new brake fluid.

2. Install the new primary cup (A, **Figure 56**) onto the tapered end of the spring. Roll the new secondary cup (B, **Figure 56**) onto the piston (C).

> *CAUTION*
> *Carefully install the piston assembly so the cups do not turn inside out. They are easily damaged.*

3. Lubricate the master cylinder bore with new DOT 4 brake fluid.

4. Install the primary cup/spring assembly (**Figure 55**) into the master cylinder bore.

5. Lubricate the piston (**Figure 54**) with new brake fluid and install it into the cylinder bore.

6. Install the washer and press the piston into the bore. Secure it in place with a new snap ring. Make sure the snap ring seats in the groove inside the cylinder bore.

7. Install the pushrod and boot by performing the following:

    a. Apply an assembly lube to each end of the push rod.

    b. Install the boot over the pushrod so the end of the boot sits within the pushrod groove (**Figure 53**).

    c. Set the pushrod/boot assembly into the cylinder bore so the round end of the pushrod engages the piston end.

    d. Press and hold the pushrod into the cylinder.

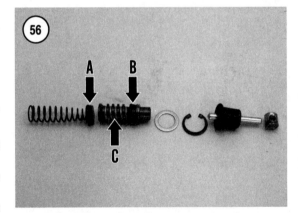

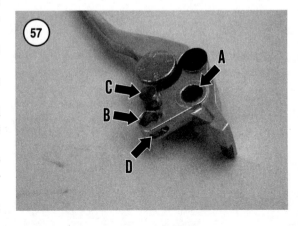

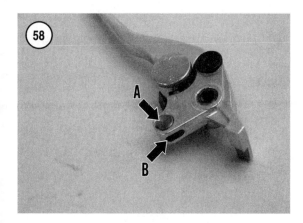

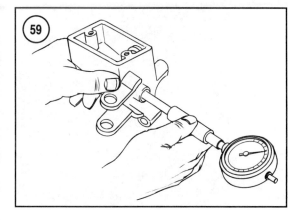

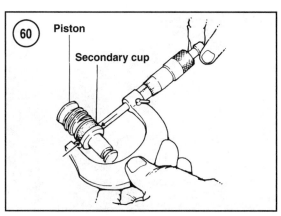

Piston

Secondary cup

Push the boot into the cylinder until its lip is seated within the bore (**Figure 52**).

    e. Slowly release the pushrod. Make sure the boot remains seated in the cylinder bore.

8. Apply a light coat of grease to the inside of the pivot-bolt hole (A, **Figure 57**) and to the bushing hole (B) in the clutch lever.

9. Install the bushing into the clutch lever by performing the following:

    a. Position the bushing (C, **Figure 57**) so its hole faces the slot (D) in the clutch lever.

    b. Lower the bushing (A, **Figure 58**) into place in the clutch lever.

    c. If necessary, rotate the bushing so its hole sits within the lever's slot (B, **Figure 58**).

10. Set the clutch lever into position in the master cylinder body. Make sure the end of the pushrod (C, **Figure 51**) passes through the lever slot and engages the hole in the bushing (B).

11. Install the lever pivot bolt (A, **Figure 51**).

12. Install the nut (**Figure 50**) onto the pivot bolt and tighten the nut securely.

13. Fit the clutch switch (B, **Figure 49**) into position and secure it with the mounting screw (A).

14. Operate the clutch lever, making sure it pivots smoothly and the pushrod engages the bushing.

15. Install the master cylinder as described in this section.

Inspection

Compare any measurements to the specifications in **Table 1**. Replace worn, damaged or out of specification parts.

1. Clean all parts in new DOT 4 brake fluid.

2. Inspect the cylinder bore surface for wear, corrosion or damage. If less than perfect, replace the master cylinder assembly. *Do not* hone the master cylinder bore.

3. Measure the cylinder bore (**Figure 59**).

4. Inspect the piston cups (A and B, **Figure 56**) for wear and damage. If less than perfect, replace the piston assembly. Cups are not available individually.

5. Inspect the contact surfaces of the piston (C, **Figure 56**) for wear and damage. If less than perfect, replace the piston assembly.

6. Check the end of the piston for wear caused by the pushrod. If worn, replace the piston assembly.

7. Measure the outside diameter of the piston with a micrometer (**Figure 60**).

8. Check the lugs (A, **Figure 61**) on the clutch lever boss for cracks or elongation.

9. Check for plugged supply (B, **Figure 61**) and relief ports in the reservoir.

10. Check the top cover, diaphragm and diaphragm plate for damage and deterioration; replace as necessary.

11. Inspect the pivot hole (A, **Figure 62**) and bushing hole (B) in the clutch lever for cracks or elongation.

12. Inspect the adjuster (C, **Figure 62**) on the hand lever. If worn or damaged replace the hand lever as an assembly.

13. Check the threads on the banjo bolt and in the master cylinder fluid port. If necessary, dress the threads or replace the banjo bolt and/or master cylinder as necessary.

14. Inspect the clutch hose/pipe assembly for damage and deterioration.

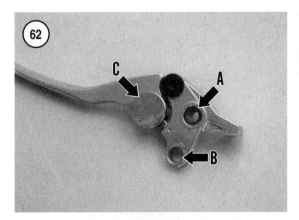

CLUTCH RELEASE CYLINDER

Refer to **Figure 45**.

Removal/Installation

1. Remove the secondary gear cover (Chapter Seven).

2A. On 1998-2004 models, perform the following:

   a. Disconnect the neutral switch single-pin connector (A, **Figure 63**) and 2-pin connector (B).

   b. Disconnect the 2-pin signal generator connector (C, **Figure 63**), the 3-pin stator connector, (D) and the 2-pin sidestand switch connector (E).

2B. On 2005-on models, perform the following:

   a. Disconnect the 3-pin gear position sensor connector (A, **Figure 64**) and the 2-pin sidestand switch connector (B).

   b. Note how each wire is routed around the clutch release cylinder.

3. Release the electrical wires from their clamp(s) and secure them out of the way.

4. Drain the fluid from the clutch system (this chapter).

5. Remove the banjo bolt (A, **Figure 65**) and disconnect the clutch hose from the release cylinder. Be prepared to catch any fluid leaking from the hose. Watch for the sealing washer on either side of the hose fitting. Insert the clutch hose end into a plastic bag.

6. Remove the release cylinder bolts (B, **Figure 65**) and lower the release cylinder from the crankcase. Watch for the spacer (A, **Figure 66**) and dowel (B) installed in each bolt boss in the crankcase.

7. Remove the left clutch push rod (C, **Figure 66**) from the transmission mainshaft so the rod will not be damaged.

8. Installation is the reverse of removal. Note the following:

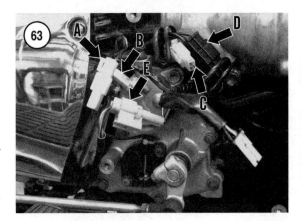

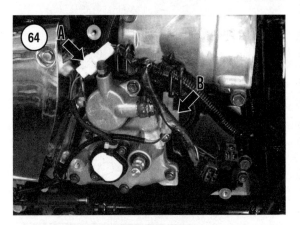

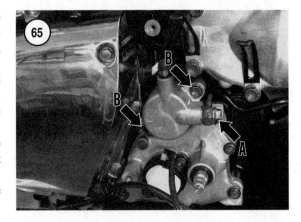

a. Apply grease to the left clutch push rod (C, **Figure 66**). Then install the rod into the mainshaft.

b. Install the dowel (B, **Figure 66**) and spacer (A) into each bolt boss in the crankcase.

c. Set the clutch release cylinder onto the crankcase so the cylinder piston engages the clutch push rod.

d. Install the release cylinder bolts (B, **Figure 65**) and tighten them securely.

e. Install the clutch hose so its neck rests against the outboard side of the post. Use a new sealing washer on each side of the hose fitting and tighten the banjo bolt (A, **Figure 65**) to 23 N•m (17 ft.-lb.).

f. Add brake fluid to the clutch reservoir and bleed the system (this chapter).

g. Install the secondary gear cover (Chapter Seven).

Disassembly/Inspection/Assembly

1. Remove the retainer (**Figure 67**) from the release cylinder.

2. Remove the piston (**Figure 68**). If necessary, use compressed air to remove the piston by performing the following:

a. Support the release cylinder on wooden block with the piston facing down.

b. Pad the area beneath the piston with a shop cloth.

WARNING
The piston may shoot out of the release cylinder with considerable force. Make sure the piston faces down onto the bench. Keep your hands out of the way.

c. Apply short bursts of low pressure compressed air to the banjo bolt fitting. Hold the air nozzle away from the fitting so excessive pressure will not be applied.

3. Remove the spring from the piston.

4. Clean all parts in new DOT 4 brake fluid. Place the components on a clean lint-free cloth after cleaning them.

NOTE
Do not remove the piston seal unless replacing it.

5. Inspect the piston seal (A, **Figure 69**) for cuts or other damage. If necessary, install a new piston seal so the lip faces toward the spring side of the piston. Coat the new piston seal with new DOT 4 brake fluid.

6. Check the piston (B, **Figure 69**) surface for scoring or damage.

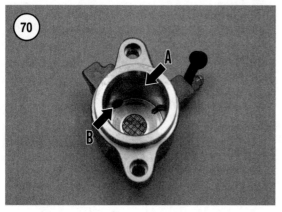

7. Check the cylinder bore (A, **Figure 70**) for scoring or damage. Replace the release cylinder body as necessary.

8. Use compressed air to clean all ports (B, **Figure 70**).

9. Clean the banjo bolt with compressed air.

10. Insert the small end of the spring onto the piston.

11. Apply new DOT 4 brake fluid to the piston seal and cylinder bore.

12. Install the spring/piston assembly (**Figure 71**) into the cylinder bore and push the piston (**Figure 68**) all the way into the cylinder. Make sure the lip of the seal does not turn inside out during installation.

13. Press the retainer (**Figure 67**) onto the release cylinder.

CLUTCH LINE

Replacement

Refer to **Figure 45**.

1. Remove the secondary gear cover (Chapter Seven).

2. Note how the clutch hose/pipe assembly is routed through the motorcycle. Route the new hose along the same path.

3. Drain the fluid from the clutch system (this chapter).

4. Remove the banjo bolt (A, **Figure 65**) and disconnect the clutch hose from the release cylinder. Be prepared to catch any fluid leaking from the hose. Watch for the sealing washer on either side of the hose fitting. Insert the clutch hose end into a plastic bag.

5. Repeat Step 4, and disconnect the hose fitting from the clutch master cylinder (B, **Figure 46**).

6. Remove any hose holder or cable ties securing the hose to the motorcycle. Note the location of each holder, clamp or cable ties. Secure the hose to the same points and with the same holder during assembly.

7. Remove the clutch hose assembly from the motorcycle.

8. Installation is the reverse of removal. Note the following:

   a. Route the new clutch hose along the same path noted during removal. Make sure the hose is routed between the fuel tank and the heat shield.

   b. Secure the hose to the frame where noted during removal. Tighten the hose holder bolt(s) securely.

   c. Install a new sealing washer onto each side of the clutch hose fittings. Tighten the banjo bolts to 23 N•m (17 ft.-lb.).

   d. Refill the clutch reservoir with new DOT 4 brake fluid and bleed the clutch (this chapter).

PRIMARY DRIVE GEAR

Removal/Installation

A rotor holder (Suzuki part No. 09930-40113), or its equivalent, is needed to remove the primary drive gear.

NOTE
The primary drive gear bolt has left-hand threads.

1. Remove the clutch cover (this chapter).
2. Hold the primary drive gear with the rotor holder.
3. Turn the primary drive gear bolt (A, **Figure 72**) clockwise and remove it from the crankshaft.

CAUTION
The primary drive gear is directional. It must be installed with its inboard side facing the crankshaft. The inboard side is marked with a painted dot. If the paint is worn away, mark the inboard side of the gear so it can be identified for installation.

4. Slide the primary drive gear (B, **Figure 72**) from the crankshaft splines. Check for the painted dot on the inboard side of the gear. If necessary, scribe a new inboard mark on the gear.
5. Inspect the teeth (A, **Figure 73**) and splines (B) on the primary drive gear for excessive wear of damage. If the teeth are damaged, also inspect the teeth on the primary driven gear. If the splines are worn, also inspect the splines on the crankshaft.
6. Installation is the reverse of removal. Note the following:
  a. Install the primary drive gear so the marked side faces inboard.
  b. Make sure the teeth of the primary drive gear (B, **Figure 24**) engage those of the primary driven gear on the clutch housing (A).
  c. Tighten the primary drive gear bolt (**Figure 74**) to 150 N•m (111 ft.-lb.).

Table 1 CLUTCH SPECIFICATIONS

Item	Standard mm (in.)	Service limit mm (in.)
Friction disc		
Total quantity	9	
Thickness	2.90-3.10 (0.114-0.122)	2.60 (0.102)
Claw width	15.6-15.8 (0.614-0.622)	14.8 (0.583)
Inside diameter		
Plain Plate		
Total quantity	8	
Plain plate warp	–	0.10 (0.004)
Clutch spring free length		
1998-2000 models	–	30.9 (1.22)
2001-on models	34.47 (1.357)	32.7 (1.29)
Clutch master cylinder		
Master cylinder bore inside diameter	14.000-14.043 (0.5512-0.5529)	–
Piston outside diameter	13.957-13.984 (0.5495-0.5506)	–
Clutch release cylinder		
Release cylinder bore inside diameter	33.600-33.662 (1.3228-1.3253)	–
Piston outside diameter	33.550-33.575 (1.3209-1.3219)	–

Table 2 CLUTCH AND PRIMARY DRIVE TORQUE SPECIFICATIONS

Item	N•m	in.-lb.	ft.-lb.
Clutch nut	95	–	70
Clutch hose banjo bolt	23	–	17
Clutch hose flare nut	14	–	10
Clutch master cylinder clamp bolt	10	89	–
Clutch spring bolt	10	89	–
Clutch spring support bolt	11	97	–
Primary drive gear bolt*	150	–	111
Release cylinder bleed valve	7.5	66	–
*Left-hand threads.			

TRANSMISSION, SHIFT MECHANISM AND SECONDARY GEAR

This chapter covers the transmission, the external and internal shift mechanisms, and the secondary drive and driven gear assemblies.

The external shift mechanism and the secondary driven gear can be serviced with the engine in the frame.

The engine must be removed and the crankcase separated to access the transmission, internal shift mechanism and secondary drive gear. Refer to Chapter 5.

During inspection, refer to the specifications at the end of the chapter. Replace worn, damaged or out of specification parts.

SHIFT LEVER

1. Remove the secondary gear cover (this chapter).
2. Note that the index dot on the shift shaft aligns with the gap in the shift lever (A, **Figure 1**). If necessary, make a new mark with a punch.
3. Loosen the clamp bolt (B, **Figure 1**) and slide the shift lever from the shift shaft splines.
4. Installation is the reverse of removal. Make sure the shift lever gap aligns with the index dot on the shift shaft.

SHIFT PEDAL/FOOTREST

Removal/Installation

1. Remove the secondary gear cover and remove the shift lever from the shift shaft (this chapter).

2. Remove the front footrest bolts (**Figure 2**) and lower the shift pedal/footrest assembly from the motorcycle.
3. If necessary, remove the shift pedal by removing the shift pedal bolt (**Figure 3**). Remove the pedal from the footrest bracket. Watch for the collar in the shift pedal pivot.
4. Install the assembly by reversing the removal procedure. Note the following:
   a. If removed, install the shift pedal onto the footrest. Make sure the collar is in place.
   b. Tighten the shift pedal bolt (**Figure 3**) to 16 N•m (12 ft.-lb.).
   c. Tighten the front footrest bolts (**Figure 2**) to 50 N•m (37 ft.-lb.).

EXTERNAL SHIFT MECHANISM

Removal/Disassembly

Refer to **Figure 4**.
1. Remove the shift lever from the shift shaft (this chapter).
2. Remove the clutch release cylinder (Chapter Six).
3A. On 1998-2004 models, remove the neutral switch (**Figure 5**) as described in Chapter Ten.
3B. On 2005-on models, remove the gear position sensor (C, **Figure 1**) as described in Chapter Ten.
4. Remove the shift mechanism cover by performing the following:

CAUTION
*On early models, gasket washers are used behind four cover bolts (A, **Figure 6**). On later models, five bolts (A and B, **Figure 6**) use gasket washers. Note the location of the gasket washers when removing the shift mechanism cover. Install new gasket washers.*

a. Remove the shift mechanism cover bolts (**Figure 6**). Note the bolts installed with a gasket washer.
b. Remove the shift mechanism cover.
c. Remove the dowels (A, **Figure 7**) and discard the gasket (B).

EXTERNAL SHIFT MECHANISM

1. Washer
2. Snap ring
3. Shift shaft spring
4. Shift shaft/shift plate
5. Pawl plate
6. Pawl plate spring
7. Oil seal
8. Boot
9. Shift lever
10. Clamp bolt
11. Shift rod locknut
12. Shift shaft stopper
13. Shift rod
14. Shift pedal
15. Spacer
16. Washer
17. Shift pedal bolt
18. Bearing retainer
19. Screw
20. Shift cam
21. Shift cam retainer
22. Spring (1998-2004 models)
23. Pin (1998-2004 models)
24. Shift cam retainer bolt
25. Stopper lever
26. Stopper lever bolt
27. Stopper lever spring
28. Washer
29. Nut
30. Gasket
31. Shift mechanism cover
32. O-ring
33. Neutral switch
34. Dowel

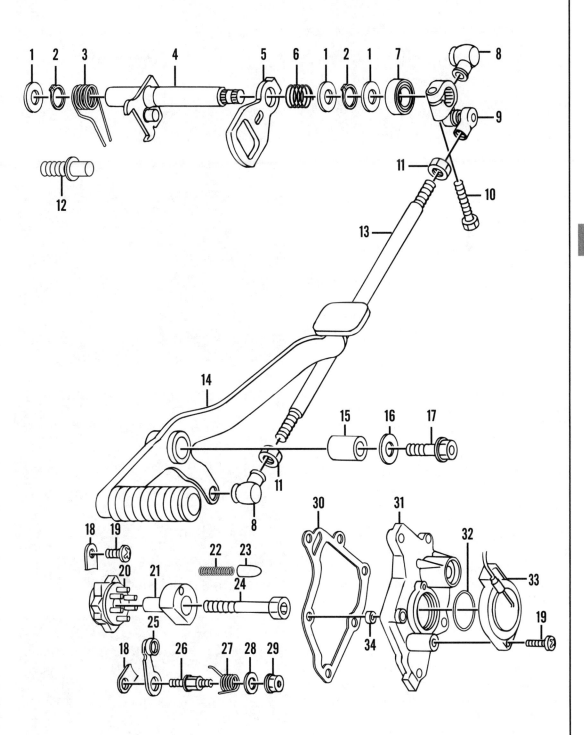

5. Remove the transmission jet (A, **Figure 8**) from the crankcase.

6. Remove the shift cam retainer bolt (B, **Figure 8**) and pull the shift cam retainer (C) from the shift cam.

7. Remove the outboard washer (A, **Figure 9**) from the shift shaft.

8. Note that the arms of the shift shaft spring straddle the shift shaft bolt (B, **Figure 9**). Pull the shift shaft assembly (C, **Figure 9**) from the crankcase. Watch for the inboard washer (**Figure 10**) on the end of the shaft.

9. Remove the nut (A, **Figure 11**) and washer (B) from the stopper lever bolt.

10. Press the stopper lever (A, **Figure 12**) forward and remove the shift cam (B) from the shift drum. Watch for the indexing pin (A, **Figure 13**) in the shift drum.

11. Remove the stopper lever spring (B, **Figure 13**) from the stopper lever. Note that one arm of the spring presses against the cutout in the stopper lever (C, **Figure 13**) while the other arm rests in the crankcase land (D).

12. Loosen the stopper lever bolt (A, **Figure 14**). Remove the bolt, stopper lever and the lower bearing retainer (B, **Figure 14**).

13. If necessary, remove the shift shaft stopper (C, **Figure 14**) from the crankcase.

Assembly/Installation

1. If removed, install the shift shaft stopper (C, **Figure 14**). Apply Suzuki Thread Lock Super 1303 to the bolt threads and tighten the shift shaft stopper to 23 N•m (17 ft.-lb.).

2. Fit the stopper lever and the bearing retainer onto the stopper lever bolt (**Figure 15**). Apply Suzuki Thread Lock 1342 to the inboard threads of the stopper lever bolt and install the bolt into the crankcase (A, **Figure 14**). Tighten the stopper lever bolt to 10 N•m (89 in.-lb.).

7

3. Slide the stopper lever spring (B, **Figure 13**) onto the stopper lever bolt. Make sure one spring arm engages the cutout in the stopper lever (C, **Figure 13**) and the other arm rests against the crankcase (D).

4. Check the operation of the stopper lever. Remove and reinstall the lever as necessary.

5. Make sure the transmission is in neutral.

6. Press the stopper lever (A, **Figure 12**) forward. Install the shift cam (B, **Figure 12**) so the hole on its inboard side engages the pin (A, **Figure 13**) in the shift drum. Release the stopper lever. Its bearing should engage the neutral detent in the shift cam.

7. Install the washer (B, **Figure 11**) onto the stopper lever bolt.

8. Apply Suzuki Thread Lock 1342 to the outboard threads of the stopper lever bolt and install the stopper lever nut (A, **Figure 11**). Tighten the nut to 10 N•m (89 in.-lb.).

9. Install the shift shaft by performing the following.

   a. Make sure a washer (**Figure 10**) sits on the inboard end of the shift shaft.

   b. Apply grease to the inboard end of the shift shaft and slide the shaft into the shift shaft bushing in the left side of the crankcase.

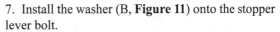

c. Position the assembly so the shift shaft spring straddles the shift shaft stopper (B, **Figure 9**). Press the shaft into the crankcase until the shaft bottoms. Rotate the shift cam as necessary so the shift pawls engage the shift cam.

d. Install the outboard washer (A, **Figure 9**) onto the shift shaft.

10. Install the shift cam retainer while aligning the notch (**Figure 16**) on the end of the retainer with the cutout in the shift cam.

11. Apply Suzuki Thread Lock 1342 to the threads of the shift cam retainer bolt. Then install and tighten the bolt (B, **Figure 8**) to 10 N•m (89 in.-lb.).

12. Apply engine oil to the O-ring on the transmission jet. Then install the jet into its gallery (A, **Figure 8**).

13. Install the dowels (A, **Figure 7**) and a new shift mechanism cover gasket (B) onto the crankcase.

14. Apply grease to the lips of the shift shaft seal in the shift mechanism cover.

15. Fit the cover into place on the crankcase. Then install the shift mechanism cover bolts (**Figure 6**). Install new gasket washers under the bolts noted during removal. Tighten the cover bolts securely.

16A. On 1999-2004 models, install the neutral switch (**Figure 5**).

16B. On 2005-on models, install the gear position sensor (C, **Figure 1**).

17. Install the clutch release cylinder and the shift lever.

Inspection

1. Clean all parts in solvent and dry them with compressed air.

2. Inspect the shift shaft seal. If necessary, replace the seal as follows:

a. Pry the oil seal from the cover (**Figure 17**).

b. Lubricate the new seal with grease.

c. Set the seal into the cover so its identification marks face out.

d. Drive the seal into place with a driver or socket (**Figure 18**) that has an outside diameter the same or slightly smaller than the seal.

3. Inspect the shift pawls on the pawl plate (A, **Figure 19**) and on shift plate (B) for excessive wear or damage.

4. Inspect the shift shaft spring (C, **Figure 19**) for cracks or other damage.

5. Inspect the shift shaft for bending, wear or other damage.

6. Inspect the splines on the end of the shift shaft for damage.

7. Inspect the ramps (A, **Figure 20**) and posts (B) on the shift cam for excessive wear.

8. Inspect the bearing (C, **Figure 20**) on the stopper lever. It should turn smoothly with no binding.

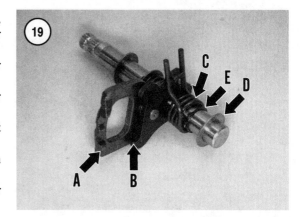

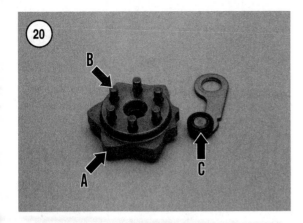

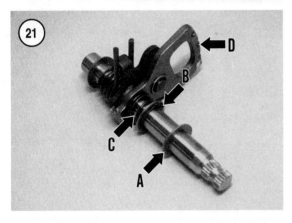

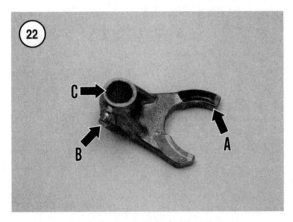

9. Inspect the stopper lever spring for cracks or fatigue.

10. Inspect the shift cam retainer and its bolt (**Figure 16**) for wear or damage.

11. Replace any worn or damaged part(s).

Shift Shaft Disassembly/Assembly

1. Remove the washer (D, **Figure 19**) and snap ring (E) from the inboard end of the shift shaft.

2. Slide the shift shaft spring (C, **Figure 19**) from the inboard end of the shift shaft. Note that the arms of the spring straddle the tang on the shift plate.

3. Remove the washer (A, **Figure 21**), snap ring (B), and washer from the outboard end of the shift shaft.

4. Slide the pawl plate spring (C, **Figure 21**) and the pawl plate (D) from the outboard end of the shift shaft. Note that the hole in the pawl plate engages the post on the shift plate.

5. Assemble the shift shaft by reversing the disassembly procedure. Note the following:

   a. Make sure the hole in the pawl plate (D, **Figure 21**) engages the post in the shift plate.

   b. Position the shift shaft spring (C, **Figure 19**) so its arms straddle the tang on the shift place.

   c. Install each snap ring so it completely sits in its groove in the shift shaft.

INTERNAL SHIFT MECHANISM

Removal/Installation

Refer to Chapter Five.

Inspection

During inspection, replace any part that is worn, damaged or out of specification.

1. Clean all parts in solvent and thoroughly dry them with compressed air.

2. Inspect each shift fork for signs of wear or cracking. Check for any burned marks on the fingers (A, **Figure 22**) of the shift forks.

3. Check the guide pin (B, **Figure 22**) on each shift fork for wear or damage.

4. Check each shift fork bore (C, **Figure 22**) for burrs, wear or pitting. Check the shift fork shafts for the same conditions.

5. Install each shift fork onto its shaft (**Figure 23**). Move each fork along the shaft and check its movement. A fork should move freely with no binding.

6. Roll each shift fork shaft over a flat surface such as a surface plate or a piece of plate glass. If a shaft is bent, replace it.

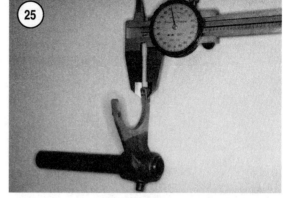

7. Install each shift fork into the groove of its respective gear. Using a flat feeler gauge, measure the clearance between the fork and the groove as shown in **Figure 24**. If the shift fork-to-groove clearance exceeds the service limit in **Table 2**, perform the following:

    a. Measure the thickness of the shift fork fingers (**Figure 25**). Replace the shift fork if the thickness is outside the range specified in **Table 2**.

    b. Measure the width of the shift fork groove in the gear (**Figure 26**). Replace the gear if the groove width is outside the range specified in **Table 2**.

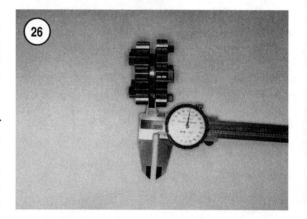

8. Check the grooves (A, **Figure 27**) in the shift drum for wear or roughness. If any of the groove profiles have excessive wear or damage, replace the shift drum.

9. Inspect the shift drum journals (B, **Figure 27**) for scoring, bluing or other signs of damage.

TRANSMISSION

The *mainshaft* refers to the transmission input shaft. The mainshaft connects to the clutch hub, which is driven by the primary drive gear. The *countershaft* refers to the output shaft of the transmission. The countershaft drives the secondary drive gear.

The manufacturer refers to the transmission input shaft as the countershaft and the output shaft as the driveshaft. If ordering parts, note the manufacturer's unconventional terminology.

Preliminary Inspection

After removing the transmission shafts from the crankcase as described in Chapter Five, clean and inspect the shafts as follows.

1. Place an assembled shaft (**Figure 28**) into a large can or plastic bucket. Thoroughly clean the assembly with solvent and a stiff brush. Dry the assembly with

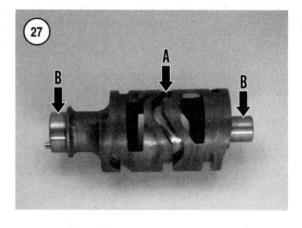

compressed air or let it sit on rags to dry. Do this for the both shaft assemblies.

2. Inspect the components for excessive wear. Any burrs, pitting or roughness on the teeth of a gear will cause wear on its mated gear. Remove minor roughness with an oilstone. Replace damaged gears and their mates together as a set.

3. Carefully check the engagement dogs. If any are chipped, worn, rounded or missing, replace the affected gear.

4. Rotate the transmission bearings. Check for roughness, noise, and radial play. Replace any worn or damaged bearing.

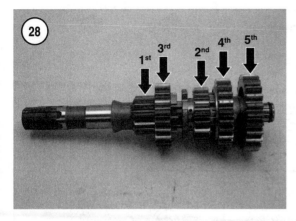

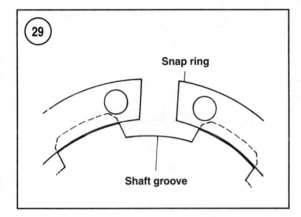

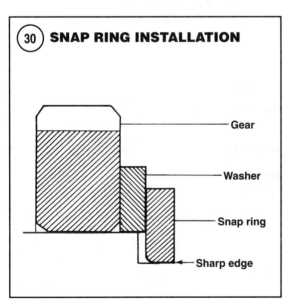

SNAP RING INSTALLATION

Gear

Washer

Snap ring

Sharp edge

Transmission Service

1. As a part is removed from a shaft, set it into an egg crate in the order of removal and with the same orientation as when installed on the shaft.

2. Snap rings may turn or fold over, making removal and installation difficult. To ease replacement, open a snap ring with snap ring pliers while at the same time holding the back of the snap ring with conventional pliers. Replace all snap rings with new ones.

3. When installing a snap ring, align the gap in the snap ring with a groove in the shaft as shown in **Figure 29**.

4. Snap rings have one flat edge and one rounded edge (**Figure 30**). Install a snap ring so the sharp edge faces away from the gear producing the thrust.

5. When installing a splined gear or a splined bushing onto a shaft, align the oil hole in the gear or bushing with the oil holes in the shaft.

6. Pay particular attention to any additional shims not shown in the drawings or photographs. These shims may have been installed during a previous repair to compensate for wear.

7. After both transmission shafts have been assembled, mesh the two assemblies together (**Figure 31**). Make sure each gear properly engages its mate on the opposite shaft. Check the shaft assemblies before installing them in the crankcase.

Mainshaft Disassembly

Refer to **Figure 32**.

1. Remove the O-ring and washer from the mainshaft.

2. Remove fifth and fourth gears.

3. Slide fourth-gear bushing, washer, and second gear from the mainshaft.

4. Remove the third-gear snap ring.

5. Remove third gear and its bushing.

6. Inspect the mainshaft components as described in this section. Keep the parts in order and with the correct orientation.

5. Slide the clutch pushrods into the mainshaft to check for binding. If binding occurs, check for a bent pushrod. Also inspect the mainshaft channel for debris. Clean out the channel. Replace the mainshaft or clutch pushrod(s) as necessary.

6. If the transmission shafts do not require disassembly, apply clean engine oil to all components and reinstall them into the crankcase.

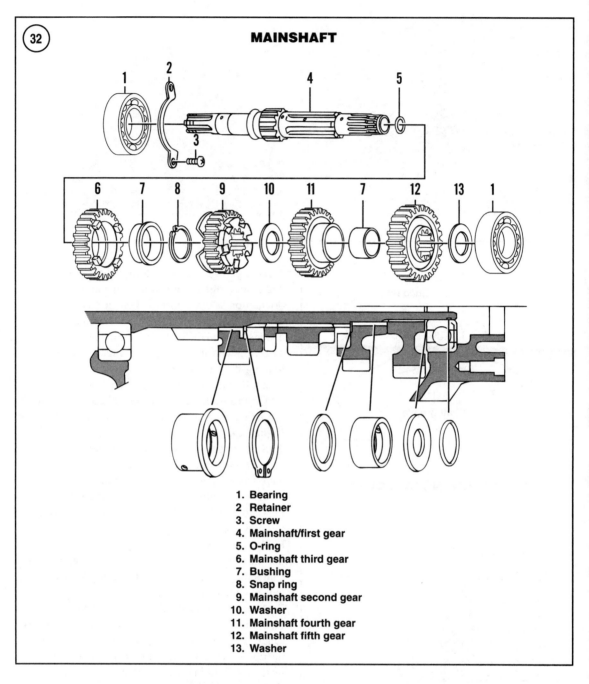

MAINSHAFT

1. Bearing
2 Retainer
3. Screw
4. Mainshaft/first gear
5. O-ring
6. Mainshaft third gear
7. Bushing
8. Snap ring
9. Mainshaft second gear
10. Washer
11. Mainshaft fourth gear
12. Mainshaft fifth gear
13. Washer

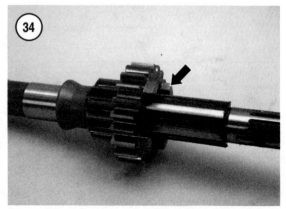

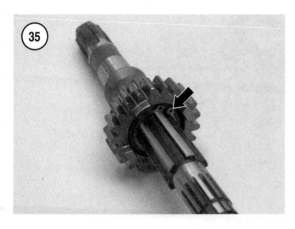

Mainshaft Assembly

Lightly coat the mainshaft, bushings, and washers with engine oil or an assembly lube before installing a gear.

1. Install third gear bushing into mainshaft third gear (**Figure 33**).
2. Slide third gear and the bushing onto the mainshaft so the gear's engagement dogs face out (**Figure 34**).
3. Install a new snap ring (**Figure 35**) so its flat side faces out away from the bushing. Seat the ring in its groove next to the bushing.
4. Slide second gear (**Figure 36**) onto the mainshaft so its shift fork groove faces in toward third gear.
5. Install the washer (A, **Figure 37**) and fourth gear bushing (B).
6. Install fourth gear onto its bushing so the gear's long center boss (**Figure 38**) faces out. (Its engagement slots face in toward second gear).
7. Install fifth gear (**Figure 39**) so its flat side faces out.
8. Install the washer (**Figure 40**) and a new O-ring (**Figure 41**). Lubricate the O-ring with grease.

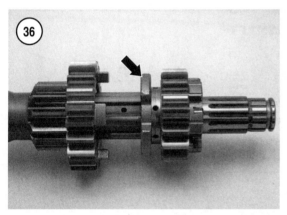

Countershaft Disassembly

Refer to **Figure 42**.

1. Remove the washer and the overdrive gear from the countershaft (**Figure 43**). Note that the gear's side with the wide center boss (**Figure 44**) faces in. Mark this for identification during assembly.
2. Remove first gear, the first gear bushing, and the splined washer.
3. Remove the snap ring, and slide third gear from the countershaft.
4. Remove the snap ring and splined washer.
5. Slide second gear and its bushing from the countershaft.
6. Rotate the lockwasher assembly and disengage lockwasher 1 from lockwasher 2. Remove both lockwashers.

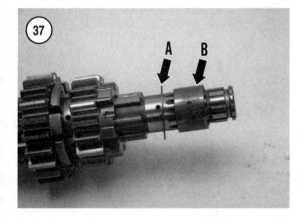

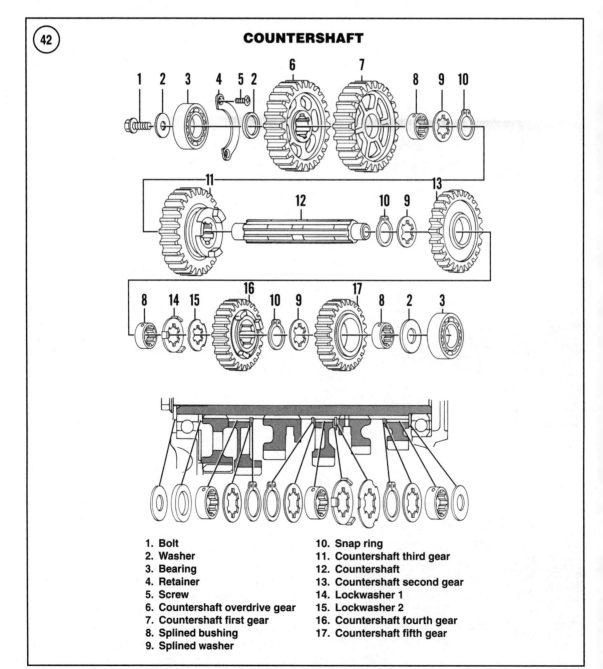

COUNTERSHAFT

1. Bolt
2. Washer
3. Bearing
4. Retainer
5. Screw
6. Countershaft overdrive gear
7. Countershaft first gear
8. Splined bushing
9. Splined washer
10. Snap ring
11. Countershaft third gear
12. Countershaft
13. Countershaft second gear
14. Lockwasher 1
15. Lockwasher 2
16. Countershaft fourth gear
17. Countershaft fifth gear

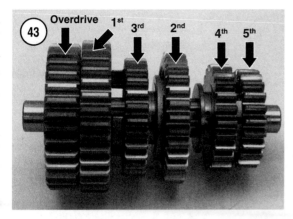

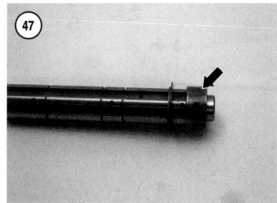

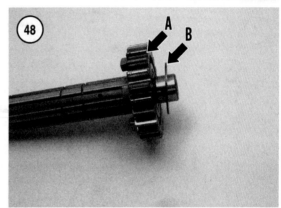

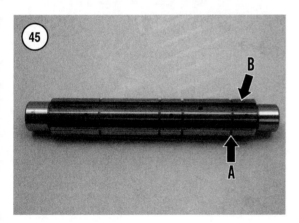

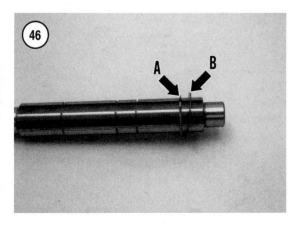

7. Remove fourth gear from the countershaft.

8. On the opposite end of the shaft, remove the washer.

9. Remove the countershaft fifth gear and its bushing.

10. Remove the splined washer and snap ring.

11. Inspect the countershaft components as described in this section. Keep the parts in order and with the same orientation.

Countershaft Assembly

Lightly coat the countershaft and bushings with engine oil or an assembly lube before installing a gear.

1. Set the countershaft on the bench so the snap ring groove closest to an end faces right as shown in A, **Figure 45**. Begin assembly from this end.

2. Install a new snap ring (A, **Figure 46**) into the groove on the right end of the shaft. The flat side of the snap ring must face left, toward the other snap ring groove in the shaft.

3. Install a splined washer (B, **Figure 46**) and seat it against the snap ring.

4. Install fifth gear bushing (**Figure 47**) so its hole aligns with the oil hole on the shaft.

5. Install fifth gear (A, **Figure 48**) so its engagement dogs face in. Seat the gear on its bushing.

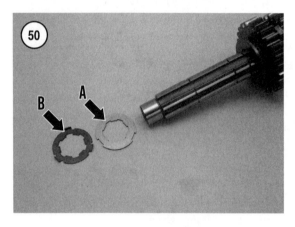

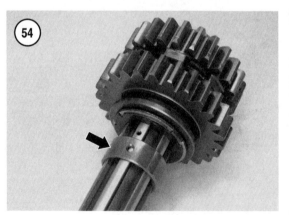

6. Install a washer (B, **Figure 48**) onto the end of the shaft.

7. Move to the opposite end of the shaft.

8. Slide fourth gear down the shaft (**Figure 49**) with its engagement dogs facing in toward fifth gear.

9. Slide lockwasher 2 (A, **Figure 50**) onto the shaft so the lockwasher 2 sits in the groove next to fourth gear. Rotate lockwasher 2 around the groove so the lockwasher's outer cutouts (**Figure 51**) align with a raised spline on the shaft.

10. Slide lockwasher 1 (B, **Figure 50**) onto the shaft so the lockwasher's tabs face inward (**Figure 52**) and align with the cutouts in lockwasher 2.

7

11. Press lockwasher 1 into place so its tabs engage the cutouts of lockwasher 2 as shown in **Figure 53**.

12. Install second gear bushing (**Figure 54**) so its oil hole aligns with the hole in the shaft.

13. Install second gear (**Figure 55**) so its engagement slots face out and seat the gear on its bushing.

14. Install the splined washer (**Figure 56**) and seat it against second gear.

15. Install a new snap ring (**Figure 57**) so its flat side faces out. The snap ring must completely seat in the groove next to second gear.

16. Install third gear (**Figure 58**) so its shift fork slot faces in toward second gear.

17. Install a new snap ring (**Figure 59**) so its flat side faces in toward third gear.

18. Slide on the washer (A, **Figure 60**) and first gear bushing (B). Make sure the hole in the bushing aligns with an oil hole in the shaft.

19. Install first gear (**Figure 61**) and seat it on its bushing. Make sure the flat side of the gear faces out.

20 Install the overdrive gear (A, **Figure 62**) so the side with the wide center boss (**Figure 44**) faces in toward first gear.

21. Install the washer (B, **Figure 62**).

Transmission Inspection

Replace worn, damaged or out of specification parts. When replacing a defective gear, also replace its mate on the opposite shaft even through the mating gear may not show as much damage or wear. The old gear will rapidly wear the new one.

1. Check each gear for excessive wear, burrs, pitting, and chipped or missing teeth (A, **Figure 63**).

2. Inspect the engagement dogs (B, **Figure 63**) and the engagement slots (A, **Figure 64**) for wear or damage.

3. Check the inner splines on sliding gears (**Figure 65**), splined bushings (**Figure 66**), and splined washers. Replace any part with excessive wear or damage.

4. Inspect the bearing surfaces (B, **Figure 64**) on rotating gears and on bushings (**Figure 67**) for wear, pitting or damage.

5. Inspect the washers for bending wear or damage. Replace if necessary.

6. Measure the shift fork-to-gear clearance as described in *Internal Shift Mechanism* in this chapter.

7. Inspect the snap ring grooves (A, **Figure 45**) and the shaft splines (B) on each shaft.

8. Inspect the teeth of first gear (A, **Figure 68**) on the mainshaft.

9. On the mainshaft, inspect the clutch hub splines

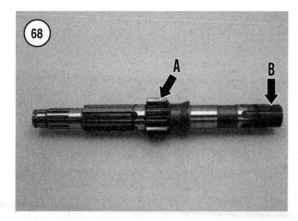

and clutch nut threads (B, **Figure 68**). If any spline is damaged, replace the shaft. If the threads have burrs or minor damage, clean them with a thread die. If the threads are excessively worn, replace the shaft.

10. Check all oil holes on the shafts, gears, and bushings. Blow them clear with compressed air as necessary.

11. Make sure all gears and bushings slide smoothly on their respective shaft splines.

SECONDARY GEAR COVER

Removal/Installation

1. Securely support the motorcycle on a level surface.

2. Remove the secondary gear cover bolts (**Figure 69**).

3. Lower the cover and turn it outward.

4A. On 1998-2004 models, disconnect the 5-pin regulator/rectifier connector (**Figure 70**).

4B. On 2005-on models, disconnect the 3-pin (A, **Figure 71**) and 4-pin (B) regulator/rectifier connectors.

5. Remove the cover.

6. Installation is the reverse of removal. Note the following:

    a. Make sure the damper/collar assembly (**Figure 72**) are in place on each cover mounting post (C, **Figure 71**).

    b. Securely connect the regulator/rectifier connector(s).

    c. Tighten the secondary gear cover bolts securely.

SECONDARY DRIVE GEAR

Removal/Installation

Separate the crankcase and remove/install the secondary drive gear assembly as described in Chapter Five.

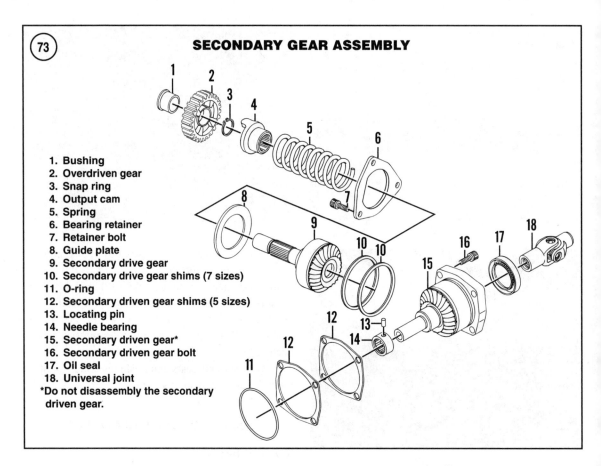

SECONDARY GEAR ASSEMBLY

1. Bushing
2. Overdriven gear
3. Snap ring
4. Output cam
5. Spring
6. Bearing retainer
7. Retainer bolt
8. Guide plate
9. Secondary drive gear
10. Secondary drive gear shims (7 sizes)
11. O-ring
12. Secondary driven gear shims (5 sizes)
13. Locating pin
14. Needle bearing
15. Secondary driven gear*
16. Secondary driven gear bolt
17. Oil seal
18. Universal joint
*Do not disassembly the secondary driven gear.

Disassembly

Refer to **Figure 73**.
1. Securely support the assembly in a press.
2. Compress the secondary drive gear assembly. Remove and discard the snap ring (**Figure 74**).
3. Slowly release the press ram. Remove the output cam and spring.

> *CAUTION*
> *Do not attempt to remove the bearing from the secondary drive gear. The bearing and gear are only available as an assembly.*

4. Remove the output cam (A, **Figure 75**), spring (B), and guide plate (C).
5. Assembly is the reverse of disassembly. Note the following:
   a. Install a new snap ring (**Figure 74**) so its flat side faces out away from the output cam.
   b. Make sure the snap ring seats within its groove in the shaft of the secondary drive gear.

Inspection

1. Inspect the teeth of the secondary drive gear (**Figure 76**) and the overdrive gear (A, **Figure 77**)

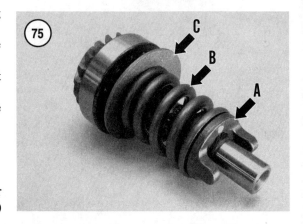

for burrs, chips or other damage.

2. Inspect the output cam (A, **Figure 75**) and the cutouts of the overdrive gear (B, **Figure 77**) for wear or damage.

3. Inspect the splines on the gear shaft and in the output cam.

4. Manually rotate the drive gear bearing. It should turn smoothly without noise or binding.

5. Inspect the damper spring (B, **Figure 75**) for cracks or signs of fatigue.

6. Measure the free length of the damper spring. Replace the damper spring if the free length is less than the service limit (**Table 1**).

7. Inspect the overdrive gear bushing (C, **Figure 77**) for scoring, bluing or other signs of damage.

8. Replace worn or damaged parts.

SECONDARY DRIVEN GEAR ASSEMBLY

Removal

Refer to **Figure 73**.

1A. Remove the engine as described in Chapter Five.

1B. If the engine is still in the frame, perform the following:

    a. Remove the secondary gear cover (this chapter).

    b. Remove the swing arm (Chapter Thirteen).

    c. Remove the boot. Then pull the universal joint from the shaft of the secondary driven gear.

2. Remove the secondary driven gear bolts (A, **Figure 78**). Note that the flange cutout in the secondary driven gear housing (B, **Figure 78**) is closest to the engine number on the crankcase.

3. Remove the secondary gearcase cover bolts (A, **Figure 79**). Note the cable holders (B, **Figure 79**) behind two of the bolts. The holders must be installed behind these bolts during installation.

4. Remove the secondary gearcase cover. Watch for the dowels (A, **Figure 80**) behind the cover.

5. Pull the secondary driven gear (B, **Figure 80**) rearward until its shaft disengages from the needle bearing (C), and remove the assembly.

6. Remove the needle bearing (A, **Figure 81**) from the bearing boss in the secondary gearcase. Remove the bearing locating pin (B, **Figure 81**).

7. Remove the secondary gear oil jet (A, **Figure 82**) from its gallery in the crankcase.

8. Inspect the secondary driven gear.

9. Installation is the reverse of removal. Note the following:

    a. Lubricate a new O-ring with grease (A, **Figure 83**). Then install the O-ring onto the secondary driven gear housing. If removed, install the shims (B, **Figure 83**) onto the secondary driven gear assembly.

    b. Apply engine oil to the O-ring on the secondary gear oil jet (A, **Figure 82**).

    c. Seat the needle bearing in the bearing boss (B, **Figure 82**) so the bearing's hole engages the locating pin (A, **Figure 81**).

    d. Install the secondary driven gear assembly so the side with the flange cutout (B, **Figure 78**) is closest to the engine number on the crankcase.

    e. Clean the mating surfaces of the secondary gearcase and the cover. Apply Suzuki Bond 1207B to the gearcase cover where shown in **Figure 84**.

    f. Evenly tighten the secondary gearcase cover bolts (**Figure 79**) in stages to 10 N•m (89 in.-lb.), and then to 22 N•m (16 ft.-lb.).

    g. Apply Suzuki Thread Lock Super 1303 to the threads of the secondary driven gear bolts (**Figure 78**) and tighten the bolts to 23 N•m (17 ft.-lb.).

    h. Install the universal joint boot so the tab marked *UP* faces up.

Inspection

CAUTION
Do not disassemble the secondary driven gear.

1. Inspect the teeth (C, **Figure 83**) of the secondary driven gear for chips or other damage.

2. Inspect the needle bearing (D, **Figure 83**) for scoring, bluing or other signs of wear.

3. Inspect the splines (A, **Figure 85**) of the secondary driven gear shaft.

4. Inspect the oil seal (B, **Figure 85**) for signs of leaks. If necessary, replace the seal by performing the following:

    a. Pry the oil seal from the bearing housing (**Figure 86**).

    b. Pack the lips of the new oil seal with grease.

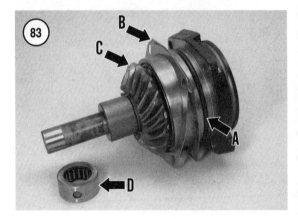

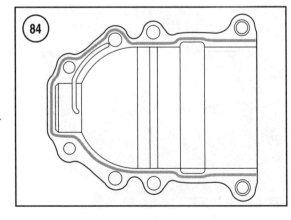

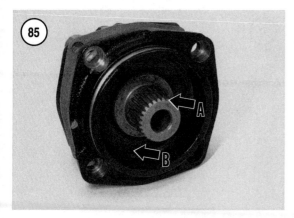

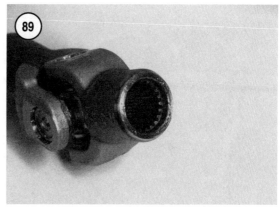

c. Install the oil seal so the manufacturer's numbers face out.

d. Drive the bearing into place with a driver or socket that matches the seal's outside diameter (**Figure 87**).

5. Blow the oil jet (**Figure 82**) clear with compressed air.

6. Replace worn or damaged parts.

Universal Joint Inspection

If the universal joint is worn or damaged, replace it. Universal joint parts are not available from the manufacturer.

1. Clean the universal joint in solvent and dry with compressed air.

2. Check the movement of the universal joint pivots (**Figure 88**). Replace the universal joint if play is excessive.

> *NOTE*
> *If the splines of the universal joint are damaged, also inspect the splines on the driveshaft and on the secondary driven shaft.*

3. Inspect the splines (**Figure 89**) at each end of the universal joint. Replace the universal joint if the splines are worn or damaged.

4. Lubricate the splines in the universal joint with molybdenum disulfide grease.

SECONDARY GEAR ASSEMBLY ALIGNMENT

Align the secondary gear assembly whenever replacing the crankcase, secondary drive gear or secondary driven gear.

1. Separate the crankcase and remove the crankshaft, transmission shafts, internal shift mechanism, and secondary drive gear assembly as described in Chapter Five.

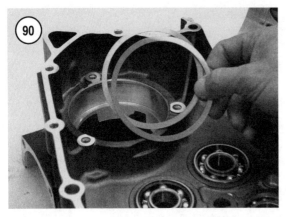

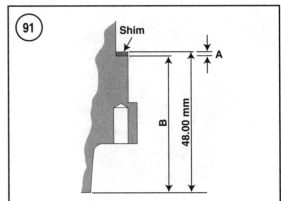

2. Measure the thickness of the secondary drive gear shims (**Figure 90**). Record the measurements.

3. If still installed, remove the secondary driven gear assembly (this chapter). Measure the thickness of the secondary driven gear shims (B, **Figure 83**). Record the measurement.

4. Measure the secondary gear assembly backlash (this chapter) and select new secondary driven gear shims. If replacing the crankcase, select new secondary drive gear shims.

Secondary Drive Gear Shim Selection

If replacing the crankcase, also replace the secondary drive gear shims. The total distance from the top of the shims to the left case half mating surface should equal 48.0 mm (1.890 in.). See **Figure 91**. Select the proper shims for the new crankcase by performing the following:

1. Set the left case half on a surface plate with its inboard side facing the surface plate.

2. Measure the distance from the lip of the secondary drive gear bearing boss to the surface plate (**Figure 92**).

3. Use the following formula to calculate the new secondary drive gear shim thickness (A, **Figure 91**):

   a. New shim thickness = (48.00 mm - B) - 0.1 mm.

   b. B equals the distance measured in Step 2.

4. Refer to **Table 3** and select two shims that together equal the new shim thickness value calculated in Step 3.

5. Install these shims with the secondary drive gear and measure secondary gear assembly backlash.

Secondary Gear Assembly Backlash

1. Install the secondary drive gear into the left case half as described in Chapter Five.

   a. If replacing the secondary drive gear and secondary driven gear components, install the removed shims for this portion of the procedure.

   b. If replacing the crankcase, select new secondary drive gear shims as described in this section. Install the new shims with the secondary drive gear.

NOTE
Check the backlash without the secondary driven gear O-ring installed in the housing. After the backlash and tooth contact are correct, install the O-ring.

2. Remove the O-ring (A, **Figure 83**) from the secondary driven gear housing. Install the secondary driven gear assembly into the left case half as described in this chapter.

3. Install the secondary gearcase cover (without sealant) onto the left case half. Tighten the secondary gearcase cover bolts to 22 N•m (16 ft.-lb.).

4. Secure a dial indicator in place so its plunger rests against a dog on the output cam as shown in **Figure 93**. Position the dial indicator so the plunger is perpendicular to a line drawn across the two dogs on the output cam.

5. Securely hold the shaft of the secondary driven gear.

6. While lifting the secondary drive gear to remove excess play, rotate the secondary drive gear in each direction. Note the reading on the dial indicator. The

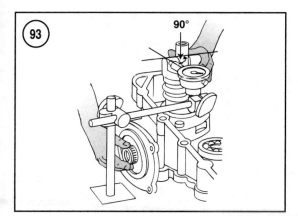

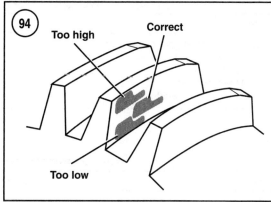

reading should be within the secondary gear backlash range specified in **Table 1**.

7. If the measurement is outside the range, select new secondary driven gear shims by performing the following:

    a. Remove the secondary driven gear assembly and measure the thickness of the existing shims (B, **Figure 83**).

NOTE
Use the thickness of the secondary driven gear shims to help with shim adjustment.

    b. If the backlash was less than 0.03 mm (0.001 in.) increase shim thickness to bring the backlash within specification. If the backlash exceeded 0.15 mm (0.006 in.), decrease shim thickness. Refer to **Table 4** and select new shims.

8. Install the secondary driven gear assembly with the new shims and without the O-ring (A, **Figure 83**). Recheck the backlash.

9. Repeat Steps 4-8 as necessary until the backlash is within specification.

10. Remove the secondary drive gear assembly from the left case half.

11. Remove all traces of oil from the teeth of the secondary drive gear and apply a coat of marking compound to the gear teeth.

12. Reinstall the secondary drive gear assembly.

13. Turn the shaft of the secondary driven gear assembly and rotate the driven gear assembly through several turns in both directions.

14. Remove the secondary drive gear assembly from the crankcase and check the tooth contact pattern. It should be centered vertically on the tooth as shown in **Figure 94**.

    a. If the contact pattern is too high on the tooth, decrease the thickness of the secondary driven gear shims or that of the secondary drive gear shims.

    b. If the contact pattern is too low on the tooth, increase the thickness of the secondary driven gear shims or that of the secondary drive gear shims.

15. Once the tooth contact pattern is correct, recheck the secondary gear assembly backlash. Repeatedly adjust the gear backlash and the tooth contact pattern as necessary until both are correct.

16. Remove the secondary driven gear assembly and install a new O-ring onto the gear housing (A, **Figure 83**). Reinstall the secondary driven gear assembly (this chapter).

Table 1 TRANSMISSION AND SECONDARY GEAR SPECIFICATIONS

Item	Standard
Transmission gear ratios	
First gear	3.000 (36/12)
Second gear	1.823 (31/17)
Third gear	1.333 (28/21)
Fourth gear	1.041 (25/24)
Top gear	0.884 (23/26)
Primary reduction ratio	1.490 (76/51)
Secondary reduction ratio	0.852 (29/34)
(continued)	

Table 1 TRANSMISSION AND SECONDARY GEAR SPECIFICATIONS (continued)

Item	Standard
Secondary drive gear damper spring	
Free length service limit	
1998 models	88.4 mm (3.48 in.)
1999-on models	73.6 mm (2.90 in.)
Secondary gear backlash	0.03-0.15 (0.001-0.006)

Table 2 SHIFT MECHANISM SPECIFICATIONS

Item	Standard mm (in.)	Service limit mm (in.)
Shift fork-to-groove clearance	0.10-0.30 (0.004-0.012)	0.50 (0.020)
Shift fork groove width	5.50-5.60 (0.217-0.220)	–
Shift fork finger thickness	5.30-5.40 (0.209-0.213)	–
Shift pedal height	82 (3.23)	–

Table 3 SECONDARY DRIVE GEAR SHIM SELECTION*

Shim Thickness mm (in.)	Part No.
1.10 (0.043)	24935-28B00-110
1.15 (0.045)	24935-28B00-115
1.20 (0.047)	24935-28B00-120
1.25 (0.049)	24935-28B00-125
1.30 (0.051)	24935-28B00-130
1.35 (0.053)	24935-28B00-135
1.40 (0.055)	24935-28B00-140
*Drive gear shim set (Suzuki part No. 24945-38810).	

Table 4 SECONDARY DRIVEN GEAR SHIM SELECTION*

Shim Thickness mm (in.)	Part No.
0.30 (0.012)	24945-38B00-030
0.35 (0.014)	24945-38B00-035
0.40 (0.016)	24945-38B00-040
0.50 (0.020)	24945-38B00-050
0.60 (0.024)	24945-38B00-060
*Driven gear shim set (Suzuki part No. 24935-38820).	

Table 5 SHIFT MECHANISM AND SECONDARY DRIVE TORQUE SPECIFICATIONS

Item	N•m	in.-lb.	ft.-lb.
Front footrest bolt	50	–	37
Secondary drive gear bearing retainer bolt	23	–	17
Secondary driven bear bolt	23	–	17
Secondary driven gear bearing stopper	105	–	77
Secondary gearcase cover bolt			
Initial	10	89	–
Final	22	–	16
Shift cam stopper bolt/nut	10	89	–
Shift cam retainer bolt	10	89	–
Shift pedal bolt	16	–	12
Shift shaft stopper	23	–	17
Stopper lever bolt	10	89	–
Stopper lever nut	10	89	–

AIR/FUEL, EXHAUST AND EMISSIONS SYSTEMS

This chapter covers the carburetors and the air, fuel delivery, exhaust and emissions systems used on carbureted models. Refer to Chapter Nine for fuel injection system specifics, including the fuel pump and emission system.

During inspection, compare measurements to the specifications at the end of this chapter. Replace worn, damaged or out of specification components.

AIR FILTER HOUSING

Removal/Installation

1. Remove the seats, meter cover, upper cover, and steering head covers (Chapter Fifteen).
2. Disconnect the crankcase breather hose (A, **Figure 1**) from the front of the air filter housing.
3A. On 1998-2004 models, loosen the clamp screw on the air filter housing clamp. A single screw loosens both clamps (**Figure 2**).
3B. On 2005-on models, perform the following:
   a. Loosen the clamp screw (**Figure 3**) on each side of housing.
   b. Disconnect the 2-pin connector (B, **Figure 1**) from the intake air temperature sensor.
4. Disengage each air filter housing port from its respective carburetor or throttle body.

5. On models with the PAIR system, lift the rear of the housing and disconnect the PAIR hose (A, **Figure 4**) from its fitting (B) on the housing.
6. Remove the air filter housing.
7. Cover each carburetor or throttle body horn to prevent debris from entering the intake system.
8. Install the air filter housing by reversing the removal steps. Note the following:
   a. On 1998-2004 models, position the clamps on the air filter housing ports so the screw head sits on the left side (**Figure 2**).
   b. On 2005-on models, position each clamp so its clamp screw head (A, **Figure 5**) faces the outboard side of its air filter housing port.
   c. Make sure each air filter housing port securely engages its carburetor or throttle body intake horn.

Inspection

1. Remove the air filter screws and lift the filter from the housing.
2. Inspect the air filter element as described in Chapter Three.
3. Wipe out the interior of the housing.
4. Inspect the air filter housing and its intake ports for cracks, wear or damage. If any damage is noted,

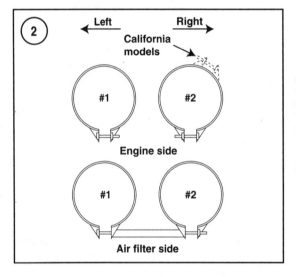

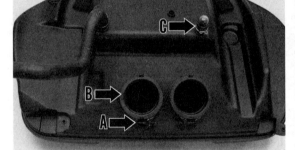

replace the housing to avoid the possibility of unfiltered air entering the engine.

5. Inspect the port fittings (B, **Figure 5**) for hardness, deterioration or damage. Replace them as necessary.

6. Remove the plug (C, **Figure 5**). Clean out all residue from the plug and air box. Reinstall the drain plug.

FUEL TANK

Removal

Refer to **Figure 6** (all models except California). Refer to *Evaporative Emissions Control System* in this chapter for California models.

1. Remove the rider's seat, steering head covers, the upper covers, and side covers (Chapter Fifteen).

2. Remove the engine side box, mufflers, and exhaust pipes (this chapter).

3. Remove the grab rail from the right side by performing the following:

   a. Evenly loosen the 8-mm (A, **Figure 7**) and 10-mm grab rail bolts (B).

   b. Remove the bolts and lower the grab rail (C, **Figure 7**) from the fender.

4A. On 1998-2004 models, perform the following:

   a. Disconnect the 2-pin fuel level sender connector (A, **Figure 8**) and 5-pin taillight/turn signal connector (B).

   b. Disconnect the fuel hose from the input fitting (A, **Figure 9**) on the fuel pump. Be prepared to catch residual fuel.

4B. On 2005-on models, perform the following:

   a. Disconnect the 3-pin fuel pump connector (A, **Figure 10**) and 3-pin tip over sensor connector (B).

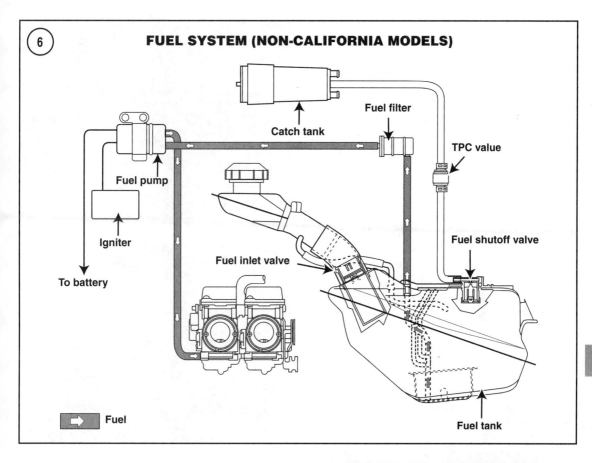

6 FUEL SYSTEM (NON-CALIFORNIA MODELS)

Catch tank

Fuel filter

TPC value

Fuel pump

Igniter

To battery

Fuel inlet valve

Fuel shutoff valve

Fuel tank

Fuel

8

7

9

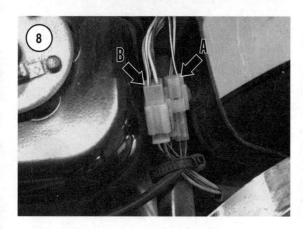

8

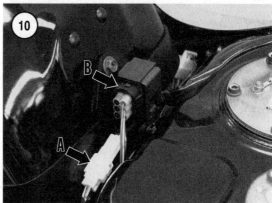

10

b. Disconnect the fuel hose (A, **Figure 11**) from its fuel pump fitting. Be prepared to catch any residual fuel.

5. Disconnect the drain hose from its fitting (**Figure 12**) on the filler neck.

6. Disconnect the breather hose from the vapor separator/fuel shutoff valve (B, **Figure 11**). On California models, this hose connects to the EVAP canister. On non-California models, it connects to the fuel catch tank.

7. Remove the upper frame bolts (A, **Figure 13**), lower frame bolts (B), and the rear frame bolts (A, **Figure 14**) from the removable frame member. Remove the frame member (B, **Figure 14**) from the right side.

8. Remove the fuel tank bolts (C, **Figure 14**). Watch for the damper and collar installed in each mount.

9. Remove the fuel tank along with the filler neck.

10. Installation is reverse of removal. Note the following:

a. Tighten the frame bolts to 50 N•m (37 ft.-lb.).

b. Apply Suzuki Thread Lock Super 1303 to threads of the grab rail bolts. Tighten all the bolts evenly and securely.

c. Tighten the 10-mm grab rail bolts to 50 N•m (37 ft.-lb.). Tighten the 8-mm bolts to 13 N•m (115 in.-lb.).

FUEL PUMP

Removal/Installation

1. Remove the rider's seat and meter cover (Chapter Fifteen).

2. Remove the steering head cover and the upper cover from the left side (Chapter Fifteen).

3. Disconnect the input hose (A, **Figure 9**) and output hose (B) from their respective fittings on the fuel pump. Catch any fuel leaking from the hoses. Label each hose and its fitting.

4. Disconnect the 2-pin fuel pump connector (C, **Figure 9**).

5. Remove the pump mounting bolts and lower the fuel pump from the left side of the motorcycle.

6. Reverse the removal procedures to install the fuel pump. Install the hoses onto the correct fittings.

Volume Test

Use a graduated container with a capacity of at least 600 ml (1.27 pt.) for this test.

1. Remove the rider's seat and meter cover (Chapter Fifteen).

2. Remove the steering head cover and the upper cover from the left side (Chapter Fifteen).

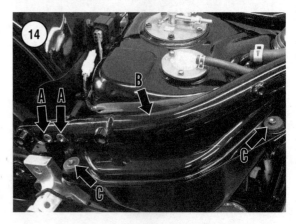

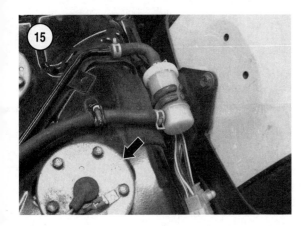

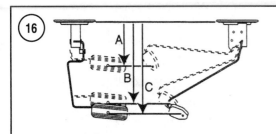

1998 Models

Float position	Height	Resistance
A	81.3 mm (3.2 in.)	10-25 ohms
B	147.8 mm (5.8 in.)	66-74 ohms
C	167.1 mm (6.6 in.)	92-102 ohms

1999-2004 models

Float position	Height	Resistance
A	63.3 mm (2.5 in.)	1-5 ohms
B	103.5 mm (4.1 in.)	28.5-36.5 ohms
C	159.1 mm (6.3 in.)	103-117 ohms

3. Disconnect the 2-pin fuel pump connector (C, **Figure 9**).

4. Disconnect the output hose (B, **Figure 9**) from its fitting on the fuel pump. Be prepared to catch residual gasoline.

5. Connect a suitable hose to the fuel pump output fitting and feed the opposite end of the hose into the graduated cylinder.

6. Operate the pump by performing the following:

   a. Use a jumper to connect the battery positive terminal to the brown/black terminal in the pump side of the fuel pump connector. Connect

the battery negative terminal to the black/white terminal with another jumper wire.

   b. After one minute, disconnect the jumpers from the connector and battery.

7. Measure the amount of fuel in the graduated cylinder. It should equal the fuel pump output volume specified in **Table 3**. If the volume is significantly less than specified, replace the fuel pump.

Resistance Test

1. Perform Steps 1-3 of the *Volume Test* described in this section.

2. Connect an ohmmeters test leads to the terminals in the pump side of the fuel pump connector.

3. Resistance should be within the range specified in **Table 3**.

FUEL LEVEL SENDER

Removal/Installation

1. Remove the rider's seat (Chapter Fifteen).

2. Disconnect the 2-pin fuel level sender connector (A, **Figure 8**).

3. Remove the bolts and lift the fuel level sender (**Figure 15**) from the fuel tank.

4. Installation is the reverse of removal. Note the following:

   a. Position a new fuel level sender gasket so its flange fits down into the fuel tank.

   b. Evenly tighten the fuel level sender bolts in a crisscross pattern to 4 N•m (35 in.-lb.).

Resistance Test

1. Remove the fuel level sender (this section).

2. Position the fuel sender so its flange parallels the floor.

3. Connect an ohmmeter test leads to the two terminals in the sender side of the fuel sender connector.

4. Move the float to position A shown in **Figure 16** and measure the resistance.

5. Move the float to position B and position C in **Figure 16**. Measure the resistance at each float position.

6. If the resistance at any float position is outside the specified range, replace the sender.

FUEL SHUTOFF VALVE

Removal/Installation

On non-California models, the fuel shutoff valve routes vapors to the catch tank on the right side of the motorcycle. On California models, the fuel shutoff valve routes vapors to the EVAP canister. The valve also closes during hard acceleration or deceleration to keep fuel inside the tank.

1. Remove the rider's seat (Chapter Fifteen).

2. Disconnect the breather hose (A, **Figure 17**) from the fitting on the fuel shutoff valve.

3. Remove the fuel shutoff valve bolts and lift the fuel shutoff valve (B, **Figure 17**) from the tank.

4. Installation is the reverse of removal. Note the following:

   a. Install the gasket so its cutout engages the tab on the fuel shutoff valve.

   b. Position the fuel shutoff valve so it breather hose fitting points forward.

   c. Evenly tighten the fuel shutoff valve bolts in a crisscross pattern to 4 N•m (35 in.-lb.).

Inspection

1. Inspect the fuel shutoff valve for leaks, cracks or other damage.

2. Fill a container with enough kerosene to float the fuel shutoff valve.

3. Check the operation of the float within the fuel shutoff valve. The float (A, **Figure 18**) should move smoothly and it should close against the valve seat (B).

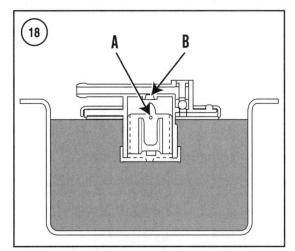

FUEL INLET VALVE

Removal/Installation

1. Remove the rider's seat, meter cover, upper covers, and side covers (Chapter Fifteen).

2. Disconnect the vent hose (A, **Figure 19**) from the tank fitting.

3. Release the clamps. Disconnect the fuel inlet hose (B, **Figure 19**) from the fuel tank and from the filler neck. Remove the hose from the motorcycle.

4. Lift the fuel inlet valve from its port in the tank.

5. Installation is the reverse of removal. Note the following:

   a. Position the clamps so their ends face down.

   b. Tighten the fuel inlet hose clamps to 2 N•m (18 in.-lb.).

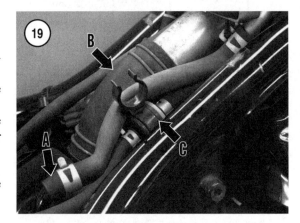

CATCH TANK

Removal/Installation

The catch tank sits on the right side of the frame. On California models, the catch tank is not used. In its place is the EVAP canister. Although the catch tank and EVAP canister look externally similar, they are different internally. Do not substitute a catch tank for an EVAP canister.

1. Remove the air filter housing (this chapter).

Inspection

1. Inspect the fuel inlet valve for leaks, cracks or other damage.

2. Fill a container with enough kerosene to float the inlet valve.

3. Check the operation of the butterfly valves (**Figure 20**). They should move smoothly.

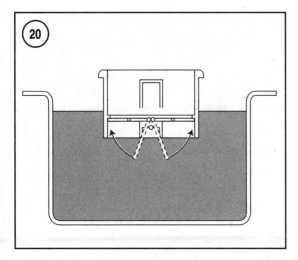

2. Note how the hoses route through the frame. Route hoses along their original paths.

3A. On non-California models, disconnect the breather hose (A, **Figure 21**) from the middle port on the catch tank.

3B. On California models, disconnect the breather hoses (A and B, **Figure 21**) from their fittings on the EVAP canister. Label each hose and its fitting.

4. Remove the mounting screw (C, **Figure 21**). Lift out the clamp and remove the catch tank (EVAP canister on California models).

5. Install the catch tank (or EVAP canister) by reversing the removal procedures. Note the following:
   a. Route the hoses as noted during removal.
   b. Connect each hose to its original fitting.
   c. On California models, the hose from the fuel shutoff valve connects to the middle port (A, **Figure 21**) on the canister. The hose to the carburetors/throttle bodies, connects to the lower port (B, **Figure 21**).

TANK PRESSURE CONTROL (TPC) VALVE

Removal/Installation

On non-California models, the TPC valve sits in-line between the fuel shutoff valve and catch tank. On California models, it is between the fuel shutoff valve and EVAP canister.

1. Remove the rider's seat, meter cover, and upper covers (Chapter Fifteen).

2. Release the clamps and pull the TPC valve (C, **Figure 19**) from the breather hose. Note that the orange side of the TPC valve faces the catch tank or EVAP canister (California models).

3. Test the pressure control valve by performing the following:
   a. Blow into the fitting on the orange side of the valve. Air should flow out the opposite side of the valve.
   b. Reverse the valve and blow into the other fitting. Air should not flow out of the orange side of the valve.
   c. Replace the valve if it fails either portion of this test.

4. Installation is the reverse of removal. Install the TPC valve so its orange side faces the catch tank or the EVAP canister (California models).

CARBURETORS

Removal/Installation

1. Disconnect the negative battery cable (Chapter Ten).

2. Remove the air filter housing (this chapter).

3. Disconnect the 3-pin connector (A, **Figure 22**) from the throttle position sensor.

4. Disconnect the fuel hose (B, **Figure 22**) from the port on the right carburetor. Be prepared to catch residual fuel.

5. Disconnect the vent hose (C, **Figure 22**) from its fitting on the top of the assembly.

6. Loosen the clamp screw on each carburetor clamp. Note the location of each clamp screw (**Figure 2**).

7. Lift the carburetors and disengage each one from its intake manifold.

8

8. Disconnect the starter cable end (**Figure 23**) from the starter bracket.

9. Disconnect the vacuum hose (**Figure 24**) from the T-fitting.

10. Loosen the locknut and turn the return cable adjuster (A, **Figure 25**) to create sufficient slack in the cable. Disconnect the return cable end (B, **Figure 25**) from the throttle wheel.

11. Repeat Step 11, and disconnect the end of the pull cable (C, **Figure 25**) from the throttle wheel.

12. Remove the carburetors from the motorcycle. Stuff a clean shop cloth into each intake manifold to keep debris out of the engine (**Figure 26**).

13. Store the carburetors by performing the following:

   a. Remove the drain screw and drain the fuel from each float bowl into a suitable container. Dispose of the fuel properly.

   b. Carefully shake the carburetors to remove as much fuel as possible.

   c. Install the drain screws.

   d. Place the carburetors in a sturdy plastic bag to protect the assembly from moisture and debris.

   e. Set the carburetors upright in a sturdy cardboard box. Set the box in a safe place away from any heat or ignition source.

14. Install the carburetors by reversing the removal procedures. Note the following:

   a. Rotate each carburetor clamp on its intake manifold so the clamp screw is in the position shown in **Figure 2**.

   b. Adjust the throttle cable free play (Chapter Three).

   c. If the carburetors were separated, synchronize the throttle valves as described in Chapter Three.

Separation

Except for the starter plunger, most carburetor parts can be replaced with the carburetors joined.

Separate the carburetors if: the starter plunger requires service, a carburetor fitting needs to be replaced, a carburetor needs to be cleaned internally or a carburetor must be replaced.

Refer to **Figure 27**.

1. Disconnect the vacuum hose (A, **Figure 28**) from the fitting on each carburetor.

2. Open the drain screw (B, **Figure 28**) and drain the fuel from each float bowl.

NOTE
The throttle position sensor is preset. Do not remove it. If the TP sensor must be removed, make alignment marks on the carburetor and on the sensor body so the sensor can be reinstalled in the same position.

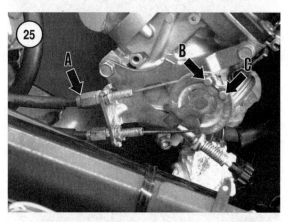

CARBURETORS

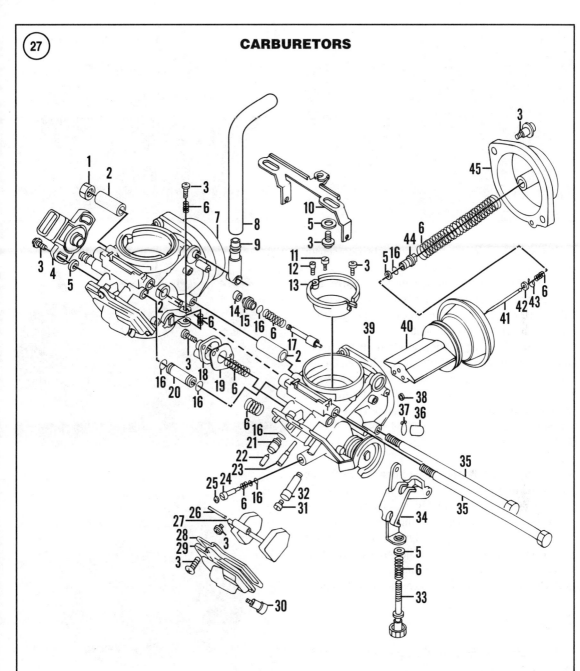

1. Nut	16. O-ring	31. Main jet
2. Spacer	17. Starter plunger	32. Main jet holder
3. Screw	18. Coasting valve cover	33. Throttle stop screw
4. Throttle position sensor	19. Coasting valve diaphragm	34. Bracket
5. Washer	20. Fuel pipe	35. Through bolt
6. Spring	21. Valve seat	36. Cap
7. Rear carb body (No. 1)	22. Needle valve	37. Clamp
8. Vent hose	23. Pilot jet	38. O-ring
9. Fitting	24. Pilot screw	39. Front carb body (No. 2)
10. Starter bracket	25. Cap	40. Piston valve
11. Pilot air jet No. 1	26. Pivot pin	41. Jet needle
12. Pilot air jet No. 2	27. Float	42. Spacer
13. Funnel	28. O-ring	43. E-clip
14. Cap	29. Float bowl	44. Jet needle stopper
15. Holder	30. Drain screw	45. Top cover

3. If necessary, remove the throttle position sensor as described in this chapter.

4. Remove the mounting screws (A, **Figure 29**), and remove the starter bracket (B) from the assembly. Note how the starter bracket fingers engage the starter plunger on each carburetor.

5. Remove the nut (A, **Figure 30**) from the upper throughbolt (B) and pull the throughbolt from the assembly. Watch for the two spacers (C, **Figure 30**).

6. Remove the lower throughbolt (A, **Figure 31**). Watch for the single spacer (C, **Figure 28**) between the carburetors.

7. Remove the bracket (B, **Figure 31**) from behind the throttle wheel.

8. Carefully separate the carburetors. Watch for the spring (A, **Figure 32**) that sits between each throttle lever in the linkage assembly. Also watch for the spring (B, **Figure 32**) between the throttle shafts.

9. Remove the vent fitting (A, **Figure 33**) from the vent port between the bodies, remove the spring (B) from the throttle shaft, and pull the fuel pipe (C) from the fuel port. Discard the O-ring from each end of the fuel pipe.

Joining

1. Place each carburetor on the bench so its butterfly faces up (**Figure 34**).

2. If still installed, remove the spring (A, **Figure 32**) from throttle linkage assembly in the right carburetor.

3. Lubricate new O-rings with grease and install them onto (**Figure 34**) the fuel pipe.

4. Press the fuel pipe (C, **Figure 33**) into the port in the left carburetor. Install the spring (B, **Figure 33**) onto the throttle shaft, and fit the vent fitting (A) into its port.

5. Press the right carburetor onto the left body so the spring engages the throttle shaft of the right carburetor, the fuel pipe seats in the fuel port on the right carburetor, and the vent fitting engages the vent port in the right carburetor. Make sure the throttle lever from the left carburetor sits above the lever on the right carburetor's assembly. Refer to **Figure 35**.

6. Set the bracket (B, **Figure 31**) behind the throttle wheel and fit in into place on the left side of the assembly.

7. Slide the lower throughbolt (A, **Figure 31**) through the bracket and left carburetor. Insert the spacer (C, **Figure 28**) between the carburetor bodies, and install the throughbolt into the right carburetor.

8. Install the spring (A, **Figure 32**) into the linkage assembly. The spring must sit between the throttle levers.

9. Insert the upper throughbolt (B, **Figure 30**) through the assembly. Install each spacer (C, **Figure 30**) and install the nut (A). Tighten the nut securely.

10. Securely tighten the lower throughbolt (A, **Figure 31**).

11. Set the starter bracket (A, **Figure 29**) across the carburetor bodies and securely install the screws. Make sure the fingers of the starter bracket engage the throttle plunger on each carburetor.

12. If removed, install the throttle position sensor as described in this chapter.

13. Connect the vacuum hose (A, **Figure 28**) to the fitting on each carburetor.

Disassembly

Disassemble, clean, and reassemble one carburetor at a time to prevent mixing parts.

NOTE
*When cleaning a carburetor, do not turn the pilot screw. It is preset and changing this setting will decrease engine performance. Refer to **Pilot Screw** in this chapter.*

1. Disconnect the vacuum hose (A, **Figure 28**) from the fitting on each carburetor.

2. Open the drain screw (B, **Figure 28**) and drain the fuel from each float bowl.

3. Remove the float bowl screws (A, **Figure 36**) and remove the float bowl (B) from the carburetor.

4. Remove and discard the float bowl O-ring (**Figure 37**).

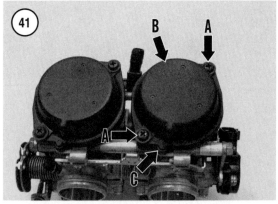

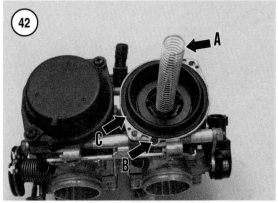

5. Pull the pin (A, **Figure 38**) from the float hinge, and lift out the float (B) with the needle valve.

6. Remove the pilot jet (**Figure 39**).

7. Remove the main jet (A, **Figure 40**) and the jet holder (B).

8. Remove the screw (C, **Figure 40**), and pull the valve seat (D) from the carburetor body.

9. Remove the cover screws (A, **Figure 41**) and lift the cover (B) from the carburetor. Watch for the spring (A, **Figure 42**) and small O-ring (B) beneath the cover. Remove the return spring from the piston valve and remove the O-ring from the carburetor body.

10. Slide the piston valve from the carburetor (**Figure 43**).

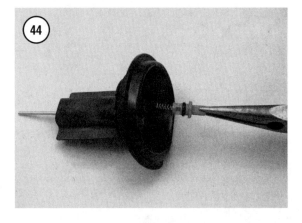

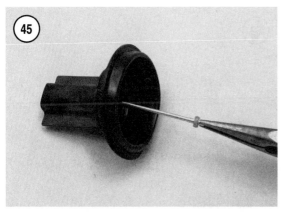

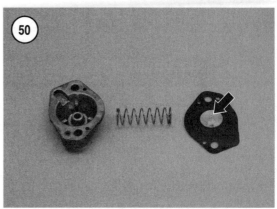

8

11. Remove the jet needle stopper (**Figure 44**) and the jet needle (**Figure 45**) from the piston valve.

12. Remove the mounting screws (A, **Figure 46**) and pull the funnel (B) from the carburetor intake horn.

13. Remove the pilot air jet No. 1 (A, **Figure 47**) and pilot jet No. 2 (B) from the intake horn.

14. Remove the screws (A, **Figure 48**) and lift the coasting valve cover (B) from the carburetor. Remove the spring (A, **Figure 49**) and the coasting valve diaphragm (B). Note that the metal cone on the diaphragm (**Figure 50**) faces down and seats against the ball valve (**Figure 51**) in the carburetor.

15. If necessary, remove the pilot screw as described under *Pilot Screw* in this chapter.

16. If necessary, remove the starter plunger as follows:
   a. Separate the carburetors.
   b. Remove the starter plunger nut (**Figure 52**) and remove the starter plunger (**Figure 53**) from the carburetor.

17. Clean and inspect the parts as described in this section.

18. Assemble the carburetor by reversing the removal procedures. Note the following:
   a. When installing the coasting valve, make sure the hole in the diaphragm and cover align with the hole in the carburetor.
   b. When installing the funnel (B, **Figure 46**), apply Suzuki Thread Lock 1342 to the threads of the funnel screws (A).
   c. Apply grease to the starter plunger O-ring (**Figure 54**).
   d. Make sure the spacer, E-clip (A, **Figure 55**) and washer (B) are in place on the jet needle (C).
   e. Position the jet needle stopper so its spring end goes into the piston valve (**Figure 44**). Press the stopper into place until it bottoms.
   f. Slide the piston valve assembly into the carburetor (**Figure 43**). Make sure the lip of the diaphragm (C, **Figure 42**) seats on the top of the body.
   g. Position a new O-ring (B, **Figure 42**) over the vent hole in the top of the carburetor.
   h. Install the top cover so its vent chamber (C, **Figure 41**) sits over the O-ring. Make sure the locating cylinder (**Figure 56**) inside the top cover sits within the return spring (A, **Figure 42**).

Cleaning and Inspection

1. Thoroughly clean and dry all parts. Clean carburetor parts in a petroleum-based solvent. Rinse them thoroughly in clean water.

> *CAUTION*
> *If compressed air is not available, allow the parts to air dry or dry them with a clean, lint-free cloth. Do not use a paper towel to dry carburetor parts. Small paper particles could plug openings in the carburetor body or jets.*

> *CAUTION*
> *Do not use a piece of wire to clean the jets. Minor gouges in a jet can affect the air/fuel mixture.*

2. With compressed air, blow through all of the jets and the jet holder.

3. Inspect the main jet (A, **Figure 57**), jet holder (B),

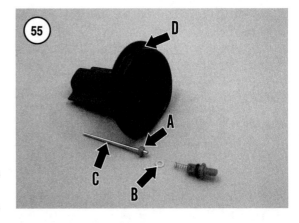

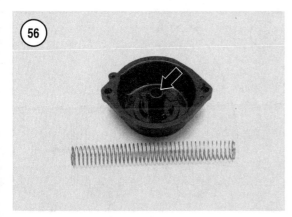

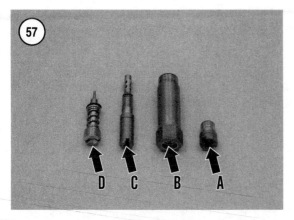

D C B A

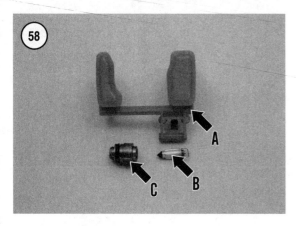

A

C B

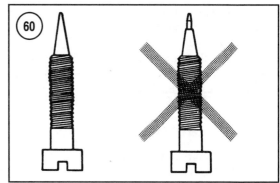

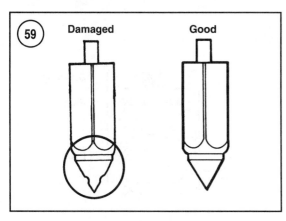

Damaged Good

pilot jet (C), and pilot screw (D). Make sure all holes and passages are clear. Clean them out if they are plugged in any way. Replace any jet or holder if it cannot be cleared.

4. Make sure all openings in the carburetor body are clear. Clean them out if they are plugged in any way.

5. Inspect the slide bore in the carburetor body. Make sure it is clean and free of any burrs or obstructions that may cause the piston valve to stick.

6. Inspect the piston valve for scoring and wear. Replace if necessary.

7. Inspect the diaphragm on the piston valve (D, **Figure 55**) for tears, cracks or other damage. If necessary, replace the piston valve.

8. Inspect the jet needle (C, **Figure 55**) for excessive wear at the tip or other damage.

9. Inspect the float (A, **Figure 58**) for deterioration or damage. Check for leaks by placing the float in a container of water. If the float sinks or if bubbles appear, replace the float.

NOTE
A worn needle valve and seat assembly can cause engine flooding. If there is any doubt about the condition of these parts, replace them as a set.

10. Inspect the needle valve assembly by performing the following:
   a. Inspect the end of the needle valve (B, **Figure 58**) for wear or damage. Refer to **Figure 59**.
   b. Check the inside of the valve seat (C, **Figure 58**). A particle of dirt or grit in the valve seat will cause the carburetor to flood.
   c. Inspect the valve seat O-ring for damage or hardness.
   d. If necessary, replace the needle valve assembly.

11. If removed, inspect the starter plunger (**Figure 54**) for wear or damage.

12. If removed, inspect the coasting enrichener diaphragm (**Figure 50**) for tears, cracks or other damage. Replace the diaphragm if any damage is found.

13. If removed, inspect the pilot screw (**Figure 60**) for wear or damage that may have occurred during

removal. If replacement is necessary, replace the pilot screws in both carburetors even if only one requires replacement.

14. Replace all O-rings during assembly. O-rings tend to harden after prolonged use and exposure to heat, which reduces their ability to seal properly.

Float Height Adjustment

The fuel shutoff valve and float maintain the fuel level in the float bowl.

1. Remove the carburetors.
2. Remove the float bowl and its O-ring.
3. Position the carburetors so the float bowl mating surfaces form a 45° angle with the floor, and the float tangs barely contact the needle valves.
4. Measure the distance from the float bowl mating surface to the top of the float (A, **Figure 61**). It should be within the float height range specified in **Table 1** or **Table 2**.
5. Adjust the float height by performing the following:
   a. Remove the pivot pin (A, **Figure 62**) from the float hinge and lift the float (B) from the float bowl. Watch for the needle valve hanging from the float tang.

   NOTE
   Decreasing the float height raises the fuel level; increasing float height lower fuel level.

   b. Carefully bend the float tang (**Figure 63**) to increase or decrease float height.
   c. Slide the needle valve onto the float tang and lower the float into the float bowl. Make sure the needle valve engages its seat.
   d. Install the pivot pin.
6. Make sure the O-ring is in place on the float bowl and install the bowl onto the carburetor.

PILOT SCREW

Removal/Installation

The pilot screw is preset and sealed with a plug to prevent adjustment. Routine adjustment is not required. However, if the carburetors were overhauled or if a pilot screw is incorrectly adjusted or damaged, adjust the screw as described.

1. Set a stop 6-mm (0.24 in.) from the end of a 1/8 inch drill bit (**Figure 64**).
2. Carefully drill a hole in the plug at the top of the pilot screw bore on the carburetor body. Do not drill too deeply. The pilot screw will be difficult to remove if the head is damaged.
3. Screw a sheet metal screw into the plug and pull

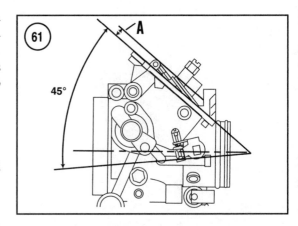

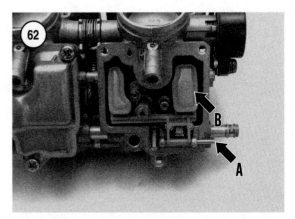

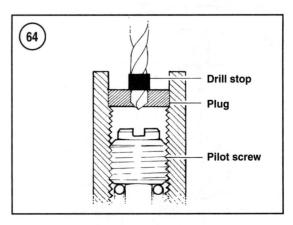

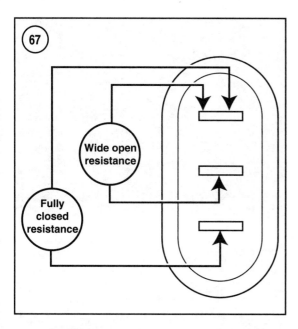

6. Inspect the O-ring and pilot screw end for wear grooves or damage. If necessary, replace the screw and/or O-ring.

7. Install the pilot screw assembly and turn the pilot screw until it *lightly* seats in the bore. Back the pilot screw out the number of turns noted during removal.

8. Install a new plug by tapping it into place with a punch.

9. Repeat this procedure for the other carburetor, if necessary. Make sure to keep each carburetor's parts separate.

THROTTLE POSITION (TP) SENSOR

Removal/Installation

The TP sensor is preset. Do not remove it unless necessary.

1. Remove the carburetors from the motorcycle as described in this chapter.

2. Draw indexing marks across the sensor body and the carburetor to mark the TP sensor's original installed position.

3. Remove the TP sensor screws (A, **Figure 66**) and remove the TP sensor (B). Note how the sensor engages the throttle valve shaft.

4. Reverse the removal procedures to install the TP sensor. Note the following:

   a. Make sure the sensor engages the throttle valve shaft.

   b. Position the sensor onto the carburetor so the indexing marks on the sensor align with those on the carburetor.

   c. Install the TP sensor screws (A, **Figure 66**) and tighten them to 3.5 N•m (31 in.-lb.).

   d. Adjust the sensor as described in this section.

Inspection/Adjustment

The TP sensor can be inspected with the carburetors installed. However, the carburetors must be removed to adjust the sensor.

1. Remove the carburetors from the motorcycle (this chapter).

2. With the throttle fully closed, measure the resistance between the two sensor terminals shown in **Figure 67**. Record the fully closed resistance.

   a. Replace the TP sensor if the fully closed resistance is outside the range specified in **Table 3**.

   b. If the resistance is within specification, continue with Step 3.

3. With the throttle wide open, measure the resistance across the two sensor terminals shown in **Figure 67**. Record the wide open resistance.

the plug from the bore.

4. While counting the number of turns, turn the pilot screw clockwise until it *lightly* seats in the bore. Record this number. Reinstall the pilot screw to this same position during assembly.

5. Remove the pilot screw, spring, washer, and O-ring from the carburetor body (**Figure 65**).

4. Compare the wide open resistance (Step 3) to the fully closed resistance (Step 2). The wide open resistance should be 76% of the fully closed resistance. For example, if the fully closed resistance equals 5 k ohms, the wide open resistance should equal 3.8 k ohms (0.76 × 5 k = 3.8 k).

5. If the wide open resistance is not 76% of the fully closed resistance, perform the following:

   a. Loosen the TP sensor screws (**Figure 66**).

   b. Slightly rotate the sensor and remeasure the wide open resistance (Step 4).

   c. Continue adjusting the sensor until the wide open resistance is 76% of the fully closed resistance.

   d. Tighten the TP sensor screws to 3.5 N•m (31 in.-lb.).

THROTTLE CABLE REPLACEMENT

The pull (or accelerator) cable and the return (or decelerator) cable are not the same. Label the cables before removing them. Replace both cables as a set.

1. Disconnect the negative battery cable (Chapter Ten).

2. Remove the air filter housing (this chapter).

3. Note the routing for the throttle cables from the right handlebar switch housing, through the fork legs and to the throttle wheel. Draw or photograph the routing, including any holders or cable ties.

4. At the throttle grip, loosen the return cable locknut (A, **Figure 68**) and turn the adjuster (B) all the way into the switch assembly to allow maximum slack in the cable. Repeat this procedure for the pull cable (C, **Figure 68**).

5A. On carbureted models, perform the following:

   a. At the carburetors, loosen both locknuts (A, **Figure 69**) on the return cable and disconnect the cable end (B) from the throttle wheel. Disengage the return cable from the throttle cable bracket.

   b. Repeat this on the pull cable.

5B. On fuel injected models, perform the following:

   a. At the throttle bodies, loosen the locknuts (A, **Figure 70**) on the return cable and disconnect the cable end from the throttle wheel. Disengage the return cable from the throttle cable bracket.

   b. Repeat this on the pull cable.

6. At the right handlebar switch, remove the screw (D, **Figure 68**) and lower the cable clamp from the switch housing.

7. Remove the switch housing screws (E, **Figure 68**) and separate the housing halves.

8. Disconnect each cable end (**Figure 71**) from the throttle drum and feed the cables through the housing half.

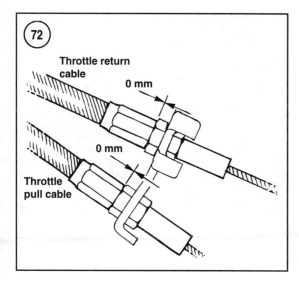

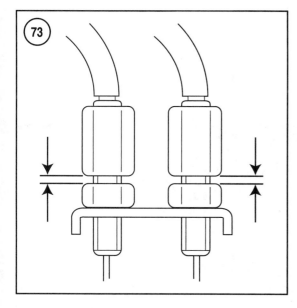

Figure 68). Make sure the clamp secures both cables in place.

13. Apply grease to the cable ends and connect each cable end to the throttle drum (**Figure 71**). Make sure each cable seats in the throttle drum channel.

14. Install the front switch half over the throttle drum and install the switch housing screws (E, **Figure 68**). Tighten the screws securely.

15. Apply grease to the ends of the throttle cables, connect the return cable end to the throttle wheel and fit the cable onto the bracket. Make sure a locknut (carbureted models: A, **Figure 69**; fuel injected models: A, **Figure 70**) sits on each side of the bracket.

16. Repeat Step 15, and install the pull cable. Make sure each cable seats in the throttle wheel channel.

17. Completely loosen both return cable locknuts (carbureted models: A, **Figure 69**; fuel injected models: A, **Figure 70**).

18A. On carbureted models, turn the cable adjuster (C, **Figure 69**) until the adjuster and the locknut rest against the bracket. There should be zero clearance between the adjuster and the forward locknut (**Figure 72**).

18B. On fuel injected models, turn the cable adjuster (B, **Figure 70**) until the clearance between the adjuster and the forward locknut equals 0-2 mm (0-0.08 in.). See **Figure 73**.

19. Tighten the locknuts.

20. Repeat Steps 17-19 for the pull cable.

21. Operate the throttle drum on the handlebar and make sure the throttle wheel operates correctly with no binding. If any drag or binding is noted, carefully check the cable for tight bends and correct installation.

22. Adjust the cable free play as described in Chapter Three.

23. Install the air filter housing.

WARNING
An improperly adjusted or incorrectly routed throttle cable can cause the throttle to remain open. Do not ride the motorcycle until throttle cable operation is correct.

24. Start the engine and let it idle. Turn the handlebar from side to side and listen to the engine speed. Make sure the idle speed does not increase. If necessary, adjust the cable or correct the cable routing.

STARTER CABLE REPLACEMENT (1998-2004 MODELS)

1. Securely support the motorcycle on a level surface.

2. Remove the steering head cover, upper covers, and meter cover (Chapter Fifteen).

CAUTION
Do not lubricate nylon-lined cables. Nylon-lined cables generally function without lubricant. Most cable lubricants will cause the liner to expand, which will pinch the liner against the cable. When installing nylon-lined or other aftermarket cables, follow the cable manufacturer's instructions.

9. Lubricate the new cables as described in Chapter Three. Do not lubricate cables with nylon liners.

10. Route the new cables along the same path as the old cables.

11. At the right handlebar switch, feed the return cable through the lower port in the switch housing.

12. Feed the pull cable through the upper port in the housing. Slide the cable clamp against the bottom of the switch housing and install the screw (D,

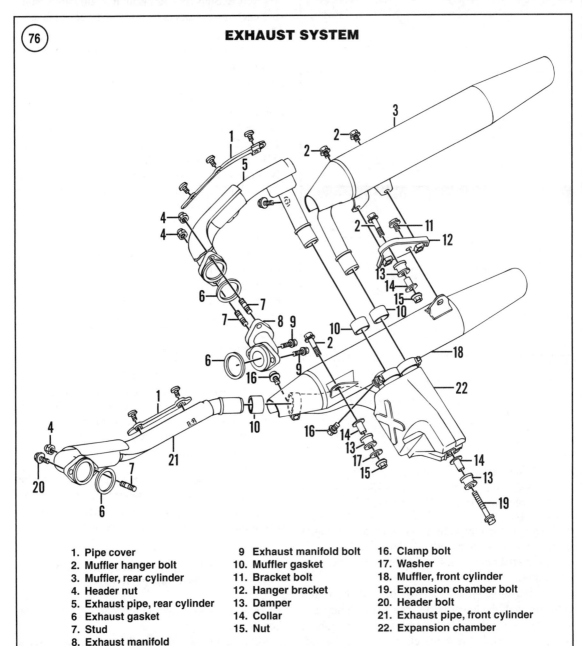

EXHAUST SYSTEM

1. Pipe cover
2. Muffler hanger bolt
3. Muffler, rear cylinder
4. Header nut
5. Exhaust pipe, rear cylinder
6. Exhaust gasket
7. Stud
8. Exhaust manifold
9. Exhaust manifold bolt
10. Muffler gasket
11. Bracket bolt
12. Hanger bracket
13. Damper
14. Collar
15. Nut
16. Clamp bolt
17. Washer
18. Muffler, front cylinder
19. Expansion chamber bolt
20. Header bolt
21. Exhaust pipe, front cylinder
22. Expansion chamber

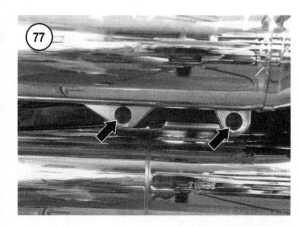

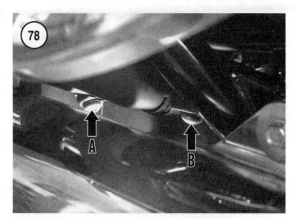

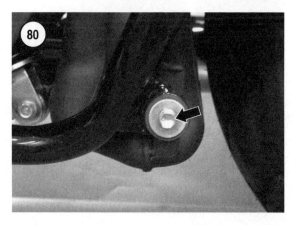

3. Remove the air filter housing and perform Steps 1-7 of *Carburetor Removal* (this chapter). Note the starter cable routing.

4. Disconnect the starter cable end (**Figure 74**) from the starter bracket.

5. Remove the rider's seat bolts (A, **Figure 75**) from the left side. Then pull the starter knob/cable assembly (B) from the motorcycle.

6. Installation is the reverse of removal. Note the following:

    a. Apply grease to the cable end.

    b. Install the cable along the route noted during removal.

EXHAUST SYSTEM

Removal

Refer to **Figure 76**.

1. Securely support the motorcycle on a level surface.

2. Remove rear muffler hanger bolts (**Figure 77**).

3. Loosen the rear muffler clamp bolt (A, **Figure 78**) at the rear port on the expansion chamber.

4. Disengage the muffler pipe from the expansion chamber and remove the rear muffler. Watch for the muffler gasket at the expansion chamber.

5. Remove the header nuts (**Figure 79**) from the rear cylinder exhaust pipe.

6. Loosen the rear exhaust pipe clamp bolt (B, **Figure 78**) at the front port on the expansion chamber.

7. Disengage the rear exhaust pipe from the front port in the expansion chamber and remove the rear cylinder exhaust pipe. Watch for the exhaust gasket at the manifold port and the muffler gasket at the expansion chamber port.

8. Remove the exhaust chamber bolt (**Figure 80**) from the left side. Watch for the damper and collar in this mount.

9. Remove the header nut (A, **Figure 81**) and header bolt (B) from the front exhaust pipe header.

10. Remove the nut and washer from the front hanger on the front muffler. Then pull the hanger bolt (**Figure 82**) out. Watch for the washer, collar and damper in the frame mount.

11. Remove the nut from the hanger bolt on the front muffler bracket. Then remove the hanger bolt (A, **Figure 83**) Watch for the collar and damper.

12. Disengage the exhaust pipe from the exhaust port on the front cylinder and remove the front exhaust pipe/muffler assembly. Watch for the exhaust gasket.

13. Remove the bracket bolt (B, **Figure 83**). Then remove the bracket (C, **Figure 83**) from the front muffler.

14. Loosen the front muffler clamp bolt (**Figure 84**). Then remove the muffler from the front exhaust pipe (**Figure 85**). Watch for the muffler gasket.

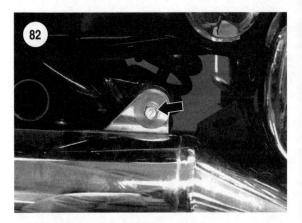

Installation

1. Apply Permatex 1372 to two new muffler gaskets. Install a gasket into the front (A, **Figure 86**) and rear ports (B) in the expansion chamber.

2. If the front muffler was removed from the front exhaust pipe, perform the following:

   a. Apply Permatex 1372 to a new muffler gasket and slide the gasket onto the front port on the front muffler.

   b. Slide the front exhaust pipe end into the front muffler (**Figure 85**).

   c. Finger-tighten the muffler clamp bolt.

3. Fit the bracket (C, **Figure 83**) in front of the hanger bracket on the front muffler and loosely install the bracket bolt (B).

4. Install a new exhaust gasket into the front cylinder exhaust port.

5. Fit the front exhaust pipe/muffler assembly into place. Install the following hardware.

   a. Loosely install the exhaust header nut (A, **Figure 81**) and bolt (B).

   b. Install the hanger bolt (A, **Figure 83**) through the muffler bracket and frame mount. Loosely install the washer and nut onto the bolt. Make sure the collar and damper are in place in the frame mount.

   c. Install the front muffler hanger bolt (**Figure 82**). Make sure the collar and damper are in place in the frame mount. Loosely install the hanger nut.

   d. Install and finger-tighten the expansion chamber bolt (**Figure 80**). Make sure a damper and collar are in place in the frame mount.

6. Install a new exhaust gasket into the rear cylinder exhaust manifold.

7. Insert the end of the rear exhaust pipe into the front port in the expansion chamber and hang the exhaust pipe from the exhaust manifold studs.

8. Install and finger-tighten the exhaust header nuts (**Figure 79**) on the exhaust manifold studs.

9. Evenly tighten all the mounting hardware installed to this point but do not tighten to final specification yet.

10. In the following order, tighten the hardware to the specifications in **Table 4**:

   a. Header bolts and nuts on the front (A and B, **Figure 81**), and rear cylinders (**Figure 79**).

   b. Bracket bolt (B, **Figure 83**), bracket hanger bolt/nut (A), and the expansion chamber bolt (**Figure 80**).

   c. Front muffler hanger bolt/nut (**Figure 82**) on the front muffler.

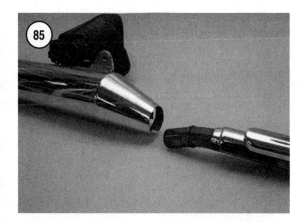

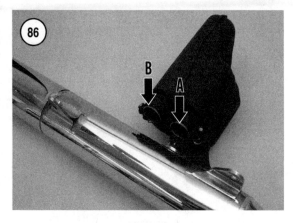

d. Front muffler clamp bolt (**Figure 84**).

e. Rear exhaust pipe clamp bolt (B, **Figure 78**) at the front port on the expansion chamber.

11. Insert the rear muffler pipe into the rear port on the expansion chamber.

12. Install the two muffler hanger bolts (**Figure 77**) into the weld nuts on the muffler bracket.

13. Tighten the muffler hanger bolts to 23 N•m (17 ft.-lb.).

14. Tighten the rear muffler clamp bolt (A, **Figure 78**) at the rear port on the expansion chamber to 23 N•m (17 ft.-lb.).

EVAPORATIVE EMISSIONS CONTROL SYSTEM (CALIFORNIA MODELS)

WARNING
The evaporative emission control system stores fuel vapors. Do not smoke or work around ignition sources.

California models are equipped with an evaporative emission control system (EVAP), which consists of a charcoal canister, fuel shutoff valve, tank pressure control valve, assorted hoses, and modified carburetors and fuel tank (**Figure 87**).

The EVAP system captures fuel tank vapor and stores them in the charcoal canister. When the motorcycle is ridden, these vapors are routed to the carburetors and drawn into the engine where they are burned.

Maintenance/Service

Inspect the hoses for damage and replace any if necessary. If system components require removal, label the hoses and connection points for reference during reassembly. On most models, the hoses and fittings are color coded with labels or bands. Due to model variances, refer to the vacuum hose routing label (**Figure 88**) inside the outer toolbox cover for specifics.

Canister Replacement

The EVAP canister mounts to the right side of the frame. Replace the canister by following the procedures described in *Catch Tank Removal/Installation* (this chapter).

8

Carburetor Surge Control Valve Removal/ Testing/Installation (1999-2004 Models)

1. Remove the meter cover, steering head covers, and upper covers (Chapter Fifteen).

2. Remove the air box (this chapter).

3. Disconnect each hose from the four fittings on the surge control valve (**Figure 89**). Label each hose and its fitting.

4. Remove the surge control valve.

5. Test the carburetor surge control valve as follows:

   a. Connect a hand-operated vacuum pump to the vacuum port on the valve (A, **Figure 90**).

   b. Operate the vacuum pump until the applied vacuum equals the surge control valve test vacuum specified in **Table 3**.

   c. Blow into the vent port (B, **Figure 90**) on the valve. Air should emerge from the valve's carburetor port (C, **Figure 90**).

   d. By hand or with a plug, seal the valve's carburetor port (C, **Figure 90**).

   e. Operate the vacuum pump until the applied vacuum equals the surge control valve test vacuum specified in **Table 3**.

   f. Blow into the vent port (B, **Figure 90**) on the valve. Air should emerge from the valve's canister port (D, **Figure 90**).

   g. Replace the carburetor surge control valve if it fails either portion of this test.

6. Install the carburetor surge control valve by reversing the removal procedures. Connect each hose to its original fitting on the valve.

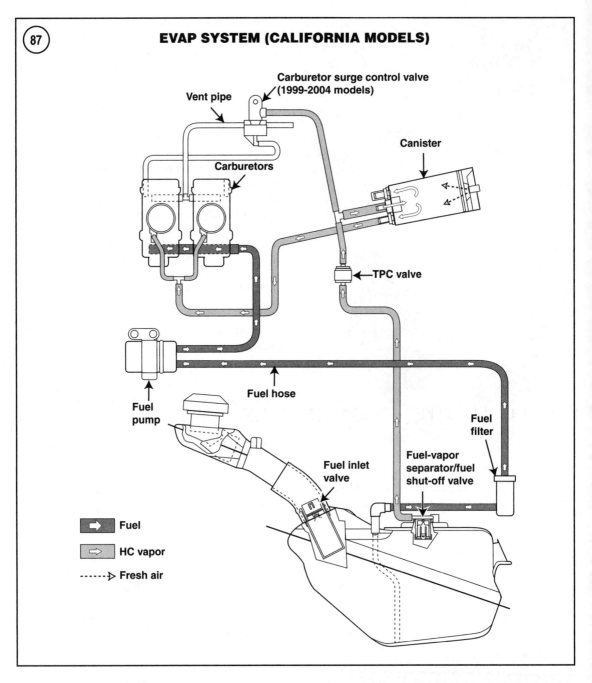

EVAP SYSTEM (CALIFORNIA MODELS)

Carburetor surge control valve
(1999-2004 models)

Vent pipe

Canister

Carburetors

TPC valve

Fuel hose

Fuel
pump

Fuel
filter

Fuel-vapor
separator/fuel
shut-off valve

Fuel inlet
valve

Fuel

HC vapor

Fresh air

ENGINE SIDE BOX

The engine side box is on the right side of the engine. On PAIR-equipped models, the control valve is inside this box.

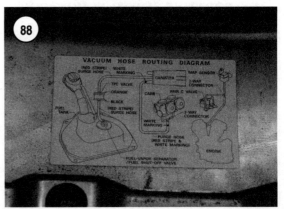

Removal/Installation

1. Remove the cover bolt (A, **Figure 91**) and lower the cover (B) from the engine side box.
2. On models with the PAIR system, remove the PAIR valve as described in this chapter.
3. Remove the engine side box bolts and their

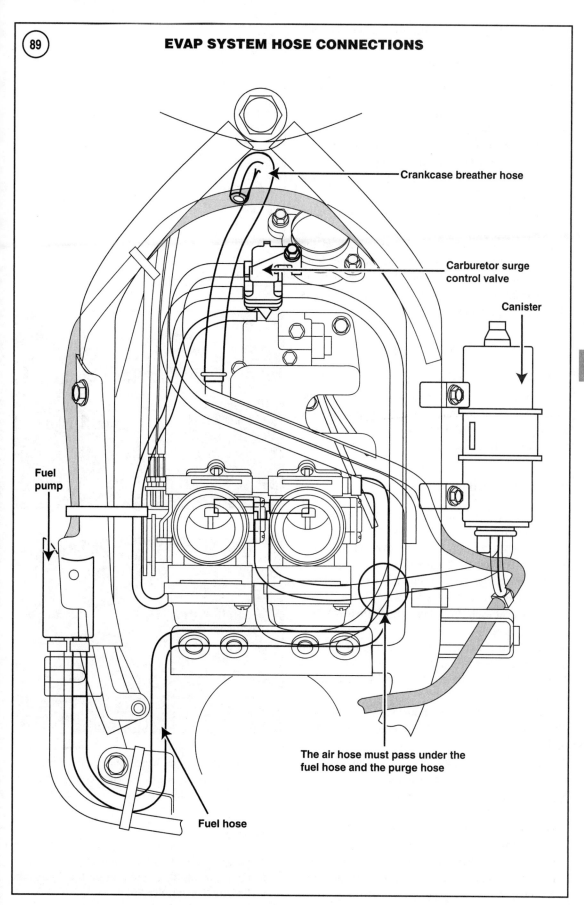

EVAP SYSTEM HOSE CONNECTIONS

Crankcase breather hose

Carburetor surge control valve

Canister

Fuel pump

The air hose must pass under the fuel hose and the purge hose

Fuel hose

washers (A, **Figure 92**). Note the damper in each mount.

4. Pull the side box from the engine. Watch for the heat shield behind the side box. On models with the PAIR system, remove the vacuum hose (B, **Figure 92**) and the air filter housing hose (C) from their ports. Remove the side box.

5. Install the engine side box by reversing the removal procedures. Note the following:

a. Install the heat guard behind the engine side box.

b. Include a damper and washer with each engine side box bolt.

c. On models with the PAIR system, feed the vacuum hose (B, **Figure 92**) and air filter housing hose (C) through the correct ports in the side box. Install the PAIR control valve as described in this chapter.

PAIR SYSTEM

The PAIR system (**Figure 93**) consists of the PAIR control valve, two reed valves, a vacuum hose and outlet hoses. The system uses momentary pressure variations created by exhaust gas pulses to introduce fresh air into the exhaust ports.

Removal/Installation

Label the each hose and fitting so they can be reinstalled correctly.

1. Remove the cover bolt (A, **Figure 91**) and lower the cover (B) from the engine side box.

2. Disconnect the PAIR vacuum hose (A, **Figure 94**) from the front of the PAIR control valve.

3. Disconnect each PAIR hose (B, **Figure 94**) from the PAIR valve.

4. Remove the mounting bolts (C, **Figure 94**) and their washers. Note the damper in each mount.

5. Partially remove the PAIR control valve from the engine side box.

6. Disconnect the air filter housing hose (C, **Figure 92**) from the back of the PAIR control valve and remove the valve.

7. Remove the mounting nuts (A, **Figure 95**) and remove each PAIR pipe (B) from its cylinder.

8. Install the PAIR system by reversing the removal procedures. Note the following:

a. Make sure a damper is in place in the housing mounts.

b. Install a washer with each housing bolt.

c. Fit the heat shield in place behind the housing.

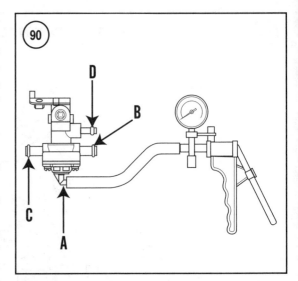

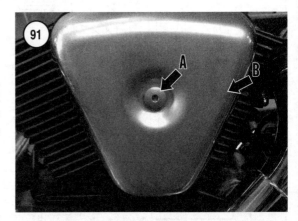

d. If the PAIR pipes were removed from each cylinder, use a new gasket when connecting each pipe to its cylinder.

Inspection

1. Inspect the PAIR valve as follows:

a. Blow air into the input port on the rear of the PAIR valve (**Figure 96**).

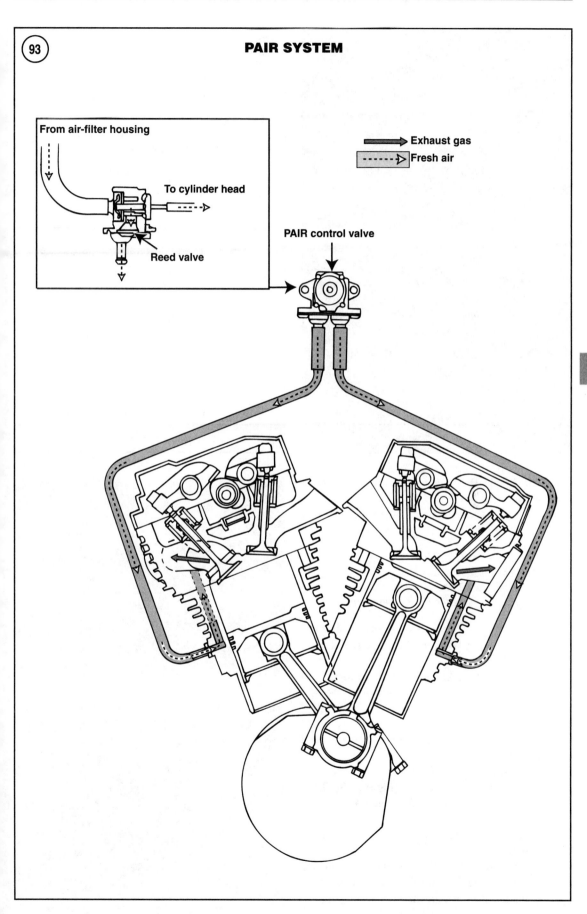

PAIR SYSTEM

93

From air-filter housing

To cylinder head

Reed valve

Exhaust gas

Fresh air

PAIR control valve

8

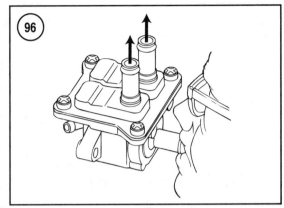

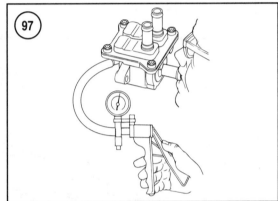

b. Air should flow from the two control-valve output ports.

c. Connect a vacuum pump to the vacuum fitting on the front of the PAIR valve (**Figure 97**).

CAUTION
*Do not exceed the specified vacuum (**Table 3**) during this test. Excessive vacuum can damage the PAIR control valve.*

d. Slowly apply vacuum to the PAIR valve until the vacuum is within the range specified in **Table 3**.

e. Blow into the PAIR control valve input port (**Figure 97**). Air should not flow from the output ports when the specified vacuum is applied to the valve.

f. Replace the PAIR valve if it fails either portion of this test.

2. Inspect the reed valve as follows:

a. Remove the cover screws (**Figure 98**). Then lift the reed valve cover from the PAIR control valve.

b. Remove each reed valve from its housing (**Figure 99**).

c. Inspect the reed valve for carbon deposits. Replace the PAIR control valve if the reeds are damaged or have deposits.

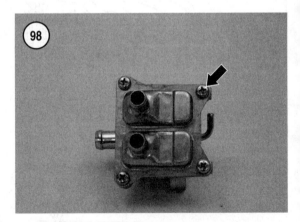

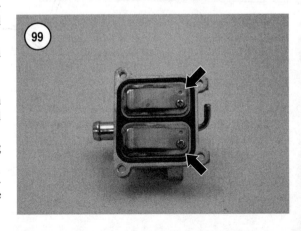

Table 1 CARBURETOR SPECIFICATIONS (1998-2000 MODELS)

Item	Front cylinder	Rear cylinder
Carburetor type	BDSR36	BDSR36
Bore size	36.5 mm (1.44 in.)	36.5 mm (1.44 in.)
ID No.		
U.S. and Canada models	10F1	10F1
California models	10F4	
1998 models	10F4	10F4
1999-2000 models	10F7	10F7
U.K. models	10F0	10F0
Float height	6.5-7.5 mm (0.26-0.30 in.)	6.5-7.5 mm (0.26-0.30 in.)
Jet needle		
U.S., California and Canada models	5D95-56	5E9-56
All models except U.S., California and Canada	5D94-56-3	5E8-56-3
Main jet*		
U.S., California and Canada models	*#112.5*	*#110*
All models except U.S., California and Canada	#112.5	#110
Needle jet*		
U.S., California and Canada models	*P-0M*	*P-0M*
All models except U.S., California and Canada	P-0	P-0
Pilot jet*		
U.S., California and Canada models	*#32.5*	*#32.5*
All models except U.S., California and Canada	#32.5	#32.5
Pilot screw		
U.S., California and Canada models	Preset	Preset
U.K. models	2 turns out	2 turns out
Throttle valve	#90	#90

*Some main, pilot and needle jets are machined to closer tolerances than their standard counterparts. The closer tolerance jets appear in italic. Do not install standard jets in place of the closer tolerance jets.

Table 2 CARBURETOR SPECIFICATIONS (2001-2004 MODELS)

Item	Front cylinder	Rear cylinder
Carburetor type	BDSR36	BDSR36
Bore size	36.5 mm (1.44 in.)	36.5 mm (1.44 in.)
ID No.		
U.S. and Canada models	10F1	10F1
California models	10F7	10F7
U.K. and Europe models	10F9	10F9
Float height	6.5-7.5 mm (0.26-0.30 in.)	6.5-7.5 mm (0.26-0.30 in.)
Jet needle		
U.S., California and Canada models	5D95-56	5E9-56
U.K. and Europe models	5D124-3	5E19-3
Main jet*		
U.S., California and Canada models	*#112.5*	*#110*
All models except U.S., California and Canada	#112.5	#110
Needle jet*		
U.S., California and Canada models	*P-0M*	*P-0M*
U.K. and Europe models	P-0M	P-0M
Pilot jet*		
U.S., California and Canada models	*#32.5*	*#32.5*
All models except U.S., California and Canada	#32.5	#32.5
Pilot screw		
U.S. and California models	Preset	Preset
Canada models	2 1/4 turns out	2 1/8 turns out
U.K. and Europe models	1 3/4 turns out	1 3/8 turns out
Throttle valve	#90	#90

* Some main, pilot and needle jets are machined to closer tolerances than their standard counterparts. The closer tolerance jets appear in italic. Do not install standard jets in place of the closer tolerance jets.

8

Table 3 FUEL SYSTEM SPECIFICATIONS

Idle speed	
1998-2000 models	900-1100 rpm
2001-2004 models	900-1100 rpm
Fuel pump output volume	More than 600 ml (1.27 pt.) per minute
Fuel pump resistance	1-2.5 ohms
Fuel tank capacity (including reserve)	
1998-1999 models	15.5 liters (4.1 U.S. gal.)
2000-2004	15.0 liters (4.0 U.S. gal.)
Fuel octane	
U.S., California and Canada models	
Pump octane: (R+M) / 2	87
Research octane	91
All models except U.S., California and Canada	
1998 models	85-95
1999-2004 models	91
PAIR control valve vacuum	30.7-40 kPa (230-300 mm Hg)
Surge control valve test vacuum	
1999-2004 California models	2.7 kPa (20 mm Hg)
Throttle cable free play	2.0-4.0 mm (0.08-0.16 in.)
Throttle position sensor	
Fully closed resistance	3.5-6.5 k ohms

Table 4 FUEL AND EXHAUST SYSTEM TORQUE SPECIFICATIONS

Item	N•m	in.-lb.	ft.-lb.
Expansion chamber bolt	23	–	17
Exhaust header bolt/nut	23	–	17
Frame bolt	50	–	37
Fuel inlet hose clamp	2	18	–
Fuel level sender mounting bolt	4	35	–
Fuel shutoff valve bolt	4	35	–
Grab rail bolt			
8 mm	13	115	–
10 mm	50	–	37
Muffler bracket bolt/nut	23	–	17
Muffler bracket hanger bolt/nut	23	–	17
Muffler/exhaust pipe clamp bolt	23	–	17
Muffler hanger bolt/nut	23	–	17
Throttle position sensor screw	3.5	31	–

FUEL INJECTION SYSTEM

9

This chapter covers the fuel injection system and emission systems specific to fuel injected models. Refer to Chapter Eight for air filter housing, fuel tank, throttle cable replacement, and exhaust system procedures that are the same on both carbureted and fuel injected machines.

During inspection, compare measurements to the specifications at the end of this chapter.

FUEL TANK

Refer to Chapter Eight.

FUEL PUMP

During removal/installation, the fuel pump must be carefully tilted and turned so it will not strike the internal baffles in the fuel tank. This can be difficult due to the pump's shape and long float arm (**Figure 1**).

Refer to **Figure 2**.

Removal/Installation

1. Disconnect the negative battery cable (Chapter Ten).
2. Remove the seats, steering head covers, meter cover, and left upper cover (Chapter Fifteen).
3. Disconnect the fuel hose (**Figure 3**) from the fuel pump. Be prepared to catch residual gasoline from the hose.
4. Disconnect the 3-pin fuel pump connector (A, **Figure 4**).
5. In a crisscross pattern, evenly loosen and remove the fuel pump bolts (B, **Figure 4**).
6. Remove the fuel pump as follows:
   a. Lift the rear of the pump mounting plate (**Figure 5**). Rotate the plate 90° counterclockwise and lift the pump plate until the pressure regulator (**Figure 6**) emerges from the fuel tank.
   b. Rotate the assembly approximately 35° counterclockwise around the tank opening.

c. Lift the pump mounting plate until the fuel filter (**Figure 7**) emerges from the tank.

d. Tilt the assembly so the pump mounting plate parallels the floor (**Figure 8**).

e. Rotate the entire assembly 90° counterclockwise around the tank opening (**Figure 9**).

f. Lift the assembly until the clamp (**Figure 10**) on the fuel pump emerges from the tank and remove the pump (**Figure 11**). Watch for the float arm (**Figure 1**) on the plate assembly.

7. Install the fuel pump by reversing the removal procedures. Note the following:

a. Install a new O-ring (**Figure 12**) into the pump mount on the fuel tank. Lubricate the O-ring with grease.

b. Apply Suzuki Thread Lock 1342 to the threads of the fuel pump bolts (B, **Figure 4**). Evenly tighten the fuel pump bolts in a crisscross pattern to 10 N•m (89 in.-lb.).

Disassembly

1. Remove the screw (A, **Figure 13**) and separate the fuel pump holder (B) from the plate assembly.

2. Remove the damper (**Figure 14**) from the pump.

3. Disconnect the 2-pin fuel pump connector (**Figure 15**).

4. Remove the clamp screw (A, **Figure 16**) and the clamp band (B).

5. Pull the fuel pump cartridge until the pump fitting (A, **Figure 17**) disengages from the port (A, **Figure 18**) in the plate assembly. Watch for the plastic collar (B, **Figure 17**) on the pump fitting.

6. Remove the grommet (B. **Figure 18**) from the plate assembly port. Note that the end of the grommet with the large hole faces out.

7. Inspect the intake filter (C, **Figure 17**) on the pump cartridge. If necessary, clear the filter with compressed air. If it cannot be cleared, replace the fuel pump cartridge.

Assembly

1. Lubricate a new grommet (B, **Figure 18**) with engine oil and press it into the port (A) in the plate assembly. The end of the grommet with the large hole must face out.

2. Make sure the plastic collar (B, **Figure 17**) on the fuel pump fitting sits flat and points to the electrical connector.

3. Set the pump cartridge on the plate assembly. Slide the fuel pump fitting (A, **Figure 17**) into the grommet in the assembly port (A, **Figure 18**). Press the fuel pump up against the plate assembly until the collar (C, **Figure 16**) bottoms against the grommet.

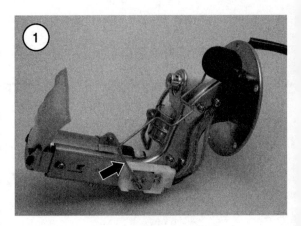

4. Fit the clamp (B, **Figure 16**) into place around the pump and tighten the clamp screw (A).

5. Plug the 2-pin connector (**Figure 15**) into the fuel pump cartridge.

6. Install the damper (**Figure 19**) onto the fuel pump.

7. Slide the pump holder (B, **Figure 13**) between the fuel pump cartridge and the plate assembly. Make sure the cutouts in the holder engage the tabs on the damper in the pump holder.

8. Install the plate screw (A, **Figure 13**).

Fuel Pressure Test

Tools

The following Suzuki tools or their equivalents are needed to perform this test:

1. Fuel pressure gauge adapter (part No. 09940-40211).

2. Fuel pressure gauge hose attachment (part No. 09940-40220).

3. Oil pressure gauge (part No. 00915-77331).

Procedure

1. Remove the seats, steering head covers, meter cover, and the left upper cover (Chapter Fifteen).

2. Disconnect the fuel hose (**Figure 3**) from the fuel pump. Be prepared to catch residual gasoline leaking from the hose.

3. Use the adapters to install the gauge inline between the fuel pump and the fuel rail. Follow the tool manufacturer's instructions. See **Figure 20**.

4. Turn the ignition switch on and read the fuel pressure. It should equal the fuel pump output pressure specified in **Table 1**.

5. If fuel pressure is less than specified, check for a leak in the fuel system, a clogged fuel filter, faulty pressure regulator or faulty fuel pump.

6. If the fuel pressure exceeds specification:

FUEL PUMP

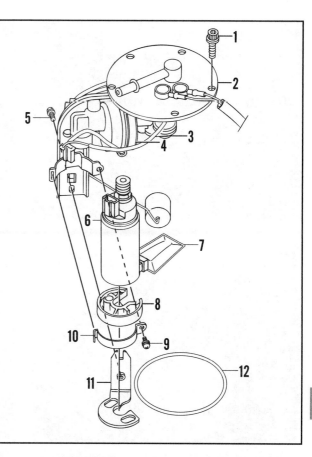

1. Plate assembly bolt
2. Plate assembly
3. Pressure regulator
4. Fuel filter
5. Fuel pump bolt
6. Fuel pump cartridge
7. Intake filter
8. Damper
9. Clamp screw
10. Clamp
11. Fuel pump holder
12. O-ring

9

a. Inspect the check valve on the fuel tank. If the
   check valve is damaged or clogged, replace it.
b. If the check valve is in working order, replace
   the fuel pump assembly.

Operation Test

1. Turn the ignition switch on and listen for fuel
pump operation.
2. If no sound is heard, test the fuel pump relay and
the tip over sensor as described in this chapter. If
both of these components are within specification,
replace the fuel pump assembly.

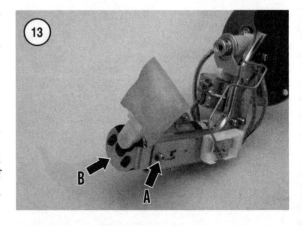

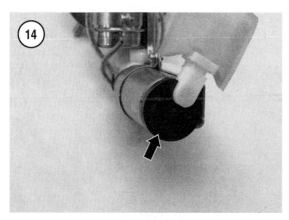

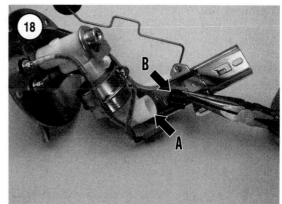

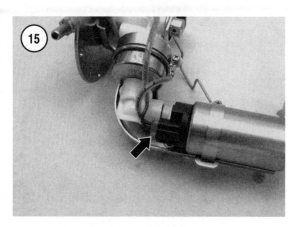

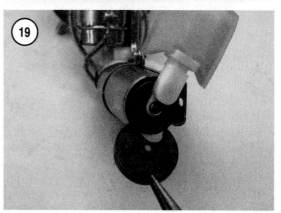

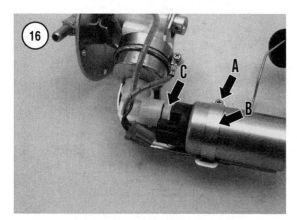

9

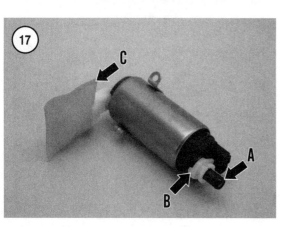

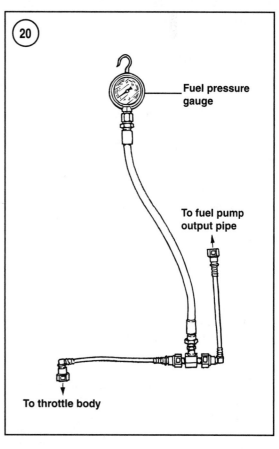

Fuel pressure gauge

To fuel pump output pipe

To throttle body

Discharge Test

1. Remove the seats, meter cover, left steering head cover, and left upper cover (Chapter Fifteen).
2. Disconnect the fuel hose (**Figure 21**) from the fuel rail. Be prepared to catch residual fuel leaking from the hose.
3. Insert the hose into a graduated cylinder.
4. Disconnect the 3-pin fuel pump connector (A, **Figure 4**).
5. Operate the pump for ten seconds by performing the following:
   a. Use a jumper wire to connect the positive battery terminal to the yellow/red wire in the pump side of the fuel pump connector. Connect the negative battery terminal to the connector's black/white terminal (pump side) with another jumper wire.
   b. The pump should operate. Collect the fuel in the graduated cylinder.
   c. After 10 seconds, disconnect the jumpers from the pump terminals.
6. Measure the amount of fuel discharged into the graduated cylinder. It should equal the fuel pump output volume specified in **Table 1**.
7. If the discharged fuel is less than the output volume, remove the fuel pump and inspect the intake filter. Clear the filter with compressed air. If the filter cannot be cleared, replace the fuel pump cartridge.

FUEL PUMP RELAY

Removal/Installation

1. Remove the left upper cover (Chapter Fifteen).
2. Disconnect the negative battery cable.
3. Pull the fuel pump relay (**Figure 22**) straight up and remove its rubber mount from the mounting tang.
4. Disconnect the 4-pin connector from the relay.
5. Install the relay by reversing the removal procedures. Make sure the rubber mount securely engages the mounting tang.

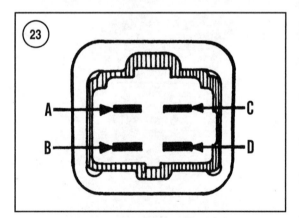

Test

1. Remove the fuel pump relay (this section).
2. Check the continuity between the A and B terminals on the relay (**Figure 23**). The relay should not have continuity.
3. Use a jumper wire to connect the positive terminal of a 12 volt battery to the C terminal on the relay (**Figure 23**). Connect the negative battery terminal to the D relay terminal with another jumper wire.
4. Check the continuity between the A and B relay

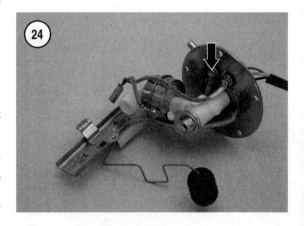

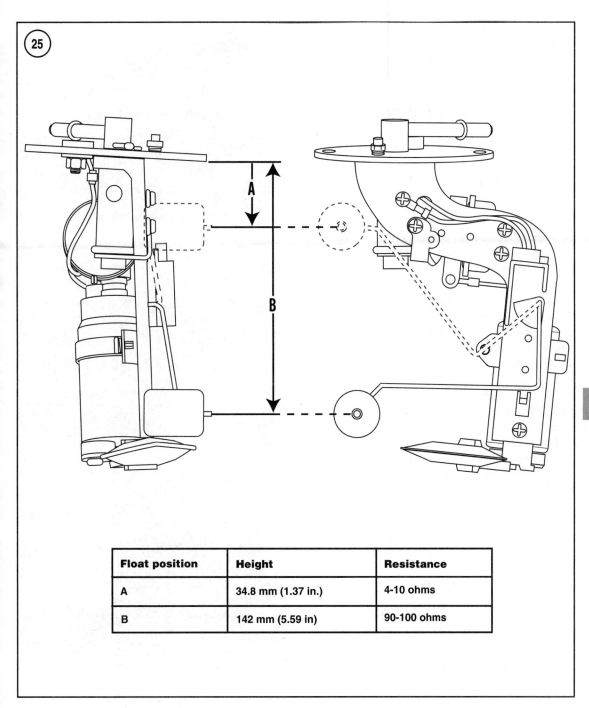

Float position	Height	Resistance
A	34.8 mm (1.37 in.)	4-10 ohms
B	142 mm (5.59 in)	90-100 ohms

terminals. The relay should have continuity when voltage is applied.

5. Replace the relay if it fails either portion of this test.

FUEL LEVEL SENDER

Removal/Installation

The fuel level sender is an integral part of the fuel pump plate assembly (**Figure 24**). If the fuel level sender must be replaced, disassemble the fuel pump (this chapter) and install a new plate assembly.

Resistance Test

1. Remove the fuel pump (this chapter).

2. Position the fuel pump so its mounting plate parallels the floor (**Figure 25**).

3. Connect an ohmmeter test probes to the red/black terminal (**Figure 24**) and the black/white terminal (C, **Figure 4**) in the plate assembly.

4. Move the float to positions A and B shown in **Figure 25**, and measure the resistance.

5. The sender is faulty if the resistance at either float position is outside the specified range.

AIR FILTER HOUSING

Refer to Chapter Eight.

THROTTLE BODIES

Removal

1. Remove the air filter housing (Chapter Eight).

2. Disconnect the fuel line (**Figure 21**) from the fuel rail. Be prepared to catch any fuel that leaks from the hose.

3. Disconnect the vacuum hose (A, **Figure 26**) from the rear cylinder intake air pressure (IAP) sensor (B), and the hose (A, **Figure 27**) from the front cylinder IAP sensor (B). Label each hose and its respective fitting.

4. Disconnect the 4-pin secondary throttle valve actuator connector (C, **Figure 27**).

5. On California models, disconnect the hose (D, **Figure 27**) from the lower fitting on the EVAP canister.

6. Disconnect the 3-pin secondary throttle position sensor connector (A, **Figure 28**).

7. Disconnect each 2-pin fuel injector connector (B, **Figure 28**).

8. Loosen the clamp screw (**Figure 29**) on each intake manifold clamp.

9. Lift the throttle bodies and disengage each body from its intake manifold. Set the assembly on the engine.

10. Disconnect the 3-pin throttle position sensor connector (**Figure 30**).

11. Loosen the locknut (A, **Figure 31**) and disconnect the pull cable end (B) from the throttle wheel. Label the cable for identification.

12. Repeat Step 11, and disconnect the return cable from the throttle wheel.

13. Remove the throttle bodies. Cover each intake manifold to keep debris out of the engine.

Installation

1. Rotate each throttle body clamp so the clamp screw faces the outboard side of its intake manifold.

2. Lubricate each intake manifold with a soap solution.

3. Set the throttle bodies onto the engine so the throttle wheel faces the left side.

4. Connect each throttle cable to the throttle wheel by performing the following:

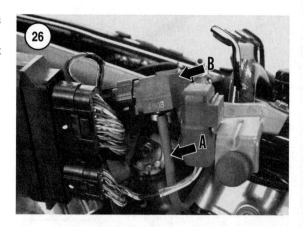

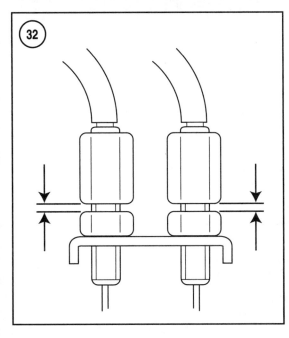

c. Repeat substep b, and connect the return cable to the throttle wheel and bracket.

d. Set each cable to its initial setting by turning the cable adjuster (C, **Figure 31**) until the clearance between the adjuster and forward locknut (A) equals 0-2 mm (0-0.08 in.) as shown in **Figure 32**. Tighten the rear locknut (D, **Figure 31**) against the bracket.

5. Connect the 3-pin throttle position sensor connector (**Figure 30**).

6. Position the assembly so each throttle body sits on its intake manifold and press the throttle bodies into place. A solid bottoming will be felt when the throttle bodies are completely seated in the manifolds.

7. Tighten the manifold clamp screws (**Figure 29**) securely.

8. Connect each 2-pin fuel injector connector (B, **Figure 28**), and connect the 3-pin secondary throttle position sensor connector (A).

9. Connect the 4-pin secondary throttle valve actuator connector (C, **Figure 27**).

10. On California models, connect the hose (D, **Figure 27**) to the EVAP canister.

11. Connect the vacuum hose (A, **Figure 26**) to the rear cylinder IAP sensor (B), and the hose (A, **Figure 27**) to the front cylinder IAP sensor (B).

12. Connect the fuel line (**Figure 21**) from the fuel rail.

13. Adjust the throttle cable free play (Chapter Three).

14. Install the air filter housing (Chapter Eight).

Disassembly

Refer to **Figure 33**.

1. Remove the throttle bodies and set the assembly on the bench so it intake manifold side faces up.

2. Remove the fuel delivery hose screw (**Figure 34**) and disconnect the fuel delivery hose (**Figure 35**) from the fuel rail fitting.

3. Turn the assembly over so the air box side faces up.

4. Remove the fuel rail screws (A, **Figure 36**). Lift the fuel rail (B, **Figure 36**) until it separates from its fuel injector and remove the fuel rail. Watch for the fuel injector O-ring (A, **Figure 37**). Note that the locating tab (B, **Figure 37**) on the injector is centered in the throttle body cutout (A, **Figure 38**).

5. Remove the fuel injector from its port in the throttle body (**Figure 39**). Watch for the fuel injector damper (C, **Figure 37**). It could come out with the injector or it may remain behind in the throttle body port.

6. Repeat Steps 2-5, and remove the fuel rail and injector from the other throttle body.

a. Apply grease to the end of each cable.

b. Connect the pull cable end (B, **Figure 31**) to the throttle wheel. Fit the cable onto the bracket so a locknut sits on each side of the bracket. Make sure the inner cable sits in the throttle wheel channel.

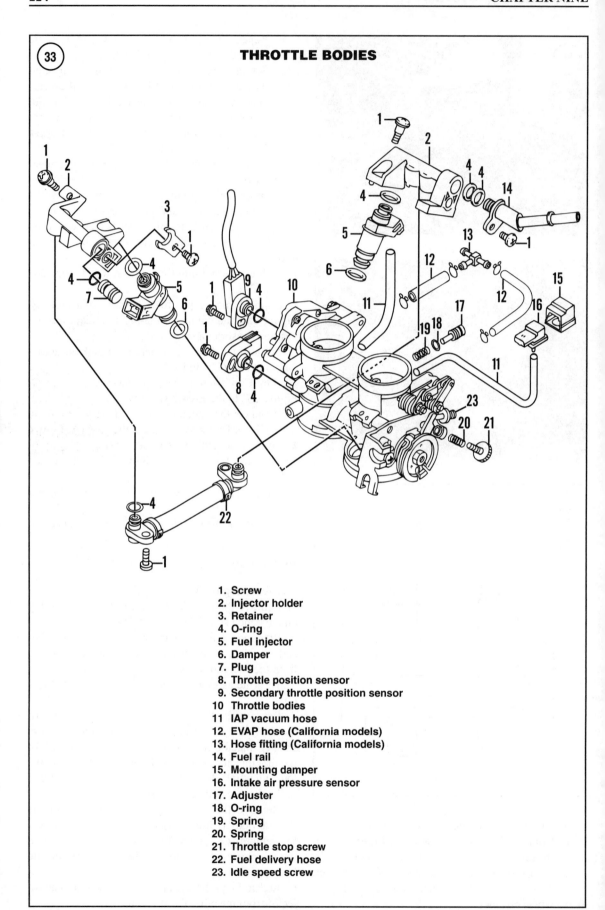

33 THROTTLE BODIES

1. Screw
2. Injector holder
3. Retainer
4. O-ring
5. Fuel injector
6. Damper
7. Plug
8. Throttle position sensor
9. Secondary throttle position sensor
10. Throttle bodies
11. IAP vacuum hose
12. EVAP hose (California models)
13. Hose fitting (California models)
14. Fuel rail
15. Mounting damper
16. Intake air pressure sensor
17. Adjuster
18. O-ring
19. Spring
20. Spring
21. Throttle stop screw
22. Fuel delivery hose
23. Idle speed screw

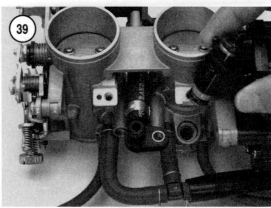

9

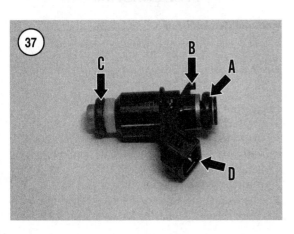

NOTE
The throttle position sensor is preset.
Do not remove it unless it is necessary.
The throttle valve, secondary throttle
valve, and the secondary throttle valve
actuator should not be removed from
the throttle bodies. The throttle stop
*screw (A, **Figure 40**) and fast idle*
screw (B) should not be turned unless
absolutely necessary.

7. If necessary, remove the throttle position sensor or the secondary throttle position sensor as described in this chapter.

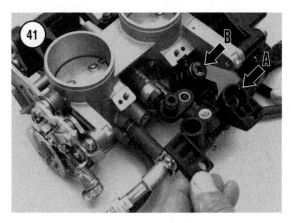

Assembly

1. If removed, install the throttle position sensor and the secondary throttle position sensor. Follow the procedure described in this chapter.

2. Install a new O-ring (A, **Figure 37**) and new damper (C) onto each fuel injector. Lubricate the O-ring and damper with engine oil.

3. Lubricate a new O-ring with engine oil and install it onto the fuel delivery pipe fitting (B, **Figure 38**).

CAUTION
Do not rotate an injector when install-ing it into its holder.

4. Align the fuel injector with its port on the throttle body. Make sure the tab (B, **Figure 37**) on the injector is centered in the throttle body cutout (A, **Figure 38**), and press the injector into the port until it bottoms.

5. Position the fuel rail so its output port (A, **Figure 41**) aligns with the fuel injector (B), and press the rail onto the injector until the rail bottoms.

6. Install the fuel rail screws (A, **Figure 36**) and tighten them to 3.5 N•m (31 in.-lb.).

7. Turn the throttle bodies over. Press the fuel delivery hose fitting (**Figure 35**) into the fuel rail port. Install the fuel delivery hose screw (**Figure 34**) and tighten it to 3.5 N•m (31 in.-lb.).

8. Repeat Steps 2-7, and install the remaining injector and fuel rail onto the other throttle body.

Inspection

CAUTION
Do not use wires to clean passages in the throttle bodies.

1. Clean the throttle bodies with an aerosol carburetor cleaner. Dry the throttle bodies and all passages with compressed air.

2. Inspect the throttle bodies (**Figure 42**) for cracks or other damage that could admit unfiltered air.

3. Operate the throttle wheel (C, **Figure 40**) and make sure both throttle valves (**Figure 43**) move smoothly.

4. Operate the secondary throttle valve lever (D, **Figure 40**) and make sure both secondary throttle valves (A, **Figure 42**) move smoothly.

5. Inspect the hoses for damage. Replace suspect hoses immediately.

6. Inspect the fuel rail and injectors as described in this chapter.

7. Replace worn or damaged parts.

FUEL INJECTORS

Removal/Installation

Remove and install the injectors as described in *Throttle Bodies, Disassembly/Assembly* (this chapter).

Inspection

1. Inspect each fuel injector (**Figure 37**) for damage. Inspect the injector nozzle for carbon buildup or damage.

2. Inspect the fuel injector filter.

3. Check each fuel injector connector (D, **Figure 37**) and each harness connector for corrosion or damage.

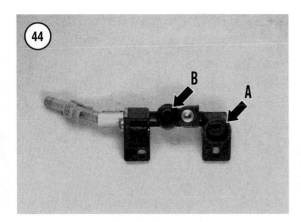

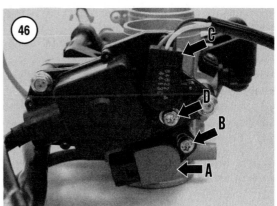

4. Blow each fuel rail clear with compressed air. Make sure the fuel injector port (A, **Figure 44**) and the fuel line port (B) are clear.

5. Inspect the injector port (B, **Figure 42**) in each throttle body for contamination.

6. Replace worn or damaged parts.

Resistance Test

1. Turn the ignition switch off.
2. Remove the air filter housing (Chapter Eight).
3. Disconnect the 2-pin fuel injector connector (B, **Figure 28**). It is not necessary to remove the injector to test its resistance.
4. Use an ohmmeter to measure the resistance between the two terminals in the fuel injector (**Figure 45**). The resistance should be within the range specified in **Table 2**.
5. Repeat this test for the remaining fuel injector.

Continuity Test

1. Perform Steps 1-3 of the injector resistance test.
2. Check the continuity between each terminal in the injector and ground. No continuity (infinity) should be indicated.

3. Repeat this test for the remaining fuel injector.

Voltage Test

1. Perform Steps 1-3 of the injector resistance test.
2. Connect the voltmeter's positive test probe to the yellow/red wire in the injector's harness connector; connect the negative test probe to a good ground.

> *NOTE*
> *Injector voltage will be present for only three seconds after the ignition switch is turned on. If necessary, turn the switch off and then back on.*

3. Turn the ignition switch on and measure the voltage. It should equal battery voltage.
4. Repeat this test for the remaining fuel injector.

THROTTLE POSITION (TP) SENSOR

Removal/Installation

A Torx wrench (Suzuki part No. 09930-11950), or its equivalent, is needed for this procedure.

> *NOTE*
> *The TP sensor is preset. Do not remove it unless necessary.*

1. Remove the throttle bodies (this chapter).
2. Scribe an index line across the TP sensor (A, **Figure 46**) and the throttle body so the sensor can be reinstalled in the same position.
3. Remove the throttle position sensor screw (B, **Figure 46**) and remove the sensor. Discard the O-ring. Note how the sensor engages the throttle shaft.
4. Lubricate the throttle shaft with grease.
5. Lubricate a new throttle valve O-ring with engine oil.
6. Close the throttle valves.

7. Align the throttle shaft with the slot in the TP sensor and slide the sensor onto the shaft.

8. Rotate the sensor so the index line on the sensor aligns with the line on the throttle body.

9. Install the throttle position sensor screw and tighten it to 3.5 N•m (31 in.-lb.).

10. Makes sure the throttle valves open and close smoothly.

11. Adjust the sensor as described in this section.

Inspection/Adjustment

The mode select switch (Suzuki part No. 09930-82710) is needed to perform this adjustment.

> *CAUTION*
> *Do not attempt this procedure without the mode select switch. Shorting the terminals in the dealer mode connector could damage the ECM.*

1. Start the engine and check the idle speed. If necessary, adjust the idle to specification as described in Chapter Three.

2. Stop the engine.

3. Remove the steering head covers (Chapter Fifteen). Remove the cover from the data link connector (**Figure 47**), and connect the mode select switch to the connector.

4. Start the engine or crank it for more than four seconds.

5. Turn the mode select switch on.

6. The diagnostic code *c00* should appear in the meter display. The dash before the code indicates the state of the TP sensor adjustment. The dash should be in the middle position as shown in **Figure 48**. If the dash is in the upper or lower position, adjust the sensor as follows:

   a. Remove the right upper cover (Chapter Fifteen).

   b. Loosen the throttle position sensor screw (A, **Figure 49**).

   c. Rotate the sensor (B, **Figure 49**) until the dash moves to the center position.

   d. Tighten the throttle position sensor screw to 3.5 N•m (31 in.-lb.).

Continuity Test

1. Turn the ignition switch off.

2. Remove the right upper cover (Chapter Fifteen).

3. Disconnect the 3-pin connector (C, **Figure 49**) from the throttle position sensor (B).

4. Check the continuity between the blue/black terminal in the sensor and a good ground.

5. Reverse the test probes and check the continuity in the opposite direction.

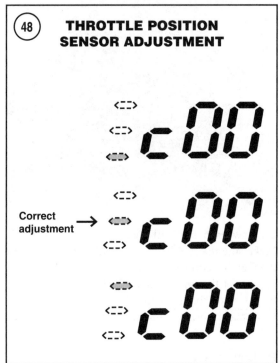

THROTTLE POSITION SENSOR ADJUSTMENT

Correct adjustment →

6. Both readings should indicate no continuity (infinity).

Resistance Test

1. Perform Steps 1-3 of the TP sensor continuity test.

2. Connect the ohmmeter's positive test probe to the blue/black terminal in the sensor; connect the negative test probe to the sensor's black/brown terminal.

3. Read the resistance when the throttle is fully closed and fully open. Record each reading. The fully closed and fully open resistance should equal the specifications in **Table 2**.

4. Connect the ohmmeter's positive test probe to the red terminal in the sensor; connect the negative test probe to the sensor's black/brown terminal.

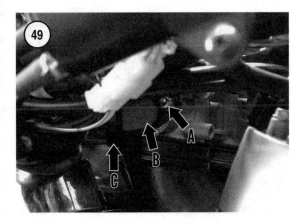

2. Make sure the throttle position sensor connector is connected to the sensor.

3. Use 0.5-mm back probe pins to back probe the harness side of the 3-pin TP sensor connector (C, **Figure 49**).

4. Connect the voltmeter's positive test probe to the blue/black terminal in the connector; connect the negative test probe to the connector's black/brown terminal.

5. Turn the ignition switch on.

6. Measure the output voltage when the throttle is fully closed and fully opened. Each measurement should equal the output voltage specified in **Table 2**.

SECONDARY THROTTLE POSITION (STP) SENSOR

Removal/Installation

A Torx wrench (Suzuki part No. 09930-11950), or its equivalent, is needed for this procedure.

NOTE
The secondary throttle position sensor is preset. Do not remove it unless sensor removal is necessary.

1. Remove the throttle bodies (this chapter).

2. Scribe an index line across the STP sensor (C, **Figure 46**) and the secondary throttle valve actuator so the sensor can be reinstalled in the same position.

3. Remove the secondary throttle position sensor screw (D, **Figure 46**) and remove the sensor. Discard the O-ring. Note how the sensor engages the secondary throttle shaft.

4. Lubricate the secondary throttle shaft with grease.

5. Lubricate a new secondary throttle valve O-ring with engine oil.

6. Manually move the secondary throttle valves to their fully opened positions (**Figure 50**).

7. Align the secondary throttle shaft with the slot in the sensor and slide the sensor onto the shaft.

8. Position the STV sensor so the index line on the sensor aligns with the line on the STV actuator.

9. Install the STP sensor screw and tighten it to 3.5 N•m (31 in.-lb.).

10. Make sure the secondary throttle valves open and close smoothly.

11. Adjust the STP sensor as described in this section.

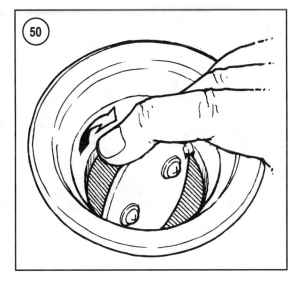

Resistance should equal the TPS resistance specified in **Table 2**.

Input Voltage Test

1. Perform Steps 1-3 of the TP sensor continuity test.

2. Connect the voltmeter's positive test probe to the red terminal in the harness side of the TP sensor connector; connect the voltmeter's negative probe to ground.

3. Turn the ignition switch on and measure the input voltage. It should be within the range specified in **Table 2**.

4. Connect the voltmeter's positive test probe to the red terminal in the harness side of the TP sensor connector; connect the negative test probe to the black/brown terminal in the harness side of the connector.

5. With the ignition switch on, the input voltage should be within the range specified in **Table 2**.

Output Voltage Test

1. Remove the right upper cover (Chapter Fifteen).

Adjustment

1. Remove the air filter housing (Chapter Eight).

2. Disconnect the 3-pin STP sensor connector (A, **Figure 51**), and the 4-pin secondary throttle valve actuator (STVA) connector (A, **Figure 52**).

3. Connect the ohmmeter's positive test probe to the yellow terminal in the sensor side of the STP sensor connector; connect the negative test probe to the black terminal in the sensor side of this connector.

4. Move the secondary throttle valve to its fully closed position (**Figure 53**).

5. Measure the resistance. It should equal the fully closed resistance specified in **Table 2**.

6. If the measured resistance is out of specification, adjust the STP sensor (B, **Figure 51**) by performing the following:

> *NOTE*
> *Perform this adjustment while the throttle bodies are installed on the engine. **Figure 46** shows the bodies removed for photographic clarity.*

   a. Loosen the STP sensor mounting screw (D, **Figure 46**).

   b. Rotate the STP sensor (C, **Figure 46**) until the resistance is within specification.

7. Tighten the mounting screw to 3.5 N•m (31 in.-lb.).

Input Voltage Test

1. Remove the air filter housing (Chapter Eight).

2. Disconnect the 3-pin STP sensor connector (A, **Figure 51**).

3. Connect the voltmeter's positive test probe to the red terminal in the harness side of the connector; connect the negative test probe to a good ground.

4. Turn the ignition switch on and measure the voltage. It should be within the input voltage range specified in **Table 2**.

5. With the voltmeter positive test probe still connected to the red terminal, connect the negative test probe to the black/brown terminal in the harness side of the connector.

6. Turn the ignition switch on and measure the voltage. It should also be within the specified input voltage range.

Continuity Test

1. Remove the air filter housing (Chapter Eight).

2. Make sure the ignition switch is off.

3. Disconnect the 3-pin STP sensor connector (A, **Figure 51**).

4. Check the continuity between ground and each terminal in the sensor side of the connector. The meter should indicate no continuity (infinity) during each portion of this test.

Resistance Test

1. Perform Step 1-3 of the STP sensor continuity test.

2. Connect the ohmmeter's positive test probe to the yellow terminal in the sensor side of the connector; connect the negative test probe to the black terminal in the sensor side of the connector.

3. Move the secondary throttle valve to its fully closed position (**Figure 53**) and measure the resistance. It should equal the fully closed resistance specified in **Table 2**.

4. Move the secondary throttle valve to its fully open position (**Figure 50**) and measure the resistance. It should equal the specified fully open resistance (**Table 2**).

5. Keep the negative test probe connected to the black terminal, but move the positive test probe to the blue wire in the sensor side of the connector.

6. Measure the resistance. It should equal the specified STPS resistance (**Table 2**).

Output Voltage Test

1. Remove air filter housing (Chapter Eight).

2. Disconnect the 4-pin STVA connector (A, **Figure 52**).

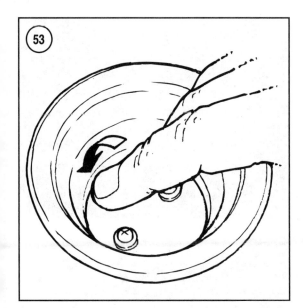

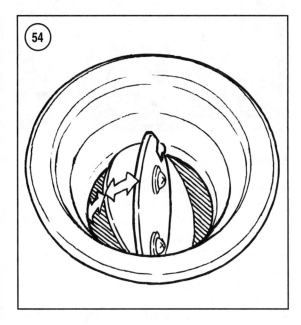

SECONDARY THROTTLE VALVE ACTUATOR (STVA)

CAUTION
Do not remove the secondary throttle valve actuator from the throttle body.

Operational Test

1. Remove the air filter housing (Chapter Eight).
2. Turn the ignition switch on and watch the movement of secondary throttle valves (**Figure 54**). Each should move to its 95% open position, to its fully open position and back to 95% open.

Continuity Test

1. Remove the air filter housing (Chapter Eight).
2. Disconnect the 4-pin STVA connector (A, **Figure 52**).
3. Check the continuity between ground and each terminal in the sensor side of the connector.
4. Each measurement should indicate no continuity.

Resistance Test

1. Perform Step 1 and Step 2 of the *Continuity Test*.
2. Measure the resistance between the black and pink terminals in the sensor side of the connector.
3. Measure the resistance between the green and white/black terminals in the sensor side of the connector.
4. Each reading should equal the specified resistance (**Table 2**).

THROTTLE CABLE REPLACEMENT

Follow the procedure in Chapter Eight.

FAST IDLE SPEED

The fuel injection system includes a fast idle cam to adjust the throttle valve position during cold starts and engine warm-up. The system closes the throttle valves once the engine has warmed up. The fast idle cam is automatically controlled by the secondary throttle valve actuator.

Adjustment

1. Securely support the motorcycle in an upright position.
2. Remove the seats, steering head covers, meter cover, and upper covers (Chapter Fifteen).

3. Make sure the 3-pin STP sensor connector (A, **Figure 51**) is connected. Connect 0.5-mm back probe pins to the harness side of the 3-pin STP sensor connector.
4. Connect the voltmeter's positive test probe to the yellow/white terminal in the STP sensor connector; connect the negative test probe to the black/brown terminal in the connector.
5. Turn the ignition switch on.
6. Move the secondary throttle valve to its fully closed position (**Figure 53**) and measure the voltage. It should equal the fully closed output voltage specified in **Table 2**.
7. Move the secondary throttle valve to its fully open position (**Figure 50**) and measure the voltage. It should equal the specified fully open output voltage.

3. Start the engine. Let it idle until the engine warms to operating temperature.

4. Use the throttle stop screw (A, **Figure 55**) to set the idle speed to 1000 rpm.

5. Check the TP sensor as described in this chapter. Adjust the sensor as necessary.

6. Turn off the engine.

7. Disconnect the 3-pin TP sensor connector (C, **Figure 49**).

8. Connect the voltmeter's positive test probe to the blue/black terminal in the TP sensor (B, **Figure 49**); connect the negative test probe to the sensor's black/brown terminal.

9. Start the engine. Measure the output voltage of the TP sensor with the engine at idle. Record the reading. This is the TP sensor idle voltage.

10. Turn off the engine and remove the air filter housing (Chapter Eight).

11. Disconnect the 4-pin STVA connector (A, **Figure 52**).

12. Move the secondary throttle valves to the fully open position (**Figure 50**).

13. Turn the ignition switch on and note the TP sensor output voltage while the secondary throttle valve is held open. Record the voltage. This is the TP sensor's STV fully open voltage.

14. Calculate the TP sensor output voltage variance by subtracting the TP sensor idle voltage from the STV fully open voltage. The variance should be within the range specified in **Table 2**.

15. If the TP sensor output voltage variance is out of specification, adjust the fast idle speed by performing the following:

   a. Turn the fast idle screw (B, **Figure 55**) to bring the TP sensor output voltage at idle within specification.

   b. Remeasure the TP sensor output voltage at idle and recalculate the TP sensor output voltage variance.

   c. Repeat substep a and substep b until the variance is within the specified range.

16. Let the engine cool to ambient temperature.

17. Start the engine and note the idle speed. The engine should idle within the specified fast idle speed range (**Table 1**). If fast idle speed is out of range, a short may exist in the oil temperature sensor, the secondary throttle valve actuator or the wiring harness.

INTAKE AIR PRESSURE (IAP) SENSOR

All models use two IAP sensors: one on the front cylinder (B, **Figure 52**) and one on the rear (A, **Figure 56**).

Removal/Installation

1A. When servicing the front cylinder IAP sensor (No. 2), remove the right upper cover (Chapter Fifteen).

1B. When servicing the rear cylinder IAP sensor (No. 1), remove the left upper cover (Chapter Fifteen).

2. Disconnect the 3-pin IAP sensor connector (B, **Figure 56**).

3. Remove the sensor's rubber damper from the mounting tang.

4. Disconnect the vacuum hose (C, **Figure 56**) from the sensor and remove the sensor from its rubber damper.

5. Install the sensor by reversing the removal procedure. Make sure the sensor is secure within its damper.

Input Voltage Test

1. Perform Step 1 and Step 2 of the IAP sensor removal procedure.

2. Connect the voltmeter's positive test probe to the red terminal in the sensor's connector; connect the negative test probe to ground.

3. Turn the ignition switch on and measure the voltage. It should be within the input voltage range specified in **Table 2**.

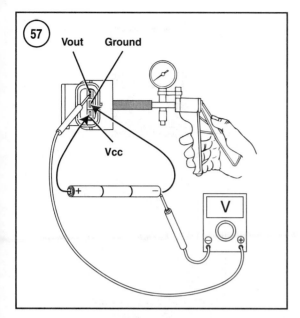

terminal in the connector; connect the negative test probe to the black/brown terminal.

4. Start the engine, run it at idle and measure the voltage. It should equal the output voltage specified in **Table 2**.

Vacuum Test

1. Remove the intake air pressure sensor as described in this section.

2. Make sure the sensor's air passage is clear, and connect a vacuum pump and gauge to the air passage (**Figure 57**).

3. Connect three new 1.5 volt batteries in series as shown in **Figure 57**. Measure the total voltage of the test batteries. The voltage must be 4.5-5.0 volts. Replace the batteries if necessary.

4. Connect the test battery's positive terminal to the Vcc terminal in the sensor; connect the test battery's negative terminal to the sensor's ground terminal.

5. Connect the voltmeter's positive test probe to the Vout terminal in the sensor; connect the voltmeter's negative test probe to the test battery's negative terminal.

6. Note the voltage reading. It should be within the Vout voltage range specified in **Table 2**.

7. Use the vacuum pump to apply vacuum to the sensor's air passage and note the changes in the voltage reading. The Vout voltage should respond to the application of vacuum as specified in **Table 3**.

INTAKE AIR TEMPERATURE (IAT) SENSOR

Removal/Installation

1. Remove the steering head cover and upper cover from the right side (Chapter Fifteen).

2. Disconnect the 2-pin connector (A, **Figure 58**) from the IAT sensor (B) on the right side of the air filter housing.

3. Remove the sensor from the housing.

4. Install the sensor by reversing the removal procedures. Note the following:
   a. Install a new O-ring.
   b. Tighten the IAT sensor to 20 N•m (15 ft.-lb.).

Resistance Test

1. Turn the ignition switch off, and perform Step 1 and Step 2 of the IAT sensor removal procedure.

2. Connect the ohmmeter positive test probe to the dark green terminal in the sensor; connect the negative test probe to the sensor's black/brown terminal.

3. Measure the resistance. It should be within specification (**Table 2**).

4. Turn the ignition switch off.

5. Connect the voltmeter's positive test probe to the red terminal in the sensor's connector; connect the negative test probe to the black/brown terminal in the sensor's connector.

6. Turn the ignition switch on and measure the voltage. It should be within the input voltage specified range.

Output Voltage Test

1. Make sure the IAP sensor connector is securely mated to the IAP sensor.

2. Connect 0.5-mm back probe pins the IAP connector during this test.

3A. For the front IAP sensor (B, **Figure 52**), connect a voltmeter's positive test probe to the green/black terminal in the connector; connect the negative test probe to the black/brown terminal.

3B. For the rear IAP sensor (A, **Figure 56**), connect a voltmeter's positive test probe to the green/white

9

Operational Test

1. Remove the IAT sensor.
2. Fill a beaker or pan with water and place it on a stove or hot plate.

NOTE
The thermometer and the sensor must not touch the container sides or bottom. If either does, it will result in a false reading.

3. Place a thermometer in the pan of water (use a cooking or candy thermometer that is rated higher than the test temperature).
4. Mount the IAT sensor so that the temperature sensing tip and the threaded portion of the body are submerged as shown in **Figure 59**.
5. Attach an ohmmeter to the sensor terminals as shown in **Figure 59**.
6. Heat the water to the test temperatures specified in **Table 2**. Note the resistance of the sensor when the water reaches each temperature.
7. Replace the IAT sensor if any reading is considerably different from the specified test resistance (**Table 2**) at a given temperature.

Input Voltage Test

1. Turn the ignition switch off, and perform Step 1 and Step 2 of the IAT sensor removal procedure.
2. Connect the voltmeter's positive test probe to the dark green terminal in the connector; connect the negative test probe to a good ground.
3. Turn on the ignition switch and measure the input voltage. It should be within the range specified in **Table 2**.
4. Connect the voltmeter's positive test probe to the dark green terminal in the connector; connect the negative test probe to the black/brown terminal in the connector.
5. Turn on the ignition switch. The input voltage should be within the specified range.

ENGINE OIL TEMPERATURE (EOT) SENSOR

Removal/Installation

1. Place a drain pan under the EOT sensor.
2. Disconnect the 2-pin EOT sensor connector (A, **Figure 60**) from its subharness mate.

CAUTION
Handle the EOT sensor carefully. It can be damaged by impact.

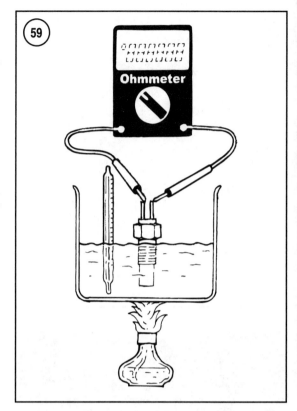

3. Remove the sensor (B, **Figure 60**) from the crankcase.
4. Installation is the reverse of removal. Note the following:
   a. Install a new sealing washer.
   b. Tighten the EOT sensor to 22 N•m (16 ft.-lb.).

Resistance Test

1. Turn the ignition switch off. Disconnect the 2-pin EOT sensor connector (A, **Figure 60**) from its subharness mate.
2. Measure the resistance across the two terminals in the sensor side of the connector. The reading should equal the specified resistance (**Table 2**).

Input Voltage Test

1. Disconnect the 2-pin EOT sensor connector (A, **Figure 60**) from its subharness mate.
2. Connect the voltmeter's positive test probe to the black/blue terminal in the subharness side of the connector; connect the negative test probe to a good ground.
3. Turn on the ignition switch and measure the input voltage. It should be within the range specified in **Table 2**.
4. Connect the voltmeter's positive test probe to the black/blue terminal in the subharness side of the con-

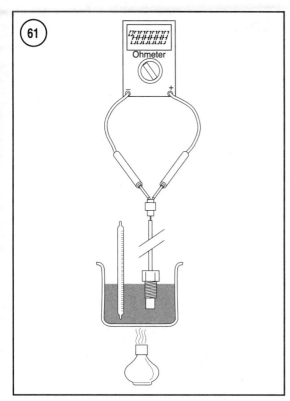

3. Place a thermometer in the pan of clean oil.

4. Mount the EOT sensor so that the temperature sensing tip and the threaded portion of the body are submerged as shown in **Figure 61**.

5. Attach an ohmmeter to the terminals in the sensor side of the connector.

6. Heat the oil to the temperatures specified in **Table 2**. Note the resistance of the sensor when the oil temperature reaches the specified values.

7. Replace the engine oil temperature sensor if any reading is considerably different than the specified test resistance (**Table 2**) at a given temperature.

HEATED OXYGEN (HO$_2$) SENSOR (U.K., EUROPE AND AUSTRALIA MODELS)

Removal/Installation

1. Remove the seats (Chapter Fifteen).

NOTE
The HO$_2$ sensor connector sits beneath the tip over sensor.

2. Disconnect the 4-pin HO$_2$ sensor connector. Note how the sensor wire is routed and secured.

WARNING
If necessary, let the exhaust system cool before removing the sensor.

3. Loosen the sensor and remove it from the exhaust chamber.

4. Install the sensor by reversing the removal procedures.

  a. Tighten the HO$_2$ sensor to 25 N•m (18 ft.-lb.).

  b. Route the wire along its original path and secure the wire to the places noted during removal.

Output voltage

1. Start the engine and warm it up to operating temperature.

2. Connect 0.5-mm back probe pins to the harness side of the 4-pin HO$_2$ sensor connector.

3. Connect the voltmeter's positive probe to the white/green terminal in the sensor connector; connect the negative test probe to the black/brown terminal.

4. Measure the output voltage at idle. Record the reading.

5. Run the engine at 5000 rpm and measure the voltage. Record the reading.

6. Each measurement should be within the specification listed in **Table 2**.

nector; connect the negative test probe to the black/green terminal (subharness side).

5. Turn on the ignition switch. The input voltage should be within the specified range.

Operational Test

1. Remove the EOT sensor.

2. Fill a beaker or pan with oil and place it on a stove or hot plate.

NOTE
The thermometer and the sensor must not touch the container sides or bottom. If either does, it will result in a false reading.

Resistance Test (Heater)

NOTE
*The temperature of the sensor's heater affects resistance readings. For accurate results, the sensor's heater must be at the indicated temperature (**Table 2**) during this test.*

1. Remove the seats (Chapter Fifteen).
2. Disconnect the 4-pin HO_2 sensor connector.
3. Measure the resistance between the two white terminals in the sensor side of the connector. The heater resistance should be within the specified range (**Table 2**).

Voltage Test (Heater)

1. Make sure the 4-pin HO_2 sensor connector is connected.
2. Connect 0.5-mm back probe pins to the harness side of the sensor connector.
3. Connect the voltmeter's positive test probe to the white/black terminal in the sensor connector; connect the negative test probe to a good ground.
4. Turn the ignition switch on and record the voltage. It should equal battery voltage.

TIP OVER (TO) SENSOR

If the TO sensor is activated, the ECM interrupts the current to the fuel pump, fuel injectors, and ignition coils.

Removal/Installation

1. Remove the seats (Chapter Fifteen), and turn the ignition switch off.
2. Disconnect the 3-pin connector (A, **Figure 62**) from the TO sensor (B).
3. Lift the sensor from the mounting tang behind the fuel tank.
4. Install the TO sensor by reversing the removal procedures. Make sure the side marked *UPPER* sits up.

Resistance Test

1. Perform Step 1 and Step 2 of *Removal/Installation* (this section).
2. Measure the resistance between the red and black/brown terminals in the sensor. It should be within the range specified in **Table 2**.

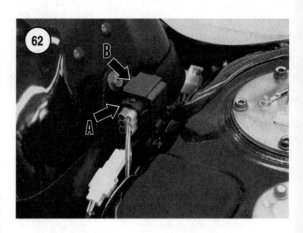

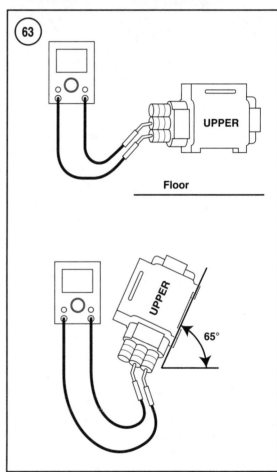

Voltage Test

1. Remove the TO sensor (B, **Figure 62**) as described in this section.
2. Reconnect the 3-pin connector to the sensor.
3. Connect 0.5-mm back probe pins to the connector.
4. Connect the voltmeter's positive test probe to the brown/white terminal in the connector; connect the negative test probe to the black/brown terminal.
5. Turn the ignition switch on.

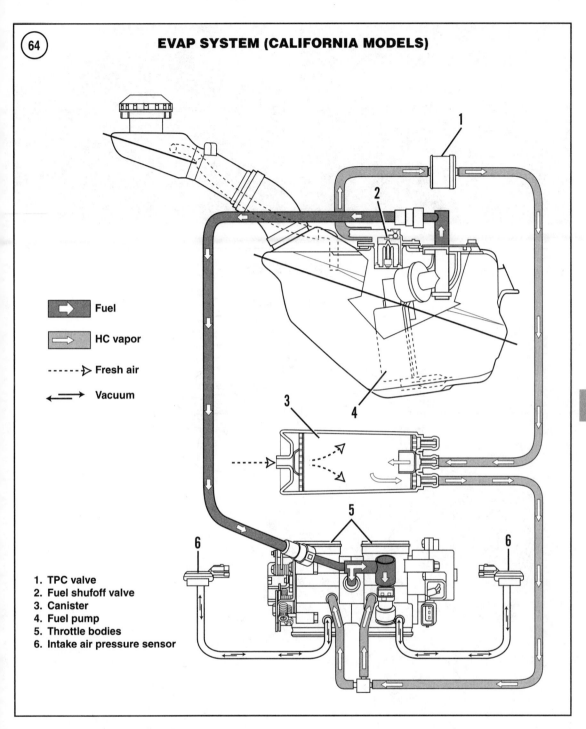

EVAP SYSTEM (CALIFORNIA MODELS)

64

- Fuel
- HC vapor
- ----▷ Fresh air
- ⟷ Vacuum

1. TPC valve
2. Fuel shufoff valve
3. Canister
4. Fuel pump
5. Throttle bodies
6. Intake air pressure sensor

6. Hold the sensor so the word *UPPER* parallels the floor (**Figure 63**) and read the voltage.

7. Rotate the sensor so the word *UPPER* forms a 65° angle with the floor and read the voltage.

8. Each reading should be within the range specified in **Table 2**.

EXHAUST SYSTEM

Refer to Chapter Eight.

EVAPORATIVE EMISSIONS CONTROL SYSTEM (CALIFORNIA MODELS)

California models are equipped with an evaporative emission control system (EVAP), which consists of a charcoal canister, fuel shutoff valve, tank pressure control valve, assorted hoses, and modified throttle bodies and fuel tank. (**Figure 64**).

Refer to *Evaporative Emissions Control System* in Chapter Eight.

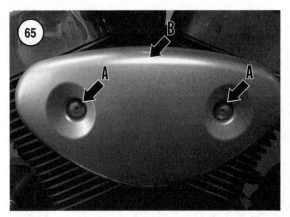

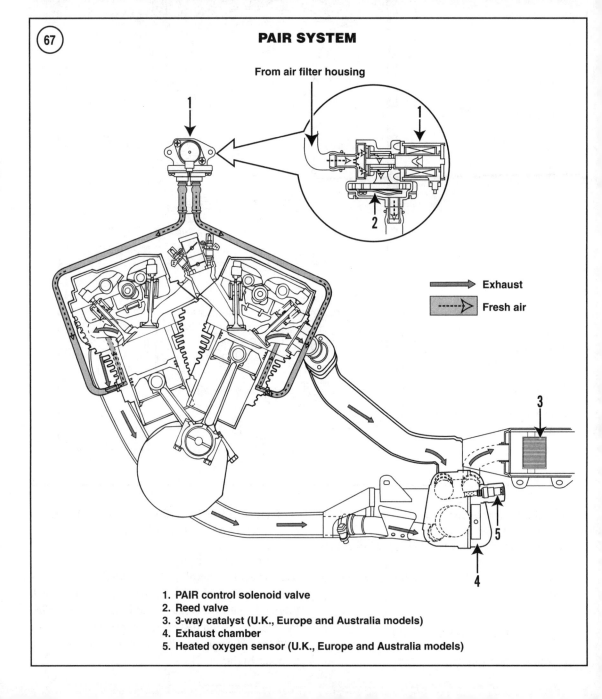

PAIR SYSTEM

From air filter housing

Exhaust

Fresh air

1. PAIR control solenoid valve
2. Reed valve
3. 3-way catalyst (U.K., Europe and Australia models)
4. Exhaust chamber
5. Heated oxygen sensor (U.K., Europe and Australia models)

ENGINE SIDE BOX

The engine side box mounts onto the right side of the engine. On models with the PAIR system, the PAIR solenoid valve sits inside this box.

1. Remove the cover bolts (A, **Figure 65**) and remove the cover (B) from the side box.

2. On models with the PAIR system, remove the PAIR solenoid valve as described in Steps 1-6 of *PAIR System, Removal/Installation* (this chapter).

3. Remove the side box bolts (A, **Figure 66**) and lower the box (B) from the engine. Watch for the damper and washer on each bolt.

4. Install the engine side box by reversing the removal procedures. Note the following:

  a. Install the heat guard behind the engine side box.

  b. Include a damper and washer with each engine side box bolt (A, **Figure 66**).

  c. On models with the PAIR system, install the PAIR control valve.

PAIR SYSTEM

The PAIR system (**Figure 67**) consists of the PAIR solenoid valve, two reed valves, a vacuum hose, and outlet hoses. The system uses momentary pressure

variations created by exhaust gas pulses to introduce fresh air into the exhaust ports.

Removal/Installation

Label each hose and fitting so they can be reinstalled correctly.

1. Remove the right upper cover (Chapter Fifteen).

2. Remove the cover bolts (A, **Figure 65**) and lower the cover (B) from the engine side box.

3. Disconnect the 2-pin PAIR solenoid valve connector (**Figure 68**).

4. Disconnect each PAIR hose (A, **Figure 69**) from the PAIR solenoid valve.

5. Remove the PAIR solenoid valve nuts (B, **Figure 69**) and slide the valve from the mounting studs.

6. Disconnect the air filter housing hose from the back of the PAIR valve and remove the valve. Pull the electrical wire (C, **Figure 69**) from the hole in the side box housing.

7. Remove the PAIR pipes as follows:

  a. Remove the mounting nut (A, **Figure 70**) from each stud. Then remove each PAIR pipe (B) from its cylinder.

  b. Remove and discard the gasket behind each pipe.

8. Install the PAIR system by reversing the removal procedures. Note the following:

  a. Fit the heat shield in place behind the engine side box.

  b. Install a damper and washer behind each side box bolt (A, **Figure 69**).

  c. Feed the electrical wire (C, **Figure 69**) through the hole in the engine side box.

  d. If the PAIR pipes were removed from the cylinders, use a new gasket when connecting each pipe to its cylinder.

Inspection

1. Inspect the PAIR valve as follows:

9

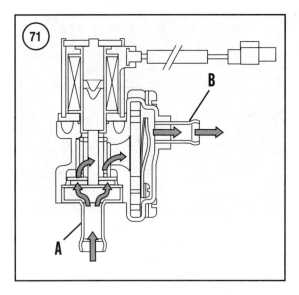

a. Blow air into the input port (A, **Figure 71**) on the rear of the PAIR solenoid valve.
b. Air should flow from the two output ports (B, **Figure 71**).
c. Energize the solenoid by connecting a battery to the terminals in the PAIR connector (**Figure 72**).
d. Blow into the input port on the PAIR solenoid valve (A, **Figure 72**). Air should not flow from the output ports (B, **Figure 72**) when the solenoid is energized.
e. Replace the PAIR solenoid valve if it fails either portion of this test.
2. Inspect the reed valve as follows:
a. Remove the cover screws (**Figure 73**) and lift the reed valve cover from the PAIR solenoid valve.
b. Remove each reed valve from its housing (**Figure 74**, typical).
c. Inspect the reed valve for carbon deposits or damage. Replace the PAIR solenoid valve if the reeds have deposits or are damaged.

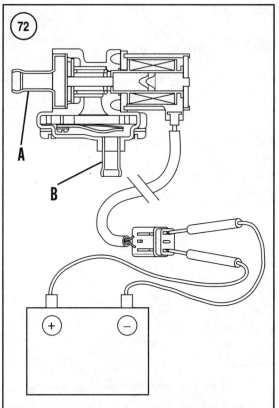

Resistance Test

1. Remove the upper cover from the right side (Chapter Fifteen).
2. Disconnect the 2-pin PAIR solenoid valve connector (**Figure 68**).
3. Measure the resistance between the two terminals in the sensor side of the connector. The resistance should be within the specified range (**Table 2**).

Continuity Test

1. Perform Step 1 and Step 2 of the *Resistance Test* (this section).

2. Check the continuity between a good ground and each terminal in the sensor side of the connector.
3. Each test should indicate no continuity (infinity).

Voltage Test

1. Perform Step 1 and Step 2 of the *Resistance Test* (this section).
2. Connect the voltmeter's positive test probe to the orange/white terminal in the harness side of the connector; connect the negative test probe to a good ground.
3. Turn the ignition switch on and measure the voltage. It should equal battery voltage.

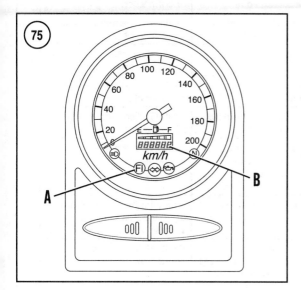

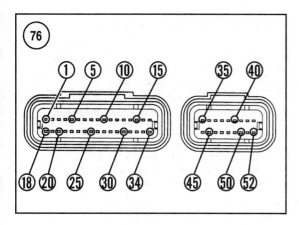

DIAGNOSTIC SYSTEM

The diagnostic system monitors the fuel injection and ignition system sensors and actuators. If an error is detected; the ECM records the malfunction and sets a malfunction code. It also turns on the FI indicator (A, **Figure 75**) in the speedometer and *FI* appears in the LCD display (B). Retrieve a stored code by entering the dealer mode as described in this section.

Electrical Component Replacement

Most motorcycle dealerships and parts suppliers will not accept the return of any electrical part. Consider any test results carefully before replacing a component that tests only slightly out of specification, especially for resistance.

If testing indicates a defective ECM verify the results carefully. If possible, install a know good replacement or have a dealership verify your test results before purchasing a new ECM.

ECM Connectors

The 34-pin and 18-pin ECM connectors use the same wire color more than once. The test procedures include a wire's color and its pin location to describe a test point. The number in parentheses after a wire's color refers to that wire's pin location number.

Refer to **Figure 76** to determine where a particular terminal is located in the relevant ECM connector. Refer to *Electronic Control Module* (Chapter Ten) for ECM test procedures.

Dealer Mode

Use the mode select switch (Suzuki part No. 09930-82710) to enter the dealer mode.

When the dealer mode is activated, the speedometer LCD (B, **Figure 75**) displays any stored malfunction code(s).

CAUTION
Do not attempt this procedure without the mode select switch. Shorting the terminals in the dealer model connector could damage the ECM.

1. Remove the steering head covers (Chapter Fifteen).
2. Remove the cover from the data link connector (**Figure 77**), and connect the mode select switch to this connector.

MALFUNCTION CODES

Malfunction code	Related item	Detected failure	Probable cause
c00	No error	–	–
c12	Crankshaft position sensor	The ECM has not received a signal from the CKP sensor 3 seconds after it received the start signal.	Faulty CKP sensor, wiring or connector.
c13, c17	Intake air pressure sensor	The sensor's voltage is outside the range of 0.1-4.8 volts.	Faulty IAP sensor, wiring or connector.
c14	Throttle position sensor	The sensor's voltage is outside the range of 0.1-4.8 volts.	Faulty TP sensor, wiring or connector.
c15	Engine oil temperature sensor	The sensor's voltage is outside the range of 0.1-4.6 volts.	Faulty EOT sensor, wiring or connector.
c18	Decompression relay	The ECM is not receiving a signal from the relay.	Faulty decompression relay, wiring or connector.
c19	Starter relay	The ECM is not receiving a signal from the relay.	Faulty starter relay, wiring or connector.
c21	Intake air temperature sensor	The sensor's voltage is outside the range of 0.1-4.6 volts.	Faulty IAT sensor, wiring or connector.
c23	Tip over sensor	The sensor's voltage is outside the range of 0.2-4.6 volts 2 seconds after the ignition switch has been turned on.	Faulty TO sensor, wiring or connector.
c24 (No. 1), c25 (No. 2)	Ignition system malfunction	The ECM does not receive a proper signal from an ignition coil.	Faulty ignition coil, wiring or connector. Faulty power supply from the battery.
c28	Secondary throttle valve actuator	Signal voltage from the ECM is not reaching the STVA, the ECM is not receiving a signal from the STVA, or load voltage is not reaching the actuator motor.	Faulty STVA, wiring or connector.
c29	Secondary throttle position sensor	The sensor's voltage is outside the range of 0.1-4.8 volts.	Faulty STP sensor, wiring or connector.
c31	Gear position signal	The gear position sensor's voltage is less than 0.6 volts for 3 or more seconds.	Faulty gear position sensor, wiring, connector or faulty shift cam.
c32 (No. 1), c33 (No. 2)	Fuel injector	The ECM does receive a proper signal from the fuel injector.	Faulty fuel injector, wiring or connector. Faulty power supply to the injector.
c41	Fuel pump relay	Load voltage flows to the fuel pump when the relay is off; load voltage does not flow to the fuel pump when the relay is on.	Faulty fuel pump relay, wiring or connector. Faulty power source to the fuel pump relay or injectors.
c42	Ignition switch signal (anti-theft)	The ECM does not receive a signal from the ignition switch.	Faulty ignition switch, wiring or connector.
c44	Heated oxygen sensor	1. The sensor's signal is not reaching the ECM. 2. The heater does not operate so its signal does not reach the ECM.	1. Faulty HO_2 sensor; the sensor circuit is open or shorted to ground. 2. Faulty HO_2 sensor, its wiring or connector; battery voltage not flowing to the sensor.
c49	PAIR solenoid valve	The ECM does not receive a signal from the valve.	Faulty PAIR solenoid valve, wiring or connector.

FAIL-SAFE ACTION

Failed item	Fail-safe action	Operation status
Intake air pressure sensor.	Intake air pressure is set to 760 mm Hg (29.92 in. Hg.).	Engine continues operating; can restart.
Throttle position sensor.	Throttle valve is set to its fully open position. Ignition timing is set to a present value.	Engine continues operating; can restart.
Engine oil temperature sensor.	Engine oil temperature is set to 80° C (176° F).	Engine continues operating; can restart.
Intake air temperature sensor.	Intake air temperature set to 40° C (104° F).	Engine continues operating; can restart.
Ignition signal cylinder No. 1.	No spark at cylinder No. 1.	Cylinder No. 2 continues operating; can restart.
Ignition signal cylinder No. 2.	No spark at cylinder No. 2.	Cylinder No. 1 continues operating; can restart.
Fuel injector No. 1.	Fuel cut-off to injector No. 1.	Cylinder No. 2 continues operating; can restart.
Fuel injector No. 2.	Fuel cut-off to injector No. 2.	Cylinder No. 1 continues operating; can restart.
Secondary throttle valve actuator.	Secondary throttle valve is fixed in any position; power from ECM cut off.	Engine continues operating; can restart.
Secondary throttle position sensor.	Secondary throttle valve is fixed in any position.	Engine continues operating; can restart.
Gear position signal.	Gear position signal set to fifth gear.	Engine continues operating; can restart.
Heated oxygen sensor	Sensor feedback compensations is interrupted. Air/fuel ration fixed to normal.	Engine continues operating; can restart.
PAIR solenoid valve	Oxygen sensor feedback control interrupted, and PAIR control valve fixed in the open position.	Engine continues operating; can restart.

9

3. Start the engine or crank it for more than four seconds.

4. After four seconds, turn the mode select switch to on. The system enters the dealer mode and displays any stored malfunction codes. If more than one code is stored, the codes display in numeric order starting with the lowest numbered code.

5. Record the malfunction codes. Refer to **Figure 78** for the codes and their probable causes.

Malfunction Code History

If a code is removed from the ECM memory, it remains as history. The on-board diagnostic system can-not retrieve history. The Suzuki Diagnostic System (part No. 09904-41010), or SDS, is required to access the history. Refer this service to a dealership.

Fail-Safe Operation

For some codes, the ECM establishes a preset value for the input so the motorcycle can still operate. This fail-safe operation gives a rider the opportunity to get home or to a service shop. Refer to **Figure 79** for the fail-safe action and operational status for each malfunction code.

If the FI indicator (A, **Figure 75**) turns on, and the LCD (B) alternately displays the odometer and *FI*,

TROUBLESHOOTING CHARTS

Diagnostic trouble code	Diagnostic flow chart
c00	No fault detected
c12	Figure 81
c13, c17	Figure 82
c14	Figure 83
c15	Figure 84
c18	Figure 85
c19	Figure 86
c21	Figure 87
c23	Figure 88
c24, c25	Figure 89
c28	Figure 90
c29	Figure 91
c31	Figure 92
c32, c33	Figure 93
c41	Figure 94
c42	Figure 95
c44	Figure 96
c49	Figure 97

the engine can be restarted. However, if the FI indicator flashes and *FI* is continuously displayed in the LCD, the engine cannot be restarted once it has been turned off.

Even if the motorcycle continues to run with a malfunction code, troubleshoot the system and eliminate the problem immediately. If the problem cannot be solved, take the motorcycle to a dealership.

Troubleshooting

1. Enter the dealer mode as described in this section.
2. Record any malfunction code(s).
3. Refer to **Figure 80**, and identify the relevant diagnostic flow chart (**Figure 81-97**) for the code.

4. Turn to the indicated diagnostic flow chart (**Figures 81-97**). Perform the test procedures in the order listed until the problem is resolved.
5. Once a fault has been corrected, reset the self-diagnostic system as described in this section.

Resetting

Perform the following to reset the diagnostic system after correcting the problem.
1. While in the dealer mode, turn the ignition switch off and then back on.
2. The LCD should display the no fault code: *c00*.
3. Turn the dealer mode switch off, and disconnect the switch from the dealer mode connector.

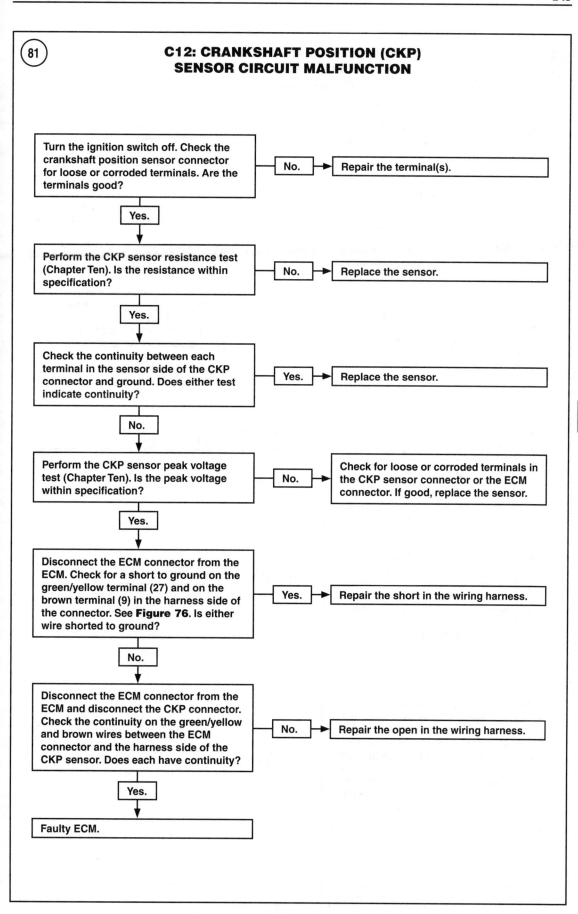

81

C12: CRANKSHAFT POSITION (CKP)
SENSOR CIRCUIT MALFUNCTION

Turn the ignition switch off. Check the crankshaft position sensor connector for loose or corroded terminals. Are the terminals good? — No. → Repair the terminal(s).

Yes.

Perform the CKP sensor resistance test (Chapter Ten). Is the resistance within specification? — No. → Replace the sensor.

Yes.

Check the continuity between each terminal in the sensor side of the CKP connector and ground. Does either test indicate continuity? — Yes. → Replace the sensor.

No.

Perform the CKP sensor peak voltage test (Chapter Ten). Is the peak voltage within specification? — No. → Check for loose or corroded terminals in the CKP sensor connector or the ECM connector. If good, replace the sensor.

Yes.

Disconnect the ECM connector from the ECM. Check for a short to ground on the green/yellow terminal (27) and on the brown terminal (9) in the harness side of the connector. See **Figure 76**. Is either wire shorted to ground? — Yes. → Repair the short in the wiring harness.

No.

Disconnect the ECM connector from the ECM and disconnect the CKP connector. Check the continuity on the green/yellow and brown wires between the ECM connector and the harness side of the CKP sensor. Does each have continuity? — No. → Repair the open in the wiring harness.

Yes.

Faulty ECM.

9

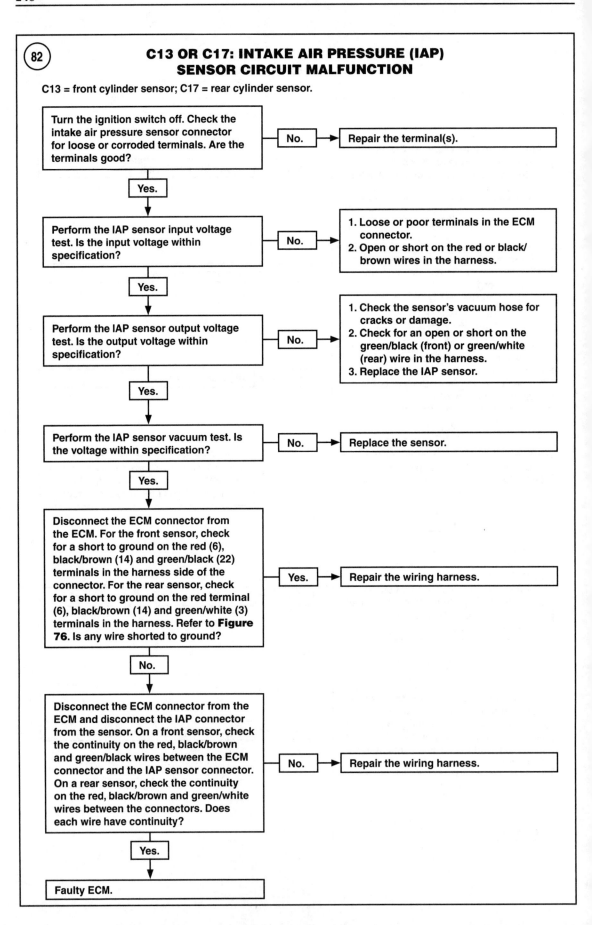

82

C13 OR C17: INTAKE AIR PRESSURE (IAP) SENSOR CIRCUIT MALFUNCTION

C13 = front cylinder sensor; C17 = rear cylinder sensor.

Turn the ignition switch off. Check the intake air pressure sensor connector for loose or corroded terminals. Are the terminals good? → No. → Repair the terminal(s).

Yes.

Perform the IAP sensor input voltage test. Is the input voltage within specification? → No. →
1. Loose or poor terminals in the ECM connector.
2. Open or short on the red or black/brown wires in the harness.

Yes.

Perform the IAP sensor output voltage test. Is the output voltage within specification? → No. →
1. Check the sensor's vacuum hose for cracks or damage.
2. Check for an open or short on the green/black (front) or green/white (rear) wire in the harness.
3. Replace the IAP sensor.

Yes.

Perform the IAP sensor vacuum test. Is the voltage within specification? → No. → Replace the sensor.

Yes.

Disconnect the ECM connector from the ECM. For the front sensor, check for a short to ground on the red (6), black/brown (14) and green/black (22) terminals in the harness side of the connector. For the rear sensor, check for a short to ground on the red terminal (6), black/brown (14) and green/white (3) terminals in the harness. Refer to **Figure 76**. Is any wire shorted to ground? → Yes. → Repair the wiring harness.

No.

Disconnect the ECM connector from the ECM and disconnect the IAP connector from the sensor. On a front sensor, check the continuity on the red, black/brown and green/black wires between the ECM connector and the IAP sensor connector. On a rear sensor, check the continuity on the red, black/brown and green/white wires between the connectors. Does each wire have continuity? → No. → Repair the wiring harness.

Yes.

Faulty ECM.

(83)

C14: THROTTLE POSITION (TP) SENSOR
CIRCUIT MALFUNCTION

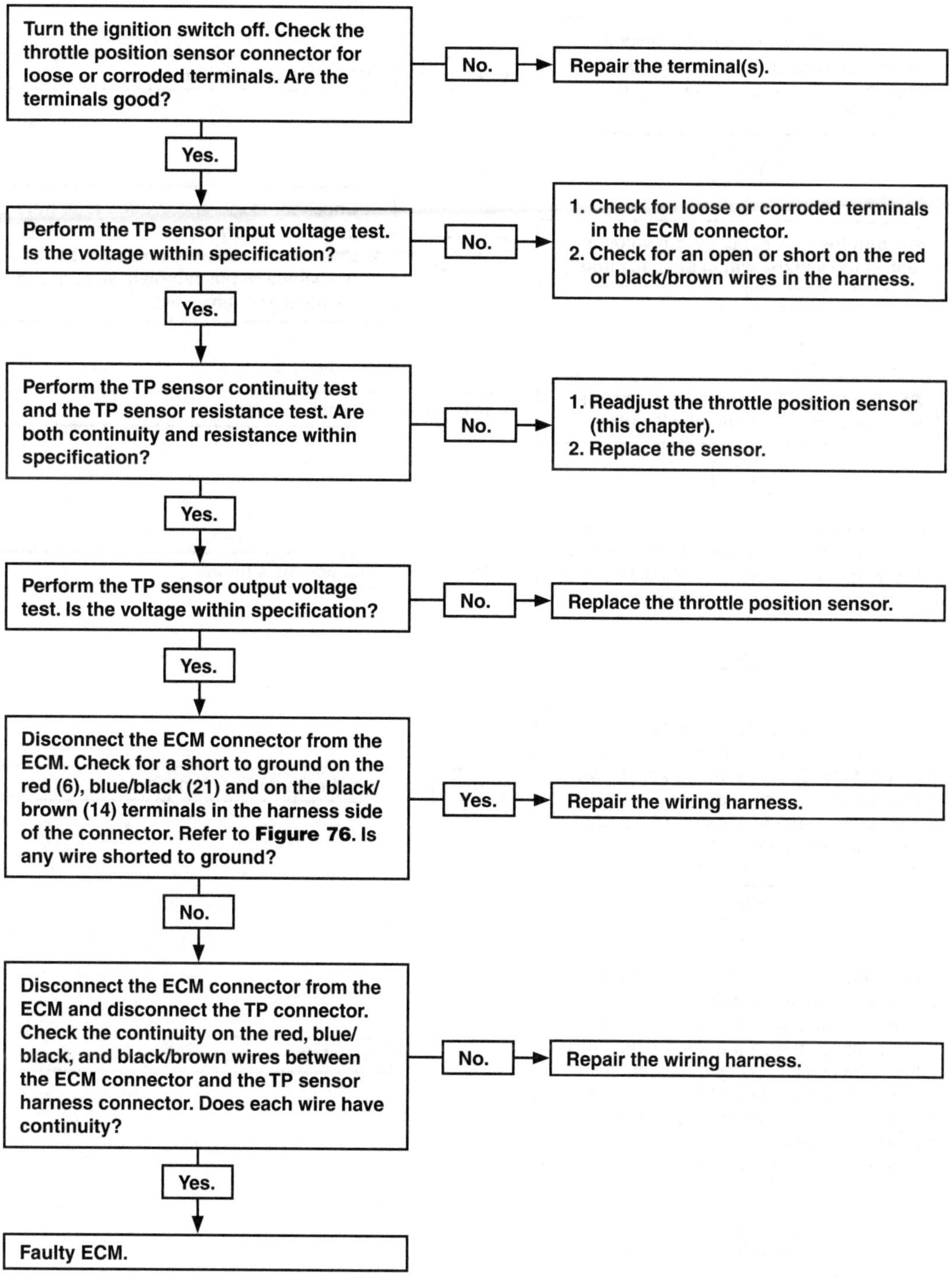

Turn the ignition switch off. Check the throttle position sensor connector for loose or corroded terminals. Are the terminals good? — **No.** → Repair the terminal(s).

Yes.

Perform the TP sensor input voltage test. Is the voltage within specification? — **No.** → 1. Check for loose or corroded terminals in the ECM connector.
2. Check for an open or short on the red or black/brown wires in the harness.

Yes.

Perform the TP sensor continuity test and the TP sensor resistance test. Are both continuity and resistance within specification? — **No.** → 1. Readjust the throttle position sensor (this chapter).
2. Replace the sensor.

Yes.

Perform the TP sensor output voltage test. Is the voltage within specification? — **No.** → Replace the throttle position sensor.

Yes.

Disconnect the ECM connector from the ECM. Check for a short to ground on the red (6), blue/black (21) and on the black/brown (14) terminals in the harness side of the connector. Refer to **Figure 76**. Is any wire shorted to ground? — **Yes.** → Repair the wiring harness.

No.

Disconnect the ECM connector from the ECM and disconnect the TP connector. Check the continuity on the red, blue/black, and black/brown wires between the ECM connector and the TP sensor harness connector. Does each wire have continuity? — **No.** → Repair the wiring harness.

Yes.

Faulty ECM.

9

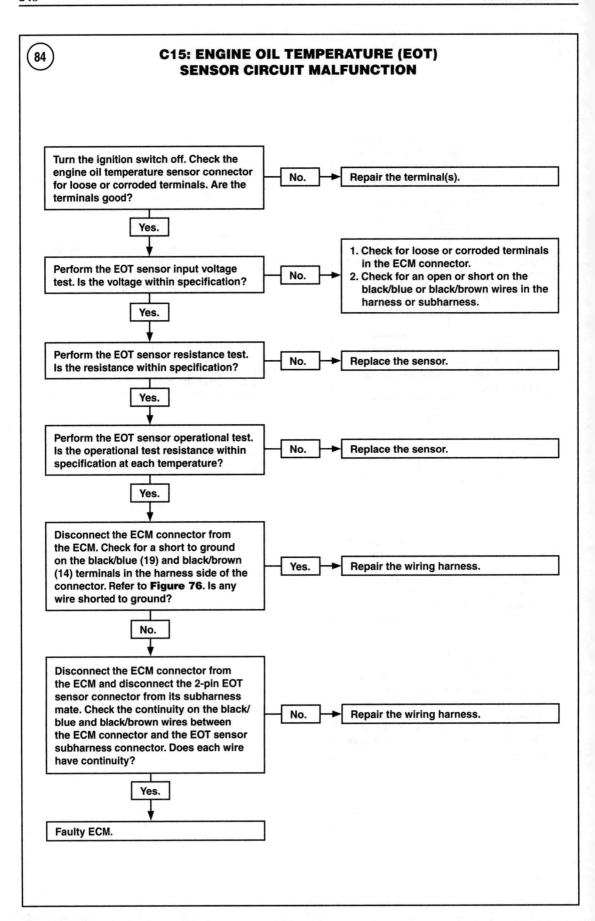

(84) **C15: ENGINE OIL TEMPERATURE (EOT)
SENSOR CIRCUIT MALFUNCTION**

Turn the ignition switch off. Check the engine oil temperature sensor connector for loose or corroded terminals. Are the terminals good? — No. → Repair the terminal(s).

Yes.

Perform the EOT sensor input voltage test. Is the voltage within specification? — No. → 1. Check for loose or corroded terminals in the ECM connector.
2. Check for an open or short on the black/blue or black/brown wires in the harness or subharness.

Yes.

Perform the EOT sensor resistance test. Is the resistance within specification? — No. → Replace the sensor.

Yes.

Perform the EOT sensor operational test. Is the operational test resistance within specification at each temperature? — No. → Replace the sensor.

Yes.

Disconnect the ECM connector from the ECM. Check for a short to ground on the black/blue (19) and black/brown (14) terminals in the harness side of the connector. Refer to **Figure 76**. Is any wire shorted to ground? — Yes. → Repair the wiring harness.

No.

Disconnect the ECM connector from the ECM and disconnect the 2-pin EOT sensor connector from its subharness mate. Check the continuity on the black/blue and black/brown wires between the ECM connector and the EOT sensor subharness connector. Does each wire have continuity? — No. → Repair the wiring harness.

Yes.

Faulty ECM.

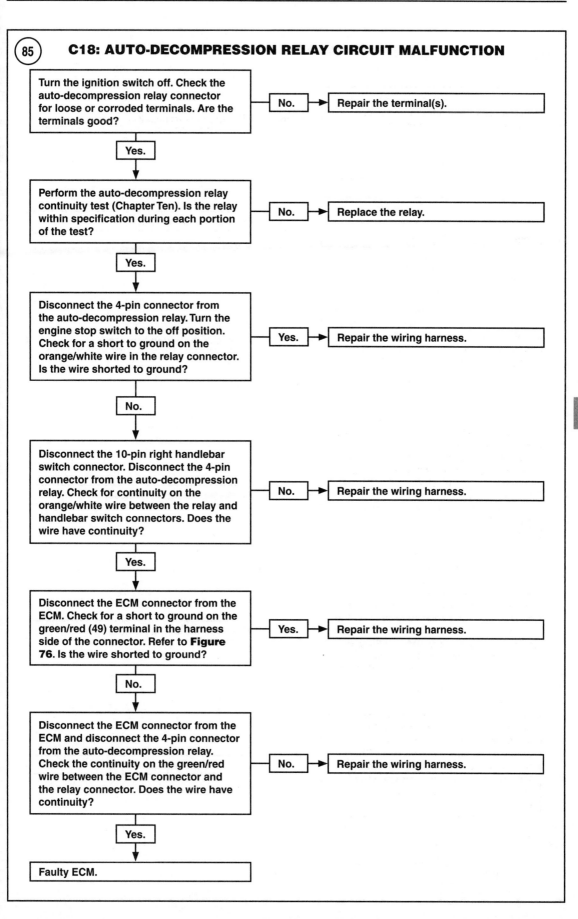

85   **C18: AUTO-DECOMPRESSION RELAY CIRCUIT MALFUNCTION**

Turn the ignition switch off. Check the auto-decompression relay connector for loose or corroded terminals. Are the terminals good? → **No.** → Repair the terminal(s).

↓ **Yes.**

Perform the auto-decompression relay continuity test (Chapter Ten). Is the relay within specification during each portion of the test? → **No.** → Replace the relay.

↓ **Yes.**

Disconnect the 4-pin connector from the auto-decompression relay. Turn the engine stop switch to the off position. Check for a short to ground on the orange/white wire in the relay connector. Is the wire shorted to ground? → **Yes.** → Repair the wiring harness.

↓ **No.**

9

Disconnect the 10-pin right handlebar switch connector. Disconnect the 4-pin connector from the auto-decompression relay. Check for continuity on the orange/white wire between the relay and handlebar switch connectors. Does the wire have continuity? → **No.** → Repair the wiring harness.

↓ **Yes.**

Disconnect the ECM connector from the ECM. Check for a short to ground on the green/red (49) terminal in the harness side of the connector. Refer to **Figure 76**. Is the wire shorted to ground? → **Yes.** → Repair the wiring harness.

↓ **No.**

Disconnect the ECM connector from the ECM and disconnect the 4-pin connector from the auto-decompression relay. Check the continuity on the green/red wire between the ECM connector and the relay connector. Does the wire have continuity? → **No.** → Repair the wiring harness.

↓ **Yes.**

Faulty ECM.

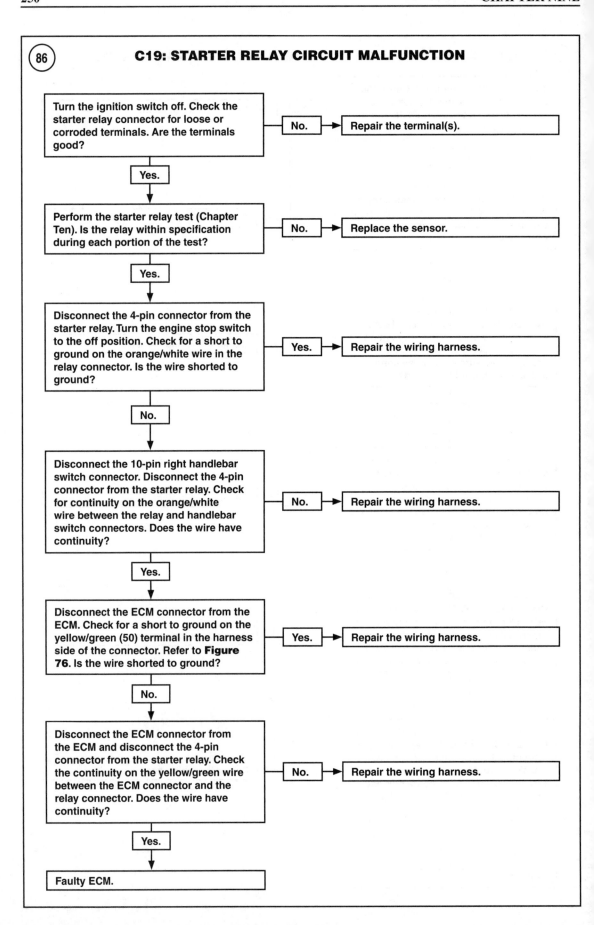

86 **C19: STARTER RELAY CIRCUIT MALFUNCTION**

Turn the ignition switch off. Check the starter relay connector for loose or corroded terminals. Are the terminals good?

No. → Repair the terminal(s).

Yes.

Perform the starter relay test (Chapter Ten). Is the relay within specification during each portion of the test?

No. → Replace the sensor.

Yes.

Disconnect the 4-pin connector from the starter relay. Turn the engine stop switch to the off position. Check for a short to ground on the orange/white wire in the relay connector. Is the wire shorted to ground?

Yes. → Repair the wiring harness.

No.

Disconnect the 10-pin right handlebar switch connector. Disconnect the 4-pin connector from the starter relay. Check for continuity on the orange/white wire between the relay and handlebar switch connectors. Does the wire have continuity?

No. → Repair the wiring harness.

Yes.

Disconnect the ECM connector from the ECM. Check for a short to ground on the yellow/green (50) terminal in the harness side of the connector. Refer to **Figure 76**. Is the wire shorted to ground?

Yes. → Repair the wiring harness.

No.

Disconnect the ECM connector from the ECM and disconnect the 4-pin connector from the starter relay. Check the continuity on the yellow/green wire between the ECM connector and the relay connector. Does the wire have continuity?

No. → Repair the wiring harness.

Yes.

Faulty ECM.

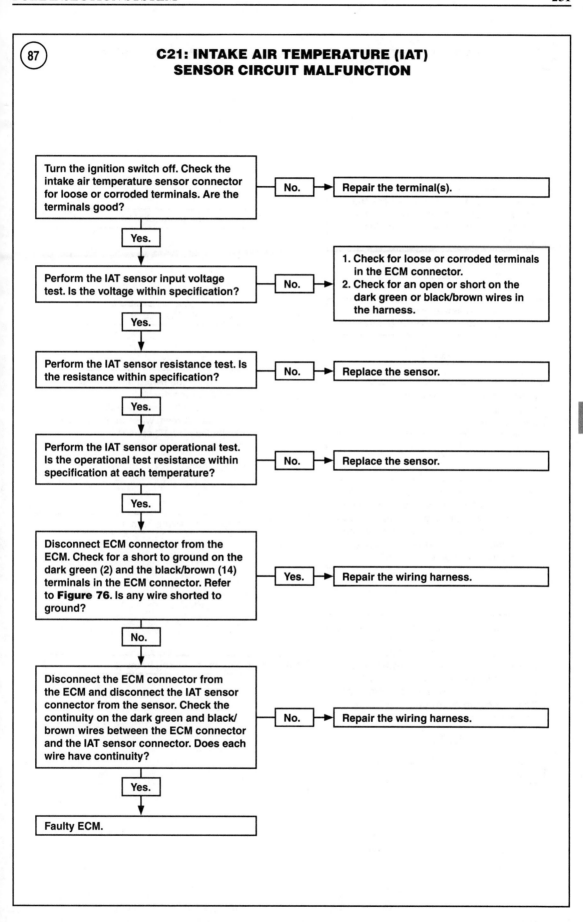

(87) **C21: INTAKE AIR TEMPERATURE (IAT) SENSOR CIRCUIT MALFUNCTION**

Turn the ignition switch off. Check the intake air temperature sensor connector for loose or corroded terminals. Are the terminals good?

→ No. → Repair the terminal(s).

↓ Yes.

Perform the IAT sensor input voltage test. Is the voltage within specification?

→ No. →
1. Check for loose or corroded terminals in the ECM connector.
2. Check for an open or short on the dark green or black/brown wires in the harness.

↓ Yes.

Perform the IAT sensor resistance test. Is the resistance within specification?

→ No. → Replace the sensor.

↓ Yes.

Perform the IAT sensor operational test. Is the operational test resistance within specification at each temperature?

→ No. → Replace the sensor.

↓ Yes.

Disconnect ECM connector from the ECM. Check for a short to ground on the dark green (2) and the black/brown (14) terminals in the ECM connector. Refer to **Figure 76**. Is any wire shorted to ground?

→ Yes. → Repair the wiring harness.

↓ No.

Disconnect the ECM connector from the ECM and disconnect the IAT sensor connector from the sensor. Check the continuity on the dark green and black/brown wires between the ECM connector and the IAT sensor connector. Does each wire have continuity?

→ No. → Repair the wiring harness.

↓ Yes.

Faulty ECM.

9

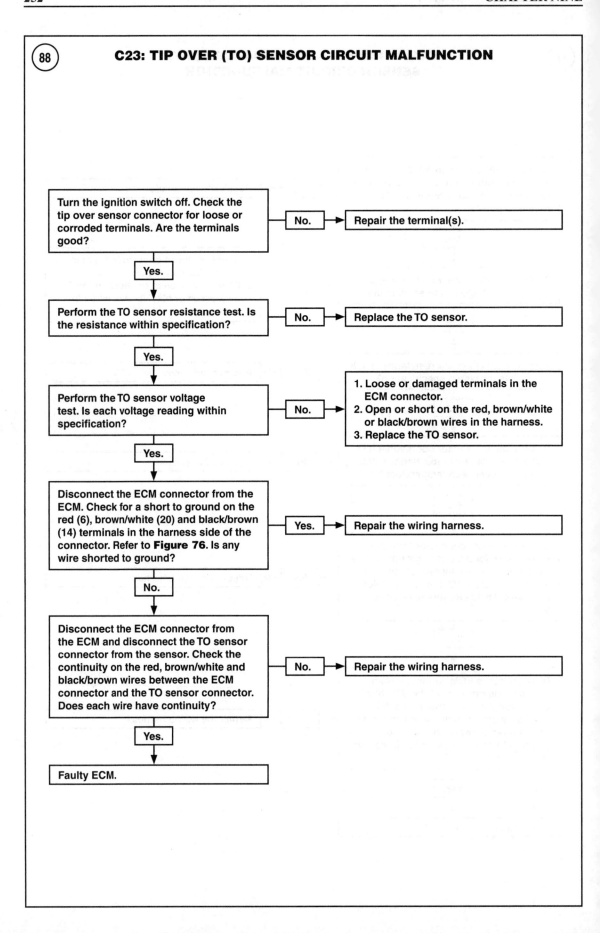

(88) **C23: TIP OVER (TO) SENSOR CIRCUIT MALFUNCTION**

Turn the ignition switch off. Check the tip over sensor connector for loose or corroded terminals. Are the terminals good? — No. → Repair the terminal(s).

Yes.

Perform the TO sensor resistance test. Is the resistance within specification? — No. → Replace the TO sensor.

Yes.

Perform the TO sensor voltage test. Is each voltage reading within specification? — No. →
1. Loose or damaged terminals in the ECM connector.
2. Open or short on the red, brown/white or black/brown wires in the harness.
3. Replace the TO sensor.

Yes.

Disconnect the ECM connector from the ECM. Check for a short to ground on the red (6), brown/white (20) and black/brown (14) terminals in the harness side of the connector. Refer to **Figure 76**. Is any wire shorted to ground? — Yes. → Repair the wiring harness.

No.

Disconnect the ECM connector from the ECM and disconnect the TO sensor connector from the sensor. Check the continuity on the red, brown/white and black/brown wires between the ECM connector and the TO sensor connector. Does each wire have continuity? — No. → Repair the wiring harness.

Yes.

Faulty ECM.

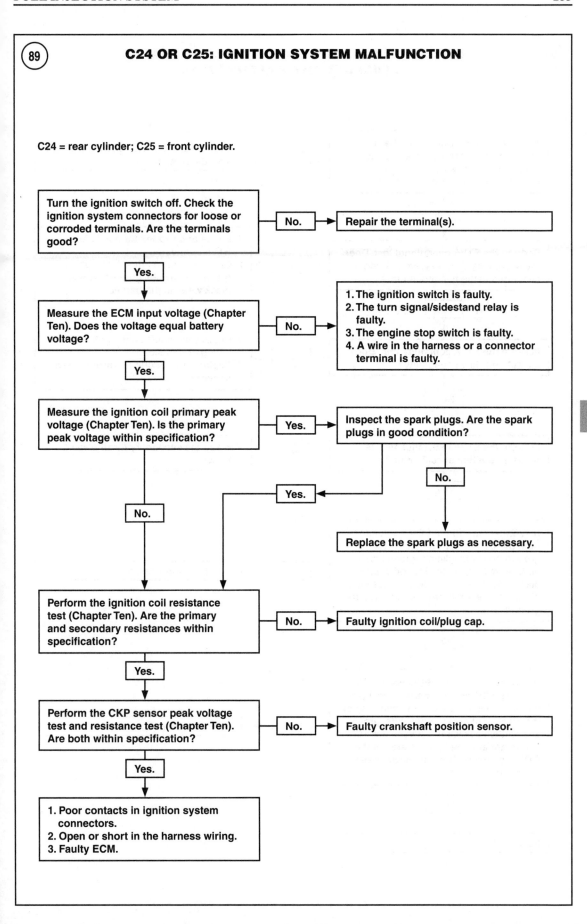

(89) **C24 OR C25: IGNITION SYSTEM MALFUNCTION**

C24 = rear cylinder; C25 = front cylinder.

Turn the ignition switch off. Check the ignition system connectors for loose or corroded terminals. Are the terminals good? — No. → Repair the terminal(s).

Yes.

Measure the ECM input voltage (Chapter Ten). Does the voltage equal battery voltage? — No. →
1. The ignition switch is faulty.
2. The turn signal/sidestand relay is faulty.
3. The engine stop switch is faulty.
4. A wire in the harness or a connector terminal is faulty.

Yes.

Measure the ignition coil primary peak voltage (Chapter Ten). Is the primary peak voltage within specification? — Yes. → Inspect the spark plugs. Are the spark plugs in good condition?

No. →

Yes. ← Yes.

Replace the spark plugs as necessary.

No.

Perform the ignition coil resistance test (Chapter Ten). Are the primary and secondary resistances within specification? — No. → Faulty ignition coil/plug cap.

Yes.

Perform the CKP sensor peak voltage test and resistance test (Chapter Ten). Are both within specification? — No. → Faulty crankshaft position sensor.

Yes.

1. Poor contacts in ignition system connectors.
2. Open or short in the harness wiring.
3. Faulty ECM.

9

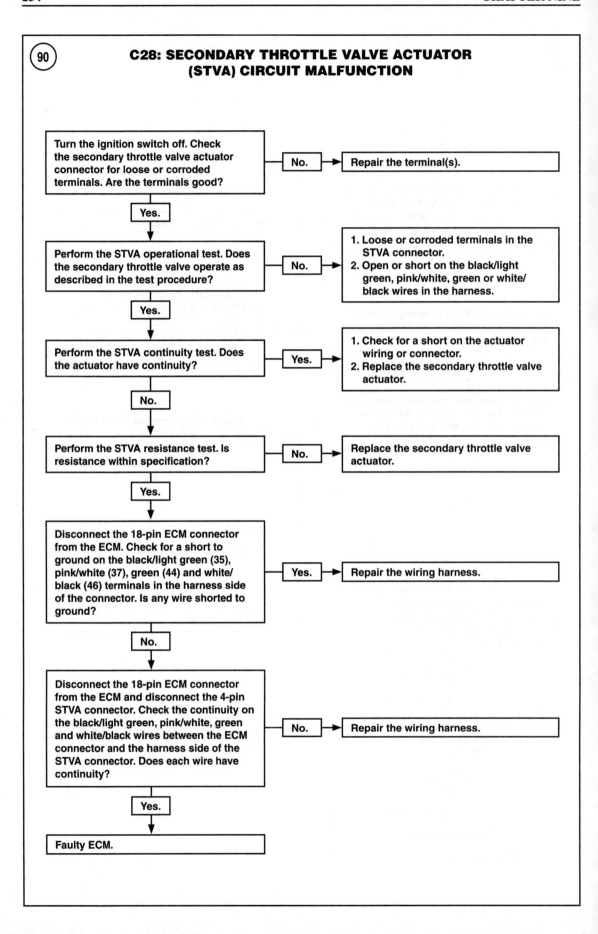

**C28: SECONDARY THROTTLE VALVE ACTUATOR
(STVA) CIRCUIT MALFUNCTION**

90

Turn the ignition switch off. Check the secondary throttle valve actuator connector for loose or corroded terminals. Are the terminals good?

No. → Repair the terminal(s).

Yes.

Perform the STVA operational test. Does the secondary throttle valve operate as described in the test procedure?

No. →
1. Loose or corroded terminals in the STVA connector.
2. Open or short on the black/light green, pink/white, green or white/black wires in the harness.

Yes.

Perform the STVA continuity test. Does the actuator have continuity?

Yes. →
1. Check for a short on the actuator wiring or connector.
2. Replace the secondary throttle valve actuator.

No.

Perform the STVA resistance test. Is resistance within specification?

No. → Replace the secondary throttle valve actuator.

Yes.

Disconnect the 18-pin ECM connector from the ECM. Check for a short to ground on the black/light green (35), pink/white (37), green (44) and white/black (46) terminals in the harness side of the connector. Is any wire shorted to ground?

Yes. → Repair the wiring harness.

No.

Disconnect the 18-pin ECM connector from the ECM and disconnect the 4-pin STVA connector. Check the continuity on the black/light green, pink/white, green and white/black wires between the ECM connector and the harness side of the STVA connector. Does each wire have continuity?

No. → Repair the wiring harness.

Yes.

Faulty ECM.

91

C29: SECONDARY THROTTLE POSITION (STP) SENSOR CIRCUIT MALFUNCTION

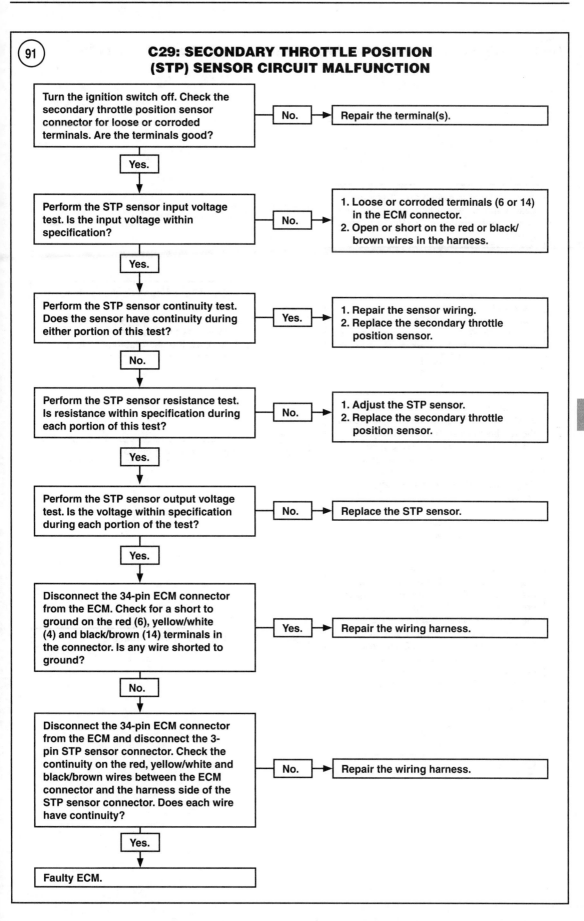

Turn the ignition switch off. Check the secondary throttle position sensor connector for loose or corroded terminals. Are the terminals good? → No. → Repair the terminal(s).

Yes. ↓

Perform the STP sensor input voltage test. Is the input voltage within specification? → No. → 1. Loose or corroded terminals (6 or 14) in the ECM connector.
2. Open or short on the red or black/brown wires in the harness.

Yes. ↓

Perform the STP sensor continuity test. Does the sensor have continuity during either portion of this test? → Yes. → 1. Repair the sensor wiring.
2. Replace the secondary throttle position sensor.

No. ↓

Perform the STP sensor resistance test. Is resistance within specification during each portion of this test? → No. → 1. Adjust the STP sensor.
2. Replace the secondary throttle position sensor.

Yes. ↓

Perform the STP sensor output voltage test. Is the voltage within specification during each portion of the test? → No. → Replace the STP sensor.

Yes. ↓

Disconnect the 34-pin ECM connector from the ECM. Check for a short to ground on the red (6), yellow/white (4) and black/brown (14) terminals in the connector. Is any wire shorted to ground? → Yes. → Repair the wiring harness.

No. ↓

Disconnect the 34-pin ECM connector from the ECM and disconnect the 3-pin STP sensor connector. Check the continuity on the red, yellow/white and black/brown wires between the ECM connector and the harness side of the STP sensor connector. Does each wire have continuity? → No. → Repair the wiring harness.

Yes. ↓

Faulty ECM.

9

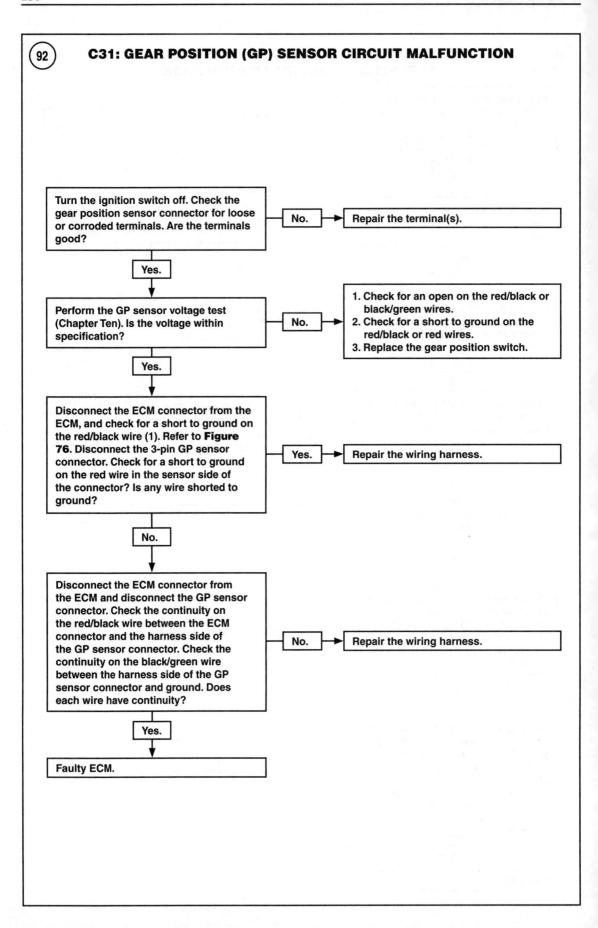

(92) **C31: GEAR POSITION (GP) SENSOR CIRCUIT MALFUNCTION**

Turn the ignition switch off. Check the gear position sensor connector for loose or corroded terminals. Are the terminals good? — No. → Repair the terminal(s).

Yes.

Perform the GP sensor voltage test (Chapter Ten). Is the voltage within specification? — No. →
1. Check for an open on the red/black or black/green wires.
2. Check for a short to ground on the red/black or red wires.
3. Replace the gear position switch.

Yes.

Disconnect the ECM connector from the ECM, and check for a short to ground on the red/black wire (1). Refer to **Figure 76**. Disconnect the 3-pin GP sensor connector. Check for a short to ground on the red wire in the sensor side of the connector? Is any wire shorted to ground? — Yes. → Repair the wiring harness.

No.

Disconnect the ECM connector from the ECM and disconnect the GP sensor connector. Check the continuity on the red/black wire between the ECM connector and the harness side of the GP sensor connector. Check the continuity on the black/green wire between the harness side of the GP sensor connector and ground. Does each wire have continuity? — No. → Repair the wiring harness.

Yes.

Faulty ECM.

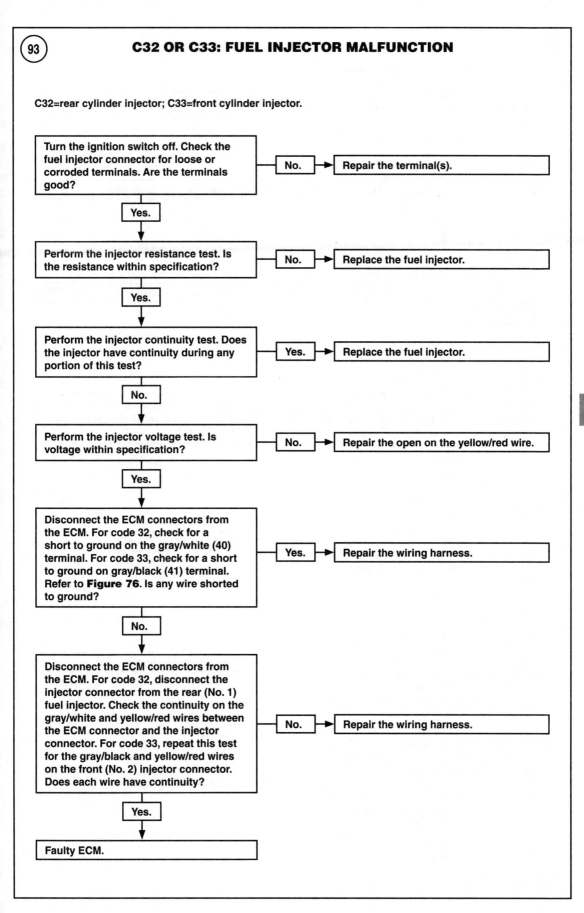

93 C32 OR C33: FUEL INJECTOR MALFUNCTION

C32=rear cylinder injector; C33=front cylinder injector.

Turn the ignition switch off. Check the fuel injector connector for loose or corroded terminals. Are the terminals good? — No. → Repair the terminal(s).

Yes.

Perform the injector resistance test. Is the resistance within specification? — No. → Replace the fuel injector.

Yes.

Perform the injector continuity test. Does the injector have continuity during any portion of this test? — Yes. → Replace the fuel injector.

No.

Perform the injector voltage test. Is voltage within specification? — No. → Repair the open on the yellow/red wire.

Yes.

Disconnect the ECM connectors from the ECM. For code 32, check for a short to ground on the gray/white (40) terminal. For code 33, check for a short to ground on gray/black (41) terminal. Refer to **Figure 76**. Is any wire shorted to ground? — Yes. → Repair the wiring harness.

No.

Disconnect the ECM connectors from the ECM. For code 32, disconnect the injector connector from the rear (No. 1) fuel injector. Check the continuity on the gray/white and yellow/red wires between the ECM connector and the injector connector. For code 33, repeat this test for the gray/black and yellow/red wires on the front (No. 2) injector connector. Does each wire have continuity? — No. → Repair the wiring harness.

Yes.

Faulty ECM.

9

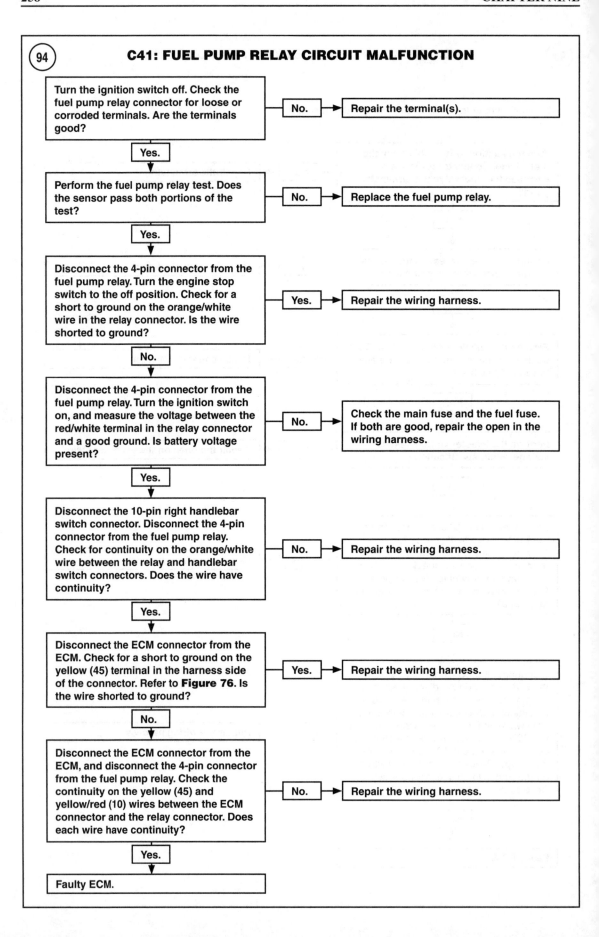

94 **C41: FUEL PUMP RELAY CIRCUIT MALFUNCTION**

Turn the ignition switch off. Check the fuel pump relay connector for loose or corroded terminals. Are the terminals good? → **No.** → Repair the terminal(s).

Yes.

Perform the fuel pump relay test. Does the sensor pass both portions of the test? → **No.** → Replace the fuel pump relay.

Yes.

Disconnect the 4-pin connector from the fuel pump relay. Turn the engine stop switch to the off position. Check for a short to ground on the orange/white wire in the relay connector. Is the wire shorted to ground? → **Yes.** → Repair the wiring harness.

No.

Disconnect the 4-pin connector from the fuel pump relay. Turn the ignition switch on, and measure the voltage between the red/white terminal in the relay connector and a good ground. Is battery voltage present? → **No.** → Check the main fuse and the fuel fuse. If both are good, repair the open in the wiring harness.

Yes.

Disconnect the 10-pin right handlebar switch connector. Disconnect the 4-pin connector from the fuel pump relay. Check for continuity on the orange/white wire between the relay and handlebar switch connectors. Does the wire have continuity? → **No.** → Repair the wiring harness.

Yes.

Disconnect the ECM connector from the ECM. Check for a short to ground on the yellow (45) terminal in the harness side of the connector. Refer to **Figure 76**. Is the wire shorted to ground? → **Yes.** → Repair the wiring harness.

No.

Disconnect the ECM connector from the ECM, and disconnect the 4-pin connector from the fuel pump relay. Check the continuity on the yellow (45) and yellow/red (10) wires between the ECM connector and the relay connector. Does each wire have continuity? → **No.** → Repair the wiring harness.

Yes.

Faulty ECM.

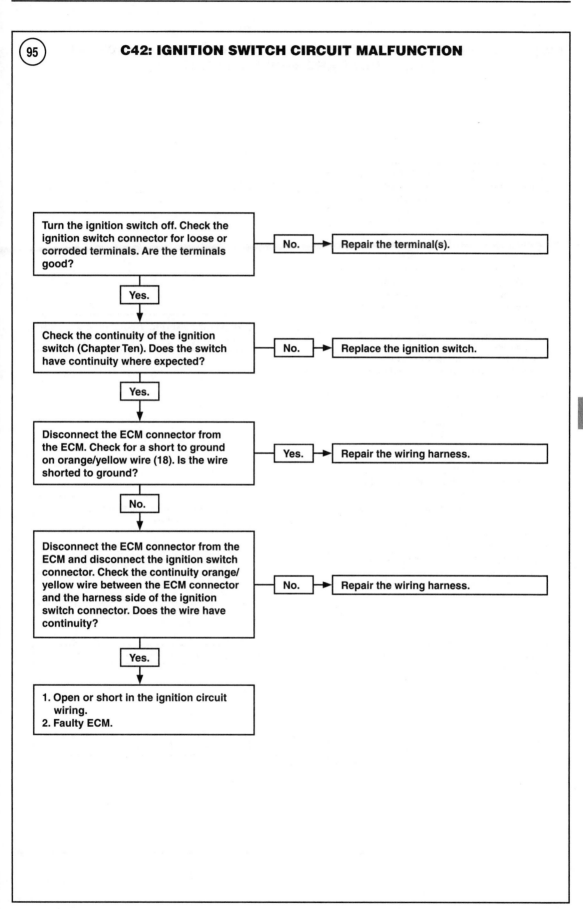

95

C42: IGNITION SWITCH CIRCUIT MALFUNCTION

Turn the ignition switch off. Check the ignition switch connector for loose or corroded terminals. Are the terminals good? → No. → Repair the terminal(s).

Yes.

Check the continuity of the ignition switch (Chapter Ten). Does the switch have continuity where expected? → No. → Replace the ignition switch.

Yes.

Disconnect the ECM connector from the ECM. Check for a short to ground on orange/yellow wire (18). Is the wire shorted to ground? → Yes. → Repair the wiring harness.

No.

Disconnect the ECM connector from the ECM and disconnect the ignition switch connector. Check the continuity orange/yellow wire between the ECM connector and the harness side of the ignition switch connector. Does the wire have continuity? → No. → Repair the wiring harness.

Yes.

1. Open or short in the ignition circuit wiring.
2. Faulty ECM.

9

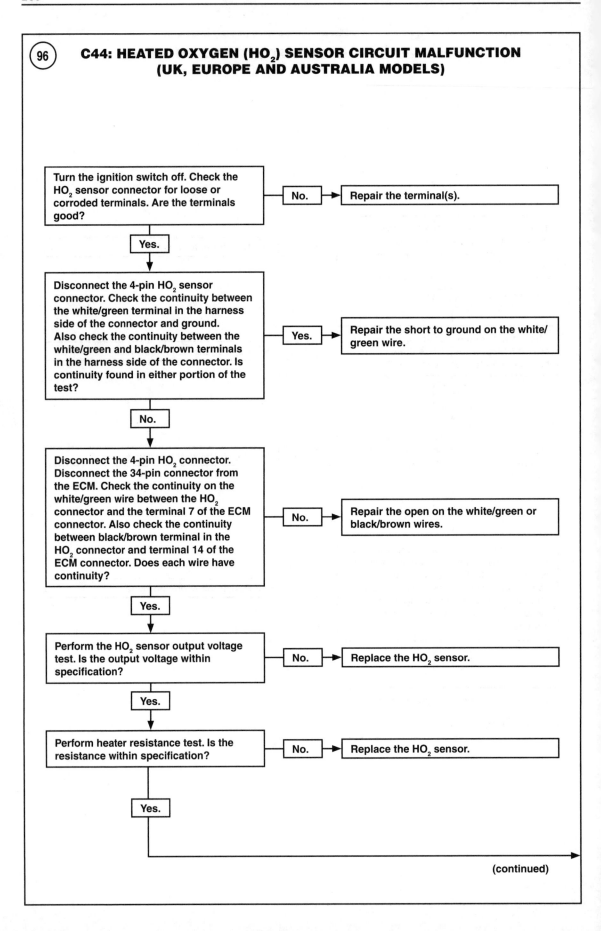

(96) **C44: HEATED OXYGEN (HO₂) SENSOR CIRCUIT MALFUNCTION
(UK, EUROPE AND AUSTRALIA MODELS)**

Turn the ignition switch off. Check the HO₂ sensor connector for loose or corroded terminals. Are the terminals good?

→ No. → Repair the terminal(s).

↓ Yes.

Disconnect the 4-pin HO₂ sensor connector. Check the continuity between the white/green terminal in the harness side of the connector and ground. Also check the continuity between the white/green and black/brown terminals in the harness side of the connector. Is continuity found in either portion of the test?

→ Yes. → Repair the short to ground on the white/green wire.

↓ No.

Disconnect the 4-pin HO₂ connector. Disconnect the 34-pin connector from the ECM. Check the continuity on the white/green wire between the HO₂ connector and the terminal 7 of the ECM connector. Also check the continuity between black/brown terminal in the HO₂ connector and terminal 14 of the ECM connector. Does each wire have continuity?

→ No. → Repair the open on the white/green or black/brown wires.

↓ Yes.

Perform the HO₂ sensor output voltage test. Is the output voltage within specification?

→ No. → Replace the HO₂ sensor.

↓ Yes.

Perform heater resistance test. Is the resistance within specification?

→ No. → Replace the HO₂ sensor.

↓ Yes.

(continued)

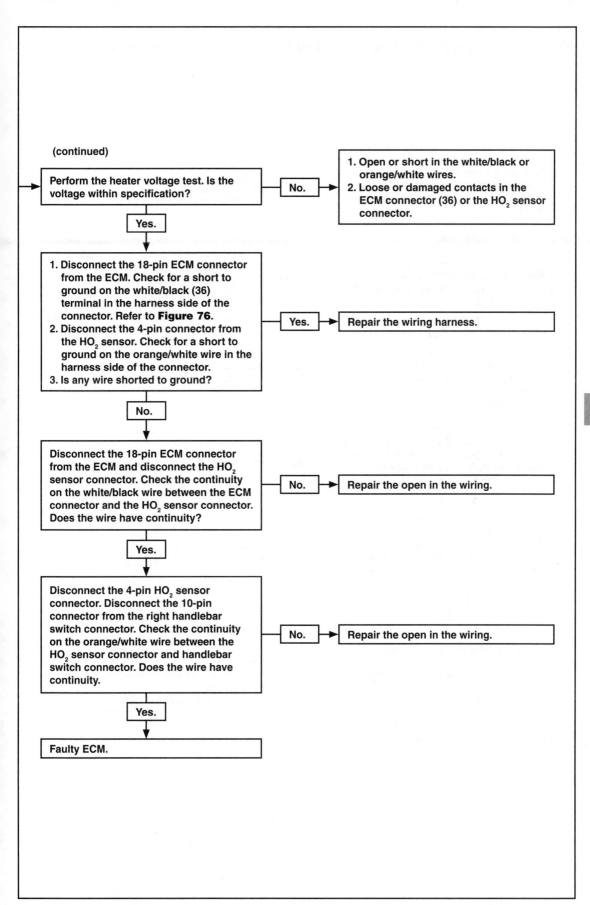

(continued)

Perform the heater voltage test. Is the voltage within specification?

→ **No.** →
1. Open or short in the white/black or orange/white wires.
2. Loose or damaged contacts in the ECM connector (36) or the HO$_2$ sensor connector.

↓ **Yes.**

1. Disconnect the 18-pin ECM connector from the ECM. Check for a short to ground on the white/black (36) terminal in the harness side of the connector. Refer to **Figure 76**.
2. Disconnect the 4-pin connector from the HO$_2$ sensor. Check for a short to ground on the orange/white wire in the harness side of the connector.
3. Is any wire shorted to ground?

→ **Yes.** → Repair the wiring harness.

↓ **No.**

Disconnect the 18-pin ECM connector from the ECM and disconnect the HO$_2$ sensor connector. Check the continuity on the white/black wire between the ECM connector and the HO$_2$ sensor connector. Does the wire have continuity?

→ **No.** → Repair the open in the wiring.

↓ **Yes.**

Disconnect the 4-pin HO$_2$ sensor connector. Disconnect the 10-pin connector from the right handlebar switch connector. Check the continuity on the orange/white wire between the HO$_2$ sensor connector and handlebar switch connector. Does the wire have continuity.

→ **No.** → Repair the open in the wiring.

↓ **Yes.**

Faulty ECM.

9

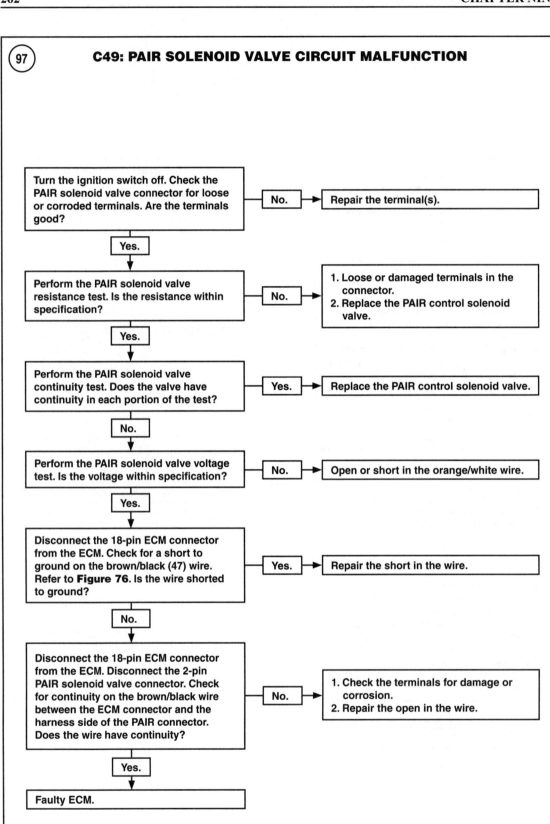

(97) **C49: PAIR SOLENOID VALVE CIRCUIT MALFUNCTION**

Turn the ignition switch off. Check the PAIR solenoid valve connector for loose or corroded terminals. Are the terminals good? → **No.** → Repair the terminal(s).

↓ **Yes.**

Perform the PAIR solenoid valve resistance test. Is the resistance within specification? → **No.** → 1. Loose or damaged terminals in the connector. 2. Replace the PAIR control solenoid valve.

↓ **Yes.**

Perform the PAIR solenoid valve continuity test. Does the valve have continuity in each portion of the test? → **Yes.** → Replace the PAIR control solenoid valve.

↓ **No.**

Perform the PAIR solenoid valve voltage test. Is the voltage within specification? → **No.** → Open or short in the orange/white wire.

↓ **Yes.**

Disconnect the 18-pin ECM connector from the ECM. Check for a short to ground on the brown/black (47) wire. Refer to **Figure 76**. Is the wire shorted to ground? → **Yes.** → Repair the short in the wire.

↓ **No.**

Disconnect the 18-pin ECM connector from the ECM. Disconnect the 2-pin PAIR solenoid valve connector. Check for continuity on the brown/black wire between the ECM connector and the harness side of the PAIR connector. Does the wire have continuity? → **No.** → 1. Check the terminals for damage or corrosion. 2. Repair the open in the wire.

↓ **Yes.**

Faulty ECM.

Table 1 FUEL SYSTEM SPECIFICATIONS

Item	Specification
Throttle body bore size	36 mm (1.42 in.)
Throttle body ID No.	
California models	10F1
All models except California	10F0
Idle speed	900-1100 rpm
Fast idle speed	1400-2000 rpm when engine is cold
Throttle cable free play	2.0-4.0 mm (0.08-0.16 in.)
Fuel pump output pressure	Approx. 300 kPa (44 psi)
Fuel pump output volume	Approx 168 ml (5.7 oz.) per 10 seconds
Fuel tank capacity (including reserve)	14.0 liter (3.7 gal.)
Recommended fuel octane	
U.S., California and Canada	
Pump octane	87
Research octane	91
All models except U.S., California and Canada	91

Table 2 FUEL SYSTEM ELECTRICAL SPECIFICATIONS

Item	Specification
Engine oil temperature sensor	
Input voltage	4.5-5.5 volts
Output voltage	0.1-4.6 volts
Resistance	
20° C (68° F)	Approx. 61.3 k ohms
50° C (122° F)	Approx. 17.8 k ohms
80° C (176° F)	Approx. 6.2 k ohms
110° C (230° F)	Approx. 2.5 k ohms
Fuel injector	
Voltage	Battery voltage
Resistance	11.7 ohms @ 20° C (68° F)
Heated oxygen sensor	
Output voltage	
At idle	0.4 volts or less
At 5000 rpm	0.6 volts or more
Heater resistance	6.5-8.9 volts @ 23° C (73.4° F)
Intake air pressure sensor	
Input voltage	4.5-5.5 volts
Output voltage	Approx. 2.53 volts @ idle
Vout voltage	4.5-5.0 volts @ 20-30° C (68-86° F)
Intake air temperature sensor	
Input voltage	4.5-5.5 volts
Output voltage	0.1-4.6 volts
Resistance	
20° C (68° F)	Approx. 2.45 k ohms
40° C (104° F)	Approx. 1.148 k ohms
60° C (140° F)	Approx. 0.587 k ohms
80° C (176° F)	Approx. 0.322 k ohms
PAIR solenoid valve resistance	20-24 ohms @20-30° C (68-86° F)
Secondary throttle position sensor	
Input voltage	4.5-5.5 volts
STPS Resistance	Approx. 4.69 k ohms
Fully closed resistance	Approx. 0.5 k ohms
Fully open resistance	Approx. 3.9 k ohms
Output voltage	
Fully closed	Approx. 0.5 volts
Fully open	Approx. 3.9 volts
Secondary throttle valve actuator resistance	Approx. 6.5 ohms
Throttle position sensor	
TPS Resistance	Approx 4.66 k ohms
Fully closed resistance	Approx. 1.12 k ohms
Fully open resistance	Approx. 4.41 k ohms
Input voltage	4.5-5.5 volts

(continued)

9

Table 2 FUEL SYSTEM ELECTRICAL SPECIFICATIONS (continued)

Item	Specification
Throttle position sensor (continued)	
Output voltage	
Fully closed	Approx. 1.12 volts
Fully open	Approx. 4.41 volts
Variance	0.064-0.096 volts
Tip over sensor	
Resistance	19.1-19.7 k ohms
Voltage	
Upright	0.4-1.4 volts
Leaning 65°	3.7-4.4 volts

Table 3 IAP SENSOR Vout VOLTAGE

Reference altitude m (ft.)	Atmospheric pressure KPa (mm Hg)	V-out voltage
0-610 (0-2000)	100-94 (750-705)	3.4-4.0
611-1524 (2001-5000)	94-85 (705-638)	2.8-3.7
1525-2438 (5001-8000)	85-76 (638-570)	2.6-3.4
2439-3048 (8001-10,000)	76-70 (570-525)	2.4-3.1

Table 4 FUEL AND EXHAUST SYSTEM TORQUE SPECIFICATIONS

Item	N•m	in.-lb.	ft.-lb.
Crankshaft position sensor mounting bolt	5	44	–
Engine oil temperature sensor	22	–	16
Fuel rail screw	3.5	31	–
Fuel delivery hose screw	3.5	31	–
Fuel pump bolt	10	89	–
Heated oxygen sensor	25	–	18
Intake air temperature sensor	20	–	15
Secondary throttle position sensor screw	3.5	31	–
Throttle position sensor screw	3.5	31	–

CHAPTER TEN

ELECTRICAL SYSTEM

This chapter covers the charging, ignition, starting, and lighting systems. Fuse and switch procedures are also covered. If necessary, refer to the wiring diagrams at the end of this manual when working on the electrical system.

Refer to *Electrical Testing* in Chapter Two. If necessary, refer to *Electrical System Fundamentals* in Chapter One.

Refer to Chapter Three for spark plug information.

During inspection, compare measurements to the specifications at the end of this chapter. Replace worn, damaged or out of specification parts.

ELECTRICAL COMPONENT REPLACEMENT

Most motorcycle dealerships and parts suppliers will not accept the return of any electrical part. If the exact cause of an electrical system malfunction cannot be determined, have a dealership retest the specific system to verify test results. If a new electrical component is installed and the system still does not work, the unit, in all likelihood, cannot be returned for a refund.

Consider any test results carefully before replacing a component that tests only slightly out of specification, especially for resistance. A number of variables can affect test results dramatically. These include: the test meter's internal circuitry, ambient temperature, and the conditions under which the machine has been operated. All instructions and specifications have been checked for accuracy. However, successful test results depend upon individual accuracy.

ELECTRICAL CONNECTORS

To prevent connector corrosion, pack electrical connectors with dielectric grease when reconnecting them. Dielectric grease seals the connector without interfering with current flow. Only use this compound or an equivalent sealant for electrical use. Do not use a material, such as silicone sealant, that will interfere with the electrical flow. Thoroughly clean and dry the connectors before applying the grease.

Also check the ground connections at the various locations on the motorcycle. Loose or dirty ground terminals are often sources of electrical problems. Make sure the ground connections are tight and free of corrosion.

The position of electrical connectors can vary between model years, and a connector may have been repositioned during a previous repair. To avoid confusion, always refer to the correct wiring diagram, and confirm the connector by the wire colors. If necessary, follow the electrical harness or wires from the connector to the electrical component.

BATTERY

A sealed, maintenance-free battery is used on all models. The battery electrolyte cannot be serviced. Never remove the sealing bar cap from a maintenance free battery.

If necessary, replace the battery with an equivalent maintenance-free type. Do not install a non-sealed battery.

Safety Precaution

Take the following precautions whenever servicing the battery.

1. Do not smoke or permit any open flame near a battery being charged, or one that has been recently charged.

2. Do not disconnect live circuits at the battery. A spark usually occurs when a live circuit is broken. Disconnect the negative cable first when working on the battery.

3. Exercise caution when connecting or disconnecting a battery charger. Turn the power switch off before making or breaking connections.

4. Keep children and pets away from the charging equipment and the battery.

Removal/Installation

The battery sits between the front downtubes at the front of the engine.

1. Turn the ignition switch off.

2. Remove the cover bolt (A, **Figure 1**) from each side of the battery box. Then lift the top cover (B) from the box.

3. Remove the terminal screw (**Figure 2**). Then disconnect the negative battery cable.

4. Remove the terminal screw (A, **Figure 3**). Then disconnect the charger connector lead (B) (where equipped) and the positive battery cable (C).

5. Remove the cover screws from the front (A, **Figure 4**) and from each side (D, **Figure 3**) of the front cover. Pull the front cover (B, **Figure 4**) from the battery box.

6. Lift the battery from the box.

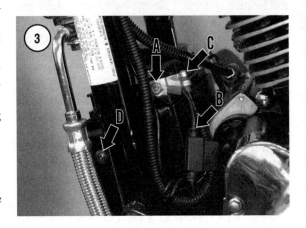

7. If necessary, remove the battery box by performing the following:

    a. Remove the battery box bolts from the inside of the box (**Figure 5**) and from the right side (C, **Figure 1**).

    b. Remove the battery box from between the frame downtubes.

8. Inspect the pads in the battery box for wear or deterioration.

9. Install the battery and its box by reversing the removal steps. Note the following:

    a. Set the battery into the battery box so the negative battery terminal (**Figure 2**) is on the right side.

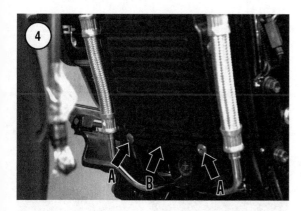

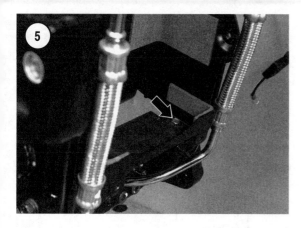

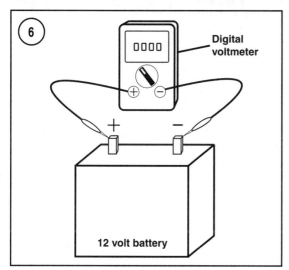

Digital
voltmeter

0000

+ −

+ −

12 volt battery

CAUTION
Connect the battery cables correctly.
Reversing the polarity will damage the
charging and ignition systems.

b. First connect the positive battery cable (C,
Figure 3) and the charger connector lead (B)
(where equipped) to the positive terminal.
Then connect the negative cable to the negative terminal (**Figure 2**).

c. Coat the battery connections with dielectric
grease to prevent corrosion.

Inspection and Testing

1. Remove the battery as described in this section.
Do not clean the battery while it is mounted in the
frame.
2. Inspect the battery pads in the battery box for contamination or damage. Clean the battery box with a
solution of baking soda and water.
3. Check the battery case for cracks or other damage. If the battery case is warped, discolored or has a
raised top, the battery has overheated.
4. Check the battery terminals and bolts for corrosion or damage. If necessary, thoroughly clean
the parts with a solution of baking soda and water.
Replace severely corroded or damaged parts.
6. If corroded, clean the top of the battery with a stiff
bristle brush using baking soda and water.
7. Check the battery cables for corrosion and damage. If corrosion is minor, clean the cable ends with a
stiff wire brush. Replace severely worn or damaged
cables.

NOTE
Measure the open circuit voltage when
battery temperature is 20° C (68° F).
Use a digital voltmeter.

8. Check the state of charge by connecting a digital
voltmeter across the battery terminals (**Figure 6**).
  a. A fully charged battery's voltage should be between 13.0-13.2 volts.
  b. If the battery voltage is less than 12.5 volts, the
  battery is undercharged and requires charging.
  c. If battery voltage is less than 12.0 volts, replace the battery.

Charging

WARNING
During charging, explosive hydrogen
gas is released from the battery. Charge
the battery in a well-ventilated area
away from open flames, including ap-
pliance pilot lights. Do not smoke in the
area. Never check the battery charge by
arcing across the terminals. The result-
ing spark can cause an explosion.

A digital voltmeter and a charger with an adjustable amperage output are required when charging
a maintenance free battery. If this equipment is not
available, have the battery charged by a shop with
the proper equipment. Excessive voltage and amper-

10

age from an unregulated charger can damage the battery and shorten its service life.

A battery will self-discharge approximately one percent of its given capacity each day. If a battery not in use (without any loads connected) loses its charge within a week after charging, the battery is defective.

If the motorcycle is not used for long periods, an automatic battery charger with variable voltage and amperage outputs is recommended for optimum battery service life.

> *CAUTION*
> *Always disconnect the battery cables from the battery. If the cables are connected during the charging procedure, the charger may damage the voltage regulator/rectifier. Some maintenance chargers can be used while the battery is connected to the motorcycle without damaging the charging system.*

1. Remove the battery from the motorcycle as described in this section.
2. Connect the positive charger lead to the positive battery terminal; connect the negative charger lead to the negative battery terminal.

> *CAUTION*
> *Do not exceed 4 amps during charging.*

3. Set the charger to 12 volts. If the amperage of the charger is variable, select the low setting.
4. The charging time depends upon the discharged condition of the battery. Use the charging amperage and length of time on the battery label. Normally, charge the battery at 1/10th of its rated capacity.
5. Turn the charger on.
6. After charging the battery, turn the charger off and disconnect the leads.
7. Wait 30 minutes. Then measure the battery voltage.
   a. If the battery voltage is between 13.0-13.2 volts, the battery is fully charged.
   b. If the battery voltage is less than 13.0 volts, the battery is undercharged and requires charging.
8. If the battery remains stable for one hour, the battery is charged.
9. Install the battery into the motorcycle as described in this section.

Initialization

When replacing the old battery, charge the new battery completely before connecting it. Using a new battery without an initial charge causes permanent battery damage. That is, the battery will not hold

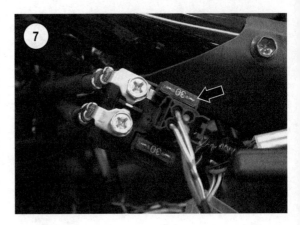

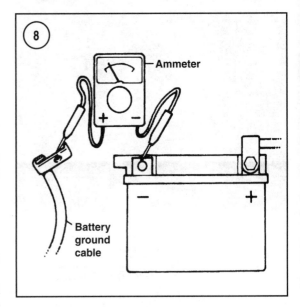

more than approximately an 80% charge. Subsequent charging will not bring its charge to 100%. When purchasing a new battery from a parts supplier, verify its charge status. If necessary, have the store perform the initial or booster charge and confirm the open circuit voltage is between 13.0-13.2 volts.

> *NOTE*
> *Recycle the old battery. Most dealerships accept old batteries in trade when purchasing a new one. Never place an old battery in the trash. It is illegal in most areas to place any acid or lead (heavy metal) contents in landfills.*

CHARGING SYSTEM

Operation and Precautions

The charging system consists of the battery, alternator, and a voltage regulator/rectifier. A 30-amp main fuse (**Figure 7**) protects the circuit.

Alternating current (AC) generated by the alternator is rectified to direct current (DC). The voltage regulator maintains the voltage to the battery and electrical loads at a constant voltage regardless of variations in engine speed and load.

To prevent charging system damage, note the following:

1. Always disconnect the negative battery cable (**Figure 2**) before removing any charging system component.

2. When charging the battery, remove it from the motorcycle, and follow the inspection and charging procedures described in this section.

3. Make sure the battery is fully charged.

4. Check the charging system wiring and connections for damage. Clean, tighten or repair any problems.

Current Draw Test

1. Turn the ignition switch off.

2. Remove the battery top cover. Then disconnect the negative battery cable (**Figure 2**).

> *CAUTION*
> *Before connecting an ammeter, set the meter to its highest amperage scale to*

prevent a possible large current flow from damaging the meter.

3. Connect the ammeter between the battery negative cable and the negative terminal (**Figure 8**).

4. Switch the ammeter from its highest to lowest amperage scale while reading the meter. The reading must not exceed the maximum current draw specified in **Table 1**.

5. If the current draw is excessive, the probable causes are:

    a. Accessory draw.

    b. Faulty electrical connector(s).

    c. Damaged battery.

    d. Short circuit in the system.

6. Disconnect the ammeter test leads and reconnect the negative battery cable.

Regulated Voltage Test

Before troubleshooting the charging system, make sure the battery is fully charged and in good condition. Inspect and test the battery as described in this section. Make sure all electrical connectors are secure and corrosion free.

1. Start the engine and let it reach normal operating temperature. Turn off the engine.

2. Remove the top cover from the battery box.

3. Turn the headlight dimmer switch to the HI position.

4. Restart the engine and let it idle.

5. Connect the voltmeter to the battery as shown in **Figure 6**.

6. Increase engine speed to 5000 rpm. The voltage reading should be within the regulated voltage range specified in **Table 1**. If the voltage is outside the specified range, inspect the alternator and the voltage regulator as described in this chapter.

7. If the charging voltage is too high; the voltage regulator/rectifier is probably faulty.

No-load Voltage Test

1. Remove the secondary gear cover (Chapter Seven).

2A. On carbureted models, disconnect the 3-pin stator connector (A, **Figure 9**).

2B. On fuel injected models:

    a. Remove the steering head covers and meter cover (Chapter Fifteen).

    b. Lift the filler neck. Then disconnect the 3-pin stator connector (A, **Figure 10**).

3. Start the engine and let it idle.

4. Connect the voltmeter test probes to a pair of terminals in the alternator side of the connector. On 1999-2004 models, the stator wires are black. On 2005-on models, these wires are white.

10

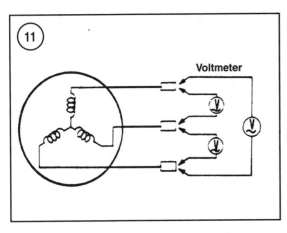

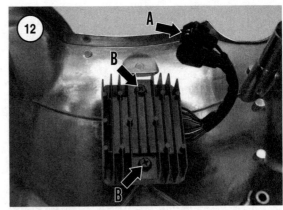

5. Increase engine speed to 5000 rpm and check the voltage on the meter. Record the voltage for that pair of terminals.

6. Repeat Step 4 and Step 5, and measure the voltage between each of the remaining terminal pairs. Take three readings. See **Figure 11**.

7. If the voltage in any test is less than the no-load voltage specified in **Table 1**, the alternator is defective.

VOLTAGE REGULATOR/RECTIFIER

Removal/Installation

1. Disconnect the negative battery cable.

2. Remove the secondary gear cover (Chapter Seven).

3. Unplug the connector (A, **Figure 12**) and remove the mounting screws (B). Then remove the regulator/rectifier from the secondary gear cover.

4. Install by reversing the removal steps. Note the following:

    a. Tighten the mounting screws (B, **Figure 12**) securely.

    b. Make sure the terminals in the connector(s) (A, **Figure 12**) are corrosion-free.

    c. Securely plug the connector(s) together.

Voltage Test

Use the multicircuit tester (Suzuki part No. 09900-25008), or its equivalent, to test the regulator/rectifier unit. Make sure the tester's battery is in good condition.

1. Perform Steps 1-3 of the regulator/rectifier removal procedures.

2. Set the tester to the diode setting.

3. On carbureted models, refer to **Figure 13** and identify the terminals in the regulator/rectifier connector. On fuel injected models, refer to **Figure 14**.

4. Connect the tester probes to the terminals indi-

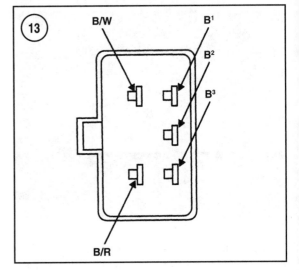

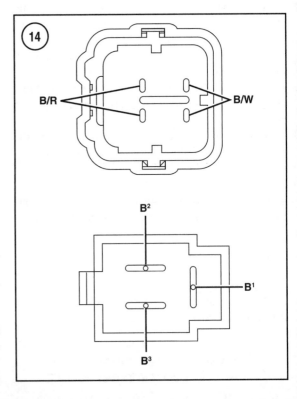

(15) REGULATOR/RECTIFIER TEST

		+ Probe of tester to:				
		B/R	B¹	B²	B³	B/W
− Probe of tester to:	B/R		0.4 ~ 0.7V	0.4 ~ 0.7V	0.4 ~ 0.7V	0.5 ~ 1.2V
	B¹	Approx. 1.5V		Approx. 1.5V	Approx. 1.5V	0.4 ~ 0.7V
	B²	Approx. 1.5V	Approx. 1.5V		Approx. 1.5V	0.4 ~ 0.7V
	B³	Approx. 1.5V	Approx. 1.5V	Approx. 1.5V		0.4 ~ 0.7V
	B/W	Approx. 1.5V	Approx. 1.5V	Approx. 1.5V	Approx. 1.5V	

B: Black; B/R: Black with red tracer; B/W: Black with white tracer

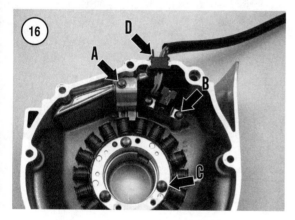

(16)

cated in **Figure 15** and note the voltage.

5. If any voltage reading differs from the given value, replace the regulator/rectifier.

STATOR

Removal/Installation

The stator assembly mounts to the inside of the alternator cover. On carbureted models, the stator assembly consists of the stator and the signal generator. On fuel injected models, it consists of the stator and crankshaft position sensor.

The stator and signal generator (carbureted models) or the stator and crankshaft position sensor (fuel injected models) must be replaced as an assembly. **Figure 16** shows a stator assembly from a 2005 model. The removal/installation procedures are the same for all models.

1. Remove the alternator cover (Chapter Five). Note how the wiring is routed through the motorcycle.

2. Place several shop cloths on the workbench and turn the alternator cover upside down.

3. Remove the stator wire clamp bolt (A, **Figure 16**) and lift out the clamp. Note how the stator wire is routed in the alternator cover.

4A. On carbureted models, remove the signal generator bolts.

4B. On fuel injected models, remove the crankshaft position sensor bolts (B, **Figure 16**).

5. Remove the stator bolts (C, **Figure 16**) from the assembly.

6. Carefully pull the rubber grommet (D, **Figure 16**) from the alternator cover, and remove the stator assembly. Note how the stator wires are routed through the cover.

7. Install the stator assembly by reversing these removal steps. Note the following:

  a. Make sure the grommet is seated.

  b. Route the stator wires along the path noted during removal.

  c. Apply Suzuki Thread Lock 1342 to the threads of all assembly bolts.

  d. Tighten the stator bolts (C, **Figure 16**) to 10 N•m (89 in.-lb.).

  e. Tighten the stator wire clamp bolt (A, **Figure 16**) to 5 N•m (44 in.-lb.).

  f. Tighten the signal generator bolts (carbureted models) or crankshaft position sensor bolts (B, **Figure 16**; fuel injected models) to 5 N•m (44 in.-1b.).

Resistance Test

1. Remove the secondary gear cover (Chapter Seven).

2A. On carbureted models, disconnect the 3-pin stator connector (A, **Figure 9**).

2B. On fuel injected models:

  a. Remove the steering head covers and meter cover (Chapter Fifteen).

10

b. Lift the filler neck. Then disconnect the 3-pin stator connector (A, **Figure 10**).

3. Connect the ohmmeter test probes to a pair of terminals in the stator side of the connector. On 1999-2004 models, the stator wires are black. On 2005-on models, these wires are white.

4. Check the reading on the meter, and record the resistance for that pair of terminals.

5. Repeat Step 3 and Step 4, and measure the resistance between each of the remaining terminal pairs. Take three readings (**Figure 17**).

6. The stator is defective if any resistance is outside the specified range (**Table 1**).

7. Check the continuity between each terminal in the stator side of the connector and ground. If any reading indicates continuity, one or more of the stator wires is shorted to ground. If so, replace the stator assembly.

IGNITION SYSTEM

On carbureted models, the ignition system consists of a signal generator, igniter with an 8-bit microprocessor (IC), two ignition coils and two park plugs. During operation, the IC in the igniter receives input from the signal generator, throttle position sensor, and MAP sensor to determine the ignition timing for the operating conditions.

The IC sends a signal to the ignition coil, the primary winding turns off and on, and a high voltage is induced in the secondary winding, which fires the spark plug.

On fuel injected models, the ignition system consists of a crankshaft position sensor, electronic control module (ECM), and two ignition coils and spark plugs. The ECM uses input from the crankshaft position sensor, throttle position sensor, engine oil temperature sensor, and gear position sensor to calculate the ignition timing for the operating conditions.

The ECM then sends a signal to the power source, which sends its energy to the primary side of the ignition coil. This induces a high voltage in the coil's secondary winding and fires the spark plug.

Both systems include an rpm limiter. On carbureted models, the igniter cuts off primary current to both ignition coils when engine speed reaches 6000 rpm. On fuel injected models, the ECM cuts off fuel to the injectors when engine speed reaches 5800-6000 rpm.

Troubleshooting

On carbureted models, refer to Chapter Two. On fuel injected models, an ignition system malfunction generates a malfunction code. Refer to Chapter Nine.

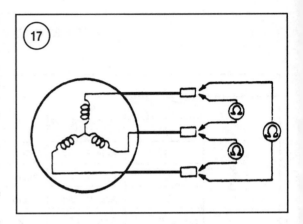

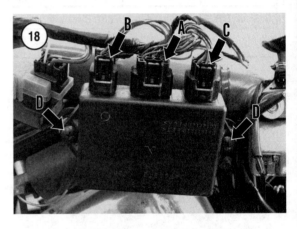

SIGNAL GENERATOR

Removal/Installation

The signal generator is part of the stator assembly. Refer to *Stator* in this chapter.

Peak Voltage Test

Use the multicircuit tester (Suzuki part No. 09900-25008) with a peak voltage adapter, or equivalent tools, to perform this test.

1. Remove the upper cover from the left side (Chapter Fifteen).

2. Disconnect the middle connector (A, **Figure 18**) from the igniter.

3. With 0.5-mm back probe pins, connect the positive test probe to the green terminal in the igniter connector; connect the negative test probe to the connector's brown terminal.

4. Shift the transmission into neutral, turn the ignition on, and pull in the clutch lever.

5. Crank the engine for a few seconds. Record the highest reading.

6. Repeat Step 5 a few times. The highest peak voltage reading should equal or exceed the value in **Table 1**. If peak voltage is lower than specified, measure

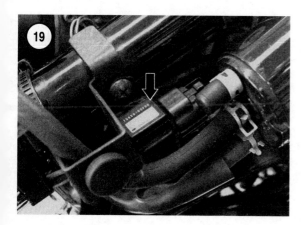

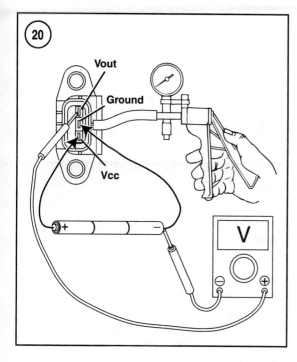

the peak voltage at the signal generator connector by performing Steps 7-9.

7. Remove the secondary gear cover (Chapter Seven), and disconnect the 2-pin signal generator connector (B, **Figure 9**).

8. Connect the positive test probe to the green terminal in the sensor side of the connector; connect the negative test probe to the blue terminal in the sensor side of the connector.

9. Crank the engine for a few seconds. Record the highest reading. Repeat this test a few times. The highest peak voltage reading should equal or exceed the value in **Table 1**.

10. Consider the following:

   a. If the peak voltage at the signal generator connector is within specification but the reading at the igniter connector is out of specification, the wiring is faulty. Locate and repair the fault or replace the wiring harness.

   b. If the peak voltage at each connector is out of specification, replace the signal generator.

Resistance Test

1. Remove the secondary gear cover (Chapter Seven), and disconnect the 2-pin signal generator connector (B, **Figure 9**).

2. Measure the resistance across the two terminals (green and blue) in the sensor side of the connector. Compare the readings to the specification in **Table 1**.

3. Check the continuity between the ground and the blue terminal in the sensor side of the connector. The meter should indicate no continuity. The sensor is shorted to ground if continuity is present.

MAP SENSOR

NOTE
On 2004 models, the MAP sensor is called the boost sensor. The sensors are identical.

Removal/Installation

1. Remove the upper cover from the right side (Chapter Fifteen).

2. Disconnect the 3-pin connector and the hose from the MAP sensor (**Figure 19**).

3. Remove the sensor from the motorcycle.

4. Installation is the reverse of removal.

Vacuum Test

1. Remove the MAP sensor as described in this section.

2. Make sure the sensor's air passage is clear, and connect a vacuum pump and gauge to the air passage (**Figure 20**).

3. Connect three new 1.5-volt batteries in series. Measure the total voltage of the batteries. The voltage must be 4.5-5.0 volts.

4. Connect the test battery's positive terminal to the Vcc terminal in the sensor; connect the negative test battery terminal to the ground terminal in the sensor.

5. Connect the voltmeter's positive test probe to the Vout terminal in the sensor; connect the negative test probe to the test battery's negative terminal.

6. Note the voltage reading. It should be within the Vout voltage range in **Table 1**.

7. Use the vacuum pump to apply vacuum to the sensor's air passage, and note the changes in the voltage reading. The Vout voltage should respond to the application of vacuum as specified in **Table 3**.

CRANKSHAFT POSITION (CKP) SENSOR

Removal/Installation

The CKP sensor is an integral part of the stator assembly. Refer to *Stator* in this chapter.

Peak Voltage Test

> *WARNING*
> *High voltage is present during ignition system operation. Do not touch ignition components, wires or test leads during this test.*

Use the multicircuit tester (Suzuki part No. 09900-25008) with a peak voltage adapter, or equivalent tools, to perform this test.
1. Remove the upper cover from the left side (Chapter Fifteen).
2. Disconnect the 34-pin connector (A, **Figure 21**) from the ECM.
3. Connect the voltmeter's positive test probe to the green/yellow terminal (27) in the ECM connector (**Figure 22**); connect the negative test probe to the connector's brown terminal (9).
4. Shift the transmission into neutral, turn the ignition on, and pull in the clutch lever.
5. Crank the engine for a few seconds. Record the highest reading.
6. Repeat Step 5 a few times. The highest peak voltage reading should equal or exceed the value in **Table 1**. If peak voltage is lower than specified, measure the peak voltage at the CKP sensor connector by performing Steps 7-9.
7. Raise the fuel-tank filler neck, and disconnect the 2-pin CKP sensor connector (B, **Figure 10**).
8. Connect the voltmeter's positive test probe to the green terminal in the sensor side of the connector; connect the negative test probe to the blue terminal in the sensor side of the connector.
9. Crank the engine for a few seconds. Record the highest reading. Repeat this test a few times. The highest peak voltage reading should equal or exceed the value in **Table 1**.
10. Consider the following:
   a. If the peak voltage at the CKP sensor connector (Step 10) is within specification but the reading taken at the ECM connector (Step 6) is out of specification, the wiring is faulty. Locate and repair the fault or replace the wiring harness.
   b. If the peak voltage at each connector (Step 6 and Step 10) is out of specification, replace the CKP sensor.

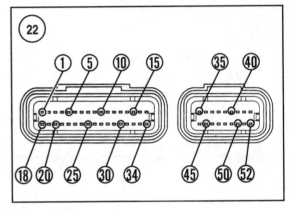

Resistance Test

1. Remove the seats, meter cover, and both upper covers (Chapter Fifteen).
2. Disconnect the 2-pin CKP sensor connector (B, **Figure 10**).
3. Connect the ohmmeter's positive test probe to the green terminal in the sensor side of the connector; connect the negative test probe to the blue terminal (sensor side).
4. The resistance should be within the range in **Table 1**.
5. Check the continuity between the each terminal in the sensor side of the connector and a good ground. No continuity (infinity) should be indicated during either test.

IGNITION COIL

Removal/Installation

1. Disconnect the negative battery cable.
2. Remove the upper cover (Chapter Fifteen) and the cylinder head side cap (Chapter Four) from the appropriate side.
3. Disconnect the spark plug cap from the spark plug (**Figure 23**).
4. Disconnect each coil lead (A, **Figure 24**) from its terminal on the ignition coil.

5. Remove the mounting bolts (B, **Figure 24**), and remove the ignition coil. Watch for the spacer on each bolt.

6. Install the ignition coil by reversing the removal procedures.

Peak Voltage Test

WARNING
High voltage is present during ignition system operation. Do not touch ignition components, wires or test leads during this test.

Use the multicircuit tester (Suzuki part No. 09900-25008) with a peak voltage adapter, or equivalent tools, to perform this test.

1. Remove the upper cover (Chapter Fifteen) and the cylinder head side cap (Chapter Four) from each side.

2. Remove the spark plug cap (**Figure 23**) from each spark plug.

3. Insert a new spark plug into each cap. Then ground the plugs to the cylinder heads.

CAUTION
Do not disconnect the wires from the ignition coil during this test.

4A. When measuring the peak voltage for the rear cylinder (No. 1) ignition coil, connect the voltmeter's positive test probe to the white terminal on the No. 1 ignition coil. Connect the negative test probe to a good ground.

4B. When measuring the peak voltage for the front cylinder (No. 2) ignition coil, connect the positive test probe to the black/yellow terminal on the No. 2 ignition coil. Connect the negative test probe to a good ground.

5. Shift the transmission into neutral, turn the ignition on, and pull in the clutch lever.

6. Crank the engine for a few seconds. Record the highest reading.

7. Repeat the previous step a few times. The highest peak voltage reading should equal or exceed the value in **Table 1**.

8. If peak voltage is lower than specified, check the ignition coil. On carbureted models, also inspect the signal generator.

Resistance Test

1. Remove the upper cover (Chapter Fifteen) and the cylinder head side cap (Chapter Four) from each side.

2. Disconnect the cap from each spark plug (**Figure 23**).

3. Disconnect both electrical connectors (A, **Figure 24**) from the respective ignition coil.

4. Use an ohmmeter to measure the primary coil resistance between the positive terminal (No. 1 coil: white or No. 2 coil: black/yellow) and the negative terminal (orange/white) on the ignition coil.

5. Use an ohmmeter to measure the secondary coil resistance between the positive terminal (No. 1 coil: white or No. 2 coil: black/yellow) on the ignition coil and the terminal in the spark plug cap.

6. Compare the test results to the specifications in **Table 1**. Replace the ignition coil(s) as necessary.

IGNITER UNIT

Removal/Installation

1. Disconnect the negative battery cable.

2. Remove the upper cover from the left side (Chapter Fifteen).

3. Disconnect the 4-pin (B, **Figure 18**), 8-pin (A) and 9-pin (C) connectors from the igniter unit.

4. Remove the nut from behind each bolt, and remove the bolts (D, **Figure 18**). Watch for the spacer and damper in each mounting hole.

5. Installation is the reverse of removal.

10

Voltage Test

1. Remove the upper cover from the left side (Chapter Fifteen).
2. Disconnect the 9-pin connector (C, **Figure 18**) from the igniter unit.
3. Connect the voltmeter's positive test probe to the orange/yellow terminal in the connector. Connect the negative test probe to the connector's black/white terminal.
4. Turn on the ignition, and measure the voltage. It should equal battery voltage.

ELECTRONIC CONTROL MODULE (ECM)

Refer to **Figure 25** for ECM terminal locations and the input/output functions for each terminal.

Some wiring colors are used more than once in the 34-pin and 18-pin connectors. To assure that the correct wire is tested, the test procedures include a wire's color and that wire's pin location number in parentheses.

Removal/Installation

1. Disconnect the negative battery cable (this chapter).
2. Remove the upper cover from the left side (Chapter Fifteen).
3. Disconnect the 34-pin connector (A, **Figure 21**) and 18-pin connector (B) from the ECM.
4. Remove the ECM damper from its mounting tangs. Then remove the ECM.
5. Installation is the reverse of removal. Secure the ECM damper to the mounting tangs.

Input Voltage Test

1. Remove the upper cover from the left side (Chapter Fifteen).
2. Disconnect the 34-pin connector (A, **Figure 21**) from the ECM.
3A. On U.S., California and Canada models, connect the voltmeter's negative test probe to the black/white terminal (13) in the 34-pin connector; connect the positive test probe to the orange/white terminal (11) in the connector.
3B. On U.K., Europe and Australia models, connect the voltmeter's negative test probe to the black/white terminal (13) in the 34-pin connector; connect the positive test probe orange/green terminal (11) in the connector.
4. Make sure the engine stop switch is in the run position and the sidestand is up.

5. Turn the ignition switch on, and measure the voltage. It should equal battery voltage.

STARTING SYSTEM

The starting system consists of the starter, starter gears, starter relay, clutch switch, neutral switch (carbureted models), gear position sensor (fuel injected models), sidestand switch, turn signal/sidestand relay, starter button, auto-decompression solenoid, and auto-decompression relay. When the starter button is pressed, it engages the starter relay and completes the circuit allowing electricity to flow from the battery to the starter.

The starting system includes an interlock system that interrupts current flow to the starter relay and the auto-decompression relay unless the transmission is in neutral and the clutch is disengaged, or the transmission is in gear, with the clutch disengaged and the sidestand up.

CAUTION
During starting, do not operate the starter for more than 5 seconds at a time. Let the starter cool for approximately 10 seconds, and try again.

STARTER

Operation Test

1. Securely support the motorcycle on level ground. Shift the transmission into neutral.
2. Pull back the rubber boot from the starter terminal.
3. Remove the starter cable nut (A, **Figure 26**) and disconnect the starter cable from the starter terminal.

WARNING
The jumper wire gauge in the next step must be as large as the battery cable. If the wire is too small, it could melt.

WARNING
The next step may produce sparks. Make sure nothing flammable is in the area.

4. Remove the top cover from the battery box (this chapter).
5. Apply battery voltage directly to the starter by connecting a jumper wire from the battery positive terminal to the starter terminal. The starter should operate.
6. If the starter does not operate when battery voltage is applied, repair or replace the starter.

㉕ ECM CIRCUIT IDENTIFICATION

TERMINAL NO.	CIRCUIT	TERMINAL NO.	CIRCUIT
1	GP switch signal (GP)	18	Ignition switch signal (AT)
2	IAT sensor signal (IAT)	19	EOT sensor signal (EOT)
3	Rear cylinder IAP sensor signal (IAP. R)	20	TO sensor signal (TOS)
4	STP sensor signal (STP)	21	TP sensor signal (TP)
5	Blank	22	Front cylinder IAP sensor signal (IAP. F)
6	Power source for sensors (VCC)	23	HO_2 control selector (EXS) [U.K., Europe and Australia models]
7	HO_2 sensor signal (HO₂S) [U.K., Europe and Australia models]	24	Mode select switch (MS)
8	Clutch lever position switch (CLP)	25	Starter switch (STA)
9	CKP sensor signal (CKP-)	26	Neutral switch (NT)
10	Power source for fuel injector (VM)	27	CKP sensor signal (CKP+)
11	Power source (B+1)	28	–
12	Power source for back-up (B+2)	29	Blank
13	ECM ground (E1)	30	Blank
14	Sensors ground (E2)	31	Serial data for speedometer (TECH)
15	–	32	Serial data for self-diagnosis (SDL)
16	–	33	–
17	–	34	–

TERMINAL NO.	CIRCUIT	TERMINAL NO.	CIRCUIT
35	STVA signal (STVA. 1B)	44	STVA signal (STVA. 2B)
36	HO_2 sensor heater (HO₂ H) [U.K., Europe and Australia models]	45	Fuel pump relay (FP Relay)
37	STVA signal (STVA. 1A)	46	STVA signal (STVA. 2A)
38	Blank	47	PAIR control solenoid valve (PAIR)
39	Ground (E01)	48	Ground (E02)
40	Rear cylinder fuel injector (#1)	49	Decomp. solenoid (DRL)
41	Front cylinder fuel injector (#2)	50	Starter relay (STR)
42	Blank	51	Blank
43	Front cylinder ignition coil (IG2)	52	Rear cylinder ignition coil (IG1)

10

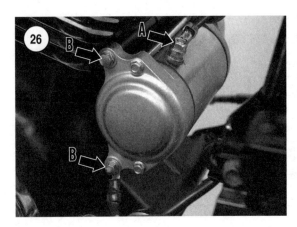

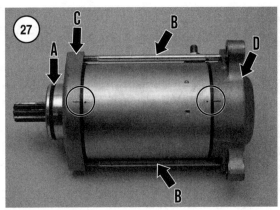

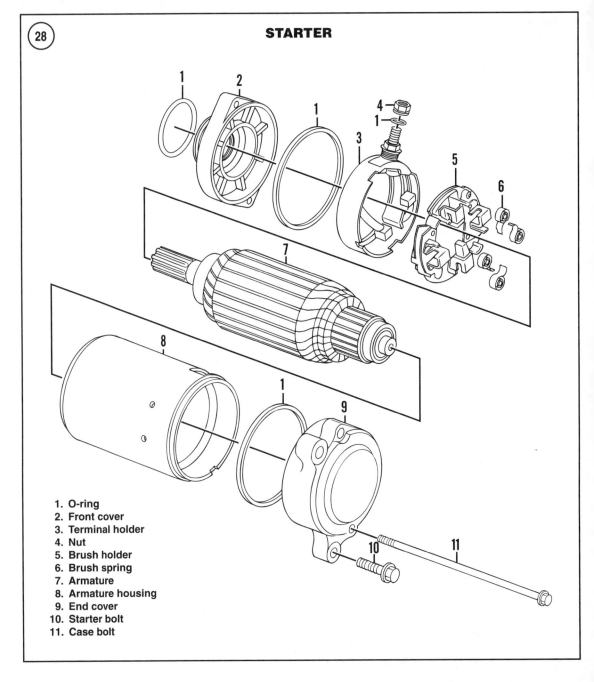

STARTER

1. O-ring
2. Front cover
3. Terminal holder
4. Nut
5. Brush holder
6. Brush spring
7. Armature
8. Armature housing
9. End cover
10. Starter bolt
11. Case bolt

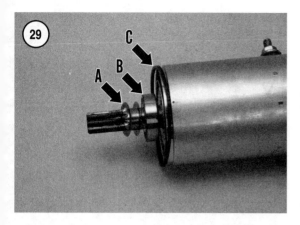

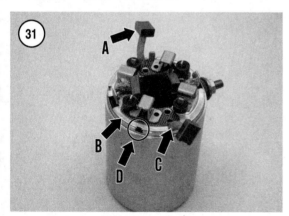

Removal/Installation

Refer to Chapter Five for starter clutch and gear service procedures.

1. Securely support the motorcycle on level ground.
2. Disconnect the negative battery cable (this chapter).
3. Remove the mufflers and exhaust pipes (Chapter Eight).
4. Pull back the rubber boot from the starter terminal.
5. Remove the nut (A, **Figure 26**) and disconnect the cable from the starter terminal.
6. Remove the starter bolts (B, **Figure 26**). Note that the battery ground lead mounts under the lower

starter bolt. Make sure it is in the same location during installation.
7. Pull the starter to the right, and then remove it from the starter gear housing.
8. Thoroughly clean the starter mounting areas on the crankcase, front cylinder, and starter. Clean the battery ground lead terminal.
9. Inspect the starter O-ring (A, **Figure 27**) in the front cover for hardness or deterioration. Replace the O-ring if necessary. Apply grease to the O-ring before installing the starter.
10. Push the starter into the crankcase so the teeth on the armature shaft engage the starter idler gear.
11. Install the starter bolts (B, **Figure 26**). Secure the battery ground lead beneath the lower starter bolt. Position the ground lead as shown in **Figure 26**.
12. On 2005-on models, tighten the starter bolts to 6 N•m (53 in.-lb.). On 1998-2004 models, tighten the starter bolts securely.
13. Place the starter cable on the starter terminal. On 2005-on models, install and tighten the starter terminal nut (A, **Figure 26**) to 6 N•m (53 in.-lb.). Press the rubber boot back into position. On 1998-2004 models, install the terminal nut and tighten it securely.
14. Install the exhaust pipes and mufflers (Chapter Eight).
15. Connect the negative battery cable (this chapter).

Disassembly

During starter (**Figure 28**) disassembly, lay out each part in order and maintain the relationship of each part to the others.

1. Remove each case bolt (B, **Figure 27**) from the starter. Note index marks on each cover and armature housing.
2. Remove the front cover (C, **Figure 27**) from the armature housing.
3. Remove the shims (A, **Figure 29**) from the armature. Note the number of shims.
4. Remove the O-ring (B, **Figure 29**) from the armature housing.
5. Remove the end cover (D, **Figure 27**) from the armature housing. Note that the slot inside the end cover engages the tab (A, **Figure 30**) on the brush holder.
6. Remove the O-ring (B, **Figure 30**).
7. Press the armature (C, **Figure 30**) from the housing.
8. Pull back the brush spring tang (D, **Figure 30**). Then remove a positive brush (A, **Figure 31**) from its holder. Repeat for the other positive brush.
9. Remove the brush holder (B, **Figure 31**) from the armature housing. Note each positive brush wire (C, **Figure 31**) sits in a cutout in the brush holder.

10. Remove the inner terminal nut (**Figure 32**), and remove the steel washer, large fiber washer, and two small fiber washers from the terminal bolt.

11. Press the terminal bolt (A, **Figure 33**) into the housing. Then remove the terminal holder assembly (**Figure 34**) from the armature housing. Remove the bolt O-ring (B, **Figure 33**).

12. Remove the insulator (A, **Figure 34**) from the terminal bolt.

13. Remove the terminal bolt (B, **Figure 34**) from the positive brush assembly (C), and lift the positive brush assembly from the terminal holder (D).

> *CAUTION*
> *Do not immerse the armature (**Figure 35**) in solvent as the insulation may be damaged. Wipe the windings with a cloth lightly moistened with solvent. Dry thoroughly.*

14. Clean all grease, dirt, and carbon from all components.

15. Inspect the starter components as described in this section.

Assembly

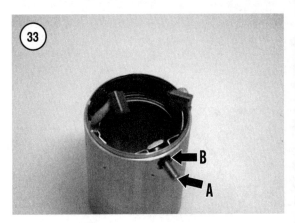

> *CAUTION*
> *To insulate the positive brush assembly from the case, reinstall all parts in the same order as noted during removal.*

1. Set the positive brush assembly (A, **Figure 36**) into the terminal holder (B) so each end of the brush assembly sits in the receptacle in the terminal holder.

2. Install the terminal bolt (B, **Figure 34**) through the brush assembly (C), and install the insulator (A) onto the terminal bolt.

3. Install a new O-ring onto the terminal bolt, and install the terminal holder assembly into the armature housing (**Figure 33**).

4. Install a new O-ring (B, **Figure 33**) onto the terminal bolt (A).

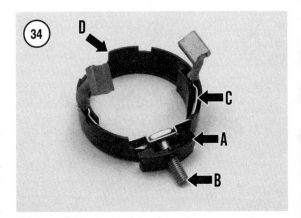

5. Install the two small fiber washers, the large fiber washer, and the steel washer (**Figure 37**) onto the terminal bolt.

6. Turn the inner nut (**Figure 32**) onto the terminal bolt. Tighten the nut securely.

7. Install the brush holder (B, **Figure 31**) into the armature housing so the tab on the holder aligns with the cutout in the housing (D). Make sure each positive brush wire (C, **Figure 31**) sits in a cutout in the brush holder.

8. Pull back the tang (D, **Figure 30**) on each brush spring, and install each brush into it holder in the brush holder.

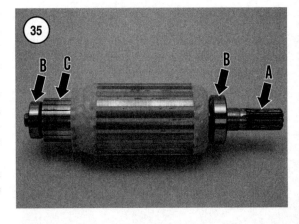

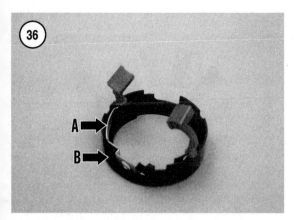

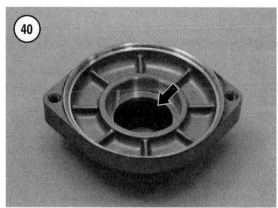

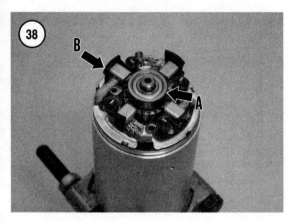

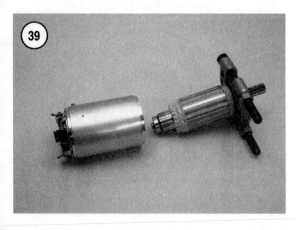

9. From a discarded engine oil bottle, cut out four plastic retainers.

10. Use the retainers to relieve the spring pressure on the brushes to install the armature. Insert a retainer (**Figure 38**) between each brush spring and its holder.

NOTE
The magnets in the armature housing pull the armature with considerable force. If necessary, use a bearing puller to control the armature when installing it into the housing.

11. Install a standard bearing puller onto the shaft end of the armature (**Figure 39**).

12. Grasp the bearing puller, and carefully install the armature into the housing until the commutator emerges past the brushes (A, **Figure 38**).

13. Remove each retainer (B, **Figure 38**) from the brush holder. Make sure each brush presses against the commutator (**Figure 30**).

14. Seat a new O-ring (B, **Figure 30**) onto the armature housing.

15. Apply grease to the end of the armature shaft (C, **Figure 30**).

16. Install the end cover (D, **Figure 27**) so the slot in the cover engages the tab (A, **Figure 30**) on the brush holder, and seat the cover on the armature housing. Make sure the index line on the end cover aligns with the index mark on the housing (**Figure 27**).

17. Install a new O-ring (B, **Figure 29**) onto the armature housing, and install the same number of shims (A) noted during removal.

18. Apply grease to the armature bearing (C, **Figure 29**) and to the lips of the oil seal (**Figure 40**) in the front cap.

19. Install the front cover (C, **Figure 27**). Make sure the index line on the front cover aligns with the index mark on the armature housing (**Figure 27**).

20. Apply Suzuki Thread Lock 1342 to the threads of the case bolts (B, **Figure 27**). Install the case bolts, and tighten them securely.

10

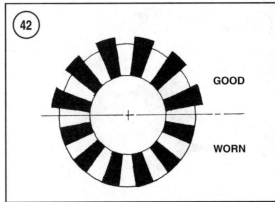

21. Apply grease to a new O-ring, and install the O-ring (A, **Figure 27**) onto the front cover.

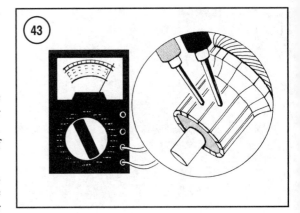

Inspection

1. Inspect each brush in the terminal holder (**Figure 34**) and brush holder (**Figure 41**) for abnormal wear or cracks. Service specifications are not available. Replace the terminal assembly and brush holder if any brush is excessively worn.

2. Inspect each end of the armature shaft for wear, burrs or damage. Pay particular attention to the splines (A, **Figure 35**). If the armature is worn or damaged, replace the starter.

3. Check the entire length of the armature assembly for straightness or heat damage.

4. Rotate the bearings (B, **Figure 35**) on the armature. Each should turn smoothly and quietly.

5. Inspect the undercut in the commutator (C, **Figure 35**). The mica in a good commentator sits below the surface of the copper bars. On a worn commutator, the mica and copper bars may be worn to the same level (**Figure 42**). If necessary, have the commutator serviced by an electrical repair shop.

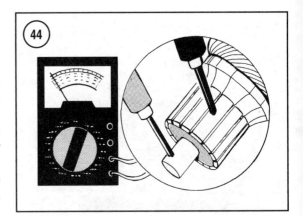

6. Inspect the commutator copper bars (C, **Figure 35**) for discoloration. If pairs of bars are discolored, grounded armature coils are indicated.

7. Use an ohmmeter and perform the following:
   a. Check for continuity between the commutator bars (**Figure 43**); there should be continuity (zero or low resistance) between pairs of bars.
   b. Check for continuity between the commutator bars and the armature shaft (**Figure 44**). There should be no continuity (infinite resistance).
   c. The armature is faulty if it fails either of these tests.

8. Inspect the front cover seal (**Figure 40**) for wear, hardness or damage. Replace the seal as necessary.

9. Inspect the magnets within the armature housing assembly. Make sure they have not picked up any metal debris. If necessary, clean the magnets. Also

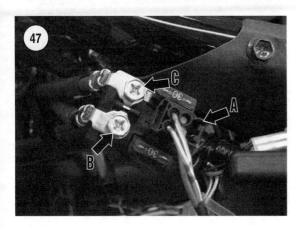

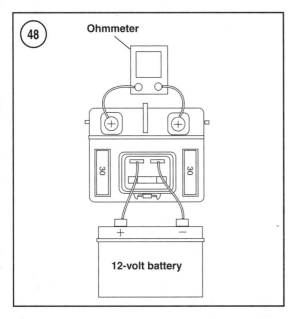

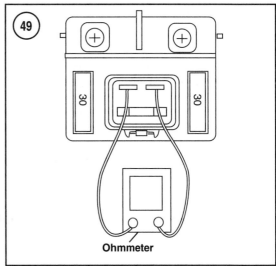

STARTER RELAY

Removal/Installation

1. Disconnect the negative battery cable.
2. Remove the upper cover from the left side (Chapter Fifteen).
3. Pull the cover (**Figure 46**) from the relay.
4. Disconnect the 4-pin primary connector (A, **Figure 47**) from the relay.
5. Disconnect the black starter lead (B, **Figure 47**) and the red battery lead (C) from the starter relay, and remove the relay.
6. Install by reversing these removal steps. Note the following:
    a. Securely install the black (B, **Figure 47**) and red cables (C) to their original terminals.
    b. Make sure the electrical connector (A, **Figure 47**) securely engages the terminals in the relay and that the cover (**Figure 46**) is properly installed to keep out moisture.

Test

1. Remove the starter relay.
2. Connect an ohmmeter and a 12 volt battery to the starter relay terminals as shown in **Figure 48**, and check the continuity.
    a. When the battery is connected, there should be continuity (zero ohms) across the two load terminals.
    b. When the battery is disconnected, there should be no continuity (infinity) across the load terminals.
3. Disconnect the battery from the starter relay.
4. Connect an ohmmeter to the starter relay terminals as shown in **Figure 49** and measure the resistance. The resistance should be within the range in **Table 1**.

inspect the armature housing for loose, chipped or damaged magnets.

10. Inspect both front (**Figure 40**) and rear covers (**Figure 45**) for wear or damage. Replace either cover as needed.
11. Check the case bolts for thread damage. If necessary, dress the threads with a die.

SIDESTAND SWITCH

Removal/Installation

1. Disconnect the negative battery cable.
2. Remove the secondary gear cover (Chapter Seven)
3. Disconnect the 2-pin sidestand switch connector (carbureted models: A, **Figure 50**; fuel injected models: A, **Figure 51**).
4. Move the sidestand to the down position.
5. Remove the sidestand switch screws, and remove the switch (B, **Figure 51**). Note how the switch wiring is routed.
6. Install a new switch. Follow the original switch wiring route noted. Apply Suzuki Thread Lock 1342 to the mounting screws and tighten them securely.
7. Move the sidestand from the down position to the up position, and make sure the switch plunger moves in.
8. Make sure the electrical connectors are clean and secure.
9. Install the secondary gear cover.

Diode Test

Use the multicircuit tester (Suzuki part No. 09900-25008), or its equivalent, to perform this test.
1. Remove the secondary gear cover (Chapter Seven).
2. Disconnect the 2-pin sidestand switch connector (carbureted models: A, **Figure 50**; fuel injected models: A, **Figure 51**).
3. Set the tester to diode.
4. Connect the tester leads to the terminals in the switch side of the connector as indicated in **Figure 52**.
5. Move the sidestand to the up position and read the voltage on the meter.
6. Move the sidestand to the down position and read the voltage.
7. If the voltage is outside the range specified in **Figure 52**, replace the sidestand switch.
8. If the diode test cannot be performed, test the continuity of the sidestand switch by performing the following:
   a. Connect the ohmmeter to the green and black/white terminals in the switch side of the connector terminals as indicated in **Figure 52**.
   b. Move the sidestand to the up position. The meter should indicate continuity.
   c. Move the sidestand to the down position. The meter should indicate no continuity.
   d. If the switch fails either of these tests, replace the switch.

SIDESTAND SWITCH TEST

Position \ Color	Green (+ probe)	Black/white (- probe)
UP	0.4 - 0.6 V	
DOWN	1.4 V or more	

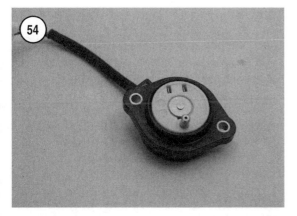

NEUTRAL SWITCH

Carbureted models use a neutral switch.

Removal/Installation

1. Remove the secondary gear cover (Chapter Seven).
2. Disconnect the 2-pin (B, **Figure 50**) and the single-pin (C) neutral switch connectors.
3. Note the wire routing and release the wires from any holders.
4. Remove the neutral switch bolts, and pull out the neutral switch (D, **Figure 50**).

5. Remove the locating pin and its spring from the shift cam retainer.
6. Install the switch by reversing the removal procedures. Note the following:
   a. Lubricate a new O-ring with grease. Then install the O-ring onto the neutral indicator light switch.
   b. Install a spring onto the locating pin. Then install the locating pin into the shift cam retainer.
   c. Follow the original switch wiring route noted.
   d. Tighten the neutral switch bolts securely.

Continuity Test

1. Remove the secondary gear cover (Chapter Seven).
2. Disconnect the single-pin neutral switch connector (C, **Figure 50**).
3. Connect the ohmmeter's positive test probe to the switch side of the connector; connect the negative test probe to a good ground.
4. The switch should have continuity when the transmission is in neutral; no continuity when the transmission is shifted into any gear.

GEAR POSITION (GP) SENSOR

Fuel injected models use a gear position (GP) sensor.

Removal/Installation

1. Remove the secondary gear cover (Chapter Seven).
2. Disconnect the 3-pin GP sensor connector (C, **Figure 51**).
3. Note the wire routing and release it from any holder.
4. Loosen out the GP sensor bolts (A, **Figure 53**), and remove the gear position sensor (B) and its O-ring.
5. Installation is the reverse of removal. Note the following:
   a. Make sure the locating pin is in place on the inboard side of the sensor (**Figure 54**).
   b. Lubricate a new O-ring (**Figure 55**) with grease, and install it onto the GP sensor.
   c. Install the sensor so its locating pin (**Figure 56**) engages the hole in the shift cam retainer.
   d. Follow the original sensor wiring route noted.
   e. Tighten the GP sensor bolts (A, **Figure 53**) securely.

Voltage Test

1. Securely support the motorcycle on a level surface.
2. Remove the secondary gear case (Chapter Seven).

3. Raise the sidestand, and make sure the engine stop switch is in the run position.

4. With 0.5-mm back probe pins, back probe the harness side of the 3-pin GP sensor connector (C, **Figure 51**), and perform the following:

    a. Connect a voltmeter positive test probe to the red/black terminal in the connector.

    b. Connect the negative test probe to the black/green terminal.

5. Turn the ignition switch on.

6. Shift the transmission into first gear, and measure the voltage. Shift the transmission to each higher gear (but not neutral), and measure the voltage. Each measurement should equal the gear position sensor voltage in **Table 1**.

Continuity Test

1. Remove the secondary gear cover (Chapter Seven), and disconnect the 3-pin GP sensor connector (C, **Figure 51**).

2. Connect an ohmmeter to the black and blue terminals in the switch side of the connector.

3. The switch should have continuity with the transmission in neutral and no continuity when the transmission is in any gear.

TURN SIGNAL/SIDESTAND RELAY

Removal/Installation

  The turn signal/sidestand relay consists of the turn signal relay, sidestand relay, and the diode. The turn signal/sidestand relay sits behind the speed sensor cover.

1. Disconnect the negative battery cable (this chapter).

2. Remove the speed sensor cover as described in *Clutch Cover* (Chapter Six).

3. Pull the turn signal/sidestand relay (**Figure 57**) straight up until the relay terminals disconnect from their mates in the mount. Remove the relay.

4. Installation is the reverse of removal. Firmly press the relay into its mount so the relay terminals engage their mates in the mount.

Relay Test

Sidestand

1. Remove the turn signal/sidestand relay.

2. Use an ohmmeter to check the continuity between terminals D and E on the relay (**Figure 58**). There should be no continuity.

3. Energize the relay and check the continuity again by performing the following:

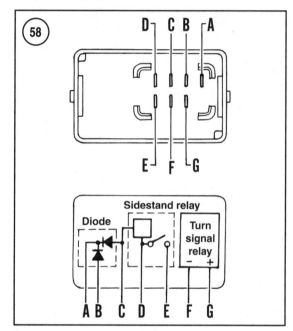

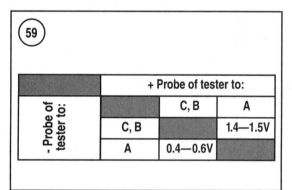

		+ Probe of tester to:	
		C, B	A
- Probe of tester to:	C, B		1.4—1.5V
	A	0.4—0.6V	

    a. Apply 12 volts to the relay by connecting the negative side of the battery to the C terminal in the relay; connect the positive battery terminal to the D terminal.

    b. Use an ohmmeter to check the continuity between terminals D and E on the relay. There should be continuity with the relay energized.

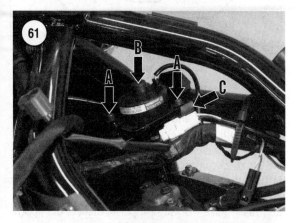

4. Replace the turn signal/sidestand relay if the relay fails either part of this test.

Diode

Use the multicircuit tester (Suzuki part No. 09900-25008), or its equivalent, to perform this test.
1. Remove the turn signal/sidestand relay.
2. Set the tester to diode test.
3. Refer to **Figure 58**. Then connect the tester probes to the terminals indicated in **Figure 59** to test the diode.
4. Replace the turn signal/sidestand relay if any measurement is outside the specified range.

Turn signal

If a turn signal light does not turn on, first inspect the bulb and socket. If they are working, check the turn signal switch as described in this chapter. Then check all electrical connections within the turn signal circuit for continuity and short-to-ground conditions.

If all of these items are working, replace the turn signal/sidestand relay.

AUTO-DECOMPRESSION SOLENOID

10

The auto-decompression solenoid automatically opens the exhaust valves during starter operation.

Removal/Installation

1. Remove the upper cover from the right side (Chapter Fifteen).
2. Remove the air filter housing (Chapter Eight).
3. Remove the outboard cylinder-head side cap from the front cylinder (Chapter Four).
4. Disconnect the 2-pin auto-decompression solenoid connector (A, **Figure 60**).

> *NOTE*
> *Two bolts (A, **Figure 61**) secure the auto-decompression solenoid (B) to the frame. A plunger limiter (C, **Figure 61**) mounts to the outboard bolt. Both mounting bolts are removed from beneath the frame.*

5. Hold the auto-decompression plunger (A, **Figure 62**) and remove the outboard mounting bolt (B). Lower the plunger limiter (C, **Figure 62**), and then lower the plunger from the auto-decompression solenoid.
6. Disconnect the plunger cable end (**Figure 63**) from the decompression lever on the front cylinder.

7. Remove the remaining inboard mounting bolt. Then remove the auto-decompression solenoid (B, **Figure 61**) from the frame.
8. Installation is the reverse of removal.
9. Adjust the auto-decompression cables (Chapter Three).

Test

1. Remove the upper cover from the right side (Chapter Fifteen).
2. Disconnect the auto-decompression solenoid 2-pin connector (A, **Figure 60**).
3. Use the ohmmeter to measure the resistance across the two terminals in the solenoid side of the connector. Resistance should equal the value in **Table 1**.

> *CAUTION*
> *Do not apply voltage to the solenoid for more than 5 seconds. The coil could be damaged.*

4. Test the operation of the solenoid as follows:
   a. Use jumper wires to apply battery voltage to the terminals in the solenoid side of the connector. Remove the jumpers within 5 seconds.
   b. The solenoid should operate when voltage is applied.
5. Replace the auto-decompression solenoid if it fails either portion of this test.

AUTO-DECOMPRESSION RELAY

Removal/Installation

1. Remove the upper cover from the right side (Chapter Fifteen).
2. Disconnect the 4-pin connector (B, **Figure 60**) from the auto-decompression relay.
3. Remove the relay from its mounting tang.
4. Installation is the reverse of removal.

Continuity Test

1. Remove the auto-decompression relay.
2. Check the continuity between the A and B terminals on the relay (**Figure 64**). The relay should not have continuity.
3. Energize the relay by connecting the positive battery terminal to the relay's C terminal (**Figure 64**); connect the negative battery terminal to the relay's D terminal.
4. Check the continuity between the A and B terminals while the relay is energized. The relay should have continuity.
5. Replace the relay if it fails either portion of this test.

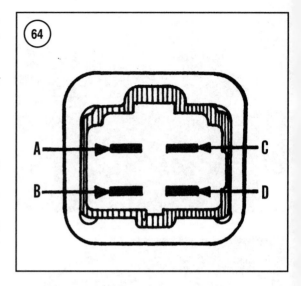

LIGHTING SYSTEM

The lighting system consists of a headlight, taillight/brake light and turn signals. Always use the correct bulb (**Table 2**) in each light.

If a light is inoperative, check the bulb for continuity. Next, check the battery condition. If the battery is fully charged, check the fuse(s) for the affected circuit. If necessary, replace the fuse(s). If the battery and fuse(s) are working properly, inspect the appropriate switch as described in this chapter.

Headlight

Bulb replacement

Refer to **Figure 65**.

> *WARNING*
> *A bulb that was just turned off or burned out will be hot. Do not remove the bulb until it cools.*

> *CAUTION*
> *All models are equipped with quartz-halogen bulbs. Do not touch the bulb glass (**Figure 66**). Oil on the bulb will reduce bulb life. In necessary, clean the bulb with a cloth moistened in alcohol or lacquer thinner.*

1. Remove the screw (A, **Figure 67**) and remove the rim/lens assembly (B) from the headlight housing.
2. Disconnect the electrical connector (**Figure 68**) by pulling it *straight out* from the headlight.
3. With the rim/lens assembly on the workbench, pull the tabs (A, **Figure 69**) and remove the dust boot. Check the boot for tears or deterioration; replace it if necessary.

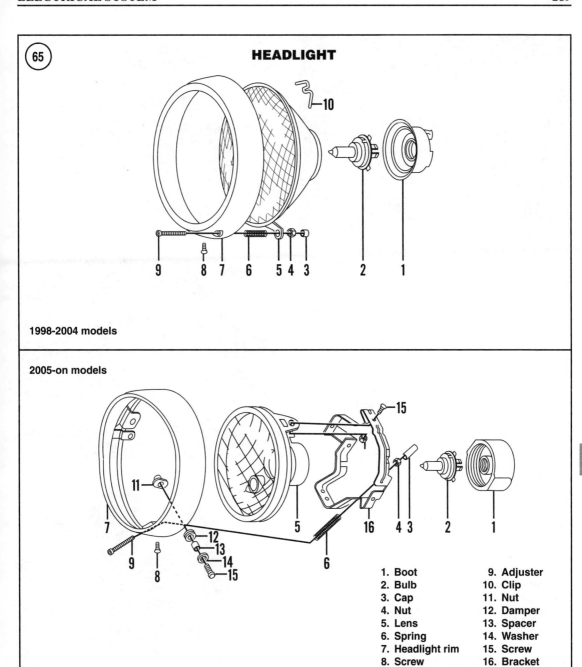

65

HEADLIGHT

10

9 8 7 6 5 4 3 2 1

1998-2004 models

2005-on models

11

7

9 8

12
13
14
15

5 16 4 3 2 1

6

10

1. Boot		9. Adjuster
2. Bulb		10. Clip
3. Cap		11. Nut
4. Nut		12. Damper
5. Lens		13. Spacer
6. Spring		14. Washer
7. Headlight rim		15. Screw
8. Screw		16. Bracket

66

67

B

A

C

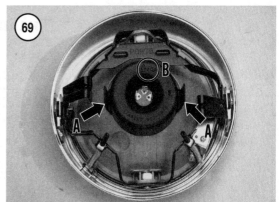

4. Unhook the bulb-retaining clip (A, **Figure 70**) and pivot it out of the way.

5. Remove the bulb.

6. Install the new bulb so the bulb tangs (B, **Figure 70**) engage the notches in the headlight housing.

7. Hook the retaining clip (A, **Figure 70**) over the bulb to hold it in place.

8. Install the dust boot so the *TOP* mark (B, **Figure 69**) sits at the top of the headlight assembly. Make sure the cover correctly seats against the lens assembly and the bulb.

9. Connect the electrical connector (**Figure 68**) to the bulb terminals. Push the connector until it bottoms on the bulb.

10. Fit the rim assembly into the headlight housing, and install the screw (A, **Figure 67**).

11. Adjust the headlight as described in this section.

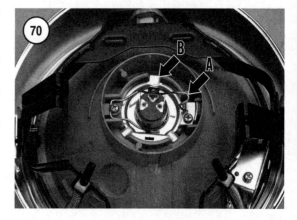

Adjustment

Proper headlight adjustment is critical to both the rider and to on-coming traffic. Always check the headlight beam adjustment whenever the motorcycle load is changed.

Adjust the headlight horizontally or vertically by turning the relevant adjuster on each side of the headlight rim. The left adjuster (C, **Figure 67**) is the vertical adjuster. The horizontal adjuster is on the right side. When adjusting a headlight, first adjust the headlight horizontally, and then vertically.

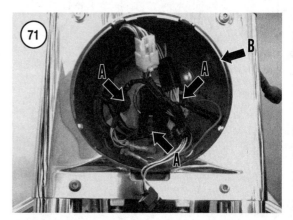

Headlight Housing
Removal/Installation

1. Perform Step 1 and Step 2 of *Bulb replacement* (this section).

2. Several electrical connectors sit within the headlight housing (1998-2004 models: **Figure 71**; 2005-on models: **Figure 72**). Disconnect each electrical connector. If necessary, label each side of a connector.

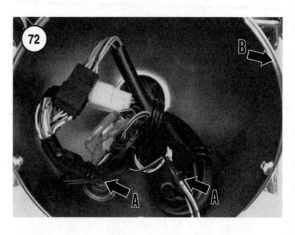

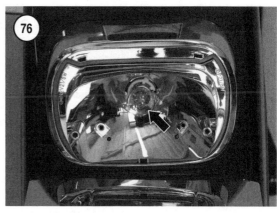

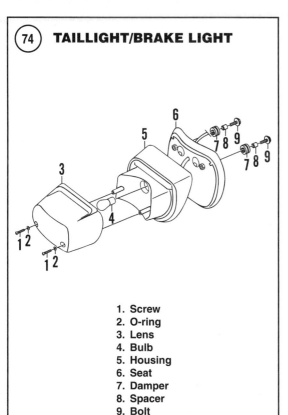

74 TAILLIGHT/BRAKE LIGHT

1. Screw
2. O-ring
3. Lens
4. Bulb
5. Housing
6. Seat
7. Damper
8. Spacer
9. Bolt

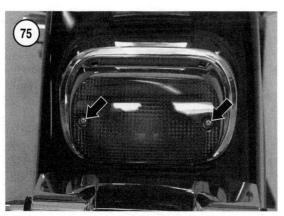

3. Note how the wires are secured by the wire clamps, and release the clamps.

4. Remove the headlight housing bolts (1998-2004 models: A, **Figure 71**; 2005-on models: A, **Figure 72**). Watch for the spacer and damper installed with each bolt.

5. Remove the headlight housing (B, **Figure 71, Figure 72**) from the housing bracket (**Figure 73**, 1998-2004 models shown). Carefully pull the wires out of the hole in the housing.

6. Install the headlight housing by reversing the removal procedures. Note the following:
   a. Make sure the damper and spacer are in place on each housing bolt.
   b. Securely connect each electrical connector.
   c. Tighten the headlight housing bolts securely.

Position Bulb Replacement (Models So Equipped)

1. Remove the position bulb socket from the headlight.

2. Pull the bulb from the socket and install a new bulb.

3. Insert the socket into the headlight housing.

Taillight/Brake Light Bulb Replacement

Refer to **Figure 74**.

1. Remove the screws (**Figure 75**) and pull the lens from the taillight housing.

2. Push the bulb (**Figure 76**) into the socket, then turn it counterclockwise and remove the bulb.

3. Press the new bulb into the socket. Then turn the bulb clockwise to lock it in place.

4. Check taillight and brake light operation.

5. Install the lens. Make sure its gasket is in place.

6. Tighten the screws securely.

10

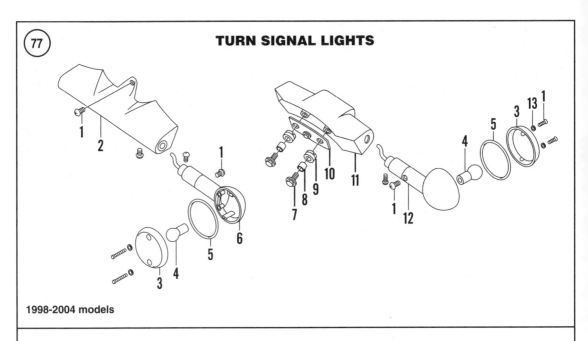

TURN SIGNAL LIGHTS

1998-2004 models

2005-on models

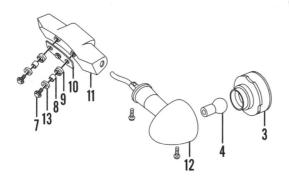

1. Screw
2. Front bracket
3. Lens/assembly
4. Bulb
5. Lens gasket
6. Front housing
7. Bolt

8. Spacer
9. Damper
10. Cover
11. Rear bracket
12. Rear housing
13. Washer

Turn Signal Bulb Replacement (Front and Rear)

Refer to **Figure 77**.

1A. On 1998-2004 models, remove the mounting screws (**Figure 78**) and lower the lens from the housing. Watch for the lens gasket.

1B. On 2005-on models, remove the lens screw (A, **Figure 79**). Turn the lens assembly (B, **Figure 79**) counterclockwise, and remove it from the housing.

2. Push the bulb into the socket (**Figure 80**), turn it counterclockwise, and remove the bulb.

3. Press the bulb into the socket, and turn the bulb clockwise to lock it in place. Check the turn signal light operation.

4. Install the lens/assembly. On carbureted models, make sure the lens gasket is in place.

HORN

Removal/Installation

On U.S., California, Canada, and Australia models, the horn is on the left side of the engine. On all other models, it is on the left side of the oil cooler. On models with dual horns, they are on the left and right side of the oil cooler. The following procedures show the horn for a 2005 California model.

1. Remove the upper covers (Chapter Fifteen).

2. Remove the bracket bolts (**Figure 81**), and lower the horn bracket from the left frame member.

3. Rotate the bracket, disconnect the electrical connectors (A, **Figure 82**) from the horn terminals, and remove the horn and bracket.

4. If necessary, remove the nut (B, **Figure 82**) and separate the horn from the bracket.

5. Installation is the reverse of removal.

Testing

1. Disconnect the negative battery cable.

2. Disconnect the connectors (A, **Figure 82**) from the horn.

3. Use jumpers to connect a 12 volt battery to the horn terminals. The horn should sound.

4. If it does not sound, replace the horn.

SPEEDOMETER (CARBURETED MODELS)

Removal/Installation

1. Remove the meter cover (Chapter Fifteen).

2. Place the meter cover upside down on the workbench.

3. Remove each mounting bolt (**Figure 83**) along with its washer.

4. Remove the speedometer from the meter cover.

10

5. Installation is the reverse of removal.

Indicator Lights

The speedometer contains several indicator lights. To test the illumination, turn signal, neutral or high beam indicator lights, perform the following:

1. Remove the speedometer from the meter cover.
2. Refer to **Figure 84** and identify the speedometer terminals by number.
3. To test a particular indicator light, refer to **Figure 85**, and connect an ohmmeter test probes to the indicated terminals in the speedometer. The indicator light should have continuity.
4. If the light does not have continuity, perform the following:
   a. Remove the rubber seal, and pull the affected socket (**Figure 86**) from the back of the speedometer.
   b. Remove the bulb from the socket, and inspect the bulb.
   c. If the bulb is burned out, replace it.
5. Recheck the continuity with the new bulb. If the light still does not have continuity, replace the speedometer.

Fuel Level Warning Light (1998 Models)

When the ignition switch is turned on, the fuel level warning light (A, **Figure 87**) turns on for 3 seconds. It then turns off if the tank contains a sufficient amount of fuel.

During operation, the fuel level warning light flashes when the fuel level drops below 3.5 liters (0.9 U.S. gal). The light turns on when the fuel level drops below 2.0 liters (0.5 U.S. gal). Perform the following tests if the light does not operate as indicated. Replace the speedometer if the warning light fails any portion of this test.

1. Turn the ignition switch on, and watch the fuel level warning light. It should turn on for 3 seconds.
2. Remove the seat, and disconnect the 2-pin fuel level sender connector (**Figure 88**).
3. Connect a 72-88 ohm resistor between the yellow/black and black/white terminals in the harness side of the fuel-level sender connector (**Figure 89**). Turn the ignition switch on, and check the fuel level warning light. It should flash after 20 seconds.
4. Remove the resistor and connect a resistor that is greater than 92 ohms between the terminals in the harness side of the connector (**Figure 89**). Turn the ignition switch on, and check the fuel level warning light. It should turn on after 20 seconds.
5. Remove the resistor, and connect a resistor that is less than 68 ohms between the terminals in the har-

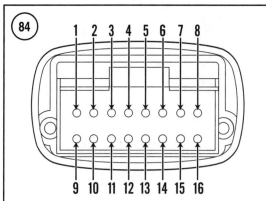

1	Ground
2	Fuel
3	Oil -
4	Neutral -
5	High beam +
6	Turn (L) +
7	Turn (R) +
8	Battery +
9	Speed sensor (signal)
10	
11	Ignition +
12	Illumination +
13	
14	Ground
15	
16	Speed sensor +

85

Indicator light	+ Probe of tester to:	– Probe of tester to:
ILLUMINATION	12	14
TURN (R)	14	7
TURN (L)	14	6
NEUTRAL	3	4
HIGH BEAM	5	14

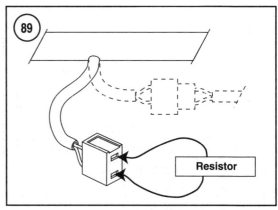

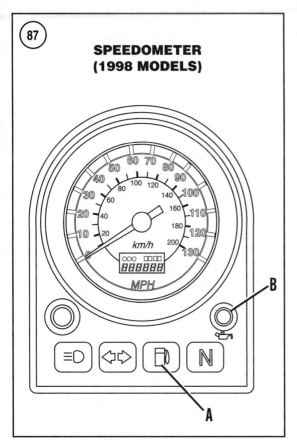

SPEEDOMETER
(1998 MODELS)

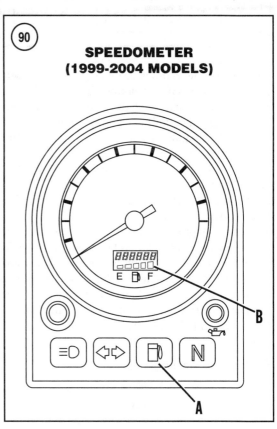

SPEEDOMETER
(1999-2004 MODELS)

10

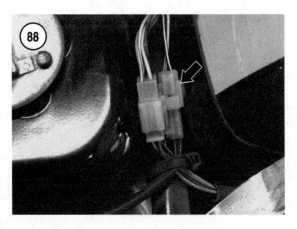

ness side of the connector (**Figure 89**). Turn the ignition switch on. The fuel level indicator should turn off after 20 seconds.

Fuel Level Warning Light and Gauge (1999-2004 Models)

When the ignition switch is turned on, the fuel level warning light (A, **Figure 90**) turns on for 3 seconds. All segments of the fuel gauge (B, **Figure 90**) also turn on for 3 seconds. They then turn off if the tank contains a sufficient amount of fuel.

During operation, the fuel level warning light turns on and the smallest segment of the fuel gauge flashes

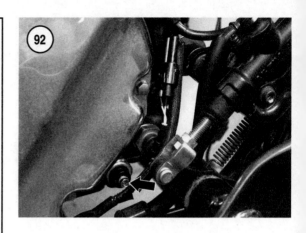

91

Resistance	Fuel gauge	Fuel level warning light
Less than 16 Ω	▪▪▪▪▪	OFF
20 - 34 Ω	▪▪▪▪▫	OFF
38 - 58 Ω	▪▪▪▫▫	OFF
62 - 87 Ω	▪▪▫▫▫	OFF
91 - 97 Ω	▪▫▫▫▫	ON
More than 103 Ω	Flashes ▪▫▫▫▫	ON

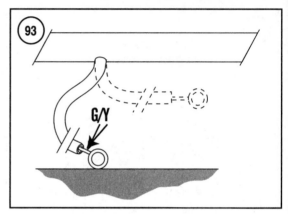

when the fuel level drops below a set level. Perform the following tests if the warning light and fuel gauge do not operate as indicated. Replace the speedometer if the warning light fails any portion of this test.

1. Turn the ignition switch on, and watch the fuel level warning light and the fuel gauge. The warning light and all segments of the fuel gauge should turn on for 3 seconds.

2. Remove the seat, and disconnect the 2-pin fuel level sender connector (**Figure 88**).

3. Refer to **Figure 91** and connect the appropriate size resistor between the yellow/black and black/white terminals in the harness side of the fuel-level sender connector (**Figure 89**). Turn the ignition switch on, and check the fuel level warning light and the fuel gauge. After 13 seconds, they should function as shown in **Figure 91**.

Oil Pressure Warning Light

WARNING
If the oil pressure warning light turns on during a ride, immediately stop and check the oil level, and determine why the light is on. Riding with the oil pressure warning light on can cause engine damage.

When the ignition switch is turned on the oil pressure warning light (B, **Figure 87**) turns on and remains on. It goes out once the engine starts.

During operation, the oil pressure warning light turns on if the oil pressure drops below normal operating range. Perform the following test if the warning light does not operate correctly.

1. Remove the screw (**Figure 92**), and disconnect the electrical lead from the oil pressure switch.

2. Ground the lead against the crankcase (**Figure 93**).

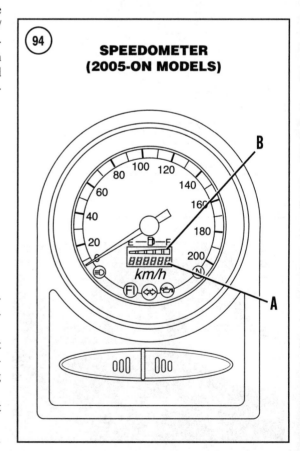

94

SPEEDOMETER (2005-ON MODELS)

3. Turn on the ignition switch. The oil pressure warning light should turn on.
4. If it does not, check the connectors in the circuit. If they are in good condition, replace the oil level warning lamp.

SPEEDOMETER (FUEL INJECTED MODELS)

On these models, the LCD (A, **Figure 94**) displays *CHEC* when the engine stop switch is turned off while the ignition switch is on. This is not a malfunction. The system returns to normal operation once the engine stop switch is set to run.

Removal/Installation

1. Remove the meter cover (Chapter Fifteen).
2. Place the meter cover upside down on the workbench.
3. Remove each mounting bolt (**Figure 95**), and lift the speedometer from the meter cover.
4. Installation is the reverse of removal.

Disassembly/Installation

If the speedometer unit (7, **Figure 96**) is defective, replace it. The unit cannot be serviced.

Indicator Lights

The indicator lights in the speedometer are LEDs, which cannot be replaced. If an indicator light does not turn on, inspect all the wiring and components in the related circuit. If they are good, replace the speedometer unit.

Fuel Gauge

The fuel gauge (B, **Figure 94**) indicates the amount of fuel in the tank. All five gauge segments turn on when the tank is full. The smallest segment flashes when the fuel level drops below 2.5 liters (0.7 U.S. gal.).

The fuel level sender is an integral part of the fuel pump on fuel-injected models. Perform the following tests if the fuel gauge does not operate as indicated.

1. Check the 3-pin fuel pump connector (**Figure 97**) and wiring.
2. Perform the *Fuel Level Sender Resistance Test* in Chapter Nine.
3. If the fuel level sender and wiring are good, replace the speedometer unit.

SPEEDOMETER

1. Screw
2. Cover plate
3. Switch cover
4. Knob
5. Damper
6. Speedometer housing
7. Speedometer unit
8. Gasket
9. Housing back

10

Oil pressure warning light

Refer to *Oil Pressure Warning Light* in *Speedometer (Carbureted Models)* in this chapter. Replace the speedometer unit if the circuit wiring is in good working order.

SPEED SENSOR

Removal/Installation

1. Remove the side cover from the right side (Chapter Fifteen).
2. Remove the speed sensor cover as described in *Clutch Cover* (Chapter Six).
3A. On carbureted models, disconnect the 3-pin speed sensor connector from the sensor (**Figure 98**).
3B. On fuel injected models, disconnect the 3-pin speed sensor connector (A, **Figure 99**).
4. Release the electrical wire from any cable holders. Note the wire routing.
5. Remove the mounting bolt, and pull the sensor (carburetor models: **Figure 98**; fuel injected models: **Figure 100**) from the clutch cover.
6. Remove and discard the sensor O-ring.
7. Installation is the reverse or removal. Note the following:
   a. Apply grease to a new O-ring, and fit the O-ring onto the speed sensor.
   b. Apply Suzuki Thread Lock 1342 to the threads of the mounting bolt. Tighten the bolt securely.
   c. Route the sensor wire along its original path and secure it to the frame where noted during removal.
   d. Tighten all fasteners securely.

Test

1. Remove the speed sensor (this chapter).
2. On carbureted models, perform the following:
   a. Arrange four 1.5 volt batteries in series.
   b. Connect the negative test battery terminal to the ground terminal in the sensor side of the connector; connect the positive test battery terminal to the connector's Vcc terminal.
   c. Connect a 1k ohm resistor and voltmeter to the Vcc and Signal terminals as shown in **Figure 101**.
3. On fuel injected models, perform the following:
   a. Use a jumper wire to connect a 12 volt negative battery terminal to the black/white terminal in the sensor side of the connector; connect the positive battery terminal to the sensor's red/black terminal with another jumper wire.
   b. Connect a 10 k ohm resistor and voltmeter to the red/black and pink terminals as shown in **Figure 102**.

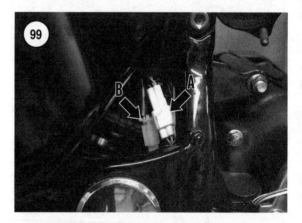

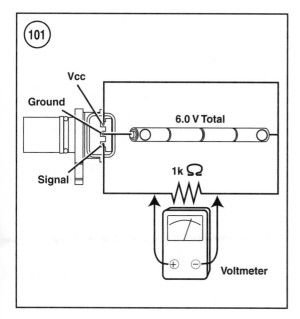

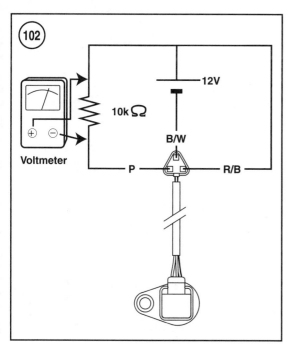

4. Touch the pick-up surface of the sensor with a screwdriver and watch the voltmeter.

5. The reading should change from 0 to test voltage or from test voltage to 0 volts. On carbureted models, test voltage is 6 volts; on fuel injected models, it is 12 volts.

SWITCHES

Testing

1. First check the fuse for the affected circuit as described in this chapter.

2. Check the battery as described in this chapter. If necessary, charge the battery.

3. Disconnect the negative battery cable if the switch connectors in the circuit are not disconnected.

4. Do not start the engine with the battery disconnected.

5. When separating two connectors, pull the connector housings and not the wires.

6. After locating a defective circuit, check the connectors to make sure they are clean and properly connected. Check all wires going into a connector to make sure each wire is secure.

7. When reconnecting electrical connectors, push them together until they click or snap into place.

Continuity Test

Refer to Chapter Two for general information on continuity testing. Refer to the wiring diagrams at the end of this manual for individual switch continuity diagrams.

Test switches as follows:

1. Disconnect the switch connector, and check continuity at the terminals on the switch side of the connector. If a connector plugs directly into the switch (like in the front brake light switch), check the continuity at the terminals on the switch.

2. Set the switch to each of its operating positions. Then connect the ohmmeter's test leads to the indicated terminals, and compare the results with the appropriate switch continuity diagram. For example:

   a. **Figure 103** shows a continuity diagram for a typical ignition switch. The horizontal lines indicate which terminals should show continuity when the switch is in a given position.

   b. In the PARK position there should be continuity between the red and brown terminals. An ohmmeter connected between these two terminals should indicate little or no resistance or a test light should light.

   c. In the OFF position, there should be no continuity between any of the terminals.

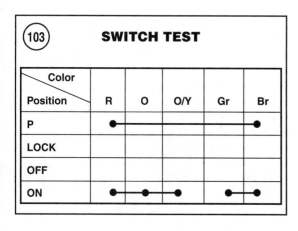

Color Position	R	O	O/Y	Gr	Br
P	●————	———	———	———	————●
LOCK					
OFF					
ON	●———	●———	●		●———	————●

Right Handlebar Switch Removal/Installation

The right handlebar switches are not available separately. If any one switch is damaged, replace the complete switch assembly. The front brake light switch is a separate unit and can be replaced independently.

1. The right handlebar switch (**Figure 104**) includes the following switches:
   a. Engine stop switch (A, **Figure 104**).
   b. Starter button (B, **Figure 104**).
   c. Hazard light switch (C, **Figure 104**) (fuel injected models only).
   d. Front brake light switch (D, **Figure 104**) (electrical connectors only—the switch is separate).
   e. Headlight switch (U.K. and Europe models).

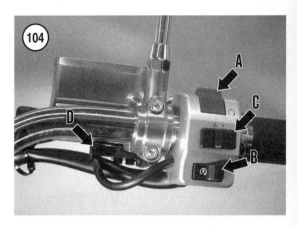

2. If replacing the right handlebar switch, perform the following:
   a. Disconnect the negative battery cable (this chapter).
   b. Remove the headlight rim/lens assembly as described in *Headlight* (this chapter).
   c. Disconnect the right handlebar switch connector (A, **Figure 105**).
   d. Remove any cable ties securing the switch wiring harness to the headlight shell and the frame. Note the wire routing through the frame.
   e. Disconnect the connector (D, **Figure 104**) from the front brake light switch.

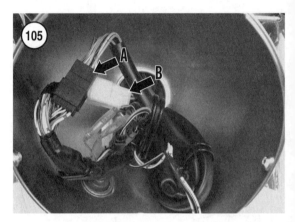

3. At the throttle grip, loosen the cable locknut (A, **Figure 106**) on the return cable and turn the adjuster nut (B) into the switch assembly to create maximum slack. Repeat this on pull cable (C, **Figure 106**).

4. Remove the screw (D, **Figure 106**) and lower the cable clamp from the switch housing.

5. Remove the switch housing screws (E, **Figure 106**) and separate the switch halves.

6. Disconnect the throttle cable ends (**Figure 107**) from the throttle drum, and remove the pull and return cables from the switch housing.

7. Install by reversing these removal steps. Note the following:
   a. Route the pull cable through the upper port in the front switch half, the return cable through lower port.
   b. Apply grease to the cable ends, and connect the throttle cable ends (**Figure 107**) to the throttle drum.
   c. Install the switch onto the handlebar and tighten the screws securely.
   d. Route the electrical cable along the path noted during removal. Make sure the electrical connectors are corrosion free and secure.
   e. Check the operation of each switch mounted in the right handlebar switch housing.
   f. Operate the throttle grip and make sure the throttle linkage operates smoothly. If any bind-

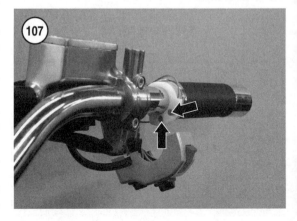

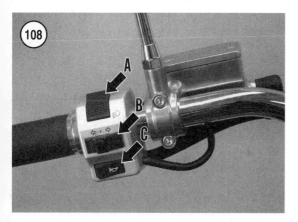

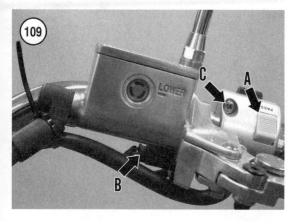

ing is noted, make sure the cable is attached correctly and there are no tight bends in the cable.

g. Adjust the throttle cable free play (Chapter Three).

Left Handlebar Switch Removal/Installation

The left handlebar switches are not available separately. If any one switch is damaged, replace the complete assembly. The clutch switch is a separate unit and can be replaced independently.

1. The left handlebar switch housing (**Figure 108**) includes the following switches:

   a. Headlight dimmer switch (A, **Figure 108**).

   b. Turn signal switch (B, **Figure 108**).

   c. Horn button (C, **Figure 108**).

   d. Clutch switch (electrical connectors only—the switch is separate).

   e. Pass switch (A, **Figure 109**) (fuel injected models only).

2. If the left handlebar switch is being replaced, perform the following:

   a. Disconnect the negative battery cable.

   b. Remove the headlight rim/lens assembly as described in *Headlight* (this chapter).

   c. Disconnect the left handlebar switch connector (B, **Figure 105**).

   d. Remove any cable ties securing the switch wiring harness to the headlight housing or frame. Note the wire routing through the frame.

   e. Disconnect the connector from the clutch switch (B, **Figure 109**).

3. Remove the housing screws (C, **Figure 109**) and separate the switch halves.

4. Install by reversing these removal steps. Note the following:

   a. Install the switch onto the handlebar and tighten the screws securely.

   b. Route the electrical cable along the path noted during removal.

   c. Check the operation of each switch mounted in the left switch housing.

Ignition Switch Removal/Installation

1. Disconnect the cable from the battery negative terminal (this chapter).

2. Remove the side cover from the left side (Chapter Fifteen).

3. Follow the ignition switch wire to its 5-pin connector, and disconnect the connector (**Figure 110**). Note how the wire is routed through the motorcycle.

4. Remove the Torx bolt (**Figure 111**) securing the ignition switch to the frame.

10

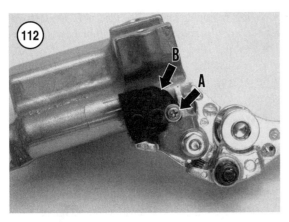

5. Install the new ignition switch, and tighten the Torx bolts securely. Apply Suzuki Thread Lock 1342 to the bolt threads.

6. Route the ignition switch wire along the path noted during removal, and connect the connector (**Figure 110**).

Front Brake Switch Removal/Installation

1. Disconnect the electrical connector (D, **Figure 104**) from the front brake switch.

2. Remove the mounting screw (A, **Figure 112**), and lower the switch (B) from the lever assembly.

3. Installation is the reverse of removal.

Rear Brake Switch Removal/Installation

1. Disconnect the 2-pin rear brake light switch connector (B, **Figure 99**). Release any clamps securing the switch cable to the frame.

2. Disconnect the switch spring (A, **Figure 113**) from the boss on the brake pedal, and remove the switch (B) from the bracket.

3. Installation is the reverse of removal. Adjust the rear brake switch as described in Chapter Three.

Clutch Switch Removal/Installation

1. Disconnect the electrical connector from the clutch switch (B, **Figure 109**) on the clutch lever assembly.

2. Remove the mounting screw (A, **Figure 114**), and lower the switch (B) from the lever assembly.

3. Installation is the reverse of removal.

FUSES

When troubleshooting an electrical problem, first check for a blown fuse. A blown fuse has a break in the element (**Figure 115**). Before replacing a blown

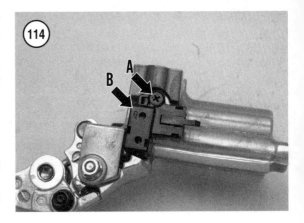

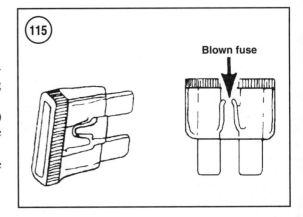

Blown fuse

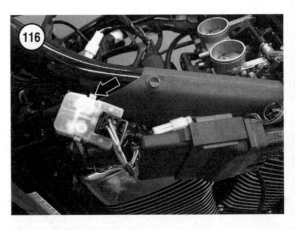

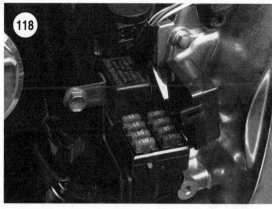

fuse, check the circuit the fuse protects and determine why the fuse blew.

Main Fuse Replacement

1. Remove the upper cover from the left side (Chapter Fifteen).
2. Pull the cover (**Figure 116**) from the starter relay.
3. Using needlenose pliers, pull out the 30-amp main fuse (A, **Figure 117**). A spare 30-amp fuse (B, **Figure 117**) is stored on the starter relay.
4. Install the new fuse into the main fuse socket. Press the fuse into the socket until it bottoms.

5. Replace the spare fuse.

Circuit Fuse Replacement

Individual circuit fuses are in the fuse box behind the speed sensor cover. The fuse box also contains two spare fuses (10A and 15A).
1. Remove the speed sensor cover as described in Step 1 and Step 2 of *Clutch Cover* in Chapter Six.
2. Open the fuse panel top cover (**Figure 118**).
3. Use needlenose pliers to remove the suspect fuse.
4. Install a replacement fuse of the same amperage and replace the spare fuse.

10

Table 1 ELECTRICAL SYSTEM SPECIFICATIONS

Item	Specification
Alternator	
Type	Three-phase AC
No-load voltage (when engine is cold)	80 volts or more (AC) @ 5000 rpm
Max output	
1998-2004 models	Approx. 340 watts @ 5000 rpm
2005-on models	Approx. 375 watts @ 5000 rpm
Regulated voltage (charging voltage)	13.5-15.0 volts @ 5000 rpm
Stator resistance	0.1-1.0 ohms
Auto-decompression solenoid resistance	0.1-1.0 ohms
Battery	
Type	
1998-2004 models	FTH 16 BS-1 Maintenance free (sealed)
2005-on models	FTZ 16 BS-1 Maintenance free (sealed)
Capacity	
1998-2004 models	12 volt 50.4 kC (14 amp hour)/10 HR
2005-on models	12 volt 64.8 kC (18 amp hour)/10 HR
Maximum current draw	Less than 1 mA
Charge rate	
Normal charge	
1998-2004 models	1.4A for 5-10 hours
2005-on models	1.8A for 5-10 hours
Quick charge	7A for 1 hour
Crankshaft position sensor (2005-on models)	
Resistance	178-242 ohms
Peak voltage (when cranking)	2.4 volts or more
Gear position sensor voltage (2005-on models)	0.6 volts or more

(continued)

Table 1 ELECTRICAL SYSTEM SPECIFICATIONS (continued)

Item	Specification
Ignition coil primary peak voltage	
1998-2004 models	
Front (No. 2 cylinder)	190 volts or more
Rear (No. 1 cylinder)	200 volts or more
2005-on models	
Front	180 volts or more
Rear	180 volts or more
Ignition coil resistance	
Primary	1-7 ohms
Secondary	18-28 k ohms
Ignition system	
Type	Electronic ignition (transistorized)
Firing order	Rear cylinder-front cylinder (1-2)
Ignition timing*	
1998-2004 models	2° BTDC @ 1000 rpm
2005-on	9° BTDC @ 1000 rpm
MAP sensor Vout voltage	4.5-5.0 volts
Sidestand switch diode test voltage	
Sidestand up	0.4-0.6 volts
Sidestand down	1.4-1.5 volts
Signal generator peak voltage (1998-2004 models)	2.4 volts or more
Signal generator resistance (1998-2004 models)	178-242 ohms
Spark plug	
Type	NGK: DPR7EA-9, Denso: X22EPR-U9
Gap	0.8-0.9 mm (0.032-0.035 in.)
Spark-test gap	Over 8 mm (0.3 in.)
Starter relay resistance	3-6 ohms

*Not adjustable.

Table 2 BULB AND FUSE SPECIFICATIONS

Item	Specification
Brake light/taillight	21/5 watts
Fuel fuse (2005-on models)	10 amp
Fuel level warning light	1.7 watts
Headlight (high/low beam)	
High beam	60 watts
Low beam	55 watts
Headlight fuse	
1999-2002 models	
High	15 amp
Low	15 amp
2003-on	
High	10 amp
Low	10 amp
High beam indicator light	1.7 watts
Ignition fuse	
1999-2002 models	10 amp
2003-on	15 amp
Main fuse	30 amp
Neut	1.7 watts
ht	LED
Europe models)	
	4 watts
	5 watts
	15 amp
004 models)	10 amp
light	
	1.7 watts
	0.84 watts

(continued)

Table 2 BULB AND FUSE SPECIFICATIONS (continued)

Item	Specification
Turn signal	
U.S., California and Canada models	
Front	21/5 watts
Rear	21
All models except U.S., California	
and Canada models	21 watts
Turn signal indicator light	1.7 watts

Table 3 MAP SENSOR Vout VOLTAGE

Reference altitude m (ft.)	Atmospheric pressure KPa (mm Hg)	V-out voltage
0-610 (0-2000)	100-94 (750-705)	3.1-3.6
611-1524 (2001-5000)	94-85 (705-638)	2.8-3.4
1525-2438 (5001-8000)	85-76 (638-570)	2.6-3.1
2439-3048 (8001-10,000)	76-70 (570-525)	2.4-2.9

Table 4 ELECTRICAL SYSTEM TORQUE SPECIFICATIONS

Item	N•m	in.-lb.	ft.-lb.
Crankshaft position sensor bolt			
(2005-on models)	5	44	–
Flywheel bolt	160	–	118
Oil pressure switch	14	–	10
Signal generator bolt			
(1998-2004 models)	5	44	–
Spark plug	18		13
Starter bolt (2005-on models)	6	53	–
Starter terminal nut			
(2005-on models)	6	53	–
Stator bolt	10	89	–
Stator wire clamp bolt	5	44	–

10

CHAPTER ELEVEN

WHEELS, HUBS AND TIRES

This chapter describes procedures for the front and rear wheels, wheel hubs, and tires. Refer to Chapter One for general bearing procedures.

When servicing components described in this chapter, compare any measurements to the specifications at the end of this chapter. Replace worn or damaged components.

MOTORCYCLE STAND

Many procedures require the wheel to be off the ground. Use a motorcycle front-end stand (**Figure 1**) or a swing arm stand to do this safely. Before using a stand, check the manufacturer's instructions to make sure the stand is designed for the model application. An adjustable centerstand can also be used to support the motorcycle with a wheel off the ground. Make sure the motorcycle is properly secured.

BRAKE ROTOR PRECAUTION

The brake rotors are easily damaged from impact. Protect the rotor when servicing a wheel or transporting a wheel for tire replacement. Do not set a wheel down on the brake rotor. If necessary, support the wheel on wooden blocks (**Figure 2**). Position the blocks along the outer circumference of the wheel so the rotor lies between the blocks, not on them.

A damaged rotor will cause a pulsation when the brakes are applied. The rotors cannot be machined to remove any imperfections or damage.

WHEEL INSPECTION

During inspection, compare all measurements to the specifications in **Table 1**. Replace damaged or out of specification parts.

1. Remove the wheel as described in this chapter.

2. Rotate each bearing. They should turn smoothly and quietly. If one is rough or noisy, inspect the bearings as described in this chapter.

3. Use a piece of fine emery cloth to remove any corrosion from the front spacer nut or axle (front: **Figure 3**, rear: **Figure 4**).

WARNING
Do not attempt to straighten a bent axle.

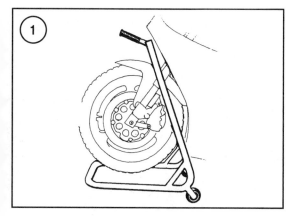

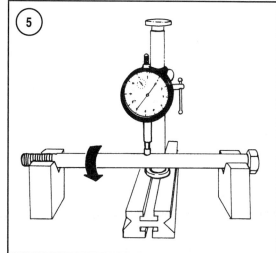

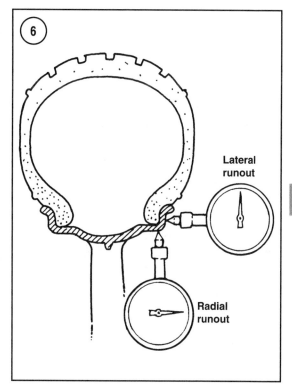

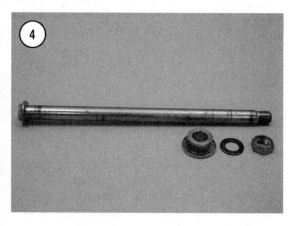

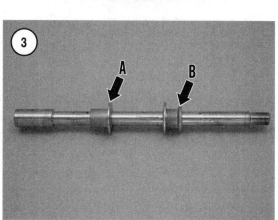

4. Check axle runout with a dial gauge and V-blocks (**Figure 5**).

5. Install the wheel on a truing stand. Measure the radial (up and down) and axial (side to side) wheel runout. Use a dial indicator as shown in **Figure 6**.

6. If the wheel runout is out of specification (**Table 1**), inspect the wheel bearings as described in this chapter.

    a. If the wheel bearings are in good condition, inspect the wheel. If necessary, replace the wheel.

    b. If either wheel bearing is worn, disassemble the hub and replace both bearings as a set.

7. Check the tightness of the brake disc bolts (A, **Figure 7**). If a bolt is loose, remove and reinstall the bolt. Apply Suzuki Thread Lock Super 1360 to the threads of the bolt. Tighten the brake disc bolts to 23 N•m (17 ft.-lb.).

8. Visually inspect the brake discs and measure the brake disc deflection as described in Chapter Fourteen. If deflection is excessive, measure wheel runout. If wheel runout is within specification, replace the brake disc (Chapter Fourteen).

9. Inspect the wheel for dents, cracks or other damage. Check the rim-sealing surface for deep scratches that may prevent tire sealing. If any of these conditions are present, replace the wheel.

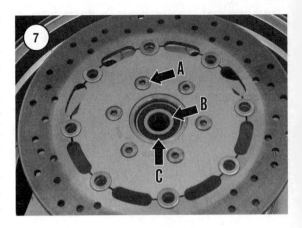

WHEEL BEARING INSPECTION

CAUTION
Do not remove the wheel bearings for inspection. Removal will damage the bearings. Remove the wheel bearings only if they require replacement.

1. Turn each bearing inner race (B, **Figure 7**) by hand. Each bearing must turn smoothly without roughness, binding or excessive noise. Some axial play (side-to-side) is normal, but radial play (up and down) must be negligible. See **Figure 8**.

2. On a sealed bearing, check the outer seal (C, **Figure 7**) for buckling or other damage that would allow dirt to enter the bearing.

3. On a non-sealed bearing, check the balls for evidence of wear, pitting or excessive heat (bluish tint).

4. Attempt to move the bearing laterally within the hub or rear coupling. The bearing should fit tightly in the bore. If a bearing is loose, inspect the hub bore for wear or damage.

5. Replace worn or damaged bearings. Compare the new bearing with the old ones to ensure the new bearings are correct.

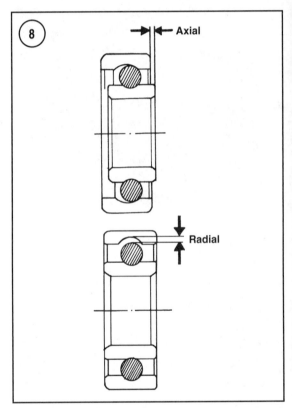

FRONT WHEEL

Refer to **Figure 9**.

Removal

Use a 12-mm Allen socket (Suzuki part No. 09900-18710), or its equivalent tool, during this procedure.

1. Support the motorcycle with the front wheel off the ground.

2. Remove the front fender (Chapter Fifteen).

3. Remove the cap from each side of the axle.

4. Loosen the front axle clamp bolt (A, **Figure 10**).

5. Remove the front axle (**Figure 11**).

6. Roll the wheel from between the fork legs.

7. Remove the spacer from each side of the wheel. Note that the left (A, **Figure 3**) and right spacers (B, **Figure 3**) are not the same.

Installation

1. Make sure the axle and the bearing surfaces of each fork leg are in good condition.

2. Install each spacer (A and B, **Figure 3**) into the correct side of the hub.

3. Position the wheel so the directional arrow points in the direction of forward wheel rotation.

4. Apply a light coat of grease to the front axle.

5. Carefully roll the wheel between the fork legs.

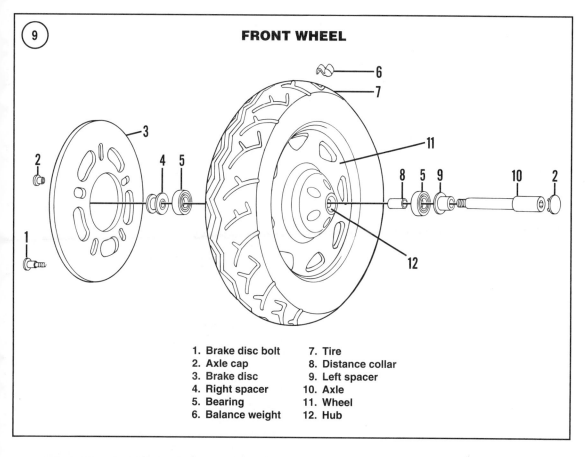

FRONT WHEEL

1. Brake disc bolt
2. Axle cap
3. Brake disc
4. Right spacer
5. Bearing
6. Balance weight
7. Tire
8. Distance collar
9. Left spacer
10. Axle
11. Wheel
12. Hub

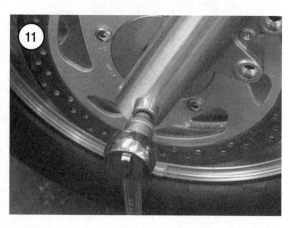

Make sure the brake disc(s) does not damage the brake pads.

6. Lift the wheel and insert the front axle (**Figure 11**) through the left fork leg and the wheel hub. Install the axle into the right fork leg.

7. Tighten the front axle so it is snug (B, **Figure 10**).

8. Remove the motorcycle support so both wheels rest on the ground.

9. Apply the front brake, and pump the fork a few times to seat the front axle.

10. Tighten the front axle (B, **Figure 10**) to 65 N•m (48 ft.-lb.).

11. Tighten the clamp bolt (A, **Figure 10**) to 23 N•m (17 ft.-lb.).

12. Roll the motorcycle back and forth several times, and apply the front brake to seat the brake pads against the brake disc.

13. Install the front fender. Securely tighten the fasteners.

FRONT HUB

Disassembly

Refer to **Figure 9**.

1. Remove the front wheel as described in this chapter.

2. If still installed, remove each spacer from the respective side of the hub.

3. If necessary, remove the brake disc bolts (A, **Figure 7**, typical) and remove the disc.

4. Inspect the wheel bearings as described in this chapter. If they require replacement, perform Step 5.

> *WARNING*
> *Wear safety glasses while using the wheel bearing remover set.*

5A. To remove the bearings with a bearing remover, perform the following:

    a. Select the correct size remover head tool, and insert it into the bearing (**Figure 12**).

    b. Turn the wheel over and insert the remover shaft into the backside of the adapter.

    c. Tap the shaft and force it into the slit in the adapter (**Figure 12**). This forces the adapter against the bearing inner race.

    d. Tap on the end of the shaft with a hammer and drive the bearing out of the hub (**Figure 13**).

    e. Remove the bearing and the distance collar.

    f. Repeat for the bearing on the other side.

5B. If a bearing remover is not available, perform the following:

    a. To remove the right and left bearings, and distance collar, insert a soft aluminum or brass drift into one side of the hub (**Figure 14**).

    b. Push the distance collar to one side and place the drift on the inner race of the lower bearing.

    c. Working around the perimeter of the inner race, tap the bearing out of the hub with a hammer.

    d. Remove the bearing and distance collar.

    e. Repeat for the other bearing.

6. Clean the hub with solvent and dry with compressed air.

Assembly

> *CAUTION*
> *Do not install removed bearings. Removal damages the bearings. Replace bearings as a set. If any one bearing in the wheel is worn, replace them both.*

1. The original equipment bearings are sealed on one side. Pack the new bearings with grease. To pack the bearings, spread some grease in the palm of your hand and scrape the open side of the bearing across the grease. Rotate the bearing a few times and repeat the process until the bearing is completely packed.

2. Blow any debris out of the hub.

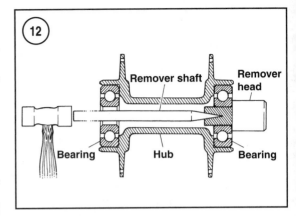

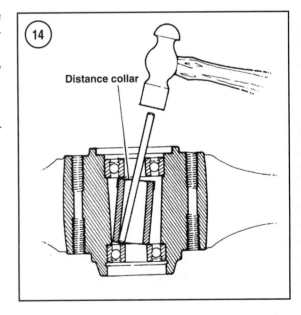

3. Apply a light coat of grease to the bearing seat in the hub.

> *CAUTION*
> *Install partially-sealed bearings with the sealed side facing outward. Be sure that the bearings are completely seated.*

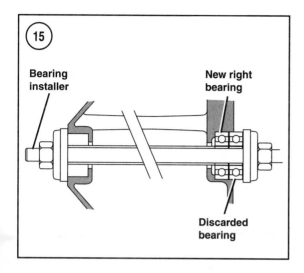

Bearing installer

New right bearing

Discarded bearing

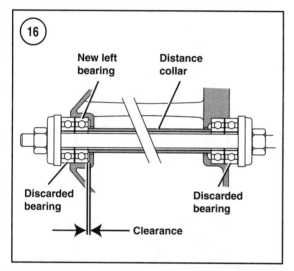

New left bearing

Distance collar

Discarded bearing

Discarded bearing

Clearance

4A. If using a bearing installer set (Suzuki part No. 09941-34513), or its equivalent, perform the following:

a. Set the right bearing into the hub with the sealed side facing out.

b. Set a discarded bearing (or a suitable size socket) against the new bearing, and assemble the bearing installer as shown in **Figure 15**.

c. Tighten the bearing installer (**Figure 15**), and slowly pull the right bearing into the hub until it is completely seated. Remove the bearing installer.

d. Turn the wheel over (left side up) on the workbench, and install the distance collar.

e. Set the left bearing into the hub with the sealed side facing out.

f. Set a discarded bearing (or a suitable size socket) against the bearing, and assemble the bearing installer as shown in **Figure 16**.

CAUTION
There is no specification for the clearance between the bearing and the distance collar. The important thing is that these two parts are not pressed against each other.

g. Tighten the bearing installer, and slowly pull the left bearing into the hub until there is a slight clearance between the inner race and the distance collar.

h. Remove the bearing installer.

4B. If a bearing installer set is not available, perform the following:

a. Set the right bearing into place in the hub so its sealed side faces out.

b. Using a bearing driver or a socket that matches the diameter of the outer bearing race, tap the first bearing squarely into place in the hub (**Figure 17**, typical). Do not tap on the inner bearing race. Make sure the bearing is completely seated in the hub.

c. Turn the wheel over on the workbench and install the distance collar.

CAUTION
There is no specification for the clearance between the bearing and the distance collar. The important thing is that these two parts are not pressed against each other.

d. Use the same tool set-up, and drive the left bearing into the hub until there is a slight clearance between the inner race and the distance collar.

5. If the brake disc was removed, perform the following:

a. Apply a small amount Suzuki Thread Lock Super 1360 to the brake disc bolt threads prior to installation.

b. Install the brake disc. Tighten the brake disc bolts (**Figure 17**, typical) to 23 N•m (17 ft.-lb.).

6. Install each spacer into the correct side of the hub.

11

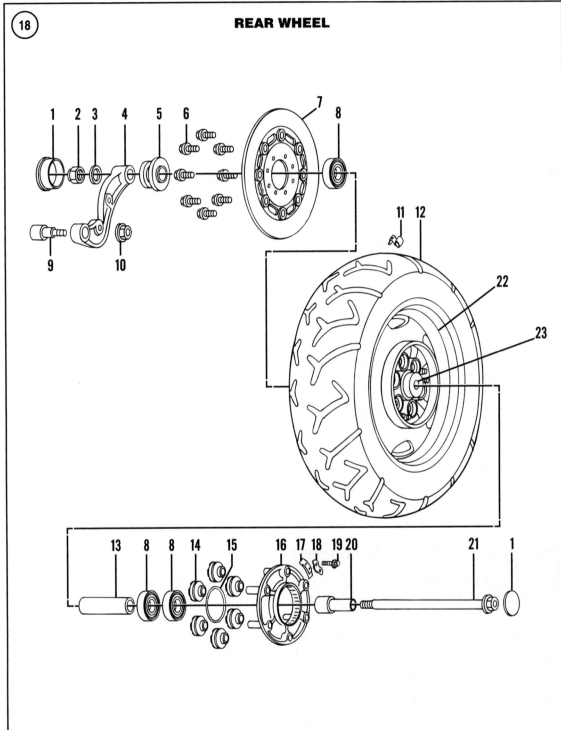

REAL WHEEL

18

1. Axle cap
2. Axle nut
3. Washer
4. Brake caliper bracket
5. Right spacer
6. Brake disc bolt
7. Brake disc
8. Bearing

9. Bracket bolt
10. Nut
11. Balance weight
12. Tire
13. Distance collar
14. Damper
15. O-ring
16. Driven coupling

17. Driven coupling stopper
18. Lockplate
19. Stopper bolt
20. Left spacer
21. Axle
22. Wheel
23. Hub

REAR WHEEL

Removal

Refer to **Figure 18**.

1. Support the motorcycle with the rear wheel off the ground.

2. Remove the rear fender (Chapter Fifteen) and the exhaust system (Chapter Eight).

3. Remove the rear brake caliper (Chapter Fourteen). Secure the caliper so it does not hang by the brake hose.

4. Remove the axle cap from each side of the wheel.

5. Remove the axle nut (**Figure 19**) and washer from the right side.

6. Partially pull out the rear axle (**Figure 20**), and remove the caliper bracket (A, **Figure 21**) and the right spacer (B).

7. Remove the axle from the left side.

8. Move the rear wheel to the right side until it disengages from the final drive. Roll the wheel from the swing arm. Make sure the left spacer clears the swing arm.

9. Remove the left spacer (**Figure 22**) from the final drive coupling.

Installation

1. Apply Suzuki Super Grease A (or its equivalent) to the splines of the driven coupling.

2. Install the left spacer into the final drive coupling (**Figure 22**).

3. Roll the wheel into place in the swing arm.

4. Position the wheel so its splines engage those of the drive coupling. Slowly move the wheel to the left until it bottoms against the final drive.

5. Install the right spacer (**Figure 23**) into the hub.

6. Install the axle so it passes into the spacer (B, **Figure 21**).

7. Position the caliper bracket (A, **Figure 21**) into place, and install the axle until it bottoms in the final drive (**Figure 20**).

8. Install the washer (**Figure 24**) and rear axle nut (**Figure 19**).

9. Tighten the rear axle nut to 110 N•m (81 ft.-lb.).

10. Install the rear brake caliper (Chapter Fourteen).

11. Pump the brake pedal and check brake operation.

12. Install the exhaust system (Chapter Eight) and rear fender (Chapter Fifteen).

REAR HUB

Refer to **Figure 18**.

Disassembly

1. Remove the rear wheel as described in this chapter.

2. If still in place, remove the spacer from the brake disc side (**Figure 23**) and from the driven coupling side (**Figure 22**) of the hub.

3. Flatten the lockplate tab away from the bolt flat on each coupling stopper bolt (A, **Figure 25**), and remove the driven coupling stopper bolts.

4. Remove each lockplate and each driven coupling stopper (B, **Figure 25**).

5. Pull the driven coupling (C, **Figure 25**) from the dampers in the hub.

6. Remove the O-ring (A, **Figure 26**).

7. Lift the dampers (B, **Figure 26**) from the hub.

8. If necessary, remove the brake disc bolts (A, **Figure 7**), and remove the disc.

9. Before proceeding further, inspect the wheel bearings (disc side: B, **Figure 7**; coupling side: C, **Figure 26**) as described in this chapter.

10. If a bearing must be replaced, remove all three bearings from the rear hub by performing Step 5A or 5B of *Front Hub, Disassembly* in this chapter. Note the following:

    a. A single bearing is used on the right side (disc side) of the hub. However, there are two bearings used on the left side (coupling side).

    b. The single bearing in the right side of the hub is a fully sealed bearing.

    c. Each bearing on the left side is sealed on one side. Note that the seal side of the inboard bearing faces into the hub. The sealed side of the outboard bearing faces out. The new bearings must be installed with this same orientation.

11. Clean the hub with solvent. Dry with compressed air.

Assembly

CAUTION
Always install new bearings. The bearings are damaged during removal and must not be reused.

1. On partially sealed bearings, pack the new bearings with grease. To pack the bearings, spread some grease in the palm of your hand and scrape the open side of the bearing across the grease. Rotate the bearing a few times and repeat until the bearing is completely full of grease.

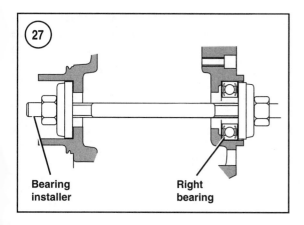

Bearing installer

Right bearing

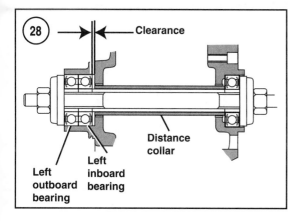

Clearance

Distance collar

Left outboard bearing

Left inboard bearing

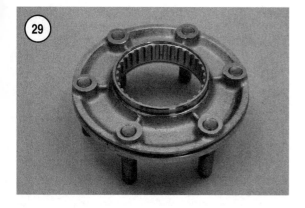

2. Blow any debris out of the hub.

3. Apply a light coat of grease to the bearing seat in the hub.

4A. If using a bearing installer (Suzuki part No. 09941-34513), or its equivalent, to install the *rear wheel bearings*, perform the following:

    a. Set the right bearing into the hub so the side with the manufacturer's marks faces out. Assemble the bearing installer as shown in **Figure 27**.

    b. Tighten the bearing installer (**Figure 27**), and slowly pull the right bearing into the hub until it is completely seated. Remove the bearing installer.

    c. Turn the wheel over (left side up) on the workbench and install the distance collar.

CAUTION
There is no specification for the clearance between the bearing and the distance collar. The important thing is that these two parts are not pressed against each other.

    d. Position the left inboard bearing so the sealed side faces into the hub (**Figure 28**). Tighten the bearing installer, and slowly pull the bearing into the hub until there is a slight clearance between the inboard bearing inner race and the distance collar.

    e. Position the outboard bearing so its sealed side faces out away from the hub. Tighten the bearing installer and slowly pull the bearing into the hub until it bottoms against the first bearing (**Figure 28**).

4B. If a bearing installer is not used, perform the following:

    a. Set the right bearing into the hub so the side with the manufacturer's mark faces out.

    b. Using a bearing driver or socket that matches the diameter of the outer bearing race, tap the bearing squarely into place in the hub. Tap on the outer race only (**Figure 17**). Do not tap on the inner race. Make sure the bearing is completely seated.

    c. Turn the wheel over on the workbench and install the distance collar.

CAUTION
There is no specification for the clearance between the bearing and the distance collar. The important thing is that these two parts are not pressed against each other.

    d. Using the same tool set-up, drive the inboard and then the outboard bearing into the hub. Make sure there is a slight clearance between the inboard bearing inner race and the distance collar. Position the inboard bearing so its sealed side faces into the hub. The sealed side of the outboard bearing must faces out of the hub. See **Figure 28**.

5. If the brake disc was removed, perform the following:

    a. Apply a small amount Suzuki Thread Lock Super 1360 to the threads of the brake disc bolts.

    b. Install the brake disc, and tighten the brake disc bolts to 23 N•m (17 ft.-lb.).

6. Lubricate the dampers (B, **Figure 26**) with soapy water, and install them into the hub.

7. Lubricate a new O-ring (A, **Figure 26**) with grease, and install it into the left side of the hub.

8. Install the driven coupling (**Figure 29**) so its posts sit in the collars in the dampers (C, **Figure 25**).

11

CAUTION
Install three new lockplates.

9. Set each driven coupling stopper (B, **Figure 25**) into place so the stopper engages the slot in the driven coupling outer rim. Install new lockplates into place, and install the stopper bolts. See **Figure 30**.

    a. Apply Suzuki Thread Lock 1303 to the threads of the stopper bolts.

    b. Tighten the driven coupling stopper bolts (A, **Figure 25**) to 10 N•m (89 in.-lb.).

10. Bend a lockplate tab against a flat on each bolt.

WHEEL BALANCE

WARNING
An unbalanced wheel may be unsafe if it affects the steering or handling. An unbalanced wheel/tire may also cause abnormal tire wear.

Before balancing a wheel, make sure the wheel bearings are in good condition. The wheel must rotate freely.

Weight kits containing adhesive backed test weights are available.

1. Remove the front or rear wheel as described in this chapter.

2. Mount the wheel on an inspection stand (**Figure 31**) so the wheel can rotate freely.

3. Spin the wheel and let it come to a stop. Mark the tire at the lowest point with chalk or light colored crayon.

4. Spin the wheel several more times. If the wheel keeps coming to rest at the same point, this spot is the heaviest part of the tire and wheel combination.

5. Attach a test weight to the upper (or light) side of the wheel.

6. Experiment with different weights until the wheel, when spun, comes to rest at a different position each time.

NOTE
After determining the balance weight amount, divide that weight in half and install it on either side of the wheel to distribute the weight evenly across the wheel. The difference between these two weights must be less than 10 grams (0.353 oz.).

7. Remove the test weights, thoroughly clean the wheel surface, and install the correct size weight (**Figure 32**) onto each side of the wheel. Make sure they are secure.

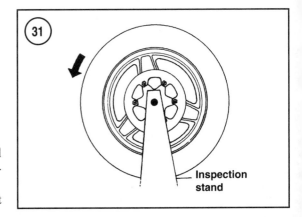

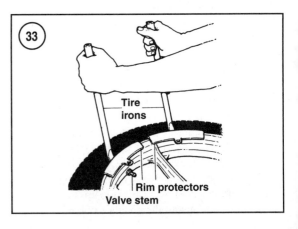

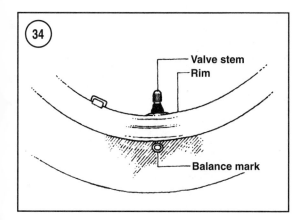

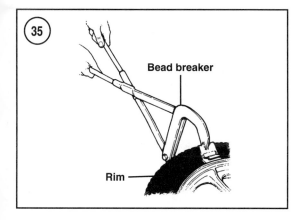

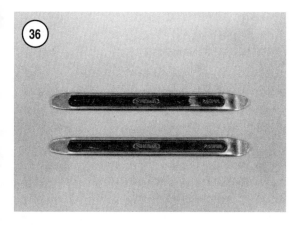

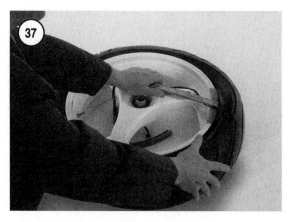

TIRES

Removal

> *CAUTION*
> *The rear tire is wide and the rigid cross section of both tires makes tire removal difficult. The manufacturer recommends the tires be removed with a tire changer. A tire changer breaks the beads loose and installs the tire while lessening the chance of damaging the wheel and tire bead-to-rim surface.*

> *CAUTION*
> *If the weather is warm, place the wheels and new tires in the sun or in an enclosed automobile to heat the tires. The softened rubber makes removal/installation easier.*

> *CAUTION*
> *Use a raised platform, a metal drum with a padded edge for example, to ease tire removal and protect the brake disc.*

The cast alloy wheels use tubeless tires. These wheels are easily damaged during tire removal. Use tire levers or flat-handle tire irons with rounded heads. Protect the rim with scraps of leather or rim protectors (**Figure 33**) inserted between the tire iron and the rim.

When removing a tubeless tire, take care not to damage the tire beads, inner liner of the tire or the wheel rim flange.

Support the wheel on two blocks of wood so the brake discs or the rear sprocket do not contact the floor.

Refer to *Tire and Wheels* in Chapter Three for tire inspection.

1. Remove the front or rear wheel as described in this chapter.
2. If not already marked by the tire manufacturer, mark the valve stem location on the tire (**Figure 34**) so the tire can be installed in the same location for easier balancing.
3. Remove the valve core from the valve stem and deflate the tire.
4. Press the entire bead on both sides of the tire away from the rim and into the center of the rim. If necessary, use a bead breaker (**Figure 35**).
5. Lubricate both beads with soapy water.
6. Insert a tire iron (**Figure 36**) under the top bead next to the valve stem. Force the bead on the opposite side of the tire into the center of the rim, and pry the bead over the rim with the tire iron (**Figure 37**).

7. Insert a second tire iron next to the first iron to hold the bead outside the rim. Work around the tire with the first tire iron, prying the bead over the rim (**Figure 38**). Work slowly, and take small bites with the tire irons.

8. Stand the wheel upright. Insert a tire iron between the second bead and the side of the rim that the first bead was pried over (**Figure 39**). Force the bead on the opposite side from the tire iron into the center of the rim. Pry the second bead off the rim working around the wheel with two rim protectors and tire irons.

9. Remove and discard the valve stem. Remove all rubber residue from the valve stem hole in the rim. Inspect the hole for cracks or other damage.

10. Remove the old balance weights from the wheel.

11. Carefully inspect the tire and wheel rim for any damage.

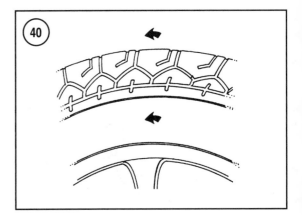

Installation

> *WARNING*
> *A new tire has poor adhesion to the road surface. Do not subject a tire to hard cornering, acceleration or braking during the first 100 miles (160 km) of use.*

1. Install a new valve stem and make sure it properly seats on the rim.

2. Lubricate both beads of the tire with soapy water.

3. Make sure the correct tire, either front or rear, is installed on the correct wheel. Install the tire so the direction arrow on the tire faces the direction of forward wheel rotation (**Figure 40**).

4. If remounting the old tire, align the mark made in Step 2 of *Removal* (this section) with the valve stem. If installing a new tire, align the colored mark near the bead (indicating the lightest point of the tire) with the valve stem. See **Figure 34**.

5. Place the backside of the tire onto the rim so the lower bead sits in the center of the rim while the upper bead remains outside the rim. (**Figure 41**). Use

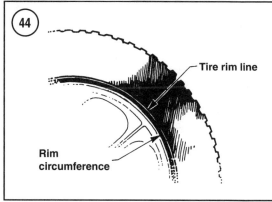

both hands to push the backside of the tire into the rim as far as possible. Use tire irons when it becomes difficult to install the tire by hand.

6. At a point opposite the valve, press the upper bead into the rim. Working on both side of this initial point, pry the bead into the rim with a tire tool and work around the rim to the valve stem (**Figure 42**). If the tire wants to pull up on one side, either use another tire iron or a knee to hold the tire in place. The last few inches are usually the toughest. If possible, continue to push the tire into the rim by hand. Relubricate the bead if necessary. If the tire bead wants to pull out from under the rim, use both your knees to hold the tire in place. If necessary, use a tire iron for the last few inches (**Figure 43**).

7. Check the bead on both side of the tire for an even fit around the rim (**Figure 44**). Align the balance mark (**Figure 34**) with the valve stem.

8. Lubricate both sides of the tire with soapy water.

> *WARNING*
> *Wear eye protection when inflating the tire. Do not exceed 400 kPa (56 psi) in-flation pressure as the tire could burst causing injury. Never stand directly over a tire while inflating it.*

9. Inflate the tire until the tire beads are pressed against the rim. A loud pop should be heard as each bead seats against the rim.

10. After inflating the tire, make sure the beads fully seat and that the rim lines are the same distance from the rim all the way around the tire (**Figure 44**). If the beads will not seat, deflate the tire and lubricate the rim and beads with soapy water.

11. Reinflate the tire to the pressure specified in **Table 1**. Install the valve stem cap.

12. Balance the wheel as described in this chapter.

Repairs

Only use tire plugs as an emergency repair. Refer to the plug manufacturer's instructions for installation. Note any weight and speed restrictions. Tire repair is a temporary measure. Replace the tire as soon as possible.

11

Table 1 WHEEL AND TIRE SPECIFICATIONS

Item	Specification
Wheel size	
Front	
1998-2001 models	16 × MT 3.50
2002-on models	16 × MT 3.50, 16M/C × MT 3.50
Rear	15M/C × MT 5.00
Wheel runout limit	
Axial	2.0 mm (0.08 in.)
Radial	2.0 mm (0.08 in.)
Axle runout limit	
Front	0.25 mm (0.010 in.)
Rear	0.25 mm (0.010 in.)
(continued)	

Table 1 WHEEL AND TIRE SPECIFICATIONS (continued)

Item	Specification
Tire Size	
Front	
1998-2001 models	150/80-16 71H
2002-on models	150/80-16 71H, 150/80-16M/C 71H
Rear	180/70-15M/C 76H
Tire tread minimum depth	
Front	1.6 mm (0.06 in.)
Rear	2.0 mm (0.08 in.)
Tire pressure (cold)*	
Front	
Solo	200 kPa (29 psi)
Rider and passenger	200 kPa (29 psi)
Rear	
Solo	250 kPa (36 psi)
Rider and passenger	250 kPa (36 psi)

*Tire inflation pressure is for original equipment tires. Aftermarket tires may require different inflation pressure. The use of tires other than those specified by the manufacturer may cause instability.

Table 2 WHEEL AND TIRE TORQUE SPECIFICATIONS

Item	N•m	in.-lb.	ft.-lb.
Brake disc bolt	23	–	17
Driven coupling stopper bolts	10	89	–
Front axle	65	–	48
Front axle clamp bolt	23	–	17
Front caliper mounting bolt	35	–	26
Rear axle nut	110	–	81
Rear caliper bracket bolt/nut	60	–	44
Rear caliper mounting bolt	35	–	26

CHAPTER TWELVE

FRONT SUSPENSION AND STEERING

This chapter covers the front fork and steering components. Refer to Chapter Eleven for wheels and tires.

Refer to **Table 1** at the end of this chapter for specifications. Replace worn, damaged or out of specification components.

FRONT FORK

To prevent the mixing of parts, remove and install each fork leg individually.

Removal (1998-2004 Models)

1. Support the motorcycle on a level surface.
2A. On 1998-2001 models, remove the front brake caliper (Chapter Fourteen) if the right fork leg is being removed.
2B. On 2002-on models, remove the front brake caliper (Chapter Fourteen) from the fork leg being removed.
3. Remove the front fender (Chapter Fifteen) and the front wheel (Chapter Eleven).
4. Remove the headlight and headlight housing (Chapter Ten).
5. Remove the mounting screws (**Figure 1**), and lower the turn signal bracket from the lower fork bridge.
6. Remove the upper fork cover bolts from the front (**Figure 2**) and rear sides (**Figure 3**) of the cover. Slide the upper fork cover (**Figure 2**) down the fork legs to expose the clamp bolts on the lower fork bridge (**Figure 4**).
7. Remove the cap bolt (**Figure 5**). Apply a single wrap or turn of electrical tape around the bolt head so the socket will not damage the cap bolt.
8. If servicing the fork leg, perform the following:
   a. Place a drain pan under the fork tube.
   b. Use an impact driver to loosen the Allen bolt (**Figure 6**) in the base of the slider. Remove the Allen bolt, and drain the fork oil. Pump the slider several times to expel most of the fork oil.

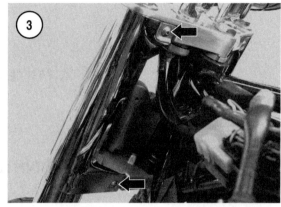

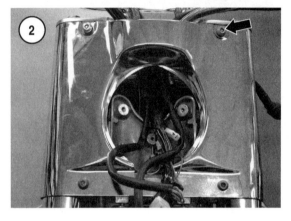

c. Use a 14-mm Allen wrench to loosen the fork spring nut (**Figure 7**).

9. Loosen the lower fork bridge clamp bolts (**Figure 4**).

10. Carefully lower the fork leg from the upper and lower fork bridges. It may be necessary to rotate the fork leg slightly while pulling it down. If the fork leg is not going to be serviced, warp it in a towel to protect the surface.

11. If both fork leg assemblies have been removed, label them to ensure they are installed correctly.

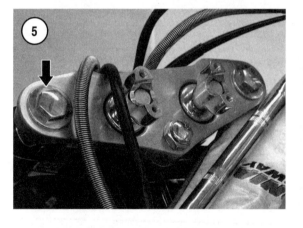

Installation (1998-2004 Models)

1. If both fork leg assemblies were removed, refer to the marks made during removal and identify the correct fork leg (left or right).

2. Slide the fork leg assembly through the lower fork bridge and into the upper fork bridge until the lower fork cover (**Figure 8**) bottoms against the lower fork bridge. The upper fork cover has been removed for photographic clarity.

3. Snug the lower fork bridge clamp bolts (**Figure 4**) enough to hold the fork leg in place.

4. If the fork leg was disassembled for service, tighten the fork spring nut (**Figure 7**) to 35 N•m (26 ft.-lb.).

5. Lubricate a new O-ring with Suzuki SS-08 fork oil

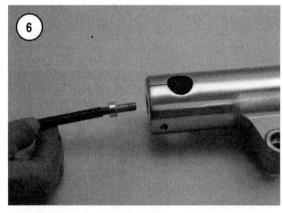

or its equivalent. Install the O-ring onto the cap bolt.

6. Install the cap bolt into the fork leg (**Figure 5**). Tighten the cap bolt to 90 N•m (66 ft.-lb.).

7. Loosen the lower fork bridge clamp bolts (**Figure 4**) to relieve any stress created by tightening the cap bolt. Tighten the clamp bolts in stages to 23 N•m (17 ft.-lb.).

8. If necessary, repeat Steps 1-7 for the other fork leg.

9. Slide the upper fork cover into place on the fork legs and install the front (**Figure 2**) and rear (**Figure 3**) upper cover bolts. Tighten the bolts securely.

10. Fit the turn signal bracket into place, and tighten the bolts securely (**Figure 1**).

11. Install the headlight housing and headlight (Chapter Ten).

12. Install the front wheel (Chapter Eleven) and front fender (Chapter Fifteen).

13. Install the brake caliper(s) (Chapter Fourteen).

12

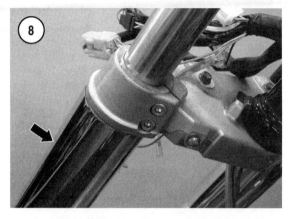

Removal (2005-on Models)

1. Support the motorcycle on a level surface.

2. Remove the front brake caliper(s) from the fork slider (Chapter Fourteen).

3. Remove the front fender (Chapter Fifteen) and the front wheel (Chapter Eleven).

4. Loosen the steering head nut (**Figure 9**).

5. Loosen the upper fork bridge clamp bolt (A, **Figure 10**), and the lower fork bridge clamp bolts (B).

6. Carefully lower the fork leg assembly from the upper fork bridge, upper fork cover, and the lower fork bridge. If necessary, rotate the fork leg slightly while pulling it down.

7. Lift the upper fork bridge slightly and remove the upper fork cover (C, **Figure 10**) from between the fork bridges.

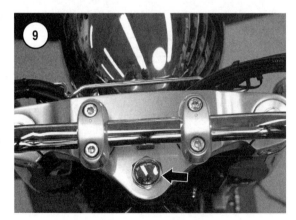

8. Remove the cover damper (A, **Figure 11**) and washer from the top of the lower fork bridge.

9. If the fork leg will be disassembled for service, perform the following:

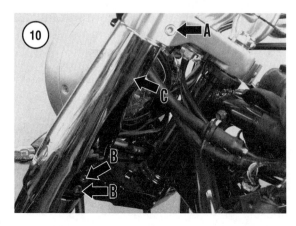

a. Slide the fork leg up through the lower and upper fork bridges. Securely tighten the lower fork bridge clamp bolts (B, **Figure 10**).

b. Place a drain pan under the fork tube.

c. Use an impact driver to loosen the Allen (**Figure 6**) bolt in the base of the slider. Remove the Allen bolt, and drain the fork oil. Pump the slider several times to expel most of the fork oil.

d. Loosen the front fork cap bolt (**Figure 12**). Apply a single wrap or turn of electrical tape around the bolt head so the socket will not damage the cap bolt.

e. Loosen the lower fork bridge clamp bolts (B, **Figure 10**), and remove the fork leg.

Installation (2005-on Models)

1. Slide the fork leg assembly through the lower fork bridge. Install the washer and damper (A, **Figure 11**) over the fork leg and onto the lower fork bridge.

2. Install the upper cover (C, **Figure 10**) so its upper lip sits inside the upper fork bridge. Also make sure the hole in the upper cover engages the tab (B, **Figure 11**) on the lower fork bridge.

3. Slide the fork tube upward until it bottoms. Make sure the tube passes through the clamp in the upper fork bridge. Snug the lower fork bridge clamp bolts (B, **Figure 10**) enough to hold the fork leg in place.

4. With the fork leg(s) positioned so the lower cover(s) bottom against the lower fork bridge, tighten the lower fork bridge clamp bolts (B, **Figure 10**) to 23 N•m (17 ft.-lb.).

5. Loosen the upper fork bridge clamp bolt (A, **Figure 10**) on each side.

6. Tighten the steering head nut (**Figure 13**) to 90 N•m (66 ft.-lb.).

7. Check the height of each fork leg. Make sure the top of each fork tube aligns with the top of the upper fork bridge (**Figure 14**). If necessary, loosen the lower clamp bolts and adjust the height. Tighten the lower fork bridge clamp bolts (B, **Figure 10**) to 23 N•m (17 ft.-lb.).

8. Tighten the upper fork bridge clamp bolt (A, **Figure 10**) on each side to 23 N•m (17 ft.-lb.).

9. Install the front wheel (Chapter Eleven) and the front fender (Chapter Fifteen).

10. Install the brake caliper(s) (Chapter Fourteen).

Disassembly (All Models)

Refer to **Figure 15**.

1. Use the following Suzuki tools, or their equivalent, to disassemble the fork leg.

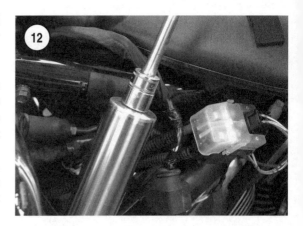

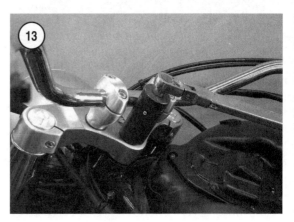

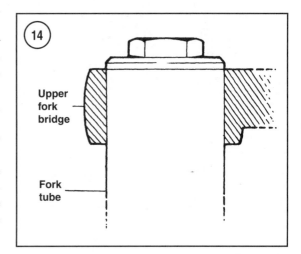

a. 14-mm Allen socket: part No. 09900-18720 (1998-2004 models).

b. Fork oil level gauge: part No. 09943-74111.

c. Attachment A: part No. 09940-34531.

d. Fork seal installer: part No. 09940-52861.

2. Slide the lower fork cover (A, **Figure 16**), the damper (B), and washer (C) from the fork leg.

3. Secure the fork vertically in a vise with soft jaws.

4A. On 1998-2004 models, use the 14-mm Allen socket and remove the fork spring nut (**Figure 17**).

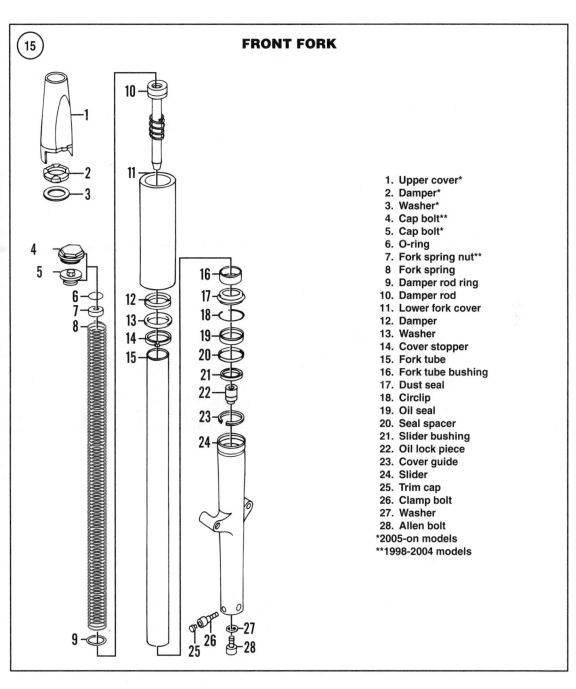

FRONT FORK

15

1. Upper cover*
2. Damper*
3. Washer*
4. Cap bolt**
5. Cap bolt*
6. O-ring
7. Fork spring nut**
8 Fork spring
9. Damper rod ring
10. Damper rod
11. Lower fork cover
12. Damper
13. Washer
14. Cover stopper
15. Fork tube
16. Fork tube bushing
17. Dust seal
18. Circlip
19. Oil seal
20. Seal spacer
21. Slider bushing
22. Oil lock piece
23. Cover guide
24. Slider
25. Trim cap
26. Clamp bolt
27. Washer
28. Allen bolt
*2005-on models
**1998-2004 models

12

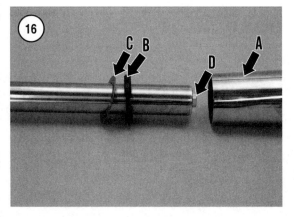

16

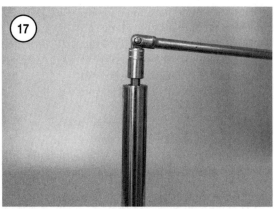

17

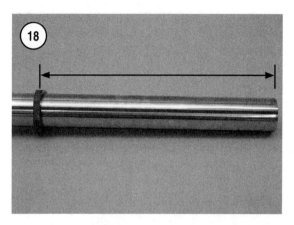

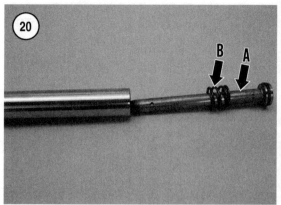

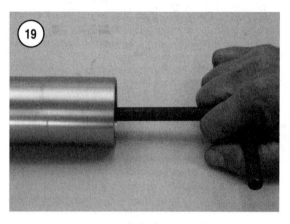

4B. On 2005-on models, remove the cap bolt (D, **Figure 16**).

5. Remove the fork spring from the fork leg.

6. Measure the distance from the upper edge of the cover stopper to the fork tube upper edge (**Figure 18**). Record the measurement, and remove the cover stopper.

7. If the Allen bolt was not removed during removal, perform the following:

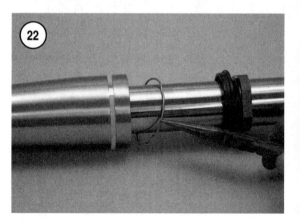

a. Invert the fork leg and pour out the fork oil. Pump the fork tube several times to expel as much oil as possible.

b. Hold the damper rod with attachment A and a T-handle (**Figure 19**).

c. Remove the Allen bolt and its washer from the bottom of the slider (**Figure 6**).

8. Remove the damper rod (A, **Figure 20**) from the fork leg. Watch for the rod spring (B, **Figure 20**). It should come out with the damper rod.

9. Pry the dust seal (**Figure 21**) from the slider, and remove the circlip (**Figure 22**).

10. Secure the slider in a vise with soft jaws.

11. There is an interference fit between the fork tube bushing and the fork slider bushing. Grasp the fork tube. Using quick in-and-out strokes, pull hard and remove the fork tube from the slider (**Figure 23**). The fork tube bushing (A, **Figure 24**), slider bushing

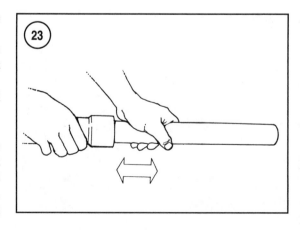

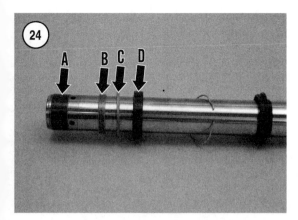

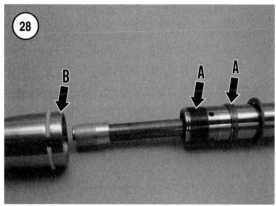

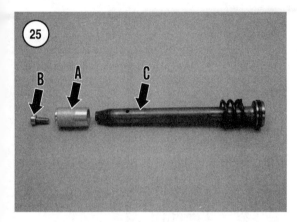

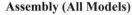

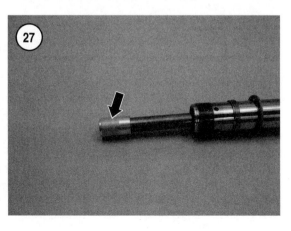

(B), seal spacer (C), and the oil seal (D) come out with the fork tube.

12. Remove the oil lock piece (A, **Figure 25**) from the slider.

13. Inspect the components as described in this section.

Assembly (All Models)

1. Coat all parts with Suzuki SS-08 fork oil, or its equivalent.

2. If removed, install a new fork tube bushing (A, **Figure 24**) onto the fork tube.

3. Slide the slider bushing (B, **Figure 24**) and the oil seal spacer (C) down the fork tube.

4. Place a piece of plastic wrap over the end of the fork tube. Lubricate the plastic wrap with fork oil.

5. Pack the lips of a new oil seal with grease. With the manufacturer's marks up, slide the oil seal (**Figure 26**), circlip, and dust seal over the plastic wrap and down the fork tube.

6. Install the spring (B, **Figure 20**) onto the damper rod (A), and install the rod into the fork tube so the rod emerges from the other end of the tube.

7. Fit the tapered end of the oil lock piece (**Figure 27**) onto the end of the damper rod.

8. Apply fork oil to both bushings (A, **Figure 28**), and install the fork tube into the slider (B).

9. Install the Allen bolt (B, **Figure 25**) as follows:

   a. Fit a new washer onto the Allen bolt.

   b. Apply Suzuki Thread Lock 1342 to the bolt threads.

   c. Insert the Allen bolt into the fork slider (**Figure 6**), and turn it into the oil lock piece.

   d. Hold the damper rod with attachment A and a T-handle (**Figure 19**), and tighten the front fork Allen bolt to 20 N•m (15 ft.-lb.).

10. Secure the slider vertically in a vise with soft jaws.

12

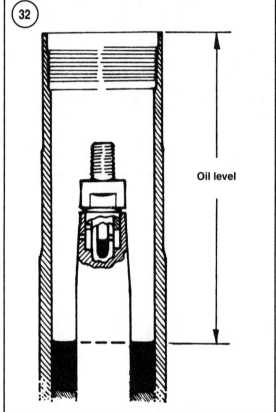

Oil level

11. Use a fork seal driver (**Figure 29**) with the correct diameter to drive the slider bushing and seal spacer into place in the slider. Make sure the bushing completely seats in the recess in the slider.

12. Use a fork seal driver to drive the oil seal into the slider until the circlip groove in the slider is visible above the top of the oil seal.

13. Install the circlip so it seats in the circlip groove in the slider (**Figure 30**).

14. Slide the dust seal down the fork tube, and seat it in the slider (**Figure 21**).

15. Slide the cover stopper down the fork tube. Position the cover stopper so the distance from the upper edge of the fork tube to the upper edge of the cover stopper (**Figure 18**) equals the cover stopper depth specified in **Table 1**. Tighten the cover stopper clamp bolt securely.

16. Fill the fork with oil, and set the oil level as described in *Fork Oil Adjustment* in this section.

Fork Oil Adjustment

1. Secure the fork leg vertically in a vise with soft jaws.

2. Push the fork tube down into fork slider until the tube bottoms.

3. Refer to **Table 1**, and add the recommended amount

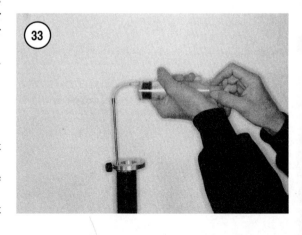

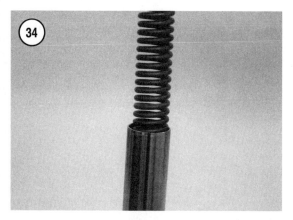

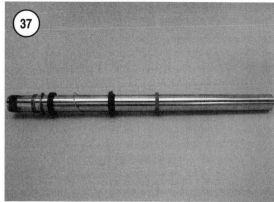

Copper surface

Fork tube bushing

Damper rod sealing ring

Check points

and type of fork oil to the fork leg (**Figure 31**).
4. Set the fork oil level by performing the following:
   a. The oil level is the distance from the top of the compressed fork tube to the upper edge of the oil (**Figure 32**).
   b. Use a ruler or oil level gauge (**Figure 33**) to set the oil level (**Table 1**).
   c. Adjust the oil level as necessary. Let the oil to settle completely and recheck.

5. Install the fork spring (**Figure 34**) so the end with the closer wound coils faces down into the slider.
6A. On 1998-2004 models, loosely install the fork spring nut (**Figure 17**).
6B. On 2005-on models, lubricate a new O-ring (**Figure 35**) with fork oil. Then install the O-ring onto the cap bolt and loosely install the cap bolt onto the fork tube.
7. Install the washer (C, **Figure 16**), damper (B), and the lower fork cover (A) onto the fork tube.
8A. On 1998-2004 models, perform the following:
   a. Slide the fork leg through the lower fork bridge until the lower fork cover bottoms against the lower fork bridge.
   b. Securely tighten the lower fork bridge clamp bolts to hold the leg in place.
   c. Tighten the fork spring nut (**Figure 7**) to 35 N•m (26 ft.-lb.).
   d. Lubricate a new O-ring (A, **Figure 4**) with fork oil. Then install the O-ring onto the cap bolt.
8B. On 2005-on models, perform the following:
   a. Slide the fork tube up through the lower fork bridge.
   b. Securely tighten the lower fork bridge clamp bolts to hold the leg in place.
   c. Tighten the front fork cap bolt (**Figure 12**) to 23 N•m (17 ft.-lb.).
9. Install the fork leg (this section).

Inspection

1. Thoroughly clean all parts in solvent and dry them.
2. Roll the damper rod (C, **Figure 25**) along a surface plate or a piece of glass. Inspect the rod and its sealing ring (**Figure 36**) for wear or damage.
3. Check the fork tube (**Figure 37**) for straightness, and inspect it for scuffing or burrs. If bent or severely scratched, replace it.
4. Inspect the threads in the top of the fork tube for wear or damage. Clean the threads with the appropriate size metric tap if necessary.

12

5. Check the slider (**Figure 38**) for dents or exterior damage that may cause the fork tube to stick. Replace the slider if necessary.

6. Check the lower fork cover guide (A, **Figure 38**) on the slider. Replace this guide as necessary.

7. Inspect the inner surfaces in the slider for scuffing or burrs. Pay particular attention to the circlip groove and the sealing surfaces. Clean the slider if necessary.

8. Inspect the mounting bosses (B, **Figure 38**) on the fork slider for cracks or other damage. If damaged, replace the slider.

9. Inspect the fork tube bushing (A, **Figure 24**) and the slider bushing (B). If either is scratched or scored, replace the bushings. Replace a bushing if the Teflon coating is so worn that the copper base material is showing on approximately 3/4 of the total bushing surface (**Figure 36**).

10. Inspect the cap bolt (**Figure 35**) for damage. If any damaged is noted, replace it.

11. On 1998-2004 models, inspect the fork spring nut for wear or damage.

12. Inspect the fork spring (**Figure 39**) for cracks or other damage.

13. Measure the uncompressed free length of the fork spring (**Figure 40**). Replace the spring if it measures less than the service limit in **Table 1**.

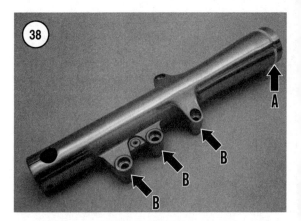

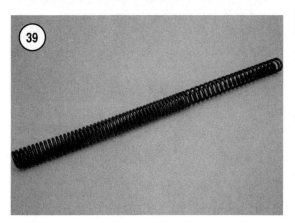

HANDLEBAR

Removal/Installation

Refer to **Figure 41**.

1. Support the motorcycle in an upright position.

2. Cover the fender and wheel to protect them from accidental brake fluid spills.

3. If the handlebar is being serviced, perform the following:

    a. Remove the front brake master cylinder (Chapter Fourteen). Suspend the master cylinder assembly from the motorcycle, keeping the reservoir upright so air does not enter the system. Do not disconnect the brake line from the master cylinder.

    b. Remove the right handlebar switch assembly (Chapter Nine).

    c. Disconnect the throttle cables from the throttle drum.

    d. Loosen the screw and remove the handlebar weight (**Figure 42**). Slide the throttle grip from the handlebar.

    e. Remove the clutch master cylinder (Chapter Six). Suspend the master cylinder assembly from the motorcycle, keeping the reservoir upright so air does not enter the system. Do not disconnect the clutch line from the master cylinder.

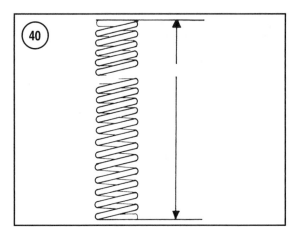

    f. Remove the left handlebar switch assembly (Chapter Nine).

    g. Remove the handlebar weight (**Figure 42**) and the left hand grip (this chapter).

4. Release any cable ties securing wires or cables to the handlebar. On 1998-2004 models, note how the cables and wires run through the upper fork cover (**Figure 43**).

5. Remove the trim cap from each handlebar clamp bolt (A, **Figure 44**), and remove the bolts.

6. Lift each upper handlebar holder (B, **Figure 44**) from its mate.

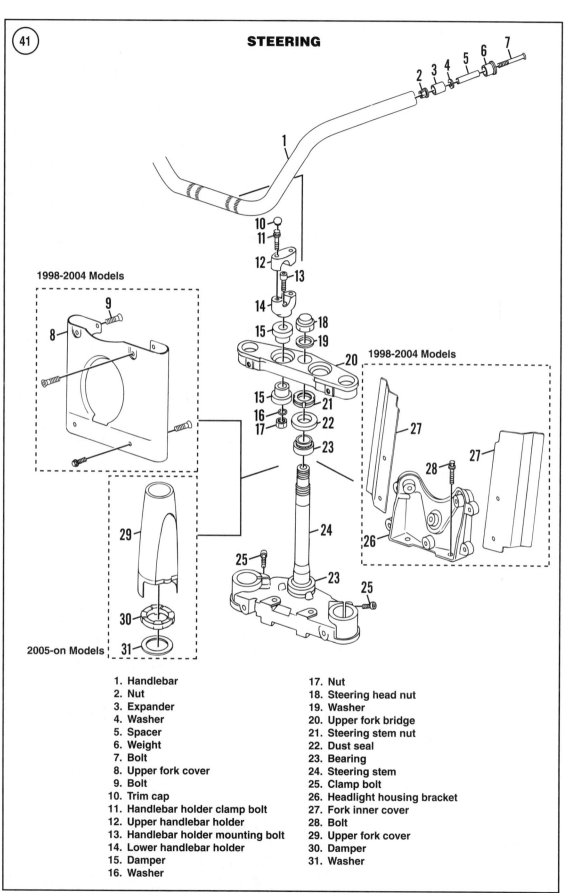

41 **STEERING**

1998-2004 Models

2005-on Models

1998-2004 Models

12

1. Handlebar
2. Nut
3. Expander
4. Washer
5. Spacer
6. Weight
7. Bolt
8. Upper fork cover
9. Bolt
10. Trim cap
11. Handlebar holder clamp bolt
12. Upper handlebar holder
13. Handlebar holder mounting bolt
14. Lower handlebar holder
15. Damper
16. Washer

17. Nut
18. Steering head nut
19. Washer
20. Upper fork bridge
21. Steering stem nut
22. Dust seal
23. Bearing
24. Steering stem
25. Clamp bolt
26. Headlight housing bracket
27. Fork inner cover
28. Bolt
29. Upper fork cover
30. Damper
31. Washer

7. Lift the handlebar from the lower handlebar holders. If the handlebar is not being serviced, rest it on the meter cover. Drape a tarp over the meter and upper covers to protect them from accidental brake fluid spills.

8. To remove the lower handlebar holders, perform the following:

    a. Remove the nut (**Figure 45**) and washer under the upper fork bridge. Then remove the handlebar holder bolt.

    b. Lift the holder from the fork bridge. Watch for the upper and lower dampers in the holder mount.

    c. Repeat the procedure for the remaining holder.

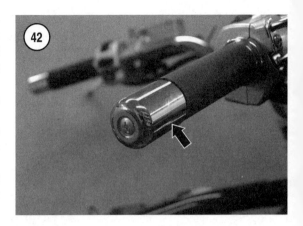

9. Installation is the reverse of removal. Note the following:

    a. If removed, install the lower handlebar holders onto the upper fork bridge. Make sure an upper and lower damper is in place in each mount. Tighten the handlebar holder nut (**Figure 45**) to 50 N•m (37 ft.-lb.) for 1998-2004 models or to 70 N•m (52 ft.-lb.) for 2005-on models.

    b. Set the handlebar onto the lower holders. Set each upper handlebar holder (B, **Figure 44**) into place and loosely install the clamp bolts (A). On handlebar holders with an index mark, position each upper holder so the index mark (C, **Figure 44**) faces forward.

    c. Position the handlebar so its punch mark faces forward, and aligns with the gap formed by the upper and lower holders (**Figure 46**).

    d. Tighten the handlebar clamp bolts evenly so the gap on the front of the holders equals the gap on the rear (**Figure 47**). Tighten the handlebar clamp bolts (A, **Figure 44**) to 16 N•m (12 ft.-lb.) for 1998-2004 models or to 23 N•m (17 ft.-lb.) for 2005-on models.

    e. Tighten the handlebar weight bolts to 50 N•m (37 ft.-lb.).

10. Adjust the throttle cable free play (Chapter Three).

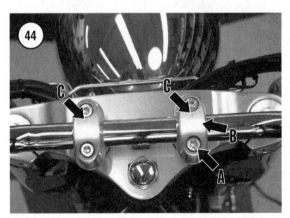

> *WARNING*
> *Make sure the brake and clutch operate correctly. If necessary, check the fluid level and/or bleed the system.*

11. Check the operation of the throttle, front brake, and clutch.

12. Check the operation of the switch functions on each switch assembly.

Inspection

1. Check the handlebar for bends, cracks or damage. Replace a bent or damaged handlebar.

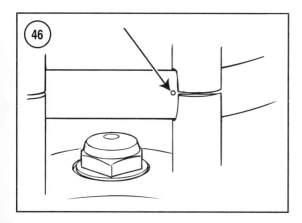

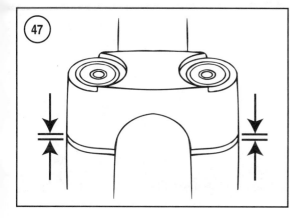

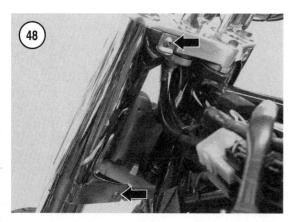

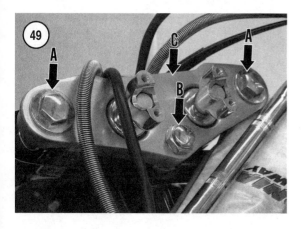

2. If the motorcycle has been crashed, thoroughly examine the handlebar, the steering stem, and front fork for damage or misalignment. Correct any problem immediately.

3. Check the bolt holes in the holders and upper fork bridge for cracks of damage.

4. Clean the knurled areas on the handlebar and holders to prevent handlebar slip.

HANDLEBAR LEFT GRIP REPLACEMENT

NOTE
The original equipment right grip is part of the throttle grip assembly and cannot be replaced separately.

1. Remove the weight from the end of the handlebar.

2. Slide a thin screwdriver between the left grip and handlebar. Then spray electrical contact cleaner into the opening under the grip.

3. Pull the screwdriver out and quickly twist the grip to break its bond with the handlebar. Then slide the grip off the handlebar.

4. Clean all rubber or sealant residue from the handlebar.

5. Install the new grip following the manufacturer's directions. Apply a grip adhesive between the grip and handlebar. Follow the adhesive manufacturer's instructions.

6. Install the handlebar weight. Tighten the handlebar weight bolt to 50 N•m (37 ft.-lb.).

STEERING HEAD AND STEM

Use a steering stem nut wrench (Suzuki part No. 09940-1491114960), or its equivalent, during this procedure.

Removal

Refer to **Figure 41**.

1. Remove the front fender (Chapter Fifteen) and front wheel (Chapter Eleven).

2. Remove the headlight and headlight housing (Chapter Ten).

3. Remove the handlebar (this chapter). Lay the handlebar over the meter cover. Protect the cover with a pad or tarp.

4A. On 1998-2004 models, perform the following:

    a. Remove the bolts from the rear of the upper fork cover (**Figure 48**).

    b. Remove the cap bolt (A, **Figure 49**) from each fork tube.

12

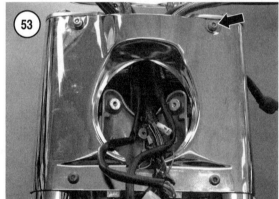

4B. On 2005-on models, loosen the clamp bolt (A, **Figure 50**) on each side of the upper fork bridge.

5. Remove the steering head nut (B, **Figure 49**) and its washer.

6. Remove the upper fork bridge (C, **Figure 49**) from the steering stem and fork tubes.

7A. On 1998-2004 models:

   a. Note how the cables and hoses are routed behind the upper fork cover (**Figure 51**).

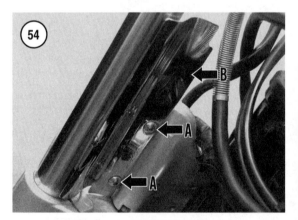

> *NOTE*
> *The upper fork cover can be removed by sliding the cover down the fork legs. However, doing this may scratch the lower fork covers (A, **Figure 52**). Removing the upper fork cover from the top of the fork legs is recommended.*

   b. Remove the bolts from the front of the upper fork cover (**Figure 53**). Slide the cover up and off the fork tubes.

   c. Remove the inner cover screws (A, **Figure 54**). Then remove the fork inner cover (B) behind each fork leg.

7B. On 2005-on models, remove the upper fork cover (B, **Figure 50**), its damper (A, **Figure 55**), and washer from each fork leg. Note that the hole in the upper cover engages the tab (B, **Figure 55**) on the upper fork bridge.

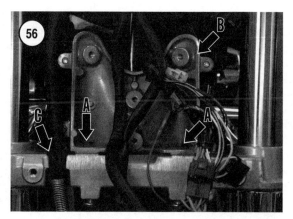

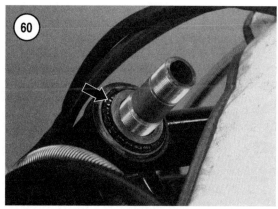

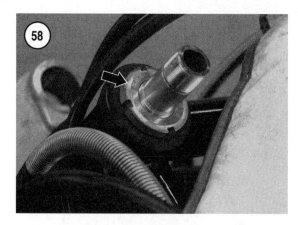

8. Remove the mounting bolts (A, **Figure 56**), and remove the headlight-housing bracket (B) from the lower fork bridge.

9. Release the brake hose from the holder (C, **Figure 56**: 1998-2004 models or **Figure 57**: 2005-on models) on the lower fork bridge.

10. Loosen the lower fork bridge clamp bolts (B, **Figure 52**: 1998-2004 models or C, **Figure 50**: 2005-on models), and remove each fork leg.

CAUTION
Support the steering stem while removing the steering stem nut.

11. Remove the steering stem nut (**Figure 58**).

12. Lower the steering stem assembly from the frame.

13. Remove the dust seal (**Figure 59**) from the top of the steering head.

14. Remove the upper bearing (**Figure 60**) from the steering head.

CAUTION
*Do not remove the lower bearing (A, **Figure 61**) and seal (B) from the steering stem unless replacing the bearing. The bearing and inner race are pressed onto the steering stem and are damaged when removed.*

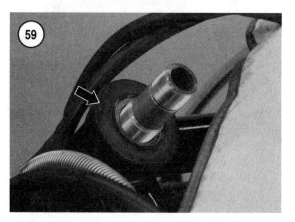

Installation

1. Make sure the bearing outer races (**Figure 62**) are clean and properly seated in the steering head.
2. Apply an even, complete coat of grease to the outer races. Also pack both bearings with grease.

> *NOTE*
> *The fork receptacles in the steering stem are offset and must face toward the front of the motorcycle. This is necessary for proper alignment with the fork receptacles in the upper fork bridge.*

3. Carefully slide the steering stem up into the frame (**Figure 63**).
4. Install the upper bearing (**Figure 60**) into the race in the top of the steering head.
5. Pack the dust seal with grease, and seat it onto the steering head (**Figure 59**).
6. Install the steering stem nut (**Figure 58**) and perform the following:
    a. Tighten the steering stem nut to the 45 N•m (33 ft.-lb.).
    b. Turn the steering stem from side-to-side (**Figure 64**) five or six times to seat the bearings.

> *NOTE*
> *The adjustment amount varies. After loosening the adjusting nut, there must be no bearing preload detected in the steering stem.*

    c. Loosen the adjusting nut 1/4 to 1/2 turn.
7. Check the steering head bearing adjustment by performing the following:
    a. Check the bearing preload by turning the steering stem from side-to-side (**Figure 64**). It should turn smoothly from lock-to-lock without drag or binding. There should be no preload. If necessary, loosen the adjuster nut in 1/8-turn increments and recheck the preload.
    b. Check for bearing free play by grasping one fork clamp area on the lower fork bridge. Try to rock the side of the lower fork bridge up and down. There should be little or no bearing free play, that is, little or no rocking in the steering head. If any play is felt, tighten the adjusting nut 1/8 turn and recheck the play.
    c. Repeatedly check the bearing free play and preload, and make any necessary adjustments.
8. Slide each fork leg through the lower fork bridge until the lower fork cover bottoms against the lower fork bridge. Tighten the lower fork bridge clamp bolts (B, **Figure 52**: 1998-2004 models or C, **Figure 50**: 2005-on models) enough to hold each fork leg in place.

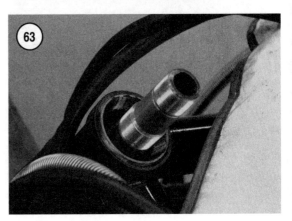

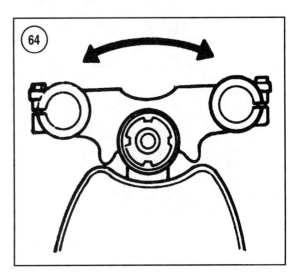

9. Set the headlight housing bracket (B, **Figure 56**) onto the lower fork bridge. Install the mounting bolts (A, **Figure 56**) and tighten securely.
10. Secure the front brake hose to the holder on the lower fork bridge (C, **Figure 56**: 1998-2004 models or **Figure 57**: 2005-on models).
11A. On 1998-2004 models perform the following:
    a. Fit an inner cover (B, **Figure 54**) behind each fork leg. Install each cover with the screws (A, **Figure 54**). Tighten the screws securely.

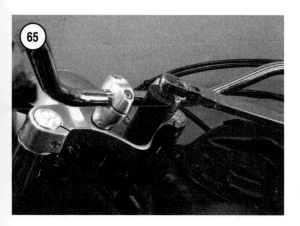

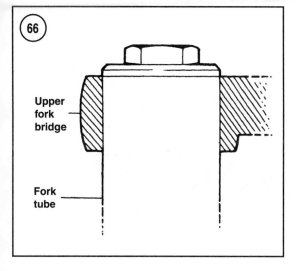

e. Snug down the cap bolts and steering head nut.

f. Loosen the lower fork bridge clamp bolts (B, **Figure 52**).

g. Tighten the cap bolts (A, **Figure 49**) and the steering head nut (B) to 90 N•m (66 ft.-lb.).

h. Tighten the lower fork bridge clamp bolts to 23 N•m (17 ft.-lb.).

i. Raise the upper fork cover into position. Install the front (**Figure 53**) and rear (**Figure 48**) fork cover bolts. Tighten the bolts securely.

11B. On 2005-on models, perform the following:

a. Install the washer and upper cover damper (A, **Figure 55**) onto the lower fork bridge.

b. Slide the upper fork cover (B, **Figure 50**) over each fork leg so the hole in the cover engages the tab (B, **Figure 55**) on the lower fork bridge.

c. Lower the upper fork bridge over the fork legs, and set the fork bridge onto the steering stem. Install the washer and steering head nut.

d. Tighten the steering head nut (**Figure 65**) to 90 N•m (66-ft.-lb).

e. Loosen the lower fork bridge clamp bolts (C, **Figure 50**) to release any stress created when the steering head nut was tightened.

f. If necessary, adjust the tube height so the top of the fork tube aligns with the top of the upper fork bridge (**Figure 66**).

g. Tighten the lower fork bridge clamp bolts (C, **Figure 50**) and the upper fork bridge clamp bolts (A) to 23 N•m (17 ft.-lb.).

12. Install the handlebar as described in this chapter.

13. Install the headlight housing, and headlight (Chapter Ten).

14. Install the front fender (Chapter Fifteen) and the front wheel (Chapter Eleven).

Inspection

1. Clean the upper (**Figure 67**) and lower bearings (A, **Figure 61**) in solvent. Make certain that the bearing degreaser is compatible with the bearing cage. Thoroughly dry the bearings with compressed air. Make sure all solvent residue is removed.

2. Wipe the old grease from the outer races (**Figure 62**) in the steering head. Then clean the outer races with a solvent soaked rag. Thoroughly dry the races with a lint-free cloth.

3. Check the races for pitting, galling and corrosion. If any race is worn or damaged, replace the race(s) and bearing as an assembly.

4. Inspect the seal (B, **Figure 61**) on the lower fork bridge.

5. Check the welds around the steering head for cracks and fractures. If any damage is found, have the frame repaired at a frame shop.

b. Slide the upper fork cover over and down the fork legs so the lower fork bridge clamp bolts are exposed.

c. Set the upper fork bridge (C, **Figure 49**) over the fork legs and steering stem. Install the washer and steering head nut (B, **Figure 49**). Finger-tighten the nut at this time.

d. Install a new O-ring onto each cap bolt (A, **Figure 49**), and install a cap bolt into each fork leg.

Upper fork bridge

Fork tube

12

6. Check the bearing rollers for pitting, scratches or discoloration indicating corrosion, wear or overheating. Replace the bearing if any rollers are less than perfect.

7. If the bearings are in good condition, pack them thoroughly with grease. Pack both sides of the cage so grease surrounds each roller.

8. Thoroughly clean all mounting parts in solvent. Dry them completely.

9. Inspect the steering head nut (B, **Figure 49**), washer, and steering stem nut (**Figure 58**) for wear or damage. Pay particular attention to the threads. If necessary, clean them with an appropriate size metric tap or replace the nut(s). If the threads are damaged, inspect the appropriate steering stem thread(s) for damage (**Figure 68**). If necessary, clean the threads with a die.

10. Inspect the steering stem nut washer for damage; replace it if necessary. If damaged, check the underside of the steering stem nut for damage; replace the nut as necessary.

11. Inspect the steering stem and the lower fork bridge for cracks or other damage. Make sure the fork bridge clamping areas are free of burrs and that the bolt holes are in good condition.

12. Inspect the upper fork bridge (**Figure 69**) for cracks or other damage. Check both the upper and lower surface of the fork bridge. Make sure the fork bridge clamping areas are free of burrs and that the bolt holes are in good condition.

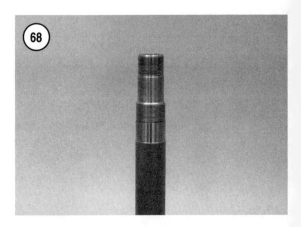

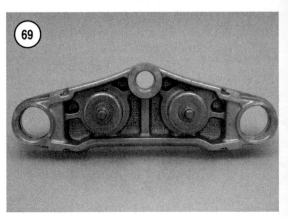

NOTE
Each bearing set consists of an inner race, an outer race and a bearing. If any part is worn or damaged, replace both the upper and lower bearing sets.

13. Replace any worn or damaged component. If any bearing or any race is worn or damaged, replace the races and bearing in both bearing sets.

STEERING HEAD BEARING RACE REPLACEMENT

Use a bearing outer race installer (Suzuki part No. 09941-34513), or its equivalent, to replace the steering head bearings.

1. Remove the steering stem as described in this chapter.

2. Insert an aluminum drift into the steering head, and carefully tap the lower race from the head (**Figure 70**). Repeat for the upper race.

3. Chill the new bearing races in a freezer for a few hours to shrink the outer diameter of the race as much as possible.

4. Clean the race seats in the steering head. Check for cracks or other damage.

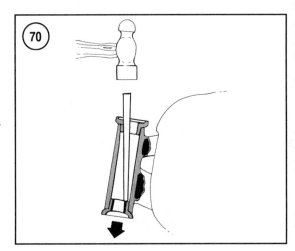

5. Set the new race into the steering head so the larger side of the taper faces out. Square the race with the bore.

CAUTION
When installing the bearing outer races do not let the tool shaft contact the face of the bearing race.

6. Assemble the installer tool through the bearing race per the manufacturer's instructions. See **Figure 71**.

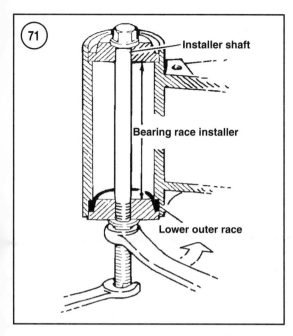

Figure 71: Installer shaft, Bearing race installer, Lower outer race

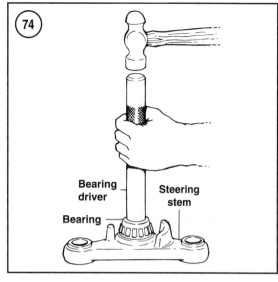

Figure 74: Bearing driver, Steering stem, Bearing

7. Hold the installer shaft and slowly turn the nut until the tool and outer race are square with the steering head bore.

8. Turn the nut, and slowly press the lower race into the bore until the race bottoms (**Figure 71**).

9. Turn the special tool over and repeat this procedure for the upper bearing race (**Figure 72**).

STEERING STEM BEARING REPLACEMENT

CAUTION
*Do not remove the lower bearing inner race (A, **Figure 61**) and seal (B) unless they will be replaced. Never reinstall a removed bearing race. It is no longer true and will damage the rest of the bearing assembly if reused.*

1. Install the steering stem nut onto the top of the steering stem to protect the threads.

2. Use a chisel to loosen the bearing from the shoulder at the base of the steering stem (**Figure 73**). Slide the bearing and seal off the steering stem.

3. Clean the steering stem with solvent, and dry it thoroughly.

4. Position the new seal with the flange side facing up.

5. Slide the seal and the new bearing onto the steering stem until they stop on the raised shoulder.

6. Align the bearing inner race with the machined shoulder on the steering stem. Slide the bearing installer (Suzuki part No. 09925-18010), an equivalent tool (**Figure 74**), or a piece of pipe over the steering stem until it seats against the inner circumference of the race. Drive the race onto the steering stem until it bottoms.

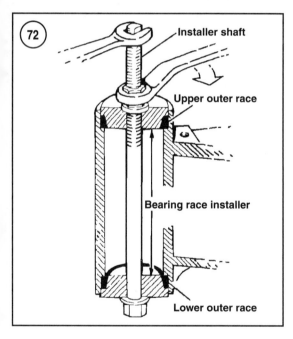

Figure 72: Installer shaft, Upper outer race, Bearing race installer, Lower outer race

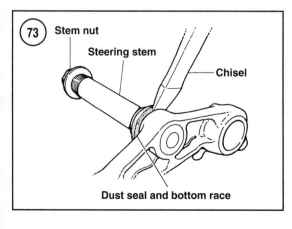

Figure 73: Stem nut, Steering stem, Chisel, Dust seal and bottom race

12

Table 1 FRONT SUSPENSION SPECIFICATIONS

Item	Specification	Service Limit
Cover stopper depth		
1998-2004 models	281.3 mm (11.07 in.)	–
2005-on models	284.3 mm (11.19 in.)	
Front fork stroke	140 mm (5.5 in.)	–
Fork spring free length		
1998-2004 models	585 mm (23.03 in.)	573 mm (22.56 in.)
2005-on models	601.5 mm (23.68 in.)	589 mm (23.19 in.)
Front fork oil level		
1998-2004 models	169.0 mm (6.65 in.)	–
2005-on models	192 mm (7.56 in.)	–
Fork oil		
Type	Suzuki SS-08 (#10) fork oil or equivalent	–
Capacity per leg		
1998-2004 models models	439 ml (14.8 oz.)	–
2005-on models	416 ml (14.1 oz.)	–

Table 2 FRONT SUSPENSION AND STEERING TORQUE SPECIFICATIONS

Item	N•m	in.-lb.	ft.-lb.
Front axle	65	–	48
Front axle clamp bolt	23	–	17
Front fork Allen bolt	20	–	15
Front fork cap bolt			
1998-2004 models	90	–	66
2005-on models	23	–	17
Front fork spring nut			
1998-2004 models	35	–	26
Handlebar clamp bolt			
1998-2004 models	16	–	12
2005-on models	23	–	17
Handlebar holder nut			
1998-2004 models	50	–	37
2005-on models	70	–	52
Handlebar weight bolt	50	–	37
Lower fork bridge clamp bolt	23	–	17
Steering head nut	90	–	66
Steering stem nut	45	–	33
Upper fork bridge clamp bolt			
2005-on models	23	–	17

CHAPTER THIRTEEN

REAR SUSPENSION AND FINAL DRIVE

This chapter covers the shock absorber, suspension linkage, swing arm, and final drive assembly.

Refer to **Table 1** at the end of this chapter for specifications. Replace any worn, damaged or out of specification components.

SHOCK ABSORBER

Removal/Installation

Refer to **Figure 1**.

1. Support the motorcycle on a level surface.
2. Remove the rear wheel (Chapter Eleven). Support the swing arm with a jack.
3. Remove each side cover and the tool box (Chapter Fifteen).
4. The shock absorber and suspension linkage nuts are on the right side (**Figure 2**). Remove the nut from the right side of the upper suspension arm bolt (A, **Figure 3**), and pull the bolt out from the left side. Lower each suspension arm (B, **Figure 3**) from the swing arm.

NOTE
The lower shock absorber bolt (10 × 54 mm) is slightly longer than the upper shock absorber bolt (10 × 50 mm). Do not confuse the two.

5. Remove the nut from the right side of the lower shock absorber bolt (C, **Figure 3**), and pull the bolt from the left side.
6. Remove the nut from the upper shock absorber bolt (**Figure 4**), pull the bolt, and lower the shock absorber from the motorcycle.
7. Reverse the removal procedure to install the shock absorber. Note the following:
   a. Apply a light coat of grease to the bolts, and to the shock absorber upper and lower mounts.
   b. Install each shock absorber bolt and the upper suspension arm bolt from the left side.
   c. Tighten each shock absorber bolt/nut to 50 N•m (37 ft.-lb.).
   d. Tighten the upper suspension arm bolt/nut (A, **Figure 3**) to 135 N•m (100 ft.-lb.).

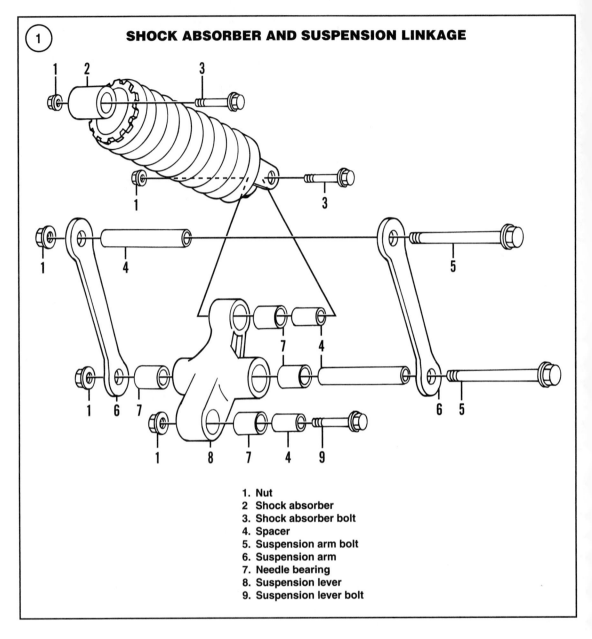

SHOCK ABSORBER AND SUSPENSION LINKAGE

1. Nut
2 Shock absorber
3. Shock absorber bolt
4. Spacer
5. Suspension arm bolt
6. Suspension arm
7. Needle bearing
8. Suspension lever
9. Suspension lever bolt

Inspection

Replacement parts are unavailable for the original equipment shock absorber. If any part of the shock absorber is faulty, replace it.

1. Inspect the shock absorber (A, **Figure 5**) for leaks.
2. Check the spring for cracks or other damage.
3. Inspect the upper and lower mounts (B, **Figure 5**) for wear or damage. Pay particular attention to the damper (**Figure 6**) in the upper mount.
4. If a part is worn or damaged, replace the shock absorber.

SUSPENSION LINKAGE

Refer to **Figure 1**.

Removal

1. Support the motorcycle on a level surface.
2. Remove the rear wheel (Chapter Eleven). Support the swing arm with a jack.
3. Remove each side cover and the tool box (Chapter Fifteen).

NOTE
The suspension arms can be installed on either side. However, after prolonged use, each develops a unique wear pattern. Before removing the suspension arms, label the outside of each arm so they can be reinstalled on the same sides. If necessary, also label the upper and lower mounting holes.

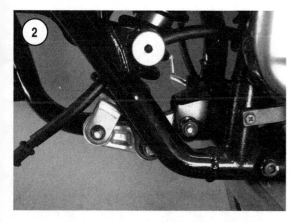

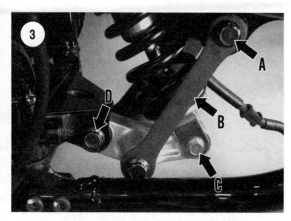

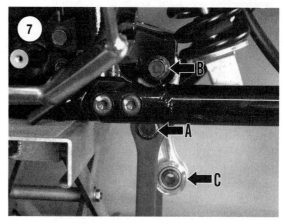

4. Remove the nut from the right side of the upper suspension arm bolt (A, **Figure 3**), and pull the bolt from the left side. Lower each suspension arm (B, **Figure 3**) from the swing arm.

5. Remove the nut from the right side of the lower shock absorber bolt (C, **Figure 3**), and pull the bolt from the left side.

6. Remove the nut from the lower suspension arm bolt (A, **Figure 7**), and pull the bolt from the left side.

7. Lower each suspension arm from the suspension lever.

8. Remove the nut from the right side of the suspension lever bolt (B, **Figure 7**).

9. Remove the suspension lever bolt (B, **Figure 7**) from the left side, and lower the suspension lever (C) from its frame mount.

Installation

1. Apply a light coat of grease to the bolts and the suspension lever's frame mount.

2. Slide the suspension lever (C, **Figure 7**) into its frame mount.

3. Insert the suspension lever bolt (B, **Figure 7**) from the left side. Loosely install the nut onto the bolt.

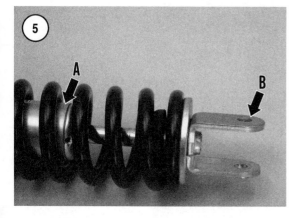

13

NOTE
*Position each suspension arm so its stamped side (**Figure 8**) faces out.*

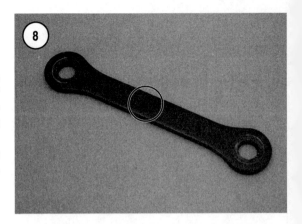

4. Position the left suspension arm so the location mark made during removal faces out. Align its lower hole with the middle mounting hole in the suspension lever, and install the lower suspension arm bolt (A, **Figure 7**) from the left side.

5. On the right side, fit the right suspension arm onto the bolt so the location mark made during removal faces out, and loosely install the nut.

NOTE
The lower suspension arm bolt/nut cannot be tightened with the suspension linkage installed.

6. Tighten the lower suspension arm bolt/nut (A, **Figure 7**) to 135 N•m (100 ft.-lb.).

7. Raise the suspension lever so its rear pivot sits between the arms of the lower shock mount.

8. Insert the lower shock absorber bolt (C, **Figure 3**) from the left side. Loosely install the nut onto the shock absorber bolt.

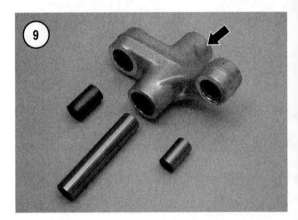

9. Pivot each suspension arm rearward until their upper mounts align with the pivot on the swing arm.

10. Install the upper suspension arm bolt (A, **Figure 3**) from the left side and loosely install the nut.

11. Tighten the mounting hardware in stages to the final torque specification, and in the following order:

    a. Suspension lever bolt/nut (D, **Figure 3**) to 135 N•m (100 ft.-lb.).

    b. Lower shock absorber bolt/nut (C, **Figure 3**) 50 N•m (37 ft.-.lb.).

    c. Upper suspension arm bolt/nut (A, **Figure 3**) to 135 N•m (100 ft.-.lb.).

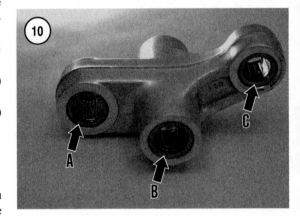

Inspection

1. Remove each spacer (**Figure 9**) from its pivot in the suspension lever. Note that three different size spacers are used. Each must be reinstalled into the correct location during assembly.

2. Inspect the spacers for wear and damage.

3. Inspect the suspension lever bearings as follows:

    a. Use a clean lint-free rag to wipe off surface grease from each suspension lever needle bearing (**Figure 10**).

    b. Rotate each bearing. The bearings should turn smoothly without excessive play or noise.

    c. Check the rollers for wear, pitting or rust.

    d. Reinstall each spacer (**Figure 11**) into its respective bearing. Slowly rotate the spacer. Each spacer must turn smoothly without excessive play or noise.

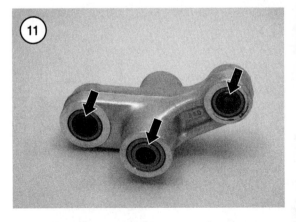

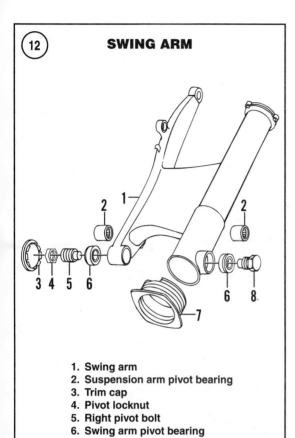

SWING ARM

1. Swing arm
2. Suspension arm pivot bearing
3. Trim cap
4. Pivot locknut
5. Right pivot bolt
6. Swing arm pivot bearing
7. Boot
8. Left pivot bolt

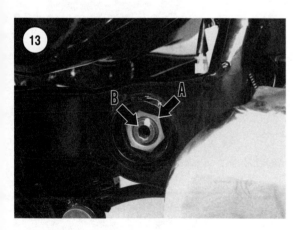

7. Replace worn or damaged parts.

8. Lubricate the bearings (**Figure 10**) and spacers (**Figure 9**) with grease. Insert each spacer (**Figure 11**) into its original pivot in the suspension lever.

SWING ARM

Refer to **Figure 12**.

Preliminary Inspection

The condition of the swing arm bearings affects motorcycle handling. Worn bearings cause wheel hop, pulling to one side under acceleration and pulling to the other side during braking. Perform the following procedure to check the condition of the swing arm bearings.

1. Remove the rear wheel (Chapter Eleven) and final drive (this chapter).

2. Remove each side cover and the tool box (Chapter Fifteen).

3. Remove the nut from the right side of the upper suspension arm bolt (A, **Figure 3**), pull the bolt from the right side, and lower the suspension arms (B) from the pivot under the swing arm.

4. On the right side, make sure the swing arm pivot locknut (A, **Figure 13**) is tight.

5. Make sure the left pivot bolt (**Figure 14**) is tight.

6. The swing arm is now free to move under its own weight.

> *WARNING*
> *Have an assistant steady the motorcycle when performing Step 7 and Step 8.*

7. Grasp both ends of the swing arm and attempt to move it from side to side in a horizontal arc. If more than a slight amount of movement is felt, the swing arm bearings are worn and must be replaced.

8. Move the ends of the swing arm up and down. The swing arm should move smoothly with no binding or abnormal noise from the bearings. If binding

e. Replace a worn or damaged suspension lever needle bearing as described in *Bearing/Race Replacement* (this chapter).

4. Inspect the suspension lever (**Figure 9**) for cracks or damage.

5. Inspect each suspension arm (**Figure 8**) for bending, cracks or damage. Replace as necessary.

6. Clean the bolts and nuts in solvent. Check each bolt for straightness. A bent bolt restricts linkage movement.

13

or noise is noted, replace the bearings as described in *Bearing/Race Replacement* (this chapter).

Removal

1. Remove each side cover and the tool box (Chapter Fifteen).
2. Remove each holder securing the rear brake hose to the swing arm.
3. Remove the rear wheel (Chapter Eleven). Suspend the rear caliper out of the way.
4. Remove the final drive as described in this chapter.
5. Use a jack to support the swing arm.
6. Remove the nut from the right side of the upper suspension arm bolt (A, **Figure 3**), pull the bolt from the left side, and lower the suspension arms (B) from the pivot under the swing arm.
7. Pull the boot (**Figure 15**) off the swing arm.
8. Remove the cap (**Figure 16**) from the swing arm pivot on each side.
9. Remove the swing arm pivot bolt locknut (A, **Figure 13**) from the right side.
10. Support the swing arm, and loosen the right swing arm pivot bolt (B, **Figure 13**) and left pivot bolt (**Figure 14**).
11. Remove the pivot bolt from each side.
12. Pull the swing arm rearward, and remove the swing arm from the motorcycle. Watch for the universal joint on the secondary driven shaft.
13. Remove the tapered roller bearing (**Figure 17**) from each side of the swing arm.
14. Remove the spacer (**Figure 18**) from the suspension arm pivot under the swing arm.

Installation

1. Make sure the boot (**Figure 15**) is in place on the secondary driven shaft. If the boot was removed, install it so its tab is up. Lubricate the splines of the universal joint with molybdenum disulfide grease, and slide the universal joint onto the splines of the secondary driven shaft.
2. Apply grease to the needle bearings in the swing arm pivot (**Figure 19**) and to the spacer (**Figure 18**). Install the spacer into the pivot bearing.
3. Pack each roller bearing (**Figure 20**) and lubricate its outer race (**Figure 21**) with grease. Install a roller bearing into each swing arm pivot (**Figure 17**).
4. Raise the swing arm into position between the frame pivots. Make sure the swing arm's drive-shaft tunnel fits over the universal joint.
5. Loosely install each swing arm pivot bolt. Finger-tighten the left pivot bolt (**Figure 14**) but not the right pivot bolt (**Figure 22**). Leave the right bolt loose for the moment.

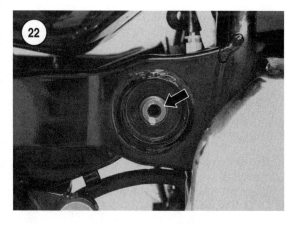

NOTE
The right swing arm pivot bolt must be
loose when the left bolt is tightened.

6. Tighten the left swing arm pivot bolt (**Figure 14**) to 100 N•m (74 ft.-lb.).

7. Tighten the right swing arm pivot bolt (**Figure 22**) to 9.5 N•m (84 in.-lb.).

8. Install the pivot bolt locknut (A, **Figure 13**) onto the right pivot bolt (B). Tighten the locknut to 100 (74 ft.-lb.).

9. Move the swing arm up and down to check for smooth movement. If the swing arm is tight or loose, the fasteners were either tightened in the wrong sequence or to the incorrect specification. Repeat Steps 5-8.

10. Align each suspension arm with the pivot boss under the swing arm. Install the upper suspension arm bolt (A, **Figure 3**) from the left side, and turn the nut onto the bolt. Tighten the suspension arm bolt/nut to 135 N•m (100 ft.-lb.).

11. Pull the boot (**Figure 15**) over the swing arm.

12. Install the final drive (this chapter) and the rear wheel (Chapter Eleven).

13. Route the rear brake hose across the swing arm, and secure the brake hose with the holders.

14. Install each side cover and the tool box (Chapter Fifteen).

Inspection

1. Wash the bolts and spacer in solvent, and thoroughly dry them.

2. Inspect the spacer (**Figure 18**) for wear, scratches or score marks.

3. Check the pivot bolts for straightness. A bent bolt restricts swing arm movement.

4. Inspect the needle bearings as follows:
   a. Use a clean lint-free rag to wipe away surface grease from the needle bearings.
   b. Turn each needle bearing (**Figure 19**) by hand. The bearing should turn smoothly without excessive play or noise. Check the rollers for evidence of wear, pitting or rust.
   c. Insert the spacer (**Figure 18**) into the bearings in the suspension arm pivot, and slowly rotate the spacer. It must turn smoothly without excessive play or noise.
   d. Replace any worn or damaged needle bearing as described in *Swing Arm Needle Bearing Replacement* (this chapter).

5. Wipe grease from the tapered roller bearings (**Figure 20**), and visually inspect the rollers for wear pitting or runs.

6. Check each bearing outer race (**Figure 21**) for pitting, galling, and corrosion. If any race is worn or

13

damaged, replace the bearing assembly as described in this chapter.

7. Check the swing arm (**Figure 23**) for cracks or fractures. Pay particular attention to the welds.

8. Inspect the threads on the pivot bolts and on the pivot bolt locknut. If damage is noted, also inspect the threads in the frame pivot. Clean minor damage with a tap or die.

9. If necessary, repair or replace any damaged part(s).

BEARING/RACE REPLACEMENT

Pivot Bearing Outer Race Replacement

Use a bearing remover (Suzuki part No. 09941-64511), or its equivalent, and a slide hammer (Suzuki part No. 09930-30102), or its equivalent, to remove the bearing outer races.

Replace the tapered roller bearing whenever replacing a bearing outer race. The bearing and its outer race must be replaced as a set.

1. Chill the new bearing races in a freezer for a few hours to shrink the outer diameter of the race as much as possible.

> *NOTE*
> *The right pivot bearing race and bearing plate are available as a single component.*

2. Use a suitable size driver to drive the bearing plate from the right bearing bore (**Figure 24**).

3. Use the bearing remover to remove the bearing outer race from the each side (**Figure 21**).

4. Clean the race seats in the swing arm. Check for cracks or other damage.

5. Set the new race into the swing arm so the larger side of the taper faces out. Square the race with the bore.

> *CAUTION*
> *When installing the bearing outer races do not let the tool contact the face of the bearing race.*

6. Use the appropriate size bearing driver to drive the outer race into the swing arm. Make sure the race is square to the swing arm bearing bore (**Figure 21**). Install the bearing race with the bearing plate into the right side of the swing arm (**Figure 24**).

Swing Arm Needle Bearing Replacement

Use a bearing remover set (Suzuki part No. 09923-74510), or an equivalent, and a slide hammer (Suzuki part No. 09930-30102), or an equivalent, to remove the bearings.

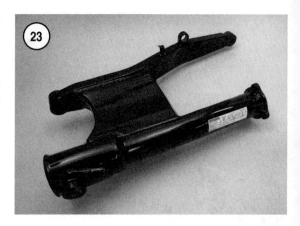

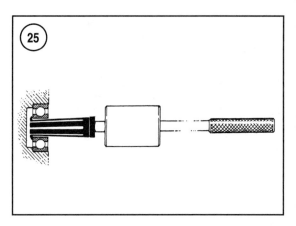

Do not remove the needle bearings unless they must be replaced. The needle bearings are damaged during removal.

> *NOTE*
> *Replace the spacer (**Figure 18**) whenever replacing the suspension arm pivot bearings (**Figure 19**). These parts should always be replaced as a set.*

1. If still installed, remove the spacer from the needle bearings.

2. Insert the bearing puller through the needle bearing, and expand it behind the bearing (**Figure 25**).

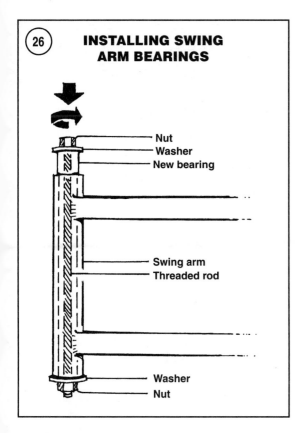

26 INSTALLING SWING ARM BEARINGS

- Nut
- Washer
- New bearing
- Swing arm
- Threaded rod
- Washer
- Nut

3. Using sharp strokes of the slide hammer, withdraw the needle bearing from the pivot boss.

4. Remove the bearing puller and the bearing.

5. Repeat for the bearing on the other side of the suspension arm pivot.

6. Thoroughly clean the inside of the pivot bore with solvent, and dry it with compressed air.

7. Apply a light coat of grease to the exterior of the new bearings and to the inner circumference of the pivot bore.

CAUTION
Install one needle bearing at a time. Make sure the bearing enters the pivot boss squarely, otherwise the bearing and the pivot boss may be damaged.

8. Position the bearing with the manufacturer's marks facing out.

9. Locate and square the new bearing in the pivot bore. Assemble the installation tool (**Figure 26**) through the pivot bore so the socket presses against the bearing.

10. Hold the nut at the bearing end of the tool.

11. Tighten the nut on the opposite end and pull the bearing into the pivot bore until the bearing sits flush with the outer surface of the pivot boss (**Figure 19**).

12. Repeat Steps 8-11 and install the bearing into the opposite side of the pivot bore.

13. Make sure the bearings are properly seated. Turn each bearing by hand. It should turn smoothly.

14. Lubricate the new bearings with grease.

Suspension Lever Needle Bearing Replacement

Use a bearing remover set (Suzuki part No. 09923-74510) or an equivalent, and a slide hammer (Suzuki part No. 09930-30102) or an equivalent, to remove the bearings. The needle bearings can be installed with a homemade tool (**Figure 26**) or a socket and hammer.

Do not remove the suspension lever needle bearings (**Figure 10**) unless they must be replaced.

CAUTION
If the needle bearings are replaced, replace the spacers at the same time. These parts should always be replaced as a set.

1. If still installed, remove the spacers (**Figure 9**) from the suspension lever.

NOTE
The bearings are different sizes. Mark the bearings front, center and rear as they are removed. The center two bearings are identical.

2. Perform the following to remove the needle bearings from the center pivot (B, **Figure 10**) in the suspension lever.

   a. Insert a blind bearing puller through a needle bearing in the center pivot. Expand the puller behind the bearing (**Figure 25**).

   b. Using sharp strokes of the slide hammer, withdraw the needle bearing from the center pivot hole.

   c. Remove the tool and the bearing.

   d. Repeat substeps a-c for the other bearing in the center pivot.

3. Use the appropriate size bearing driver or socket to drive the bearing from the front pivot (A, **Figure 10**) and from the rear pivot (C).

4. Thoroughly clean out the inside of the pivot bores with solvent. Dry them with compressed air.

5. Apply a light coat of grease to the exterior of the new bearings and to the inner circumference of the pivot bores.

6. Locate and square the new bearing in the pivot bore. When installing bearings in the center pivot bore (B, **Figure 10**), position the bearings so the manufacturer's marks face out.

7A. Install each bearing with the tool by performing Steps 9-11 of *Swing Arm Needle Bearing Replacement*.

7B. If this tool is unavailable, install the bearings with a hammer and socket that matches the outer race diameter. Tap the bearings into place.

13

8. Make sure each bearing is properly seated in the suspension lever. Refer to **Figure 10**. Turn each bearing by hand. The bearing should turn smoothly.

9. Lubricate the needles of the new bearing with grease.

FINAL DRIVE

Removal

1. If servicing the final drive assembly, drain the gear oil as described in Chapter Three.

2. Remove the rear wheel (Chapter Eleven).

3. Remove the final drive nuts (**Figure 27**) and washers.

4. Pull the final drive rearward until the drive shaft disengages from the universal joint, and remove the final drive along with the drive shaft from the swing arm (**Figure 28**). Watch for the stopper plate (**Figure 29**) between the final drive and the swing arm mount.

Installation

1. Apply Suzuki Bond 1207B to the mating surfaces of the final drive and swing arm.

2. Install the stopper plate (**Figure 29**) onto the final drive studs. Align the slots in the stopper plate with the splines of the bearing holder.

3. Apply molybdenum disulfide grease to the splines of the drive shaft.

4. Insert a screwdriver (**Figure 30**) between the boot and the end of the swing arm.

5. While an assistant uses a screwdriver to hold the U-joint as far down into the swing arm as possible, slide the final drive assembly into the drive shaft tunnel on the swing arm (**Figure 28**).

6. Slide the drive shaft through the tunnel until the end of the drive shaft reaches the universal joint. Carefully align the splines of the drive shaft with those on the universal joint, and slide the drive shaft

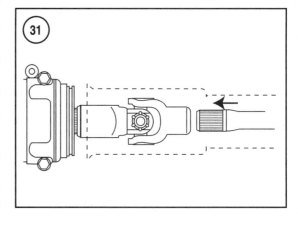

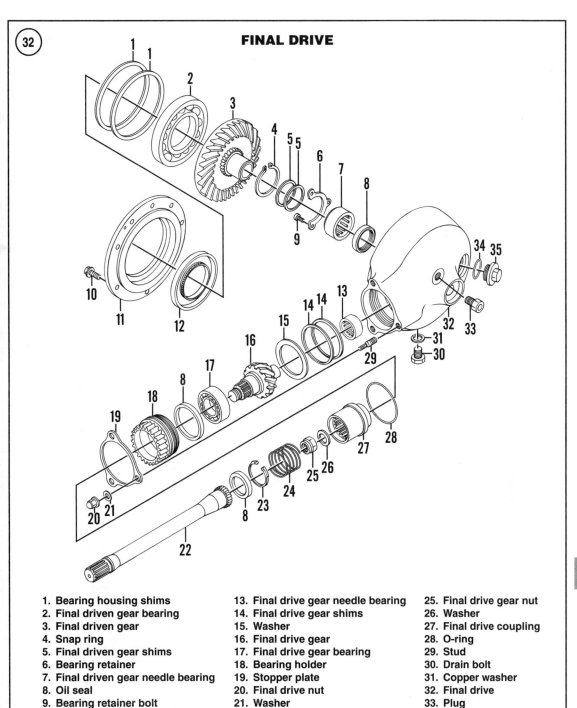

FINAL DRIVE

1. Bearing housing shims
2. Final driven gear bearing
3. Final driven gear
4. Snap ring
5. Final driven gear shims
6. Bearing retainer
7. Final driven gear needle bearing
8. Oil seal
9. Bearing retainer bolt
10. Bearing housing bolt
11. Bearing housing
12. Oil seal
13. Final drive gear needle bearing
14. Final drive gear shims
15. Washer
16. Final drive gear
17. Final drive gear bearing
18. Bearing holder
19. Stopper plate
20. Final drive nut
21. Washer
22. Drive shaft
23. Snap ring
24. Spring
25. Final drive gear nut
26. Washer
27. Final drive coupling
28. O-ring
29. Stud
30. Drain bolt
31. Copper washer
32. Final drive
33. Plug
34. O-ring
35. Filler bolt

into the U-joint (**Figure 31**).

7. Apply Suzuki Thread Lock 1342 to the threads of the final drive studs, and install the final drive nuts (**Figure 27**) and washers. Tighten the nuts to 40 N•m (29.5 ft.-lb.).

8. If the oil was drained, add gear oil to the final drive (Chapter Three).

Disassembly

Refer to **Figure 32**.

1. Use the following Suzuki tools (or their equivalent) to disassemble and assemble the final drive.

   a. Service final drive gear coupling holder (part No. 09924-64510).

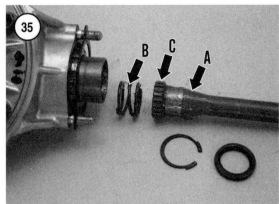

b. Final drive gear bearing holder wrench (part No: 09924-62410).

c. Final driven gear remover/installer (part No. 09924-74570).

d. Backlash measuring tool (27-50 mm): (part No. 09924-34510).

e. Bearing puller: (part No. 0913-60910).

f. Final drive gear bearing installer (part No. 09913-84510).

g. Final drive needle bearing installer, drive shaft side (part No. 09913-75821).

h. Final drive needle bearing installer, wheel side (part No. 09913-76010).

i. Bearing remover (part No. 09941-64511).

j. Slide hammer (part No. 09930-30102).

2. Remove the stopper plate (**Figure 29**) from the gearcase studs.

3. Remove the drive shaft oil seal (**Figure 33**) from the final drive coupling, and remove snap ring (**Figure 34**). This seal must be replaced.

4. Pull the drive shaft (A, **Figure 35**) from the coupling, and remove the spring (B).

5. Unstake the final drive gear nut (**Figure 36**).

6. Hold the final drive coupling with the final drive gear coupling holder (**Figure 37**), and loosen the final drive gear nut.

7. Remove the final drive gear nut (A, **Figure 38**), its washer (B), and the final drive coupling (C).

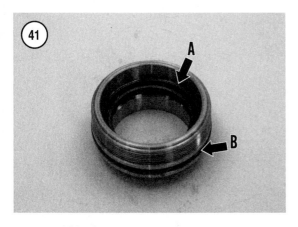

8. Use the bearing holder wrench to loosen the bearing holder in the final drive (**Figure 39**). Remove the bearing holder (**Figure 40**). Watch for the oil seal (A, **Figure 41**) and O-ring (B) on the bearing holder.

9. Remove the final drive gear (A, **Figure 42**) and its shim (B).

10. Remove the bearing housing bolts. Note the two 10-mm bolts (**Figure 43**). The remaining eight are 8-mm bolts.

11. Install two 5-mm bolts (**Figure 44**) into the bearing housing. Tighten the bolts and drive the bearing housing from the final drive.

12. Remove the bearing housing (A, **Figure 45**) from the final drive. Watch for the final driven gear shims (B, **Figure 45**).

13

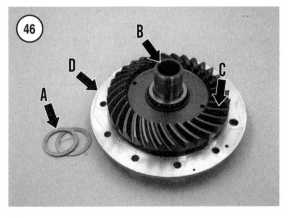

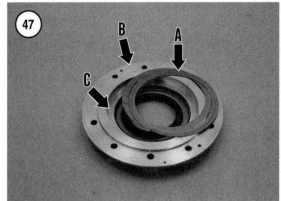

13. If still installed, remove the final driven gear shims (A, **Figure 46**) from the shaft (B) of the final driven gear.

14. Remove the final driven gear (C, **Figure 46**) from the bearing housing (D).

15. Remove the bearing housing shims (A, **Figure 47**) from the bearing housing (B).

Assembly

1. Install the bearing housing shims (A, **Figure 47**) into the bearing housing (B).

2. Install the final driven gear (C, **Figure 46**) into the bearing housing (D).

3. Set the final driven gear shims (A, **Figure 46**) onto the shaft of the final driven gear (B).

4. Apply Suzuki Bond 1207B to the mating surfaces of the final drive and the bearing housing.

5. Set the bearing housing into place, and install the bearing housing bolts. Apply Suzuki Thread Lock 1342 to the threads of the bolts, and snug all bolts down evenly. Tighten the two 10-mm (**Figure 43**) to 50 N•m (37 ft.-lb.). Then tighten the 8-mm bolts to 23 N•m (17 ft.-lb.).

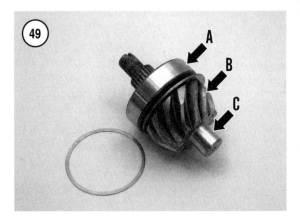

6. Install the shim (B, **Figure 42**) onto the final drive gear (A), and install the gear into the gearcase.

7. Install the bearing holder (**Figure 40**) into the final drive. Use the bearing holder wrench (**Figure 39**) to tighten the bearing holder to 110 N•m (81 ft.-lb.).

8. Install the final drive coupling (**Figure 48**) so its inner splines engages those on the final drive gear (**Figure 38**).

9. Install the washer (B, **Figure 38**) and final drive gear nut (A). Apply Suzuki Thread Lock 1342 to the threads of the nut.

10. Hold the final drive coupling with the final drive gear coupling holder (**Figure 37**), and tighten the final drive gear nut to 100 N•m (74 ft.-lb.).

11. Stake the nut to the gear shaft (**Figure 36**).

12. Apply molybdenum disulfide grease to the drive shaft splines (C, **Figure 35**) and the coupling.

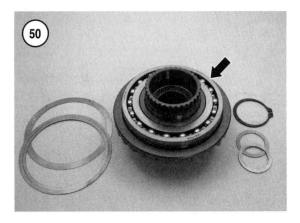

13. Fit the spring (B, **Figure 35**) into the coupling, and install the drive shaft (A) so its splines engage those of the coupling.

14. Install the snap ring (**Figure 34**), and seat it in the groove in the coupling.

15. Rotate the drive shaft and check for noise or binding.

16. Apply grease to the lips of a new oil seal (**Figure 33**), and install the seal with the manufacturer's marks facing out.

17. Install the stopper plate (**Figure 29**) so its tab engages a groove in the bearing holder.

18. Measure the final drive backlash and the tooth contact as described in this section.

Inspection

1. Rotate the final drive gear bearing (A, **Figure 49**) and final driven gear bearing (**Figure 50**) by hand. If a bearing is noisy, binding or has excessive play, replace it as described in this section.

2. Inspect the final driven gear needle bearing (A, **Figure 51**) and the final drive gear needle bearing (B). Replace either as necessary (this section).

3. Inspect the needle bearing contact area on the shaft (B, **Figure 46**) of the final driven gear and on the nose (C, **Figure 49**) of the final drive gear for nicks, scoring or other damage.

4. Inspect the oil seal (A, **Figure 41**) and O-ring (B) in the bearing holder. Replace either as necessary. When replacing this oil seal, drive the seal into the holder so the seal's spring side faces up (**Figure 52**)

5. Inspect the oil seal (**Figure 53**) in the bearing housing. Replace the seal if any leaking is noted.

6. Inspect teeth of the final drive gear (B, **Figure 49**) and final driven gear (C, **Figure 46**). If the teeth on either gear are chipped or worn, replace both the final drive gear and the final driven gear as a set.

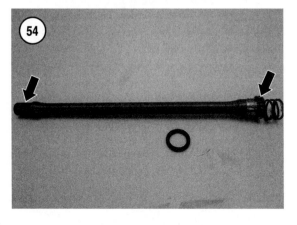

7. Inspect the splines of the drive shaft (**Figure 54**) and final drive coupling (**Figure 55**) for wear or damage.

8. Replace worn, damaged, or out of specification parts.

13

Bearing Housing Shim Clearance

1. Set the bearing housing onto the bench so the side with the oil seal faces the bench (**Figure 47**).
2. Set two pieces of Plastigage on opposite sides of the shim seat (C, **Figure 47**) in the bearing housing.
3. Install the original bearing housing shims (A, **Figure 47**) into the bearing housing (B). Make sure the shims sit on the Plastigage.
4. Install the final driven gear (C, **Figure 46**) into the bearing housing (D).
5. Install the original final driven gear shims (A, **Figure 46**) onto the shaft (B) of the final driven gear.
6. Set the bearing housing into place. Install and evenly snug down the bearing housing bolts. Tighten the two 10-mm bolts (**Figure 43**) to 50 N•m (37 ft.-lb.), Then tighten the 8-mm bolts (**Figure 43**) to 23 N•m (17 ft.-lb.).
7. Remove and disassemble the bearing housing by performing Steps 10-15 of *Final Drive, Disassembly*.
8. Measure the thickness of the Plastigage per the manufacturer's instructions. It should equal the bearing housing shim clearance specified in **Table 1**.
9. If the bearing housing shim clearance is out of specification, refer to **Table 2** and select new shims to bring the clearance within specification.

Backlash

Measurement

1. Install the backlash measuring tool onto the final drive coupling.
2. Position the dial indicator so its plunger rests against the index mark on the backlash tool. (**Figure 56**).
3. Securely hold the final driven gear. Gently rotate the final drive gear coupling in each direction from tooth engagement to tooth engagement.
4. Record the backlash on the dial indicator. It should be within the final drive backlash range (**Table 1**).
5. If the backlash is not within specification, adjust the backlash as described in this section.

Adjustment

1. Remove the final driven gear shims (A, **Figure 46**) and the bearing housing shims (A, **Figure 47**) by performing Steps 10-15 of *Final Drive, Disassembly*.
2. Measure and record the thickness of each original final driven gear shim.

3. Add the measured thicknesses of all the final drive gear shims to attain the stack thickness. See the example in **Figure 57**.
4. Repeat Step 2 and Step 3 for the bearing housing shims.
5. Add the stack thickness of the final driven gear shims (Step 3) to the stack thickness of the bearing housing shims (Step 4). This sum equals the total shim thickness.

> *CAUTION*
> *Backlash is adjusted by increasing or decreasing the thickness of the final driven gear shims and the bearing housing shims. The total shim thickness must be the same before and after the adjustment so the clearance between the bearing and bearing housing remains constant. If thickness of one stack is increased, the thickness of the other stack must be reduced by the same amount. See* ***Figure 57****.*

6. If the measured backlash is too large, decrease the thickness of the final driven gear shim stack (A, **Figure 58**) and increase the thickness of the bearing housing shim stack (B) by the same amount. See **Figure 57**.
7. If the measured backlash is too small, increase the thickness of the final driven gear shim stack (A, **Figure 58**) and decrease the thickness of the bearing housing shim stack (B) by the same amount. See **Figure 57**.
8. Refer to **Table 2** and **Table 3** to select new shims.
9. Reassemble the gearcase with the correct shims by performing Steps 1-5 of *Final Drive, Assembly*.
10. Recheck the backlash. Adjust the backlash as needed to bring it within specification.
11. Once backlash is within specification, check the tooth contact.

57 **BACKLASH ADJUSTMENT**

	Shim 1 (mm)	Shim 2 (mm)	Stack thickness (mm)	Total shim thickness (mm)
Original size	–	–	–	3.80
Final driven gear shims	1.45	1.40	2.85	–
Bearing housing shims	0.35	0.60	0.95	–
Backlash too large	–	–	–	3.80
Final driven gear shims	1.45	1.35	2.80	–
Bearing housing shims	0.40	0.60	1.00	–
Backlash too small	–	–	–	3.80
Final driven gear shims	1.50	1.40	2.90	–
Bearing housing shims	0.40	0.50	0.90	–

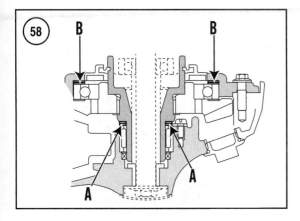

58

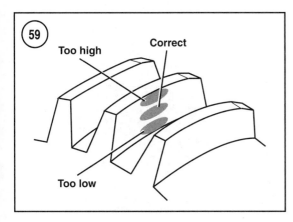

59

Too high   Correct

Too low

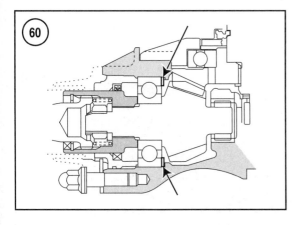

60

Tooth Contact

1. Remove the bearing housing from the gearcase by performing Steps 9-12 of *Final Drive, Disassembly*.

2. Degrease several teeth (C, **Figure 46**) on the final driven gear.

3. Apply a coat of marking compound to both sides of the teeth.

4. Reinstall the bearing housing assembly by performing the following:

    a. If removed, install the final driven gear shim(s) (A, **Figure 46**) onto the shaft (B) of the final driven gear.

    b. Set the bearing housing into place in the final drive. *Do not* apply sealant at this time.

    c. Install and snug down the bearing housing bolts. Tighten the two 10-mm bolts (**Figure 43**) to 50 N•m (37 ft.-lb.). Then tighten the 8-mm bolts to 23 N•m (17 ft.- lb.).

5. Fit a socket onto the final drive gear nut (**Figure 36**), and rotate the final drive gear through several rotations in each direction. Grasp the final driven gear to load the gear during this step.

6. Remove the bearing housing from the gearcase, and examine the impression on the coated teeth of the final driven gear (C, **Figure 46**). The impression should be centered on each tooth (**Figure 59**).

7. If the tooth impression is too low or too high, adjust the size of the final drive gear shim (**Figure 60**) by performing the following:

    a. Remove the final drive gear shim(s) by performing Steps 4-9 of *Final Drive, Disassembly*.

    b. Measure and record the thickness of the final drive gear shim.

    c. If the tooth impression is too high, refer to **Table 4** and select a thinner final drive gear shim.

    d. If the tooth impression is too low, select a thicker final drive gear shim.

    e. Reassemble the gearcase with the new final drive gear shim.

13

8. Recheck the tooth contact pattern and adjust the shim size as necessary until the tooth contact pattern is centered on the teeth.

> *CAUTION*
> *Changing the tooth contact pattern also affects gear backlash. Repeatedly adjust the backlash and tooth contact pattern until each is correct. Operating the motorcycle with one or both of these out of specification will rapidly wear the final drive and driven gears.*

9. Once tooth contact is correct, recheck backlash. Repeatedly adjust both backlash and tooth contact until each is within specification.

Bearing Replacement

Replace the final drive and final driven bearings as a set.

Final drive gear bearing

Use a general bearing puller and the drive gear bearing installer (Suzuki part No. 09913-84510), or an equivalent tool, to replace the bearing.
1. Using a bearing puller, remove the bearing from the final drive gear (**Figure 61**).
2. If necessary, remove the inner race from the gear shaft.
3. Make sure the washer is installed on the gear.
4. Set a new bearing onto the gear shaft so the manufacturer's marks face out. Use the bearing installer to drive the bearing onto the gear shaft.

Final Driven Gear Bearing

Use the final driven gear remover/installer (Suzuki part No. 09924-74570), or an equivalent, to drive the shaft from the gear.

1. Use two bolts or a drift to drive the bearing from the driven gear (**Figure 62**).

2. If necessary, remove the final driven gear from its shaft by performing the following:

    a. Remove the snap ring (**Figure 63**) from the final driven gear.

    b. Drive the shaft from the gear with gear remover/installer.

3. If removed, install the final driven gear onto its shaft by performing the following:

    a. Use the final driven gear remover/installer to drive the final driven gear onto the shaft (**Figure 64**).

    b. Install the snap ring (**Figure 63**) onto the shaft. Make sure the snap ring is completely seated in its groove.

4. Set a new bearing onto the final driven gear with the manufacturer's marks facing out. Install the bearing by tapping the bearing inner race with a soft face mallet (**Figure 65**).

Final Drive Needle Bearings

Use bearing installers (Suzuki part Nos. 09913-76010 and 09913-75821), or their equivalents, in the following procedure.

1. Chill the new needle bearing in a freezer to ease installation.

2. Replace the final driven gear needle bearing as follows:

    a. Remove the retainer screws, and remove the bearing retainer (C, **Figure 51**) from the driven side of the gearcase.

    b. Use the blind bearing puller to remove the needle bearing (**Figure 66**), and remove the oil seal from behind the bearing. Discard the oil seal.

    c. Install a new oil seal into the gearcase so the spring side of the seal faces out (toward the final drive gear needle bearing).

    d. With a bearing installer, install the needle bearing into the gearcase (**Figure 67**). The bearing manufacturer's marks must face out (toward the final driven gear).

    e. Install the bearing retainer (C, **Figure 51**). Apply Suzuki Thread Lock 1342 to the threads of the bearing retainer bolts, and tighten the bolts to 9 N•m (80 in.-lb.).

3. Replace the final drive gear needle bearing as follows:

    a. Use a blind bearing puller to remove the needle bearing from the drive side of the gearcase (**Figure 68**).

    b. With a bearing installer, install the new needle bearing (**Figure 69**). Install the bearing with its manufacturer's marks facing out (toward the drive shaft).

13

Table 1 REAR SUSPENSION AND FINAL DRIVE SPECIFICATIONS

Item	Specification mm (in.)
Bearing housing shim clearance	0.10 (0.004)
Final drive backlash	0.03-0.64 (0.001-0.025)
Rear wheel travel	118 (4.6)
Shock absorber spring preload	
Standard preload (spring length)	222 (8.74)
Maximum preload (min. spring length)	217 (8.54)
Minimum preload (max. spring length)	227 (8.94)

Table 2 BEARING HOUSING SHIMS

Part No.	Shim thickness mm (in.)
27327-38B00-035	0.35 (0.014)
27327-38B00-040	0.40 (0.016)
27327-38B00-050	0.50 (0.020)
27327-38B00-060	0.60 (0.024)

Table 3 FINAL DRIVEN GEAR SHIMS

Part No.	Shim thickness mm (in.)
09160-35008	0.95 (0.037)
09181-35141	1.05 (0.041)
09181-35144	1.10 (0.043)
09181-35148	1.20 (0.047)
09181-35151	1.25 (0.049)
27326-45104	1.35 (0.053)
09181-35154	1.40 (0.055)
27326-45100-145	1.45 (0.057)
09181-35156	1.50 (0.059)

Table 4 FINAL DRIVE GEAR SHIMS

Part No.	Shim thickness mm (in.)
27445-24A01-030	0.30 (0.012)
27445-24A01-035	0.35 (0.014)
27445-24A01-040	0.40 (0.016)
27445-24A01-050	0.50 (0.020)
27445-24A01-060	0.60 (0.024)

Table 5 REAR SUSPENSION AND FINAL DRIVE TORQUE SPECIFICATIONS

Item	N•m	in.-lb.	ft.-lb.
Bearing holder	110	–	81
Bearing housing bolt			
8 mm	23	–	17
10 mm	50	–	37
Bearing retainer bolts	9	80	–
Brake disc bolt	23	–	17
Final drive gear nut	100	–	74
Final drive drain bolt	23	–	17
Final drive nut	40	–	29.5

(continued)

Table 5 REAR SUSPENSION AND FINAL DRIVE TORQUE SPECIFICATIONS (continued)

Item	N•m	in.-lb.	ft.-lb.
Rear axle nut	110	–	81
Rear caliper bracket bolt/nut	60	–	44
Rear caliper mounting bolt	35	–	26
Shock absorber mounting bolt/nut	50	–	37
Suspension arm bolt/nut	135	–	100
Suspension lever bolt/nut	135	–	100
Swing arm			
Pivot bolt			
Left	100	–	74
Right	9.5	84	–
Pivot bolt locknut	100	–	74

13

CHAPTER FOURTEEN

BRAKES

This chapter covers the brake system. During brake service, compare measurements to the specifications at the end of this chapter. Replace worn, damaged or out of specification parts.

The brake system on 1998-2001 models consists of a single disc brake in the front and one in the rear. On 2002-on models, the system consists of dual disc brakes up front and a single disc brake in the rear.

BRAKE SERVICE

Safety and Service Fundamentals

1. Brake fluid will damage most painted and plastic surfaces. Observe the following to prevent brake fluid damage:
   a. Control the flow of brake fluid when refilling the reservoirs. Place a small hole into the seal of a new container. Put this hole next to the edge of the pour spout.
   b. Protect the motorcycle with a cover before beginning any service requiring draining, bleeding or handling of brake fluid.
   c. Keep a bucket of soapy water on hand while working on the brake system. If brake fluid spills on any surface, immediately wash the area.
2. When adding brake fluid, only use DOT 4 brake fluid from a sealed container.
3. Do not use silicone-based brake fluids.
4. If possible, do not mix different brands of brake fluids. One manufacturer's brake fluid may not be compatible with another's.
5. Brake fluid absorbs moisture from the air. Purchase brake fluid in small containers, and properly discard any small leftover quantities. Do not store brake fluid in a container with less than 1/4 of the fluid remaining. This small amount absorbs moisture very rapidly.
6. Never reuse brake fluid expelled during brake bleeding. Contaminated brake fluid can cause brake failure.
7. Dispose of used brake fluid in a safe manner.
8. Always keep the master cylinder reservoir cover installed. It keeps dust and moisture out of the system.

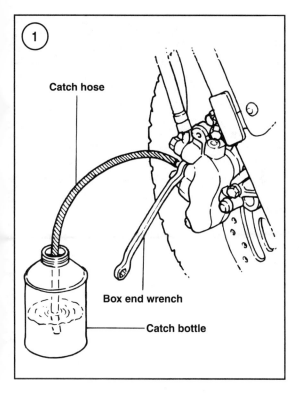

Catch hose

Box end wrench

Catch bottle

9. Keep the work area and all tools clean. Caliper or master cylinder components can be damaged by tiny particles of grit.

10. Do not use sharp tools inside the master cylinder, calipers or on the pistons. Sharp tools can damage brake components, and these defects can interfere with brake operation.

11. Use DOT 4 brake fluid to clean hydraulic parts. Never use petroleum-based solvents on the brake system's internal components. The seals will swell and distort, and require replacement if contaminated.

12. Use an aerosol brake parts cleaner to clean components without leaving a residue.

13. Whenever any brake banjo bolt or brake line nut is loosened, the system is opened and must be bled to remove air. If the brakes feel spongy, this usually means air has entered the system. Refer to *Brake Bleeding* in this chapter.

14. Do not inhale brake dust. If necessary, wear an appropriate facemask to prevent inhalation of debris.

15. After completing any brake service, test ride the motorcycle slowly and carefully. Ensure the brake system is functioning correctly.

BRAKE BLEEDING

Bleeding the brakes removes air from the brake system. Air in the brakes increases brake-lever or brake-pedal travel, and it makes the brakes feel soft

or spongy. Under extreme circumstances, it can cause complete loss of brake pressure.

Bleed the brakes manually or with a vacuum pump.

Preliminary Information

1. Clean the area around the bleed valve. Make sure the valve opening is clear.

2. To prevent valve damage, use a box end wrench to open and close the bleed valve.

3. Replace a bleed valve with damaged threads or a rounded hex head. A damaged valve is difficult to remove and cannot be properly tightened.

4. Use a clear catch hose (**Figure 1**) so the fluid can be seen as it leaves the bleed valve. Air bubbles in the catch hose indicate air exiting the brake system.

5. Open the bleed valve just enough to allow fluid to pass through the valve and into the catch bottle. If a bleed valve is too loose, air can be drawn into the system through the valve threads.

6. If air does enter through the valve threads, apply silicone brake grease around the valve where it emerges from the caliper. Use just enough grease to seal the valve. Clean the grease from the valve once the brakes have been bled. If necessary, remove the bleed valve and apply Teflon tape to the valve threads. Make sure the Teflon tape does not cover the passage in the bleed valve.

7. When bleeding the front brakes, turn the handlebars to level the front master cylinder.

8. The setting on the front brake lever adjuster affects bleeding. Initially bleed the front brakes with the adjuster turned to the No. 4 setting. Once the brakes feel solid, check the feel with the adjuster in several different settings. If the lever feels soft at any setting or if the lever hits the handlebar, air is still trapped in the system. Continue bleeding.

9. If the front brakes are difficult to bleed, remove the master cylinder assembly and tilt the assembly so the brake-hose banjo bolt sits below reservoir. Hold the master cylinder assembly in this position, and pump the brake lever several times. Any trapped air will be expelled into the reservoir. Reinstall the master cylinder assembly and continue conventional bleeding.

10. Tapping on the banjo bolts at the calipers, master cylinders and at any other hose connections in the brake line also may help remove trapped air bubbles.

11. As brake fluid enters the system, the level in the reservoir drops. Add brake fluid as necessary to keep the fluid level 10 mm (3/8 in.) below the reservoir top so air will not be drawn into the system. The fluid level will drop rapidly when using a vacuum pump.

14

Manual Bleeding

1. Remove the dust cap from the bleed valve (**Figure 2**) on the caliper assembly.

2. Connect a length of clear tubing to the bleed valve (**Figure 1**, typical). Place the other end of the tube into a clean container. Fill the container with enough fresh brake fluid to keep the hose end submerged. The tube should be long enough so that its loop is higher than the bleed valve. This prevents air from being drawn into the caliper during bleeding.

3. If bleeding the front brakes, turn the handlebars to level the front master cylinder.

4. Clean all debris from the top of the master cylinder reservoir, and remove the top cover, diaphragm plate (front brake) and the diaphragm from the reservoir.

5. Add brake fluid to the reservoir until the fluid level reaches the reservoir upper limit. Loosely install the diaphragm and the cover. Leave them in place during bleeding to keep dirt out of the system and so brake fluid cannot spurt from the reservoir.

6. Pump the brake lever or brake pedal a few times. Then release it.

7. Apply the brake lever or pedal until it stops, and hold it in this position.

8. Open the bleed valve with a wrench. Let the brake lever or pedal move to the limit of its travel. Then close the bleed valve. Do not release the brake lever or pedal while the bleed valve is open.

9. Repeat Steps 6-8 until the brake fluid flowing from the hose is clear and free of air. If the system is difficult to bleed, tap the master cylinder or caliper with a soft mallet to release trapped air bubbles.

10. Test the feel of the brake lever or pedal. It should feel firm and offer the same resistance each time it is operated. If the lever or pedal feels soft, air is still trapped in the system. Continue bleeding.

11. When bleeding is complete, disconnect the hose from the bleed valve. Tighten the bleed valve to 7.5 N•m (66 in.-lb.).

12. When bleeding the front brakes on 2002-on models, repeat Steps 2-11 on the opposite front caliper.

13. Add brake fluid to the master cylinder to correct the fluid level.

14. Install the diaphragm, diaphragm plate (front brake) and top cap. Make sure the cap is secured in place. Install the top-cover clamp onto the front master cylinder reservoir.

Vacuum Bleeding

1. Remove the dust cap from the bleed valve (**Figure 2**) on the caliper assembly.

2. Clean all debris from the top of the master cylinder reservoir. Remove the top cover, diaphragm plate (front brake) and diaphragm from the reservoir.

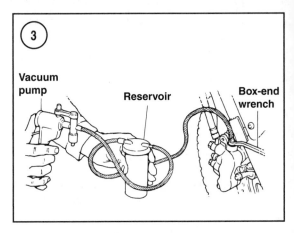

Vacuum pump   Reservoir   Box-end wrench

3. Add brake fluid to the reservoir until the fluid level reaches the reservoir upper limit. Loosely install the diaphragm and the cover. Leave them in place during bleeding to keep dirt out of the system and so brake fluid cannot spurt out of the reservoir.

4. Assemble the vacuum tool following the manufacturer's instructions.

5. Connect the pump's catch hose to the bleed valve on the brake caliper (**Figure 3**).

6. Operate the vacuum pump to create vacuum in the hose.

7. Use a wrench to open the bleed valve. The vacuum pump should pull fluid from the system. Close the bleed valve before the brake fluid stops flowing from the system or before the master cylinder reservoir runs empty. Add fluid to the reservoir as necessary.

8. Operate the brake lever or brake pedal a few times, and release it.

9. Repeat Steps 6-7 until the fluid leaving the bleed valve is clear and free of air bubbles. If the system is difficult to bleed, tap the master cylinder and caliper housing with a soft mallet to release trapped air bubbles.

10. Test the feel of the brake lever or brake pedal. It should feel firm and offer the same resistance each time it is operated. If the lever or pedal feels soft, air is still trapped in the system. Continue bleeding.

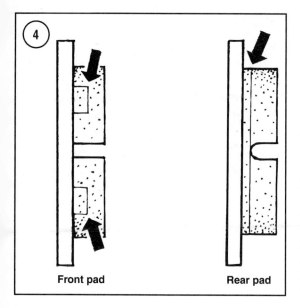

Front pad   Rear pad

11. When bleeding is complete, disconnect the hose from the bleed valve, and tighten the valve to 7.5 N•m (66 in.-lb.).

12. When bleeding the front brakes on 2002-on models, repeat Steps 2-11 on the opposite front caliper.

13. Add brake fluid to the master cylinder to correct the fluid level.

14. Install the diaphragm, diaphragm plate (front brake) and top cap. Be sure the cap is secured in place. Install the clamp onto the front brake master cylinder.

BRAKE FLUID DRAINING

Before disconnecting a brake hose, drain the brake fluid from the front or rear brakes as described in this section. Draining the fluid reduces the amount of fluid that can spill out when system components are removed.

This section describes two methods for draining the brake system: manual and vacuum.

Manual Draining

An empty bottle, a length of clear hose, and a wrench is required when performing this procedure.

1. Remove the dust cap from the bleed valve (**Figure 2**). Remove all dirt from the valve and its outlet port.

2. Connect a length of clear hose to the bleed valve on the caliper. Insert the other end into a container (**Figure 1**, typical).

3. Apply the front brake lever or the rear brake pedal until it stops. Hold the lever or pedal in this position.

4. Open the bleed valve with a wrench, and let the lever or pedal move to the limit of its travel. Close the bleed valve.

5. Release the lever or pedal, and repeat Step 3 and Step 4 until brake fluid stops flowing from the bleed valve.

6. If draining the front brakes on 2002-on models, repeat this on the other brake caliper.

7. Dispose of the brake fluid in a responsible manner.

Vacuum Draining

A hand-operated vacuum pump is required when performing this procedure.

1. Remove the dust cap from the bleed valve (**Figure 2**). Remove all dirt from the valve and its outlet port.

2. Connect the pump's catch hose to the bleed valve on the brake caliper (**Figure 3**).

3. Operate the vacuum pump to create vacuum in the hose.

4. Use a wrench to open the bleed valve. The vacuum pump should pull fluid from the system.

5. When fluid has stopped flowing through the hose, close the bleed valve.

6. Repeat Steps 2-4 until brake fluid no longer flows from the bleed valve.

7. If draining the front brake system on 2002-on models, repeat this procedure on the opposite caliper.

8. Dispose of the brake fluid in a responsible manner.

BRAKE PAD INSPECTION

To maintain even brake pressure on the disc, always replace all pads in a caliper at the same time. When replacing the front brake pads on 2002-on models, replace all pads in *both front calipers* at the same time.

The brake hose does not need to be disconnected from the caliper during brake pad replacement. If the hose is removed, bleed the brakes.

Refer to *Brake Service* in this chapter.

14

> *WARNING*
> *Check the pads more frequently as the brake pads approach the end of the wear mark (**Figure 4**, typical). On some pads, the wear limit marks are very close to the metal backing plate. If pad wear is uneven, the backing plate may contact the disc and cause damage.*

1. Remove the brake pads as described in this chapter.

2. Inspect the brake pads by performing the following. See **Figure 5**, typical.

   a. Inspect the friction material for dirt, grease and oil contamination. If possible, remove light contamination with sandpaper. If contamination has penetrated the pad surface, replace the brake pads.

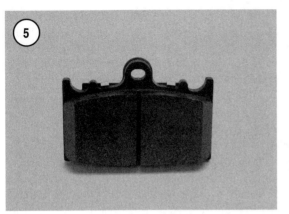

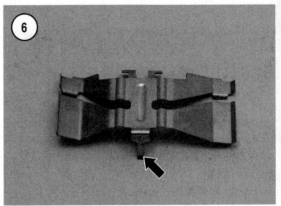

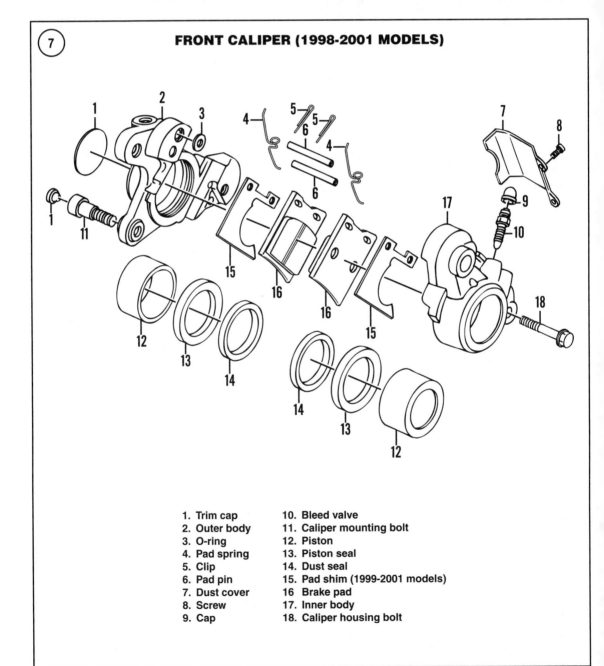

FRONT CALIPER (1998-2001 MODELS)

1. Trim cap
2. Outer body
3. O-ring
4. Pad spring
5. Clip
6. Pad pin
7. Dust cover
8. Screw
9. Cap
10. Bleed valve
11. Caliper mounting bolt
12. Piston
13. Piston seal
14. Dust seal
15. Pad shim (1999-2001 models)
16. Brake pad
17. Inner body
18. Caliper housing bolt

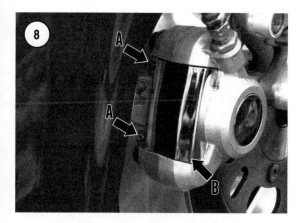

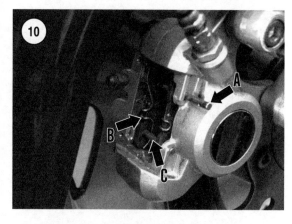

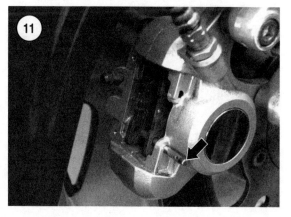

b. Inspect the brake pads for excessive wear or damage. Replace the brake pads if either pad is worn to the bottom of the wear groove.

c. Inspect the friction material for uneven wear, damage or contamination. All pads in a caliper should show approximately the same amount of wear. If the pads are wearing unevenly, the caliper may not be operating correctly.

d. Inspect the metal plate on the back of each pad for corrosion and damage.

3. Check the friction surface of the new pads for any debris or manufacturing residue. If necessary, clean the pads with an aerosol brake cleaner.

4. Check the pad spring(s) (**Figure 6**, typical) for wear or fatigue. Replace the pad spring(s) if any shows sign of damage or excessive wear.

5. Thoroughly clean any corrosion or road debris from the pad spring(s) and pad pin (where installed).

6. Inspect the pad pin. Replace a bent or worn pin.

7. Service the brake disc as follows:

a. Use an aerosol brake parts cleaner and a piece of fine-grade emery cloth to remove all brake pad residue and any rust from the brake disc. Clean both sides of the disc. If the brake pad compound is different, removing the old pad residue is critical.

b. Inspect the brake disc for wear as described in this chapter.

FRONT BRAKE CALIPER (1998-2001 MODELS)

Refer to *Brake Service* in this chapter. Refer to **Figure 7**.

Pad Removal/Installation

1. Secure a spacer between the brake lever and the throttle grip. With a spacer in place, the pistons will not be forced out of their cylinders if the lever is inadvertently squeezed.

2. Remove the screws (A, **Figure 8**) and lift the dust cover (B) from the caliper.

3. Remove the clip (A, **Figure 9**) from the upper pad pin. Note that the clip sits between the outboard pad and the caliper.

4. Remove the upper pad pin (A, **Figure 10**) from the caliper, and remove each pad spring (B). Note that the arms of the pad springs press against the bottom of the pad pins (C, **Figure 10**). If necessary, release the spring tension on a pad pin by pressing the spring arm into the caliper.

5. Remove the lower pad pin (**Figure 11**) by repeating Step 3 and Step 4.

14

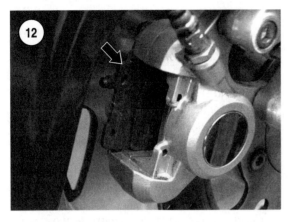

6. Lift each brake pad (**Figure 12**) from the caliper. Watch for the pad shim on 1999-2001 models.

7. Inspect the brake pads (**Figure 13**) as described in *Brake Pad Inspection* (this chapter).

8. When new pads are installed in the calipers, the fluid level in the master cylinder reservoir rises. Remove some brake fluid from the reservoir and reposition the caliper pistons by performing the following:

 a. Clean the top of the master cylinder reservoir.
 b. Remove the top cover, plate, and diaphragm.
 c. Use a syringe to remove approximately half of the fluid from the reservoir.
 d. Temporarily install one of the old brake pads into the caliper and seat it against the piston.
 e. Press the pad against the piston, and slowly push the caliper piston all the way into the caliper. Constantly check the reservoir to make sure brake fluid does not overflow. Remove additional brake fluid as necessary.
 f. The piston should move freely. If it does not, remove the caliper and service it as described in this chapter.
 g. Remove the old brake pad and repeat this process for the piston on the other side.

9. Slide the inboard (**Figure 12**) and outboard brake pads into the caliper so the brake material faces the brake disc.

10. Insert the lower pad pin (**Figure 11**) so it passes through both brake pads and sits in the boss in the inboard side of the caliper. Rotate the pad pin so its clip hole sits vertically relative to the caliper.

11. Install the clip (**Figure 14**) into the lower pad pin so the clip sits between the caliper and the outboard brake pad (B, **Figure 9**).

12. Install the outboard pad spring so its arm fits under the lower pad pin (**Figure 15**). Make sure the hook of the spring rests on the brake pad (A, **Figure 16**).

13. Press the arm of the pad spring into the caliper, and partially install the upper pad pin (B, **Figure 16**). The pin must sit above the pad spring arm.

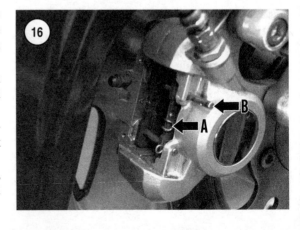

14. Install the inboard pad spring so its arm fits under the lower pad pin. Seat its hook (B, **Figure 10**) on the brake pad.

15. Press the arm of the pad spring into the caliper. Install the upper pad pin so it passes over the pad spring arm, through the hole in the inboard brake pad, and seats in the caliper. Refer to **Figure 17**.

16. Rotate the pad pin so its clip hole sits vertically. Install the clip (A, **Figure 9**) into the pad pin so the clip sits between the caliper and the outboard brake pad.

17. Install the dust cover (B, **Figure 8**) and screws (A).

Caliper Removal

1. If the caliper will be serviced, perform the following:
   a. Remove the brake pads as described in this section.
   b. Slowly operate the brake lever and push the pistons from their cylinders. Do not let the pistons contact the brake disc.
   c. Drain the front brakes as described in this chapter.
   d. Hold the brake hose fitting (A, **Figure 18**), and loosen the joint nut (B). Disconnect the brake hose from the caliper.
   e. Insert the hose end into a plastic bag so brake fluid will not leak onto the motorcycle.
2. Remove the reflector from its mount.
3. Remove the caliper mounting bolts (**Figure 19**) and lift the caliper from the brake disc. Note that the caliper sits against the inboard side of the mounting bosses.

Caliper Installation

1. Carefully set the caliper onto the inboard side of the mounting bosses. Avoid contact with the brake pads.
2. Install the caliper mounting bolts (**Figure 19**). Tighten the bolts to 35 N•m (26 ft.-lb.).
3. If the caliper was serviced, connect the brake hose to the caliper.
   a. Install a new sealing washer with the adaptor nut (C, **Figure 18**).
   b. Tighten the brake hose joint nut (B, **Figure 18**) to 15 N•m (11 ft.-lb.).
   c. Tighten the brake hose adapter nut (C, **Figure 18**) to 23 N•m (17 ft.-lb.).
4. Install the reflector.
5. Install the brake pads as described in this section.

Caliper Disassembly/Assembly

1. Remove the caliper housing bolts (**Figure 20**), and separate the caliper halves.

14

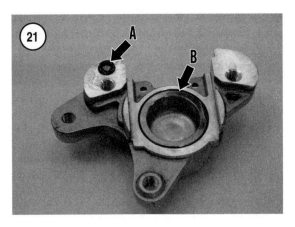

2. Remove the fluid port O-ring (A, **Figure 21**). It must be replaced during assembly.

> *NOTE*
> *If the pistons were partially forced out of the caliper body during removal, Steps 3-5 may not be necessary. If the pistons or caliper bores are corroded or very dirty, a small amount of compressed air may be necessary to completely remove the pistons from the body bores.*

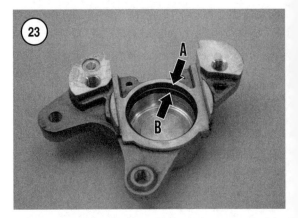

3. Place a piece of soft wood or a folded shop cloth over the end of the piston(s) and into the caliper body. Turn this assembly over with the piston facing down onto the workbench top.

> *WARNING*
> *In the next step, the piston may shoot out of the caliper body with considerable force. Keep your hands and fingers out of the way. Wear shop gloves and safety goggles when using compressed air to remove the pistons.*

4. Apply air pressure in short bursts to the fluid passageway and force the piston out of the caliper bore.

5. Repeat for the other caliper body half.

6. Remove the piston (**Figure 22**) from the bore in each caliper half.

7. Use a piece of wood or plastic scraper and carefully push the dust seal (A, **Figure 23**) and the piston seal (B) in toward the caliper cylinder bore and out of their grooves. Remove the dust and piston seals from the other caliper half and discard all seals.

8. If necessary, remove the bleed valve.

9. Inspect the caliper assembly as described in this section.

10. Coat the new seals, pistons, and cylinders with brake fluid.

11. Carefully install the new piston seal (**Figure 24**) into the inner groove in the cylinder bore.

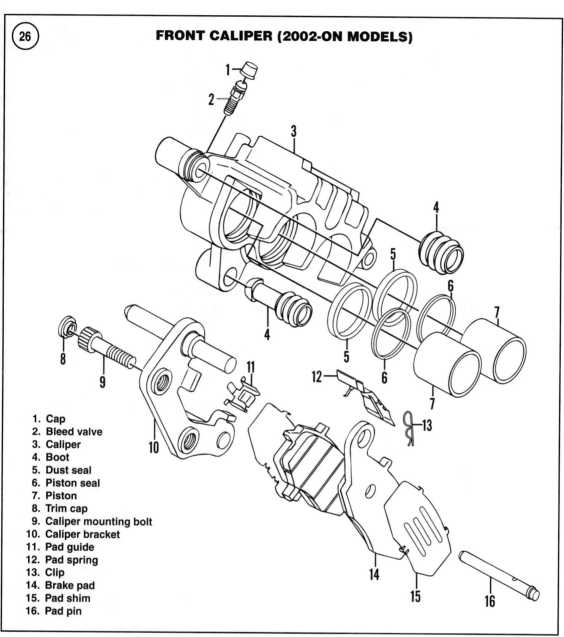

FRONT CALIPER (2002-ON MODELS)

1. Cap
2. Bleed valve
3. Caliper
4. Boot
5. Dust seal
6. Piston seal
7. Piston
8. Trim cap
9. Caliper mounting bolt
10. Caliper bracket
11. Pad guide
12. Pad spring
13. Clip
14. Brake pad
15. Pad shim
16. Pad pin

12. Install the new dust seal (**Figure 25**) into the outer groove. Make sure both seals are properly seated in their respective grooves (**Figure 23**).

13. Repeat Step 11 and Step 12 for the other caliper half.

14. Position the piston with the open end facing out. To prevent seal damage, carefully turn the piston into the caliper cylinder. Press the piston into the cylinder bore until it bottoms (B, **Figure 21**). Repeat for the other caliper half.

15. Coat a *new* O-ring with brake fluid, and install the O-ring (A, **Figure 21**) into the depression in the inboard caliper half.

16. Set the outboard caliper half onto the inboard half. Make sure the O-ring is still in place.

17. Install the two caliper housing bolts (**Figure 20**). Tighten the front caliper housing bolts to 33 N•m (24 ft.-lb.).

18. Install the bleed valve and tighten it to 7.5 N•m (66 in.-lb.).

19. Install the caliper and brake pads as described in this section.

20. Bleed the brake as described in this chapter.

FRONT BRAKE CALIPER
(2002-ON MODELS)

Refer to *Brake Service* in this chapter. Refer to **Figure 26**.

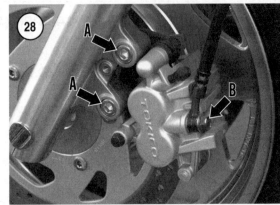

Pad Removal/Installation

1. Secure a spacer between the brake lever and the throttle grip. With a spacer in place, the pistons will not be forced out of their cylinders if the lever is inadvertently squeezed.

2. Remove the reflector (A, **Figure 27**) from the fork leg. Carefully pry the trim cap (B, **Figure 27**) from each caliper mounting bolt.

3. Remove the caliper mounting bolts (A, **Figure 28**), and lift the caliper from the brake disc.

4. Remove the clip (A, **Figure 29**) from the pad pin, and pull the pin (B) from the caliper. Note that the clip sits between the caliper and inboard pad (**Figure 30**).

5. Rotate the inboard pad from the caliper (**Figure 31**), and slide if off the caliper bracket post. Watch for the pad shim on the pad.

6. Remove the outboard pad (**Figure 32**) along with its shim.

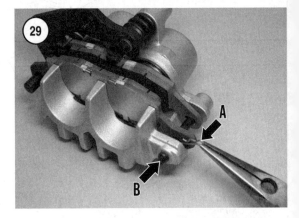

> *NOTE*
> *The pad spring is directional. The side with the single tang (**Figure 33**) faces the outboard side of the caliper.*

7. Grasp the pad spring tang at the back of the caliper (**Figure 34**). Lift the tang up and forward, and remove pad spring from the caliper (**Figure 35**).

8. Inspect the brake pad (**Figure 36**), pad pin and pad spring (**Figure 33**) as described in *Brake Pad Inspection* (this chapter). Also inspect the caliper bracket (10, **Figure 26**). Make sure it moves smoothly within the caliper. If necessary, remove and lubricate the bracket as described in *Caliper Disassembly/Assembly* (this section).

9. When new pads are installed in a caliper, the fluid level in the master cylinder reservoir rises. Remove some hydraulic fluid from the reservoir and reposition the caliper pistons by performing the following:

    a. Clean the top of the master cylinder reservoir.

    b. Remove the top cover, plate, and diaphragm.

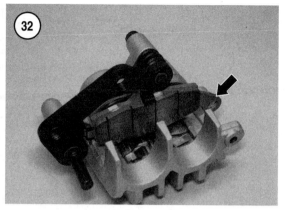

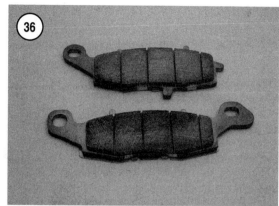

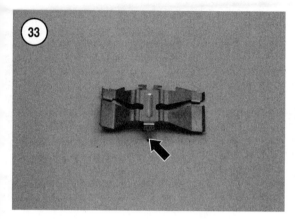

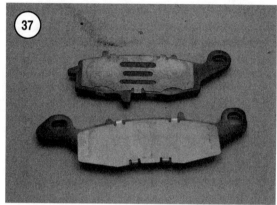

c. Use a syringe to remove approximately half of the fluid from the reservoir.

d. Temporarily install an old outboard pad into the caliper and seat it against the piston(s).

e. Press the pad against the pistons, and slowly push the caliper piston(s) all the way into the caliper. Constantly check the reservoir to make sure brake fluid does not overflow. Remove additional fluid as necessary.

f. The pistons should move freely. If one or both do not, remove the caliper and service it as described in this chapter.

g. Remove the old brake pad.

10. Position the pad spring so the side with the single tang faces the outboard side of the caliper (**Figure 35**). Install the pad spring so this single tang engages the cutout in the caliper (**Figure 34**).

11. Install the pad shim onto the back of each new pad (**Figure 37**).

12. Install the outboard pad into the caliper (**Figure 32**).

13. Slide the inboard pad over the caliper bracket post (**Figure 31**), and rotate the pad into the caliper (**Figure 38**).

14. Install the pad pin (B, **Figure 29**) so it passes through both brake pads and seats in the caliper boss.

14

15. Install the clip (A, **Figure 29**) through the pad pin hole. Make sure the clip sits between the inboard pad and the caliper (**Figure 30**).

16. Install the caliper as described in this section.

Caliper Removal

1. Remove the reflector (A, **Figure 27**) from the fork leg, and pry the trim clip (B) from each caliper mounting bolt.

2. Remove the caliper mounting bolts (A, **Figure 28**), and lift the caliper from the motorcycle.

3. If the caliper will be disassembled for service, perform the following:

   a. Remove the brake pads and pad spring as described in this section.

   b. Fit the caliper back onto the fork slider. Install the caliper mounting bolts.

   c. Operate the brake lever and press the pistons from their cylinders. Make sure the pistons do not contact the brake disc.

   d. Drain the front brakes (this chapter).

   e. Remove the banjo bolt (B, **Figure 28**), and separate the brake hose from the caliper port. Watch for the sealing washer on each side of the hose fitting. Insert the hose end in a plastic bag so fluid will not leak onto the motorcycle.

   f. Remove the caliper mounting bolts, and remove the caliper.

4. Disassemble the caliper as described in this section.

Caliper Installation

1. If removed, install the brake pads as described in this section.

2. Fit the caliper onto the fork slider so the caliper bracket sits against the inboard side of the mounting bosses.

3. Install the caliper mounting bolts (A, **Figure 28**). Tighten them to 35 N•m (26 ft.-lb.).

4. If removed, fit the brake hose onto the caliper fluid port and install the banjo bolt (B, **Figure 28**). Install a seal washer onto each side of the brake hose fitting, and tighten the banjo bolt to 23 N•m (17 ft.-lb.).

5. If the brake hose was removed, bleed the brakes.

6. Install the trim clip (B, **Figure 27**) into each caliper mounting bolt, and install the reflector (A).

Caliper Disassembly/Assembly

Refer to **Figure 26**.

1. Remove the caliper, brake pads and pad spring.

2. Slide the caliper bracket (**Figure 39**) from the boots in the caliper.

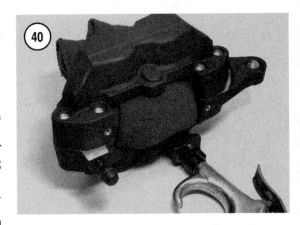

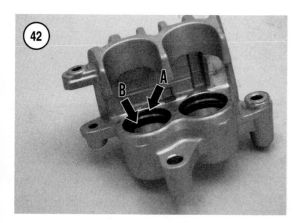

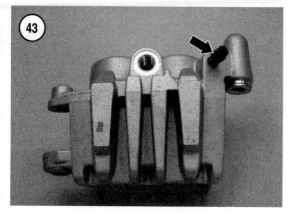

NOTE
If the pistons were partially forced out of the caliper body during removal, Step 3 and Step 4 may not be necessary. If the pistons or caliper bores are corroded or very dirty, a small amount of compressed air may be necessary to completely re-move the pistons from the body bores.

3. Insert a piece of soft wood or a folded shop cloth over the end of the piston(s) and into the caliper body. Turn this assembly over with the piston facing down onto the workbench top.

WARNING
In the next step, the pistons may shoot out of the caliper body with consider-able force. Keep your hands and fingers out of the way. Wear shop gloves and safety goggles when using compressed air to remove the pistons.

4. Apply air pressure in short bursts to the fluid pas-sageway and force the pistons out of the caliper bore (**Figure 40**, typical).

5. Remove each piston (**Figure 41**) from its cylinder.
6. Use a piece of wood or plastic scraper and care-fully push the dust seal (A, **Figure 42**) and the piston seal (B) in toward the caliper cylinder bore and out of their grooves. Remove the dust and piston seals from each cylinder and repeat for the other caliper half.
7. If necessary, remove the bleed valve (**Figure 43**).
8. If the boots (**Figure 44**) are torn or worn, remove them.
9. Refer to *Front Brake Caliper Inspection (All Models)*.
10. If the boots were removed, install new ones.
11. Coat the new seals, pistons, and cylinders with brake fluid.
12. Carefully install the new piston seal (**Figure 45**) into the inner groove in the cylinder bore.
13. Install the new dust seal (**Figure 46**) into the outer groove. Make sure both seals are properly seat-ed in their respective grooves (**Figure 42**).

14

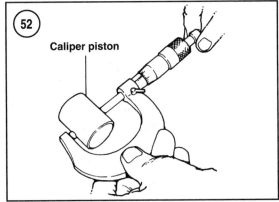

Caliper piston

14. Position the piston with the open end facing out. To prevent seal damage, carefully turn each piston into its cylinder bore (**Figure 41**). Press the piston into the cylinder until it bottoms (**Figure 47**). Repeat for the other piston.

15. Apply grease to the caliper bracket posts and slide the holder into the caliper boots (**Figure 39**).

16. Install the bleed valve (**Figure 43**) and tighten to 7.5 N•m (66 in.-lb.).

17. Install the brake pads and caliper as described in this section.

18. Bleed the brake as described in this chapter.

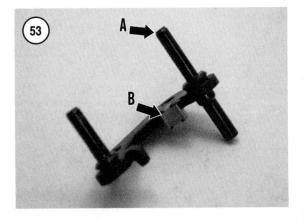

FRONT MASTER CYLINDER

1. Cover screw
2. Top cover
3. Plate
4. Diaphragm
5. Protector
6. Bolt
7. Clamp
8. Reservoir
9. Boot
10. Piston assembly

FRONT BRAKE CALIPER INSPECTION (ALL MODELS)

When inspecting brake components, compare any measurements to the specifications in **Table 1** or **Table 2**. Replace worn, damaged or out of specification parts.

1. Clean both caliper body halves and the pistons. Dry the parts with compressed air.

2. Inspect the fluid passageways (A, **Figure 48**) in each cylinder bore and in each caliper body (B). Apply compressed air to the openings to make sure they are clear. Clean them with an aerosol brake cleaner if necessary.

3. Inspect the piston and dust seal grooves (C, **Figure 48**) in each cylinder for damage or corrosion.

4. Inspect the threads in the bolt holes and fluid ports of each caliper body. If worn or damaged, dress the threads with a metric tap or replace the caliper assembly.

5. Inspect the bleed valve, banjo bolt (2002-on models), or adapter fitting (**Figure 49**, 1998-2001 models). Apply compressed air to the openings and make sure each is clear. Clean each part with brake parts cleaner if necessary.

6. Inspect the caliper bodies for damage. Check the threads of the caliper mounting holes for wear or damage. Clean the threads with an appropriate size metric tap or replace the caliper assembly.

7. Inspect the cylinder bore walls (**Figure 48**) and pistons (**Figure 50**) for scratches, scoring or other damage.

8. Measure the inside diameter of each cylinder bore (**Figure 51**).

9. Measure the outside diameter of the pistons (**Figure 52**).

10. On a front caliper from 2002-on models, inspect the brake caliper bracket (A, **Figure 53**). Make sure its bracket posts (A, **Figure 53**) are smooth. Inspect the boots for tears or other damage. Make sure the pad guide (B, **Figure 53**) is secure.

FRONT BRAKE MASTER CYLINDER

Refer to *Brake Service* in this chapter. Refer to **Figure 54**.

Removal

1. If the master cylinder will be serviced, perform the following:

   a. Drain the brake fluid from the front brakes as described in this chapter.

   b. Clean the top of the master cylinder.

   c. Remove the top cover, diaphragm plate and diaphragm from the master cylinder reservoir.

14

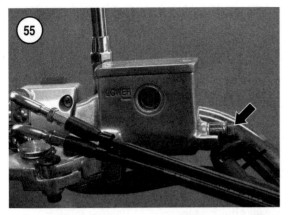

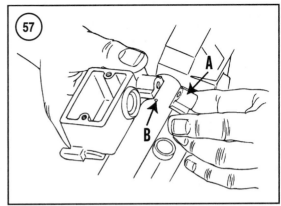

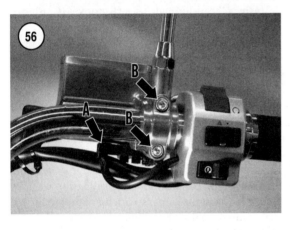

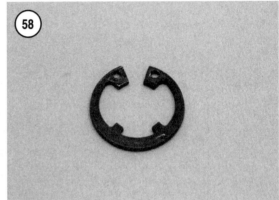

d. Place a rag beneath the banjo bolt (**Figure 55**), remove the bolt, and separate the brake hose from the master cylinder. Watch for the two sealing washers, one on each side of the brake hose fitting.

e. Place the brake hose end into a plastic bag so brake fluid will not leak onto the motorcycle. Seal the bag with a rubber band.

2. Disconnect the electrical connectors (A, **Figure 56**) from the brake switch.

3. Remove the master cylinder clamp bolts (B, **Figure 56**), and lower the master cylinder from the handlebar.

4. If the master cylinder will be serviced, drain any residual brake fluid from the master cylinder and reservoir. Watch for the protector inside the reservoir.

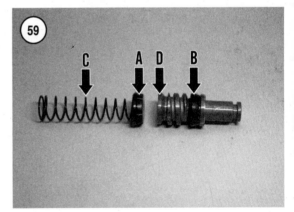

Installation

1. Set the front master cylinder onto the right handlebar so its clamp mating surface (A, **Figure 57**) aligns with the indexing dot on the handlebar (B).

2. Mount the clamp with the UP mark facing up, and install the master cylinder clamp bolts (B, **Figure 56**). Tighten the upper mounting bolt first. Then tighten the lower bolt, leaving a gap at the bottom. Tighten the front master cylinder clamp bolts to 10 N•m (89 in.-lb.).

3. Connect the electrical connectors (A, **Figure 56**)

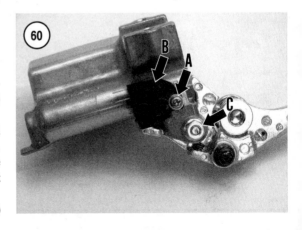

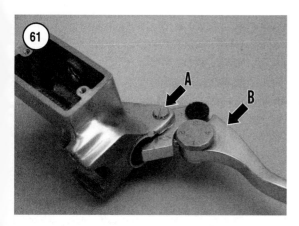

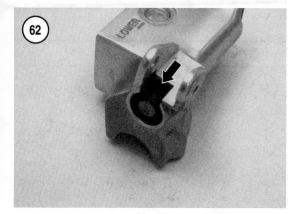

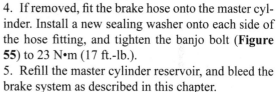

to the brake light switch.

4. If removed, fit the brake hose onto the master cylinder. Install a new sealing washer onto each side of the hose fitting, and tighten the banjo bolt (**Figure 55**) to 23 N•m (17 ft.-lb.).

5. Refill the master cylinder reservoir, and bleed the brake system as described in this chapter.

Disassembly

> *WARNING*
> *Install a new snap ring (**Figure 58**), primary cup (A, **Figure 59**), and secondary cup (B) whenever the master cylinder has been disassembled. Reinstalling used parts could cause brake failure.*

1. Remove the master cylinder as described in this section.

2. Remove the mounting screw (A, **Figure 60**), and lift the front brake light switch (B) from the reservoir.

3. Remove the nut (C, **Figure 60**) from the brake lever pivot bolt.

4. Remove the brake lever pivot bolt (A, **Figure 61**), and slide the lever assembly (B) from the master cylinder bracket.

5. Roll the rubber boot (**Figure 62**) from the piston in cylinder bore.

6. Press the piston into the cylinder bore, and use snap ring pliers to remove the snap ring (**Figure 63**).

7. Remove the piston (**Figure 64**) and the spring assembly (**Figure 65**) from the cylinder bore.

8. Note the position of the protector and remove it from the bottom of the reservoir. It must be reinstalled with this same orientation.

Assembly

1. Soak new cups in brake fluid for at least 15 minutes to make them pliable. Coat the inside of the cylinder bore with brake fluid.

14

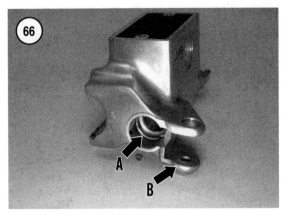

2. Install the new primary cup (A, **Figure 59**) onto the new spring (C). Install the new secondary cup (B, **Figure 59**) onto the new piston (D).

> *WARNING*
> *When installing the piston assembly, do not allow the cups to turn inside out. They will be damaged, and brake fluid will leak within the cylinder bore.*

3. Install the spring/primary cup assembly (**Figure 65**) into the master cylinder bore.
4. Install the piston (**Figure 64**) into the cylinder bore.
5. Press the piston into the bore, and secure it in place with a new snap ring (**Figure 63**). The snap ring must be completely seated in the groove (A, **Figure 66**) inside the cylinder bore.
6. Lubricate the new boot with brake fluid. Carefully roll the boot over the piston so the boot seals the master cylinder bore. See **Figure 62**.
7. Install the brake lever as follows:
   a. Lubricate the pivot bolt with waterproof grease.
   b. Fit the brake lever assembly (B, **Figure 61**) into place in the lever boss, and install the pivot bolt (A).
   c. Turn the nut (C, **Figure 60**) onto the pivot bolt, and tighten the nut securely. Check that the brake lever moves freely. If there is any binding or roughness, remove the brake lever. Inspect the parts.
8. Set the front brake light switch (B, **Figure 60**) in place so its knob engages the dimple in the housing, and tighten the screw (A) securely.
9. Seat the protector in the reservoir port as noted during removal.

Inspection

Compare any measurements to the specifications in **Table 1** or **Table 2**. Replace worn, damaged or out of specification parts.

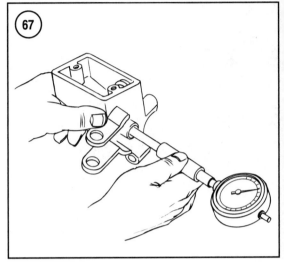

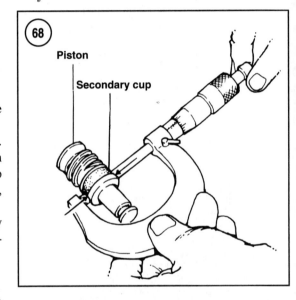

Piston

Secondary cup

1. Clean all hydraulic parts in brake fluid. Use an aerosol brake parts cleaner on other components. Inspect the cylinder bore surface (A, **Figure 66**) for wear, corrosion or damage. If less than perfect, replace the master cylinder assembly. *Do not* hone the master cylinder bore to remove imperfections.
2. Measure the cylinder bore (**Figure 67**).
3. Inspect the contact surfaces of the piston (D, **Figure 59**) for wear and damage. If less than perfect, replace the piston assembly.
4. Measure the outside diameter of the piston (**Figure 68**).
5. Check the lugs on the brake lever boss (B, **Figure 66**) for cracks or elongation.
6. Inspect the threads in the brake hose port (A, **Figure 69**). Clean the threads with a tap or replace the master cylinder assembly.
7. Make sure the port (B, **Figure 69**) in the bottom of the reservoir is clear.

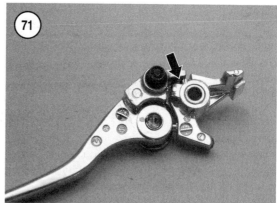

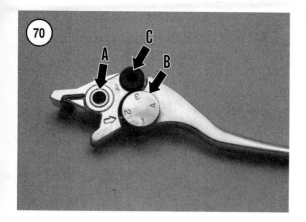

8. Inspect the pivot hole (A, **Figure 70**) in the brake lever for cracks or elongation.

9. Inspect the adjuster (B, **Figure 70**) on the lever. If worn or damaged replace the hand lever as an assembly.

10. If necessary, remove the nut and the pivot bolt (C, **Figure 70**), and separate the brake lever from the knocker. During assembly, make sure the spring (**Figure 71**) engages the hole in the lever and the post on the knocker.

11. Check the top cover, diaphragm and diaphragm plate for damage and deterioration; replace as necessary.

REAR BRAKE CALIPER

Refer to *Brake Service* in this chapter. Refer to **Figure 72** or **Figure 73**.

Pad Removal/Installation

1. Securely support the motorcycle on a level surface.

2. Tie the brake pedal to the frame so the pistons will not be forced out of their cylinders if the pedal is inadvertently pressed.

3A. To remove the pads from 1998-2001 models:

  a. Remove the pad cover (**Figure 74**) from the caliper.

  b. Remove the clip (**Figure 75**) from the forward pad pin.

  c. Press the spring arm (A, **Figure 76**) into the caliper to release spring tension on the pad pin (B), and pull the pin from the caliper.

  d. Remove the pad spring (**Figure 77**) from each pad.

  e. Remove the clip (A, **Figure 78**) and pull the rear pad pin (B).

  f. Lift the brake pad (**Figure 79**) from each side of the brake disc.

3B. To remove the pads from 2002-on models:

  a. Remove the screws (A, **Figure 80**), and lift the pad spring (B) from the caliper.

  b. Remove the pad pin (C, **Figure 80**).

  c. Remove the outboard brake pad (**Figure 81**) and the inboard pad (**Figure 82**).

  d. Remove the pad shim (A, **Figure 83**) and damper shim (B) from the back of each pad (C).

4. Inspect the brake pads (1998-2001 models: **Figure 84**, 2002-on models: **Figure 85**) and pad spring (2002-on models: **Figure 86**). Refer to *Brake Pad Inspection* in this chapter.

5. When new pads are installed in the calipers, the fluid level rises in the rear master cylinder reservoir. Remove the brake fluid from the reservoir and reposition the caliper pistons by as follows:

  a. Clean the top of the master cylinder reservoir.

  b. Remove the top cover, plate, and diaphragm.

  c. Use a syringe to remove approximately half of the fluid from the reservoir.

  d. Temporarily install one of the old brake pads into the caliper and seat it against the piston(s).

  e. Press the pad against the piston(s), and slowly push the caliper piston all the way into the caliper. Constantly check the reservoir to make sure brake fluid does not overflow. Remove fluid as necessary.

14

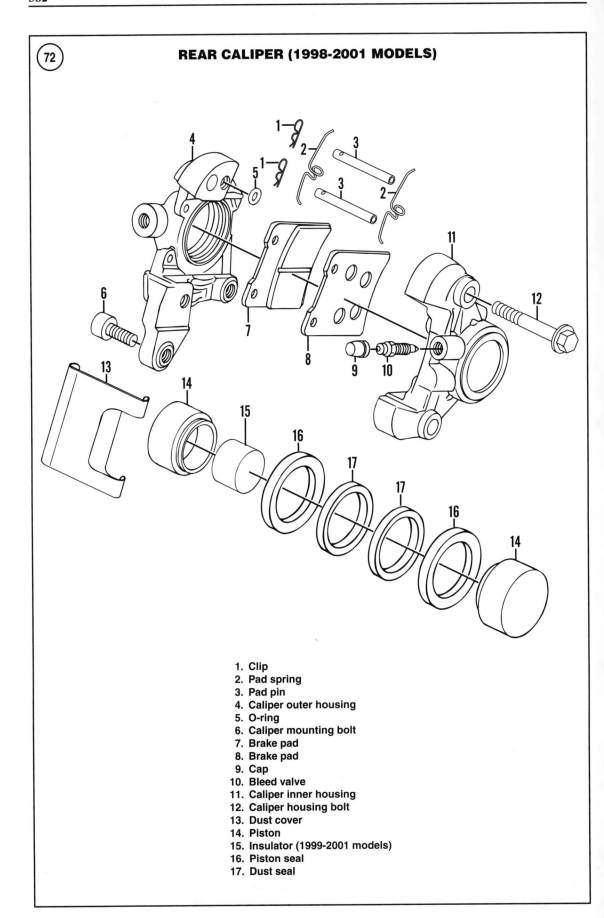

REAR CALIPER (1998-2001 MODELS)

1. Clip
2. Pad spring
3. Pad pin
4. Caliper outer housing
5. O-ring
6. Caliper mounting bolt
7. Brake pad
8. Brake pad
9. Cap
10. Bleed valve
11. Caliper inner housing
12. Caliper housing bolt
13. Dust cover
14. Piston
15. Insulator (1999-2001 models)
16. Piston seal
17. Dust seal

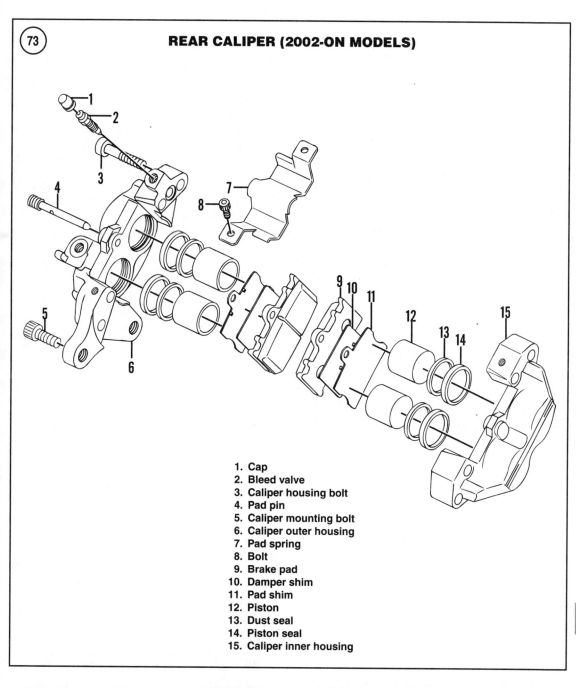

REAR CALIPER (2002-ON MODELS)

1. Cap
2. Bleed valve
3. Caliper housing bolt
4. Pad pin
5. Caliper mounting bolt
6. Caliper outer housing
7. Pad spring
8. Bolt
9. Brake pad
10. Damper shim
11. Pad shim
12. Piston
13. Dust seal
14. Piston seal
15. Caliper inner housing

14

f. The piston(s) should move freely. If not, remove and service the caliper as described in
   this chapter.

g. Remove the old brake pad and repeat this process for the piston(s) on the other side.

6A. To install the pads on 1998-2001 models:

a. Slide the inboard and outboard brake pads
   (**Figure 79**) into the caliper so the pad material
   faces the brake disc.

b. Insert the rear pad pin (B, **Figure 78**) so it
   passes through both brake pads and sits in the
   boss in the inboard side of the caliper.

c. Rotate the pad pin so its clip hole sits vertically
   relative to the caliper, and install the clip (A,
   Figure 78).

d. Install each pad spring (**Figure 87**) so its arm
   fits under the rear pad pin. Make sure the hook
   of each spring engages the brake pad (**Figure
   77**).

e. Install the forward pad pin (B, **Figure 76**).
   Press the arm of each pad spring (A, **Figure
   76**) into the caliper as necessary to ease pin installation.

f. Install the clip (**Figure 75**) into the forward
   pad pin so the clip sits between the caliper and
   the outboard brake pad.

6B. To install the pads on 2002-on models:

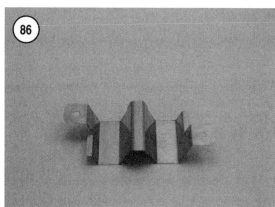

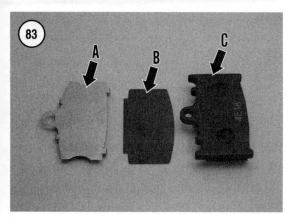

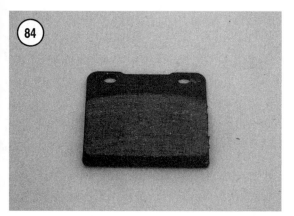

14

a. Install the damper shim (B, **Figure 83**), and then the pad shim (A) onto the back of each pad (C). Make sure the fingers of the pad shim grasp the back of the pad (**Figure 88**).

b. Install the inboard brake pad (**Figure 82**) and outboard pad (**Figure 81**) so the pad material faces the brake disc.

c. Install the pad pin (C, **Figure 80**) so it passes through both pads and sits in the boss on the inboard housing half. Tighten the pad pin to 16 N•m (12 ft.-lb.).

d. Install the pad spring (B, **Figure 80**), and tighten the screws (A) securely.

Removal

The following procedure shows a 2002-on caliper (**Figure 73**). Except for the number of pistons,
the earlier-model caliper (**Figure 72**) is serviced the
same way as the later caliper. Any procedural differences are noted in the text.

1. Remove the rear cylinder (upper) muffler from
the motorcycle (Chapter Eight).
2. If the caliper will be serviced, perform the following:

    a. Remove the brake pads as described in this
       section.

    b. Slowly press the brake pedal and force the pis-
       tons from their cylinders. Stop before the pis-
       tons contact the brake disc.

    c. Drain the rear brake as described in this chap-
       ter.

    d. Remove the banjo bolt (A, **Figure 89**) and dis-
       connect the brake hose from the caliper. Insert
       the hose end in a plastic bag so brake fluid will
       not leak onto the motorcycle.

    e. Loosen the caliper housing bolts (B, **Figure
       89**) so they can be removed easily.

3. Loosen the rear axle nut (A, **Figure 90**).
4. Remove the nut from the caliper bracket bolt (C,
Figure 89). Pull the bolt, and pivot the caliper bracket upward to expose the caliper mounting bolts (B,
Figure 90).
5. Remove the caliper mounting bolts, and lift the
caliper from the bracket. Note how the caliper mounts
to the inboard side of the caliper bracket.
6. If the caliper will not be serviced, use a bungee
cord or wire to suspend the caliper from the motorcycle.

Installation

1. Fit the brake caliper onto the brake disc. If the
brake pads are installed, be careful so the leading
edges of the pads are not damaged.
2. Rotate the caliper bracket upward, and align the
mounting holes with those in the caliper. Make sure
the caliper sits on the inboard side of the bracket.
3. Install the rear caliper mounting bolts (B, **Figure
90**), and tighten them to 35 N•m (26 ft.-lb.).
4. Lower the rear caliper bracket into place, and install the bracket bolt. (C, **Figure 89**).
5. Turn the nut onto the bracket bolt, and tighten
the rear caliper bracket bolt/nut (C, **Figure 89**) to 60
N•m (44 ft.-lb.).
6. Tighten the rear axle nut (A, **Figure 90**) to 110
N•m (81 ft.-lb.).
7. If the caliper was disassembled, perform the following:

    a. Tighten the rear caliper housing bolts (B,

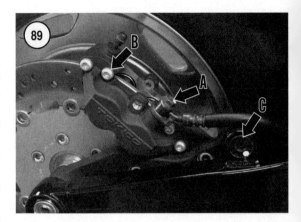

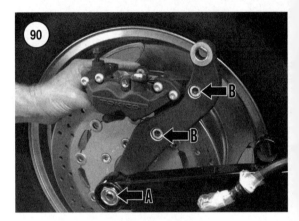

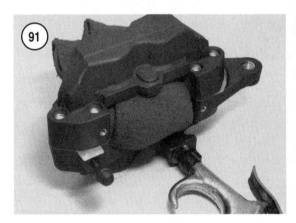

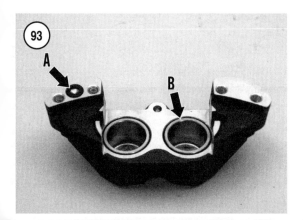

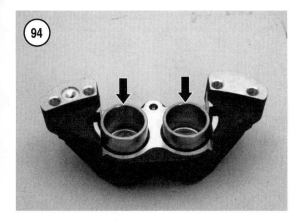

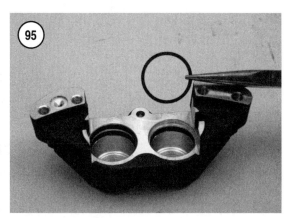

Figure 89) to 33 N•m (24 ft.-lb.) for 1998-2001 models or to 21 N•m (15 ft.-lb.) for 2002-on models.

b. Install the brake pads as described in this section.

c. Fit the brake hose onto the caliper fluid port and install the banjo bolt (A, **Figure 89**). Include a washer on each side of the fitting, and tighten the banjo bolt to 23 N•m (17 ft.-lb.). Make sure the brake hose neck sits against the inboard side of the stop post.

d. Add brake fluid and bleed the brakes as described in this chapter.

8. Install the rear cylinder (upper) muffler as described in Chapter Eight.

Disassembly/Assembly

NOTE
If the pistons were partially forced out of the caliper body during removal, Step 1 and Step 2 may not be necessary. If the pistons or caliper bores are corroded or very dirty; compressed air may be necessary to completely remove the pistons from the body bores.

1. Place a piece of soft wood or a folded shop cloth over the end of the piston(s) and into the caliper body. Turn this assembly over with the piston facing down onto the workbench top.

WARNING
In the next step, the piston may shoot out of the caliper body with considerable force. Keep your hands and fingers out of the way. Wear shop gloves and safety goggles when using compressed air to remove the pistons.

2. Apply air pressure in short bursts to the fluid passageway (**Figure 91**) and force the piston(s) out of the caliper bore.

3. Remove the caliper housing bolts (**Figure 92**), and separate the caliper halves.

4. Remove and discard the fluid port O-ring (A, **Figure 93**). It must be replaced during assembly.

5. Remove the piston(s) (**Figure 94**) from each bore in the caliper half.

6. Repeat Step 5 for the other caliper half.

7. On 1999-2001 models, remove the insulator (15, **Figure 72**).

8. Use a piece of wood or plastic scraper and carefully push the dust seal (**Figure 95**) and piston seal (**Figure 96**) into the caliper cylinder bore and out of their grooves.

14

9. Remove the dust seal and piston seal from each caliper cylinder bore and repeat for the other caliper half.

10. If necessary, remove the bleed valve (A, **Figure 97**) from the caliper half.

11. Inspect the caliper assembly as described in this section.

12. Coat the new seals, pistons, and cylinders with brake fluid.

13. Carefully install the new piston seal (**Figure 96**) into the inner groove in the cylinder bore.

14. Install the new dust seal (**Figure 95**) into the outer groove. Make sure both seals are properly seated in their respective grooves.

15. Repeat Step 14 and Step 15 for each remaining caliper cylinder.

16. Position the piston with the open end facing out. Carefully turn the piston into the cylinder bore (**Figure 94**) so the seals are not damaged. Press the piston into the cylinder until it bottoms (B, **Figure 93**). Repeat for each remaining piston.

17. On 1999-2001 models, install the insulator (15, **Figure 72**).

18. Coat the *new* fluid port O-ring with brake fluid, and install the O-ring (A, **Figure 93**) into the port depression in the inboard caliper half.

19. Set the outboard caliper half onto the inboard half. Make sure the O-ring is still in place.

20. Install the rear caliper housing bolts (**Figure 92**). Tighten the rear caliper housing bolts to 33 N•m (24 ft.-lb.) for 1998-2001 models or to 21 N•m (15 ft.-lb.) for 2002-on models.

21. If removed, install the bleed valve (A, **Figure 97**). Tighten it to 7.5 N•m (66 in.-lb.).

22. Install the caliper and brake pads as described in this section.

23. Bleed the brakes (this chapter).

Inspection

When inspecting brake components, compare any measurements to the specifications in **Table 1** or **Table 2**. Replace worn, damaged or out of specification parts.

1. Clean both caliper body halves and the pistons. Dry the parts with compressed air.

2. Inspect the fluid passageways in the cylinder bores (A, **Figure 98**) and in the caliper bodies (B, **Figure 98**; A and B, **Figure 97**). Apply compressed air to the openings to make sure they are clear. Clean them with an aerosol brake cleaner if necessary.

3. Inspect the piston and dust seal grooves in the cylinder bores (C, **Figure 98**) for damage or corrosion.

4. Inspect the threads in the bolt holes and fluid ports of the caliper halves. If worn or damaged, dress the threads with a tap or replace the caliper assembly.

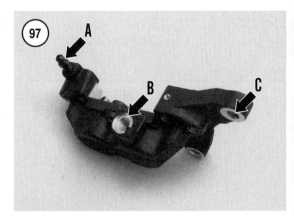

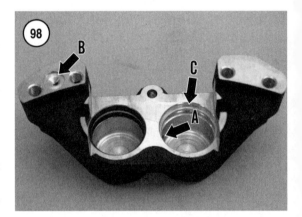

5. Inspect the bleed valve (A, **Figure 97**) and banjo bolt. Apply compressed air to the openings and make sure each is clear. Clean either part with brake cleaner if necessary.

6. Inspect both caliper halves for damage. Check the threads of the caliper mounting holes (C, **Figure 97**) for wear or damage. Clean the threads with a tap or replace the caliper assembly.

7. Inspect the walls of each cylinder (A, **Figure 98**) and the pistons (**Figure 99**) for scratches, scoring or other damage.

8. Measure the inside diameter of each cylinder bore (**Figure 100**).

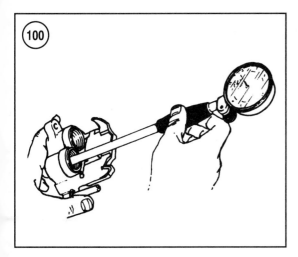

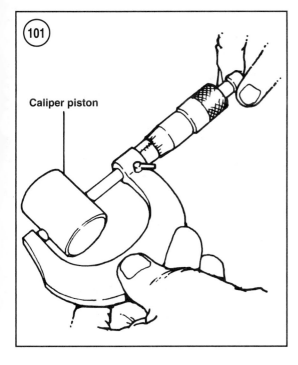

Caliper piston

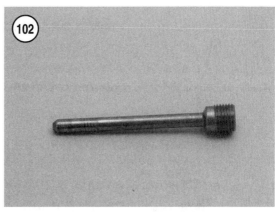

9. Measure the outside diameter of the each piston (**Figure 101**).

10. Inspect the pad pin(s) (**Figure 102**) for corrosion or other damage that would impede the movement of the pads. Remove minor corrosion with fine emery cloth.

REAR BRAKE MASTER CYLINDER

Refer to *Brake Service* in this chapter. Refer to **Figure 103**.

Removal

1. Securely support the motorcycle on a level surface.

2. Drain the brake fluid from the rear brake as described in this chapter.

3. Remove the brake hose banjo bolt (**Figure 104**), and separate the brake hose from the port on the master cylinder. Discard the sealing washer from each side of the brake hose fitting. Be prepared to catch residual brake fluid that leaks from the brake hose.

4. Insert the brake hose end into a plastic bag. Seal the bag around the hose with a rubber band.

5. Remove the cotter pin (A, **Figure 105**) and washer (B) from the end of the clevis pin.

6. Withdraw the clevis pin (A, **Figure 106**) from the pushrod clevis (B).

7. Remove the hose cover bolt (**Figure 107**) and the reservoir bolt (**Figure 108**). Remove the hose cover.

8. Remove the master cylinder mounting bolts (**Figure 109**), and lift the master cylinder and reservoir assembly from the motorcycle.

Installation

1. Correctly position the rear master cylinder onto the inboard side of its mount (**Figure 109**). Make sure the push rod clevis (B, **Figure 106**) engages the brake pedal boss.

2. Install the master cylinder mounting bolts (**Figure 109**). Tighten them to 10 N•m (89 in.-lb.).

3. Set the reservoir into place so it indexing knob engages its hole in the frame.

4. Fit the hose cover in place. Install the reservoir bolt (**Figure 108**) and the hose cover bolt (**Figure 107**). Tighten each bolt securely.

5. Route the brake hose along the path noted during removal.

6. Install the brake hose onto the master cylinder. Fit a new sealing washer onto each side of the brake hose fitting, and turn in the banjo bolt (**Figure 104**). Tighten the banjo bolt to 23 N•m (17 ft.-lb.).

7. Align the pushrod clevis (B, **Figure 106**) with the hole in the brake pedal boss, and install the clevis pin (A) through both parts.

8. Slip the washer (B, **Figure 105**) over the end of the clevis pin, and install a *new* cotter pin (A).

14

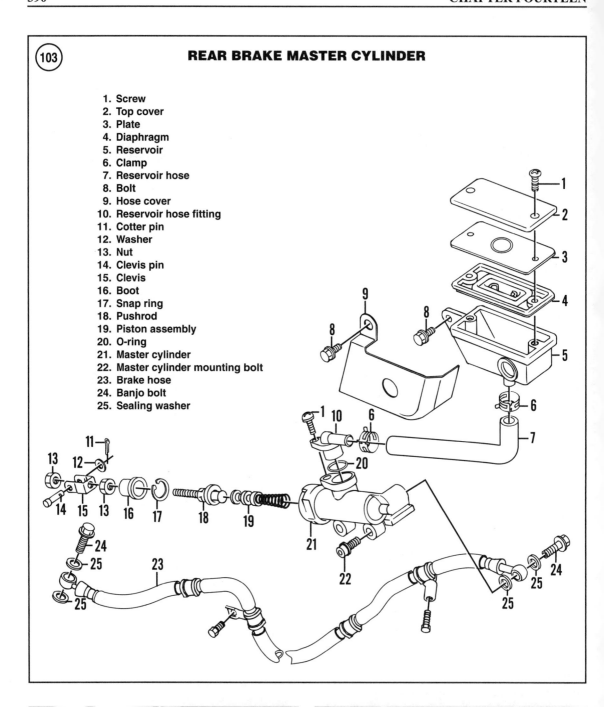

REAR BRAKE MASTER CYLINDER

103

1. Screw
2. Top cover
3. Plate
4. Diaphragm
5. Reservoir
6. Clamp
7. Reservoir hose
8. Bolt
9. Hose cover
10. Reservoir hose fitting
11. Cotter pin
12. Washer
13. Nut
14. Clevis pin
15. Clevis
16. Boot
17. Snap ring
18. Pushrod
19. Piston assembly
20. O-ring
21. Master cylinder
22. Master cylinder mounting bolt
23. Brake hose
24. Banjo bolt
25. Sealing washer

104

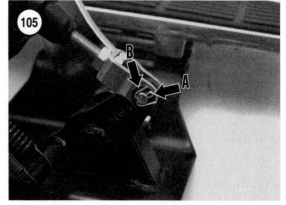

105

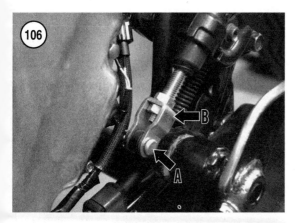

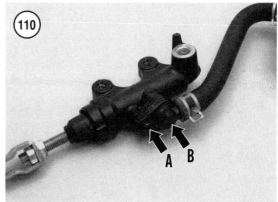

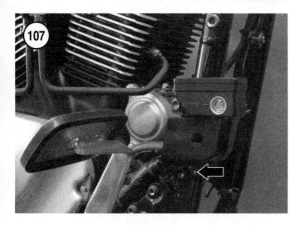

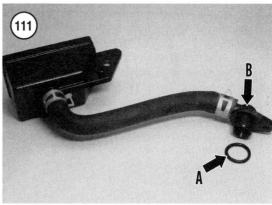

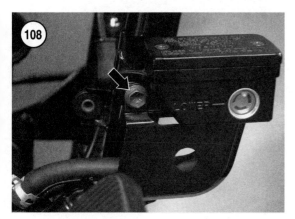

9. Add brake fluid to the reservoir, and bleed the rear brake as described in this chapter.

10. Install the diaphragm, diaphragm plate and cover onto the reservoir.

Disassembly

1. Remove the screw (A, **Figure 110**) and separate the reservoir hose fitting (B) from the port on the master cylinder. Discard the O-ring (A, **Figure 111**).

2. Remove the top cover (**Figure 112**), plate and diaphragm from the fluid reservoir. Pour out any residual brake fluid and discard it.

14

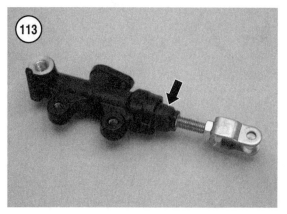

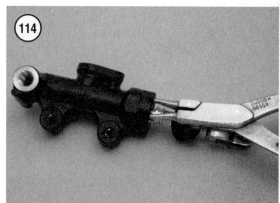

3. Roll the rubber boot (**Figure 113**) down the push-rod.

4. Using snap ring pliers to remove the pushrod snap ring from the master cylinder body (**Figure 114**).

5. Pull the pushrod assembly (**Figure 115**) and the piston assembly (**Figure 116**) from the master cylinder.

6. If necessary, loosen the clevis locknut (A, **Figure 117**), and remove the clevis (B) and adjuster nut (C) from the pushrod.

Assembly

1. If removed, install the clevis (B, **Figure 117**) and adjuster nut (C) onto the pushrod.

2. Soak the new piston assembly in brake fluid to make the cups (A, **Figure 118**) pliable.

3. Coat the inside of the cylinder bore with brake fluid.

4. If necessary, install the tapered end of the spring (B, **Figure 118**) onto the piston.

> *WARNING*
> *When installing the piston assembly, do not allow the cups to turn inside out. They will be damaged and allow brake fluid leaks within the cylinder bore.*

5. Insert the piston assembly (**Figure 116**) into the cylinder bore. Press the assembly into the cylinder until it bottoms.

6. Install the pushrod assembly (**Figure 115**) so the push rod engages the end of the piston, and press the pushrod assembly all the way into the cylinder.

7. Hold the pushrod assembly in this position, and install the snap ring (**Figure 114**). Make sure the snap ring is correctly seated in its groove.

8. Roll the rubber boot (**Figure 113**) into the body so it is completely seated in the master cylinder.

9. Install a new O-ring (A, **Figure 111**) into the hose port on the master cylinder body. Apply a light coat of brake fluid to the O-ring.

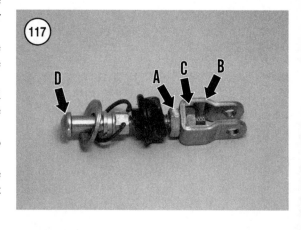

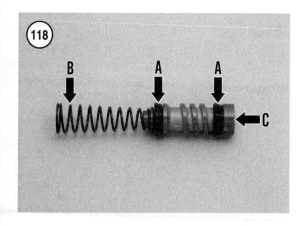

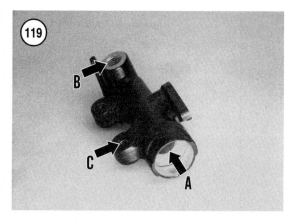

10. Install the reservoir hose fitting (B, **Figure 110**) onto the master cylinder. Secure the fitting in place with the mounting screw (A, **Figure 110**). Tighten the screw securely.

11. Install the master cylinder as described in this chapter.

12. Adjust the brake pedal height (Chapter Three).

Inspection

During inspection, compare any measurements to the specifications in **Table 1** and **Table 2**. Replace worn, damaged or out of specification parts.

1. Clean all hydraulic brake parts in brake fluid. Use an aerosol brake parts cleaner on other components.

2. Inspect the cylinder bore surface (A, **Figure 119**). If it is less than perfect, replace the master cylinder assembly. The body cannot be replaced separately.

3. Make sure all fluid passages (**Figure 120**) in the master cylinder body are clear. Clean them if necessary.

4. Measure the cylinder bore (A, **Figure 119**).

5. Measure the outside diameter of the piston (**Figure 121**).

6. Check the entire master cylinder body for wear or damage. If damaged in any way, replace the master cylinder assembly.

7. Inspect the piston cups (A, **Figure 118**) for wear and damage. If less than perfect, replace the piston assembly. The cups cannot be replaced separately.

8. Check the end of the piston (C, **Figure 118**) for wear caused by the pushrod.

9. Inspect the pushrod assembly (**Figure 117**) for wear or damage. Pay particular attention to the push rod end (D, **Figure 117**) and the boot.

10. Inspect the banjo bolt threads (B, **Figure 119**) and the mounting bolt threads (C) in the master cylinder. If damaged, clean the threads with a tap or replace the master cylinder.

11. Check the reservoir hose fitting (B, **Figure 111**) for damage.

12. Inspect the reservoir, top cover, plate and diaphragm for wear or damage.

13. Inspect the brake hose and reservoir hose for wear or deterioration.

BRAKE HOSE REPLACEMENT

Refer to *Brake Service* in this chapter.

Front Brakes Hose(s)

Refer to **Figure 122**.

1. Drain the front brakes as described in this chapter.

14

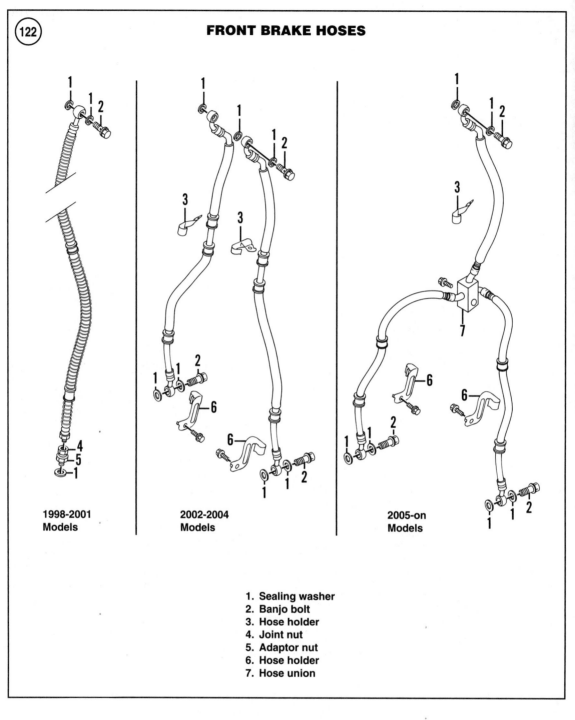

(122) FRONT BRAKE HOSES

1998-2001
Models

2002-2004
Models

2005-on
Models

1. Sealing washer
2. Banjo bolt
3. Hose holder
4. Joint nut
5. Adaptor nut
6. Hose holder
7. Hose union

2. Note how the hose(s) are routed from the master cylinder, through the steering head, and along the fork legs. The hose(s) must be rerouted along the same path.

3. Release the brake hose(s) from the holder(s) (**Figure 123**) on the fender.

CAUTION
The upper fork cover on 1998-2004 models can be removed by sliding the cover down the fork legs. However, this

*will most likely scratch the lower fork covers (**Figure 124**). Removing the upper fork cover from the top of the fork legs is highly recommended.*

4. On 1998-2004 models, remove the upper fork cover by performing the following:
   a. Remove the handlebar (Chapter Twelve) and lay it on the meter cover.
   b. Remove the headlight and headlight housing (Chapter Ten).

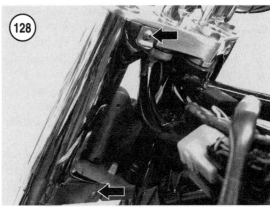

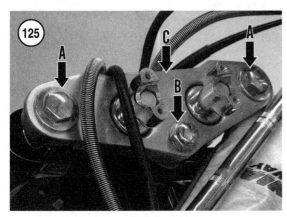

14

c. Remove the cap bolt (A, **Figure 125**) from each fork leg.

d. Remove the steering head nut (B, **Figure 125**) and its washer. Remove the upper fork bridge (C, **Figure 125**) from the steering stem and fork tubes.

e. Note how the cables and wires are routed behind the upper fork cover (**Figure 126**).

f. Remove the upper fork cover bolts (front: **Figure 127**; rear: **Figure 128**), and slide the upper fork cover up and off the fork legs.

g. Release the brake hose(s) from the holder(s) (**Figure 129**) in the lower fork bridge.

5A. On 1998-2001 models, perform the following:

    a. Hold the brake hose fitting (A, **Figure 130**), and loosen the joint nut (B). Disconnect the brake hose from the caliper.

    b. Insert the hose end into a plastic bag so brake fluid will not leak onto the motorcycle.

5B. On 2002-2004 models, perform the following:

    a. Remove the banjo bolt (**Figure 131**) and disconnect the brake hose from the caliper. Watch for the two sealing washers, one on each side of the brake hose fitting. Insert the hose end into a plastic bag. Seal the bag with a rubber band so brake fluid will not leal onto the motorcycle.

    b. Repeat for the other caliper.

5C. On 2005-on models, perform the following:

    a. Remove the screws and lower the cable holder (**Figure 132**) from the lower fork bridge.

    b. Remove the banjo bolt (**Figure 131**) and disconnect the brake hose from the caliper. Watch for the two sealing washers, one on each side of the brake hose fitting. Insert the hose end into a plastic bag.

    c. Repeat for the other caliper.

    d. Remove the mounting screw (**Figure 133**) and separate the brake hose union from the bracket on the lower fork bridge.

6A. On 1998-2001 models and on 2005-on models, remove the banjo bolt (**Figure 134**) and disconnect the brake hose from the master cylinder. Watch for the two sealing washers, one on each side of the hose fitting.

6B. On 2002-2004 models, remove the banjo bolt and separate the two hoses from the master cylinder. Watch for the three sealing washers. Refer to **Figure 122**.

7. Secure the hose end(s) in a plastic bag and remove them from the motorcycle.

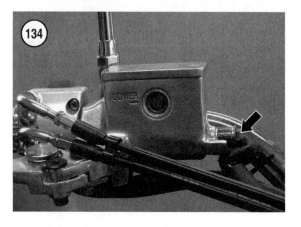

8. Installation is the reverse of removal. Note the following:

    a. Route the new hose(s) along the paths noted during removal.

    b. Install new sealable washers.

    c. Tighten each banjo bolt (**Figure 134**) to 23 N•m (17 ft.-lb.).

    d. Tighten the joint nut (B, **Figure 130**) to 15 N•m (11 ft.-lb.).

    e. Tighten the adaptor nut (C, **Figure 130**) to 23 N•m (17 ft.-lb.).

Rear Brake Hose

Refer to **Figure 103**.

NOTE
Refer to the rear master cylinder removal/installation procedure when replacing a reservoir hose.

1. Note how the brake hose travels rearward from the master cylinder, along the frame member and over the swing arm. The new hose must be rerouted along the same path.

2. Drain the brake fluid as described in this chapter.

3. Remove the banjo bolt (**Figure 135**), and disconnect the brake hose from the rear master cylinder. Be prepared to catch residual brake fluid that leaks from the brake hose. Insert the hose end into a plastic bag, and seal the bag with a rubber band. Remove and discard the sealing washer installed on each side of the hose fitting.

4. Remove the banjo bolt (**Figure 136**) and disconnect the brake hose from the rear caliper. Take the precautions mentioned in Step 3 so brake fluid does not leak onto the motorcycle.

5. Remove the holders that secure the brake hose to the frame (A, **Figure 137** and **Figure 138**) and swing arm.

6. Carefully pull the rear the brake hose from the motorcycle.

7. Install the new hose by reversing the removal procedures. Note the following:

    a. Route the brake hose along the path noted during removal.

    b. Install new sealing washers on each side of the brake hose fittings.

    c. Tighten the banjo bolts to 23 N•m (17 ft.-lb.).

    d. Install the holders securing the brake hose to the frame and swing arm.

    e. Refill the master cylinder reservoir and bleed the rear brake system as described in this chapter.

14

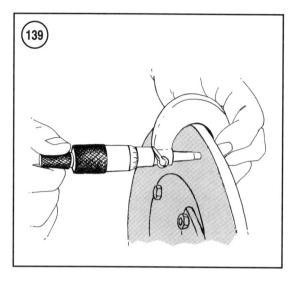

BRAKE DISC

The brake discs are independent of the wheel hubs and can be removed once the wheel is off the motorcycle.

Inspection

Refer to **Table 1** and **Table 2** for standard and service limit brake disc specifications. The minimum (MIN) thickness is stamped on the disc face. If the specification stamped on the disc differs from the service limit in the table, use to the specification stamped on the disc.

The discs cannot be machined to remove imperfections or wear grooves.

1. Measure the thickness of the disc at several locations around the disc (**Figure 139**). Replace the disc if the thickness in any area is less than the service limit.

2. Make sure the disc mounting bolts are tight.

NOTE
When checking the front disc, turn the handlebar all the way to one side, and then to the other side.

3. Slowly rotate the wheel and measure the disc runout with a dial indicator (**Figure 140**). If runout is excessive, and the mounting bolts are tight, inspect the wheel bearings, and examine the surface of the brake disc. If these are in good condition, replace the brake disc.

4. Clean any rust or corrosion from the disc, and wipe it clean with brake parts cleaner. Never use a solvent that may leave an oily residue on the disc.

5. Inspect the floating disc fasteners (A, **Figure 141**) between the outer and the inner rings of the discs. If damaged, replace the disc.

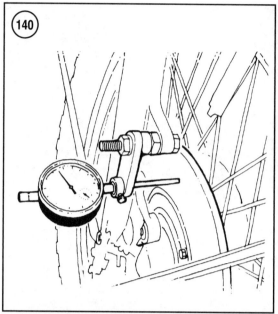

Removal/Installation

1. Remove the front or rear wheel as described in Chapter Eleven.

CAUTION
Do not set the wheel down on the disc surface, as it may get scratched or warped. Set the wheel on two wooden blocks.

NOTE
Insert a piece of wood or vinyl tube between the pads in the caliper(s). This way, if the brake lever or pedal is inadvertently applied, the pistons will not be forced out of the cylinders. If they are, the caliper might have to be disassembled to reseat the pistons and the system will have to be bled.

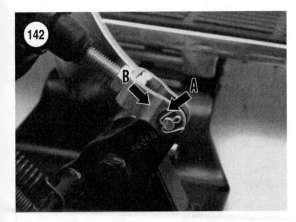

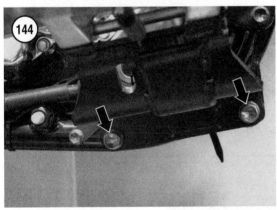

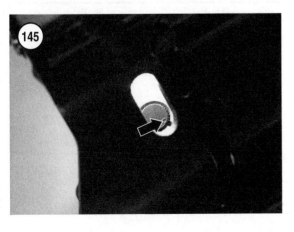

2. Remove the brake disc bolts (B, **Figure 141**), and remove the disc from the hub.

3. Install by reversing these removal steps while noting the following:

    a. Position the disc so its direction arrow points in the direction of forward wheel rotation.

    b. Apply Suzuki Thread Lock Super 1360 to the threads of the disc bolts.

    c. Tighten the brake disc bolts to 23 N•m (17 ft.-lb.).

BRAKE PEDAL/FOOTREST

Removal/Installation

1. Disconnect the pushrod clevis from the pedal by performing the following:

    a. Remove the cotter pin (A, **Figure 142**) and the washer (B) from the end of the clevis pin.

    b. Remove the clevis pin (B, **Figure 137**) from the pushrod clevis (C).

2. Disconnect the brake light spring (A, **Figure 143**) and the return spring (B) from the post on the brake pedal.

3. Remove the front footrest bolts (**Figure 144**) and lower the brake pedal/footrest assembly from the motorcycle.

> *NOTE*
> *The brake pedal can be removed while the pedal/footrest is installed on the motorcycle.*

4. If necessary, remove the brake pedal by performing the following:

    a. Note that the index dot (**Figure 145**) on the pivot shaft aligns with the gap in the brake pedal clamp.

    b. Loosen the brake pedal clamp bolt (D, **Figure 137**).

    c. Slide the pedal from the pivot shaft.

5. Install the assembly by reversing the removal procedure. Note the following:

    a. If removed, install the brake pedal onto the pivot shaft so the index dot (**Figure 145**) aligns with the gap on the brake pedal clamp.

    b. Tighten the brake pedal bolt to 16 N•m (12 ft.-lb.).

    c. Tighten the front footrest bolts (**Figure 144**) to 50 N•m (37 ft.-lb.).

    d. Adjust the brake pedal height as described in Chapter Three.

14

Table 1 BRAKE SPECIFICATIONS (1998-2001 MODELS)

Item	Standard mm (in.)	Service limit mm (in.)
Brake fluid	DOT 4	–
Brake disc runout	–	0.30 (0.12)
Brake disc thickness		
Front	5.8-6.2 (0.228-0.244)	5.5 (.217)
Rear	6.6-7.0 (0.260-0.276)	6.2 (.244)
Front master cylinder		
Cylinder bore	12.700-12.743 (0.5000-0.5017)	–
Piston diameter	12.657-12.684 (0.4983-0.4994)	–
Front brake caliper		
Cylinder bore	45.000-45.076 (1.7717-1.7746)	–
Piston diameter	44.930-44.980 (1.7689-1.7709)	
Rear master cylinder		
Cylinder bore	12.700-12.743 (0.5000-0.5017)	–
Piston diameter	12.657-12.684 (0.4983-0.4994)	–
Rear brake caliper		
Cylinder bore	42.850-42.926 (1.6870-1.6900)	–
Piston diameter	42.770-42.820 (1.6839-1.6858)	–
Brake pedal height	98 (3.86)	–

Table 2 BRAKE SPECIFICATIONS (2002-ON MODELS)

Item	Standard mm (in.)	Service limit mm (in.)
Brake fluid	DOT 4	–
Brake disc runout	–	0.30 (0.12)
Brake disc thickness		
Front	4.8-5.2 (0.189-0.205)	4.5 (.177)
Rear	6.6-7.0 (0.260-0.276)	6.2 (.244)
Front master cylinder		
Cylinder bore	15.870-15.913 (0.6248-0.6265)	–
Piston diameter	15.827-15.854 (0.6231-0.6242)	–
Front brake caliper		
Cylinder bore	30.230-30.306 (1.1902-1.1931)	–
Piston diameter	30.150-30.200 (1.1870-1.1890)	–
Rear master cylinder		
Cylinder bore	12.700-12.743 (0.5000-0.5017)	–
Piston diameter	12.657-12.684 (0.4983-0.4994)	–
Rear brake caliper		
Cylinder bore	30.230-30.306 (1.1902-1.1931)	–
Piston diameter	30.150-30.200 (1.1870-1.1890)	–
Brake pedal height	98 (3.86)	–

Table 3 BRAKE TORQUE SPECIFICATIONS

Item	N•m	in.-lb.	ft.-lb.
Bleed valve	7.5	66	–
Brake disc bolt	23	–	17
Brake pedal bolt	16	–	12
Brake hose banjo bolt	23	–	17
Front brake hose adapter nut			
1998-2001 models	23	–	17
Front brake hose joint nut			
1998-2001 models	15	–	11
Front caliper housing bolt			
1998-2001 models	33	–	24
2002-on models	35	–	26
Front caliper mounting bolt	35	–	26
Front footrest bolt	50	–	37

(continued)

Table 3 BRAKE TORQUE SPECIFICATIONS (continued)

Item	N•m	in.-lb.	ft.-lb.
Front master cylinder clamp bolt	10	89	–
Rear axle nut	110	–	81
Rear brake pedal bolt	16	–	12
Rear caliper bracket bolt/nut	60	–	44
Rear caliper mounting bolt	35	–	26
Rear caliper housing bolt			
1998-2001 models	33	–	24
2002-on models	21	–	15
Rear caliper pad pin (2002-on models)	16	–	12
Rear master cylinder mounting bolt	10	89	–
Rear master cylinder pushrod locknut	18	–	13

14

CHAPTER FIFTEEN

BODY AND FRAME

This chapter describes the removal and installation of the seats, covers and other body parts.

TRIM CLIPS

Quick release trim clips are used at several locations on the motorcycle. The plastic trim clips deteriorate over time. Installing a worn trim clip can be difficult. The ends may break off or distort so they will not close down enough for insertion into the holes. If necessary, replace trim clips.

To remove a trim clip, push the center pin into the head with a Phillips screwdriver (**Figure 1**). This releases the inner lock so the trim clip can be withdrawn from the body panel.

To install a trim clip, push the center pin outward so it protrudes from the head (**Figure 2**), and insert the clip through the mounting holes. Lock the trim clip in place by pushing the pin into the clip (**Figure 3**) so the pin sits flush with the top of the head.

SEATS

Removal/Installation

1. Securely support the motorcycle on a level surface.

2. Remove the passenger seat bolt (**Figure 4**).
3. Pull the passenger seat rearward until it clears the strap and disengages from the tongue (A, **Figure 5**) on the passenger seat bracket.
4. Remove the bracket screws (B, **Figure 5**). Then remove the passenger seat bracket from the rear fender.
5. Remove the screw (**Figure 6**) from each side of the rider's seat. Then remove the rider's seat from the motorcycle.
6. Installation is the reverse of removal. Note the following:
   a. Set the passenger seat bracket onto the rear fender so the bracket screws (B, **Figure 5**) pass through the passenger seat bracket and through the bracket (**Figure 7**) on the rider's seat.
   b. Install the passenger seat by sliding the seat forward through the strap until the tongue (A, **Figure 5**) on the passenger seat bracket engages the slot in the seat (**Figure 8**).
   c. Tighten all the screws securely.

STEERING HEAD COVER

Removal/Installation

Refer to **Figure 9**.

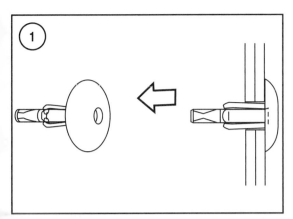

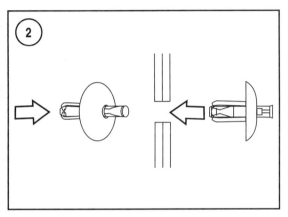

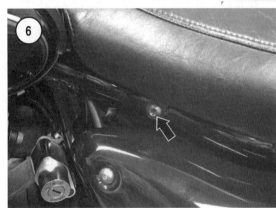

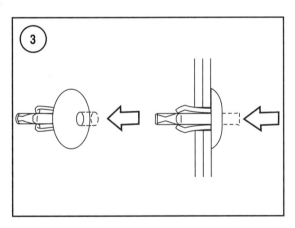

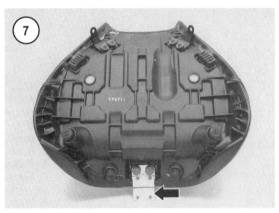

15

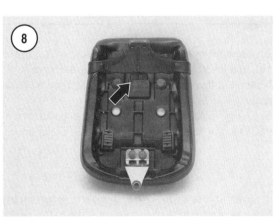

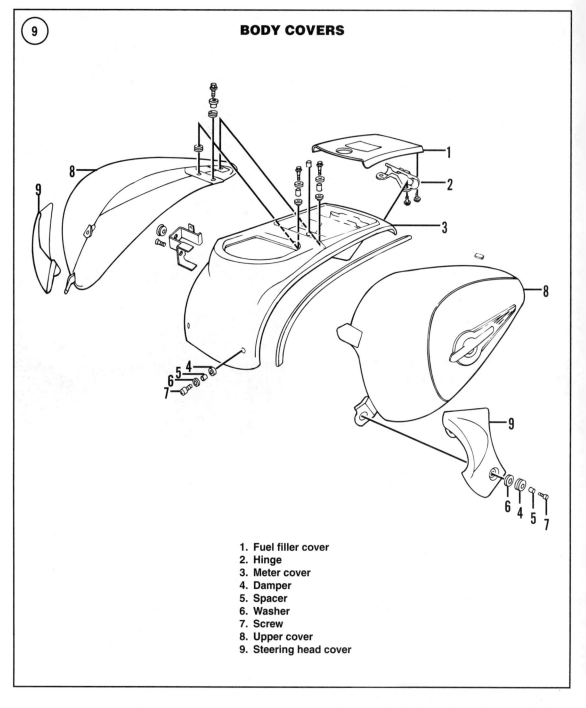

BODY COVERS

9

1. Fuel filler cover
2. Hinge
3. Meter cover
4. Damper
5. Spacer
6. Washer
7. Screw
8. Upper cover
9. Steering head cover

1. Remove the steering head cover screw (A, **Figure 10**), and lower the cover (B) from the steering head. Note the collar, damper and washer installed with the screw.

2. During installation, make sure the cover screw passes through the forward mount in the upper cover.

METER COVER

Several types of fasteners, dampers, spacers, collars and washers are used to secure the meter cover and upper covers. These vary from model to model. To ensure correct reinstallation, keep the hardware together and organized during disassembly. If necessary, photograph or draw the assembly.

Refer to **Figure 9**.

Removal

1. Remove the seats (this chapter).

2. Use the key to open the fuel filler cover (**Figure 11**), and remove the fuel filler cap (**Figure 12**).

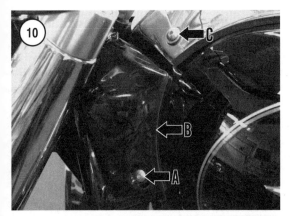

3. Stuff a rag into the filler neck (A, **Figure 13**) so hardware will not fall into the fuel tank.

4. Remove each Phillips screw and its washer (B, **Figure 13**).

5. Remove the rear meter cover bolts (C, **Figure 13**) along with any related hardware.

6. Remove the outer meter cover bolts (**Figure 14**) along with any related hardware.

7. Remove the front screw (C, **Figure 10**) and related hardware from each side of the meter cover.

8. Raise the meter cover, disconnect the harness connector (**Figure 15**) from its mate on the meter assembly, and remove the cover from the motorcycle.

15

Installation

1. Set the meter cover onto the motorcycle. Firmly plug the harness connector (**Figure 15**) into the meter. The motorcycle will not start if this connector does not securely engage the meter assembly.

2. Lower the meter cover into place atop the upper covers.

3. Install the front screw (C, **Figure 10**) onto each side of the meter cover. Make sure the screw passes through the meter cover and the top mount of the upper cover.

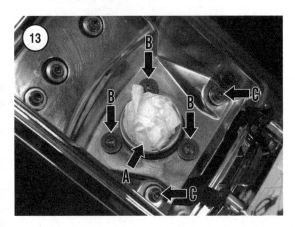

4. Install the outer meter cover bolts (**Figure 14**) along with any hardware noted during removal. Each bolt must pass through the meter cover, through the frame bracket (A, **Figure 16**) and through the tongue on the upper cover.

5. Install the rear meter cover bolts (B, **Figure 13**) along with any hardware noted during removal. Each bolt passes through the meter cover and upper cover.

6. Install each Phillips screw with its washer (A, **Figure 13**). Each screw passes through the meter cover and the filler neck.

7. Install the filler cap (**Figure 12**) and close the fuel filler cover (**Figure 11**).

UPPER COVER

Removal/Installation

Refer to **Figure 9**.

1. Remove the steering head covers and the meter cover (this chapter).

2. Remove the upper cover bolt (B, **Figure 16**) from the frame bracket (A). Note the hardware installed with this bolt.

3. Pull the upper cover outward until its tongue slides out from beneath the frame bracket (A, **Figure 16**), and remove the upper cover.

4. On 2005-on models, remove the mounting bolt, and lower the upper cover damper (**Figure 17**) from the frame.

5. Repeat Steps 2-4 and remove the opposite cover.

6. Installation is the reverse of removal. Note the following:

    a. Fit the upper cover onto the frame so its tongue slides under the frame bracket (A, **Figure 16**).

    b. Install the upper cover bolt(s) (B, **Figure 16**) through the frame bracket (A) and into the weld nut(s) on the upper cover tongue. Tighten securely.

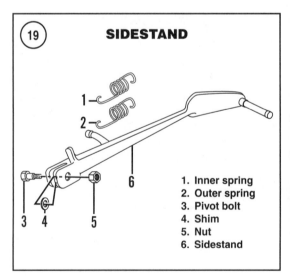

SIDESTAND

1. Inner spring
2. Outer spring
3. Pivot bolt
4. Shim
5. Nut
6. Sidestand

SIDE COVER

Removal/Installation

1. Remove the side cover screws from the side (A, **Figure 18**) and rear of the cover.

2. Remove the side cover (B, **Figure 18**) from the frame.

3. Reverse the removal procedure to install the side cover.

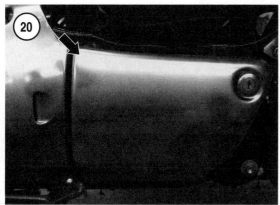

b. Install the pivot bolt from the inboard side.

c. Make sure the shim sits between the frame mount and the sidestand.

TOOL BOX

Removal/Installation

1. Use the key to remove the outer tool box cover (**Figure 20**).

2. Remove the tool box cover (**Figure 21**).

3. Remove the contents from the tool box.

4. Remove the mounting screws (**Figure 22**), and pull the tool box from the frame.

5. Installation is the reverse of removal.

FRONT FENDER

Removal/Installation

1. On 2002-on models, remove the hose holder bolt (A, **Figure 23**) and lift the hose holder from the fender. Note that the tang on each hose holder sits in a hole in the fender. Repeat on the other side. On 1998-2001 models, remove the hose holder from the right side of the fender.

2. Pry the trim caps from the fender bolts, and remove the bolts (B, **Figure 23**).

3. Remove the fender bolts from the other side, and carefully remove the front fender from between the fork legs.

4. Install the front fender by reversing the removal procedures. Make sure the tang on each hose holder engages the hole in the fender.

5. Tighten all fasteners securely.

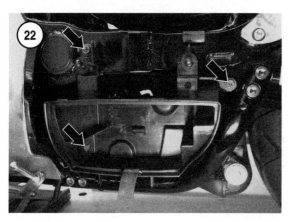

SIDESTAND

Refer to **Figure 19**.

1. Release the inner and outer spring from the post on the sidestand.

2. Remove the nut from the pivot bolt.

3. Remove the pivot bolt and lower the sidestand from its frame mount. Watch for the shim between the frame mount and the sidestand.

4. Installation is the reverse of removal. Note the following:

    a. Set the sidestand in place so the frame mount sits between the arms of the sidestand.

REAR FENDER

Removal/Installation

1. Remove the seats.

15

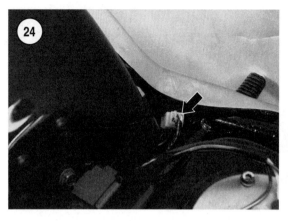

2. Disconnect the 5-pin taillight/rear turn signal connector (**Figure 24**) on the left side of the rear fender.

3. Remove the grab rail from one side by performing the following:

    a. Evenly loosen the 8-mm grab rail bolts (A, **Figure 25**) and the 10-mm grab rail bolts (B).

    b. Remove the bolts and lower the grab rail (C, **Figure 25**) from the fender.

4. Have an assistant support the fender, and move to the opposite side.

5. Remove the 10-mm grab rail bolts (A, **Figure 26**), and remove the fender and grab rail (B) from the motorcycle.

6. If necessary, remove the 8-mm grab rail bolts (C, **Figure 26**), and remove this grab rail from the fender.

7. Reverse the installation procedure to install the fender. Note the following:

    a. Apply Suzuki Thread Lock Super 1303 to threads of the grab rail bolts.

    b. Tighten the 10-mm grab rail bolts to 50 N•m (37 ft.-lb.) and the 8-mm grab rail bolts to 13 N•m (115 in.-lb.).

Table 1 FRAME AND BODY TORQUE SPECIFICATIONS

Item	N•m	in.-lb.	ft.-lb.
Grab rail bolt			
8 mm	13	115	–
10 mm	50	–	37

INDEX

16

16

16

16

1998 VL1500 U.S., CALIFORNIA AND CANADA

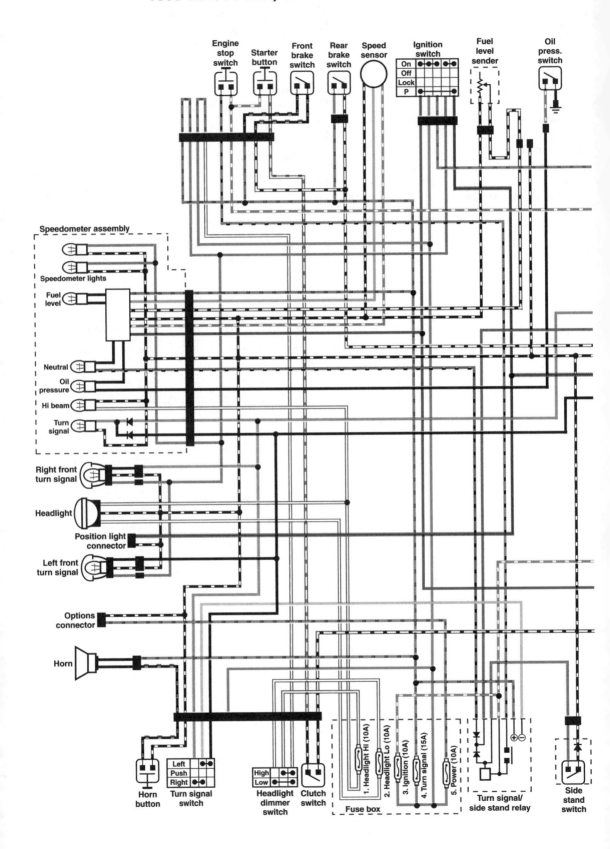

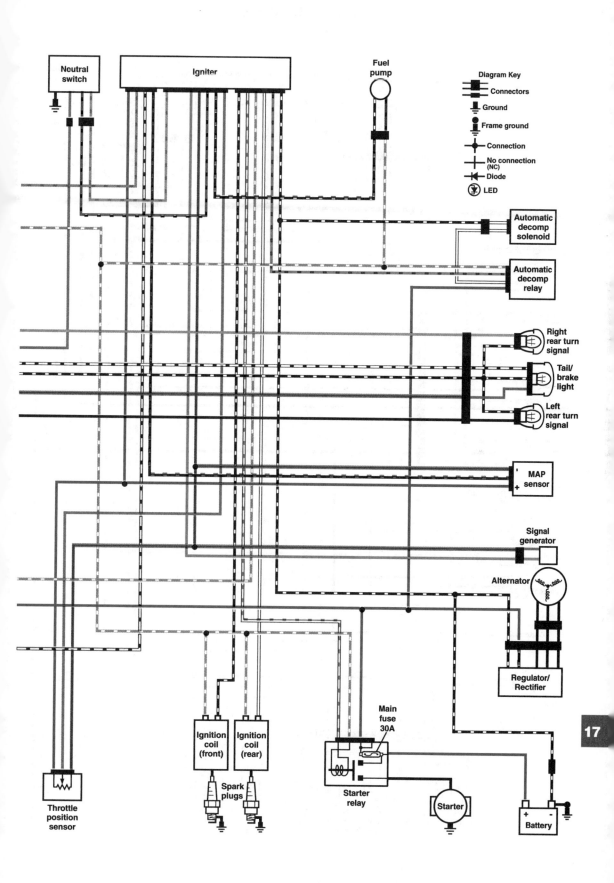

1998 VL1500 U.K. AND EUROPE

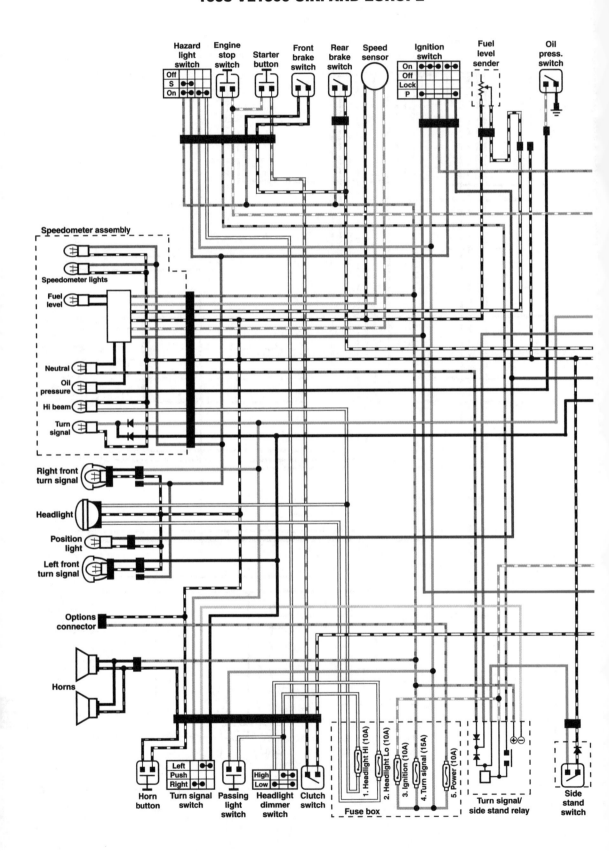

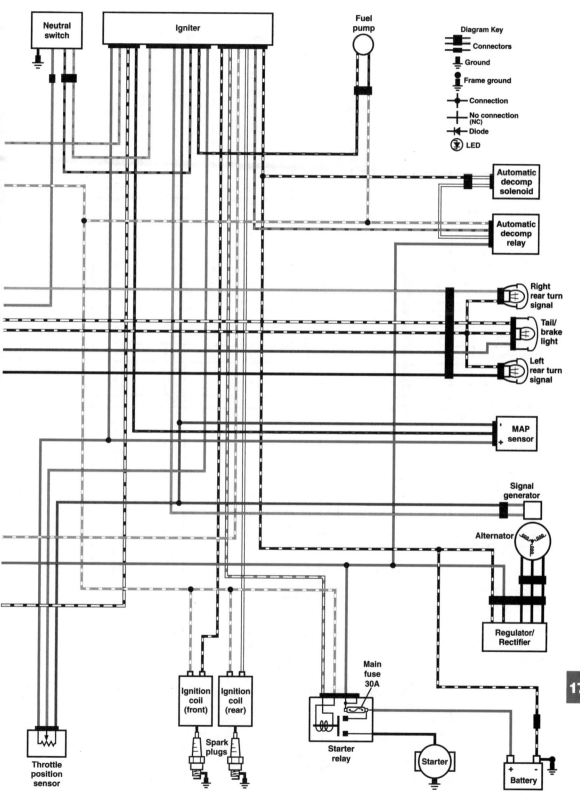

17

1999-2003 VL1500 U.S., CALIFORNIA, CANADA

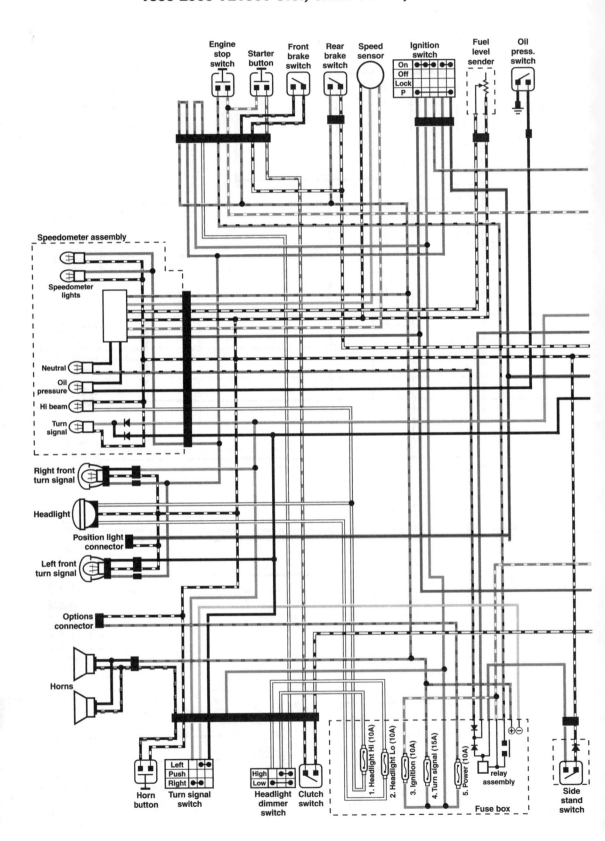

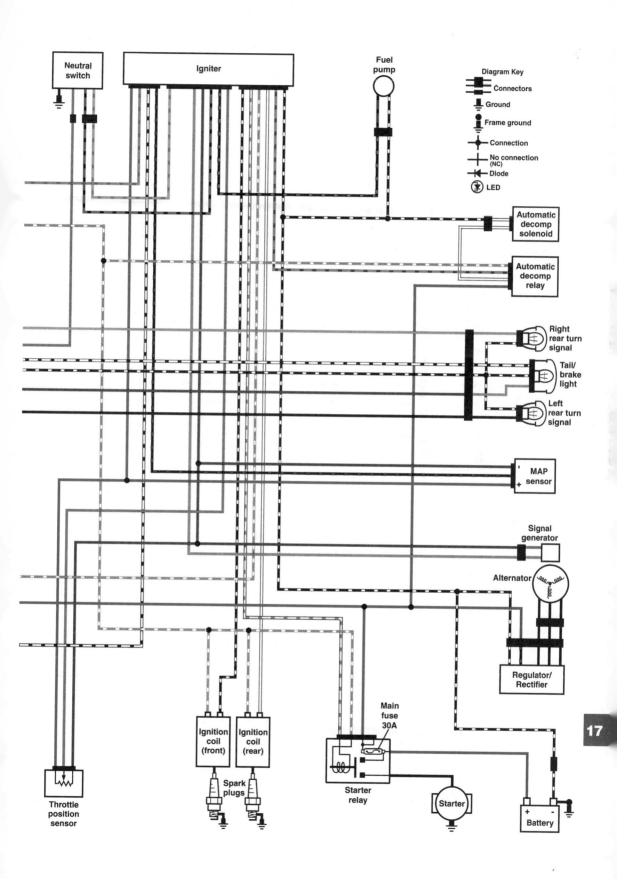

1999-2004 VL1500 U.K., EUROPE AND BRAZIL

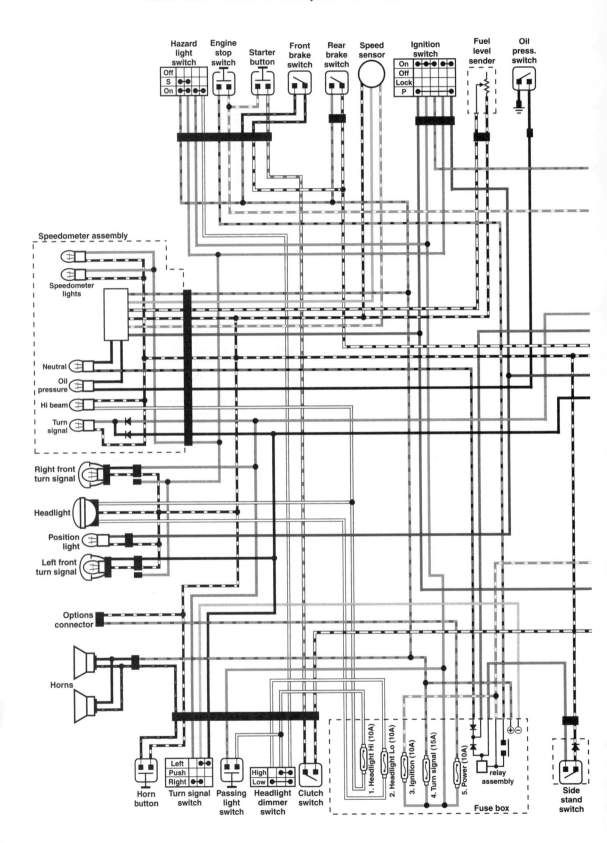

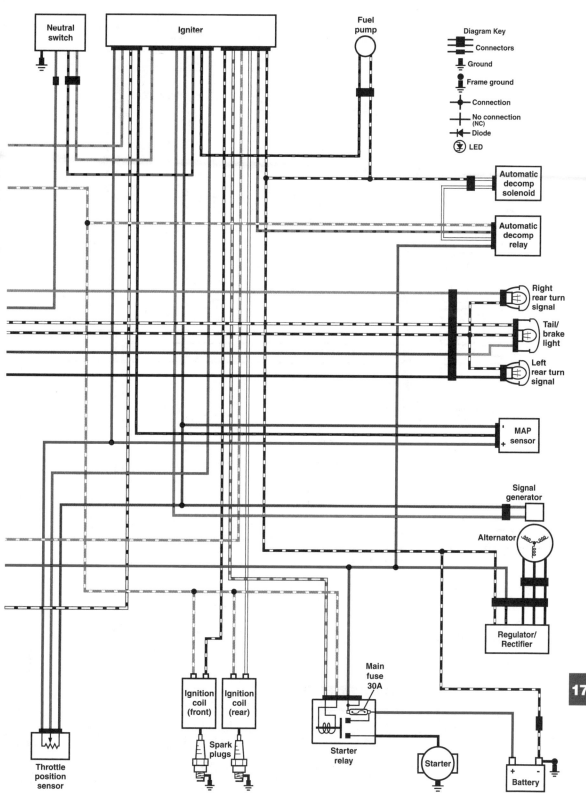

17

2004 VL1500 U.S., CALIFORNIA AND CANADA

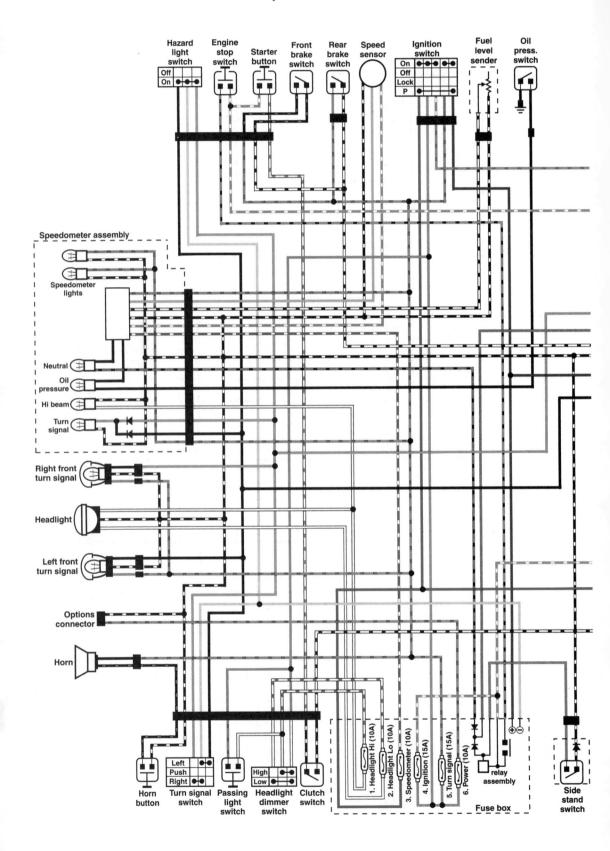

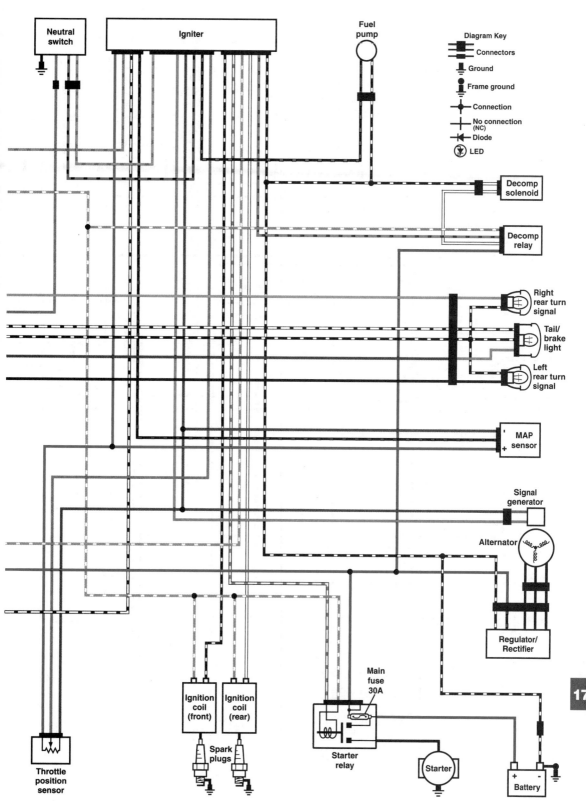

2005-2006 VL1500 (C90) U.S., CALIFORNIA AND CANADA

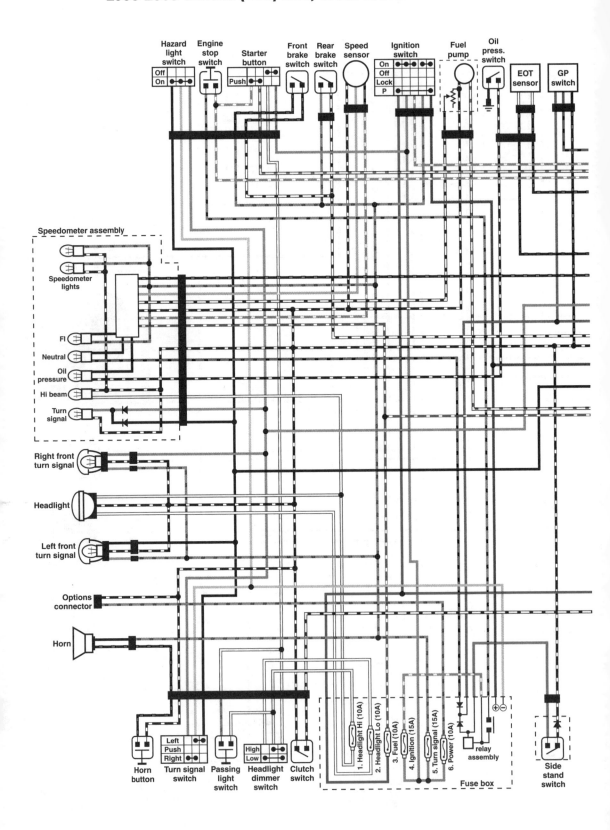

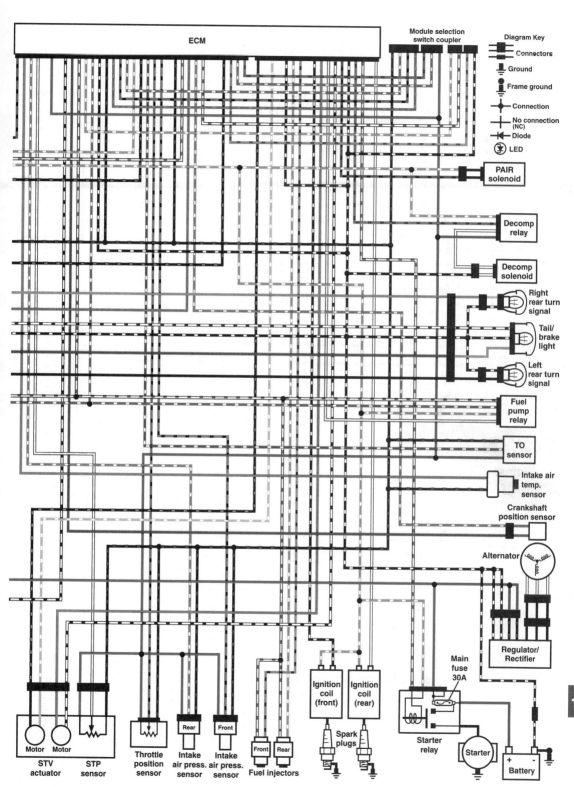

2005-2007 VL1500 (C90) U.K., EUROPE & AUSTRALIA

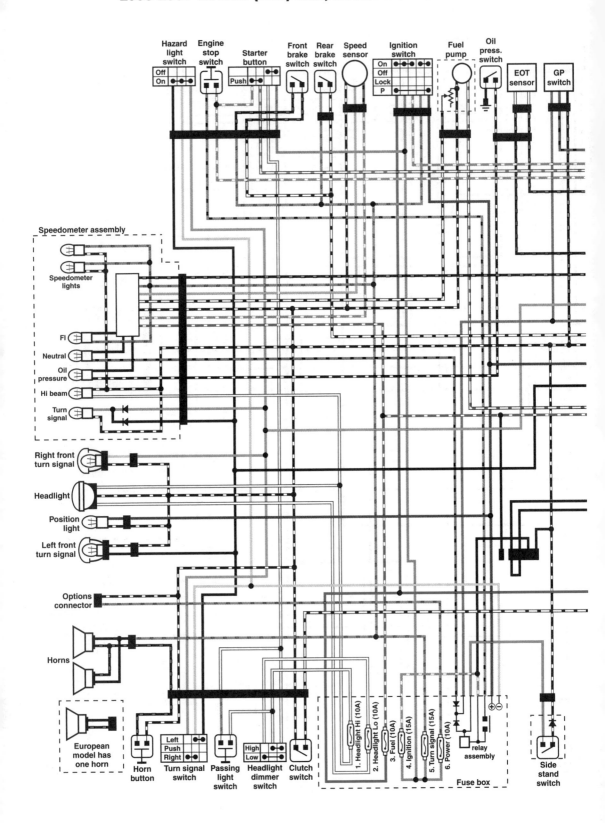

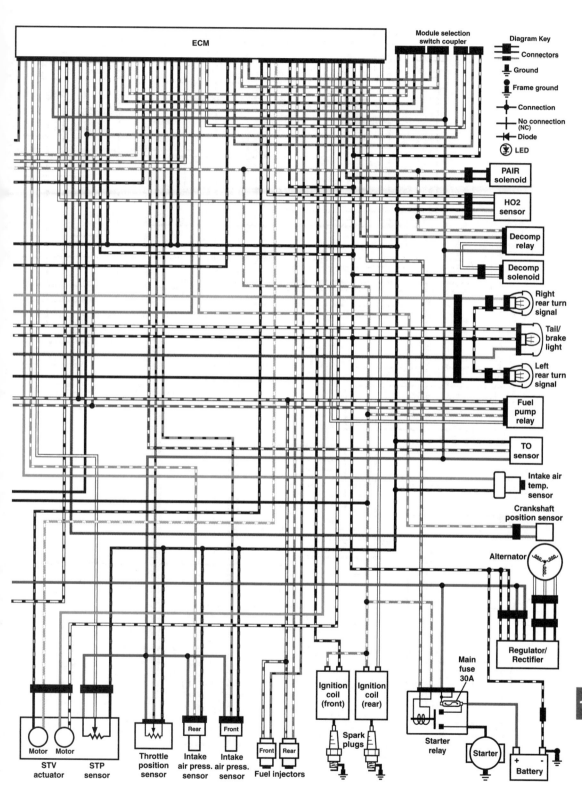

2007-ON VL1500 (C90) U.S., CALIFORNIA AND CANADA

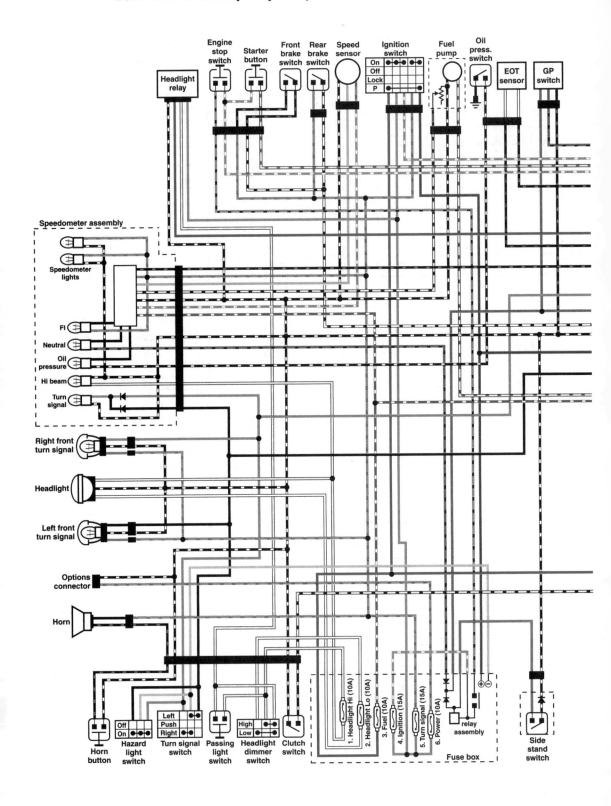

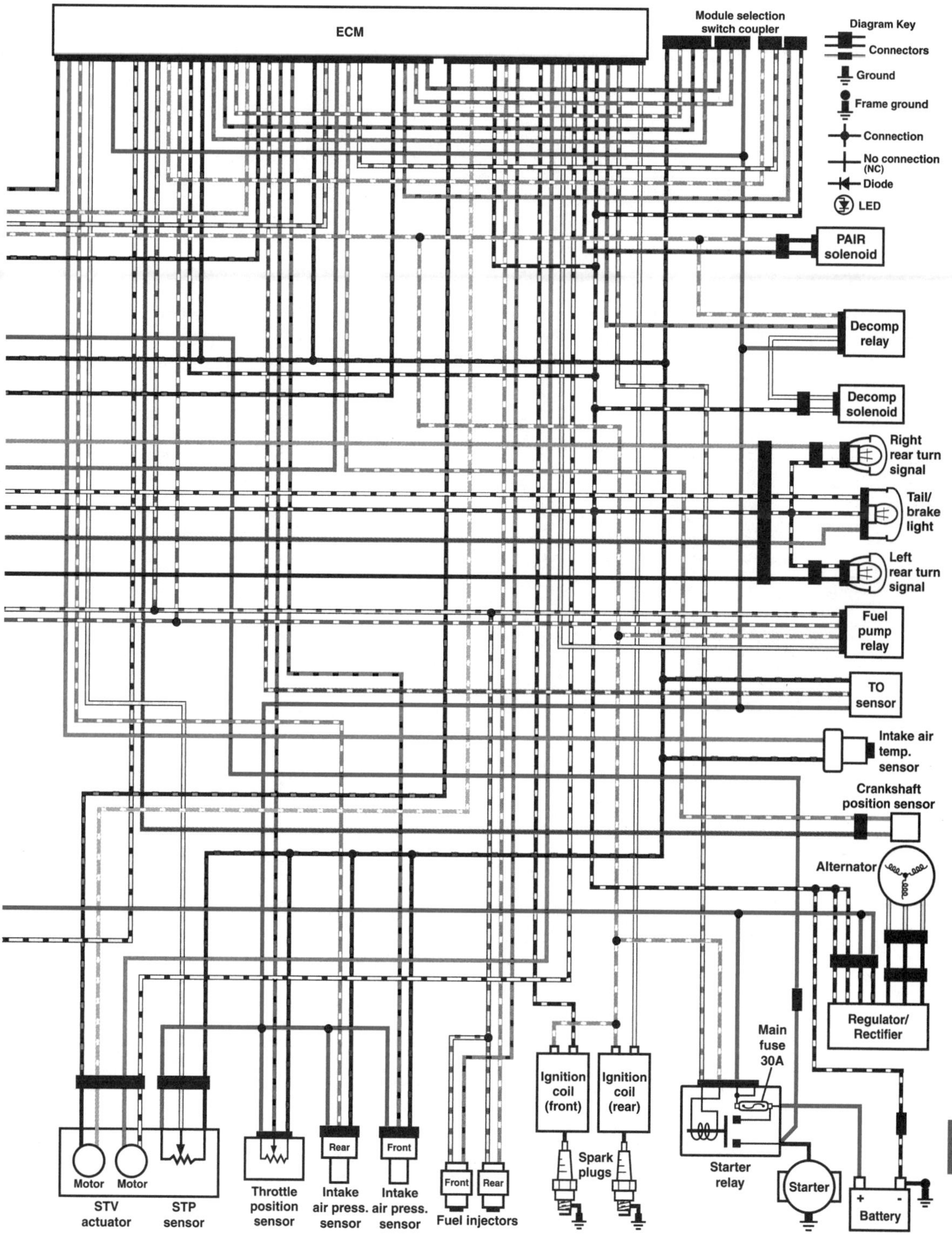

ECM

Module selection switch coupler

Diagram Key

Connectors

Ground

Frame ground

Connection

No connection (NC)

Diode

LED

PAIR solenoid

Decomp relay

Decomp solenoid

Right rear turn signal

Tail/ brake light

Left rear turn signal

Fuel pump relay

TO sensor

Intake air temp. sensor

Crankshaft position sensor

Alternator

Regulator/ Rectifier

Main fuse 30A

Ignition coil (front)

Ignition coil (rear)

Spark plugs

Starter relay

Starter

Battery

Motor Motor

STV actuator

STP sensor

Throttle position sensor

Rear Front

Intake air press. sensor

Intake air press. sensor

Front Rear

Fuel injectors

17

NOTES

NOTES

NOTES

MAINTENANCE LOG

Date	Miles	Type of Service

Check out *clymer.com* for our full line of powersport repair manuals.

BMW

M308	500 & 600cc Twins, 55-69
M502-3	BMW R50/5-R100GS PD, 70-96
M500-3	BMW K-Series, 85-97
M501-2	K1200RS, GT & LT, 98-08
M503-3	R850, R1100, R1150 & R1200C, 93-05
M309	F650, 1994-2000

HARLEY-DAVIDSON

M419	Sportsters, 59-85
M429-5	XL/XLH Sportster, 86-03
M427-2	XL Sportster, 04-09
M418	Panheads, 48-65
M420	Shovelheads,66-84
M421-3	FLS/FXS Evolution,84-99
M423-2	FLS/FXS Twin Cam, 00-05
M250	FLS/FXS/FXC Softail, 06-09
M422-3	FLH/FLT/FXR Evolution, 84-98
M430-4	FLH/FLT Twin Cam, 99-05
M252	FLH/FLT, 06-09
M426	VRSC Series, 02-07
M424-2	FXD Evolution, 91-98
M425-3	FXD Twin Cam, 99-05

HONDA

ATVs

M316	Odyssey FL250, 77-84
M311	ATC, TRX & Fourtrax 70-125, 70-87
M433	Fourtrax 90, 93-00
M326	ATC185 & 200, 80-86
M347	ATC200X & Fourtrax 200SX, 86-88
M455	ATC250 & Fourtrax 200/250, 84-87
M342	ATC250R, 81-84
M348	TRX250R/Fourtrax 250R & ATC250R, 85-89
M456-4	TRX250X 87-92; TRX300EX 93-06
M446-3	TRX250 Recon & Recon ES, 97-07
M215	TRX250EX, 01-05
M346-3	TRX300/Fourtrax 300 & TRX300FW/Fourtrax 4x4, 88-00
M200-2	TRX350 Rancher, 00-06
M459-3	TRX400 Foreman 95-03
M454-4	TRX400EX 99-07
M201	TRX450R & TRX450ER, 04-09
M205	TRX450 Foreman, 98-04
M210	TRX500 Rubicon, 01-04
M206	TRX500 Foreman, 05-11

Singles

M310-13	50-110cc OHC Singles, 65-99
M315	100-350cc OHC, 69-82
M317	125-250cc Elsinore, 73-80
M442	CR60-125R Pro-Link, 81-88
M431-2	CR80R, 89-95, CR125R, 89-91
M435	CR80R &CR80RB, 96-02
M457-2	CR125R, 92-97; CR250R, 92-96
M464	CR125R, 1998-2002
M443	CR250R-500R Pro-Link, 81-87
M432-3	CR250R, 88-91 & CR500R, 88-01
M437	CR250R, 97-01
M352	CRF250R, CRF250X, CRF450R & CRF450X, 02-05
M319-3	XR50R, CRF50F, XR70R & CRF70F, 97-09
M312-14	XL/XR75-100, 75-91
M222	XR80R, CRF80F, XR100R, & CRF100F, 92-09
M318-4	XL/XR/TLR 125-200, 79-03
M328-4	XL/XR250, 78-00; XL/XR350R 83-85; XR200R, 84-85; XR250L, 91-96
M320-2	XR400R, 96-04
M221	XR600R, 91-07; XR650L, 93-07
M339-8	XL/XR 500-600, 79-90
M225	XR650R, 00-07

Twins

M321	125-200cc Twins, 65-78
M322	250-350cc Twins, 64-74
M323	250-360cc Twins, 74-77
M324-5	Twinstar, Rebel 250 & Nighthawk 250, 78-03
M334	400-450cc Twins, 78-87
M333	450 & 500cc Twins, 65-76
M335	CX & GL500/650, 78-83
M344	VT500, 83-88
M313	VT700 & 750, 83-87
M314-3	VT750 Shadow Chain Drive, 98-06
M440	VT1100C Shadow, 85-96
M460-4	VT1100 Series, 95-07
M230	VTX1800 Series, 02-08
M231	VTX1300 Series, 03-09

Fours

M332	CB350-550, SOHC, 71-78
M345	CB550 & 650, 83-85
M336	CB650,79-82
M341	CB750 SOHC, 69-78
M337	CB750 DOHC, 79-82
M436	CB750 Nighthawk, 91-93 & 95-99
M325	CB900, 1000 & 1100, 80-83
M439	600 Hurricane, 87-90
M441-2	CBR600F2 & F3, 91-98
M445-2	CBR600F4, 99-06
M220	CBR600RR, 03-06
M434-2	CBR900RR Fireblade, 93-99
M329	500cc V-Fours, 84-86
M349	700-1000cc Interceptor, 83-85
M458-2	VFR700F-750F, 86-97
M438	VFR800Fl Interceptor, 98-00
M327	700-1100cc V-Fours, 82-88
M508	ST1100/Pan European, 90-02
M340	GL1000 & 1100, 75-83
M504	GL1200, 84-87

Sixes

M505	GL1500 Gold Wing, 88-92
M506-2	GL1500 Gold Wing, 93-00
M507-3	GL1800 Gold Wing, 01-10
M462-2	GL1500C Valkyrie, 97-03

KAWASAKI

ATVs

M465-3	Bayou KLF220 & KLF250, 88-10
M466-4	Bayou KLF300, 86-04
M467	Bayou KLF400, 93-99
M470	Lakota KEF300, 95-99
M385-2	Mojave KSF250, 87-04

Singles

M350-9	80-350cc Rotary Valve, 66-01
M444-2	KX60, 83-02; KX80 83-90
M448-2	KX80, 91-00; KX85, 01-10 & KX100, 89-09
M351	KDX200, 83-88
M447-3	KX125 & KX250, 82-91; KX500, 83-04
M472-2	KX125, 92-00
M473-2	KX250, 92-00
M474-3	KLR650, 87-07
M240	KLR650, 08-09

Twins

M355	KZ400, KZ/Z440, EN450 & EN500, 74-95
M360-3	EX500, GPZ500S, & Ninja 500R, 87-02
M356-5	Vulcan 700 & 750, 85-06
M354-3	Vulcan 800 & Vulcan 800 Classic, 95-05
M357-2	Vulcan 1500, 87-99
M471-3	Vulcan 1500 Series, 96-08

Fours

M449	KZ500/550 & ZX550, 79-85
M450	KZ, Z & ZX750, 80-85
M358	KZ650, 77-83
M359-3	Z & KZ 900-1000cc, 73-81
M451-3	KZ, ZX & ZN 1000 &1100cc, 81-02
M452-3	ZX500 & Ninja ZX600, 85-97
M468-2	Ninja ZX-6, 90-04
M469	Ninja ZX-7, ZX7R & ZX7RR, 91-98
M453-3	Ninja ZX900, ZX1000 & ZX1100, 84-01
M409	Concours, 86-04

POLARIS

ATVs

M496	3-, 4- and 6-Wheel Models w/250-425cc Engines, 85-95
M362-2	Magnum & Big Boss, 96-99
M363	Scrambler 500 4X4, 97-00
M365-4	Sportsman/Xplorer, 96-10
M366	Sportsman 600/700/800 Twins, 02-10
M367	Predator 500, 03-07

SUZUKI

ATVs

M381	ALT/LT 125 & 185, 83-87
M475	LT230 & LT250, 85-90
M380-2	LT250R Quad Racer, 85-92
M483-2	LT-4WD, LT-F4WDX & LT-F250, 87-98
M270-2	LT-Z400, 03-08
M343	LT-F500F Quadrunner, 98-00

Singles

M369	125-400cc, 64-81
M371	RM50-400 Twin Shock, 75-81
M379	RM125-500 Single Shock, 81-88
M386	RM80-250, 89-95
M400	RM125, 96-00
M401	RM250, 96-02
M476	DR250-350, 90-94
M477-3	DR-Z400E, S & SM, 00-09
M384-4	LS650 Savage/S40, 86-07

Twins

M372	GS400-450 Chain Drive, 77-87
M484-2	GS500E Twins, 89-02
M361	SV650, 1999-2002
M481-5	VS700-800 Intruder/S50, 85-07
M261	1500 Intruder/C90, 98-07
M260-2	Volusia/Boulevard C50, 01-08
M482-3	VS1400 Intruder/S83, 87-07

Triple

M368	GT380, 550 & 750, 72-77

Fours

M373	GS550, 77-86
M364	GS650, 81-83
M370	GS750, 77-82
M376	GS850-1100 Shaft Drive, 79-84
M378	GS1100 Chain Drive, 80-81
M383-3	Katana 600, 88-96 GSX-R750-1100, 86-87
M331	GSX-R600, 97-00
M264	GSX-R600, 01-05
M478-2	GSX-R750, 88-92; GSX750F Katana, 89-96
M485	GSX-R750, 96-99
M377	GSX-R1000, 01-04
M266	GSX-R1000, 05-06
M265	GSX1300R Hayabusa, 99-07
M338	Bandit 600, 95-00
M353	GSF1200 Bandit, 96-03

YAMAHA

ATVs

M499-2	YFM80 Moto-4, Badger & Raptor, 85-08
M394	YTM200, 225 & YFM200, 83-86
M488-5	Blaster, 88-05
M489-2	Timberwolf, 89-00
M487-5	Warrior, 87-04
M486-6	Banshee, 87-06
M490-3	Moto-4 & Big Bear, 87-04
M493	Kodiak, 93-98
M287	YFZ450, 04-09
M285-2	Grizzly 660, 02-08
M280-2	Raptor 660R, 01-05
M290	Raptor 700R, 06-09

Singles

M492-2	PW50 & 80 Y-Zinger & BW80 Big Wheel 80, 81-02
M410	80-175 Piston Port, 68-76
M415	250-400 Piston Port, 68-76
M412	DT & MX Series, 77-83
M414	IT125-490, 76-86
M393	YZ50-80 Monoshock, 78-90
M413	YZ100-490 Monoshock, 76-84
M390	YZ125-250, 85-87 YZ490, 85-90
M391	YZ125-250, 88-93 & WR250Z, 91-93
M497-2	YZ125, 94-01
M498	YZ250, 94-98; WR250Z, 94-97
M406	YZ250F & WR250F, 01-03
M491-2	YZ400F, 98-99 & 426F, 00-02; WR400F, 98-00 & 426F, 00-01
M417	XT125-250, 80-84
M480-3	XT350, 85-00; TT350, 86-87
M405	XT/TT 500, 76-81
M416	XT/TT 600, 83-89

Twins

M403	650cc Twins, 70-82
M395-10	XV535-1100 Virago, 81-03
M495-6	V-Star 650, 98-09
M281-4	V-Star 1100, 99-09
M283	V-Star 1300, 07-10
M282	Road Star, 99-05

Triple

M404	XS750 & XS850, 77-81

Fours

M387	XJ550, XJ600 & FJ600, 81-92
M494	XJ600 Seca II/Diversion, 92-98
M388	YX600 Radian & FZ600, 86-90
M396	FZR600, 89-93
M392	FZ700-750 & Fazer, 85-87
M411	XS1100, 78-81
M461	YZF-R6, 99-04
M398	YZF-R1, 98-03
M399	FZ1, 01-05
M397	FJ1100 & 1200, 84-93
M375	V-Max, 85-03
M374	Royal Star, 96-03

VINTAGE MOTORCYCLES

Clymer® Collection Series

M330	Vintage British Street Bikes, BSA 500–650cc Unit Twins; Norton 750 & 850cc Commandos; Triumph 500-750cc Twins
M300	Vintage Dirt Bikes, V. 1 Bultaco, 125-370cc Singles; Montesa, 123-360cc Singles; Ossa, 125-250cc Singles
M305	Vintage Japanese Street Bikes Honda, 250 & 305cc Twins; Kawasaki, 250-750cc Triples; Kawasaki, 900 & 1000cc Fours